Double-Chocolate Cream Tart, page 350

*Orange-and-Maple Roasted Turkey with
Giblet Gravy, page 326*

$\mathcal{M}$eet the *Cooking Light* Foods Staff

On these pages we present the *Cooking Light* Foods Staff, from left in each photograph.

Sitting: John Stark, Jill Melton
Standing: Becky Luigart-Stayner,
Kellie Kelley, Doug Crichton

Sitting: Cynthia LaGrone; Standing: Martha Condra,
Julie Walton, Leigh Fran Jones, Becky Pate, Billy Sims,
Mary Creel, Kathleen Kanen

Sitting: Kate Nicholson, Ellen Carroll, Nathalie Dearing
Standing: John Kirkpatrick, Maureen Callahan, Cathy Muir, Lee
Puckett. Not pictured: Cindy Barr, Susan Dendy, Fonda Shaia

3

Rigatoni with Bell Peppers, Olives, and Feta, page 125

Cooking Light

ANNUAL RECIPES
1998

Oxmoor
House

Library of Congress Catalog Number: 96-71335
ISBN: 0-8487-1598-5
ISSN: 1091-3645

Manufactured in the United States of America
First printing 1997

Be sure to check with your health-care provider
before making any changes in your diet.

WE'RE HERE FOR YOU!

We at Oxmoor House are dedicated to serving you with
reliable information that expands your imagination and
enriches your life. We welcome your comments and
suggestions. Please write us at:

Oxmoor House, Inc.
Editor, *Cooking Light® Annual Recipes*
2100 Lakeshore Drive
Birmingham, AL 35209

To order additional publications, call 1-205-877-6560.

Cover: *Italian Cream Cake* (page 90)

Back cover: *Spaghetti with Rhu's Marinara Sauce*
(page 41); *Beef Meatballs* (page 42)

Cooking Light®

Editor: Doug Crichton
Art Director: Susan Waldrip Dendy
Executive Editor: Nathalie Dearing
Managing Editor: Billy R. Sims
Senior Food Editor: Jill G. Melton, M.S., R.D.
Senior Editor: John Stark
Senior Editor–Projects: Ellen Templeton Carroll,
    M.S., R.D.
Food Editor: Mary S. Creel, M.S., R.D.
Associate Editor: Polly Pabor Linthicum
Associate Food Editors: Maureen Callahan, M.S., R.D.,
    Cynthia Nicholson LaGrone
Photo Stylists: Cindy Manning Barr, Cathy Muir
Senior Photographer: Howard L. Puckett
Photographer: Becky Luigart-Stayner
Studio Assistant: Fonda Shaia
Test Kitchens Director: Rebecca J. Pate
Food Stylist: Kellie Gerber Kelley
Test Kitchens Staff: Martha Condra, Leigh Fran Jones,
    M. Kathleen Kanen, John Kirkpatrick, Julie Walton
Copy Chief: Tim W. Jackson
Copy Editors: Lisa C. Bailey, Ritchey Halphen
Production Editors: Hazel R. Eddins, Matthew Solan
Editorial Coordinator: Carol C. Noe
Editorial Assistants: Kate Nicholson, Stacey L. Strawn
Editor-at-Large: Graham Kerr

Oxmoor House, Inc.

Editor-in-Chief: Nancy Fitzpatrick Wyatt
Senior Foods Editor: Katherine M. Eakin
Senior Editor, Editorial Services: Olivia Kindig Wells
Art Director: James Boone

Cooking Light® Annual Recipes 1998

Foods Editor: Cathy A. Wesler, R.D.
Copy Editor: Jacqueline B. Giovanelli
Editorial Assistants: Kaye Howard Smith, Catherine S. Ritter
Designer: Faith Nance
Production Director: Phillip Lee
Associate Production Manager: Theresa L. Beste
Production Assistant: Faye Porter Bonner
Indexer: Mary Ann Laurens

CONTENTS

Welcome

Welcome to *Cooking Light Annual Recipes 1998!* We've included more recipes for you than ever before: nearly 900 irresistible creations from the 10 issues published in 1997—all from the world's largest epicurean magazine.

It was a very special year for us—our 10th anniversary—and we celebrated the weekend of April 18–20 by inviting all 5.7 million of our readers home to Birmingham, Alabama. We hosted a major outdoor festival called the *Cooking Light* Reader Reunion. There is a true relationship between *Cooking Light*'s editors and readers, and that proved to be especially true during the reunion. We featured the best of American chefs at the event, and their spectacular recipes are included here (page 94). And so is the grand-prize-winning reader recipe from the Reunion's $20,000 Recipe of the Decade contest: Priscilla Yee's Brownie Cheesecake Torte (page 222).

But there's more: In the April anniversary issue we showcased many of our "Best-Ever" recipes including our foods editors' all-time favorite *Cooking Light* recipes (page 107), our most-requested recipe (page 90), as well as our 10 best recipes ever (page 86).

 Plus, throughout the year we identified the 10 hottest food trends that you'll find highlighted with our "Hot Trends" logo. As we researched these trends, it became clear that we're in the Age of Flavor: big, bold, spicy, sweet, sour, tart, and fresh.

If your family's like mine, holidays wouldn't be complete without a few special recipes. So in keeping with our tradition, we've got sumptuous holiday feasts with classic recipes we've lightened and updated. And don't miss our mix-and-match selection of recipes for your holidays (page 322).

I hope you enjoy this special edition of the *Cooking Light Annual Recipes* series. We have a lot of great cooking going on!

Best Regards,

Vice President/Editor

Our Favorite Recipes of the Year

For a recipe to make it into the pages of *Cooking Light* magazine, it has to be pretty special. After all, each recipe is tested several times by our Test Kitchens staff, who, along with our foods staff, judge its merits on many factors: taste, ease of preparation, broadness of appeal, relevancy to today's way of eating, and that indefinable quality that we call "yum appeal." Of all the recipes we passed in 1997, we've highlighted the following. We think of them as the most delicious of the delicious. But don't forget to look through the April issue, which includes the top recipes in the history of the magazine (page 86) and our all-time favorites (page 107).

◆ HOPPIN' JOHN CAKES WITH TOMATILLO-TOMATO SALSA (page 18): One of the South's most beloved vegetables, black-eyed peas, comes of age in these patties, complete with a Mexican-style salsa.

◆ FUDGY SOUFFLÉ CAKE WITH WARM TURTLE SAUCE (page 19): So versatile, this cake can be served warm, at room temperature, or chilled. Once it's fallen, it takes on the consistency of a dense fudge cake. And the two-ingredient Turtle Sauce also tastes great on low-fat ice cream and fat-free pound cake.

◆ SPAGHETTI WITH BEEF MEATBALLS AND RHU'S MARINARA SAUCE (pages 41 and 42): Spicy meatballs top a rich marinara sauce brimming with garlic flavor. Definitely a lightened favorite.

◆ PERFECT PASTA AND CHEESE (page 63): A smooth Cheddar cheese sauce with chives smothers penne pasta and mushrooms; then this comforting dish is sprinkled with breadcrumbs and baked until bubbly. Umm, so good.

◆ ULTIMATE CHOCOLATE LAYER CAKE (page 108): This layer cake tastes like a high-fat luxury, but the analysis reveals the surprising truth. You won't want to miss its luscious silky frosting.

◆ BANANA PUDDING (page 133): With its creamy filling, meringue peaks, and chewy crust, this pudding just seems to say, "Dig in."

◆ SPICY APPLE-GLAZED CHICK 'N' GRITS GORGONZOLA (page 148): This winner of our Wisconsin Cheese Recipe Contest is a twist on a Southern favorite. The combo of grits, cheese, and sweet and spicy chicken will make a grits fan out of anyone!

◆ POLENTA WITH ROASTED RED PEPPERS AND FONTINA CHEESE (page 148): As first runner-up in the Wisconsin Cheese Recipe Contest, this vegetarian entrée is a winner with just four ingredients: bell peppers, tomatoes, polenta, and fontina cheese.

◆ GARLICKY TOMATO TART (page 193): Fresh-from-the-vine tomatoes take center stage in this vegetarian entrée. It's a casual dish, but don't hesitate to serve it at a dinner party—the flavors will impress your guests.

◆ GRILLED SALMON WITH NECTARINE-RED ONION RELISH (page 234): Fresh salmon and nectarines are the basics in this culinary combination. A touch of orange juice and red onion, jalapeño pepper, sliced basil, and garlic turn plain fish into a spectacular entrée.

◆ LINGUINE WITH TWO SAUCES (page 276): Like its name implies, this entrée showcases two favorites in the sauce category—creamy cheese and rich tomato.

◆ PROVENÇALE POTATO GRATIN (page 292): A key ingredient here is Asiago cheese. And because of its intense flavor, a little goes a long way in this potato, tomato, and onion gratin.

◆ CINNAMON-APPLE CAKE (page 294): A double layer of apple-cinnamon streusel flavors this cake, which stays moist because of the cream cheese in the batter.

◆ HAMANTASCHEN (page 295): Don't let the name intimidate you. These cookies are tender pastries filled with a moist fig filling.

◆ CHOCOLATE SOUFFLÉS WITH WHITE CHOCOLATE-RUM SAUCE (page 351): Drizzle these semisweet, chocolatey soufflés with warm white chocolate sauce for a flavor match that's made in heaven.

◆ FUDGY CHOCOLATE BROWNIES (page 351): There's nothing more satisfying than brownies, especially those with an intense chocolate flavor. Enjoy!

◆ BITTERSWEET CHOCOLATE PUDDING (page 352): When you want deep, rich chocolate—no wimpy milk chocolate stuff—try this satiny pudding. Whether served warm or chilled, this delectable dessert provides pure enjoyment.

HOW TO USE IT AND WHY Glance at the end of any *Cooking Light* recipe, and you'll see how committed we are to helping you make the best of today's light cooking. With four registered dietitians, four test kitchens professionals, three chefs, and a computer system that analyzes every ingredient we use, *Cooking Light* gives you authoritative dietary detail like no other magazine. We go to such lengths so you can see how our recipes fit into your healthy eating plan. If you're trying to lose weight, the calorie and fat figures will help most. But if you're keeping a close eye on the sodium, cholesterol, and saturated fat in your diet, we provide those numbers, too. Many women don't get enough iron or calcium; we can also help there. Finally, there's a fiber analysis for those of us who don't get enough roughage.

What it means and how we get there: We list calories, protein, fat, fiber, iron, and sodium at the end of each recipe, but there are a few things we abbreviate for space.

- *sat* for saturated fat
- *g* for gram
- *CHOL* for cholesterol
- *mono* for monounsaturated fat

- *CARB* for carbohydrates
- *poly* for polyunsaturated fat
- *mg* for milligram
- *CALC* for calcium

We get numbers for those categories based on a few assumptions: When we give a range for an ingredient, we calculate the lesser amount. Some alcohol calories evaporate during heating; we reflect that. And only the amount of marinade absorbed by the food is calculated.

Your Daily Nutrition Guide

	WOMEN AGES 25 TO 50	WOMEN OVER 50	MEN OVER 24
Calories	2,000	2,000 or less	2,700
Protein	50g	50g or less	63g
Fat	67g or less	67g or less	90g or less
Saturated Fat	22g or less	22g or less	30g or less
Carbohydrates	299g	299g	405g
Fiber	25g to 35g	25g to 35g	25g to 35g
Cholesterol	300mg or less	300mg or less	300mg or less
Iron	15mg	10mg	10mg
Sodium	2,400mg or less	2,400mg or less	2,400mg or less
Calcium	1,000mg	1,200mg	1,000mg

Calorie requirements vary according to your size, weight, and level of activity. This chart is a good general guide; additional nutrients are needed during some stages of life. For example, children's calorie and protein needs are based on height and vary greatly as they grow. Compared to adults, teenagers require less protein but more calcium and slightly more iron. Pregnant or breast-feeding women need more protein, calories, and calcium. Also, the need for iron increases during pregnancy but returns to normal after birth.

JANUARY FEBRUARY

Hot Plates

Be prepared with Cooking Light's 10 hottest food trends. Big, bold flavors are coming your way!

To identify the 10 hottest food trends, we looked at various indicators: What are trendy restaurants serving? What are the latest ethnic ingredients to go mass-market? We checked out new cookbook titles and supermarket products; talked with chefs, nutritionists, food writers, and recipe developers across the country; even tuned in to the TV Food Network.

Factoring in the 4,000 recipes we sampled in our Test Kitchens last year with the above information, it became clear that this is the Age of Flavor: big, bold, spicy, sweet, sour, tart, fresh, full-throttle flavor.

At no time in America has eating been so exciting as now. Today's supermarkets are international food emporiums: mangoes, won ton wrappers, ginger, tortillas—what foreign cuisine shall we eat tonight, or shall we go fusion?

The 10 trends that we've identified support our Big Flavor theory while reflecting America's newfound passion for healthy living. As the saying goes, the proof is in the pudding—or, in this case, the pasta, pilaf, scones, or other dishes that we've created to showcase each trend. Besides the following story, we'll be spotlighting our top 10 trends throughout the year. We predict that all these trends are here to stay. Indeed, the year promises to leave a very flavorful impression.

ONE DISH MEALS If you're tired after work or need to rush off to an appointment, you probably don't have the time or inclination to cook a balanced dinner featuring meat, potatoes, and a vegetable.

More and more, home-cooked one-dish meals are helping you satisfy several food groups in one fell swoop. Add a salad and some bread, and you're all set.

WHITE BEAN-AND-SAGE CASSOULET

2 teaspoons olive oil
1 cup diced carrot
1 cup chopped fennel bulb
1 cup diced onion
6 garlic cloves, minced
2 (16-ounce) cans cannellini beans, drained
4 ounces thinly sliced prosciutto or ham
¼ cup low-salt chicken broth or water
1 (14.5-ounce) can peeled tomato wedges (such as Del Monte Fresh Cut)
2 tablespoons thinly sliced fresh sage or 2 teaspoons dried sage
½ to 1 teaspoon freshly ground pepper
2 (1-ounce) slices diagonally cut French bread (about 1 inch thick)
Vegetable cooking spray
Fresh sage leaves (optional)

1. Preheat oven to 425°.
2. Heat oil in a large nonstick skillet over medium-high heat. Add carrot, fennel, onion, and garlic; sauté 5 minutes. Spoon carrot mixture into an 11 x 7-inch baking dish. Stir in beans and next 5 ingredients.
3. Trim crusts from bread. Cut bread into 1-inch cubes. Lightly coat cubes with cooking spray. Arrange bread cubes in a single layer over carrot mixture pressing bread cubes gently into mixture. Cover with aluminum foil, and bake at 425° for 25 minutes. Uncover and bake 5 additional minutes or until croutons are golden. Garnish with sage leaves, if desired. Yield: 6 servings (serving size: 1⅓ cups).

CALORIES 272 (20% from fat); FAT 6g (sat 1.1g, mono 2.6g, poly 1.6g); PROTEIN 14.9g; CARB 41.7g; FIBER 5.9g; CHOL 11mg; IRON 3.9mg; SODIUM 753mg; CALC 89mg

ASIAN NOODLES It used to be that all you could buy in the supermarket were egg noodles. Then came Italian pasta. And now, Asian noodles are filling supermarket shelves from coast to coast. Just like their Italian counterparts, Asian noodles are high in carbohydrates, low in fat, and extremely versatile. Nutty and dense, they're able to stand up to stronger, hotter flavors.

The popularity of Asian noodles coincides with America's yen for spicier, more exotic foods—i.e., dishes made with such signature Asian flavorings as soy sauce, ginger, coconut milk, and curry paste. Just when you thought you would run out of healthy pasta and noodle recipes, a whole new world opens.

SPICY SHRIMP WITH UDON NOODLES

Spaghetti can be used in place of udon noodles. You can find red curry paste at Asian markets; made primarily from chiles and very concentrated, it imparts a spicy, salty flavor.

     2 pounds large shrimp, peeled and deveined
     1 teaspoon grated lime rind
     3 tablespoons fresh lime juice
     3 tablespoons low-sodium soy sauce
     1 to 3 tablespoons red curry paste
     3 tablespoons brown sugar
     1 tablespoon chili oil or vegetable oil
  1½ cups (2 x ¼-inch) julienne-cut red bell pepper
     ½ cup thinly sliced green onions
     ⅓ cup minced fresh cilantro
     1 cup fresh bean sprouts (about 2 ounces)
     6 cups cooked udon noodles (thick, round fresh Japanese wheat noodles) or spaghetti (about 8 ounces uncooked)
Vegetable cooking spray
     ¼ cup plus 2 tablespoons chopped peanuts

1. Starting at the tail end, butterfly each shrimp, cutting to, but not through, outside of shrimp. Set aside.
2. Combine lime rind and next 5 ingredients; stir well. Combine ⅓ cup lime mixture and shrimp in a large zip-top plastic bag; seal bag, and marinate shrimp in refrigerator for 30 minutes.
3. Combine remaining ⅓ cup lime mixture, bell pepper, and next 4 ingredients in a large bowl, tossing to coat.
4. Place a large nonstick skillet coated with cooking spray over medium-high heat until hot. Add shrimp; sauté 5 minutes or until done. Combine shrimp and noodle mixture; toss gently. Sprinkle each serving with 1 tablespoon nuts. Serve warm or chilled. Yield: 6 servings (serving size: 1⅓ cups).

CALORIES 372 (23% from fat); FAT 9.6g (sat 1.5g, mono 3.3g, poly 3.6g); PROTEIN 31.3g; CARB 39.3g; FIBER 2.6g; CHOL 172mg; IRON 5.3mg; SODIUM 470mg; CALC 93mg

---

OLIVES Americans are catching on that these small, flavor-packed fruits are, as the ancient Greeks believed, gifts from the gods. With so many health benefits linked to the Mediterranean diet and its use of olive oil, it's only natural that olives are popping up all over the place, from breads to pizzas to salsas. Although olives are high in monounsaturated fats, they are so intense in flavor that a little goes a long way.

Mostly from Greece, Italy, Spain, France, and now California, olives, be they green or black, have a plethora of varieties and curing methods—so many, in fact, that one could easily become an olive snob. In these health-conscious times, one of mankind's oldest foods is new again.

PAN-SEARED TUNA WITH OLIVE-WINE SAUCE

The flavors in this dish are pure Mediterranean. The sweetness of the fennel and the fruity aroma of the orange balance with the saltiness of the olives. Greek olives are the big, meaty variety—simply slice the olive away from the pit.

Vegetable cooking spray
     1 teaspoon fennel seeds
     2 garlic cloves, minced
     ¾ cup dry white wine
     3 tablespoons pitted, chopped Greek black olives
     3 tablespoons pitted, chopped green olives
     2 tablespoons fresh lemon juice
     1 teaspoon grated orange rind
     ¼ teaspoon dried crushed red pepper
     ¼ teaspoon black pepper
     ⅛ teaspoon salt
     4 (6-ounce) tuna steaks (about 2 inches thick)
     2 cups hot cooked couscous
Orange rind (optional)

1. Place a large nonstick skillet coated with cooking spray over medium heat until hot. Add fennel seeds and garlic; sauté 3 minutes or until seeds are lightly toasted. Spoon mixture into a bowl. Add wine and next 5 ingredients; stir well, and set aside.
2. Sprinkle black pepper and salt over tuna. Coat skillet with cooking spray; place over medium-high heat until very hot. Add tuna; sauté 5 minutes on each side or until medium-rare or to desired degree of doneness. Remove tuna from skillet. Spoon ½ cup couscous into each of 4 large shallow bowls; arrange tuna to the side. Set aside; keep warm.
3. Add wine mixture to skillet; cook 2 minutes or until sauce is slightly reduced. Pour sauce evenly over tuna steaks. Garnish with orange rind, if desired. Yield: 4 servings (serving size: 1 tuna steak, ½ cup couscous, and about ¼ cup sauce).
Note: Substitute kalamata olives for Greek black olives, if desired.

CALORIES 365 (25% from fat); FAT 10.2g (sat 2.4g, mono 3.4g, poly 3.1g); PROTEIN 43.6g; CARB 23.1g; FIBER 1.5g; CHOL 65mg; IRON 3.1mg; SODIUM 258mg; CALC 25mg

GRAINS When it comes to cooking with grains, there are far more choices today than white rice: there's amaranth, brown and wild rice, bulgur, grits, oats, pearl barley, quinoa, and wheat berries. All are loaded with protein and are high in fiber. Because of their variety and healthfulness, these grains are moving more and more toward center stage in American cooking.

Like rice and pasta, grains are really economical to buy. They can extend other ingredients in a recipe or relegate them to supporting roles. Once considered a peasant food, grain-based dishes are now the stuff of upscale, trendy restaurants.

TWO-GRAIN PILAF WITH VEAL

Wild rice and pearl barley star in this osso buco-type dish.

- 1   (1-pound) veal or beef shank
- ¼   teaspoon salt
- ¼   teaspoon pepper
- 1   tablespoon all-purpose flour
- 2   teaspoons vegetable oil, divided
- 1   cup diced carrot
- 1   cup diced celery
- 1   cup diced yellow onion
- 2   garlic cloves, minced
- ½   cup dry white wine
- 1   (14½-ounce) can fat-free beef broth, divided
- 1   (14.5-ounce) can no-salt-added whole tomatoes, undrained and chopped
- 1   cup water
- 1   teaspoon dried basil
- ⅔   cup wild rice
- ⅓   cup uncooked pearl barley
- Carrot curls (optional)
- Basil sprigs (optional)

1. Preheat oven to 350°.
2. Trim fat from veal. Sprinkle salt and pepper over veal; dredge in flour.

Heat 1 teaspoon oil in a large oven-proof Dutch oven over medium-high heat. Add veal; cook 2½ minutes on each side or until browned. Remove from Dutch oven; set aside. Add 1 teaspoon oil, diced carrot, celery, onion, and garlic to Dutch oven; cook over medium heat for 5 minutes or until tender. Add wine, scraping Dutch oven to loosen browned bits. Return veal to Dutch oven; add 1 cup broth, tomato, water, and dried basil. Cover and bake at 350° for 30 minutes. Add rice, barley, and remaining broth; cover and bake 1½ hours or until veal is tender and rice is done.
3. Remove veal from Dutch oven. Remove meat from bone; discard bone. Shred meat with 2 forks; return shredded veal to Dutch oven. If desired, garnish with carrot curls and basil sprigs. Yield: 5 servings.

CALORIES 258 (19% from fat); FAT 5.4g (sat 1.8g, mono 1.7g, poly 1.3g); PROTEIN 14g; CARB 38.9g; FIBER 5.1g; CHOL 30mg; IRON 2.1mg; SODIUM 238mg; CALC 107mg

FLAVORS OF THE SUN The closer you get to the equator, the sunnier, the more radiant the flavors. Intense spices, salsas, and tropical fruits define the exciting, colorful dishes of Mexico, Central and South America, and the Caribbean. Chefs in this country, meanwhile, have begun creating their own flavors-of-the-sun recipes with such tropical fruits as mangoes, plantains, and tamarind. Formerly unheard of in supermarkets, they're now spilling out of bins—and perfect for today's light eating.

CALYPSO CHICKEN WITH SAUTÉED PLANTAINS AND DOWN-ISLAND SALSA

This entrée is similar to the famous chicken dish called country captain, but the fiery seasonings and sides make it uniquely Caribbean. Plantains are a large, firm variety of banana. If you can't find plantains, the dish is equally good without them.

- 2½   cups chopped onion
- ½   cup minced green bell pepper
- 2   tablespoons fresh lime juice
- 1   teaspoon minced fresh thyme
- 2   garlic cloves, minced
- 6   (4-ounce) skinned, boned chicken breast halves
- ¾   teaspoon salt, divided
- ½   teaspoon pepper
- 2   teaspoons vegetable oil
- Vegetable cooking spray
- 1   (14.5-ounce) can diced tomatoes, undrained
- ½   cup water
- 1   serrano chile
- Down-Island Salsa
- Sautéed Plantains
- 3   cups hot cooked long-grain rice
- Fresh thyme sprigs (optional)
- Lime wedges (optional)

1. Combine first 6 ingredients in a bowl; toss to coat. Cover and refrigerate 1 hour, turning occasionally.
2. Remove chicken from marinade, reserving marinade; sprinkle chicken with ½ teaspoon salt and ½ teaspoon pepper. Heat oil in a large nonstick skillet coated with cooking spray over medium-high heat until hot. Add chicken; sauté 1 minute per side or until browned. Add reserved marinade, ¼ teaspoon salt, tomato, water, and serrano chile; bring to a boil. Cover, reduce heat, and simmer 1 hour. Discard chile.
3. Top each chicken breast half with tomato mixture; serve with Down-Island Salsa, Sautéed Plantains, and rice. If desired, garnish with thyme sprigs and lime wedges. Yield: 6 servings (serving size: 1 chicken breast,

⅓ cup sauce, ⅔ cup salsa, plantain half, and ½ cup rice).

CALORIES 606 (10% from fat); FAT 6.8g (sat 1.1g, mono 1.6g, poly 1.3g); PROTEIN 32.4g; CARB 104g; FIBER 5.3g; CHOL 66mg; IRON 3.8mg; SODIUM 554mg; CALC 84mg

Down-Island Salsa:

- ¼ cup firmly packed brown sugar
- 3 tablespoons white rum
- 2 tablespoons fresh lime juice
- 1 teaspoon seeded, minced serrano chile
- 4 cups (1-inch) fresh pineapple cubes
- 1 cup peeled, diced ripe mango
- 1 cup carambola (star fruit), halved lengthwise and thinly sliced

1. Combine first 3 ingredients in a large bowl; stir well. Add chile and remaining ingredients; toss to coat. Chill at least 2 hours. Yield: about 4 cups (serving size: ⅔ cup).
Note: Increase the mango to 2 cups if carambola is unavailable.

CALORIES 121 (4% from fat); FAT 0.6g (sat 0.1g, mono 0.1g, poly 0.2g); PROTEIN 0.7g; CARB 25.5g; FIBER 2.2g; CHOL 0mg; IRON 0.6mg; SODIUM 5mg; CALC 17mg

Sautéed Plantains:

- 1 tablespoon vegetable oil
- 3 ripe plantains, peeled and halved lengthwise

1. Heat oil in a large nonstick skillet over medium-high heat. Add plantains; sauté 1½ minutes per side or until browned. Slice, if desired. Yield: 6 servings.

CALORIES 181 (14% from fat); FAT 2.8g (sat 0.4g, mono 0.7g, poly 1.1g); PROTEIN 1.7g; CARB 41.9g; FIBER 0.7g; CHOL 0mg; IRON 0.8mg; SODIUM 5mg; CALC 4mg

ROASTING THE UNEXPECTED

The technique that your mom used to employ for Sunday-night pot roast is back, only this time it's not just for big hunks of meat—it's for fruits and vegetables, too.

Roasting concentrates flavors without fat (courtesy of caramelization) and adds a butter-soft texture. If roasting can bring out the sweetness in savory dishes like chicken, fish, and beef, think of what it can do for asparagus, tomatoes, peaches, apricots, or whatever else is in season. By roasting the unexpected, vegetarians can also enjoy this flavorful cooking technique.

POLENTA CAKE WITH ROASTED NECTARINES

For this simple dessert, use nectarines from Chile, which are in season in January. Pears also work great.

- ⅓ cup stick margarine, softened
- ⅔ cup firmly packed dark brown sugar, divided
- 2 large eggs
- ¼ cup skim milk
- ½ teaspoon grated lemon rind
- 1⅔ cups all-purpose flour
- ¼ cup yellow cornmeal
- 1 teaspoon baking powder
- ¼ teaspoon baking soda
- ¼ teaspoon salt
- 1¼ cups peeled, finely chopped Granny Smith apple
- Vegetable cooking spray
- ¼ cup water
- 1 teaspoon ground cinnamon
- 8 medium-size firm nectarines, halved (about 1½ pounds)
- 1 tablespoon turbinado sugar or granulated sugar
- Cinnamon sticks (optional)

1. Preheat oven to 350°.
2. Beat margarine and ⅓ cup brown sugar at medium speed of an electric mixer until well-blended. Add eggs, 1 at a time, beating well after each addition. Add milk and lemon rind; beat well. Combine flour and next 4 ingredients; add to creamed mixture, and beat well. Stir in chopped apple.
3. Spoon batter into a 9-inch round cake pan coated with cooking spray. Bake at 350° for 28 minutes or until a wooden pick inserted in center comes out clean. Cool in pan 5 minutes; remove from pan. Let cool completely on a wire rack.
4. Preheat oven to 475°.
5. Combine ⅓ cup brown sugar, water, and ground cinnamon in a 2-cup glass measure; stir well. Microwave at HIGH 30 seconds or until sugar dissolves. Combine nectarines and brown sugar mixture; toss well. Arrange nectarines, cut sides down, in a 13 x 9-inch baking dish. Bake at 475° for 15 minutes or until tender. Turn nectarines over; sprinkle with turbinado sugar. Bake 5 additional minutes. Serve with cake. Garnish with cinnamon sticks, if desired. Yield: 8 servings (serving size: 1 cake wedge and 2 nectarine halves).
Pear Variation: Substitute 6 small, firm Bosc pears, cored and quartered (about 2¼ pounds), for nectarines, if desired.

CALORIES 303 (29% from fat); FAT 9.8g (sat 2g, mono 4g, poly 2.9g); PROTEIN 5.5g; CARB 49.8g; FIBER 3.4g; CHOL 55mg; IRON 2.3mg; SODIUM 224mg; CALC 67mg

THE NEW SOUL FOOD To bring this down-home culinary tradition in step with healthy living, there's a nationwide movement among African-Americans to lighten their comfort food. This healthier, redefined soul food is being served in upscale restaurants and is the subject of several new cookbooks. Everywhere you go, Southern staples such as collards, grits, and pinto beans can be found souffléed, creamed, gratinéed, or roasted.

HOPPIN' JOHN CAKES WITH TOMATILLO-TOMATO SALSA

One of the South's most beloved vegetables, black-eyed peas, comes of age in these '90s patties, complete with a refreshing Mexican-style salsa.

2   cups well-drained canned black-eyed peas, divided
Vegetable cooking spray
¾ cup diced onion
1   tablespoon seeded, diced jalapeño pepper
3   garlic cloves, minced
4   cups fresh breadcrumbs, divided (about 8 slices)
1   cup cooked basmati rice
2   tablespoons all-purpose flour
1   large egg, lightly beaten
1   large egg white, lightly beaten
2   tablespoons vegetable oil, divided
Tomatillo-Tomato Salsa
Cherry tomatoes (optional)

1. Mash 1 cup black-eyed peas. Set aside.
2. Place a large nonstick skillet coated with cooking spray over medium-high heat until hot. Add onion, jalapeño, and garlic; sauté 3 minutes or until onion is lightly browned.
3. Combine mashed black-eyed peas, 1 cup whole peas, onion mixture, 1 cup breadcrumbs, and next 4 ingredients in

a bowl; stir well. Divide mixture into 8 equal portions. Shape into ½-inch-thick cakes, using wet hands. Pat 3 cups breadcrumbs over cakes.
4. Heat 1 tablespoon oil in a large nonstick skillet over medium-high heat. Add 4 cakes, and cook 4 minutes. Carefully turn cakes over, and cook 4 minutes or until golden. Repeat procedure with remaining oil and cakes. Serve with Tomatillo-Tomato Salsa. Garnish with cherry tomatoes, if desired. Yield: 4 servings (serving size: 2 cakes and ½ cup salsa).

CALORIES 432 (23% from fat); FAT 10.8g (sat 2.2g, mono 3.2g, poly 4.4g); PROTEIN 16.5g; CARB 68g; FIBER 5.8g; CHOL 57mg; IRON 4mg; SODIUM 952mg; CALC 86mg

Tomatillo-Tomato Salsa:

1   cup diced tomato
¼ cup chopped green onions
2   tablespoons chopped fresh cilantro
2   tablespoons seeded, minced jalapeño pepper
¼ teaspoon pepper
1   (11-ounce) can green tomatoes (tomatillos), drained and chopped
1   garlic clove, minced

1. Combine all ingredients in a bowl; stir well. Let stand at room temperature 2 to 4 hours. Yield: 2 cups (serving size: ½ cup).

CALORIES 46 (4% from fat); FAT 0.2g (sat 0g, mono 0g, poly 0.1g); PROTEIN 1g; CARB 10.2g; FIBER 2.5g; CHOL 0mg; IRON 0.5mg; SODIUM 689mg; CALC 12mg

VEGETARIAN MEALS As more people trade in beef for barley and pork for polenta, the challenge of creating interesting meatless entrées grows. Nowadays, there's more to life than sprouts and soyburgers: Supermarket shelves are full of exciting grains, pastas, spices, and other vegetarian-friendly items. And America's new love affair with ethnic flavors makes the options for meatless eating almost limitless.

LINGUINE WITH POTATOES, GREEN BEANS, AND SPINACH PESTO

(pictured on page 38)

Packed with spinach, green beans, and potatoes, this dish is loaded with calcium and beta carotene and has plenty of protein to boot.

¼ cup plus 2 tablespoons toasted pine nuts, divided
7   cups packaged spinach leaves, trimmed
⅓ cup grated fresh Parmesan cheese
¼ cup chopped fresh basil
2   tablespoons lemon juice
½ teaspoon salt
¼ teaspoon pepper
2   garlic cloves, minced
2   tablespoons water
1   tablespoon olive oil
8   ounces uncooked linguine
3   cups (½-inch) peeled, cubed red potato (about 3 medium)
2   cups (2-inch) cut green beans (about ¼ pound)
Shaved fresh Parmesan cheese (optional)

1. Place 3 tablespoons pine nuts, spinach, and next 6 ingredients in a food processor; process until smooth, scraping sides of processor bowl once. With food processor on, slowly pour water and oil through food chute; process until well-blended. Set aside.

2. Cook linguine and potato in boiling water 6 minutes. Add green beans; cook 5 additional minutes or until potato is tender. Drain. Combine 3 tablespoons pine nuts, spinach mixture, and pasta mixture in a large bowl. Toss well to coat. Garnish with shaved Parmesan cheese, if desired. Yield: 4 servings (serving size: 2 cups).

CALORIES 524 (30% from fat); FAT 17.3g (sat 5g, mono 6.9g, poly 4.2g); PROTEIN 23.9g; CARB 73.9g; FIBER 8.8g; CHOL 13mg; IRON 7.8mg; SODIUM 689mg; CALC 372mg

NEW COMFORT DESSERTS

From apple pie to cheesecake to chocolate cake, few things are more satisfying (or comforting) than classic American desserts, which chefs across the country are redefining with contemporary ingredients and low-fat expectations. In the new year, you'll be able to have your cake, pie, brownie, ice cream, or cobbler and eat it, too. There, there, don't you feel better already?

FUDGY SOUFFLÉ CAKE WITH WARM TURTLE SAUCE

No more dashing from oven to table—just bake the soufflé; then serve warm, at room temperature, or chilled. Once it's fallen, it takes on the consistency of a dense fudge cake.

Butter-flavored vegetable cooking spray
¼ teaspoon sugar
½ cup unsweetened cocoa
¼ cup plus 2 tablespoons hot water
2 tablespoons stick margarine
3 tablespoons all-purpose flour
¾ cup 1% low-fat milk
¼ cup sugar
⅛ teaspoon salt
4 large egg whites (at room temperature)
3 tablespoons sugar
Warm Turtle Sauce

1. Preheat oven to 375°.
2. Coat a 1½-quart soufflé dish with cooking spray; sprinkle with ¼ teaspoon sugar. Set aside.
3. Combine cocoa and hot water in a bowl. Stir well; set aside.
4. Melt margarine in a small heavy saucepan over medium heat. Add flour; cook, stirring constantly with a whisk, 1 minute. Add milk, ¼ cup sugar, and salt; cook, stirring constantly, 3 minutes or until thick. Remove from heat. Add cocoa mixture; stir well. Spoon into a large bowl; let cool slightly.
5. Beat egg whites at high speed of an electric mixer until foamy. Add 3 tablespoons sugar, 1 tablespoon at a time, beating until stiff peaks form. Gently fold 1 cup egg white mixture into cocoa mixture; gently fold in remaining egg white mixture. Spoon into prepared soufflé dish.
6. Bake at 375° for 35 minutes or until puffy and set. Remove from oven; serve warm, at room temperature, or chilled with Warm Turtle Sauce. Yield: 6 servings.

CALORIES 241 (29% from fat); FAT 7.8g (sat 1.7g, mono 3.3g, poly 1.9g); PROTEIN 6.1g; CARB 58.6g; FIBER 0.4g; CHOL 2mg; IRON 1.6mg; SODIUM 182mg; CALC 54mg

Warm Turtle Sauce:

¼ cup plus 2 tablespoons fat-free caramel-flavored sundae syrup
3 tablespoons chopped pecans, toasted

1. Place caramel syrup in a small bowl; microwave at HIGH 30 seconds or until warm. Stir in pecans. Yield: ½ cup (serving size: about 1½ tablespoons).

CALORIES 79 (28% from fat); FAT 2.5g (sat 0.2g, mono 1.5g, poly 0.6g); PROTEIN 0.2g; CARB 35.6g; FIBER 0.2g; CHOL 0mg; IRON 0.1mg; SODIUM 35mg; CALC 1mg

COFFEE BREAKS

Gourmet coffee breaks are becoming increasingly popular, even replacing the traditional after-work happy hour. As for what to serve at your next coffee break, try wholesome, low-fat offerings such as biscotti and scones.

GINGERSNAP SCONES WITH ESPRESSO GLAZE

1¾ cups all-purpose flour
¼ cup gingersnap crumbs (about 6 cookies, finely crushed)
¼ cup sugar
1½ teaspoons baking powder
½ teaspoon baking soda
¼ teaspoon salt
¼ cup chilled stick margarine, cut into small pieces
½ cup low-fat buttermilk
1 large egg, lightly beaten
Vegetable cooking spray
1½ tablespoons hot water
1½ teaspoons instant coffee granules
¾ cup sifted powdered sugar
10 walnut halves

1. Preheat oven to 400°.
2. Combine first 6 ingredients in a bowl; cut in margarine with a pastry blender until mixture resembles coarse meal. Add buttermilk and egg, stirring just until moist (dough will be sticky).
3. Turn dough out onto a lightly floured surface; with floured hands, knead lightly 4 times. Pat dough into a 10-inch circle on a baking sheet coated with cooking spray. Cut dough into 10 wedges, cutting into, but not through, dough. Bake at 400° for 15 minutes or until golden.
4. Combine hot water and coffee granules; stir well. Add powdered sugar; stir well. Drizzle over scones. Cut into 10 wedges; top each with 1 walnut half. Yield: 10 servings.

CALORIES 220 (30% from fat); FAT 7.4g (sat 1.4g, mono 2.8g, poly 2.5g); PROTEIN 4g; CARB 34.7g; FIBER 0.7g; CHOL 24mg; IRON 1.4mg; SODIUM 194mg; CALC 73mg

Dark Clouds

When egg whites are whipped and added to a dish, heavenly textures emerge. Add cocoa and you receive a devilish surprise.

When it comes to eating healthfully, egg whites may be a dessert's best friend. Besides being fat-free, egg whites take on billowing proportions when whipped. As you beat them, air becomes trapped within, enabling you to create light, fluffy confections and desserts.

When it comes to flavorings, cocoa also makes a good companion to desserts, seeing as it's almost fat-free. So what happens when egg whites meet cocoa? You get something that's completely irresistible: chocolate clouds.

Although you don't think of chocolate as being particularly light, you will with these recipes. The whipped egg whites give these desserts a variety of rich textures, from a creamy mousse to crisp meringue shells. With the addition of cocoa, even the queen of lightness herself, angel food cake, shows an unexpected, sinful side. With our step-by-step instructions, you'll have no trouble mastering these elegant, diaphanous desserts. These are dark clouds you don't want to avoid.

COCOA MERINGUE SHELLS WITH GLAZED FRESH FRUITS

Any combination of fruits can be used with these airy meringues.

- 3 large egg whites (at room temperature)
- ½ teaspoon vanilla extract
- ⅛ teaspoon cream of tartar
- ½ cup sugar
- 2 tablespoons sifted unsweetened cocoa
- Pastry Cream
- 8 orange sections
- 8 thin slices peeled kiwifruit
- ¼ cup blueberries
- 1 tablespoon red currant jelly, melted
- Unsweetened cocoa (optional)

1. Preheat oven to 225°.
2. Place parchment paper over a large baking sheet. Draw 8 (3-inch) circles on parchment paper. Turn parchment paper over, and secure with masking tape. Beat egg whites, vanilla, and cream of tartar at high speed of an electric mixer until foamy. Gradually add sugar, 1 tablespoon at a time, beating until stiff peaks form (do not underbeat). Fold 2 tablespoons cocoa into mixture.
3. Divide egg white mixture evenly among the 8 circles. Using the back of a spoon, shape egg white mixture into nests with 1-inch sides. Bake at 225° for 1½ hours or until dry. Turn oven off; let meringues cool in oven at least 12 hours.
4. Carefully remove meringue nests from paper. Fill each meringue with Pastry Cream; top with fruit. Gently brush fruit with jelly. Sprinkle each serving with cocoa, if desired. Yield: 8 servings (serving size: 1 meringue, 2 tablespoons Pastry Cream, 1 orange section, 1 kiwi slice, and 1½ teaspoons blueberries).

CALORIES 130 (9% from fat); FAT 1.3g (sat 0.1g, mono 0g, poly 0g); PROTEIN 3.8g; CARB 26.2g; FIBER 1.3g; CHOL 0mg; IRON 28.9mg; SODIUM 45mg; CALC 53mg

Pastry Cream:

- 1 cup 1% low-fat milk
- 3 tablespoons sugar
- 1 tablespoon plus 1 teaspoon cornstarch
- 1 large egg
- ½ teaspoon vanilla extract

1. Combine first 4 ingredients in top of a double boiler; cook over simmering water, stirring constantly with a whisk, 8 minutes or until thick. Remove from heat; stir in vanilla. Pour into a bowl; cover surface of cream with plastic wrap. Chill. Yield: 1 cup.

CHOCOLATE-ALMOND MERINGUE COOKIES

- ⅓ cup slivered almonds, ground
- ½ teaspoon cornstarch
- ½ teaspoon ground cinnamon
- 1 (1-ounce) square semisweet chocolate, grated
- 2 large egg whites (at room temperature)
- ⅛ teaspoon cream of tartar
- ¾ cup sifted powdered sugar
- ¼ teaspoon almond extract
- Vegetable cooking spray

1. Preheat oven to 300°.
2. Combine ground almonds, cornstarch, cinnamon, and grated chocolate in a bowl; set aside.

TIPS FOR WHIPPING UP CHOCOLATE CLOUD DESSERTS

- Eggs are easier to separate when cold, but beat up to a greater volume at room temperature. For best results, separate eggs as soon as you take them out of the refrigerator, then let them come to room temperature.
- When the humidity is high, add 1 teaspoon of cornstarch along with the sugar when making a meringue. This will help stabilize the egg whites.
- Cream of tartar increases volume and stabilizes the egg whites, especially during baking.
- The best way to remove a bit of yolk is by dabbing it with a small piece of bread; the speck will usually cling to the bread. Egg whites that contain even a speck of yolk will not whip up to maximum volume.
- Always use a clean bowl and beaters to beat egg whites. Even the smallest speck of dirt or grease will prevent the whites from achieving full volume.

3. Beat egg whites and cream of tartar at high speed of an electric mixer until foamy. Gradually add sugar, beating until stiff peaks form. Add almond extract, and beat until blended. Gently fold in chocolate mixture.

4. Drop egg white mixture by level tablespoons 2 inches apart onto a baking sheet coated with cooking spray. Bake at 300° for 45 minutes. Remove cookies from baking sheet; let cool on wire racks. Yield: 2 dozen (serving size: 1 cookie).

CALORIES 33 (35% from fat); FAT 1.3g (sat 0.3g, mono 0.7g, poly 0.2g); PROTEIN 0.8g; CARB 4.8g; FIBER 0.3g; CHOL 0mg; IRON 0.2mg; SODIUM 4mg; CALC 6mg

CHOCOLATE-COCONUT CUPCAKES

- 3 tablespoons unsweetened cocoa
- 1 teaspoon ground cinnamon
- ½ cup boiling water
- ⅔ cup plain fat-free yogurt
- 1 teaspoon baking soda
- ½ cup sugar
- 2 tablespoons margarine, melted
- 1 large egg yolk
- 1 cup all-purpose flour
- 3 tablespoons shredded sweetened coconut
- 1 teaspoon vanilla extract
- ½ teaspoon almond extract
- 1 large egg white (at room temperature)
- ¼ teaspoon salt
- 1½ tablespoons water
- 1 teaspoon margarine
- ½ ounce semisweet chocolate, chopped
- 1 cup sifted powdered sugar
- ½ teaspoon ground cinnamon
- ½ teaspoon vanilla extract

1. Preheat oven to 350°.
2. Place 12 paper muffin cup liners in muffin cups; set aside.
3. Combine cocoa and 1 teaspoon cinnamon in a small bowl. Add boiling water, stirring until cocoa dissolves; set aside.
4. Combine yogurt and baking soda.
5. Combine ½ cup sugar, 2 tablespoons margarine, and yolk. Beat at

STEP-BY-STEP TO PERFECT EGG WHITES

❶ *Beat egg whites and cream of tartar at high speed of an electric mixer until foamy.*

❷ *Gradually add sugar, 1 tablespoon at a time, beating at high speed of mixer.*

❸ *At soft-peak stage, the egg whites will gently fold over when beaters are pulled away.*

❹ *When glossy peaks form, the egg whites are stiff, and they'll stand up when the beaters are pulled away.*

high speed of an electric mixer 1 minute. Add cocoa mixture, yogurt mixture, flour, coconut, 1 teaspoon vanilla, and almond extract; mix well.
6. Beat egg white and salt at high speed until stiff peaks form; fold into batter. Spoon batter evenly into prepared muffin cups. Bake at 350° for 20 minutes or until cupcakes spring back when touched lightly in center.
7. Combine 1½ tablespoons water, 1 teaspoon margarine, and chocolate in a small saucepan. Cook over medium-low heat, stirring constantly, until chocolate melts. Remove saucepan from heat; stir in powdered sugar, ½ teaspoon cinnamon, and ½ teaspoon vanilla. Spread 2 teaspoons glaze over each warm cupcake. Let cool on wire racks. Yield: 1 dozen (serving size: 1 cupcake).

CALORIES 164 (21% from fat); FAT 3.9g (sat 1.4g, mono 1.3g, poly 0.8g); PROTEIN 2.9g; CARB 29.6g; FIBER 0.4g; CHOL 18mg; IRON 1mg; SODIUM 199mg; CALC 36mg

DEVILISH ANGEL FOOD CAKE

(pictured on page 38)

⅔ cup sifted cake flour
⅓ cup unsweetened cocoa
¼ cup sugar
½ teaspoon ground cinnamon
12 large egg whites (at room temperature)
1 teaspoon cream of tartar
2 teaspoons warm water
1 teaspoon vanilla extract
½ teaspoon salt
1 cup sugar

1. Preheat oven to 350°.
2. Sift together first 4 ingredients in a bowl, and set aside.
3. Beat egg whites, cream of tartar, warm water, vanilla extract, and salt in a large bowl at high speed of an electric mixer until foamy. Gradually add 1 cup sugar, 2 tablespoons at a time, beating mixture until stiff peaks form. Sift flour mixture, ¼ cup at a time, over egg white mixture, gently folding until combined.
4. Spoon batter into an ungreased 10-inch tube pan, spreading evenly. Break air pockets by cutting through batter with a knife. Bake at 350° for 45 minutes or until cake springs back when lightly touched. Invert pan; let cool completely. Loosen cake from sides of pan using a narrow spatula. Remove cake from pan; place on plate. Yield: 8 servings.

CALORIES 196 (3% from fat); FAT 0.6g (sat 0.3g, mono 0g, poly 0.1g); PROTEIN 6.9g; CARB 41g; FIBER 0g; CHOL 0mg; IRON 1.4mg; SODIUM 227mg; CALC 12mg

CHOCOLATE-SOUFFLÉED CRÊPES

These crêpes are best served immediately from the oven.

½ cup all-purpose flour
½ cup 1% low-fat milk
2 teaspoons sugar
2 teaspoons vegetable oil
1 large egg
Vegetable cooking spray
2 tablespoons sugar
2 tablespoons unsweetened cocoa
2 teaspoons all-purpose flour
¼ cup 1% low-fat milk
1 large egg yolk
1 teaspoon vanilla extract
3 large egg whites (at room temperature)
1 tablespoon sugar
Chocolate Sauce
1 tablespoon powdered sugar
Orange rind strips (optional)

1. Place ½ cup flour in a medium bowl. Combine ½ cup milk, 2 teaspoons sugar, oil, and 1 egg; add milk mixture to flour, stirring with a whisk until almost smooth. Cover and chill 1 hour.
2. Coat an 8-inch crêpe pan or non-stick skillet with cooking spray; place over medium-high heat until hot. Remove pan from heat. Pour a scant ¼ cup batter into pan; quickly tilt pan in all directions so batter covers pan with a thin film. Cook about 1 minute. Carefully lift edge of crêpe with a spatula to test for doneness. Crêpe is ready to turn when it can be shaken loose from pan and underside is lightly browned. Turn crêpe over; cook 30 seconds.
3. Place crêpe on a towel; let cool. Repeat procedure until all of batter is used. Stack crêpes between single layers of wax paper or paper towels to prevent sticking.
4. Preheat oven to 350°.
5. Combine 2 tablespoons sugar, cocoa, and 2 teaspoons flour in a small saucepan; stir well. Add ¼ cup milk and yolk; stir with a whisk. Place milk mixture over low heat; cook 5 minutes or until thick. Remove from heat. Stir in vanilla. Pour mixture into a large bowl; let cool.

6. Beat egg whites at high speed of an electric mixer until foamy. Gradually add 1 tablespoon sugar, beating until stiff peaks form. Gently fold one-fourth of egg white mixture into chocolate mixture, and gently fold in remaining egg white mixture.
7. Spoon ⅓ cup soufflé mixture into center of each crêpe; fold in half. Place filled crêpes on a baking sheet. Bake at 350° for 10 minutes or until puffy. Spoon Chocolate Sauce over each crêpe; sprinkle with powdered sugar. Garnish with orange rind strips, if desired. Yield: 6 servings (serving size: 1 filled crêpe and 3 tablespoons Chocolate Sauce).

CALORIES 200 (22% from fat); FAT 4.8g (sat 1.6g, mono 1.3g, poly 1.1g); PROTEIN 7.8g; CARB 30.6g; FIBER 0.3g; CHOL 76mg; IRON 1.4mg; SODIUM 76mg; CALC 104mg

Chocolate Sauce:

3 tablespoons sugar
1 tablespoon cornstarch
2 tablespoons unsweetened cocoa
1 cup 1% low-fat milk
½ teaspoon vanilla extract

1. Combine first 4 ingredients in a small saucepan. Bring sugar mixture to a boil, and cook, stirring constantly, 1 minute. Remove from heat. Stir in vanilla. Cover and chill. Yield: 1 cup plus 2 tablespoons (serving size: 3 tablespoons).

CALORIES 55 (11% from fat); FAT 0.7g (sat 0.4g, mono 0.1g, poly 0g); PROTEIN 1.9g; CARB 10.3g; FIBER 0g; CHOL 2mg; IRON 0.3mg; SODIUM 21mg; CALC 53mg

CHILLED CHOCOLATE-BANANA SOUFFLÉ

Once this soufflé chills, it deflates and takes on the consistency of a mousse.

Vegetable cooking spray
2 teaspoons sugar
½ cup sugar
¼ cup all-purpose flour
3 tablespoons unsweetened cocoa
1 cup 1% low-fat milk
2 large egg yolks
½ cup mashed ripe banana
1 tablespoon margarine, melted
1 tablespoon dark rum
1 teaspoon vanilla extract
6 large egg whites (at room temperature)
¼ teaspoon salt
2 tablespoons sugar
½ cup frozen reduced-calorie whipped topping, thawed

1. Preheat oven to 350°.
2. Coat a 2-quart soufflé dish with cooking spray; sprinkle with 2 teaspoons sugar. Set aside.
3. Combine ½ cup sugar, flour, and cocoa in a medium saucepan; gradually add milk, stirring with a whisk until blended. Cook over medium heat, stirring constantly with a whisk, 5 minutes or until thick and bubbly.
4. Beat yolks in a bowl with a whisk. Gradually add chocolate mixture to yolks, stirring constantly with a whisk. Stir in banana and next 3 ingredients.
5. Beat egg whites and salt at high speed of an electric mixer until foamy. Gradually add 2 tablespoons sugar, 1 tablespoon at a time, beating until stiff peaks form. Gently fold one-fourth of egg white mixture into chocolate mixture; gently fold in remaining egg white mixture. Spoon into soufflé dish. Place soufflé dish in a 9-inch square baking pan; add hot water to pan to a depth of 1 inch. Bake at 350° for 55 minutes or until puffy and set. Remove from water; let cool to room temperature. Cover and chill 8 hours. Top with whipped topping. Yield: 8 servings.

CALORIES 169 (21% from fat); FAT 4g (sat 1.5g, mono 1.2g, poly 0.8g); PROTEIN 5.5g; CARB 26.7g; FIBER 0.5g; CHOL 56mg; IRON 0.8mg; SODIUM 151mg; CALC 53mg

Those Harbor Lights

Nantucketers feel that their scallops are the sweetest of them all. Take a culinary journey into Nantucket Harbor with our New England-style recipes.

BOURBON-BACON SCALLOPS

(pictured on page 39)

Serve over rice with a side of snow peas and broccoli.

3 tablespoons minced green onions
2 tablespoons bourbon
2 tablespoons maple syrup
1 tablespoon low-sodium soy sauce
1 tablespoon Dijon mustard
¼ teaspoon pepper
24 large sea scallops (about 1½ pounds)
6 low-sodium bacon slices (4 ounces)
Vegetable cooking spray

1. Combine first 6 ingredients in a bowl. Add scallops; stir gently to coat. Cover and marinate scallops in refrigerator 1 hour, stirring occasionally.
2. Remove scallops from bowl, reserving marinade. Cut each slice of bacon into 4 pieces. Wrap 1 bacon piece around each scallop (bacon might only wrap halfway around scallops if they are very large). Thread scallops onto 4 (12-inch) skewers, leaving some space between scallops so bacon will cook. Place skewers on a broiler pan coated with cooking spray; broil 8 minutes or until bacon is crisp and scallops are done, basting occasionally with reserved marinade (cooking time will vary greatly with size of scallops). Yield: 4 servings (serving size: 6 scallops).

CALORIES 245 (26% from fat); FAT 7g (sat 2g, mono 2.5g, poly 1.1g); PROTEIN 32.4g; CARB 11.3g; FIBER 0.1g; CHOL 68mg; IRON 0.7mg; SODIUM 642mg; CALC 51mg

SCALLOP-AND-VEGETABLE NEWBURG

1 cup diced carrot
1 cup diced zucchini
1½ pounds bay scallops
⅓ cup all-purpose flour
2 cups 2% low-fat milk
1 tablespoon dry sherry
½ teaspoon salt
⅛ teaspoon pepper
Vegetable cooking spray
¾ cup fresh breadcrumbs
3 tablespoons grated fresh Parmesan cheese
1½ tablespoons margarine, melted
3½ cups hot cooked rice

1. Arrange carrot in a steamer basket over boiling water; cover and steam 2 minutes. Add zucchini; steam, covered, 2 minutes or until tender. Set aside.
2. Pat scallops dry with paper towels.
3. Place flour in a large saucepan. Gradually add milk, stirring with a whisk until blended. Place over medium heat; cook, stirring constantly, 5 minutes or until thick. Add scallops; cover and cook 5 minutes or until scallops are done, stirring occasionally. Stir in carrot, zucchini, sherry, salt, and pepper; cook, uncovered, 2 minutes or until thoroughly heated.
4. Spoon mixture into a 2-quart shallow baking dish coated with cooking spray. Combine breadcrumbs, cheese, and margarine; stir well. Sprinkle over scallop mixture. Broil 2 minutes or until golden. Serve over rice. Yield: 7 servings (serving size: 1 cup casserole and ½ cup rice).

CALORIES 308 (16% from fat); FAT 5.6g (sat 1.9g, mono 1.8g, poly 1.2g); PROTEIN 23g; CARB 39.7g; FIBER 1.4g; CHOL 39mg; IRON 1.8mg; SODIUM 458mg; CALC 161mg

SCALLOP-CORN CHOWDER

1 tablespoon margarine
1 cup chopped onion
½ cup diced celery
⅓ cup diced red bell pepper
1 garlic clove, minced
¼ cup all-purpose flour
1½ cups diced red potatoes
1 cup frozen whole-kernel corn
¼ teaspoon salt
¼ teaspoon dried thyme
⅛ teaspoon pepper
3 (8-ounce) bottles clam juice
½ cup water
1 pound bay scallops
¼ cup chopped fresh parsley

1. Melt margarine in a Dutch oven over medium heat. Add onion and next 3 ingredients; sauté 8 minutes or until tender. Sprinkle with flour; stir well. Cook, stirring constantly, 1 minute. Add potato and next 6 ingredients, stirring well. Bring to a boil; cover, reduce heat, and simmer 20 minutes or until potato is tender.
2. Add scallops; cover and cook 4 minutes or until scallops are done. Sprinkle with parsley. Yield: 7 servings (serving size: 1 cup).

CALORIES 150 (14% from fat); FAT 2.3g (sat 0.4g, mono 0.8g, poly 0.8g); PROTEIN 13.5g; CARB 19.4g; FIBER 2g; CHOL 21mg; IRON 0.9mg; SODIUM 428mg; CALC 45mg

COQUILLES ST. JACQUES

Although it's not a New England recipe, you can't have scallops without the classic Coquilles St. Jacques.

½ cup all-purpose flour
1½ pounds sea scallops
2 tablespoons margarine
⅓ cup finely chopped onion
2 tablespoons minced shallots
1 garlic clove, minced
¾ cup dry white wine
⅛ teaspoon salt
⅛ teaspoon dried thyme
⅛ teaspoon ground white pepper
1 bay leaf
¼ cup (1 ounce) shredded Swiss cheese

1. Place flour in a zip-top plastic bag; add scallops. Seal and shake to coat. Remove scallops from bag, shaking off excess flour; set aside.
2. Melt margarine in a large nonstick skillet over medium heat. Add onion, and sauté 3 minutes or until lightly browned. Add shallots and garlic; sauté 1 minute.
3. Add scallops, wine, and next 4 ingredients. Cover, reduce heat, and simmer 4 minutes. Uncover, bring to a boil, and cook 1 minute. Discard bay leaf. Divide scallop mixture evenly among 4 individual gratin dishes. Top each with 1 tablespoon cheese; broil 30 seconds or until cheese melts. Serve scallops immediately. Yield: 4 servings.
Note: Substitute ¾ cup low-salt chicken broth for wine, if desired.

CALORIES 297 (28% from fat); FAT 9.1g (sat 2.5g, mono 3.1g, poly 2.4g); PROTEIN 32.7g; CARB 19.2g; FIBER 0.7g; CHOL 63mg; IRON 1.6mg; SODIUM 437mg; CALC 124mg

PARMESAN-CRUSTED BROILED SCALLOPS

Place the broiler pan on the second rack position in the oven to keep the scallops from burning.

⅓ cup finely crushed onion-flavored Melba toast rounds (about 9)
1 tablespoon grated Parmesan cheese
1 tablespoon minced fresh parsley
¼ teaspoon paprika
¼ teaspoon pepper
1½ pounds sea scallops
1 tablespoon margarine, melted
Vegetable cooking spray
Lemon wedges

1. Combine first 5 ingredients in a large zip-top plastic bag; set aside. Brush scallops with margarine. Add scallops to bag, and seal; shake to coat.
2. Place scallops on a broiler pan coated with cooking spray; broil 10 minutes or until done. Serve with lemon wedges. Yield: 4 servings.

CALORIES 209 (22% from fat); FAT 5.2g (sat 0.9g, mono 1.4g, poly 1.4g); PROTEIN 30.1g; CARB 8.9g; FIBER 0.1g; CHOL 57mg; IRON 0.9mg; SODIUM 390mg; CALC 61mg

CREAMED SCALLOPS, CORN, AND TOMATOES

1 tablespoon margarine
1 cup sliced green onions
1½ pounds bay scallops
2 tablespoons all-purpose flour
1 teaspoon dried basil
½ teaspoon salt
½ teaspoon dried thyme
Dash to ¼ teaspoon ground red pepper
1½ cups frozen whole-kernel corn, thawed
½ cup whole milk
1 (14½-ounce) can diced tomatoes, drained

1. Melt margarine in a large nonstick skillet over medium-high heat. Add green onions and scallops; sauté 3 minutes. Add flour and next 4 ingredients, stirring until blended. Stir in corn, milk, and tomato; bring to a boil, and cook, stirring constantly, 2 minutes or until slightly thick. Yield: 4 servings (serving size: 1¼ cups).

CALORIES 301 (17% from fat); FAT 5.8g (sat 1.5g, mono 1.7g, poly 1.5g); PROTEIN 33.5g; CARB 30.7g; FIBER 3.5g; CHOL 60mg; IRON 7.8mg; SODIUM 797mg; CALC 220mg

WINE PICKS

- *Atlas Peak Napa Valley Chardonnay 1995 (California white), $16*
- *Bernardus Sauvignon Blanc 1995 (California white), $12*

ENTERTAINING

Long Nights, Little Bites

A cold winter's evening is the perfect time for an imaginative, easy-to-do Russian buffet.

Who knows better than the Russians how to get through a long, cold winter night? Think of thick novels, five-hour operas, four-act plays, and candlelight dinners in which all the guests arrive via horse-drawn sleighs.

In honor of the Russians, and the season, we've put together a menu of *zakuski*, or "little bites." These easy-to-make appetizers are perfect for entertaining guests.

RUSSIAN BEAN SALAD

2 small tomatoes, each cut into 4 wedges
Vegetable cooking spray
½ teaspoon salt, divided
⅛ teaspoon pepper
3 tablespoons red wine vinegar
2 tablespoons low-salt chicken broth
2 teaspoons olive oil
¼ teaspoon Dijon mustard
Dash of sugar
1 garlic clove
1 teaspoon minced fresh cilantro
1 cup diced red onion
1 cup diced yellow bell pepper
¼ cup minced fresh cilantro
1 (19-ounce) can kidney beans, drained
1 (19-ounce) can cannellini beans or other white beans, drained

1. Preheat oven to 350°.
2. Place tomato wedges on a baking sheet coated with cooking spray. Lightly coat tomatoes with cooking spray; sprinkle with ¼ teaspoon salt and ⅛ teaspoon pepper. Bake at 350° for 1 hour.
3. Place tomatoes, ¼ teaspoon salt, vinegar, and next 5 ingredients in a blender; cover and process until smooth. Pour into a bowl. Stir in 1 teaspoon cilantro; set aside.
4. Combine diced onion, bell pepper, ¼ cup cilantro, and beans in a bowl; stir well. Add tomato mixture, and toss well. Yield: 10 servings (serving size: ½ cup).

CALORIES 124 (15% from fat); FAT 2.1g (sat 0.3g, mono 0.9g, poly 0.6g); PROTEIN 6.7g; CARB 20.9g; FIBER 3.3g; CHOL 0mg; IRON 2.4mg; SODIUM 265mg; CALC 35mg

POOR MAN'S CAVIAR

2 (1-pound) eggplants
2 tablespoons olive oil
1½ cups finely chopped onion
1 cup finely chopped green bell pepper
1 cup finely chopped red bell pepper
3 garlic cloves, minced
⅓ cup chopped fresh parsley
1 tablespoon sugar
2 tablespoons tomato paste
2 tablespoons lemon juice
1 teaspoon salt
1 teaspoon dried basil
⅛ teaspoon pepper
1 (16-ounce) can crushed tomatoes, undrained

1. Preheat oven to 400°.
2. Pierce eggplants with a fork; place on an aluminum foil-lined baking sheet. Bake at 400° for 45 minutes or until tender. Let cool slightly; peel and finely chop. Place eggplant in a colander; let drain.
3. Heat oil in a large nonstick skillet over medium-high heat. Add onion, bell peppers, and garlic; sauté 8 minutes or until tender. Stir in eggplant, parsley, and remaining ingredients. Cover, reduce heat, and simmer 1 hour, stirring occasionally. Serve warm or chilled with assorted raw vegetables or toasted pumpernickel bread triangles. Yield: 5 cups (serving size: ¼ cup).

CALORIES 42 (34% from fat); FAT 1.2g (sat 0.2g, mono 1g, poly 0.2g); PROTEIN 1.2g; CARB 7g; FIBER 1.4g; CHOL 0mg; IRON 0.8mg; SODIUM 152mg; CALC 32mg

CELERIAC SALAD

Celeriac is also known as celery root. To keep it from turning brown, peel and grate just before adding the dressing.

   2 whole garlic heads
Vegetable cooking spray
   ½ teaspoon salt, divided
   ¼ teaspoon pepper, divided
   ½ cup low-fat sour cream
   ⅓ cup low-salt chicken broth
   ¼ cup white wine vinegar
   1 teaspoon Dijon mustard
   ½ teaspoon sugar
   6 cups peeled, shredded celeriac
      (about 1½ pounds)
   ¼ cup minced fresh chives

1. Preheat oven to 400°.
2. Remove white papery skin from garlic heads (do not peel or separate cloves). Cut ¼ inch from top of each head; lightly coat cut surfaces with cooking spray. Sprinkle with ¼ teaspoon salt and ⅛ teaspoon pepper. Wrap each head separately in aluminum foil. Bake at 400° for 45 minutes; let cool 10 minutes. Separate cloves, and squeeze to extract garlic pulp; discard skins.
3. Place garlic pulp, ¼ teaspoon salt, ⅛ teaspoon pepper, sour cream, and next 4 ingredients in a blender; cover and process until smooth. Pour dressing into a bowl; cover and chill 2 hours.
4. Combine celeriac and chives in a large bowl; add dressing, and toss well. Serve immediately. Yield: 8 servings (serving size: ½ cup).

CALORIES 95 (23% from fat); FAT 2.4g (sat 1.2g, mono 0.6g, poly 0.3g); PROTEIN 3.4g; CARB 17.2g; FIBER 1.8g; CHOL 6mg; IRON 1.2mg; SODIUM 295mg; CALC 97mg

---

> **MENU SUGGESTION**
>
> *Meat loaf*
>
> RICE-STUFFED CABBAGE
> LEAVES
>
> *Caramel banana splits**
>
> *Place 6 peeled, halved bananas on a baking sheet coated with cooking spray. Brush with fat-free caramel sundae syrup; broil 4 minutes. Serve with fat-free frozen yogurt and additional syrup.

RICE-STUFFED CABBAGE LEAVES

This dish is considered an appetizer, but it can be served as a side dish.

  12 large green cabbage leaves
   1 tablespoon olive oil
   2 cups thinly sliced leek
1½ cups finely chopped celery
   1 cup finely chopped carrot
   2 garlic cloves, minced
   1 cup uncooked basmati rice
1⅔ cups low-salt chicken broth, divided
   ¼ teaspoon fennel seeds, crushed
   2 tablespoons chopped fresh parsley
   ½ teaspoon salt
   2 cups chopped onion
   2 tablespoons chopped fresh parsley
   1 tablespoon lemon juice
   1 teaspoon sugar
   ½ teaspoon salt
   1 garlic clove, minced
   1 (28-ounce) can plum tomatoes, undrained and chopped
   ⅓ cup finely chopped pimento-stuffed green olives
   ¼ teaspoon pepper
Vegetable cooking spray

1. Arrange cabbage leaves in a steamer basket over boiling water. Cover and steam 3 minutes; set aside.
2. Heat oil in a nonstick skillet over medium heat. Add leek and next 3 ingredients; sauté 7 minutes. Add rice, 1 cup broth, and fennel seeds; cover and cook 7 minutes or until liquid is nearly absorbed.
3. Combine rice mixture, 2 tablespoons parsley, and ½ teaspoon salt in a bowl; toss well, and set aside.
4. Add ⅓ cup broth to skillet; place over medium heat until hot. Add onion; cook 10 minutes, stirring occasionally. Add remaining ⅓ cup broth, 2 tablespoons parsley, lemon juice, and next 4 ingredients; bring to a boil. Cover, reduce heat, and simmer 10 minutes. Remove from heat; stir in olives and pepper. Set sauce aside.
5. Preheat oven to 400°.
6. Spoon ⅓ cup rice mixture onto each cabbage leaf; roll up jelly-roll fashion. Place rolls in a 13 x 9-inch baking dish coated with cooking spray. Spoon sauce over rolls. Cover and bake at 400° for 1 hour. Yield: 12 servings (serving size: 1 cabbage roll and ⅓ cup sauce).

CALORIES 137 (14% from fat); FAT 2.2g (sat 0.4g, mono 1.2g, poly 0.4g); PROTEIN 3.9g; CARB 26.9g; FIBER 3.9g; CHOL 0mg; IRON 2.4.mg; SODIUM 383mg; CALC 89mg

---

BLINI WITH SMOKED SALMON AND DILLED ONION COMPOTE

Although traditional blini (buckwheat pancakes) are served with butter, this low-fat version calls for smoked salmon and onion relish. If you don't have buckwheat flour, use all-purpose flour.

   ½ teaspoon sugar
   1 package dry yeast
   2 tablespoons warm water (105° to 115°)
2½ cups low-fat buttermilk
   1 tablespoon vegetable oil
   1 large egg
1½ cups all-purpose flour
   ½ cup buckwheat flour
   1 tablespoon sugar
   ½ teaspoon baking powder
   ½ teaspoon baking soda
Dash of salt
   2 large egg whites (at room temperature)
   8 ounces thinly sliced smoked salmon, cut into ¼-inch-wide strips
Dilled Onion Compote

1. Combine ½ teaspoon sugar and yeast in warm water in a large bowl; let stand 5 minutes. Add buttermilk, oil, and 1 egg; stir with a whisk until smooth. Combine all-purpose flour and next 5 ingredients; stir well. Add to yeast mixture; stir until smooth. Cover and chill 8 hours.

2. Beat egg whites at high speed of an electric mixer until stiff peaks form. Gently fold egg whites into batter. Spoon about 1 tablespoon batter for each pancake onto a hot nonstick griddle or nonstick skillet. Turn pancakes when tops are covered with bubbles and edges look cooked.

3. Divide salmon strips evenly among pancakes, and top each with about 1 teaspoon Dilled Onion Compote. Yield: 6 dozen (serving size: 1 appetizer).

CALORIES 29 (22% from fat); FAT 0.7g (sat 0.2g, mono 0.2g, poly 0.2g); PROTEIN 1.6g; CARB 4.2g; FIBER 0.2g; CHOL 4mg; IRON 0.2mg; SODIUM 58mg; CALC 17mg

Dilled Onion Compote:

    2 cups chopped red onion
    ¼ cup fresh lemon juice
    ¼ cup water
    2 tablespoons sugar
    ½ teaspoon salt
    ⅓ cup low-fat sour cream
    3 tablespoons minced fresh
          dillweed

1. Combine first 5 ingredients in a heavy-duty, zip-top plastic bag, and seal; shake to coat. Marinate in refrigerator 8 hours; turn bag occasionally.

2. Drain onion, and rinse under cold water; drain well. Combine onion, sour cream, and dillweed in a bowl, stirring well. Store in an airtight container in refrigerator up to 3 days. Yield: 1½ cups (serving size: 1 teaspoon).

PIROSHKI

Piroshki are little turnovers that can be either sweet or savory. This version uses a commercial bread dough which dramatically cuts the fat.

    6 cups thinly sliced napa
          (Chinese) cabbage
    1 tablespoon salt
    1 tablespoon olive oil
    1¾ cups chopped onion
    ½ cup finely chopped carrot
    1 pound lean ground lamb
    ¼ cup chopped fresh cilantro
    2 garlic cloves, minced
    2 tablespoons low-fat sour cream
    1 (2-pound) package frozen
          white bread dough, thawed
Vegetable cooking spray
    1 large egg white, lightly beaten

1. Combine cabbage and salt in a large bowl; toss well. Let stand 1 hour. Drain well. Pat cabbage dry with a paper towel. Return to bowl; set aside.

2. Heat oil in a large nonstick skillet over medium heat. Add onion; sauté 4 minutes. Stir in carrot; cover, reduce heat to low, and cook 8 minutes. Add lamb, cilantro, and garlic; cook, uncovered, over medium-high heat until lamb is browned, stirring to crumble. Drain lamb mixture in a colander; pat dry with paper towels. Add lamb mixture and sour cream to cabbage; toss well.

3. Preheat oven to 350°.

4. Divide dough into 30 equal portions. Working with 1 portion at a time (cover remaining portions to keep from drying out), roll into a 4-inch circle on a lightly floured surface. Spoon 2 heaping tablespoons cabbage mixture onto half of circle. Fold dough over filling; press edges together with a fork to seal. Place turnover on a baking sheet coated with cooking spray, and brush with egg white. Repeat procedure with remaining dough, cabbage mixture, and egg white.

5. Bake at 350° for 25 minutes or until golden. Serve warm. Yield: 2½ dozen (serving size: 1 appetizer).

CALORIES 105 (22% from fat); FAT 2.6g (sat 0.7g, mono 1.1g, poly 0.4g); PROTEIN 6g; CARB 14.3g; FIBER 0.4g; CHOL 10mg; IRON 1mg; SODIUM 276mg; CALC 37mg

Castle Cuisine

Philip McGrath remembers his first sight of the historic Castle at Tarrytown in Tarrytown, New York, (a private residence at the time) when he was 10. "It looked gigantic standing on top of Westchester County's highest hill. I wondered how I could ever get in. I was convinced there must be a moat and a dungeon." He found neither—but, luckily, he did find the kitchen when he was hired last May as executive chef. And there's no Henry VIII-type cuisine here; instead, McGrath prepares low-fat and vegetarian dishes, as well as personalized menus with touches of light fare.

"We've developed lighter recipes that taste full and complete—not skimpy or spa-type food," he says. Examples include appetizers like Smoked Salmon in Endive Leaves and Roasted New Potatoes Filled with Corn and Shrimp.

SMOKED SALMON IN ENDIVE LEAVES

    1 tablespoon chopped fresh
          parsley
    2 tablespoons fresh lemon juice
    1 tablespoon capers
    1 teaspoon minced onion
    ½ teaspoon Dijon mustard
    ⅛ teaspoon pepper
    4 ounces smoked salmon,
          chopped
   24 Belgian endive leaves
Parsley sprigs (optional)

1. Combine first 7 ingredients in a bowl; stir well. Spoon 1½ teaspoons mixture onto each endive leaf. Garnish with parsley sprigs, if desired. Yield: 2 dozen (serving size: 2 appetizers).

CALORIES 28 (19% from fat); FAT 0.6g (sat 0.2g, mono 0.2g, poly 0.2g); PROTEIN 2.8g; CARB 3.8g; FIBER 0g; CHOL 2mg; IRON 0.6mg; SODIUM 144mg; CALC 2mg

ROASTED NEW POTATOES FILLED WITH CORN AND SHRIMP

12 small red potatoes (about 1½ pounds)
¼ teaspoon salt
¼ teaspoon pepper
Vegetable cooking spray
1 tablespoon olive oil
1½ cups frozen whole-kernel corn, thawed and drained
3 tablespoons minced green onions
2 tablespoons cider vinegar
1 teaspoon chopped fresh or ¼ teaspoon dried tarragon
24 small shrimp, cooked and peeled
Fresh tarragon (optional)

1. Cut each potato in half crosswise; scoop out pulp, leaving a ¼-inch-thick shell; reserve pulp for another use. Sprinkle insides of potato shells with salt and pepper. Place potato shells upside down on a baking sheet coated with cooking spray. Bake at 450° for 15 minutes; set aside.
2. Heat oil in a medium skillet over medium-high heat. Add corn and green onions; sauté 2 minutes. Add vinegar and chopped tarragon; cook 1 minute. Divide corn mixture evenly among potato shells; top each with 1 shrimp. Garnish with fresh tarragon, if desired. Yield: 2 dozen (serving size: 2 appetizers).

CALORIES 90 (16% from fat); FAT 1.6g (sat 0.2g, mono 1g, poly 0.2g); PROTEIN 5.6g; CARB 14g; FIBER 1.6g; CHOL 34mg; IRON 1.4mg; SODIUM 94mg; CALC 18mg

Souper Bowl Champs

You'll keep plenty warm this winter with these prize-winning soups and stews.

When we invited readers to send us a low-fat soup or stew recipe to warm us in the winter, we were bowled over: Almost 2,000 recipes poured in to our Souper Bowl Contest. After evaluating each recipe for lightness, ease of preparation, originality, and taste, we crowned the following Souper Bowl champs.

For Grand Prize Winner Beda Lovitt of Helena, Montana, combining flavors for her stew wasn't as difficult as measuring ingredients. "I'm more of a dump-and-pinch cook. I think measuring my ingredients was the hardest thing I had to do." Her stew reflects her love of combining regional tastes. "I have lived in a lot of places and tried many different dishes, and the sweet-and-sour taste of the Caribbean is one of my favorites. Adding the molasses and vinegar provided just the right touch."

ISLAND BEEF STEW

—Grand Prize Winner Beda Lovitt, Helena, Montana

3 pounds lean, boned chuck roast
3 tablespoons all-purpose flour
1 tablespoon olive oil
2 (14.5-ounce) cans no-salt-added whole tomatoes, undrained and chopped
3 cups vertically sliced onion
1¼ teaspoons pepper
1 teaspoon salt
2 cups water
⅓ cup molasses
⅓ cup white vinegar
2½ cups thinly sliced carrot (about 1 pound)
½ cup raisins
½ teaspoon ground ginger

1. Trim fat from beef. Dredge beef in flour. Heat oil in a large Dutch oven; add beef, browning on all sides. Add tomato, onion, pepper, and salt. Combine water, molasses, and vinegar; stir into beef mixture. Cover, reduce heat, and simmer 1 hour and 15 minutes or until beef is tender. Stir in carrot, raisins, and ginger; simmer 30 additional minutes or until carrot is tender.
2. Remove roast from Dutch oven. Separate roast into bite-size pieces, and shred with 2 forks. Return shredded roast to Dutch oven. Yield: 9 servings (serving size: 1 cup).

CALORIES 277 (24% from fat); FAT 7.3g (sat 2.4g, mono 3.3g, poly 0.5g); PROTEIN 26.1g; CARB 27.3g; FIBER 2.2g; CHOL 68mg; IRON 4.3mg; SODIUM 365mg; CALC 82mg

GINGERED WINTER SQUASH-AND-ROOT VEGETABLE SOUP

Jan Greenberg of Rhinebeck, New York, says she's forever creating new soups. She decided to send in this particular recipe to urge people to use winter vegetables. "Winter squashes and root vegetables are so delicious when flavored properly. They should be used much more than they are."

- 2 tablespoons vegetable oil
- 1 large onion, cut into 1-inch pieces
- 1 teaspoon ground ginger
- ½ teaspoon salt
- ½ teaspoon ground cumin
- ½ teaspoon dry mustard
- ¼ teaspoon ground mace
- ¼ teaspoon ground cinnamon
- ¼ teaspoon black pepper
- ⅛ teaspoon ground red pepper
- 6 cups peeled, cubed butternut squash (about 2 pounds)
- 2½ cups peeled, cubed sweet potato (about ¾ pound)
- ¾ cup (1-inch-thick) sliced parsnip
- 5 (10½-ounce) cans low-salt chicken broth
- 1 cup skim milk

1. Heat oil in a large stockpot over medium heat. Add onion and next 8 ingredients; sauté 2 minutes. Reduce heat to low; cover and cook 5 minutes or until onion is tender. Add squash, sweet potato, parsnip, and broth. Bring to a boil; reduce heat, and simmer, partially covered, 30 minutes or until tender.
2. Place one-third of vegetable mixture in a blender or food processor; cover and process until smooth. Pour puréed mixture into a large bowl. Repeat procedure with remaining vegetable mixture. Return puréed mixture to stockpot; stir in milk. Cook over low heat 5 minutes or until thoroughly heated, stirring occasionally. Yield: 11 servings (serving size: 1 cup).

CALORIES 128 (26% from fat); FAT 3.7g (sat 0.8g, mono 1.1g, poly 1.4g); PROTEIN 3.6g; CARB 21.7g; FIBER 2.5g; CHOL 0mg; IRON 1.5mg; SODIUM 172mg; CALC 69mg

SALMON BISQUE

Marilou Robinson of Portland, Oregon, considers lightening her heavier dishes a labor of love: "I started cooking lighter when I found out my husband had heart trouble. Lightening recipes like this bisque was a challenge—but if you have the heavier version loaded with bacon and butter, you wish you'd never eaten it. I think we simply feel better when we eat lighter."

- 1 tablespoon vegetable oil
- 1 cup chopped onion
- 1 cup chopped celery
- 4 cups peeled, chopped baking potato
- ¼ cup finely chopped fresh parsley
- 1 teaspoon white pepper
- ½ teaspoon salt
- 2 (14¼-ounce) cans no-salt-added chicken broth
- ¼ cup dry white wine
- 2 (12-ounce) cans evaporated skim milk
- 1 teaspoon lemon juice
- 1 (1-pound) salmon fillet, skinned and cut into ½-inch pieces
- 2 tablespoons chopped fresh parsley

1. Heat oil in a Dutch oven over medium heat. Add onion and celery; sauté 10 minutes or until tender. Add potato and next 4 ingredients. Bring to a boil; reduce heat, and simmer 20 minutes or until tender.
2. Place potato mixture in container of an electric blender or food processor; cover and process until smooth. Return puréed mixture to Dutch oven; stir in wine and milk. Cover and cook over medium-low heat 15 minutes, stirring occasionally. Add lemon juice and fish; cook 10 minutes or until fish flakes easily when tested with a fork, stirring frequently. Sprinkle with 2 tablespoons parsley. Yield: 10 servings (serving size: 1 cup).

CALORIES 186 (18% from fat); FAT 3.8g (sat 0.6g, mono 0.9g, poly 1.3g); PROTEIN 16.4g; CARB 20.8g; FIBER 1.6g; CHOL 26mg; IRON 1.3mg; SODIUM 287mg; CALC 214mg

CARAMELIZED ONION-AND-ROASTED GARLIC BISQUE

Runner-up Barbara Lento of Aliquippa, Pennsylvania, was feeling adventurous when she created this bisque.

- 1 large whole garlic head
- 1½ tablespoons olive oil, divided
- 9 cups thinly sliced Vidalia or other sweet onion (about 4 large)
- 2½ cups sliced leek (about 2 medium)
- 1 teaspoon salt, divided
- 1 teaspoon dried thyme
- 2 tablespoons all-purpose flour
- ⅓ cup dry white wine
- 3 (10½-ounce) cans low-salt chicken broth
- 2 cups 2% low-fat milk
- ¼ cup plus 2 tablespoons fat-free sour cream

1. Preheat oven to 350°.
2. Remove white papery skin from garlic head (do not peel or separate cloves). Rub 1½ teaspoons oil over garlic head; wrap in aluminum foil. Bake at 350° for 1 hour; let cool 10 minutes. Separate cloves; squeeze to extract pulp. Discard skins. Set pulp aside.
3. Heat remaining 1 tablespoon oil in a Dutch oven over medium heat. Add onion and leek; cook 30 minutes, stirring often. Add ½ teaspoon salt and thyme. Cook 30 minutes or until onion is golden, stirring occasionally. Stir in flour. Add wine and broth; bring mixture to a boil. Reduce heat, and simmer 30 minutes. Add garlic pulp, remaining ½ teaspoon salt, and milk; simmer 8 minutes or until thoroughly heated.
4. Place half of onion mixture in a blender. Cover and process until smooth; pour mixture into a bowl. Repeat procedure with remaining onion mixture. Garnish with sour cream. Yield: 6 servings (serving size: 1 cup soup and 1 tablespoon sour cream).

CALORIES 249 (24% from fat); FAT 6.6g (sat 1.8g, mono 3.4g, poly 0.8g); PROTEIN 9.8g; CARB 40.1g; FIBER 5.5g; CHOL 7mg; IRON 2.8mg; SODIUM 510mg; CALC 200mg

GRUBBIN' SPICY CHICKEN SOUP

As a graphic designer, Patty McNally of Portland, Oregon, finds that her natural creativity tends to flow into her kitchen. "Cooking is an artistic and creative outlet for me. It mellows me out after work," she says. Her flair for the unique and an ability to appeal to friends' palates led to the creation of her Grubbin' Spicy Chicken Soup. "It's not your straightforward chili—I wanted something different. Now every time I have company, they want my chicken soup."

 1 tablespoon olive oil
 1 cup diced sweet onion
 2 tablespoons chili powder
 1 tablespoon grated orange rind
 1 teaspoon dried crushed red
   pepper
 4 garlic cloves, minced
 2 cups shredded cooked
   chicken breast
 ½ cup fresh orange juice
 4 (10½-ounce) cans low-salt
   chicken broth, divided
 2 cups red bell pepper strips
 ⅓ cup (1-inch) julienne-cut carrot
 ⅓ cup seeded, diced Anaheim
   chile
 2 tablespoons seeded, diced
   jalapeño pepper
 ½ teaspoon salt
 4 cups coarsely chopped green
   cabbage
 4 cups vegetable juice
 1 cup uncooked wild rice
 1 tablespoon chili powder
 4 plum tomatoes, each cut into
   8 wedges
 3 cups drained canned navy beans
 ½ cup low-fat sour cream

1. Heat oil in a large nonstick skillet over medium heat. Add onion and next 4 ingredients; sauté 4 minutes or until onion is tender. Stir in chicken and orange juice; bring to a boil. Cook, stirring constantly, 2 minutes or until liquid is almost evaporated.
2. Add 1 can broth, and bring to a boil. Stir in bell pepper and next 4 ingredients. Cook over medium heat

15 minutes or until vegetables are tender. Set aside.
3. Combine 3 cans broth, cabbage, and next 4 ingredients in a large Dutch oven; bring to a boil. Reduce heat, and simmer 20 minutes. Add chicken mixture and beans; cook 45 additional minutes. Serve with sour cream. Yield: 8 servings (serving size: 1½ cups soup and 1 tablespoon sour cream).
Note: Make this soup 1 day ahead of time—the flavors meld and become more intense the next day.

CALORIES 383 (22% from fat); FAT 9.3g (sat 2.6g, mono 3.5g, poly 2g); PROTEIN 22.4g; CARB 56.1g; FIBER 10.9g; CHOL 37mg; IRON 4.7mg; SODIUM 990mg; CALC 109mg

---

THE KERR PACKAGE

Sitting Pretty

Pull up a chair (a very special chair) to learn the secrets of healthy living.

This column begins a new series—based on a chair metaphor—that will examine what can happen when you adopt a more interconnected approach to lifestyle change. I'll also share a recipe in each column.

Picture, if you will, a sturdy dining-room chair with four legs, a seat, and an upright back, and see how each element of its construction complements the others. The four legs, for our purposes, represent food, exercise, reflection, and friendship. They are equal in length and spaced evenly to carry the weight. If one of the legs were missing, the chair would be quite useless. The seat should comfortably fit the need and, because each of us is different, let's visualize this seat as a way to settle in, set reasonable goals, and adjust comfortably to change. The chair back, which also helps support us, represents a caring, responsible perception of life that will help us live our lives in compassionate balance with those around us.

Together, we'll explore some practical ways to make creative changes—ones that last a lifetime. And now, here's that recipe I promised.

SLOPPY JOES

 1 teaspoon olive oil
 2 cups chopped mushrooms
 1 cup chopped onion
 ½ cup chopped green bell pepper
 ¼ cup chopped celery
 ¼ cup chopped carrot
 2 garlic cloves, minced
 6 ounces ground turkey breast
 6 ounces ground round
 ¼ cup ketchup
 1 tablespoon red wine vinegar
 1 tablespoon Worcestershire
   sauce
 1 teaspoon dried oregano
 ¼ teaspoon salt
 ¼ teaspoon pepper
 1 (8-ounce) can no-salt-added
   tomato sauce
 6 (1½-ounce) whole-wheat
   hamburger buns, toasted

1. Heat oil in a large skillet over medium-high heat. Add mushrooms and next 7 ingredients; sauté 5 minutes or until meat is browned, stirring to crumble. Stir in ketchup and next 6 ingredients; bring to a boil. Cover, reduce heat, and simmer 20 minutes, stirring occasionally. Serve on toasted hamburger buns. Yield: 6 servings (serving size: 1 bun and ¾ cup meat mixture).

CALORIES 266 (30% from fat); FAT 9g (sat 3g, mono 3.7g, poly 1.1g); PROTEIN 17.1g; CARB 29.8g; FIBER 2.7g; CHOL 49mg; IRON 2.5mg; SODIUM 518mg; CALC 51mg

Once Is Not Enough

Like movies, dinners can also come in sequels. Take our sweet-and-spicy Apricot-Glazed Pork Roast. We've created several days' worth of meals for two from the leftovers. You'll have quick and exciting new dishes, such as a succotash-and-spinach salad, tangy barbecue sandwiches, a pork-and-vegetable fettuccine stir-fry, and Persian rice. Not only does this pork roast have a happy beginning, but it has a happy ending, too.

APRICOT-GLAZED PORK ROAST

(pictured on page 39)

1 (2- to 2¼-pound) boned, rolled pork loin roast
½ cup apricot preserves
1 tablespoon Dijon mustard
1 teaspoon dried thyme
Vegetable cooking spray

1. Preheat oven to 325°.
2. Unroll roast; trim fat. Reroll roast; secure at 1-inch intervals with heavy string. Combine preserves, mustard, and thyme in a bowl; stir. Brush 1 tablespoon apricot mixture over roast. Place on a broiler pan coated with cooking spray. Insert meat thermometer into thickest portion of roast.
3. Bake at 325° for 1 hour and 45 minutes or until meat thermometer registers 160° (slightly pink), basting once with apricot mixture. Let stand 15 minutes before slicing. Bring remaining apricot mixture to a boil; reduce heat, and cook 2 minutes. Serve with roast. Yield: 6 servings (serving size: 3 ounces pork and about 2 teaspoons sauce).

CALORIES 266 (31% from fat); FAT 9.2g (sat 3.1g, mono 4g, poly 1.1g); PROTEIN 27.3g; CARB 18g; FIBER 0g; CHOL 83mg; IRON 1mg; SODIUM 156mg; CALC 19mg

PORK-AND-VEGETABLE ALFREDO

½ teaspoon vegetable oil
1 cup sliced mushrooms
1 cup chopped broccoli
⅓ cup chopped onion
2 cups hot cooked fettuccine (about 4 ounces uncooked pasta)
⅔ cup thinly sliced Apricot-Glazed Pork Roast (about 3 ounces)
⅛ teaspoon pepper
Dash of salt
½ cup light alfredo sauce

1. Heat oil in a nonstick skillet over medium-high heat. Add mushrooms, broccoli, and onion; sauté 5 minutes. Add fettuccine and next 3 ingredients; sauté 2 minutes. Stir in alfredo sauce; cook 1 minute or until heated. Yield: 2 servings (serving size: 1½ cups).

CALORIES 427 (28% from fat); FAT 13.3g (sat 5.4g, mono 2.5g, poly 1.6g); PROTEIN 26.2g; CARB 50.6g; FIBER 4.5g; CHOL 62mg; IRON 3.1mg; SODIUM 345mg; CALC 142mg

PERSIAN RICE

¾ cup finely chopped onion
½ cup uncooked long-grain parboiled rice (such as Uncle Ben's)
¼ teaspoon ground cinnamon
¼ teaspoon ground cloves
Dash of ground nutmeg
½ cup no-salt-added chicken broth
½ cup orange juice
2 tablespoons golden raisins
1 tablespoon lemon juice
¼ teaspoon salt
⅛ teaspoon pepper
¾ cup diced Apricot-Glazed Pork Roast (about 4 ounces)
3 cups chopped fresh spinach
2 tablespoons finely chopped fresh parsley
1 tablespoon slivered almonds, toasted

1. Cook onion in a nonstick skillet over medium-high heat until tender. Add rice and next 3 ingredients; cook 3 minutes, stirring occasionally. Add broth and next 5 ingredients; bring to a boil. Cover; reduce heat. Simmer 20 minutes or until rice is tender and liquid is absorbed. Remove from heat; add pork and spinach. Let stand, covered, 10 minutes. Spoon rice mixture onto individual plates; top with parsley and almonds. Yield: 2 servings (serving size: 1½ cups).

CALORIES 430 (20% from fat); FAT 9.5g (sat 2.5g, mono 4.2g, poly 1.5g); PROTEIN 26.6g; CARB 61g; FIBER 6.6g; CHOL 56mg; IRON 5.2mg; SODIUM 451mg; CALC 159mg

---

MENU SUGGESTION

BARBECUED-PORK SANDWICHES

Potato wedges *

Quick coleslaw *

*Brush potato wedges with olive oil; sprinkle with salt and pepper. Bake at 425° for 45 minutes or until done.
*Toss a bag of angel hair slaw with reduced-fat coleslaw dressing.

BARBECUED-PORK SANDWICHES

¼ cup barbecue sauce
2 teaspoons brown sugar
½ teaspoon lemon juice
½ teaspoon vegetable oil
1 cup sliced onion
½ cup green bell pepper strips
2 (2-ounce) sandwich rolls
¾ cup thinly sliced Apricot-Glazed Pork Roast (about 4 ounces)

1. Preheat oven to 400°.
2. Combine first 3 ingredients in a small bowl. Stir well; set aside.
3. Heat oil in a nonstick skillet over medium-high heat. Add onion and pepper; sauté 6 minutes or until tender. Spread barbecue sauce over cut sides of rolls. Arrange onion mixture and pork on roll bottoms; top with roll tops. Wrap tightly in aluminum foil; bake at 400° for 15 minutes. Yield: 2 servings.

CALORIES 388 (26% from fat); FAT 11.1g (sat 3g, mono 4.5g, poly 2.9g); PROTEIN 25.5g; CARB 46.1g; FIBER 1.7g; CHOL 56mg; IRON 4mg; SODIUM 678mg; CALC 39mg

PORK-AND-SUCCOTASH SPINACH SALAD

4 cups prepackaged spinach
½ cup orange juice
2 tablespoons lime juice
2 teaspoons vegetable oil
½ teaspoon garlic powder
¼ teaspoon ground cumin
¼ teaspoon pepper
4 ounces Apricot-Glazed Pork Roast, cut into strips (about ¾ cup)
¼ cup chopped red onion
1 (8½-ounce) can lima beans, drained
1 (7-ounce) can whole-kernel corn with sweet peppers, drained

1. Remove large stems from spinach; discard stems. Tear spinach into small pieces. Place in a medium bowl, and set aside.
2. Combine orange juice and next 5 ingredients in a 2-cup glass measure. Microwave at HIGH 2 minutes or until mixture boils. Add to spinach, and toss. Add pork and remaining ingredients; toss. Yield: 2 servings (serving size: 2 cups).

CALORIES 426 (25% from fat); FAT 11.9g (sat 3g, mono 4.1g, poly 3.1g); PROTEIN 30g; CARB 52.2g; FIBER 7.4g; CHOL 56mg; IRON 6.8mg; SODIUM 845mg; CALC 163mg

IN SEASON

Perfectly Pears

One of nature's most graceful and polished couplings is wintertime and pears. Think of a whole pear—so firm, so perfect in form—sitting on a plate, lit by candlelight or the distant sun. Or wrapped in paper, as if posing.

When cut in half and cored, a pear is equally stunning, especially when poached in red wine or cranberry juice. Now if a pear had only its good looks to get by on, that would suffice, but it has everything across the board. Tastewise, pears are sweet and spicy, with a subtle, intoxicating perfume.

Although a pear is usually thought of as a fruit to be eaten in its natural state, it's actually as versatile as the apple, especially this time of year. In season in January are the Bosc, Anjou, and Comice pears—the latter considered the Cadillac of pears because of its juiciness. In these recipes, Bosc and Anjou pears can be used interchangeably; firmer than the fall Bartlett, they hold their shapes well when baked (the Comice is better for eating out of hand than for baking).

OLD MAID CAKE

The inspiration for this dessert is tarte Tatin, *the French upside-down apple tart that was created by two unmarried sisters.*

1 cup all-purpose flour
¼ cup firmly packed brown sugar
1 teaspoon baking powder
1 teaspoon ground ginger
1 teaspoon ground cinnamon
½ teaspoon baking soda
¼ teaspoon salt
¼ teaspoon ground cloves
½ cup low-fat buttermilk
¼ cup egg substitute
¼ cup molasses
2 tablespoons stick margarine, melted
2 tablespoons stick margarine
⅓ cup firmly packed brown sugar
3 tablespoons chopped walnuts
2 medium pears (about 1 pound)
Cinnamon sticks (optional)
Pear slices (optional)

1. Preheat oven to 375°.
2. Combine first 8 ingredients in a bowl; stir well. Combine buttermilk, egg substitute, molasses, and 2 tablespoons melted margarine in a bowl; stir well. Add to flour mixture, stirring until smooth.
3. Melt 2 tablespoons margarine in a 9-inch cast-iron skillet. Stir in ⅓ cup brown sugar; cook over medium heat 1 minute. Remove from heat; sprinkle with walnuts.

4. Peel and core pears. Cut each in half lengthwise. Cut each half into thin slices, cutting to, but not through, stem end. Fan pear halves; place, core sides up, on top of brown sugar mixture in skillet.
5. Pour batter over pears; bake at 375° for 35 minutes or until a wooden pick inserted in center comes out clean. Let cool in skillet 5 minutes on a wire rack. Loosen cake from sides of skillet using a narrow metal spatula. Invert onto a cake plate. If desired, garnish with cinnamon sticks and pear slices. Yield: 8 servings (serving size: 1 wedge).

CALORIES 250 (28% from fat); FAT 8g (sat 1.4g, mono 2.9g, poly 3g); PROTEIN 3.9g; CARB 42.5g; FIBER 1.8g; CHOL 0mg; IRON 2mg; SODIUM 248mg; CALC 105mg

QUICK-AND-EASY PEAR COFFEECAKE

Served with a dollop of light whipped topping, this cake is as good for dessert as it is for breakfast.

1¼ cups firmly packed brown sugar
⅓ cup vegetable oil
½ teaspoon almond extract
2 large egg whites
1 large egg
2 cups all-purpose flour
2 teaspoons baking powder
1 teaspoon ground cinnamon
½ teaspoon ground nutmeg
¼ teaspoon salt
¼ teaspoon ground cloves
1¼ cups diced pear
¼ cup dried currants
Vegetable cooking spray

1. Preheat oven to 350°.
2. Combine first 5 ingredients in a large bowl; beat at low speed of an electric mixer until well-blended. Combine flour and next 5 ingredients in a medium bowl; stir well. Gradually add flour mixture to brown sugar mixture; beat just until blended. Stir in pear and currants.
3. Pour batter into a 9-inch square baking pan coated with cooking spray.

Bake at 350° for 40 minutes or until a wooden pick inserted in center comes out clean. Let cool in pan 10 minutes on a wire rack. Yield: 16 servings.

CALORIES 157 (30% from fat); FAT 5.2g (sat 1g, mono 1.5g, poly 2.3g); PROTEIN 2.5g; CARB 25.8g; FIBER 0.8g; CHOL 13mg; IRON 1.1mg; SODIUM 53mg; CALC 41mg

PEAR-WALNUT MUFFINS

A sprinkling of sugar on top gives these muffins a sweet, crispy crust.

1½ cups all-purpose flour
⅔ cup firmly packed brown sugar
½ cup whole-wheat flour or all-purpose flour
1 tablespoon baking powder
½ teaspoon salt
½ teaspoon ground cinnamon
1¼ cups finely chopped pear
⅓ cup coarsely chopped walnuts, toasted
¾ cup 2% low-fat milk
2 tablespoons vegetable oil
1 large egg, lightly beaten
Vegetable cooking spray
1 tablespoon granulated sugar

1. Preheat oven to 400°.
2. Combine first 6 ingredients in a medium bowl; stir well. Add pear and walnuts; toss gently to coat. Make a well in center of mixture. Combine milk, oil, and egg; stir well. Add to flour mixture, stirring just until moist (dough will be sticky).
3. Divide batter evenly among 12 muffin cups coated with cooking spray; sprinkle with granulated sugar. Bake at 400° for 20 minutes or until a wooden pick inserted in center comes out clean. Remove muffins from pans immediately; let cool on a wire rack. Yield: 1 dozen.

CALORIES 175 (27% from fat); FAT 5.3g (sat 0.9g, mono 1.4g, poly 2.6g); PROTEIN 4.3g; CARB 28.6g; FIBER 1.7g; CHOL 20mg; IRON 1.5mg; SODIUM 115mg; CALC 104mg

STEP-BY-STEP FOR PHYLLO PASTRIES

❶ *Spoon pear mixture onto one end of each phyllo stack.*

❷ *Fold left bottom corner over pear mixture, forming a triangle.*

❸ *Keep folding back and forth into triangle to end of phyllo strip.*

PEAR PHYLLO PASTRIES

¼ cup dry breadcrumbs
¼ cup firmly packed brown sugar
3 tablespoons stick margarine, melted
1 tablespoon vegetable oil
½ cup granulated sugar
½ teaspoon ground cinnamon
½ teaspoon almond extract
¼ teaspoon ground nutmeg
4 cups peeled, coarsely chopped pear (about 4 pears)
½ cup dried cranberries
¼ cup chopped almonds, toasted
12 sheets frozen phyllo dough, thawed
Vegetable cooking spray

1. Preheat oven to 350°.
2. Combine breadcrumbs and brown sugar in a bowl. Stir well; set aside. Combine melted margarine and oil in another bowl. Stir well; set aside.
3. Combine granulated sugar and next 3 ingredients in a bowl. Add pear, cranberries, and almonds; toss gently.
4. Working with 1 phyllo sheet at a time (cover remaining dough to keep from drying), brush 1 sheet lightly with margarine mixture. Stack 1 phyllo sheet on top of the first; brush top sheet lightly with melted margarine mixture. Repeat procedure with a third sheet of phyllo, forming a stack of 3 sheets. Sprinkle 2 tablespoons breadcrumb mixture over top of stack. Using a sharp knife or pizza cutter, cut stack lengthwise into 3 (4½-inch-wide) strips.
5. Spoon about ⅓ cup pear mixture onto 1 end of each phyllo strip. For each strip, fold left bottom corner over pear mixture, forming a triangle. Keep folding back and forth into triangle to end of strip. Repeat procedure with remaining sheets of phyllo, margarine mixture, breadcrumb mixture, and pear mixture.
6. Place triangles, seam sides down, on a baking sheet coated with cooking spray. Bake at 350° for 25 minutes or until golden. Serve warm or at room temperature. Yield: 12 servings.
Note: If dried cranberries are unavailable, substitute dried currants or raisins.

CALORIES 216 (12% from fat); FAT 6.6g (sat 1.1g, mono 2.6g, poly 2.4g); PROTEIN 2.5g; CARB 38.4g; FIBER 2.1g; CHOL 0mg; IRON 1.2mg; SODIUM 150mg; CALC 27mg

PEPPER-PEAR RELISH

¾ cup rice vinegar
½ cup firmly packed brown sugar
½ cup chopped red bell pepper
¼ cup minced fresh onion
1 teaspoon seeded, minced jalapeño pepper
⅛ teaspoon black pepper
⅛ teaspoon dried crushed red pepper
3 cups peeled, chopped pear (about 3 medium)

1. Combine first 7 ingredients in a large saucepan, and bring to a boil. Reduce heat to medium, and cook vinegar mixture 10 minutes, stirring occasionally. Stir in pear. Partially cover, reduce heat to low, and simmer 45 minutes or until most of liquid evaporates. Serve warm with chicken or pork. Yield: 6 servings (serving size: ¼ cup).

CALORIES 128 (3% from fat); FAT 0.4g (sat 0g, mono 0.1g, poly 0.1g); PROTEIN 0.5g; CARB 31.7g; FIBER 2.5g; CHOL 0mg; IRON 0.8mg; SODIUM 11mg; CALC 27mg

PEAR COBBLER

If you make the fruit mixture and dough ahead of time, you can assemble the cobbler just before dinner and serve it warm from the oven.

6 cups peeled, sliced pear (about 3 pounds)
⅓ cup firmly packed brown sugar
1 tablespoon all-purpose flour
1 tablespoon lemon juice
½ teaspoon apple pie spice
Vegetable cooking spray
½ cup all-purpose flour
½ cup whole-wheat flour or all-purpose flour
3 tablespoons brown sugar
1 teaspoon baking powder
¼ teaspoon salt
2 tablespoons chilled stick margarine, cut into small pieces
½ cup skim milk
2 teaspoons margarine, melted
1 tablespoon brown sugar

1. Preheat oven to 350°.
2. Combine first 5 ingredients in a large bowl; toss gently to coat. Spoon pear mixture into an 8-inch square baking dish coated with cooking spray.
3. Combine ½ cup all-purpose flour and next 4 ingredients in a medium bowl; cut in 2 tablespoons chilled margarine with a pastry blender or 2 knives until mixture resembles coarse meal. Add milk, and toss with a fork until flour mixture is moist.
4. Drop dough by heaping tablespoons onto pear mixture. Brush melted margarine over dough; sprinkle with 1 tablespoon brown sugar. Bake at 350° for 45 minutes or until lightly browned and bubbly. Yield: 8 servings.

CALORIES 232 (18% from fat); FAT 4.6g (sat 0.8g, mono 1.8g, poly 1.4g); PROTEIN 3g; CARB 47.7g; FIBER 4.4g; CHOL 0mg; IRON 1.4mg; SODIUM 133mg; CALC 86mg

CRANBERRY-POACHED PEARS

Use a melon baller to core the pears.

3 large pears (about 2 pounds)
2 cups cranberry juice cocktail
¼ cup firmly packed brown sugar
1 teaspoon whole cloves
1 (3-inch) cinnamon stick
3 tablespoons low-fat sour cream

1. Peel and core pears. Cut each pear in half lengthwise; set aside.
2. Combine cranberry juice and next 3 ingredients in a large nonaluminum saucepan; bring to a boil. Place pears, cut sides up, in a single layer in pan; cover, reduce heat, and simmer 8 minutes or until pears are tender. Remove from heat; let stand, covered, 20 minutes. Remove pears with a slotted spoon; place in a shallow dish. Cover and chill.
3. Bring juice mixture to a boil; cook 5 minutes or until reduced to 1 cup. Strain juice mixture through a sieve into a small bowl; cover and chill. Discard spices.
4. Arrange 1 pear half, cut side up, on each of 6 dessert plates. Drizzle 2½ tablespoons juice mixture over each pear half; top each with 1½ teaspoons sour cream. Yield: 6 servings.

CALORIES 156 (8% from fat); FAT 1.4g (sat 0.6g, mono 0.4g, poly 0.2g); PROTEIN 0.7g; CARB 37.7g; FIBER 3.2g; CHOL 3mg; IRON 0.6mg; SODIUM 9mg; CALC 29mg

SPICY PEPPERED PEARS IN RED WINE

We used a vanilla bean instead of vanilla extract in the poaching liquid. That's because extracts evaporate when heated, which means the pears won't pick up the vanilla flavor.

4 medium pears (about 2 pounds)
1 (6-inch) vanilla bean, split lengthwise (optional)
⅓ cup sugar
1 tablespoon black peppercorns
5 whole cloves
1 (3-inch) cinnamon stick
1 (750-milliliter) bottle dry red wine
¼ cup crumbled blue cheese

1. Peel and core pears. Cut each pear in half lengthwise; set aside.
2. Scrape seeds from vanilla bean, and place seeds and bean in a large nonaluminum skillet. Add sugar and next 4 ingredients to skillet; bring to a boil over medium heat. Arrange pears, cut sides down, in a single layer in skillet; cover, reduce heat, and simmer 10 minutes. Turn pears over; simmer, covered, 10 additional minutes or until tender. Remove pears with a slotted spoon. Place in a large shallow dish; set aside.
3. Bring wine mixture to a boil; cook 20 minutes or until reduced to ¾ cup. Strain through a sieve into the dish of pears; discard spices. Cover and chill 8 hours, turning pears occasionally. Remove pears with a slotted spoon, reserving wine mixture.
4. Arrange 2 pear halves in each of 4 compotes. Drizzle 3 tablespoons wine mixture over each serving, and top each with 1 tablespoon blue cheese. Yield: 4 servings.

CALORIES 200 (12% from fat); FAT 2.7g (sat 1.4g, mono 0.7g, poly 0.2g); PROTEIN 2.5g; CARB 44.4g; FIBER 4.3g; CHOL 5mg; IRON 1.2mg; SODIUM 114mg; CALC 71mg

Getting Back to Your Roots

When the calendar flips to winter, it's prime time to dig into dishes made with flavorful root vegetables.

While you may be hip to many of the standard root vegetables (plants whose underground parts are edible)—carrots, onions, sweet potatoes—there are many other unique and flavorful varieties out there, such as fennel, rutabagas, leeks, parsnips, and celeriac. Root vegetables are traditionally more robust than spring and summer vegetables, and because of their various textures, they lend themselves to several cooking methods, including sautéing, boiling, baking, and even microwaving.

THE ROOT OF THE MATTER

• **Celeriac:** This rather unattractive vegetable—knobby, hairy, and brown—is also known as celery root. Trim off the ends and peel away the rough exterior and you'll find a creamy, white flesh with a mild flavor. Its intriguing texture combines the crunch of celery with the smoothness of potatoes. Pick small- to medium-size roots that are firm and relatively clean.

• **Fennel:** Resembling a flattened bunch of celery, this root vegetable has a large, white bulb base and feathery green leaves. Fennel is often mislabeled "sweet anise" because it has a licorice flavor, which becomes milder when the vegetable is cooked. Look for firm, white bulbs that show no signs of browning; the stalks should have a fresh, green color.

• **Leeks:** A mild-flavored member of the onion family, leeks resemble giant scallions. Choose ones with clean, white bottoms; the flat green leaves on top should be crisp and wrapped tightly around each other. Cut off the root ends and discard; trim the tops, leaving about three inches of green leaves. Strip away any coarse outer leaves.

• **Parsnips:** A fair-skinned cousin of the carrot, this creamy-white root has a pleasantly sweet and nutty flavor. Avoid parsnips that are limp, shriveled, or spotted.

• **Rutabagas:** This root vegetable is part of the cabbage family. Although sometimes mistaken for turnips, they are larger, more rounded, denser, and sweeter tasting. Look for smooth, firm rutabagas that feel heavy for their size; lightweight ones may be woody.

• **Turnips:** A globe-shaped root, turnips have a reddish-purple skin, crisp white flesh, and a sweet-to-hot flavor. Like rutabagas, choose ones that are firm and feel heavy for their size. Preparation is simple: just rinse and peel like a potato.

BARBECUED EGGPLANT AND LENTILS

6 cups cubed eggplant
1 tablespoon olive oil
1 tablespoon low-sodium soy sauce
1 tablespoon lemon juice
2 teaspoons paprika
1 teaspoon dried oregano
2 garlic cloves, minced
Vegetable cooking spray
2 cups chopped leek
2 cups diced carrot
2 cups no-salt-added tomato juice
1 tablespoon white wine vinegar
1 tablespoon honey
¼ teaspoon salt
1 (28-ounce) can no-salt-added whole tomatoes, undrained and chopped
2 cups cooked lentils
½ cup dry breadcrumbs
½ cup grated Parmesan cheese

1. Preheat oven to 375°.
2. Combine first 7 ingredients in a large bowl; toss well to coat. Arrange eggplant mixture in a single layer on a baking sheet coated with cooking spray. Bake at 375° for 30 minutes.
3. Coat a nonstick skillet with cooking spray; place over medium-high heat until hot. Add leek and carrot; sauté 5 minutes or until lightly browned. Add tomato juice and next 4 ingredients; bring to a boil. Stir in lentils and eggplant mixture. Reduce heat; simmer 35 minutes or until thick.
4. Spoon 2 cups mixture into each of 4 individual gratin dishes or entire mixture into a 3-quart casserole coated with cooking spray. Combine breadcrumbs and cheese; sprinkle over top. Bake at 375° for 10 minutes. Yield: 4 servings.

CALORIES 403 (21% from fat); FAT 9.3g (sat 3.5g, mono 4.1g, poly 1g); PROTEIN 20.9g; CARB 63.5g; FIBER 7.2g; CHOL 11mg; IRON 6.8mg; SODIUM 688mg; CALC 364mg

ROASTED ROOT VEGETABLES

2 cups (½-inch-thick) diagonally sliced parsnip
2 cups (½-inch-thick) diagonally sliced carrot
1 small rutabaga (about ¾ pound), peeled and cut into 1-inch pieces
2 tablespoons lemon juice
2 teaspoons dried thyme
2 teaspoons olive oil
½ teaspoon salt
½ teaspoon pepper

1. Preheat oven to 425°.
2. Arrange first 3 ingredients in a steamer basket over boiling water; cover and steam 5 minutes or until crisp-tender.
3. Combine vegetables, lemon juice, and remaining ingredients in a 13 x 9-inch baking dish; toss. Bake at 425° for 40 minutes or until tender, stirring occasionally. Yield: 4 servings (serving size: 1 cup).

CALORIES 141 (18% from fat); FAT 2.8g (sat 0.4g, mono 1.8g, poly 0.4g); PROTEIN 2.7g; CARB 28.9g; FIBER 5g; CHOL 0mg; IRON 2.1mg; SODIUM 337mg; CALC 99mg

BUTTERNUT SQUASH RAGOÛT

2 teaspoons olive oil
2 cups chopped onion
4 cups peeled, cubed butternut or acorn squash (about 1½ pounds)
2 cups sliced carrot
1 cup peeled, chopped celeriac
1 teaspoon curry powder
2 garlic cloves, minced
1 cup drained canned chickpeas
1 cup canned vegetable broth
1 cup no-salt-added tomato juice
½ cup chopped dried apricots
¼ cup chopped almonds, toasted
Chopped fresh parsley
3 cups cooked couscous

1. Heat oil in a nonstick saucepan over medium heat. Add onion and next 5 ingredients; sauté 2 minutes. Add chickpeas, broth, and juice; bring to a boil. Reduce heat; simmer, uncovered, 30 minutes or until tender. Top with apricots, almonds, and parsley. Serve over couscous. Yield: 6 servings (serving size: 1½ cups ragoût with ½ cup couscous).

CALORIES 337 (13% from fat); FAT 4.9g (sat 0.5g, mono 2.7g, poly 0.9g); PROTEIN 9.9g; CARB 68.9g; FIBER 9.7g; CHOL 0mg; IRON 3.5mg; SODIUM 174mg; CALC 101mg

BARLEY-VEGETABLE STUFFED ACORN SQUASH

3 medium acorn squash (about 12 ounces each)
1 tablespoon water
1 tablespoon dark sesame oil
1 cup sliced fresh shiitake mushroom caps
1 cup diced onion
1 cup diced carrot
1 cup sliced leek
2 garlic cloves, minced
2 cups chopped fresh spinach
2 cups cooked pearl barley
2 tablespoons low-sodium soy sauce
¼ teaspoon salt
¼ to ½ teaspoon ground red pepper
1 tablespoon toasted sesame seeds

1. Cut squash in half lengthwise; discard seeds and stringy pulp. Place squash halves, cut sides up, on a 12-inch round glass platter; sprinkle with water. Cover loosely with plastic wrap; microwave at HIGH 15 minutes or until tender, rotating platter a half-turn every 5 minutes. Let cool slightly. Scoop pulp from shells to equal 2 cups, reserving pulp and shells; set aside.

2. Heat oil in a large nonstick skillet over medium heat. Add mushrooms and next 4 ingredients; sauté 5 minutes. Stir in reserved squash pulp, spinach, and next 4 ingredients. Spoon 1 cup spinach mixture into each squash shell half; sprinkle with sesame seeds. Yield: 6 servings.

CALORIES 139 (23% from fat); FAT 3.5g (sat 0.5g, mono 1.2g, poly 1.5g); PROTEIN 3.8g; CARB 24.7g; FIBER 5.3g; CHOL 0mg; IRON 2mg; SODIUM 256mg; CALC 71mg

MULTI-GRAIN PILAF WITH ROOT VEGETABLES

Almost like a fried rice, this entrée is high in soluble fiber, the type that helps lower blood cholesterol levels.

1 tablespoon plus 1 teaspoon olive oil, divided
1 cup chopped onion
1 cup chopped red bell pepper
1 cup chopped carrot
½ cup peeled, chopped turnip
½ cup peeled, chopped celeriac
2 teaspoons peeled, grated fresh gingerroot
2 cups cooked basmati or other long-grain rice
2 cups cooked pearl barley
1 cup drained canned pinto beans
3 cups torn spinach
1 tablespoon low-sodium soy sauce
¼ teaspoon salt

1. Heat 2 teaspoons oil in a large nonstick skillet over medium heat. Add onion and next 5 ingredients; sauté 5 minutes. Stir in rice, barley, and beans; cook 2 minutes. Add 2 teaspoons oil, spinach, soy sauce, and salt; cook 1 minute or just until spinach begins to wilt. Yield: 4 servings (serving size: 2 cups).

CALORIES 347 (15% from fat); FAT 5.6g (sat 0.8g, mono 3.4g, poly 0.8g); PROTEIN 10g; CARB 65.8g; FIBER 12.2g; CHOL 0mg; IRON 4.5mg; SODIUM 572mg; CALC 113mg

---

MENU SUGGESTION

PASTA ROOTANESCA

Italian bread

*Greens-and-Gorgonzola salad**

*Combine ½ ounce Gorgonzola cheese, 2 tablespoons strong brewed tea, 1 tablespoon vinegar, 1 tablespoon oil, and 1 teaspoon Dijon mustard. Toss with red leaf lettuce and watercress.

PASTA ROOTANESCA

2 teaspoons olive oil
2 cups diced onion
1 cup diced carrot
1 cup diced fennel bulb
3 garlic cloves, minced
½ teaspoon dried oregano
¼ to ½ teaspoon dried crushed red pepper
1 cup water
¼ cup pitted, chopped kalamata olives
2 tablespoons capers
2 tablespoons balsamic vinegar
1 (25.5-ounce) jar fat-free marinara sauce
6 cups hot cooked vermicelli (about 12 ounces uncooked)

1. Heat oil in a large nonstick skillet over high heat. Add onion and next 5 ingredients; sauté 5 minutes. Add water and next 4 ingredients; bring to a simmer over medium heat, stirring frequently. Serve over vermicelli. Yield: 4 servings (serving size: 1½ cups sauce and 1½ cups pasta).

CALORIES 291 (15% from fat); FAT 4.9g (sat 0.7g, mono 3g, poly 0.8g); PROTEIN 9.5g; CARB 51.3g; FIBER 7.5g; CHOL 0mg; IRON 4.8mg; SODIUM 805mg; CALC 74mg

Mostaccioli-Spinach Bake, page 43

Peach-and-Walnut Salad, page 43

*Linguine with Potatoes, Green Beans, and
Spinach Pesto, page 18*

Devilish Angel Food Cake, page 22

Apricot-Glazed Pork Roast, page 31

Bourbon-Bacon Scallops, page 23

Spaghetti with Rhu's Marinara Sauce, page 41

Beef Meatballs, page 42

Twist and Shout

Thinking back to the good old days, a daughter updates her mom's unparalleled spaghetti and meatballs.

Most of us have memories of at least one meal that our mom would prepare faithfully—one that nobody could ever top. For Alyson Moreland Haynes, that comfort and joy was "a plate of spaghetti and meatballs topped with fresh Parmesan cheese." Her mom's secret? A homemade marinara sauce "heavy on the herbs and garlic," Alyson says. "When mom made it, all the scents from the spices and seasonings would envelop the house."

When Alyson set out to lighten Rhunette Moreland's spaghetti and meatballs, her goal was to come down on the fat and calories without compromising one bit of flavor. While careful to keep the sauce's rich, garlicky taste, she decreased the oil. Along with beef meatballs, she created turkey and lamb alternatives. And instead of frying them, she baked them to trim the calories of her mom's spaghetti and meatballs by more than one-third. She also cut the fat, cholesterol, and sodium by about half. Best of all, when Alyson served her lightened version, Rhu approved—more than that, she asked for the recipe.

RHU'S MARINARA SAUCE

(pictured on page 40)

The sauce gets better after the flavors blend in the refrigerator a few days. The sauce and the meatballs should be frozen separately.

1   tablespoon olive oil
1   cup diced onion
1   cup sliced mushrooms
¼   cup diced green bell pepper
6   garlic cloves, crushed
¾   cup dry red wine
¾   cup water
¼   cup chopped fresh parsley
1   tablespoon sugar
1   teaspoon dried oregano
1   teaspoon dried basil
½   teaspoon dried rosemary, crushed
½   teaspoon pepper
¼   teaspoon salt
2   bay leaves
1   (28-ounce) can whole tomatoes, undrained and chopped
1   (6-ounce) can tomato paste

1. Heat olive oil in a Dutch oven over medium-high heat. Add onion, mushrooms, bell pepper, and garlic; sauté 5 minutes or until tender. Add wine and remaining ingredients; bring to a boil. Cover, reduce heat, and simmer 30 minutes, stirring occasionally. Yield: 6 servings (serving size: 1 cup).

CALORIES 102 (26% from fat); FAT 3g (sat 0.4g, mono 1.8g, poly 0.5g); PROTEIN 3.3g; CARB 18.4g; FIBER 3.2g; CHOL 0mg; IRON 2.5mg; SODIUM 338mg; CALC 72mg

TURKEY-VEGGIE MEATBALLS

For moister, more flavorful meatballs, use ground turkey that contains light and dark meat rather than just breast meat.

1½   pounds ground turkey
½   cup dry breadcrumbs
½   cup finely shredded fresh Parmesan cheese
⅓   cup finely chopped green onions
¼   cup coarsely shredded carrot
¼   cup coarsely shredded zucchini
¼   cup chopped fresh parsley
¼   teaspoon salt
¼   teaspoon pepper
1   large egg white
2   garlic cloves, crushed
Vegetable cooking spray

1. Preheat oven to 400°.
2. Combine all ingredients except cooking spray in a large bowl; stir well. Shape mixture into 30 (1½-inch) meatballs. Place meatballs on a broiler pan coated with cooking spray. Bake at 400° for 15 minutes or until done. Yield: 30 meatballs (serving size: 5 meatballs).

CALORIES 228 (29% from fat); FAT 7.3g (sat 3.1g, mono 1.8g, poly 1.4g); PROTEIN 30.3g; CARB 8.5g; FIBER 0.8g; CHOL 71mg; IRON 2.5mg; SODIUM 399mg; CALC 166mg

---

RELIABLE SAUCES

If you are in a hurry, you might want to make the meatballs and not the sauce. If so, you can always pick up one of the light sauces that are now in your supermarket. Read the label carefully, of course, making sure that one cup has about 100 calories and no more than 3 to 4 grams of fat.

SERVING SIZE

1 cup cooked spaghetti
1 cup Rhu's Marinara Sauce
5 Beef Meatballs
1 tablespoon finely shredded
Parmesan cheese

CALORIES	
792	556

FAT	
43g	14.6g

PERCENT OF TOTAL CALORIES	
49%	24%

CHOLESTEROL	
169mg	73mg

SODIUM	
2,979mg	822mg

HOW WE DID IT

- Used lean ground meat
- Boiled pasta without oil and salt
- Omitted whole eggs in meatballs
- Decreased the amount of cheese in meatballs and sprinkled over the top
- Baked the meatballs instead of frying in butter and oil
- Decreased oil in sauce

BEEF MEATBALLS

(pictured on page 40)

Because the meatballs are baked and not fried, they won't fall apart when turned over.

1½ pounds ground round
½ cup dry breadcrumbs
⅓ cup chopped fresh parsley
¼ cup finely shredded fresh Parmesan cheese
¼ cup tomato sauce
1 teaspoon dry mustard
¾ teaspoon dried Italian seasoning
¼ teaspoon salt
¼ teaspoon dried crushed red pepper
2 garlic cloves, crushed
Vegetable cooking spray

1. Preheat oven to 400°.
2. Combine all ingredients except cooking spray in a large bowl; stir well. Shape mixture into 30 (1½-inch) meatballs. Place meatballs on a broiler pan coated with cooking spray. Bake at 400° for 15 minutes or until done. Yield: 30 meatballs (serving size: 5 meatballs).

CALORIES 228 (35% from fat); FAT 8.8g (sat 3.4g, mono 3.5g, poly 0.5g); PROTEIN 27.4g; CARB 8.2g; FIBER 0.8g; CHOL 73mg; IRON 3.4mg; SODIUM 370mg; CALC 95mg

HERBED LAMB MEATBALLS

Baking the meatballs on a broiler rack or pan prevents them from being cooked in fat. For the easiest cleanup, line the rack or pan with aluminum foil, and simply discard the foil when you're done.

1½ pounds lean ground lamb
½ cup dry breadcrumbs
½ cup crumbled feta cheese
3 tablespoons chopped fresh parsley
1 teaspoon dried mint flakes
¼ teaspoon salt
¼ teaspoon pepper
2 garlic cloves, crushed
Vegetable cooking spray

1. Preheat oven to 400°.
2. Combine all ingredients except cooking spray in a large bowl, and stir well. Shape mixture into 30 (1½-inch) meatballs. Place meatballs on a broiler pan coated with cooking spray. Bake at 400° for 15 minutes or until meatballs are done. Yield: 30 meatballs (serving size: 5 meatballs).

CALORIES 247 (39% from fat); FAT 10.8g (sat 4.5g, mono 4.3g, poly 0.8g); PROTEIN 28.1g; CARB 7.4g; FIBER 0.5g; CHOL 89mg; IRON 2.5mg; SODIUM 353mg; CALC 88mg

SPAGHETTI TWISTS

Although our recipes for Herbed Lamb Meatballs and Beef Meatballs are over 30% of calories from fat, the complete dishes (with pasta and marinara sauce) are below that percentage. Balancing the total meal is what's important.

WINE PICKS

- *Boutari Naoussa Xinomavro 1994 (Greek red), $8*
- *Francis Coppola Family Napa Valley Cabernet Franc 1994 (California red), $18*
- *Angelo Gaja Cremes Dolcetto 1995 (Italian red), $25*
- *Nozzole Chianti Classico 1993 (Italian red), $16*

Starting Over

To help get you over that post-holiday slump and into the new year on the right foot, we've created five weekday dinner menus that are healthy (nothing is over 30% calories from fat), economical (no over-priced ingredients), and quick (no prep time over 30 minutes).

If the holidays have left you feeling overfed, overspent, and overworked, then your problems are over—and that's no overstatement. It's our goal to get you over the post-holiday slump and back on track for the new year. After all, the thought of planning and cooking one more dinner right now could drive anyone over the edge.

MONDAY

Who wants to spend the weekend in the grocery store? This meatless menu uses staples in your pantry, freezer, and refrigerator.

Cost: $1.65 per serving
Calories: 503
Prep time: 30 minutes
Cook time: 30 minutes

MOSTACCIOLI-SPINACH BAKE

(pictured on page 37)

8   ounces uncooked mostaccioli (about 3 cups uncooked tubular-shaped pasta)
2   tablespoons reduced-calorie stick margarine, divided
1   cup vertically sliced onion
2   teaspoons bottled minced garlic
¼   cup all-purpose flour
2½ cups skim milk
1¼ cups preshredded Parmesan cheese, divided
1½ teaspoons dried Italian seasoning
½   teaspoon pepper
1   (14.5-ounce) can diced tomatoes with basil, garlic, and oregano
1   (10-ounce) package frozen chopped spinach, thawed and drained
Vegetable cooking spray
¼   cup dry breadcrumbs
2   tablespoons preshredded Parmesan cheese

1. Preheat oven to 350°.
2. Cook pasta according to package directions, omitting salt and fat. Drain; set aside.
3. Melt 1 tablespoon margarine in a heavy saucepan over medium-high heat. Add onion and garlic; sauté 5 minutes or until tender. Add flour; cook, stirring constantly, 30 seconds. Gradually add milk; cook 4 minutes or until bubbly. Stir in ¼ cup cheese, Italian seasoning, and pepper; remove from heat.
4. Combine pasta, cheese sauce, 1 cup cheese, tomatoes, and spinach in a bowl; stir well. Spoon mixture into a 13 x 9-inch baking dish coated with cooking spray. Combine breadcrumbs, 2 tablespoons cheese, and 1 tablespoon margarine; sprinkle over pasta mixture. Bake at 350° for 30 minutes or until thoroughly heated. Yield: 6 servings (serving size: 1½ cups).

CALORIES 372 (26% from fat); FAT 10.6g (sat 5.1g, mono 3.3g, poly 1.4g); PROTEIN 21g; CARB 48.4g; FIBER 3.6g; CHOL 20mg; IRON 3.8mg; SODIUM 884mg; CALC 525mg

PEACH-AND-WALNUT SALAD

(pictured on page 37)

1   (29-ounce) can sliced peaches in heavy syrup, undrained and chilled
¾   cup tub fat-free cream cheese, softened
¼   cup coarsely chopped walnuts
Curly-leaf lettuce leaves
Ground cinnamon

1. Drain peaches in a colander over a bowl, reserving ¼ cup syrup. Combine reserved syrup and cream cheese; stir well with a whisk. Stir in nuts.
2. Divide peaches among 6 lettuce-lined bowls. Drizzle 3 tablespoons cream cheese mixture over each serving; sprinkle with cinnamon. Yield: 6 servings.

CALORIES 131 (20% from fat); FAT 2.9g (sat 0.2g, mono 0.7g, poly 2g); PROTEIN 5.3g; CARB 19.6g; FIBER 1.1g; CHOL 5mg; IRON 0.2mg; SODIUM 178mg; CALC 83mg

WINE PICKS

MONDAY
• *Dunnewood Gamay Beaujolais 1995 (California red), $5.99*

TUESDAY
• *Louis M. Martini North Coast Merlot 1994 (California red), $10.50*

WEDNESDAY
• *Frick Winery Dry Creek Valley Zinfandel 1992 (California red), $15*

THURSDAY
• *Dunnewood North Coast Sauvignon Blanc 1995 (California white), $7*

FRIDAY
• *Boutari Santorini Assyrtiko 1995 (Greek white), $10*

The week's not even half over, and you need some comforting. Try smothered pork chops and garlic mashed potatoes.

Cost: $1.95 per serving
Calories: 505
Prep time: 25 minutes
Cook time: 45 minutes

PORK CHOPS WITH CHUNKY TOMATO SAUCE

1   teaspoon ground cumin
1   teaspoon chili powder
2   teaspoons cider vinegar
½   teaspoon ground cinnamon
4   (6-ounce) lean center-cut pork chops (about ¾ inch thick)
1   teaspoon vegetable oil
1   (16-ounce) package frozen whole-kernel corn, thawed
1½ cups chopped red bell pepper
½   cup chopped green onions
2   tablespoons finely chopped pickled jalapeño pepper
1   tablespoon plus 1 teaspoon bottled minced garlic
1   teaspoon dried oregano
1   (14.5-ounce) can diced tomatoes, drained
Parsley sprigs (optional)

1. Combine first 4 ingredients; stir well. Rub cumin mixture over both sides of chops.
2. Heat oil in a large nonstick skillet over medium-high heat until hot. Add pork chops; cook 3 minutes on each side or until browned. Add corn and next 6 ingredients, scraping bottom of skillet to loosen browned bits.
3. Cover, reduce heat, and simmer 45 minutes or until pork is tender. Garnish with parsley sprigs, if desired. Yield: 4 servings (serving size: 1 chop and 1 cup sauce).

CALORIES 325 (28% from fat); FAT 10g (sat 3.1g, mono 4.1g, poly 1.7g); PROTEIN 30.1g; CARB 32.2g; FIBER 4.8g; CHOL 71mg; IRON 3.3mg; SODIUM 179mg; CALC 61mg

GARLIC MASHED POTATOES

2   pounds medium baking potatoes, quartered
¾   cup 2% low-fat milk
1   tablespoon margarine
1½ teaspoons garlic powder
½   teaspoon onion powder
½   teaspoon salt
¼   teaspoon pepper

1. Place potatoes in a saucepan; cover with water. Bring to a boil. Reduce heat; simmer 25 minutes or until tender. Drain in a colander over a bowl, reserving ½ cup cooking liquid. Return potatoes to pan. Add reserved cooking liquid, milk, and remaining ingredients; beat at medium speed of an electric mixer until smooth. Yield: 6 servings (serving size: 1 cup).

CALORIES 180 (13% from fat); FAT 2.6g (sat 0.8g, mono 1g, poly 0.7g); PROTEIN 4.1g; CARB 34.7g; FIBER 2.3g; CHOL 2mg; IRON 0.6mg; SODIUM 241mg; CALC 47mg

Get the burrito ingredients ready the night before so you can just turn on the slow cooker in the morning.

Cost: $1.65 per serving
Calories: 419
Prep time: 30 minutes
Cook time: 9 hours

SLOW-COOKER BEEF-AND-BEAN BURRITOS

1   (2-pound) London broil
1   (1.25-ounce) package taco seasoning mix
Vegetable cooking spray
1   cup chopped onion
1   tablespoon white vinegar
1   (4.5-ounce) can chopped green chiles
1   (16-ounce) can fat-free refried beans
12 (8-inch) fat-free flour tortillas
1½ cups (6 ounces) shredded Monterey Jack cheese
1½ cups chopped plum tomato
¾   cup fat-free sour cream

1. Trim fat from meat; rub seasoning mix over both sides of meat. Place meat in an electric slow cooker coated with cooking spray; add onion, vinegar, and green chiles. Cover with lid; cook on low-heat setting for 9 hours. Remove meat from slow cooker, reserving cooking liquid; shred meat with two forks. Combine meat and reserved cooking liquid; stir well.
2. Warm beans and tortillas according to package directions. Spread 2 tablespoons beans down the center of each tortilla. Spoon a heaping ⅓ cup meat mixture on top of beans on each tortilla. Top each with 2 tablespoons cheese, 2 tablespoons tomato, and 1 tablespoon sour cream; roll up. Yield: 12 servings.

CALORIES 350 (30% from fat); FAT 11.8g (sat 6.1g, mono 4.1g, poly 0.5g); PROTEIN 24g; CARB 31.3g; FIBER 3.3g; CHOL 49mg; IRON 4mg; SODIUM 839mg; CALC 175mg

RANCH SLAW

½   cup sliced green onions
2   (10-ounce) bags angel hair slaw
⅔   cup fat-free ranch dressing
2   (11-ounce) cans mandarin oranges in light syrup, well-drained
1   ripe peeled avocado, pitted and coarsely chopped

1. Combine green onions and slaw in a large bowl. Add dressing; toss to coat. Add oranges and avocado; toss gently. Serve immediately. Yield: 12 servings (serving size: ¾ cup).
Note: Unless you plan to serve all of the salad at one time, it's best to make half the recipe because it will water out if stored in the refrigerator for any length of time.

CALORIES 69 (30% from fat); FAT 2.3g (sat 0.4g, mono 1.4g, poly 0.3g); PROTEIN 1.5g; CARB 11.1g; FIBER 0.9g; CHOL 0mg; IRON 0.7mg; SODIUM 168mg; CALC 54mg

So you're working overtime and have resigned yourself to picking up some Chinese take-out. Try our healthy, quick, take-in version instead.

Cost: $1.80 per serving
Calories: 359
Prep time: 15 minutes
Cook time: 15 minutes

ORANGE-GINGER CHICKEN LO MEIN

½ cup low-salt chicken broth
¼ cup thawed orange juice concentrate, undiluted
¼ cup low-sodium soy sauce
2 tablespoons cornstarch
2 tablespoons brown sugar
1 tablespoon bottled minced garlic
½ teaspoon ground ginger
¼ teaspoon salt
¼ teaspoon dried crushed red pepper
6 cups water
1 (8-ounce) package Chinese-style noodles
1 tablespoon vegetable oil
1 (16-ounce) package fresh stir-fry vegetables (not frozen)
¾ pound skinned, boned chicken breasts, cut into strips
1 cup diagonally sliced green onions
¼ cup chopped unsalted, dry-roasted peanuts

1. Combine first 9 ingredients in a small bowl; stir well with a whisk. Set aside.
2. Bring water to a boil in a large saucepan. Add noodles; cook 3 minutes. Drain and set aside.
3. Heat oil in a large nonstick skillet or wok over medium-high heat. Add vegetables; stir-fry 2 minutes. Add chicken and green onions; stir-fry 3 minutes or until chicken is done. Add broth mixture; cook, stirring constantly, 1 minute or until thick.
4. Combine chicken mixture and noodles in a large bowl, and toss well. Spoon onto plates, and sprinkle with peanuts. Yield: 6 servings (serving size: 1⅓ cups chicken mixture and 2 teaspoons peanuts).

CALORIES 345 (18% from fat); FAT 6.9g (sat 1.1g, mono 2.4g, poly 2.5g); PROTEIN 23.2g; CARB 47.8g; FIBER 6.9g; CHOL 33mg; IRON 2.6mg; SODIUM 490mg; CALC 64mg

GREEN ONION-MUSHROOM BROTH

½ cup water
2 (14½-ounce) cans Oriental broth (such as Swanson's)
½ teaspoon ground ginger
¼ teaspoon pepper
¼ cup plus 2 tablespoons chopped green onions
¼ cup plus 2 tablespoons presliced mushrooms

1. Combine water and broth in a medium saucepan; bring to a simmer. Stir in ginger and pepper. Ladle ⅔ cup soup into each cup; top each with 1 tablespoon green onions and 1 tablespoon mushrooms. Yield: 6 servings.

CALORIES 14 (0% from fat); FAT 0g; PROTEIN 0.9g; CARB 2.8g; FIBER 0.2g; CHOL 0mg; IRON 0.2mg; SODIUM 713mg; CALC 5mg

Fish for Friday—but of course!

Cost: $2.45 per serving
Calories: 408
Prep time: 10 minutes
Cook time: 20 minutes

TUNA-AND-WILD RICE SALAD

1 (6.2-ounce) package fast-cooking recipe long-grain and wild rice (such as Uncle Ben's)
2 (6-ounce) cans low-sodium albacore tuna in water, drained
1 (14-ounce) can quartered artichoke hearts, drained
1 (4.5-ounce) jar sliced mushrooms, drained
⅓ cup sliced green onions
2 tablespoons white wine vinegar
1 tablespoon olive oil
2 teaspoons Dijon mustard
¼ teaspoon pepper
8 romaine lettuce leaves
12 cherry tomatoes, halved

1. Prepare rice according to package directions, omitting fat. Let cool slightly.
2. Combine rice, tuna, artichokes, and mushrooms in a large bowl; toss gently. Combine green onions and next 4 ingredients in a bowl; stir with a whisk until blended. Add dressing to tuna mixture, tossing gently. Serve salad in lettuce-lined dishes; top with tomatoes. Yield: 4 servings (serving size: 1¼ cups).

CALORIES 298 (15% from fat); FAT 5g (sat 0.7g, mono 2.6g, poly 0.6g); PROTEIN 22.4g; CARB 43.7g; FIBER 2.3g; CHOL 17mg; IRON 3.7mg; SODIUM 1208mg; CALC 77mg

LEMON-GARLIC PITA CHIPS

3 (6-inch) pita bread rounds, split in half horizontally
2 teaspoons olive oil
1½ teaspoons lemon pepper
¼ teaspoon garlic powder

1. Preheat oven to 400°.
2. Cut each pita half into 4 wedges; place on a baking sheet. Drizzle oil evenly over wedges. Combine lemon pepper and garlic powder; sprinkle evenly over wedges. Bake at 400° for 5 minutes or until crisp. Yield: 4 servings (serving size: 6 chips).

CALORIES 108 (28% from fat); FAT 3.3g (sat 0.6g, mono 2g, poly 0.6g); PROTEIN 2.9g; CARB 16.7g; FIBER 0.8g; CHOL 1mg; IRON 1mg; SODIUM 308mg; CALC 26mg

If you feel dinner's not over until you've had dessert, here are two quick-and-easy ones. Both use ingredients that are often on hand.

ICE CREAM WITH RUM-RAISIN APPLE SAUCE

1 (6-ounce) can thawed apple juice concentrate, undiluted
1 teaspoon ground cinnamon
⅛ teaspoon ground cloves
⅛ teaspoon ground ginger
3 medium Granny Smith apples, each cut into ¼-inch wedges and halved (about 1¾ pounds)
½ cup raisins
2 tablespoons white rum or
¼ teaspoon vanilla extract
3½ cups vanilla low-fat ice cream

1. Combine first 4 ingredients in a large nonstick skillet. Bring to a boil. Reduce heat, and simmer, stirring constantly, 2 minutes.
2. Add apples and raisins; simmer 8 minutes or until apples are crisp-tender. Remove from heat; stir in rum. Serve warm over ice cream. Yield: 7 servings (serving size: ½ cup sauce and ½ cup ice cream).

CALORIES 243 (13% from fat); FAT 3.4g (sat 1.8g, mono 0.8g, poly 0.3g); PROTEIN 3.2g; CARB 50.7g; FIBER 4.1g; CHOL 9mg; IRON 0.8mg; SODIUM 64mg; CALC 114mg

PEACH-AND-BLUEBERRY COBBLER

1 cup reduced-fat baking mix
½ cup regular oats
¼ cup firmly packed brown sugar
½ teaspoon ground cinnamon
¼ cup chilled reduced-calorie stick margarine, cut into small pieces
4 cups frozen sliced peaches
2 cups frozen blueberries
¼ cup granulated sugar
Vanilla low-fat frozen yogurt (optional)

1. Preheat oven to 350°.
2. Combine first 4 ingredients in a bowl; cut in margarine with a pastry blender or 2 knives until mixture resembles coarse meal. Set aside.
3. Combine peaches and blueberries in a 2-quart casserole; sprinkle ¼ cup sugar evenly over fruit. Crumble oat mixture evenly over fruit. Bake at 350° for 45 minutes or until cobbler is bubbly. Top with frozen yogurt, if desired. Yield: 6 servings (serving size: 1 cup).

CALORIES 282 (19% from fat); FAT 6g (sat 1.1g, mono 2.3g, poly 1.8g); PROTEIN 3.9g; CARB 60.6g; FIBER 3.7g; CHOL 0mg; IRON 1.5mg; SODIUM 417mg; CALC 19mg

Carnival Pleasures in Quebec

Picture Mardi Gras with snow, and you'll have a good idea of what the Quebec Winter Carnival is like. The annual festival in Quebec City features sparkling nighttime parades, endless oompah music, ice sculpting, and the traditional swimsuit-clad "roll in the snow." And, of course, there's plenty of food. Quebec City is known for its hearty and artistic—and sometimes light—cuisine. And most chefs are experimenting more and more with low-fat fare. "Today, we're obligated to do that," says Jean-Marc Bass, owner and chef of Café de la Paix. "Clients want it."

PIONEER KETCHUP

If you can't make it to Quebec's Winter Carnival, this chutneylike mixture will bring a taste of it to you. Serve it with beef, pork, or—as the Québeçois like it—with a pâté.

6 medium tomatoes, peeled and quartered (about 3 pounds)
1 tablespoon salt
1 teaspoon whole cloves
1 teaspoon whole allspice
1 (3-inch) cinnamon stick, broken
1½ cups sugar
2 cups finely chopped onion
1 cup chopped celery
1½ cups white vinegar
1 tablespoon maple syrup
2 medium Rome apples, peeled, cored, and quartered
1 medium pear, peeled, cored, and quartered
1 (8.25-ounce) can sliced peaches in light syrup, drained

1. Place a colander in a 2-quart glass measure or medium bowl. Place quartered tomato in colander; sprinkle salt over tomato. Cover with plastic wrap; refrigerate 12 hours. Discard liquid.
2. Place cloves, allspice, and cinnamon on a small piece of cheesecloth. Gather edges of cheesecloth together; tie with string to make a pouch.
3. Combine quartered tomato, cheesecloth pouch, sugar, and remaining ingredients in a large Dutch oven. Bring to a simmer over medium heat; cook, uncovered, 1½ hours, stirring frequently. Discard cheesecloth pouch. Yield: 7 cups (serving size: ¼ cup).
Note: Pioneer Ketchup can be stored in an airtight container in your refrigerator for up to 1 month.

CALORIES 72 (4% from fat); FAT 0.3g (sat 0g, mono 0g, poly 0.1g); PROTEIN 0.7g; CARB 18.4g; FIBER 1.4g; CHOL 0mg; IRON 0.3mg; SODIUM 260mg; CALC 9mg

MARCH

The Great Noodle Revolution

Supermarket shelves are now filled with all kinds of Asian noodles. Healthy, fast, and economical, they offer a delicious change from pasta.

Revolutions aren't always noisy. Sometimes they just happen quietly. Take noodles, for example. At one time, all you could buy in the supermarket were egg noodles. Then came Italian pasta. *And now . . .* Asian noodles are everywhere. And for good reason: They are an extremely versatile main component in soups, salads, and stir-fries.

Asian noodles are made with buckwheat flour, rice, and other substantial ingredients, so they can handle strong flavors such as soy sauce, cilantro, and ginger. Available in varying textures, shapes, and sizes, they can, like any noodle, be served hot, at room temperature, or cold. They are equally appropriate at informal or formal gatherings, and they take a mere two to six minutes to cook—now that's quick and easy.

Because so many Americans are demanding healthy, spicy tastes, supermarkets are stocking more and more Asian products on their shelves and in their produce sections: oyster and fish sauces; sumptuous arrays of Asian vegetables, mushrooms, and herbs. With this kind of momentum, there's no stopping the noodle revolution. Only from now on, it won't be so quiet—not with us shouting its praises.

VEGETABLE-SMOTHERED NOODLE PANCAKE

- 1 (.75-ounce) package dried black mushrooms
- 2 cups boiling water
- ½ pound Chinese egg noodles or vermicelli
- 1¼ teaspoons dark sesame oil, divided
- 1 tablespoon vegetable oil, divided
- 2½ tablespoons low-sodium soy sauce
- 1 tablespoon cornstarch
- 1 tablespoon oyster sauce
- 1 tablespoon peeled, minced fresh gingerroot
- 5 garlic cloves, minced
- 1¾ cups thinly sliced leek
- 1¾ cups shredded carrot
- 1 tablespoon mirin (sweet rice wine)

1. Combine mushrooms and 2 cups boiling water in a bowl; let stand 20 minutes or until soft. Drain mushrooms in a colander over a bowl, reserving liquid; set mushroom liquid aside. Discard mushroom stems, and thinly slice mushroom caps. Set aside.
2. Cook noodles in boiling water 3 minutes; drain. Rinse noodles under cold water; drain well. Combine noodles and ½ teaspoon sesame oil, and toss well.
3. Heat 2 teaspoons vegetable oil in a 12-inch nonstick skillet. Press noodle mixture into skillet to form a pancake; cook 10 minutes or until crisp and golden. Turn pancake over; cook 10 additional minutes. Invert noodle pancake onto a serving platter. Set aside; keep warm.
4. Combine reserved mushroom liquid, ¾ teaspoon sesame oil, soy sauce, cornstarch, and oyster sauce in a bowl; stir well, and set aside.
5. Heat 1 teaspoon vegetable oil in a large nonstick skillet over high heat. Add mushrooms, gingerroot, and garlic; stir-fry 2 minutes. Add leek, carrot, and mirin; stir-fry 1 minute. Add cornstarch mixture. Bring to a boil; cook, stirring constantly, 1 minute. Serve vegetable mixture over noodle pancake. Yield: 6 servings (serving size: ½ cup vegetable mixture and ⅙ noodle pancake).

CALORIES 228 (16% from fat); FAT 4.1g (sat 0.7g, mono 1.3g, poly 1.8g); PROTEIN 6g; CARB 40g; FIBER 1.9g; CHOL 0mg; IRON 2.2mg; SODIUM 288mg; CALC 32mg

WINE PICKS

- *Château Souverain Sonoma County Chardonnay 1994 (California white), $12*
- *Columbia Crest Johannisberg Riesling Columbia Valley 1994 (Washington state white), $6*
- *Geyser Peak Sonoma County Sauvignon Blanc 1995 (California white), $8*
- *Tyrrell's Long Flat White South Eastern Australia 1995 (white), $6*

MOO SHU VEGETABLE ROLLS

You may substitute flour tortillas or steamed wrappers for moo shu wrappers.

  2 tablespoons vegetable oil, divided
  2 large eggs, lightly beaten
 12 moo shu wrappers
  3 tablespoons peeled, minced fresh gingerroot
 15 garlic cloves, minced
  5 cups thinly sliced napa (Chinese) cabbage
  4 cups thinly sliced shiitake mushroom caps (about ¾ pound mushrooms)
  3 cups (3-inch) julienne-cut leek
 ⅓ cup mirin (sweet rice wine)
 ¼ cup low-sodium soy sauce
  1 teaspoon sugar
  1 teaspoon cornstarch
 ¼ teaspoon pepper
 ¾ cup hoisin sauce
  3 tablespoons water
  1 tablespoon low-sodium soy sauce

1. Heat 1 teaspoon oil in a large non-stick skillet or wok over medium-high heat. Add eggs; stir-fry 2 minutes or until soft-scrambled. Remove from skillet; set aside, and keep warm.
2. Wrap moo shu wrappers in heavy-duty plastic wrap; microwave at HIGH 3 minutes, rotating a half-turn after 1½ minutes. Set aside; keep warm.
3. Heat 1 tablespoon plus 2 teaspoons oil in skillet over medium-high heat. Add gingerroot and garlic; stir-fry 30 seconds. Add cabbage, mushrooms, and leek; stir-fry 2 minutes. Add eggs, mirin, and next 4 ingredients; stir-fry 2 minutes. Remove from heat. Set aside; keep warm.
4. Combine hoisin sauce, water, and 1 tablespoon soy sauce; stir well. Place ⅓ cup vegetable mixture on each warm moo shu wrapper. Drizzle 1 tablespoon hoisin sauce mixture over each; roll up. Yield: 6 servings (serving size: 2 rolls).

CALORIES 341 (23% from fat); FAT 8.9g (sat 4.3g, mono 4.3g, poly 1.7g); PROTEIN 11.3g; CARB 57.4g; FIBER 4.6g; CHOL 74mg; IRON 3.1mg; SODIUM 1,111mg; CALC 143mg

CHILE NOODLES

Because of the hot-and-sour dressing, these stir-fried noodles complement grilled meats and seafood.

  1 (8.8-ounce) package uncooked soba (buckwheat noodles)
 ½ cup low-sodium soy sauce
 ¼ cup mirin (sweet rice wine)
  2 tablespoons sugar
  3 tablespoons Chinese black vinegar or Worcestershire sauce
  2 teaspoons dark sesame oil
  1 teaspoon vegetable oil
 2½ tablespoons peeled, minced fresh gingerroot
 10 garlic cloves, minced
 ½ teaspoon dried crushed red pepper
  2 cups vertically sliced red onion
 2½ cups julienne-cut zucchini (about 2 medium)
 2½ cups julienne-cut yellow squash (about 3 small)
 ¼ cup minced fresh parsley
    Fresh parsley sprigs (optional)

1. Cook soba in boiling water 4 minutes; drain. Rinse under cold water; drain and set aside.
2. Combine soy sauce, mirin, sugar, and black vinegar in a small bowl; stir well, and set aside.
3. Heat oils in a large nonstick skillet or wok over medium-high heat. Add gingerroot, garlic, and red pepper; stir-fry 15 seconds. Add onion; stir-fry 1 minute. Add zucchini and squash; stir-fry 1½ minutes or until crisp-tender. Remove from heat; add noodles, soy sauce mixture, and minced parsley, tossing gently to coat. Garnish with parsley sprigs, if desired. Yield: 8 servings (serving size: 1 cup).

CALORIES 189 (12% from fat); FAT 2.5g (sat 0.4g, mono 0.8g, poly 1g); PROTEIN 5.7g; CARB 34g; FIBER 1.6g; CHOL 0mg; IRON 1.2mg; SODIUM 451mg; CALC 40mg

SPICY PESTO SOBA

(pictured on page 75)

Cooked angel hair pasta can be used in place of the soba noodles.

  1 (8.8 ounce) package uncooked soba (buckwheat noodles)
  3 cups snow peas (about 10 ounces), trimmed
  1 cup fresh basil leaves
 ½ cup fresh mint leaves
  2 tablespoons fresh lemon juice
 1½ tablespoons dark sesame oil
  1 teaspoon dried crushed red pepper
  6 garlic cloves
 ¼ cup plus 2 tablespoons low-sodium soy sauce
 ⅓ cup rice vinegar
  3 tablespoons sugar
  2 tablespoons mirin (sweet rice wine)
  3 cups shredded cooked chicken (about 1 pound)
 ¾ cup sliced green onions
    Small red chile peppers (optional)

1. Cook soba in boiling water 4 minutes. Add snow peas; cook 1 additional minute. Drain; rinse under cold water. Drain and set aside.
2. Place basil, mint leaves, lemon juice, sesame oil, crushed red pepper, and garlic cloves in a food processor; process until well-blended. Set aside.
3. Combine soy sauce, vinegar, sugar, and mirin in a small bowl; stir well.
4. Combine soba mixture, pesto, soy sauce dressing, chicken, and green onions in a large bowl; toss well. Garnish with chiles, if desired. Yield: 6 servings.

CALORIES 364 (17% from fat); FAT 7g (sat 1.4g, mono 2.5g, poly 2.3g); PROTEIN 31.1g; CARB 41g; FIBER 1.7g; CHOL 64mg; IRON 3.1mg; SODIUM 546mg; CALC 63mg

SAUCY GARLIC BEEF
LO MEIN

Cucumber salad*

*Vanilla low-fat ice cream
with crystallized ginger*

*Combine 4 small peeled, seeded, sliced cucumbers with 2 small seeded, chopped red chiles. Toss with ½ cup rice vinegar, ¼ cup chopped fresh cilantro, 2 tablespoons sugar, and ½ teaspoon salt.

SAUCY GARLIC BEEF LO MEIN

1 pound green beans
1½ pounds lean flank steak
1 tablespoon sugar
2 tablespoons low-sodium soy sauce
1½ tablespoons mirin (sweet rice wine)
7 garlic cloves, minced
4 quarts water
1 (10-ounce) package Chinese noodles
Vegetable cooking spray
2¼ cups low-salt chicken broth
½ cup low-sodium soy sauce
2½ tablespoons cornstarch
3 tablespoons mirin (sweet rice wine)
1½ teaspoons sugar
1½ teaspoons dark sesame oil
¼ teaspoon pepper
2 teaspoons vegetable oil
3 cups thinly sliced shiitake mushroom caps (about ½ pound mushrooms)
2 cups (1-inch) sliced green onions
3 tablespoons peeled, minced fresh gingerroot
1½ tablespoons minced garlic (about 7 cloves)

1. Trim ends from beans; remove strings. Cut beans into 3-inch pieces. Set aside.
2. Trim fat from steak. Cut across grain into thin slices; cut slices in half crosswise. Combine steak, 1 tablespoon sugar, and next 3 ingredients; stir well. Set aside.
3. Bring 4 quarts water to a boil in a large Dutch oven. Add beans; cook 5 minutes or until tender. Remove with a slotted spoon; place in a colander. Rinse under cold water; drain well. Set aside. Add noodles to boiling water. Cook 3 minutes; drain. Rinse under cold water. Drain; set aside.
4. Coat a large nonstick skillet or wok with cooking spray, and place over medium-high heat until hot. Add steak mixture; stir-fry 5 minutes or until browned. Spoon steak mixture into a bowl; set aside. Wipe skillet clean with a paper towel.
5. Combine broth and next 6 ingredients in a bowl. Stir well; set aside. Heat vegetable oil in skillet over medium-high heat. Add mushroom caps and remaining 3 ingredients; stir-fry 2 minutes. Add broth mixture. Bring to a boil; cook, stirring constantly, 1 minute. Return steak to skillet; add beans and noodles. Stir-fry 1 minute. Yield: 6 servings (serving size: 2 cups).

CALORIES 516 (30% from fat); FAT 17.1g (sat 6.4g, mono 6.9g, poly 2.5g); PROTEIN 33g; CARB 57g; FIBER 3.1g; CHOL 60mg; IRON 6.9mg; SODIUM 925mg; CALC 86mg

STIR-FRIED JAPANESE NOODLES WITH PORK

This is the "spaghetti and meatballs" of Japan, popular with everyone. The noodles are cooked briefly, tossed with a mélange of colorful vegetables, then seasoned with a spunky dressing. Cooked vermicelli can be substituted for the Chinese egg noodles.

1 pound lean, boned pork loin
¼ cup plus 2 tablespoons low-sodium soy sauce, divided
1½ tablespoons peeled, minced fresh gingerroot
5 garlic cloves, minced
4 quarts water
¾ pound uncooked Chinese egg noodles
1 tablespoon plus 2 teaspoons vegetable oil, divided
4 cups thinly sliced napa (Chinese) cabbage
2 cups vertically sliced onion
1 cup shredded carrot
1 teaspoon dried crushed red pepper
¼ cup plus 2 tablespoons mirin (sweet rice wine)
1½ tablespoons sugar
½ teaspoon dark sesame oil

1. Trim fat from pork; cut pork into 2 x ¼-inch strips. Combine pork, 2 tablespoons soy sauce, gingerroot, and garlic in a bowl; stir well. Cover and marinate in refrigerator for 30 minutes.
2. Bring 4 quarts water to a boil in a large Dutch oven. Add noodles. Cook 6 minutes or until tender; drain. Rinse under cold water; drain well, and set noodles aside.
3. Heat 2 teaspoons vegetable oil in a large nonstick skillet or wok over high heat. Add pork mixture, and stir-fry 5

minutes or until done. Remove pork from skillet; set aside.

4. Heat 1 tablespoon vegetable oil in skillet over medium-high heat. Add cabbage and next 3 ingredients; stir-fry 4 minutes. Add ¼ cup soy sauce, mirin, sugar, and sesame oil; stir-fry 1 minute. Return pork to skillet. Add noodles; stir-fry 1 minute. Yield: 6 servings (serving size: 2 cups).

CALORIES 447 (29% from fat); FAT 14.6g (sat 4g, mono 5.5g, poly 3.7g); PROTEIN 25.5g; CARB 52.9g; FIBER 3.5g; CHOL 105mg; IRON 4.2mg; SODIUM 576mg; CALC 96mg

SPICY SLIPPERY NOODLES

As the cellophane noodles cook, they swell, soaking up the hearty broth which is liberally seasoned with garlic, gingerroot, and chile paste.

  4 ounces uncooked cellophane noodles (bean threads)
  2 cups boiling water
  4 green onions
  ½ pound lean ground pork
4½ tablespoons soy sauce, divided
  1 teaspoon vegetable oil
  2 tablespoons peeled, minced fresh gingerroot
  1 teaspoon chile paste
 10 garlic cloves, minced
1½ cups thinly sliced leek
  ½ cup finely shredded carrot
3½ tablespoons mirin (sweet rice wine), divided
1½ cups low-salt chicken broth
  1 teaspoon sugar
  1 teaspoon dark sesame oil

1. Combine noodles and boiling water in a bowl; let stand 5 minutes or until soft. Drain; set aside.
2. Remove tops from green onions; chop tops to measure 1 tablespoon. Set aside. Mince white part of green onions to measure 3 tablespoons; set aside.
3. Combine pork and 1 tablespoon soy sauce in a bowl. Cook pork mixture in a large nonstick skillet or wok over medium-high heat until browned, stirring to crumble. Drain in a colander. Wipe skillet clean with a paper towel.

4. Heat vegetable oil in skillet over high heat. Add 3 tablespoons minced onions, gingerroot, chile paste, and garlic; stir-fry 1 minute. Add leek, carrot, and 2 tablespoons mirin; stir-fry 2 minutes. Add 3½ tablespoons soy sauce, 1½ tablespoons mirin, chicken broth, sugar, and sesame oil; bring mixture to a boil. Return pork to skillet, and add noodles; cook 4 minutes or until liquid is absorbed. Spoon noodle mixture onto a serving platter, and sprinkle with 1 tablespoon chopped green onion tops. Yield: 4 servings (serving size: 1½ cups).

CALORIES 324 (29% from fat); FAT 10.4g (sat 2.7g, mono 3.8g, poly 2g); PROTEIN 16.2g; CARB 41.9g; FIBER 1.5g; CHOL 40mg; IRON 3.3mg; SODIUM 1,013mg; CALC 96mg

TYPES OF ASIAN NOODLES

The range of Asian noodles is extraordinary. But don't worry; it's not necessary to be familiar with every type on the market, just the main varieties. Although most supermarkets stock several kinds of these noodles, a wider selection is available at Asian markets. The following noodles are used in our recipes. Where possible, substitutions are included.

CELLOPHANE NOODLES   Also called bean threads, these translucent dried noodles are made from the starch of mung beans, potatoes, or green peas. When softened in warm water, they absorb the flavor of the foods they are cooked with and become slippery. Serve them in soups, stews, stir-fries, and salads. These noodles are commonly deep-fried in hot oil to create crisp noodle nests. You may substitute ultrathin rice sticks in most recipes.

CHINESE EGG NOODLES   These are labeled simply as egg noodles or instant egg noodles. Because egg noodles are not made with eggs, the Food and Drug Administration requires that they be labeled "imitation." Egg noodles are primarily used in stir-fried and pan-fried dishes and soups. In most recipes, you can substitute capellini (angel hair) or vermicelli.

CHINESE WHEAT-FLOUR NOODLES   Made with flour and water, these are labeled Chinese noodles. Many stores offer a wide variety of "flavored" noodles (shrimp, crab, and chicken) and they may be round or flat. Generally, wheat-flour noodles are used in soups and in some stir-fried dishes. As with egg noodles, any Italian pasta that has a similar thickness and shape can be substituted.

MOO SHU WRAPPERS   These are also called lumpia wrappers or spring roll skins. Lumpia wrappers are often deep-fried. They are usually sold frozen. In some recipes calling for a steamed wrapper, tortilla wrappers may be substituted.

RICE STICKS   The most popular of all Asian noodles, rice sticks (as they are labeled) are made from rice flour and water. Although any type of rice-flour noodle may be called rice sticks, we use this term for flat rice noodles, which are sold mainly in three forms. Thin flat rice noodles are used mainly in soups and in some stir-fried dishes. Medium-thick rice sticks (called *pho* in Vietnamese) are all-purpose and may be used in soups, stir-fries, and salads (a slightly wider Thai version is called *jantaboon*). The widest rice sticks (*sha he fen* in Chinese) are found in meat, seafood, and vegetable stir-fries. Vermicelli can be substituted for rice sticks.

SOBA   Soba noodles from Japan are made with a combination of buckwheat flour, wheat flour, and water.

SOMEN   The most delicate of noodles, they are made with wheat flour, a dash of oil, and water. Somen are served cold with a dipping sauce or hot in soups. The closest substitution would be a very fine pasta such as capellini (angel hair) or vermicelli.

PAD THAI (THAI FRIED RICE NOODLES)

In this quintessential Thai dish, vermicelli can be used in place of the rice sticks, if desired.

- ½ pound uncooked rice sticks (rice-flour noodles)
- 4 cups boiling water
- 3 tablespoons fish sauce
- ¼ cup ketchup
- 1½ tablespoons sugar
- 3 tablespoons water
- ¼ cup chopped unsalted dry-roasted peanuts
- 3 tablespoons chopped green onions
- 2½ tablespoons chopped fresh cilantro
- ½ teaspoon dried crushed red pepper
- 1 tablespoon vegetable oil, divided
- 1 pound medium-size shrimp, peeled and deveined
- 10 garlic cloves, minced
- 3 large eggs, lightly beaten
- 2 cups bean sprouts
- 1 lime, cut into 6 wedges

1. Combine rice sticks and boiling water in a bowl; let stand 10 minutes or until soft. Drain; set aside.
2. Combine fish sauce and next 3 ingredients in a bowl; stir well. Set aside.
3. Combine peanuts and next 3 ingredients in a bowl; stir well. Set aside.
4. Heat 1 teaspoon oil in a large nonstick skillet or wok over medium-high heat. Add shrimp; stir-fry 1½ minutes. Remove from skillet. Set aside; keep warm.
5. Heat 2 teaspoons oil over medium-high heat. Add garlic; stir-fry 30 seconds. Add eggs; stir-fry 2 minutes. Add rice sticks and fish sauce mixture; stir-fry 3 minutes. Return shrimp to skillet; add bean sprouts, and stir-fry 30 seconds. Spoon 1⅓ cups shrimp mixture onto each of 6 plates; top each with 2 tablespoons peanut mixture. Serve with lime wedges. Yield: 6 servings (serving size: 1⅓ cups).

CALORIES 345 (29% from fat); FAT 9.6g (sat 1.9g, mono 3.4g, poly 3.0g); PROTEIN 22.9g; CARB 41.4g; FIBER 1.4g; CHOL 197mg; IRON 3.8mg; SODIUM 1,280mg; CALC 77mg

THAI CLAM POT

If you'd like, use cooked angel hair pasta in place of the somen noodles. The substantial quantity of mirin makes this dish surprisingly sweet.

- 3 pounds small clams in shells (about 48), scrubbed
- 2 tablespoons cornmeal
- 6 ounces uncooked somen (wheat-flour noodles)
- 1 teaspoon vegetable oil
- 1 teaspoon dried crushed red pepper
- 8 garlic cloves, thinly sliced
- 8 green onions, cut into 2-inch pieces
- 1½ cups water
- ¾ cup mirin (sweet rice wine)
- 1 cup thinly sliced fresh basil
- 2 tablespoons fish sauce

1. Place clams in a large bowl; cover with cold water. Sprinkle with cornmeal; let stand 30 minutes. Drain; rinse.
2. Cook somen in boiling water 5 minutes; drain. Rinse under cold water. Drain; set aside.
3. Heat oil in a large Dutch oven over medium-high heat. Add pepper, garlic, and green onions; stir-fry 30 seconds. Add 1½ cups water and mirin; bring to a boil. Add clams; cover, reduce heat, and simmer 8 minutes or until clams open. Discard any unopened shells. Stir in basil and fish sauce; cook 1 additional minute.
4. Spoon ½ cup noodles into each of 6 bowls; top each with ¾ cup cooking liquid and 8 clams in shells. Yield: 6 servings.

CALORIES 142 (10% from fat); FAT 1.6g (sat 0.3g, mono 0.4g, poly 0.6g); PROTEIN 6.8g; CARB 24.1g; FIBER 0.6g; CHOL 6mg; IRON 3.6mg; SODIUM 705mg; CALC 44mg

Bread, They Said

These savory breads represent a world of flavors, from Pesto Baguettes to Garden Tomato Upside-Down Corn Bread. And for a colorful experience, try breadsticks made from a variety of pureed vegetables, including tomatoes, spinach, beets, and sweet potatoes.

PESTO BAGUETTES

I brought four loaves of this bread to a friend's birthday party. She tore it into pieces and served it in little baskets. It made a nice hors d'oeuvre. Sometimes I make it into breadsticks with a warm marinara sauce for dipping.
—Elaine H. Wacholtz, Richardson, Texas

- 1 package dry yeast
- 1 tablespoon sugar
- 1 cup warm water (105° to 115°)
- 3 cups bread or all-purpose flour
- 2 tablespoons nonfat dry milk
- 1 tablespoon dried basil
- 1 tablespoon dried oregano
- 1 tablespoon freeze-dried chives
- 1 teaspoon garlic powder
- 1 teaspoon salt
- Vegetable cooking spray

1. Sprinkle yeast and sugar over warm water in a 2-cup glass measure; let stand 5 minutes. Place flour and next 6 ingredients in a food processor, and pulse 5 times. With processor on, slowly add yeast mixture through food chute, and process until dough forms a ball. Process dough 1 additional minute. (Dough will be sticky.) Turn dough out onto a lightly floured surface, and knead lightly 4 or 5 times.
2. Place dough in a large bowl coated with cooking spray, turning to coat top. Cover and let rise in a warm place (85°), free from drafts, 1 hour and 15 minutes or until doubled in bulk. Punch dough

down; roll dough into a 15 x 10-inch rectangle on a lightly floured surface. Cut dough into 4 (15 x 2½-inch) strips. Roll up each strip tightly, starting with long edge and pressing firmly to eliminate air pockets; pinch seam and ends to seal. Place rolls, seam sides down, on a large baking sheet coated with cooking spray. Cover and let rise 35 minutes or until doubled in bulk.

3. Preheat oven to 375°.

4. Uncover bread dough. Bake dough at 375° for 15 minutes or until loaves sound hollow when tapped. Remove loaves from baking sheet, and let cool on a wire rack. Cut each loaf diagonally into ¾-inch slices. Yield: 4 baguettes, 10 servings per loaf (serving size: 1 slice).

CALORIES 41 (4% from fat); FAT 0.2g (sat 0g, mono 0g, poly 0.1g); PROTEIN 1.5g; CARB 8.2g; FIBER 0.1g; CHOL 0mg; IRON 0.6mg; SODIUM 61mg; CALC 10mg

VEGETABLE BREADSTICKS

(pictured on page 73)

Baking bread is one of my favorite things to do, and my daughter is a breadstick fanatic. So I just make them out of anything—like pureed vegetables. It's a terrific snack, and I make my own spaghetti sauce for dipping.
— Gloria Weichs, Frontenac, Minnesota

    1 cup instant potato flakes
    1 cup water
    ¼ cup plus 2 tablespoons skim milk
    1 teaspoon onion powder
    1 teaspoon garlic powder
    1 package dry yeast
    2 tablespoons sugar
    ¾ cup warm skim milk (105° to 115°)
    5 cups bread or all-purpose flour, divided
    ¼ cup stick margarine, softened
    1 teaspoon salt
    1 teaspoon cider vinegar
    1 large egg
Vegetable cooking spray

1. Combine potato flakes, water, ¼ cup plus 2 tablespoons skim milk, onion powder, and garlic powder; set aside.

2. Sprinkle yeast and sugar over ¾ cup warm milk in a large bowl; let stand 5 minutes. Add 2 cups flour, potato mixture, margarine, salt, vinegar, and egg; beat at medium speed of an electric mixer until smooth. Stir in 1 cup flour to form a sticky dough.

3. Turn dough out onto a lightly floured surface. Knead dough until smooth and elastic (about 10 minutes), adding enough of remaining 2 cups flour to prevent dough from sticking to hands.

4. Place dough in a large bowl coated with cooking spray, turning to coat top. Cover dough, and let rise in a warm place (85°), free from drafts, 1 hour or until doubled in bulk.

5. Punch dough down, and divide in half. Working with one portion at a time (cover remaining dough to keep from drying), roll dough into a 10 x 7-inch rectangle. Cut dough crosswise into 20 (7 x ½-inch strips). Gently twist strips of dough. Repeat with remaining dough. Place dough twists 1 inch apart on two baking sheets coated with cooking spray. Cover dough twists, and let rise in a warm place (85°), free from drafts, 30 minutes or until doubled in bulk.

6. Preheat oven to 350°.

7. Uncover dough twists. Bake at 350° for 18 to 20 minutes. Remove from baking sheets, and let cool on wire racks. Yield: 40 breadsticks (serving size: 1 breadstick).

Note: To make 2 loaves of bread instead of breadsticks, roll each portion into a 10 x 7-inch rectangle on a lightly floured surface. Roll up rectangles tightly, starting with a long edge and pressing firmly to eliminate air pockets; pinch seams and ends to seal. Place each roll, seam side down, in a 9 x 5-inch loaf pan coated with cooking spray. Cover and let rise 45 minutes or until doubled in bulk. Bake for 30 minutes or until loaves sound hollow when tapped. Remove from pans; let cool on wire racks.

CALORIES 183 (13% from fat); FAT 2.7g (sat 0.5g, mono 1g, poly 0.8g); PROTEIN 5.5g; CARB 33.7g; FIBER 0.1g; CHOL 9mg; IRON 1.5mg; SODIUM 141mg; CALC 27mg

VARIATIONS: *You can substitute the following vegetable mixtures for the mashed-potato mixture (the first 5 ingredients) called for in the original recipe.*

Tomato Variation:

    2 (6-ounce) cans no-salt-added tomato paste
    2 teaspoons dried Italian seasoning

CALORIES 142 (17% from fat); FAT 2.7g (sat 0.5g, mono 1g, poly 0.8g); PROTEIN 4.6g; CARB 25g; FIBER 0.1g; CHOL 9mg; IRON 1.7mg; SODIUM 133mg; CALC 24mg

Spinach Variation:

    1 (10-ounce) package frozen chopped spinach, thawed and drained
    1½ teaspoons dried oregano

CALORIES 134 (18% from fat); FAT 2.7g (sat 0.5g, mono 1g, poly 0.9g); PROTEIN 4.4g; CARB 22.8g; FIBER 0.5g; CHOL 9mg; IRON 1.6mg; SODIUM 136mg; CALC 30mg

Beet Variation:

    1 (16-ounce) jar sliced beets, drained and pureed
    1 teaspoon caraway seeds

CALORIES 134 (18% from fat); FAT 2.7g (sat 0.5g, mono 1g, poly 0.8g); PROTEIN 4.4g; CARB 23g; FIBER 0.2g; CHOL 9mg; IRON 1.4mg; SODIUM 147mg; CALC 18mg

Sweet Potato Variation:

    1½ cups mashed cooked sweet potato
    2 teaspoons pineapple extract or vanilla extract

CALORIES 154 (16% from fat); FAT 2.7g (sat 0.5g, mono 1g, poly 0.9g); PROTEIN 4.4g; CARB 27.3g; FIBER 0.7g; CHOL 9mg; IRON 1.5mg; SODIUM 130mg; CALC 20mg

GARDEN TOMATO UPSIDE-DOWN CORN BREAD

I'm single and a nuclear scientist. For me, cooking is really a social thing. After all, there's no better way to get a girl over for dinner than to cook for her.

—Stan Stewart, La Jolla, California

 1 tablespoon vegetable oil
 1 teaspoon dried Italian
 seasoning
 2 garlic cloves, minced
 4 to 6 plum tomatoes, cut into
 ¼-inch-thick slices
 ½ teaspoon salt
 ½ teaspoon pepper
 1 cup all-purpose flour
 1 cup yellow cornmeal
 3 tablespoons sugar
 1 tablespoon baking powder
 ½ to 1 teaspoon garlic-pepper
 seasoning
 ½ teaspoon chili powder
 ¼ cup minced fresh onion
 ½ cup (2 ounces) grated sharp
 Cheddar cheese
 1 cup skim milk
 3 tablespoons ketchup
 2 tablespoons vegetable oil
 2 large egg whites, lightly beaten

1. Preheat oven to 400°.
2. Heat 1 tablespoon oil in a 9-inch cast-iron skillet over medium heat. Add Italian seasoning and garlic; sauté 1 minute. Arrange tomato slices in a circular pattern in skillet. Sprinkle with salt and pepper. Reduce heat to low.
3. Combine flour and next 7 ingredients in a large bowl. Add milk and remaining 3 ingredients, stirring until moist. Pour batter into skillet. Bake at 400° for 30 minutes or until a wooden pick inserted in center comes out clean. Place a plate upside down on top of skillet, and invert onto plate. Yield: 10 servings (serving size: 1 wedge).

CALORIES 196 (30% from fat); FAT 6.5g (sat 2g, mono 1.8g, poly 2.2g); PROTEIN 5.8g; CARB 29g; FIBER 1.6g; CHOL 6mg; IRON 1.7mg; SODIUM 182mg; CALC 164mg

ENTERTAINING

Moroccan Bound

This Passover, try a light, flavorful Moroccan menu that is steeped in history.

For a departure from the traditional Eastern European-style Passover menu, we've prepared an authentic Moroccan feast. Spicy and flavorful, the following recipes are steeped in history. When the Jews were expelled from Spain in 1492, many crossed the narrow Strait of Gibraltar to settle in Morocco.

Today, the Sephardic Jews who live there maintain a full-flavored cooking style that reflects local methods and ingredients. This delicious, exotic repast is not only light and healthy, but also is compatible with Jewish dietary laws.

PASSOVER VEGETABLE SOUP

 8 cups fat-free chicken broth
 6 cups chopped leek
 3 cups diced carrot
 3 cups peeled, diced
 turnip
 ½ teaspoon salt
 ¼ teaspoon pepper
 ⅛ teaspoon ground saffron
 (optional)
 2 tablespoons plus 1 teaspoon
 chopped fresh cilantro

1. Combine first 6 ingredients in a large Dutch oven; stir in saffron, if desired. Bring mixture to a boil over medium-high heat; cover, reduce heat, and simmer 1 hour or until vegetables are tender.
2. Ladle soup into bowls, and sprinkle with cilantro. Yield: 14 servings (serving size: 1 cup soup and ½ teaspoon cilantro).

CALORIES 62 (3% from fat); FAT 0.2g (sat 0g, mono 0.1g, poly 0.1g); PROTEIN 5.2g; CARB 10.5g; FIBER 1.8g; CHOL 0mg; IRON 1.1mg; SODIUM 217mg; CALC 42mg

┌─────────────────────────┐
│   MENU   │
│ PASSOVER VEGETABLE   │
│   SOUP   │
│   │
│ CHICKEN WITH PRUNE   │
│   SAUCE   │
│ AND BRAISED TURNIPS   │
│   │
│ FRESH TOMATO-AND-   │
│   PEPPER SALAD   │
│   │
│ SWEET CARROT SALAD   │
│   │
│ CHOPPED-EGGPLANT   │
│   RELISH   │
│   │
│ CARAMELIZED SWEET   │
│   POTATO PUDDING   │
│   │
│ About 671 calories and │
│   10 grams fat   │
│ (13% calories from fat)│
└─────────────────────────┘

CHICKEN WITH PRUNE SAUCE AND BRAISED TURNIPS

 ¼ teaspoon salt
 ¼ teaspoon pepper
 8 (4-ounce) skinned, boned
 chicken breast halves
 2 teaspoons olive oil
 ½ cup coarsely chopped green
 onions
 4 cups water
 1 tablespoon chopped fresh
 parsley
 1 tablespoon chopped fresh
 cilantro
 Braised Turnips
 Prune Sauce

1. Sprinkle salt and pepper over chicken; set aside. Heat oil in a large nonstick skillet over medium-high heat. Add green onions, and sauté until tender. Add chicken, and cook 3 minutes on each side or until browned. Add water, parsley, and cilantro; bring mixture to a boil. Cover, reduce heat, and simmer 35 minutes or until chicken is done. Remove chicken from skillet. Set chicken aside, and keep warm. Reserve 3 cups cooking liquid from skillet for Braised Turnips and Prune Sauce.

2. Place chicken and Braised Turnips on plates. Spoon Prune Sauce over chicken. Yield: 8 servings (serving size: 1 chicken breast half, 4 turnip quarters, and 3 tablespoons sauce).

CALORIES 276 (18% from fat); FAT 5.4g (sat 1.2g, mono 2.1g, poly 0.9g); PROTEIN 30.1g; CARB 27.2g; FIBER 3.2g; CHOL 72mg; IRON 2.3mg; SODIUM 576mg; CALC 79mg

Braised Turnips:

2   cups cooking liquid (reserved from chicken)
1   tablespoon sugar
⅛   teaspoon salt
⅛   teaspoon pepper
8   small turnips, peeled and quartered

1. Combine first 4 ingredients in a large nonstick skillet, and bring to a boil. Add turnips. Cover; reduce heat to medium-low. Cook 25 minutes or until tender. Drain. Yield: 8 servings (serving size: 4 quarters).

Prune Sauce:

1   cup kosher Concord grape wine (such as Manischewitz)
20 pitted prunes (about 6 ounces)
1   cup cooking liquid (reserved from chicken)
1   tablespoon honey
Dash of ground cinnamon

1. Combine wine and prunes in a small saucepan, and bring to a boil. Cover, reduce heat, and simmer 20 minutes or until tender.
2. Place prune mixture in a food processor or blender; process until smooth. Add cooking liquid, honey, and cinnamon; process until blended. Yield: 8 servings (serving size: 3 tablespoons).

FRESH TOMATO-AND-PEPPER SALAD

2   cups diced tomato
1   cup diced green bell pepper
1   cup diced yellow bell pepper
1   cup diced onion
¼   cup chopped fresh parsley
¼   cup fresh lemon juice
3   tablespoons capers
2   teaspoons olive oil
¼   teaspoon salt
¼   teaspoon pepper

1. Combine all ingredients in a medium bowl, and stir well. Yield: 4 cups (serving size: ¼ cup).

CALORIES 20 (33% from fat); FAT 0.8g (sat 0.1g, mono 0.4g, poly 0.2g); PROTEIN .6g; CARB 3.4g; FIBER .9g; CHOL 0mg; IRON 0.5mg; SODIUM 166mg; CALC 6mg

SWEET CARROT SALAD

5   cups (½-inch-thick) carrot slices
2   garlic cloves, halved
⅔   cup fresh lemon juice
¼   cup chopped fresh parsley
2   tablespoons sugar
1   teaspoon ground cinnamon
½   teaspoon ground cumin
½   teaspoon paprika

1. Combine carrot and garlic in a large saucepan. Cover with water; bring to a boil. Cook 8 minutes or until tender; drain. Discard garlic.
2. Combine lemon juice and remaining 5 ingredients in a medium bowl, stirring well. Add carrot to juice mixture; toss to coat. Serve at room temperature or chilled. Yield: 4 cups (serving size: ½ cup).

CALORIES 30 (3% from fat); FAT 0.1g (sat 0.1g, mono 0g, poly 0g); PROTEIN .6g; CARB 8g; FIBER .9g; CHOL 0mg; IRON 0.5mg; SODIUM 31mg; CALC 19mg

CHOPPED-EGGPLANT RELISH

2   medium eggplants (about 2 pounds)
2   tablespoons chopped fresh parsley
1   tablespoon fresh lemon juice
½   teaspoon paprika
½   teaspoon ground cumin
¼   teaspoon salt
⅛   teaspoon pepper
2   garlic cloves, minced

1. Preheat oven to 400°.
2. Pierce eggplants several times with a fork. Place eggplants on a baking sheet, and bake at 400° for 40 minutes or until tender (eggplants should be tender yet firm enough to chop). Cut each eggplant lengthwise into quarters; drain well. Peel eggplant; chop pulp.
3. Combine chopped eggplant, parsley, and remaining ingredients in a medium bowl; stir mixture gently. Yield: 2 cups (serving size: ¼ cup).

CALORIES 26 (3% from fat); FAT 0.1g (sat 0g, mono 0g, poly 0.1g); PROTEIN 1.1g; CARB 6.3g; FIBER 1.5g; CHOL 0mg; IRON 0.7mg; SODIUM 78mg; CALC 37mg

CARAMELIZED SWEET POTATO PUDDING

    3 medium-size sweet potatoes
       (about 2 pounds)
 ½ cup sliced almonds
    1 cup sugar, divided
Vegetable cooking spray
    2 egg whites (at room
       temperature)
    1 teaspoon vanilla extract

1. Preheat oven to 400°.
2. Wrap sweet potatoes in aluminum foil; bake at 400° for 1 hour or until tender. Let cool slightly; peel.
3. Combine sweet potatoes and sliced almonds in a food processor; process until smooth. Spoon mixture into a large nonstick skillet, and keep warm over low heat.
4. Place ¾ cup sugar in a medium nonstick skillet. Cook over medium-high heat 5 minutes or until golden. Immediately pour three-fourths of caramelized sugar into sweet potato mixture, stirring constantly. Set remaining caramelized sugar aside.
5. Spoon sweet potato mixture into a 1½-quart casserole coated with cooking spray. Beat egg whites at high speed of an electric mixer until foamy. Add ¼ cup sugar, 1 tablespoon at a time, beating until stiff peaks form. Add vanilla; beat well. Spread meringue evenly over sweet potato mixture, sealing to edge of dish. Bake at 400° for 15 minutes or until golden. Place remaining caramelized sugar over low heat until melted (caramel will have hardened); drizzle over meringue. Serve warm. Yield: 8 servings (serving size: ¾ cup).

CALORIES 257 (12% from fat); FAT 3.5g (sat 0.4g, mono 2g, poly 0.8g); PROTEIN 3.9g; CARB 53.9g; FIBER 4.1g; CHOL 0mg; IRON 0.9mg; SODIUM 29mg; CALC 40mg

---

A GOOD SPORT

It's All Downhill

Start a high-carb, low-fat breakfast with these high-energy pancakes, and round it out with granola and skim milk.

MULTIGRAIN PANCAKES

 ½ cup all-purpose flour
 ½ cup whole-wheat flour
 ¼ cup quick-cooking oats
    2 tablespoons yellow cornmeal
    2 tablespoons brown sugar
1½ teaspoons baking powder
 ½ teaspoon salt
    1 cup 2% milk
 ¼ cup plain fat-free yogurt
    1 tablespoon vegetable oil
    1 large egg

1. Combine first 7 ingredients. Combine milk and remaining 3 ingredients. Add to flour mixture; stir until smooth. Spoon about ¼ cup batter for each pancake onto a hot nonstick griddle. Turn pancakes when tops are covered with bubbles and edges look cooked. Yield: 4 servings (serving size: 3 pancakes).

CALORIES 246 (25% from fat); FAT 6.9g (sat 1.8g, mono 2.1g, poly 2.1g); PROTEIN 9.3g; CARB 38.1g; FIBER 3.3g; CHOL 60mg; IRON 2.1mg; SODIUM 354mg; CALC 225mg

---

THE ENLIGHTENED CHEF

A California Creation

Russell Jackson, executive chef at The Dining Room in Beverly Hills' Regent Beverly Wilshire Hotel, says that the person who had the greatest influence on his career was his future wife. Jackson asked what she liked to eat. "Anything without sugar, salt, butter, or oil" was her answer. He incorporated unique ingredients in his recipes, seeking intense flavor

from Asian, Thai, Indian, French, Pakistani, Latin, and Southwestern cultures.

ROASTED CORN-AND-ASPARAGUS RISOTTO

    1 medium-size red bell pepper
    1 ear shucked corn
 10 asparagus spears
    1 cup water
    2 (14½-ounce) cans vegetable
       broth
    2 tablespoons olive oil
    1 cup minced onion
    2 tablespoons minced shallots
    1 garlic clove, minced
    2 cups uncooked Arborio rice
    1 cup dry white wine
 ¼ cup grated fresh Parmesan cheese
    1 tablespoon minced fresh chives
    1 tablespoon minced fresh parsley
    2 teaspoons dried oregano
    2 teaspoons dried thyme

1. Cut pepper in half lengthwise; discard seeds and membranes. Place pepper, skin sides up, on an aluminum foil-lined baking sheet; flatten with hand. Add corn; broil 5 minutes. Add asparagus; broil 10 minutes or until pepper is blackened, turning corn and asparagus after 5 minutes. Place pepper in a zip-top plastic bag; seal. Let stand 15 minutes; peel and chop. Cut kernels from corn. Cut asparagus into ¼-inch pieces.
2. Bring water and broth to a simmer in a medium saucepan (do not boil). Keep warm over low heat.
3. Heat oil in a large saucepan over medium-high heat. Add onion, shallots, and garlic; sauté 3 minutes. Add rice; cook, stirring constantly, 2 minutes. Add wine; cook, stirring constantly, 5 minutes or until nearly absorbed. Add broth, 1 cup at a time, stirring constantly; cook until each portion of broth is absorbed before adding the next cup (about 20 minutes). Stir in vegetables, cheese, and remaining ingredients; cook, stirring constantly, 2 minutes. Yield: 8 servings (serving size: 1 cup).

CALORIES 263 (19% from fat); FAT 5.5g (sat 1.2g, mono 2.9g, poly 0.5g); PROTEIN 6g; CARB 47.6g; FIBER 2g; CHOL 2mg; IRON 3.3mg; SODIUM 224mg; CALC 69mg

Yes Can Do

Healthier and tastier than you may think, canned vegetables are shedding their dowdy image. After evaluating their flavors and textures, we picked our favorites and updated their look with these jazzy recipes.

We were surprised at how well canned vegetables held up and how good they tasted when cooked, even the spinach and okra. We found that canned produce works well in dishes seasoned with herbs and spices, especially those that call for several different vegetables.

Even cooks who would never consider canned vegetables probably do use canned tomatoes, by far the most popular canned vegetable. We use them in less-predictable ways than in spaghetti sauces. Seeing how far we could push the canned-veggie envelope, we tried them in a dessert and got spectacular results. Our moist Sweet Potato Cake earned a near-perfect taste-test score.

FOUR-CORN PIE

There's hardly any preparation for this dish—a little chopping and opening a few cans. It's like a quiche but easier because you don't have to make a crust.

Vegetable cooking spray
1 cup chopped onion
2 (8¾-ounce) cans no-salt-added whole-kernel corn, drained
1 (8.5-ounce) can no-salt-added cream-style corn
1 (15.5-ounce) can white hominy, drained
1 (4.5-ounce) can chopped green chiles, drained
¼ cup chopped fresh cilantro
¾ cup (3 ounces) shredded colby-Jack cheese, divided
¾ cup egg substitute
1 cup cornflakes, finely crushed
¼ cup fat-free sour cream

1. Preheat oven to 400°.
2. Place a small nonstick skillet coated with cooking spray over medium heat until hot. Add onion; sauté 5 minutes or until lightly browned.
3. Combine onion, whole-kernel corn, and next 4 ingredients in a large bowl; stir in ½ cup cheese and egg substitute. Spoon mixture into a 9-inch pie plate coated with cooking spray. Combine ¼ cup cheese and cornflakes; toss well. Sprinkle cornflake mixture over corn mixture.
4. Bake at 400° for 50 minutes or until top is browned and mixture is set. Serve with sour cream. Yield: 4 servings.

CALORIES 352 (24% from fat); FAT 9.3g (sat 4.5g, mono 2.3g, poly 0.8g); PROTEIN 16.2g; CARB 51.2g; FIBER 4.7g; CHOL 20mg; IRON 2.8mg; SODIUM 561mg; CALC 188mg

SPINACH, HAM, AND GRITS SOUFFLÉ

Use quick-cooking grits, not instant grits, for this soufflé.

Vegetable cooking spray
¼ pound lean country ham, finely chopped
1½ cups skim milk
1 (10½-ounce) can low-salt chicken broth
¾ cup uncooked quick-cooking grits
1 cup (4 ounces) shredded reduced-fat sharp Cheddar cheese
¼ teaspoon garlic powder
¼ teaspoon pepper
1 (13½-ounce) can chopped spinach, drained and squeezed dry
4 large egg whites

1. Preheat oven to 375°.
2. Place a large saucepan coated with cooking spray over medium-high heat until hot. Add ham, and sauté 2 minutes or until lightly browned. Remove from pan; set aside.
3. Combine milk and broth in pan; bring to a boil, stirring constantly. Stir in grits; reduce heat, and simmer 7 minutes or until thick, stirring frequently. Combine grits mixture, ham, cheese, garlic powder, pepper, and spinach in a large bowl. Stir well; set aside.
4. Beat egg whites at high speed of an electric mixer until stiff peaks form. Gently fold one-fourth of egg whites into grits mixture; gently fold in remaining egg whites. Spoon mixture into a 2-quart casserole or soufflé dish coated with cooking spray. Bake at 375° for 40 minutes or until set and lightly browned. Yield: 6 servings (serving size: 1 cup).
Note: Substitute cured ham or cooked smoked pork chops for country ham, if desired.

CALORIES 198 (25% from fat); FAT 5.5g (sat 2.5g, mono 1g, poly 0.1g); PROTEIN 16.6g; CARB 20.9g; FIBER 1.2g; CHOL 23mg; IRON 1.9mg; SODIUM 623mg; CALC 278mg

TOMATO-GREEN BEAN RISOTTO WITH FETA CHEESE

We used the liquid from the can of green beans to add flavor and nutrients.

½ ounce sun-dried tomatoes, packed without oil (about 8)
1 (14½-ounce) can cut green beans, undrained
⅔ cup dry white wine
3 (10½-ounce) cans low-salt chicken broth
2 teaspoons olive oil
1 cup chopped onion
2 garlic cloves, crushed
1½ cups uncooked Arborio or other short-grain rice
1 teaspoon dried basil
⅛ teaspoon salt
¾ cup crumbled feta cheese with peppercorns

1. Cut sun-dried tomatoes into thin strips; set aside.
2. Drain beans in a colander over a medium saucepan; set beans aside. Add wine and broth to reserved canned liquid; bring to a simmer (do not boil). Combine ½ cup warm broth mixture and tomatoes in a bowl. Cover; set aside. Keep remaining broth mixture warm over low heat.
3. Heat oil in a large saucepan over medium heat. Add onion and garlic; sauté 3 minutes. Add rice; cook, stirring constantly, 1 minute. Add warm broth mixture, 1 cup at a time, stirring constantly until each portion of broth mixture is absorbed (about 20 minutes total). Add tomato mixture, beans, basil, and salt; cook, stirring constantly, 2 minutes. Remove from heat; stir in cheese. Yield: 6 servings (serving size: 1 cup).

CALORIES 280 (19% from fat); FAT 6g (sat 2.4g, mono 1.9g, poly 0.4g); PROTEIN 8.2g; CARB 48.6g; FIBER 1.8g; CHOL 13mg; IRON 3.8mg; SODIUM 514mg; CALC 104mg

---

CANNED CAN BE BETTER

"Consumers can feel good about choosing canned vegetables along with fresh and frozen," says Barbara Klein, a University of Illinois professor of foods and nutrition. After comparing current nutritional data on food labels with that of government data for fresh-cooked food, she found that canned food is nutritionally quite similar to fresh-cooked. In her review, she even discovered that some brands of canned carrots, potatoes, spinach, and pumpkin are slightly higher in vitamins A and C than their fresh-cooked counterparts.

SWEET POTATO CAKE

This cake is so moist that it doesn't need a frosting or glaze.

2 cups sugar
¾ cup stick margarine, softened
¾ cup egg substitute
2 (14½-ounce) cans unsweetened mashed sweet potatoes
3 cups sifted cake flour
1½ teaspoons ground cinnamon
1 teaspoon baking powder
1 teaspoon baking soda
½ teaspoon ground nutmeg
½ teaspoon salt
2 teaspoons vanilla extract
Vegetable cooking spray
¼ cup flaked sweetened coconut
2 tablespoons finely chopped pecans

1. Preheat oven to 350°.
2. Beat sugar and softened margarine at medium speed of an electric mixer until well-blended (about 5 minutes). Gradually add egg substitute, beating well. Add 2½ cups sweet potatoes (about 1½ cans), and beat well. Reserve remaining sweet potatoes for another use.
3. Combine sifted flour and next 5 ingredients; stir well. Gradually add flour mixture to sweet potato mixture,

beating well after each addition. Stir in vanilla.
4. Pour batter into a 10-inch tube pan coated with cooking spray. Sprinkle coconut and pecans over batter. Bake at 350° for 1 hour and 25 minutes or until a wooden pick inserted in center comes out clean. Let cool in pan 10 minutes; remove from pan. Let cool completely on a wire rack. Yield: 16 servings.
Note: Substitute 6 egg whites (about ¾ cup) for egg substitute, if desired.

CALORIES 298 (30% from fat); FAT 10g (sat 2.3g, mono 4.2g, poly 3g); PROTEIN 3.6g; CARB 50.7g; FIBER 1.3g; CHOL 0mg; IRON 2.4mg; SODIUM 261mg; CALC 36mg

---

BEEF-VEGETABLE RAGOÛT WITH SOFT POLENTA

2 pounds lean, boned round steak, cut into 1-inch cubes
2 tablespoons all-purpose flour
Vegetable cooking spray
1 cup chopped onion
1 cup no-salt-added tomato sauce, divided
2 cups water
1 teaspoon dried thyme
¾ teaspoon dried rosemary
½ teaspoon garlic salt
¼ teaspoon pepper
2 (14¼-ounce) cans fat-free beef broth
1 bay leaf
⅓ cup all-purpose flour
1 (15¼-ounce) can no-salt-added sweet peas, drained
1 (15-ounce) can whole white potatoes, drained and halved
1 (15-ounce) can tender baby whole carrots, drained
Soft Polenta

1. Combine steak and 2 tablespoons flour in a large zip-top plastic bag. Seal; toss to coat. Remove steak from bag. Place a large Dutch oven coated with cooking spray over medium-high heat until hot. Add steak and onion; cook 2 minutes on all sides or until steak is browned. Add ½ cup tomato sauce, water, and next 6 ingredients; bring to a boil. Cover, reduce heat, and

simmer 45 minutes or until steak is tender, stirring occasionally. Discard bay leaf.

2. Combine ½ cup tomato sauce and ⅓ cup flour in a small bowl; stir well. Add tomato sauce mixture, peas, potatoes, and carrots to steak mixture in Dutch oven; bring to a boil. Cover, reduce heat, and simmer 5 minutes or until thick, stirring occasionally. Serve over Soft Polenta. Yield: 8 servings (serving size: 1½ cups ragoût and 1 cup polenta).

CALORIES 425 (12% from fat); FAT 5.8g (sat 1.9g, mono 2.1g, poly 0.6g); PROTEIN 33.4g; CARB 56.0g; FIBER 3.7g; CHOL 65mg; IRON 5.8mg; SODIUM 656mg; CALC 31mg

Soft Polenta:

2½   cups yellow cornmeal
¾   teaspoon salt
8   cups water

1. Place cornmeal and salt in a large saucepan. Gradually add water, stirring constantly with a whisk. Bring to a boil, and reduce heat to medium. Cook 15 minutes, stirring frequently. Serve immediately. Yield: 8 servings (serving size: 1 cup).

CALORIES 158 (4% from fat); FAT 0.7g (sat 0.1g, mono 0.2g, poly 0.3g); PROTEIN 3.7g; CARB 33.5g; FIBER 2.2g; CHOL 0mg; IRON 1.8mg; SODIUM 221mg; CALC 2mg

FRIED-CHICKEN SALAD

¼   cup dry breadcrumbs
¼   cup all-purpose flour
1   teaspoon garlic powder
1   teaspoon dried thyme
½   teaspoon salt
½   teaspoon pepper
¾   pound skinned, boned chicken breasts, cut into thin strips
½   cup low-fat buttermilk
   Vegetable cooking spray
1   tablespoon olive oil
4   cups thickly sliced romaine lettuce (cut across rib)
1   (15-ounce) can whole baby beets, drained and halved
½   cup fat-free honey-Dijon mustard salad dressing
½   cup crumbled blue cheese

1. Combine first 6 ingredients in a shallow dish. Stir well; set aside. Combine chicken and buttermilk in a small bowl; stir. Cover and marinate in refrigerator 30 minutes. Drain chicken, and dredge a few strips at a time in breadcrumb mixture, tossing well to coat.

2. Coat a nonstick skillet with cooking spray. Add oil; place over medium heat until hot. Add chicken; cook 3 minutes on each side or until done.

3. Arrange 1 cup lettuce on each plate; divide chicken and beets among plates. Top each with 2 tablespoons dressing and 2 tablespoons cheese. Yield: 4 servings.

CALORIES 287 (27% from fat); FAT 7.4g (sat 2.2g, mono 3.4g, poly 0.8g); PROTEIN 25.8g; CARB 28.3g; FIBER 2.0g; CHOL 60mg; IRON 2.9mg; SODIUM 710mg; CALC 116mg

MENU SUGGESTION

TUSCAN TOMATO SOUP

Grilled pepper-cheese sandwich*

Red grapes

*On sliced Italian bread, layer bottled roasted red bell peppers, pepperoncini peppers, and part-skim mozzarella. Grill in skillet coated with cooking spray until cheese melts.

TUSCAN TOMATO SOUP

2½   cups (1-inch) cubes French bread (about 2½ [1-ounce] slices)
   Olive oil-flavored vegetable cooking spray
1   teaspoon olive oil
4   garlic cloves, crushed
2   (14.5-ounce) cans no-salt-added whole tomatoes, undrained and chopped
1   (14½-ounce) can chicken broth (such as Swanson's)
1   tablespoon balsamic vinegar
1½   teaspoons dried parsley flakes
1   teaspoon dried oregano
½   teaspoon pepper
1   tablespoon plus 2 teaspoons grated Parmesan cheese

1. Preheat oven to 400°.

2. Arrange bread cubes in a single layer on a jelly-roll pan. Lightly coat bread with cooking spray. Bake at 400° for 10 minutes or until dry and toasted. Set aside.

3. Heat oil in a large saucepan over medium-low heat. Add garlic, and sauté 2 minutes. Add tomatoes and next 5 ingredients; bring to a boil. Reduce heat; simmer 10 minutes, stirring occasionally.

4. Divide croutons among 5 bowls; ladle 1 cup soup over croutons in each bowl, and sprinkle with 1 teaspoon cheese. Yield: 5 servings.

CALORIES 108 (19% from fat); FAT 2.3g (sat 0.7g, mono 1.2g, poly 0.4g); PROTEIN 5.2g; CARB 16.9g; FIBER 0.5g; CHOL 2mg; IRON 1.5mg; SODIUM 397mg; CALC 97mg

WINE PICKS

• SPINACH, HAM, AND GRITS SOUFFLÉ; FOUR-CORN PIE: *Gloria Ferrer Blanc de Noirs Sonoma County Nonvintage (California sparkling), $14*

• TOMATO-GREEN BEAN RISOTTO WITH FETA CHEESE: *Livio Felluga Pinot Grigio Colli Orientali del Friuli 1994 (Italian white), $15*

• BEEF-VEGETABLE RAGOÛT WITH SOFT POLENTA: *Michele Chiarlo Barbera d'Asti 1993 (Italian red), $9*

• FRIED-CHICKEN SALAD: *Chappellet Chenin Blanc Napa Valley Dry 1995 (California white), $10*

LAMB AND OKRA WITH INDIAN SPICES

1½ pounds lean, boned leg of lamb
2 tablespoons all-purpose flour
1 tablespoon pumpkin-pie spice
¼ teaspoon salt
⅛ teaspoon black pepper
Vegetable cooking spray
1½ cups chopped onion
3 large garlic cloves, crushed
2 bay leaves
1 (14.5-ounce) can whole tomatoes, undrained and chopped
1 teaspoon ground cumin
1 teaspoon brown sugar
¼ teaspoon salt
¼ teaspoon ground red pepper
1 (14½-ounce) can sliced okra, well drained
6 cups hot cooked rice
2 tablespoons flaked sweetened coconut, toasted

1. Trim fat from lamb; cut lamb into ¾-inch cubes. Combine lamb and next 4 ingredients in a large zip-top plastic bag; seal and toss well. Set aside.
2. Place a large nonstick skillet coated with cooking spray over medium-high heat until hot. Add lamb; cook 5 minutes or until browned on all sides. Drain lamb; set aside. Coat skillet with cooking spray. Add onion, garlic, and bay leaves; sauté 5 minutes or until onion is tender. Return lamb to skillet. Add tomatoes and next 4 ingredients; cover, reduce heat, and simmer 10 minutes, stirring occasionally. Gently stir in okra; cover and simmer 5 additional minutes. Discard bay leaves. Serve over rice; sprinkle with coconut. Yield: 6 servings (serving size: 1 cup lamb mixture, 1 cup rice, and 1 teaspoon coconut).

CALORIES 456 (14% from fat); FAT 7g (sat 2.7g, mono 2.5g, poly 0.6g); PROTEIN 27.5g; CARB 69.6g; FIBER 4g; CHOL 63mg; IRON 4.9mg; SODIUM 511mg; CALC 132mg

QUICK & EASY WEEKNIGHTS

A Touch of Irish

Now here's something to parade about: In honor of St. Patrick's Day, we present three Irish menus with creative interpretations. We've included a corned beef–potato hash, trout in a traditional sour cream sauce, and a lamb soup made with barley. How lucky can you get?

> ### MENU
>
> HOT CORNED BEEF-
> POTATO HASH
>
> *or*
>
> IRISH LAMB-AND-BARLEY
> SOUP
>
> CARAWAY SCONES

HOT CORNED BEEF-POTATO HASH

8 ounces thinly sliced lean deli corned beef
1 pound small red potatoes (about 8 potatoes), thinly sliced
1 cup thinly sliced leek (about 1 medium)
1 (10-ounce) bag angel hair slaw
1 tablespoon vegetable oil
¼ cup plus 2 tablespoons red wine vinegar
2 teaspoons spicy brown mustard
1 teaspoon sugar
½ teaspoon salt
½ teaspoon garlic powder
½ teaspoon pepper

1. Cut corned beef slices crosswise into thin strips; set aside.
2. Place potatoes in a saucepan. Cover with water; bring to a boil. Cook 5 minutes. Add leek; cook 2 additional minutes. Drain well. Combine potato mixture and slaw in a bowl; toss well. Set aside.

3. Heat oil in a large nonstick skillet over medium heat. Add corned beef; sauté 2 minutes. Add vinegar and remaining 5 ingredients; cook 1 minute, stirring frequently. Pour vinaigrette over potato mixture; toss until well-blended and wilted. Serve immediately. Yield: 4 servings (serving size: 2 cups).

CALORIES 218 (24% from fat); FAT 5.9g (sat 1.7g, mono 1g, poly 1.8g); PROTEIN 5.9g; CARB 28.7g; FIBER 4.2g; CHOL 40mg; IRON 2.6mg; SODIUM 913mg; CALC 68mg

IRISH LAMB-AND-BARLEY SOUP

Vegetable cooking spray
1¼ pounds boneless lean lamb leg, cut into 1-inch cubes
2 (10½-ounce) cans beef broth
1 cup water
2 cups coarsely chopped green cabbage
1 cup chopped carrot
1 cup chopped onion
1 cup peeled, chopped rutabaga
⅓ cup uncooked quick-cooking barley
1 teaspoon dried thyme
¼ teaspoon garlic powder
¼ teaspoon ground allspice
¼ teaspoon pepper
1 bay leaf

1. Place a Dutch oven coated with cooking spray over medium-high heat until hot. Add lamb; cook 5 minutes or until browned. Add broth and remaining ingredients; bring to a boil. Cover, reduce heat, and simmer 20 minutes or until lamb is tender, stirring occasionally. Discard bay leaf. Yield: 4 servings (serving size: 2 cups).

CALORIES 331 (18% from fat); FAT 7g (sat 2.4g, mono 2.6g, poly 0.8g); PROTEIN 38.6g; CARB 27.9g; FIBER 5.8g; CHOL 119mg; IRON 4.7mg; SODIUM 1,084mg; CALC 70mg

CARAWAY SCONES

2 cups all-purpose flour
1½ tablespoons sugar
2 teaspoons baking powder
1 teaspoon caraway seeds
½ teaspoon salt
3 tablespoons stick margarine, chilled and cut into small pieces
⅔ cup 1% low-fat milk
1 large egg, lightly beaten
Vegetable cooking spray

1. Preheat oven to 400°.
2. Combine first 5 ingredients; cut in margarine with a pastry blender or 2 knives until mixture resembles coarse meal. Combine milk and egg; add to flour mixture, stirring just until moist (dough will be sticky). Turn dough out onto a lightly floured surface, and knead 4 or 5 times. Pat dough into an 8-inch circle on a baking sheet coated with cooking spray. Cut dough into 12 wedges, cutting into, but not through, dough. Bake at 400° for 15 minutes. Serve scones warm. Yield: 12 servings.

CALORIES 120 (27% from fat); FAT 3.6g (sat 0.8g, mono 1.5g, poly 1.1g); PROTEIN 3.2g; CARB 18.5g; FIBER 0.6g; CHOL 19mg; IRON 1.2mg; SODIUM 144mg; CALC 69mg

---

TROUT WITH SOUR CREAM-CUCUMBER SAUCE

½ cup peeled, chopped cucumber
½ cup fat-free sour cream
½ cup plain fat-free yogurt
½ teaspoon grated lemon rind
2 teaspoons fresh lemon juice
½ teaspoon dried dillweed
¼ teaspoon pepper
⅛ teaspoon salt
4 (6-ounce) rainbow trout fillets
Vegetable cooking spray

1. Combine first 6 ingredients in a bowl; stir well, and set aside.
2. Sprinkle pepper and salt over trout; place trout on a broiler pan coated with cooking spray. Broil 8 minutes or until fish flakes easily when tested with a fork. Spoon ¼ cup cucumber mixture over each fillet. Yield: 4 servings.

CALORIES 293 (35% from fat); FAT 11.5g (sat 2g, mono 4.1g, poly 4g); PROTEIN 39.1g; CARB 5.2g; FIBER 0.1g; CHOL 99mg; IRON 2.7mg; SODIUM 204mg; CALC 136mg

---

MASHED ROOTS

4 cups peeled, cubed baking potato (about 1½ pounds)
2 cups peeled, sliced parsnip (about 12 ounces)
2 cups peeled, cubed turnip (about 12 ounces)
2 bay leaves
¼ cup plus 1 tablespoon reduced-calorie stick margarine
¼ cup skim milk
½ teaspoon salt
¼ teaspoon pepper

1. Place first 4 ingredients in a large saucepan; cover with water, and bring to a boil. Cook 20 minutes or until vegetables are very tender. Drain well; discard bay leaves. Return vegetables to pan; add margarine, milk, salt, and pepper. Beat at medium speed of an electric mixer until smooth. Yield: 6 servings (serving size: 1 cup).

CALORIES 221 (26% from fat); FAT 6.4g (sat 1.3g, mono 2.7g, poly 2g); PROTEIN 3.7g; CARB 38.7g; FIBER 3.9g; CHOL 0mg; IRON 0.9mg; SODIUM 342mg; CALC 56mg

---

CORNED BEEF-CABBAGE PIZZA

1 (10-ounce) can refrigerated pizza crust dough
Vegetable cooking spray
2 ounces thinly sliced lean deli corned beef
1 (10-ounce) bag angel hair slaw
¼ teaspoon salt
⅛ teaspoon pepper
¾ cup fat-free traditional pasta sauce
½ cup (2 ounces) finely shredded part-skim mozzarella cheese
¼ cup grated Parmesan cheese

1. Preheat oven to 425°.
2. Unroll dough; pat dough into bottom and ½ inch up sides of a 13 x 9-inch baking dish coated with cooking spray. Bake at 425° for 7 minutes or until crust begins to brown. Remove from oven; set aside.
3. Cut corned beef slices crosswise into thin strips; set aside.
4. Coat a large nonstick skillet with cooking spray; place over medium heat until hot. Add slaw, salt, and pepper; sauté 7 minutes or until wilted. Set aside.
5. Spread pasta sauce over pizza crust; spread slaw mixture over sauce. Top with corned beef, and sprinkle with cheeses. Bake at 425° for 14 minutes or until crust is golden. Serve immediately. Yield: 4 servings.

CALORIES 323 (25% from fat); FAT 8.8g (sat 3.3g, mono 2.4g, poly 0.3g); PROTEIN 11.7g; CARB 43.2g; FIBER 1.7g; CHOL 26mg; IRON 0.8mg; SODIUM 1,082mg; CALC 195mg

PUB SALAD

- 4 cups torn Boston lettuce (about 2 small heads)
- ½ cup pickled sliced beets
- ½ cup peeled, thinly sliced cucumber
- 1 hard-cooked large egg, sliced
- ¼ cup diced celery
- ¼ cup diced onion
  Creamy Tarragon Dressing
- ½ cup (2 ounces) shredded reduced-fat sharp Cheddar cheese

1. Arrange lettuce on salad plates; top with beets and next 4 ingredients. Drizzle 2 tablespoons salad dressing over each; sprinkle evenly with cheese. Yield: 4 servings.

CALORIES 109 (36% from fat); FAT 4.4g (sat 2g, mono 1.3g, poly 0.4g); PROTEIN 8.1g; CARB 10.2g; FIBER 1.2g; CHOL 63mg; IRON 0.7mg; SODIUM 410mg; CALC 172mg

Creamy Tarragon Dressing:

- ¼ cup fat-free mayonnaise
- ¼ cup plain fat-free yogurt
- 1 tablespoon white wine vinegar
- ¾ teaspoon Dijon mustard
- ½ teaspoon dried tarragon

1. Combine all ingredients. Yield: ½ cup (serving size: 2 tablespoons).

CALORIES 22 (4% from fat); FAT 0.1g; (sat 0.0g, mono 0.0g, poly 0.1g) PROTEIN 0.8g; CARB 4.2g; FIBER 0g; CHOL 0mg; IRON 0mg; SODIUM 229mg; CALC 172mg

WINE PICKS

- **IRISH LAMB-AND-BARLEY SOUP:** *Guinness Stout*

- **TROUT WITH SOUR CREAM-CUCUMBER SAUCE:** *Joh. Hos. Prum Riesling Kabinett Mosel Ürziger Würzgarten 1993 (German white), $12*

- **CORNED BEEF-CABBAGE PIZZA:** *Black Opal Shiraz South Eastern Australia 1994 (red), $9*

Make the White Decision

If you've never made a béchamel sauce, it's easy and light—if you make it our way. To show you just how versatile this basic white sauce is, we've applied it to five recipes from renowned cooking instructor Anne Willan.

A béchamel sauce (pronounced "bay-shah-MEHL") is one of the foundations of creative cooking. It's traditionally made by stirring milk or cream into a butter-flour mixture called a roux. You can use this sauce on its own or to build other sauces (add cheese, for example, and you have a Mornay sauce).

Once you've learned to make it, you can use a béchamel sauce in many dishes. We made a difference, however, by lightening Willan's béchamel sauce and the recipes that call for it. We replaced the cream with 1% low-fat milk and used margarine instead of butter, and in a smaller quantity. Yet all of the rich taste of a béchamel sauce is still there—that's because we've followed Willan's method of steeping savory flavorings such as whole peppercorns, onion, and bay leaf in the warm milk.

Whereas an average béchamel sauce contains about 76% calories from fat, our lightened version has 46%. And lest you think a French sauce is *trop difficile* to make, we provide step-by-step instructions to show you just how easy it is.

BÉCHAMEL SAUCE

- 2½ cups 1% low-fat milk
- 8 black peppercorns
- 1 (½-inch-thick) slice onion
- 1 bay leaf
- 2 tablespoons stick margarine
- ¼ cup all-purpose flour
- ¼ teaspoon salt
- ⅛ teaspoon ground white pepper
  Dash of ground nutmeg

1. Combine first 4 ingredients in a heavy saucepan; cook over medium-high heat to 180° or until tiny bubbles form around edge (do not boil). Remove from heat. Cover; let stand 10 minutes. Strain mixture through a sieve into a bowl; discard solids. Set milk aside.

2. Melt margarine in saucepan over medium heat. Add flour, stirring with a whisk until blended. Cook, stirring constantly, 1 minute. Gradually add strained milk; cook over medium-low heat 5 minutes or until thick. Stir in salt, pepper, and nutmeg. Yield: 2¼ cups (serving size: ¼ cup).

CALORIES 64 (46% from fat); FAT 3.3g (sat 1g, mono 1.3g, poly 0.8g); PROTEIN 2.6g; CARB 5.9g; FIBER 0.1g; CHOL 3mg; IRON 0.2mg; SODIUM 129mg; CALC 85mg

HOW TO MAKE A LIGHT WHITE SAUCE

❶ *Willan steeps peppercorns, onion, and bay leaf in the milk over medium heat for about 5 minutes. This flavor combination infuses the milk with sweet, nutty tones.*

❷ *A smooth roux is the key to a creamy white sauce. Carefully whisk the flour into the melted margarine, and cook 1 minute. Watch carefully, because an overcooked roux will make the white sauce taste burned.*

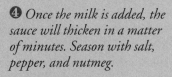

❸ *Another key to a smooth sauce is to slowly but vigorously whisk the milk into the roux.*

❹ *Once the milk is added, the sauce will thicken in a matter of minutes. Season with salt, pepper, and nutmeg.*

PERFECT PASTA AND CHEESE

One serving of Anne's Perfect Pasta and Cheese has almost 50% more calcium than a cup of milk.

Béchamel Sauce (page 62)
- 2 teaspoons margarine
- ½ cup minced shallots
- 2 cups sliced mushrooms
- 1½ cups sliced shiitake mushroom caps (about 4 ounces)
- ¼ teaspoon salt
- ¼ teaspoon pepper
- 3 garlic cloves, minced
- ¾ cup fresh breadcrumbs
- 2 cups (8 ounces) shredded reduced-fat sharp Cheddar cheese, divided
- ¼ cup chopped chives, divided
- 3½ cups uncooked penne (tubular-shaped pasta)

1. Preheat oven to 350°.
2. Prepare Béchamel Sauce; set aside, and keep warm.
3. Melt margarine in a large nonstick skillet over medium-high heat. Add shallots; sauté 1 minute. Stir in mushrooms, salt, pepper, and garlic; sauté 3 minutes or until liquid has evaporated. Set aside.
4. Combine breadcrumbs, ¼ cup cheese, and 1 tablespoon chives. Stir well; set aside. Add 1¾ cups cheese to Béchamel Sauce; stir until cheese melts. Cook pasta according to package directions, omitting salt and fat. Drain well; return pasta to pan. Add mushroom mixture, cheese sauce, and 3 tablespoons chives; stir well.
5. Spoon pasta mixture into a 3-quart casserole; sprinkle with breadcrumb mixture. Bake at 350° for 30 minutes. Yield: 7 servings (serving size: 1 cup).

CALORIES 403 (28% from fat); FAT 12.5g (sat 5.2g, mono 4.1g, poly 2g); PROTEIN 20.6g; CARB 51.8g; FIBER 2g; CHOL 25mg; IRON 3mg; SODIUM 527mg; CALC 419mg

CANNELLONI STUFFED WITH VEAL AND HERBS

2 cups Béchamel Sauce (page 62), divided
8 uncooked cannelloni
¾ pound lean ground veal
¼ cup chopped fresh parsley
2 tablespoons grated Parmesan cheese
1 tablespoon chopped fresh thyme
1 tablespoon chopped fresh sage
1 large egg, lightly beaten
Vegetable cooking spray
2 tablespoons grated Parmesan cheese

1. Preheat oven to 350°. Prepare Béchamel Sauce; keep warm.
2. Cook pasta according to package directions, omitting salt and fat.
3. Combine 1 cup Béchamel Sauce, veal, and next 5 ingredients in a bowl.
4. Spoon veal mixture into cooked cannelloni. Arrange stuffed cannelloni in a 13 x 9-inch baking dish coated with cooking spray. Spoon 1 cup Béchamel Sauce over cannelloni. Cover and bake at 350° for 40 minutes. Uncover; sprinkle with 2 tablespoons cheese. Bake an additional 10 minutes or until cheese is golden. Yield: 4 servings (serving size: 2 cannelloni).

CALORIES 523 (29% from fat); FAT 17.1g (sat 5.9g, mono 6.1g, poly 2.5g); PROTEIN 33.2g; CARB 55.2g; FIBER 0.6g; CHOL 135mg; IRON 1.9mg; SODIUM 472mg; CALC 295mg

CRÊPES WITH WILD MUSHROOMS AND HERBS

We suggest cooking the crêpes before making the béchamel sauce.

1¼ cups all-purpose flour
1½ cups skim milk
1 tablespoon margarine, melted
1 large egg, lightly beaten
Vegetable cooking spray
Béchamel Sauce (page 62)
2 teaspoons margarine
3½ cups sliced mushrooms
3½ cups sliced shiitake mushroom caps (about 8 ounces)
½ cup minced shallots
2 tablespoons dry sherry
3 garlic cloves, minced
¼ cup chopped fresh parsley or 1 tablespoon dried parsley
3 tablespoons minced chives

1. Place flour in a medium bowl. Combine milk, 1 tablespoon margarine, and egg; add to flour, stirring with a whisk until almost smooth. Cover; chill 1 hour.
2. Coat an 8-inch crêpe pan or nonstick skillet with cooking spray; place over medium-high heat until hot. Remove pan from heat. Pour a scant ¼ cup batter into pan; quickly tilt pan in all directions so batter covers pan with a thin film. Cook about 1 minute.
3. Carefully lift edge of crêpe with a spatula to test for doneness (crêpe is ready to turn when it can be shaken loose from pan and underside is lightly browned). Turn crêpe over; cook 30 seconds on other side. Place crêpe on a towel; allow to cool. Repeat procedure until all batter is used. Stack crêpes between single layers of wax paper or paper towels to prevent sticking.
4. Preheat oven to 350°.
5. Prepare Béchamel Sauce. Set aside, and keep warm.
6. Melt 2 teaspoons margarine over medium-high heat in a large nonstick skillet. Add mushrooms, shallots, sherry, and garlic; sauté 5 minutes.
7. Add parsley and chives to Béchamel Sauce; stir well. Add 1 cup béchamel mixture to mushroom mixture, and stir well.
8. Spoon ¼ cup mushroom mixture onto center of each crêpe. Bring 2 opposite sides to center; fold over filling. Beginning at 1 short side, roll up crêpe tightly, jelly-roll fashion. Place stuffed crêpes, seam sides down, in a 13 x 9-inch baking dish coated with cooking spray. Pour remaining béchamel mixture over crêpes. Bake at 350° for 20 minutes. Yield: 6 servings (serving size: 2 crêpes).

CALORIES 289 (31% from fat); FAT 9.8g (sat 2.5g, mono 3.8g, poly 2.6g); PROTEIN 12g; CARB 38.8g; FIBER 2.2g; CHOL 42mg; IRON 0.2mg; SODIUM 280mg; CALC 229mg

GRATIN OF LEEKS AND HAM

Béchamel Sauce (page 62)
4 medium leeks (about 2½ pounds)
16 very thin slices lean smoked ham (about ¾ pound)
Vegetable cooking spray
1 tablespoon grated Parmesan cheese

1. Preheat oven to 350°. Prepare Béchamel Sauce; keep warm.
2. Remove roots, outer leaves, and tops from leeks, leaving 8 inches of each leek. Cut each leek in half lengthwise to, but not through, root end. Rinse under cold water; drain. Tie leeks securely with string.
3. Place leeks in a medium saucepan. Cover leeks with water, and bring to a boil. Reduce heat, and simmer, uncovered, 15 minutes or until leeks are tender. Rinse leeks under cold water; drain and squeeze dry. Remove and discard string. Finish cutting each leek lengthwise through root end; cut each half crosswise. Wrap each quarter with a slice of ham.
4. Place ham rolls in a 13 x 9-inch baking dish coated with cooking spray. Pour Béchamel Sauce over ham rolls; sprinkle with cheese. Bake at 350° for 25 minutes. Broil 3 minutes or until browned. Yield: 4 servings (serving size: 4 ham rolls).

CALORIES 350 (33% from fat); FAT 13g (sat 4g, mono 5.3g, poly 2.5g); PROTEIN 26g; CARB 32.2g; FIBER 1.7g; CHOL 52mg; IRON 4.3mg; SODIUM 1,361mg; CALC 289mg

CREAMED COD WITH MUSHROOMS AND SHRIMP

Béchamel Sauce (page 62)
2 pounds cod fillets
Vegetable cooking spray
½ cup minced shallots
¼ cup dry white wine
¼ teaspoon salt
⅛ teaspoon pepper
2 cups sliced mushrooms
½ cup bottled clam juice
2 tablespoons fresh lemon juice
12 large shrimp, peeled and deveined (about ½ pound)
¼ cup dry breadcrumbs
1 teaspoon margarine, melted

1. Preheat oven to 350°. Prepare Béchamel Sauce; keep warm.
2. Place fish in a 13 x 9-inch baking dish coated with cooking spray. Sprinkle with shallots and next 3 ingredients; cover loosely with aluminum foil. Bake at 350° for 25 minutes. Let fish cool to room temperature. Transfer fish to a bowl, reserving cooking liquid. Shred fish with 2 forks; set aside. Strain cooking liquid through a sieve into a bowl; discard solids.
3. Combine cooking liquid, mushrooms, clam juice, and lemon juice in a nonstick skillet. Cover; cook over medium-high heat for 3 minutes. Stir mushroom mixture and fish into Béchamel Sauce; pour into six gratin dishes coated with cooking spray. Place shrimp on béchamel mixture; sprinkle with breadcrumbs. Drizzle with margarine. Broil on second shelf 5 minutes or until shrimp are done. Yield: 6 servings (serving size: 1 cup).

CALORIES 322 (22% from fat); FAT 8g (sat 2g, mono 2.7g, poly 2.3g); PROTEIN 43.9g; CARB 16.6g; FIBER 0.8g; CHOL 306mg; IRON 3mg; SODIUM 549mg; CALC 202mg

FOR TWO

Cold Comfort

The cruciferous vegetables of winter make flavorful, robust salads that are good for you . . . and that's the truth.

The problem with dark green vegetables like broccoli, Brussels sprouts, and Swiss chard is that they're so nutritious—so much so, you can't believe how flavorful they are. Even their family name, Cruciferae, sounds daunting, as if they could help prevent diseases. As a matter of fact, they do: Scientific studies have shown that they can actually decrease the risk of many kinds of cancer, especially breast cancer.

Because cruciferous vegetables are so plentiful in the winter months, we used them to make some salads that incorporate other bold vegetables and citrus fruits. As you enjoy these salads, which are all served warm or at room temperature, don't think about all the vitamin A and C you're getting. Or all the fiber they provide. Or that they're natural sources of folates, which play an ancillary role in blocking cancer. Just ignore all that and say, "Mmmm."

BROCCOLI, ORANGE, AND WATERCRESS SALAD

(pictured on page 74)

2 medium oranges
1 teaspoon vegetable oil
1 teaspoon prepared horseradish
1 teaspoon honey
⅛ teaspoon salt
Dash of pepper
2 cups small broccoli florets
¼ cup thinly sliced red onion, separated into rings
2 cups trimmed watercress

1. Peel and section oranges over a large bowl, and squeeze membranes to extract juice. Set orange sections aside, and reserve 1 tablespoon juice. Discard orange membranes.
2. Add oil and next 4 ingredients to reserved orange juice. Stir well, and set aside.
3. Arrange broccoli in a steamer basket over boiling water. Cover and steam 1½ minutes or until crisp-tender. Rinse broccoli under cold water; drain well.
4. Add broccoli, orange sections, onion, and watercress to orange juice mixture; toss well. Divide salad evenly between 2 plates. Yield: 2 servings.

CALORIES 121 (29% from fat); FAT 3.9g (sat 0.7g, mono 1.1g, poly 1.8g); PROTEIN 4.5g; CARB 20.9g; FIBER 7.8g; CHOL 0mg; IRON 1mg; SODIUM 181mg; CALC 124mg

AFRICAN-SPICED BROCCOLI-AND-CAULIFLOWER SALAD

Toasting the spices in a skillet brings out their sweet and hot flavors.

¾ cup small broccoli florets
¾ cup small cauliflower florets
½ cup (¼-inch) diagonally sliced carrot
⅛ teaspoon salt
¼ teaspoon ground ginger
¼ teaspoon ground cumin
⅛ teaspoon ground coriander
⅛ teaspoon ground nutmeg
⅛ teaspoon dried crushed red pepper
3 tablespoons fat-free sour cream
2 teaspoons cider vinegar
½ teaspoon honey
2 tablespoons sliced green onions

1. Arrange first 3 ingredients in a steamer basket over boiling water. Cover and steam 2 minutes. Rinse broccoli mixture under cold water; drain well.
2. Combine salt and next 5 ingredients in a small skillet; cook over medium heat, stirring constantly, 2 minutes or until lightly browned.
3. Combine spice mixture, sour cream, vinegar, and honey in a bowl; stir well. Add broccoli mixture; toss well to coat. Stir in green onions just before serving. Yield: 2 servings (serving size: 1 cup).

CALORIES 57 (6% from fat); FAT 0.4g (sat 0.2g, mono 0.1g, poly 0.1g); PROTEIN 3.8g; CARB 10.7g; FIBER 3g; CHOL 0mg; IRON 0.9mg; SODIUM 194mg; CALC 40mg

BRUSSELS SPROUTS, ORANGE, AND FENNEL SALAD

2 tablespoons white wine
   vinegar
1 teaspoon grated orange rind
2 teaspoons water
1 teaspoon vegetable oil
¼ teaspoon ground ginger
⅛ teaspoon salt
⅛ teaspoon freshly ground
   pepper
2 cups trimmed Brussels sprouts
   (about ½ pound)
¾ cup thinly sliced fennel
2 small oranges, peeled,
   quartered, and thinly sliced

1. Combine first 7 ingredients in a
bowl. Stir well; set aside.
2. Arrange Brussels sprouts in a steamer
basket over boiling water. Cover and
steam 8 minutes. Rinse sprouts under
cold water; drain well. Cut sprouts in
half lengthwise. Add sprouts, fennel,
and orange slices to vinegar mixture;
toss well. Yield: 2 servings (serving
size: 1½ cups).

CALORIES 102 (25% from fat); FAT 2.8g (sat 0.5g, mono 0.7g,
poly 1.3g); PROTEIN 4.6g; CARB 17.8g; FIBER 6.9g;
CHOL 0mg; IRON 2.3mg; SODIUM 167mg; CALC 100mg

CHILE-SPIKED CAULIFLOWER SALAD

2 tablespoons chopped fresh
   parsley
2½ tablespoons lemon juice
2 teaspoons anchovy paste
1 teaspoon olive oil
⅛ teaspoon bottled minced garlic
2½ cups small cauliflower florets
⅓ cup thinly sliced radishes
1 jalapeño pepper, halved
   lengthwise, seeded, and thinly
   sliced (about 1½ teaspoons)

1. Combine first 5 ingredients; stir.
2. Arrange cauliflower in a steamer
basket over boiling water. Cover and
steam 1½ minutes or until cauliflower
is crisp-tender. Rinse cauliflower under cold water; drain well.
3. Combine cauliflower, radishes, and
jalapeño in a bowl; toss with lemon
juice mixture. Yield: 2 servings (serving size: 1 cup).

CALORIES 67 (30% from fat); FAT 2.3g (sat 0.6g, mono 0.9g,
poly 0.2g); PROTEIN 4.3g; CARB 9.9g; FIBER 3.4g;
CHOL 0mg; IRON 0.9mg; SODIUM 731mg; CALC 41mg

WINTER-GREENS SLAW WITH WARM BACON DRESSING

½ cup sliced onion
¼ cup fat-free cream cheese,
   softened
¼ cup skim milk
2 teaspoons white wine
   vinegar
1 teaspoon Dijon mustard
½ teaspoon dried dillweed
½ teaspoon honey
⅛ teaspoon pepper
2 cups thinly sliced kale
2 cups thinly sliced beet greens
2 cups thinly sliced Swiss
   chard
2 slices turkey-bacon, cooked
   and chopped

1. Heat a large nonstick skillet over
medium-high heat. Add onion; sauté 5
minutes or until golden. Reduce heat
to low. Add cream cheese and next 6

ingredients; stir until blended. Remove skillet from heat.
2. Add kale, beet greens, and Swiss
chard to skillet; toss to coat. Cover and
let stand 30 seconds. Divide slaw evenly
between 2 plates; top each with chopped
bacon. Serve immediately. Yield: 2 servings (serving size: 2 cups).

CALORIES 141 (19% from fat); FAT 2.9g (sat 0.6g, mono 1.1g,
poly 0.8g); PROTEIN 11.8g; CARB 17.8g; FIBER 2.2g;
CHOL 15mg; IRON 2.8mg; SODIUM 582mg; CALC 297mg

SESAME SPINACH SALAD

2 tablespoons low-sodium soy
   sauce
1 tablespoon sesame seeds,
   toasted and crushed
1 tablespoon honey
½ pound fresh turnip greens
1 (10-ounce) bag fresh spinach
2 quarts water

1. Combine first 3 ingredients in a
bowl, stirring until well-blended.
2. Remove stems from turnip greens
and spinach. Bring 2 quarts water to a
boil in an 8-quart stockpot or Dutch
oven. Add turnip greens; cover and
cook 1 minute. Add spinach, and cook
until wilted. Drain and rinse greens
mixture under cold water; drain and
pat dry. Toss with sesame dressing.
Yield: 2 servings (serving size: 2 cups).
Note: Mustard greens can be substituted for turnip greens.

CALORIES 118 (23% from fat); FAT 3g (sat 0.5g, mono 0.9g,
poly 1.3g); PROTEIN 5.5g; CARB 19.9g; FIBER 7g;
CHOL 0mg; IRON 4.7mg; SODIUM 517mg; CALC 363mg

Dip Dip Hooray!

On a quest for a light chile con queso? Look no further: We've got this creamy Tex-Mex dip and healthy nachos to go along with it.

To each era its dip. Today it's the inescapable chile con queso, found not only in such expected locales as Tex-Mex restaurants but in movie theaters, ballparks, and service stations.

Obviously there's a reason for chile con queso's popularity that goes beyond the comfort factor. It's the swashbuckling duel that takes place between the hot green chiles and the soothing melted cheeses. Put this flavor punch on chips, and you've created a crispy mini pizza with a Southwestern accent.

The problem with chile con queso is the high fat content, and the same goes for the fried chips that usually accompany the dip. So we set out to change all that by creating a light chile con queso based on the classic recipe that appears on some cans of diced tomatoes and chiles. Our lightened version cuts the fat by two-thirds—reason enough to shout olé!

BEFORE & AFTER	
SERVING SIZE	
¼ cup	
CALORIES	
88	63
FAT	
6g	1.7g
PERCENT OF TOTAL CALORIES	
61%	24%

HOW WE DID IT

- Substituted fat-free cream cheese for some of the processed cheese
- Used light processed cheese in place of the regular

CHILE CON QUESO DIP

1 (14.5-ounce) can diced tomatoes, undrained
1 (10-ounce) can diced tomatoes and green chiles, undrained
1 teaspoon olive oil
½ cup chopped onion
2 garlic cloves, minced
1 (8-ounce) block fat-free cream cheese, softened
1 teaspoon chili powder
6 ounces light processed cheese, cubed (such as Velveeta Light)
Cilantro sprigs (optional)

1. Drain tomatoes and tomatoes with chiles in a colander over a bowl, reserving ⅓ cup liquid; set tomatoes and reserved liquid aside.
2. Heat oil in a medium saucepan over medium heat. Add onion and garlic; sauté 4 minutes. Add cream cheese; cook, stirring constantly, until cheese melts. Add tomatoes, reserved liquid, and chili powder; bring to a boil. Add processed cheese; reduce heat, and simmer, stirring constantly, 3 minutes or until cheese melts. Garnish with cilantro, if desired. Serve warm with baked tortilla chips. Yield: 3½ cups (serving size: ¼ cup).

CALORIES 63 (24% from fat); FAT 1.7g (sat 0.9g, mono 0.2g, poly 0.1g); PROTEIN 5.5g; CARB 6.4g; FIBER 0.3g; CHOL 7mg; IRON 0.3mg; SODIUM 400mg; CALC 132mg

QUICK NACHOS

For this simple nacho recipe we used canned beans, which increased the sodium significantly. If this is a problem for you, use your own refried beans recipe and leave out the salt.

5 cups baked tortilla chips (about 4 ounces)
1 (16-ounce) can fat-free refried beans
1 cup warm Chile Con Queso Dip
2 cups thinly sliced iceberg lettuce
¼ cup sliced green onions
¼ cup fat-free sour cream

1. Place chips on a large serving platter. Heat refried beans according to label directions, and spread warm beans over chips. Pour Chile Con Queso Dip over beans, and top with lettuce, green onions, and sour cream. Yield: 4 servings.

CALORIES 335 (9% from fat); FAT 3.3g (sat 1g, mono 0.3g, poly 0.4g); PROTEIN 18.9g; CARB 59.8g; FIBER 7.9g; CHOL 7mg; IRON 3.1mg; SODIUM 1,057mg; CALC 199mg

A NACHO ABOVE

Homemade chips are a snap to make and, in our opinion, much better than the commercial baked varieties. Simply stack corn or flour tortillas and cut into wedges. Then place cut tortillas on a baking sheet in a single layer and bake at 350° for 10 minutes.

The New Iron Age

Are the oldest pots in your kitchen made of cast iron? If so, they're probably well-seasoned and have been used for practically everything—from fried chicken, chili, and hamburgers to pineapple upside-down cake. Of course you can make an upside-down cake in any ol' cake pan you have, but the gooey, caramelized edges won't turn out nearly so crunchy as when made in a cast-iron skillet. The same goes for corn bread. Everything browns better in cast iron.

FRENCH ONION BURGERS

French Onion Burgers get their sweetness from caramelized onions.

- 2 teaspoons vegetable oil
- 2 cups chopped onion
- 1 pound ground round
- ¼ teaspoon pepper
- 1 large egg white, lightly beaten
- 1 teaspoon salt
- 4 (1½-ounce) French bread rolls or hamburger buns, split and toasted
- 1 tablespoon plus 1 teaspoon fat-free French or blue cheese salad dressing

1. Heat oil in a 12-inch cast-iron skillet over medium-high heat. Add onion; sauté 10 minutes or until tender. Spoon onion into a bowl; let cool.
2. Add beef, pepper, and egg white to onion, and stir well. Divide beef mixture into 4 equal portions, shaping into ¾-inch-thick patties.
3. Sprinkle salt evenly over surface of skillet. Heat salt in skillet over high heat 2 minutes. Add patties; cook patties 5 minutes on each side or until done. Place patties on bottom halves of rolls; top each with 1 teaspoon French dressing and top half of a bun. Yield: 4 servings.

CALORIES 340 (21% from fat); FAT 7.8g (sat 2.4g, mono 3g, poly 1.8g); PROTEIN 31.6g; CARB 33.1g; FIBER 2.3g; CHOL 66mg; IRON 3.5mg; SODIUM 957mg; CALC 40mg

---

APRICOT-GLAZED PORK TENDERLOIN

- 1 (1-pound) pork tenderloin
- ¼ cup all-purpose flour
- 1 tablespoon plus 1 teaspoon vegetable oil, divided
- ¼ cup minced shallots
- 2 teaspoons peeled, grated fresh gingerroot
- ¾ cup apricot nectar
- ¼ cup dry sherry
- 1 (3-inch) cinnamon stick
- 2 tablespoons low-sodium soy sauce
- 2 teaspoons cornstarch
- ¾ cup low-salt chicken broth
- ½ teaspoon lemon juice
- ½ teaspoon dark sesame oil
- ¼ teaspoon salt
- ⅛ teaspoon pepper

1. Trim fat from pork; cut crosswise into ¼-inch-thick slices. Combine pork and flour in a large zip-top plastic bag. Seal and shake to coat; set aside.
2. Heat a 10-inch cast-iron skillet over medium-high heat. Add 1½ teaspoons vegetable oil; swirl to coat bottom of skillet. Add half of pork; cook 2 minutes on each side or until done. Remove from skillet; set aside. Repeat procedure with 1½ teaspoons vegetable oil and remaining pork. Let skillet cool slightly.
3. Heat skillet over medium heat. Add 1 teaspoon vegetable oil, swirling to coat. Add shallots and gingerroot; sauté 30 seconds. Stir in apricot nectar, sherry, and cinnamon stick, scraping skillet to loosen browned bits. Combine soy sauce and cornstarch in a small bowl; stir well. Add cornstarch mixture to skillet. Stir in broth and lemon juice.

Bring to a boil; cook, stirring constantly, 1 minute. Return pork to skillet; reduce heat, and simmer 3 minutes or until thoroughly heated. Stir in remaining ingredients. Discard cinnamon stick. Yield: 4 servings (serving size: 3 ounces pork and ¼ cup sauce).

CALORIES 252 (30% from fat); FAT 8.3g (sat 1.9g, mono 2.9g, poly 2.8g); PROTEIN 25.5g; CARB 16.9g; FIBER 0.6g; CHOL 74mg; IRON 2.4mg; SODIUM 416mg; CALC 18mg

---

SICILIAN SWEET-AND-SOUR SWORDFISH

- 2 (6-ounce) swordfish steaks (about ½ inch thick), skinned
- 1 tablespoon all-purpose flour, divided
- 2 teaspoons olive oil, divided
- 1 cup finely chopped onion
- 1 tablespoon capers
- 1 tablespoon raisins
- ½ cup bottled clam juice
- 2 tablespoons dry white wine
- 2 tablespoons tomato paste
- 1 tablespoon water
- 2 tablespoons chopped kalamata olives
- 1 tablespoon red wine vinegar
- 2 teaspoons sugar
- 2 tablespoons chopped fresh parsley

1. Combine swordfish and 2½ teaspoons flour in a large zip-top plastic bag; seal and shake gently to coat.
2. Heat 1 teaspoon oil in a 10-inch cast-iron skillet over high heat. Add swordfish; cook 1½ minutes on each side or until done. Remove from skillet; keep warm.
3. Heat 1 teaspoon oil in skillet over medium heat. Add onion; sauté 3 minutes. Add ½ teaspoon flour, capers, and raisins; cook, stirring constantly, 1 minute. Stir in clam juice and next 3 ingredients; bring to a boil. Add olives, vinegar, and sugar; cook 1 minute. Stir in parsley. Serve sauce with swordfish. Yield: 2 servings (serving size: 5 ounces fish and ¼ cup sauce).

CALORIES 351 (32% from fat); FAT 12.6g (sat 2.7g, mono 6.7g, poly 2.2g); PROTEIN 36.5g; CARB 22.7g; FIBER 3.1g; CHOL 66mg; IRON 2.9mg; SODIUM 708mg; CALC 54mg

PAN-SEARED SCALLOPS WITH CHILI CREAM SAUCE

Pan-Seared Scallops with Chili Cream Sauce is best served over angel hair pasta.

1½ pounds sea scallops
2 tablespoons plus 2 teaspoons all-purpose flour, divided
1 teaspoon vegetable oil
1 teaspoon margarine
1 teaspoon chili powder
¼ teaspoon salt
⅛ teaspoon ground cumin
¾ cup 1% low-fat milk
2 tablespoons chopped fresh cilantro
Fresh cilantro sprigs (optional)

1. Combine scallops and 2 tablespoons flour in a large zip-top plastic bag; seal bag, and shake gently to coat scallops.
2. Heat oil in a 10-inch cast-iron skillet over high heat, swirling to coat bottom of skillet. Add scallops; cook 2 minutes on each side or until lightly browned. Remove scallops from skillet; keep warm.
3. Melt margarine in skillet over medium heat. Add 2 teaspoons flour, and cook, stirring constantly, 30 seconds. Add chili powder, salt, and cumin; cook 30 seconds, stirring frequently. Gradually stir in milk, and cook 2½ minutes or until thick, stirring frequently. Return scallops to skillet; add chopped cilantro, stirring gently to coat. Garnish with cilantro sprigs, if desired. Yield: 4 servings (serving size: 5 ounces scallops and 2 tablespoons sauce).

CALORIES 209 (17% from fat); FAT 4g (sat 0.9g, mono 1g, poly 1.4g); PROTEIN 30.7g; CARB 10.7g; FIBER 0.4g; CHOL 58mg; IRON 1mg; SODIUM 462mg; CALC 103mg

---

MENU SUGGESTION

SKILLET TORTILLA CASSEROLE

Jicama-mango slaw*

Cinnamon-dusted rice pudding

*Combine shredded cabbage, shredded jicama, chopped mango, and fresh lime juice in a bowl. Sprinkle with chopped green onions.

SKILLET TORTILLA CASSEROLE

2 teaspoons olive oil
1 cup chopped onion
1 cup frozen whole-kernel corn, thawed and divided
1 teaspoon dried oregano
¼ teaspoon ground cumin
1 garlic clove, crushed
2 tablespoons all-purpose flour
1 (14.5-ounce) can no-salt-added whole tomatoes, undrained and chopped
1 (15-ounce) can black beans, drained
1 (4.5-ounce) can chopped green chiles
6 (6-inch) corn tortillas, quartered
½ cup sliced green onions
½ cup chopped fresh cilantro, divided
½ cup (2 ounces) shredded sharp Cheddar cheese
½ teaspoon paprika
¼ cup sliced radishes
¼ cup low-fat sour cream

1. Preheat oven to 375°.
2. Heat oil in a 10-inch cast-iron skillet over medium heat. Add 1 cup onion; sauté 5 minutes. Add ¾ cup corn; sauté 5 minutes or until lightly browned. Add oregano, cumin, and garlic; sauté 30 seconds. Add flour; cook, stirring constantly, 1 minute. Add tomatoes, beans, and chiles; cook 2 minutes or until thick. Remove from heat; spoon bean mixture into a bowl.
3. Spread ½ cup bean mixture over bottom of skillet. Arrange half of tortilla quarters over bean mixture, overlapping slightly. Spread half of remaining bean mixture over tortilla quarters; sprinkle with green onions and ¼ cup cilantro. Repeat with remaining tortillas and bean mixture. Top with ¼ cup corn, cheese, and paprika.
4. Bake at 375° for 30 minutes or until thoroughly heated. Remove from oven; let stand 10 minutes. Spoon onto 4 plates; top evenly with ¼ cup cilantro, radishes, and sour cream. Yield: 4 servings (serving size: one-fourth casserole, 1 tablespoon cilantro, 1 tablespoon radishes, and 1 tablespoon sour cream).

CALORIES 365 (27% from fat); FAT 10.8g (sat 4.7g, mono 3.9g, poly 1.2g); PROTEIN 15.3g; CARB 56.6g; FIBER 7.6g; CHOL 21mg; IRON 3.9mg; SODIUM 415mg; CALC 276mg

---

A PAN FOR ALL SEASONS

Cast iron can rust if neglected. By following some basic rules, your skillet should remain rust-free and last for generations:

◆ As soon as food is removed, scrub the skillet under hot water, then place on a warm burner for a few minutes to dry. After the skillet is dry, drizzle some vegetable oil in it. Rub the oil all over the inside of the skillet with a paper towel so that it shines. Let the skillet cool.

◆ Cast iron does not like to be wet when not in use. Never put your cast-iron skillet in the dishwasher.

◆ Cast iron can corrode when acidic foods are added. But when the skillet is well-seasoned, corrosion is unlikely. Just be sure to remove acidic food from the skillet as soon as it has finished cooking.

◆ Rusted cast iron can be saved by scouring the rust away with steel wool. Scrub the skillet with hot, soapy water, then scour with steel wool again before drying. Reseason by adding oil and baking or heating on the burner.

◆ Foods cooked in a cast-iron skillet could contain twice as much or more of the amount of iron they would contain otherwise.

SUKIYAKI-STYLE MIXED GRILL

1 medium zucchini (about 6 ounces)
1 medium carrot (about 3 ounces)
2 teaspoons vegetable oil, divided
1 (6-ounce) package presliced portobello mushrooms
1 medium-size green bell pepper, seeded and cut into ½-inch strips (about 6 ounces)
1 medium-size red onion, cut into ½-inch-thick slices (about ½ pound)
1 medium-size sweet potato, peeled and cut into ¼-inch-thick slices (about 6 ounces)
5 (⅛-inch-thick) slices peeled fresh gingerroot
1 cup sake (rice wine)
¼ cup water
¼ cup low-sodium soy sauce
2 tablespoons sugar
1 teaspoon cornstarch
1 tablespoon water
2 green onions, cut into 2-inch pieces
½ teaspoon dark sesame oil
4 cups hot cooked Chinese-style noodles (about 8 ounces uncooked)

1. Cut zucchini and carrot lengthwise into quarters; cut each quarter crosswise in half. Set aside.
2. Heat a 10-inch cast-iron skillet over high heat. Add ½ teaspoon vegetable oil; swirl to coat bottom of skillet. Add zucchini; sauté over medium-high heat 3 minutes or until browned. Place zucchini in a bowl. Add ½ teaspoon vegetable oil to skillet; swirl to coat. Add mushrooms; sauté 2 minutes or until browned. Add mushrooms to zucchini.
3. Add ½ teaspoon vegetable oil to skillet; swirl to coat. Add pepper and red onion; sauté 5 minutes or until browned. Place pepper mixture in a bowl. Add ½ teaspoon vegetable oil to skillet; swirl to coat. Add carrot and sweet potato; sauté 2 minutes or until browned. Add to pepper mixture. Add gingerroot to skillet; sauté 30 seconds. Stir in sake and next 3 ingredients; scrape skillet to loosen browned bits.

Add pepper mixture; bring to a boil. Cover, reduce heat, and simmer 5 minutes or until tender. Combine cornstarch and 1 tablespoon water in a bowl; stir well. Add cornstarch mixture and zucchini mixture to skillet. Bring to a boil; cook, stirring constantly, 1 minute. Stir in green onions and sesame oil. Serve over noodles. Yield: 4 servings (serving size: 1 cup vegetable mixture and 1 cup noodles).

CALORIES 376 (11% from fat); FAT 4.5g (sat 0.7g, mono 1.1g, poly 2g); PROTEIN 10.7g; CARB 73.2g; FIBER 5.9g; CHOL 0mg; IRON 4.2mg; SODIUM 418mg; CALC 55mg

GOLDEN POTATOES WITH CARROTS

3 medium baking potatoes, peeled and cut crosswise into ¼-inch-thick slices (about 1½ pounds)
1½ cups (¼-inch-thick) sliced carrot
1 tablespoon vegetable oil
1 cup finely chopped onion
¾ teaspoon dried thyme
½ teaspoon salt
⅛ teaspoon pepper

HOW TO SEASON A CAST-IRON SKILLET

Because a well-seasoned cast-iron skillet requires little oil for cooking, it's right at home preparing light and healthy meals. The more you use a cast-iron skillet, the more nonstick the surface becomes. That's because cast iron is porous, and when it's heated it absorbs a bit of the oil, protecting it against future moisture.

When a cast-iron skillet is new it must be seasoned before use. That means it must be cleaned well, then dried, oiled, and heated for a length of time. To season it repeat this process several times before using.

1) Simply rinse under warm sudsy water. 2) Dry skillet well. 3) Rub the skillet generously with oil. 4) Leave it on a burner turned to low heat for about 1 hour, or bake it in a 350° oven for 2 hours. Let the skillet cool, then pour out any residual oil.

1. Cook potatoes and carrot in boiling water 5 minutes; drain.
2. Heat oil in a 10-inch cast-iron skillet over medium-high heat, swirling to coat bottom of skillet. Add potato mixture; sauté 5 minutes. Add onion and remaining ingredients; sauté 10 minutes or until tender. Yield: 4 servings (serving size: 1 cup).

CALORIES 138 (24% from fat); FAT 3.7g (sat 0.7g, mono 1g, poly 1.7g); PROTEIN 4.2g; CARB 23.7g; FIBER 4.4g; CHOL 0mg; IRON 4.7mg; SODIUM 321mg; CALC 63mg

APPLE-GLAZED DESSERT PANCAKE

This dessert is a variation on a classic Dutch Baby.

 1 tablespoon margarine
 3 cups sliced Rome apple (about 1 pound)
 1 tablespoon brown sugar
 ¾ teaspoon ground cinnamon
 ¼ teaspoon ground nutmeg
 ½ cup apple juice
 ¼ cup water
 1 teaspoon cornstarch
 1 cup all-purpose flour
 2 cups 1% low-fat milk, divided
 2 teaspoons vanilla extract
 ¼ teaspoon salt
 ⅓ cup sugar
 2 large eggs
 2 large egg whites
Vegetable cooking spray
 1 tablespoon powdered sugar

1. Preheat oven to 425°.
2. Melt margarine in a 10-inch cast-iron skillet over medium-high heat. Add apple; sauté 3 minutes. Stir in brown sugar, cinnamon, and nutmeg; cook 2 minutes. Combine juice, water, and cornstarch, stirring well; add to skillet. Bring to a boil; cook 1 minute or until thick, stirring gently. Remove from skillet; set aside, and keep warm. Wipe skillet clean with a paper towel.
3. Place skillet in oven for 5 minutes. Combine flour and 1 cup milk in a large bowl; stir well with a whisk. Stir in 1 cup milk, vanilla, and next 4 ingredients; set aside. Coat skillet with cooking spray;

pour batter into preheated skillet. Bake at 425° for 25 minutes or until puffy and brown around edges. Remove from oven; sprinkle with powdered sugar. Cut into wedges; top with apple mixture. Serve immediately. Yield: 8 servings (serving size: 1 wedge and ¼ cup topping).

CALORIES 196 (17% from fat); FAT 3.8g (sat 1.2g, mono 1.3g, poly 0.8g); PROTEIN 6.2g; CARB 34.2g; FIBER 1.8g; CHOL 58mg; IRON 1.2mg; SODIUM 151mg; CALC 93mg

APRICOT UPSIDE-DOWN CAKE

 1¼ cups pineapple juice
 ¾ cup dried apricots, quartered
 2 tablespoons stick margarine
 ⅓ cup firmly packed dark brown sugar
 2 tablespoons finely chopped walnuts
 ¾ cup all-purpose flour
 1 teaspoon baking powder
 ½ cup granulated sugar, divided
 ⅓ cup 1% low-fat milk
 1 large egg yolk
 1 teaspoon vanilla extract
 3 large egg whites (at room temperature)

1. Preheat oven to 350°.
2. Combine pineapple juice and apricots in a saucepan; bring to a boil. Reduce heat; simmer 8 minutes or until plump. Drain apricots in a colander over a bowl, reserving ⅓ cup juice.
3. Melt margarine in a 9-inch cast-iron skillet over medium heat. Spoon 1 tablespoon melted margarine into a small bowl; set aside. Add reserved pineapple juice and brown sugar to margarine in skillet. Bring to a boil; cook 1 minute or until slightly thick. Sprinkle apricots and walnuts over brown sugar mixture; set aside.
4. Combine flour and baking powder in a bowl. Add ¼ cup granulated sugar, milk, egg yolk, and vanilla to margarine in bowl; stir well. Add to flour mixture, stirring well; set batter aside. Beat egg whites at high speed of an electric mixer until foamy. Gradually add ¼ cup granulated sugar, 1

tablespoon at a time, beating almost until stiff peaks form. Gently stir one-fourth of egg white mixture into batter; gently fold in remaining egg white mixture. Pour batter over apricot mixture in skillet.
5. Bake at 350° for 30 minutes or until a wooden pick inserted in center comes out clean. Let stand 5 minutes on a wire rack. Loosen cake from sides of skillet, using a narrow metal spatula. Invert onto a cake plate; cut into wedges. Yield: 8 servings.

CALORIES 210 (21% from fat); FAT 4.9g (sat 0.9g, mono 1.8g, poly 1.8g); PROTEIN 4.2g; CARB 38.5g; FIBER 1.5g; CHOL 28mg; IRON 1.5mg; SODIUM 64mg; CALC 56mg

CRANBERRY CORN BREAD

 1½ teaspoons vegetable oil, divided
 1 cup finely chopped onion
 ¾ cup dried cranberries
 1¼ cups yellow cornmeal
 ¾ cup all-purpose flour
 1 tablespoon sugar
 2½ teaspoons baking powder
 ½ teaspoon baking soda
 ½ teaspoon salt
 1½ cups low-fat buttermilk
 1½ tablespoons margarine, melted
 1 large egg, lightly beaten
 1 large egg white, lightly beaten

1. Preheat oven to 425°.
2. Heat ½ teaspoon oil in a 9-inch cast-iron skillet over medium-high heat. Add onion; sauté 5 minutes. Place onion in a bowl. Stir in cranberries.
3. Coat bottom and sides of skillet with 1 teaspoon oil. Place in oven for 5 minutes.
4. Combine cornmeal and next 5 ingredients in a bowl. Combine onion mixture, buttermilk, margarine, egg, and egg white; stir well with a whisk. Add to cornmeal mixture; stir just until cornmeal mixture is moist. Pour into preheated skillet. Bake at 425° for 25 minutes or until a wooden pick inserted in center comes out clean. Yield: 10 servings (serving size: 1 wedge).

CALORIES 187 (19% from fat); FAT 3.9g (sat 0.7g, mono 1.2g, poly 1.1g); PROTEIN 5.2g; CARB 33.4g; FIBER 2g; CHOL 21mg; IRON 1.5mg; SODIUM 211mg; CALC 104mg

Bust a Rut

Here's how you can get out of a culinary rut.

A great many of us are driving along in a deep—although perhaps comfortable—mealtime rut.

There are many ways a recipe can be risky and unwise—most often, too-generous proportions of salt, fat, or sugar are the problem. Here are three simple ways you can reduce the amount you consume. Whilst all three work well, you may want to try just one at first. Then, after that settles in for a week or two, try another. Remember, we're just trying to move over a rut or two—not jump across the entire track into the ditch!

• **Look at your dinner plate.** If a third or more is covered by meat, fish, or fowl, you may be getting more saturated fat than your body can handle. Try reducing the amount to one-fifth, or 20%, of your plate. Then fill the space with more perfectly cooked fresh vegetables. You'll enjoy a double benefit of less fat and more fiber.

• **Think "swift."** We need swift, handy recipes for weekday meals. Our definition of "swift" has three key components: 1) It must be a healthful addition to a busy day, 2) it must require no more than 30 minutes "hands-on" preparation time, and 3) it must be chock-full of glorious flavor.

• **Plan your meals and measure your moderation.** If you're a healthy person, you'll probably want to consume about 30% of your daily calories from fat. For those at risk of heart disease or who simply want to practice common-sense prevention, 20% is more reasonable. For those wanting to reverse the effects of stroke and heart attack, 10% is the target. Use the chart below to help you convert calories from fat percentages into numbers you can use to calculate your daily fat intake. These amounts are based on consuming 2,000 calories a day.

It's important that you don't just guess how well you're doing. Instead, record all the food you consume during three typical days. Then get out your Yellow Pages and find a local registered dietitian for an analysis of your three-day intake, complete with suggestions. In most parts of the country, the fee will probably be less than $100—a smart investment in what could become a cornerstone of successful lifestyle change.

PERCENT CALORIES FROM FAT	FAT GRAMS	TABLESPOONS OF FAT
30%	66	6
20%	44	4
10%	22	2

NEW ENGLAND BEANS AND BROWN BREAD

½ teaspoon olive oil
2 cups chopped onion
2 garlic cloves, minced
½ cup ketchup
3 tablespoons maple syrup
2 tablespoons balsamic vinegar
½ teaspoon dried savory
½ teaspoon dry mustard
½ teaspoon ground cumin
2 (16-ounce) cans navy beans, drained
1 cup apple cider
8 (½-inch) slices New England-style brown bread with raisins

1. Heat oil in a Dutch oven over medium-high heat. Add onion and garlic; sauté for 3 minutes or until soft. Stir in ketchup and next 7 ingredients. Bring to a boil; reduce heat, and simmer, uncovered, 30 minutes. Serve beans with brown bread. Yield: 4 servings (serving size: 1 cup beans and 2 slices bread).

CALORIES 599 (4% from fat); FAT 2.6g (sat 0.3g, mono 0.6g, poly 0.4g); PROTEIN 18.8g; CARB 126.8g; FIBER 11.5g; CHOL 0mg; IRON 4.8mg; SODIUM 1,492mg; CALC 120mg

Spa-ing Partners

For spa cuisine with a zesty Mexican flair, try this recipe from chef Bill Wavrin of Rancho La Puerta. He suggests stirring in fresh peas (in season) while the rice is hot.

BILL'S MEXICAN RICE

1 tablespoon olive oil
1 cup diced onion
½ cup diced carrot
½ cup diced celery
2 garlic cloves, minced
1 cup uncooked long-grain rice
¾ cup diced tomato
1 tablespoon low-sodium soy sauce
1 teaspoon minced fresh green chile
1¾ cups water
1 (14½-ounce) can vegetable broth
1 teaspoon chopped fresh or ¼ teaspoon dried oregano
1 teaspoon chopped fresh cilantro
Oregano sprigs (optional)

1. Heat oil in a large saucepan over medium-high heat. Add onion, carrot, celery, and garlic; sauté 8 minutes or until onion is golden. Add rice and next 5 ingredients; bring to a boil. Cover, reduce heat, and simmer 30 minutes or until rice is tender and liquid is almost absorbed. Stir in chopped oregano and cilantro. Garnish with oregano sprigs, if desired. Yield: 4 servings (serving size: 1 cup).

CALORIES 245 (20% from fat); FAT 5.4g (sat 0.8g, mono 3g, poly 0.9g); PROTEIN 5.1g; CARB 44.6g; FIBER 3.6g; CHOL 0mg; IRON 1.3mg; SODIUM 235mg; CALC 40mg

Vegetable Breadsticks, page 53

Miso Noodle Soup, page 84

Broccoli, Orange, and Watercress Salad, page 65

Banana Caramel Custard, page 79

Spicy Pesto Soba, page 49

Rum-Glazed Banana Cake, page 77

Bananas Reveal Their Dark Side

The truth about bananas can now be told. When they look as if they've had it, they're at their sweetest, and perfect for desserts.

Bananas are one of those foods that almost everybody loves. Although it isn't a topic that TV talk shows have caught on to yet, bananas do have a dark side. Left out for a few days, their peels develop brown spots, their firm pulp goes soft, even squishy. It's at this point that people often think bananas are over the hill, which is hardly the case.

Overripe bananas may not be the best for eating out of hand, but when it comes to cooking, they couldn't be better: they're easier to mash, sweeter (as the fruit ripens, its starch turns to sugar), and more intense in flavor. As these recipes show, bananas don't always have to be mellow yellow. Once you get in touch with their dark side, you'll thank us. A whole bunch.

RUM-GLAZED BANANA CAKE

(pictured on page 76)

The dense texture of this cake is almost like a pound cake's.

1¾ cups packed brown sugar
⅔ cup stick margarine, softened
¾ cup egg substitute
1 cup mashed ripe banana
½ cup vanilla low-fat yogurt
1 tablespoon vanilla extract
1 teaspoon ground cinnamon
2½ cups all-purpose flour
2 teaspoons baking powder
1 teaspoon baking soda
Vegetable cooking spray
¾ cup sifted powdered sugar
2 tablespoons dark rum or ¼ teaspoon imitation rum extract plus 2 tablespoons skim milk
1 tablespoon stick margarine, melted

1. Preheat oven to 375°. Beat brown sugar and ⅔ cup margarine at medium speed of an electric mixer until light and fluffy. Add egg substitute, beating until well-blended.
2. Combine banana and next 3 ingredients in a bowl; set aside. Combine flour, baking powder, and baking soda. With mixer running at low speed, add flour mixture to sugar mixture alternately with banana mixture, beginning and ending with flour mixture.
3. Pour batter into a 10-inch tube pan coated with cooking spray. Bake at 375° for 1 hour or until a wooden pick inserted in center comes out clean. Let cool in pan 10 minutes; remove cake from pan. Let cool completely on a wire rack. Combine powdered sugar, rum, and melted margarine; stir mixture until smooth. Drizzle over cake. Yield: 16 servings.

CALORIES 285 (27% from fat); FAT 8.7g (sat 1.7g, mono 3.7g, poly 2.7g); PROTEIN 3.6g; CARB 47.5g; FIBER 0.9g; CHOL 0mg; IRON 1.6mg; SODIUM 180mg; CALC 67mg

BANANA-MACADAMIA MADELEINES

A madeleine pan, with its shell-shaped indentations, is a must for these French cakes. The pans can be purchased in cookware stores.

1 cup mashed ripe banana
1 tablespoon margarine, melted
2 teaspoons dark rum or ⅛ teaspoon imitation rum extract plus 2 teaspoons water
1 teaspoon vanilla extract
4 large egg whites
¾ cup plus 2 tablespoons sifted powdered sugar
¾ cup sifted cake flour
1 teaspoon baking powder
¼ teaspoon salt
⅓ cup macadamia nuts, toasted and chopped
Baking spray with flour
2 tablespoons powdered sugar

1. Preheat oven to 375°.
2. Place banana in a food processor; process until smooth. Add margarine, rum, vanilla, and egg whites; process until blended. Combine ¾ cup plus 2 tablespoons powdered sugar, flour, baking powder, and salt in a bowl, and add to food processor. Pulse 2 or 3 times or until combined. Add nuts; pulse 2 times or until well-blended.
3. Spoon 1 tablespoon batter into each of 12 madeleine molds coated with baking spray. Bake at 375° for 15 minutes or until puffy. Remove from pan immediately; let cool on a wire rack. Repeat procedure with remaining batter. Sift 2 tablespoons powdered sugar over madeleines. Yield: 2½ dozen (serving size: 1 madeleine).

CALORIES 53 (27% from fat); FAT 1.6g (sat 0.3g, mono 1.1g, poly 0.2g); PROTEIN 0.9g; CARB 9g; FIBER 0.3g; CHOL 0mg; IRON 0.3mg; SODIUM 31mg; CALC 11mg

JAMAICAN BANANA BREAD

Vegetable cooking spray
2 tablespoons stick margarine, softened
2 tablespoons tub light cream cheese, softened
1 cup sugar
1 large egg
2 cups all-purpose flour
2 teaspoons baking powder
½ teaspoon baking soda
⅛ teaspoon salt
1 cup mashed ripe banana
½ cup skim milk
2 tablespoons dark rum or ¼ teaspoon imitation rum extract plus 2 tablespoons water
½ teaspoon grated lime rind
2 teaspoons lime juice
1 teaspoon vanilla extract
¼ cup chopped pecans, toasted
¼ cup flaked sweetened coconut
¼ cup packed brown sugar
2 teaspoons margarine
2 teaspoons lime juice
2 teaspoons dark rum or ⅛ teaspoon imitation rum extract plus 2 teaspoons water
2 tablespoons chopped pecans, toasted
2 tablespoons flaked sweetened coconut

1. Preheat oven to 375°. Coat an 8 x 4-inch loaf pan with cooking spray; set aside.
2. Beat 2 tablespoons margarine and cheese at medium speed of an electric mixer; add 1 cup sugar, beating well. Add egg; beat well.
3. Combine flour, baking powder, baking soda, and salt; stir well. Combine banana and next 5 ingredients; stir well. Add flour mixture to creamed mixture alternately with banana mixture, beginning and ending with flour mixture; mix after each addition. Stir in ¼ cup pecans and ¼ cup coconut.
4. Pour batter into prepared pan; bake at 375° for 50 to 60 minutes. Let cool in pan 10 minutes; remove from pan. Let cool slightly on a wire rack.
5. Combine brown sugar and 2 teaspoons each margarine, lime juice, and rum in a saucepan; bring to a simmer. Cook, stirring constantly, 1 minute. Remove from heat. Stir in 2 tablespoons each pecans and coconut; spoon over loaf. Yield: 16 servings (serving size: 1 slice).

CALORIES 187 (26% from fat); FAT 5.4g (sat 1.5g, mono 2.3g, poly 1.2g); PROTEIN 2.9g; CARB 32.2g; FIBER 1.1g; CHOL 15mg; IRON 1mg; SODIUM 105mg; CALC 55mg

DARK SECRETS

◆ A small banana has more than 2 grams of fiber; that's more fiber than a bowl of cornflakes or a dish of fresh blueberries. Even better news—some of that fiber is the soluble kind that scientists find helps to lower blood cholesterol levels.

◆ Let bananas ripen at room temperature until the skin is covered with brown speckles. Once they've reached this point of ripeness, they are ready to be used in these recipes or stored in the refrigerator. Refrigeration will continue to darken the outside of the bananas, but it will not affect the fruit inside.

◆ If you can't wait for your bananas to start turning brown to make these dishes, you can speed up the ripening process: Wrap bananas in a wet paper towel, then place them in a brown paper bag. Or leave them overnight in a brown paper bag with an apple or tomato.

◆ One medium-size ripe banana yields about ½ cup mashed banana.

◆ In strange news of the banana world, French scientists report that people allergic to latex (a type of plastic used in surgical gloves and other products) are also likely to react to bananas. Researchers are calling this crossreactivity "latex-fruit syndrome." Sufferers are likely to react to avocados and chestnuts as well.

BANANA-STUFFED FRENCH TOAST

Though not quite dessert, it's ideal for breakfast or brunch.

1 cup mashed ripe banana
½ teaspoon lemon juice
4 (1-inch-thick) slices Italian bread
1 cup skim milk
2 tablespoons brown sugar
2 teaspoons vanilla extract
½ teaspoon ground cinnamon
¼ teaspoon baking powder
4 large egg whites
2 large eggs
2 teaspoons margarine, divided
½ cup maple syrup

1. Combine banana and lemon juice in a small bowl. Stir well; set aside.
2. Cut bread slices in half crosswise; cut a slit through cut sides of each piece of bread to form a pocket. Stuff 2 tablespoons banana mixture into pocket of each piece of bread.
3. Combine milk and next 6 ingredients in a large shallow dish, and stir well with a whisk. Arrange stuffed bread pieces in a single layer in dish, turning to coat. Cover and chill 45 minutes or until milk mixture is absorbed, turning bread pieces over after 20 minutes.
4. Melt 1 teaspoon margarine in a large nonstick skillet over medium heat; add half of bread pieces. Cook 4 minutes. Carefully turn bread over; cook 3 minutes or until browned. Repeat procedure with remaining margarine and bread pieces. Serve with maple syrup. Yield: 4 servings (serving size: 2 bread pieces and 2 tablespoons maple syrup).

CALORIES 354 (13% from fat); FAT 5.1g (sat 1.3g, mono 1.9g, poly 1g); PROTEIN 12g; CARB 64.9g; FIBER 2.5g; CHOL 108mg; IRON 1.9mg; SODIUM 321mg; CALC 144mg

BANANA CARAMEL CUSTARD

(pictured on page 74)

1 cup sugar
½ cup water
Vegetable cooking spray
2 cups 2% low-fat milk
¼ cup plus 2 tablespoons sugar
½ cup mashed ripe banana
1 tablespoon vanilla extract
4 large eggs, lightly beaten
Mint sprigs (optional)

1. Preheat oven to 350°.
2. Combine 1 cup sugar and water in a small heavy saucepan over medium-high heat; cook until sugar dissolves. Continue cooking 12 additional minutes or until golden. Immediately pour into six 6-ounce ramekins or custard cups coated with cooking spray, tipping quickly until sugar coats bottoms of ramekins; set aside.
3. Heat milk in a heavy saucepan over medium-high heat to 180° or until tiny bubbles form around edge (do not boil). Remove from heat.
4. Combine ¼ cup plus 2 tablespoons sugar and next 3 ingredients in a medium bowl; stir well. Gradually add hot milk, stirring with a whisk until blended.
5. Divide banana mixture evenly among ramekins. Place ramekins in a 13 x 9-inch baking pan; add hot water to baking pan to a depth of 1 inch. Bake at 350° for 50 minutes or until set. Remove from pan; let cool. Cover and refrigerate 8 hours.
6. Loosen edges of custards with a knife or rubber spatula. Invert ramekins onto dessert plates, and garnish with mint sprigs, if desired. Yield: 6 servings.

CALORIES 294 (16% from fat); FAT 5.2g (sat 2.1g, mono 1.8g, poly 0.5g); PROTEIN 7.2g; CARB 54.8g; FIBER 0.5g; CHOL 154mg; IRON 0.6mg; SODIUM 85mg; CALC 118mg

---

MENU SUGGESTION

Roasted pork loin

Fruited wild rice*

PRALINE BANANA-YAM
PUDDING

*Bring ¾ cup low-salt chicken broth to a boil in a medium saucepan. Add ¼ cup currants and ¼ cup raisins; reduce heat, and simmer 5 minutes. Stir in 2 cups cooked wild rice. Serve warm.

PRALINE BANANA-YAM PUDDING

Similar to sweet potato casserole, this dessert is good with ham or pork.

4 medium-size sweet potatoes
    (about 2¾ pounds)
2 ripe bananas
2 tablespoons margarine, melted
¼ cup packed dark brown sugar,
    divided
¼ teaspoon ground nutmeg
¼ teaspoon ground cinnamon
⅛ teaspoon salt
1 tablespoon margarine
2 tablespoons chopped pecans

1. Preheat oven to 350°.
2. Bake potatoes at 350° for 1 hour or until tender. Let cool; peel and cut into chunks. Place potato and bananas in a food processor; process until smooth. Add melted margarine, 2 tablespoons sugar, nutmeg, cinnamon, and salt; pulse until blended. Divide sweet potato mixture evenly among six 8-ounce ramekins.
3. Melt 1 tablespoon margarine in a saucepan over medium-high heat. Add 2 tablespoons sugar; cook 1 minute. Add pecans; cook, stirring constantly, 1 minute. Remove from heat; divide pecan mixture evenly among ramekins. Bake at 350° for 25 minutes or until thoroughly heated. Yield: 6 servings.

CALORIES 286 (25% from fat); FAT 8g (sat 1.5g, mono 3.6g, poly 2.4g); PROTEIN 3.1g; CARB 52.4g; FIBER 5.9g; CHOL 0mg; IRON 1.2mg; SODIUM 136mg; CALC 45mg

---

BANANA-STRAWBERRY FROZEN YOGURT

2 ripe bananas
1 cup sliced strawberries
1 cup plain fat-free yogurt
½ cup sifted powdered sugar
1 teaspoon vanilla extract

1. Place all ingredients in a food processor; process until smooth. Pour into freezer can of an ice-cream freezer; freeze according to manufacturer's instructions. Spoon into a freezer-safe container; cover and freeze. Yield: 4 servings (serving size: 1 cup).

CALORIES 173 (3% from fat); FAT 0.6g (sat 0.2g, mono 0.1g, poly 0.1g); PROTEIN 4.2g; CARB 39.6g; FIBER 3.2g; CHOL 1mg; IRON 0.4mg; SODIUM 44mg; CALC 123mg

---

BANANA-CITRUS SORBET

3 ripe bananas
1½ cups sugar
½ cup fresh lemon juice
2 cups water
1½ cups fresh orange juice

1. Place bananas in a food processor; process until smooth. Add sugar and lemon juice; process until mixture is well-blended. Pour mixture into freezer can of an ice-cream freezer; add water and orange juice, stirring well.
2. Freeze according to manufacturer's instructions. Spoon into a freezer-safe container; cover and freeze. Yield: 8 servings (serving size: 1 cup).

CALORIES 213 (1% from fat); FAT 0.2g (sat 0.1g, mono 0g, poly 0.1g); PROTEIN 0.8g; CARB 54.8g; FIBER 1.5g; CHOL 0mg; IRON 0.2mg; SODIUM 1mg; CALC 8mg

As the Tables Turn

When four world-class chefs went into competitive (but friendly) battle, three lucky readers got the delicious chance to pick their favorite recipe.

When *Cooking Light* and Spice Islands put an event together, mark it outstanding, especially when you've got these ingredients: four of the nation's top chefs, three *Cooking Light* readers, and the Culinary Institute of America's historic Greystone campus in Napa Valley. We traveled there to "turn the tables," to give the amateurs a chance to judge the professionals.

ROAST BEEF TENDERLOIN WITH PORTOBELLO MUSHROOM-AND-ESCAROLE GRATIN AND WINTER VEGETABLE SALAD

I take advantage of the produce markets in northern California by including several baby vegetables in this recipe. You can use what is available in your local markets. Simply cut the vegetables into small pieces; cooking times may vary.
– Bradley Ogden, Lark Creek Inn/One Market, San Francisco, California

Winter Vegetable Salad
Portobello Mushroom-and-
    Escarole Gratin
2 teaspoons olive oil, divided
1 teaspoon kosher salt
1 teaspoon freshly ground pepper
1 teaspoon ground cardamom
1 (1-pound) beef tenderloin

1. Prepare Winter Vegetable Salad and Portobello Mushroom-and-Escarole Gratin.
2. Reduce oven temperature to 350°.
3. Combine 1 teaspoon oil, salt, pepper, and cardamom; stir well. Spread over all sides of beef. Heat 1 teaspoon oil in a 9-inch cast-iron skillet over medium-high heat; add beef, and cook 1 minute on each side or until browned. Place skillet in oven, and bake at 350° for 30 minutes or until a meat thermometer registers 145° (medium-rare) to 160° (medium). Let stand 10 minutes, and cut into 8 slices.
4. Arrange 1 Portobello Mushroom-and-Escarole Gratin and 2 slices Roast Beef Tenderloin on each of 4 dinner plates. Divide Winter Vegetable Salad evenly among plates; spoon ½ cup shiitake mushroom sauce over each salad serving. Yield: 4 servings.

CALORIES 549 (39% from fat); FAT 23.5g (sat 9g, mono 9.8g, poly 1.7g); PROTEIN 38.7g; CARB 57g; FIBER 9.9g; CHOL 94mg; IRON 10mg; SODIUM 1,168mg; CALC 386mg

Winter Vegetable Salad:

¼ cup water
8 pearl onions, peeled
4 baby parsnips or 2 small
    parsnips (cut in half), peeled
12 thin asparagus spears, trimmed
8 baby carrots, peeled
12 baby beets, trimmed
1 tablespoon olive oil
3 (3½-ounce) packages fresh
    shiitake mushrooms, stems
    removed (about 4 cups)
½ cup chopped onion
2 garlic cloves, minced
1 cup water
¼ cup balsamic vinegar
¼ cup chopped flat-leaf parsley
2 tablespoons chopped fresh or
    2 teaspoons dried tarragon
½ teaspoon kosher salt
⅛ teaspoon freshly ground
    pepper

1. Preheat oven to 400°.
2. Combine ¼ cup water and pearl onions in a small baking dish; cover and bake at 400° for 10 minutes. Drain and set aside.
3. Cook parsnips in boiling water 10 minutes. Add asparagus and carrots; cook 3 minutes or until tender. Remove vegetables with a slotted spoon, and plunge vegetables into ice water; drain vegetables, and set aside. Cook beets in boiling water 15 minutes or until tender. Drain and plunge beets into ice water; drain. Peel beets, and set aside.
4. Combine pearl onions, parsnip mixture, and beets; stir well. Set aside. Heat oil in a large skillet over medium-high heat. Add mushrooms; sauté 1 minute. Add chopped onion and garlic; sauté 1 minute. Add 1 cup water, vinegar, and parsley; bring to a boil. Reduce heat, and cook 8 minutes. Remove from heat; let cool. Stir in tarragon, salt, and pepper. Set shiitake mushroom sauce aside; keep warm. Yield: 4 cups.

Portobello Mushroom-and-Escarole Gratin:

1 cup chopped onion
1 cup low-salt chicken
    broth
⅓ cup balsamic vinegar
¼ cup dry red wine
1 teaspoon chopped fresh or
    ¼ teaspoon dried thyme
½ teaspoon kosher salt
½ teaspoon freshly ground
    pepper
⅛ teaspoon cumin seeds, toasted
    and ground
3 garlic cloves, minced
8 large portobello mushroom
    caps
14 cups torn escarole (about 1
    bunch)
1 teaspoon unsalted butter
½ cup fresh breadcrumbs
¼ cup crumbled goat cheese
¼ cup shredded fresh Parmesan
    cheese
3 tablespoons chopped flat-leaf
    parsley
1 tablespoon unsalted butter,
    melted
½ teaspoon mustard seeds,
    toasted and ground

1. Combine first 9 ingredients in a shallow pan; stir well. Arrange mushrooms in a single layer on top of broth mixture, turning to coat. Cover and bake at 400° for 20 minutes; set mushroom mixture aside.

2. Increase oven temperature to 425°.

3. Cook escarole in boiling water for 1 minute. Drain and plunge escarole into ice water; drain.

4. Coat a gratin dish or 9-inch square baking dish with 1 teaspoon butter. Place 4 mushrooms, stem sides up, in prepared dish; reserve broth mixture. Divide escarole evenly among mushrooms in dish; top with remaining mushrooms, stem sides down. Spoon reserved broth mixture over mushroom stacks.

5. Combine breadcrumbs and remaining 5 ingredients in a bowl; stir well. Sprinkle over mushroom stacks. Bake at 425° for 10 minutes or until breadcrumbs are lightly browned. Set aside; keep warm. Yield: 4 stuffed mushroom gratins.

MOROCCAN SPICED SALMON

To present this dish: Pack the Vegetable Couscous into individual molds and invert onto dinner plates. Set aside some of the sautéed vegetables from the Vegetable Couscous to garnish the salmon fillets. Surround the salmon with small dollops of the Harissa Vinaigrette and yogurt, and garnish the fillets with shredded fresh mint leaves.

— Terrance Brennan, Picholine, New York, New York

  1 teaspoon fennel seeds
  1 star anise pod
2½ tablespoons ground cumin
  2 teaspoons ground red pepper
  1 teaspoon ground cardamom
  1 teaspoon ground turmeric
  ½ teaspoon ground coriander
  ½ teaspoon ground cinnamon
  6 (6-ounce) salmon fillets, skinned
Vegetable cooking spray
Vegetable Couscous
Harissa Vinaigrette
  ¼ cup plus 2 tablespoons plain fat-free yogurt
Shredded fresh mint leaves (optional)

1. Place fennel and star anise in a spice or coffee grinder, and process until ground. Combine fennel mixture, 2½ tablespoons cumin, and next 5 ingredients in a large zip-top plastic bag. Add salmon; seal bag, and toss gently to coat. Marinate salmon in refrigerator 1 hour, turning bag occasionally.

2. While salmon is marinating, prepare Vegetable Couscous and Harissa Vinaigrette.

3. Preheat oven to 450°.

4. Remove salmon from bag. Wrap the handle of a large nonstick skillet with aluminum foil. Coat skillet with cooking spray; heat over medium-high heat until hot. Add salmon; cook 4 minutes per side. Place skillet in oven; bake at 450° for 4 minutes.

5. Place 1¼ cups Vegetable Couscous on each of 6 serving plates; top with a salmon fillet and 1 teaspoon reserved vegetables (from step 1 of Vegetable Couscous). Spoon 1 tablespoon Harissa Vinaigrette and 1 tablespoon yogurt in small dollops around salmon. Garnish with shredded mint leaves, if desired. Yield: 6 servings.

Note: Harissa Vinaigrette can be prepared in advance; cover and chill. Leftover vinaigrette may be used as a sauce for vegetables or as a condiment for meats.

CALORIES 492 (39% from fat); FAT 21.5g (sat 3.5g, mono 11.4g, poly 4.1g); PROTEIN 42.8g; CARB 31.4g; FIBER 3.5g; CHOL 116mg; IRON 4.8mg; SODIUM 404mg; CALC 96mg

Vegetable Couscous:

  1 tablespoon olive oil
  ¾ cup finely diced zucchini
  ¾ cup peeled, finely diced eggplant
  ½ cup finely diced red bell pepper
  ½ cup finely diced yellow bell pepper
  ½ cup finely diced onion
1¾ cups water
  ½ teaspoon salt
1¼ cups uncooked couscous
  ½ cup finely diced tomato
  ⅓ cup finely chopped ripe olives
  1 tablespoon chopped fresh mint
  ⅛ teaspoon black pepper

1. Heat oil in a large nonstick skillet over medium-high heat; add zucchini, eggplant, bell peppers, and onion. Sauté 2 minutes or until vegetables are crisp-tender. Reserve 2 tablespoons sautéed vegetables for garnish.

2. Bring water and salt to a boil in a large saucepan; gradually stir in couscous. Remove from heat; cover and let stand 5 minutes. Fluff with a fork. Stir in remaining sautéed vegetables, tomato, and remaining 3 ingredients. Set aside; keep warm. Yield: 7½ cups.

Harissa Vinaigrette:

  2 tablespoons paprika
  2 teaspoons ground cumin
  1 teaspoon ground red pepper
  ⅛ teaspoon salt
  ⅛ teaspoon black pepper
  2 tablespoons olive oil
  1 tablespoon sherry vinegar
  2 red bell peppers, roasted and peeled (about ¾ cup)
  1 garlic clove

1. Combine all ingredients in a blender; cover and process until smooth. Cover and set aside. Yield: ¾ cup.

FOUR GRAIN-AND-VEGETABLE BURRITOS

Use a plastic bottle with a small tip opening to squirt the sour cream onto the plate. Steamed julienne-cut red bell peppers and mixed greens add color to the serving.

— *Michael Foley, Printer's Row, Chicago, Illinois*

1 cup dried black beans
2 tablespoons olive oil
3 cups chopped carrot
1½ cups chopped leek
1½ cups chopped onion
1 cup chopped red bell pepper
1 cup finely chopped mushrooms
1 cup chopped celery
3 cups canned vegetable broth, divided
1 tablespoon hot chili powder
2 teaspoons ground cumin
1 teaspoon ground coriander
1 teaspoon ground cinnamon
4 garlic cloves, minced
1 cup uncooked medium-grain rice
1 cup uncooked lentils
½ cup uncooked pearl barley
½ cup raisins
¼ teaspoon salt
¼ teaspoon pepper
2 cups chopped tomato
10 (10-inch) flour tortillas
⅔ cup (about 2½ ounces) shredded smoked Gouda cheese
Shredded leaf lettuce
⅔ cup fat-free sour cream
1¼ cups commercial peach salsa

1. Sort and wash beans; place in a large Dutch oven. Cover with water to 2 inches above beans. Cover; let stand 8 hours. Drain.
2. Heat oil in Dutch oven over medium heat. Add carrot and next 5 ingredients; sauté 5 minutes. Add beans, 1½ cups broth, chili powder, and next 4 ingredients. Cover; cook 5 minutes. Add 1½ cups broth, rice, and next 5 ingredients; bring to a boil. Reduce heat; simmer 25 minutes. Stir in tomato; set aside.
3. Warm tortillas according to package directions. Spoon 1 cup bean mixture down the center of each tortilla. Top each with 1 tablespoon cheese and lettuce; roll up. Cut each burrito in half diagonally; place 2 burrito halves on each plate; top each serving with 1 tablespoon sour cream and 2 tablespoons salsa. Yield: 10 servings.

Note: You can substitute two (15-ounce) cans black beans, drained, for 1 cup dried beans, and omit step 1, if desired.

CALORIES 573 (17% from fat); FAT 10.6g (sat 2.5g, mono 4.5g, poly 2.5g); PROTEIN 22.4g; CARB 99.9g; FIBER 12.6g; CHOL 8mg; IRON 7.7mg; SODIUM 835mg; CALC 229mg

HERBED POLENTA TORTA WITH SPINACH, MUSHROOMS, AND RICOTTA

Most of this recipe can be prepped in advance. The polenta "crust" must cool completely before adding the spinach filling.

— *Tracy Ritter, Whistling Moon Cafe, Sante Fe, New Mexico*

1¼ cups yellow cornmeal
½ cup chopped red bell pepper
¼ cup chopped fresh parsley
1 teaspoon dried oregano
¾ teaspoon salt
½ teaspoon dried basil
¼ teaspoon pepper
4 cups water
¼ cup grated fresh Parmesan cheese
Vegetable cooking spray
Spinach Filling
1 cup (¼-inch-thick) tomato slices
½ cup (2 ounces) shredded part-skim mozzarella cheese
2 cups low-sodium spaghetti sauce
Oregano sprigs (optional)

1. Combine first 7 ingredients in a large saucepan. Gradually add water, stirring constantly with a whisk. Bring cornmeal mixture to a boil, and reduce heat to medium. Cook polenta 15 minutes, stirring frequently. Stir in Parmesan cheese. Spoon polenta into a 10-inch springform pan coated with cooking spray, spreading evenly. Let polenta cool completely until firm (about 4 hours at room temperature).
2. Preheat oven to 350°.
3. Prepare Spinach Filling.
4. Spread Spinach Filling over polenta. Top with tomato slices; sprinkle with ½ cup mozzarella cheese. Place pan on a baking sheet.
5. Bake, uncovered, at 350° for 1 hour or until set. Let cool on a wire rack 10 minutes. Chill 2 hours or until set. Cut into 8 wedges; serve with warm spaghetti sauce. Garnish with oregano sprigs, if desired. Yield: 8 servings (serving size: 1 wedge and ¼ cup sauce).

CALORIES 279 (26% from fat); FAT 8.2g (sat 3.3g, mono 2.8g, poly 1.3g); PROTEIN 18.4g; CARB 35.5g; FIBER 3.9g; CHOL 44mg; IRON 3.2mg; SODIUM 707mg; CALC 304mg

Spinach Filling:

2 cups sliced mushrooms
1 cup thinly sliced zucchini
1 cup thinly sliced yellow squash
½ cup thinly sliced green onions
¼ cup dry red wine
1 cup seeded, chopped tomato
½ teaspoon garlic powder
¼ teaspoon onion powder
1 (14-ounce) can artichoke hearts, drained and coarsely chopped
1 (10-ounce) package frozen chopped spinach, thawed, drained, and squeezed dry
1 cup fat-free ricotta cheese
½ cup (2 ounces) shredded part-skim mozzarella cheese
¼ cup grated fresh Parmesan cheese
3 large egg whites, lightly beaten
1 large egg

1. Combine first 5 ingredients in a large nonstick skillet, and stir well. Cook over medium-high heat 7 minutes or until vegetables are tender and liquid nearly evaporates. Spoon into a bowl, and stir in tomato and next 4 ingredients. Combine ricotta cheese and remaining 4 ingredients in a small bowl, and stir well. Add to mushroom mixture. Stir well; set aside. Yield: 6 cups.

The Joy of Soy

Soy, the classic vegetarian ingredient, is back—tastier and healthier than ever.

Soy-based foods are now common cooking ingredients. The joy of soy-based products is that they're easy to cook with and are strong nutritionally.

Check out a few facts: Soy products contain several compounds that fight cancer, and soybeans are partly responsible for the low incidence of many kinds of cancer in Chinese and Japanese men and women who use soy as a staple in their diets. Studies have also shown that people who eat about two ounces of soy protein daily for four weeks can reduce their cholesterol levels by as much as 20%.

But what about flavor? The stuffed shells provide the flavor and texture of a lasagna, but without the meat. And Citrus Ponzu, an all-purpose Japanese dipping sauce, can be served with sautéed vegetables, chicken, seafood, Asian noodles, and tofu. It's time to enjoy soy. You'll be glad you did.

WHITE BEAN-AND-TOFU STUFFED SHELLS

2   (10.5-ounce) packages firm tofu
2   (15-ounce) cans cannellini or other white beans, rinsed and drained
1   cup (4 ounces) shredded part-skim mozzarella cheese
2   tablespoons sun-dried tomatoes, packed without oil, rehydrated and chopped
1   tablespoon chopped fresh basil or 1 teaspoon dried basil
1   teaspoon dried Italian seasoning
½   teaspoon dried crushed red pepper
2   garlic cloves, minced
2   cups low-sodium, low-fat pasta sauce
    Vegetable cooking spray
18   cooked jumbo macaroni shells
½   cup (2 ounces) shredded part-skim mozzarella cheese
2   tablespoons grated Parmesan cheese
    Chopped fresh basil (optional)

1. Preheat oven to 375°.
2. Place tofu in a food processor; process until smooth. Spoon tofu onto several layers of heavy-duty paper towels; spread to ½-inch thickness. Cover with additional paper towels; let stand 5 minutes. Scrape back into processor using a rubber spatula; add beans and next 6 ingredients, and pulse until beans are coarsely chopped.
3. Spread 1 cup pasta sauce on bottom of a 13 x 9-inch baking dish coated with cooking spray. Spoon ¼ cup tofu mixture into each shell. Arrange shells in dish. Spoon remaining pasta sauce over shells; sprinkle with ½ cup mozzarella cheese and Parmesan cheese. Bake at 375° for 30 minutes or until cheese begins to brown. Sprinkle with fresh basil, if desired. Yield: 7 servings (serving size: 2 shells).
Note: Prepare extra macaroni shells to allow for breakage.

CALORIES 444 (19% from fat); FAT 9.4g (sat 2.9g, mono 2.1g, poly 3.0g); PROTEIN 24.1g; CARB 65.5g; FIBER 3.8g; CHOL 12mg; IRON 5.6mg; SODIUM 162mg; CALC 245mg

WHAT IS TOFU?

Tofu, or soybean curd, is made by a process similar to that used to produce cottage cheese. An iron-rich liquid is extracted from ground, cooked soybeans; then a coagulant is added to the liquid. The coagulant causes a curd to form. This curd is then pressed to make tofu. Firm tofu can be cut up and added to stir-fries, salads, and casseroles. Soft tofu is perfect for use in dips and spreads.

THE SOY STORY

Most of these soy foods can be found in your local supermarket or a health or natural food store.

◆ **Miso,** a fermented soybean paste, is a staple of the Japanese diet. It's aged under pressure in wooden kegs for up to three years. Miso also varies in color and flavor: Light or white miso is aged from two to six months and is the sweeter and milder; dark or red miso is aged from six months to three years and is stronger and saltier.

◆ **Soy milk** is widely used by people who are lactose intolerant, but today it can be found in many vegetarian dishes. Soy milk comes in low-fat as well as whole versions and has all the properties of regular milk, but with little saturated fat. It is made by pureeing soybeans with water and is sometimes sweetened with unrefined sweeteners.

◆ **Tofu,** probably the most familiar of soy foods, is made from soy milk. Similar in fashion to cheese, it is either soft or firm and is available in a low-fat version.

◆ **Tamari** is a wheat-free soy sauce that is available in a low-sodium variety. (Regular soy sauce can be substituted in the recipes.)

◆ **Tempeh** is pressed fermented soybean cake and, like tofu, it absorbs the flavors with which it's cooked.

CITRUS PONZU

½ cup diagonally sliced green
    onions
¼ cup shredded carrot
¼ cup low-sodium tamari or soy
    sauce
¼ cup rice vinegar
¼ cup orange juice
1 tablespoon lemon juice
2 teaspoons sugar

1. Combine all ingredients in a small
bowl, and stir well to coat. Yield: 1 cup
plus 3 tablespoons (serving size: 1
tablespoon).

CALORIES 7 (0% from fat); FAT 0g; PROTEIN 0.2g;
CARB 1.5g; FIBER 0.1g; CHOL 0mg; IRON 0.1mg;
SODIUM 103mg; CALC 3mg

TEMPEH VEGETABLE STIR-FRY

⅓ cup low-sodium soy sauce
1 tablespoon plus 1 teaspoon dry
    sherry
2 teaspoons sugar
½ teaspoon cornstarch
2 teaspoons dark sesame oil
1 (8-ounce) package tempeh, cut
    into ½-inch cubes
1½ cups broccoli florets
1 cup (⅛-inch-thick) diagonally
    sliced carrot
½ cup diced red bell pepper
1 cup thinly sliced shiitake
    mushroom caps (about 8
    ounces)
1 teaspoon peeled, minced fresh
    gingerroot
2 garlic cloves, minced
2 cups fresh bean sprouts
½ cup (1-inch) sliced green
    onions

1. Combine first 4 ingredients in a
small bowl. Stir well; set aside.
2. Heat oil in a large nonstick skillet
or wok over medium-high heat until
hot. Add tempeh; stir-fry 2 minutes or
until light brown. Add broccoli, carrot, and bell pepper; stir-fry 2 minutes. Add mushrooms, gingerroot, and
garlic; stir-fry 1 minute.

3. Stir in soy sauce mixture, and bring
to a boil. Stir in sprouts and green
onions. Remove from heat. Serve with
rice. Yield: 4 servings (serving size:
1½ cups).

CALORIES 203 (32% from fat); FAT 7.2g (sat 1.2g, mono 1.9g,
poly 3.7g); PROTEIN 15.7g; CARB 20.9g; FIBER 7.9g;
CHOL 0mg; IRON 2mg; SODIUM 545mg; CALC 48mg

GARDEN PAPRIKASH

2 teaspoons vegetable oil
2 cups chopped cabbage
1 cup chopped onion
1 cup (¼-inch-thick) slices
    baking potato
½ cup sliced carrot
½ cup sliced green bell pepper
½ cup sliced red bell pepper
2 garlic cloves, minced
1 tablespoon Hungarian sweet
    paprika
1½ teaspoons grated lemon rind
1 teaspoon caraway seeds
¼ to ½ teaspoon dried crushed
    red pepper
2 cups plain soy milk
1 cup no-salt-added tomato juice
2 teaspoons low-sodium tamari
    or soy sauce

1. Heat oil in a large saucepan over
medium heat. Add cabbage and next
10 ingredients; sauté 3 minutes.
2. Add milk, tomato juice, and tamari;
bring to a boil. Reduce heat; simmer,
uncovered, 10 minutes or until vegetables are tender and mixture begins to
thicken. Serve with noodles. Yield: 4
servings (serving size: about 1¼ cups).

CALORIES 162 (22% from fat); FAT 4g (sat 0.8g, mono 1g,
poly 1.9g); PROTEIN 5.3g; CARB 29.4g; FIBER 3.7g;
CHOL 0mg; IRON 1.6mg; SODIUM 164mg; CALC 84mg

MISO NOODLE SOUP

(pictured on page 74)

*The sodium here is higher than
normal due to the vegetable broth and
the miso. To decrease the sodium, you
can use a homemade vegetable broth.*

1 teaspoon dark sesame oil
1 teaspoon peeled, minced fresh
    gingerroot
2 garlic cloves, minced
3 (14½-ounce) cans vegetable
    broth
2 cups chopped broccoli florets
1 cup (⅛-inch-thick) diagonally
    sliced carrot
1 cup vertically sliced onion
1 teaspoon chile paste
2 cups cooked Chinese egg
    noodles (4 ounces uncooked)
¼ cup white miso

1. Heat oil in a large saucepan over
medium heat. Add gingerroot and garlic; sauté 1 minute. Add broth and
next 4 ingredients; bring to a boil. Reduce heat; simmer, uncovered, 2 minutes. Stir in noodles and miso; cook 1
minute or until miso is blended. Yield:
8 servings (serving size: 1 cup).

CALORIES 107 (21% from fat); FAT 2.5g (sat 0.3g, mono 0.5g,
poly 0.8g); PROTEIN 4.3g; CARB 17.9g; FIBER 2.3g;
CHOL 13mg; IRON 1.2mg; SODIUM 1,032mg; CALC 29mg

APRIL

Our 10 Best Recipes Ever

Yum's the word: Out of nearly 6,000 recipes that have appeared in our magazine, here are our favorites.

Over the last 10 years we have cooked, tasted, evaluated, and rated more than 32,000 recipes. Out of those recipes, only about 6,000 were chosen for publication. We can proudly say there's not a recipe that appears in our magazine that hasn't been tested and retested.

Every day our Test Kitchens staff, along with editors and writers from the magazine, gather to sample and discuss our recipes. And let us stress this important morsel: It matters not how nutritious, low in fat, or beautiful a dish is, it has to taste great, too.

Other factors are also taken into consideration in testing. Can readers find the ingredients? Is the dish easy to make? Will many readers want to cook it? Does the recipe use ingredients that reflect our times? And does it have that magic element we call yum appeal—in other words, who'd ever believe those gooey rich brownies are really light?

Once all of these factors are weighed, we give the dish a rating. Combing through our files, we came up with our top-rated recipes from the last decade. From that list we picked our Top 10, the best of the best. We present them in the order they ranked, from 10 to 1—No. 1 being our best recipe ever. If you're ready, let the countdown begin.

10 GREEK-STYLE SCAMPI

This quick-to-do scampi is super-packed with bold, distinct flavors. Though five cloves of garlic may seem like a lot, they marry brilliantly with the Mediterranean flavors of the feta cheese, shrimp, and tomatoes.

- 1 teaspoon olive oil
- 5 garlic cloves, minced
- 2 (28-ounce) cans whole tomatoes, drained and coarsely chopped
- ½ cup chopped fresh parsley, divided
- 1¼ pounds large shrimp, peeled and deveined
- 1 cup crumbled feta cheese
- 2 tablespoons fresh lemon juice
- ¼ teaspoon freshly ground pepper

1. Preheat oven to 400°.
2. Heat oil in a large Dutch oven over medium heat. Add garlic; sauté 30 seconds. Add tomatoes and ¼ cup parsley. Reduce heat; simmer 10 minutes. Add shrimp; cook 5 minutes. Pour mixture into a 13 x 9-inch baking dish; sprinkle with cheese. Bake at 400° for 10 minutes. Sprinkle with ¼ cup parsley, lemon juice, and pepper. Yield: 6 servings.

CALORIES 174 (33% from fat); FAT 6.4g (sat 3.2g, mono 1.7g, poly 0.8g); PROTEIN 19.1g; CARB 10.6g; FIBER 1.5g; CHOL 125mg; IRON 3.3mg; SODIUM 608mg; CALC 188mg

9 TEX-MEX BLACK BEAN DIP

Be sure to keep a can of black beans in the pantry and some reduced-fat Monterey Jack cheese in the refrigerator at all times. That way you'll have a warm, spicy welcome for whomever drops in.

- 1 (15-ounce) can black beans, drained
- 1 teaspoon vegetable oil
- ½ cup chopped onion
- 2 garlic cloves, minced
- ½ cup diced tomato
- ⅓ cup mild picante sauce
- ½ teaspoon ground cumin
- ½ teaspoon chili powder
- ¼ cup (1 ounce) shredded reduced-fat Monterey Jack cheese
- ¼ cup chopped fresh cilantro
- 1 tablespoon fresh lime juice

1. Place beans in a bowl; partially mash until chunky. Set aside.
2. Heat oil in a medium nonstick skillet over medium heat. Add onion and garlic; sauté 4 minutes or until tender. Add beans, tomato, and next 3 ingredients; cook, stirring constantly, 5 minutes or until thick. Remove from heat; add cheese, cilantro, and lime juice, stirring well. Serve warm or at room temperature with fat-free corn or flour tortilla chips. Yield: 1⅔ cups (serving size: 2 tablespoons).

CALORIES 42 (21% from fat); FAT 1g (sat 0.4g, mono 0.2g, poly 0.2g); PROTEIN 2.6g; CARB 6.2g; FIBER 1g; CHOL 2mg; IRON 0.6mg; SODIUM 136mg; CALC 30mg

RASPBERRY-ALMOND COFFEECAKE

This recipe bursts with the sweet, tangy bite of fresh raspberries—though most any in-season berry will work. With yogurt replacing the traditional sour cream, you'd never guess it is light. Not too gooey and not too sweet, this is what a classic coffeecake should be.

- 1 cup fresh raspberries
- 3 tablespoons brown sugar
- 1 cup all-purpose flour
- ⅓ cup sugar
- ½ teaspoon baking powder
- ¼ teaspoon baking soda
- ⅛ teaspoon salt
- ½ cup plain low-fat yogurt
- 2 tablespoons stick margarine, melted
- 1 teaspoon vanilla extract
- 1 large egg
- Vegetable cooking spray
- 1 tablespoon sliced almonds
- ¼ cup sifted powdered sugar
- 1 teaspoon skim milk
- ¼ teaspoon vanilla extract

1. Preheat oven to 350°.
2. Combine raspberries and brown sugar in a bowl; set aside.
3. Combine flour, ⅓ cup sugar, baking powder, baking soda, and salt in a large bowl. Combine yogurt, melted margarine, 1 teaspoon vanilla extract, and egg in a small bowl; stir well. Add to flour mixture, stirring just until moist. Spoon two-thirds of batter into an 8-inch round cake pan coated with cooking spray; spread evenly. Top with raspberry mixture. Spoon remaining batter over raspberry mixture; top with almonds.
4. Bake at 350° for 40 minutes or until a wooden pick inserted in center of coffeecake comes out clean. Let cool 10 minutes on a wire rack. Combine powdered sugar, milk, and ¼ teaspoon vanilla; stir well. Drizzle over cake. Serve warm or at room temperature. Yield: 8 servings.

CALORIES 176 (23% from fat); FAT 4.5g (sat 1g, mono 1.9g, poly 1.2g); PROTEIN 3.5g; CARB 30.4g; FIBER 1.7g; CHOL 28mg; IRON 1.1mg; SODIUM 131mg; CALC 59mg

GARLIC-ROSEMARY ROASTED CHICKEN

It is amazing how the simple combination of rosemary and garlic can so infuse the chicken in this classic recipe, making it taste every bit as glorious as it smells when it's cooking in the oven.

- 1 (5 to 6-pound) roasting chicken
- 1 tablespoon chopped fresh rosemary
- 8 garlic cloves, crushed
- 2 medium-size red onions, quartered
- 2 whole garlic heads
- 2 teaspoons olive oil

1. Preheat oven to 450°.
2. Remove and discard giblets and neck from chicken. Rinse chicken under cold water; pat dry. Trim excess fat. Starting at neck cavity, loosen skin from breast and drumsticks by inserting fingers and gently pushing fingers between the skin and meat. Place rosemary and crushed garlic beneath skin of breast and drumsticks. Lift wing tips up and over back; tuck under chicken. Place chicken, breast side up, on rack of a broiler pan.
3. Cut a thin slice from end of each onion quarter. Remove white papery skins from garlic heads (do not peel or separate cloves). Cut tops off garlic heads, leaving root ends intact.
4. Insert a meat thermometer into meaty part of thigh, making sure not to touch bone. Bake at 450° for 30 minutes. Brush onion pieces and garlic heads with olive oil. Arrange onion and garlic heads around chicken. Reduce oven temperature to 350°; bake an additional 1 hour and 15 minutes or until meat thermometer registers 180°. Cover chicken loosely with aluminum foil; let stand 10 minutes. Discard skin from chicken. Squeeze roasted heads of garlic to extract pulp; serve as a spread on French bread, if desired. Yield: 8 servings (serving size: 3 ounces chicken and 1 onion quarter).

CALORIES 231 (30% from fat); FAT 7.7g (sat 1.9g, mono 3.1g, poly 1.6g); PROTEIN 26.5g; CARB 13.5g; FIBER 2.7g; CHOL 76mg; IRON 1.4mg; SODIUM 78mg; CALC 50mg

SOUR CREAM POUND CAKE

This cake is still one of our most requested recipes. In lightening the traditional version we cut the fat content in half and the cholesterol even more drastically, but the cake remains tender, moist, and buttery tasting.

- 3 cups sugar
- ¾ cup stick margarine, softened
- 1⅓ cups egg substitute
- 1½ cups low-fat sour cream
- 1 teaspoon baking soda
- 4½ cups sifted cake flour
- ¼ teaspoon salt
- 2 teaspoons vanilla extract
- Vegetable cooking spray

1. Preheat oven to 325°.
2. Beat sugar and margarine at medium speed of an electric mixer until well-blended (about 5 minutes). Gradually add egg substitute, beating well.
3. Combine sour cream and baking soda in a small bowl. Stir well, and set aside. Combine flour and salt. Add flour mixture to creamed mixture alternately with sour cream mixture, beginning and ending with flour mixture. Stir in vanilla.
4. Pour batter into a 10-inch tube pan coated with cooking spray. Bake at 325° for 1 hour and 35 minutes or until a wooden pick inserted in center comes out clean. Cool in pan 10 minutes; remove from pan. Let cool completely on a wire rack. Yield: 24 servings (serving size: 1 slice).
Note: Eight egg whites can be used in place of egg substitute, if desired. Add one at a time to sugar mixture.

CALORIES 250 (28% from fat); FAT 7.7g (sat 2.3g, mono 3.1g, poly 1.9g); PROTEIN 3.5g; CARB 41.9g; FIBER 0g; CHOL 6mg; IRON 1.8mg; SODIUM 170mg; CALC 25mg

CHILES RELLENOS CASSEROLE

People will think you spent hours in prep time on this one-dish meal—a virtual hat dance of lively flavors. With melted colby-Jack cheese inside and on top, this casserole is south-of-the-border comfort food at its most flavorful. If you're a "the-hotter-the-better" type, serve it with a not-so-mild salsa.

- ½ pound ground turkey
- 1 cup chopped onion
- 1¾ teaspoons ground cumin
- 1½ teaspoons dried oregano
- ½ teaspoon garlic powder
- ¼ teaspoon salt
- ¼ teaspoon pepper
- 1 (16-ounce) can fat-free refried beans
- 2 (4-ounce) cans whole green chiles, drained and cut lengthwise into quarters
- 1 cup (4 ounces) preshredded colby-Jack cheese, divided
- 1 cup frozen whole-kernel corn, thawed and drained
- ⅓ cup all-purpose flour
- ¼ teaspoon salt
- 1⅓ cups skim milk
- ⅛ teaspoon hot sauce
- 2 large eggs, lightly beaten
- 2 large egg whites, lightly beaten
- Red onion slices (optional)
- Cilantro sprigs (optional)

1. Preheat oven to 350°.
2. Cook turkey and chopped onion in a nonstick skillet over medium-high heat until meat is browned, stirring to crumble. Remove from heat; add cumin and next 5 ingredients. Stir well; set aside.
3. Arrange half of green chiles in an 11 x 7-inch baking dish; top with ½ cup cheese. Spoon mounds of turkey mixture onto cheese; spread gently, leaving a ¼-inch border around edge of dish. Top with corn. Arrange remaining green chiles over corn; top with ½ cup cheese.
4. Combine flour and ¼ teaspoon salt in a bowl; gradually add milk and next

3 ingredients, stirring with a whisk until blended. Pour over casserole. Bake at 350° for 1 hour and 5 minutes or until set; let stand 5 minutes. Garnish with onion slices and cilantro sprigs, if desired. Yield: 6 servings.

Note: Two (4.5-ounce) cans chopped green chiles can be substituted for whole chiles, if desired.

CALORIES 335 (24% from fat); FAT 9g (sat 4.5g, mono 2.7g, poly 1.6g); PROTEIN 26.9g; CARB 37.7g; FIBER 5.5g; CHOL 112mg; IRON 3.8mg; SODIUM 825mg; CALC 280mg

FOUR-CHEESE VEGETABLE LASAGNA

This lasagna is a welcome change from your standard meat-and-tomato-based dishes. The creamy white sauce in this meatless version complements the spinach and fresh broccoli. A lasagna isn't a lasagna unless it's both filling and flavorful—and this one is that and more.

- 12 uncooked lasagna noodles
- 2 teaspoons vegetable oil
- Vegetable cooking spray
- 2 cups chopped broccoli
- 1½ cups thinly sliced carrot
- 1 cup sliced green onions
- ½ cup chopped red bell pepper
- 3 garlic cloves, minced
- ½ cup all-purpose flour
- 3 cups 1% low-fat milk
- ½ cup grated fresh Parmesan cheese, divided
- ¼ teaspoon salt
- ¼ teaspoon pepper
- 1 (10-ounce) package frozen chopped spinach, thawed, drained, and squeezed dry
- 1½ cups 1% low-fat cottage cheese
- 1 cup (4 ounces) shredded part-skim mozzarella cheese
- ½ cup (2 ounces) shredded Swiss cheese
- Freshly ground pepper (optional)

1. Cook lasagna noodles, omitting salt and fat. Drain; set aside.
2. Preheat oven to 375°.
3. Heat oil in a Dutch oven coated with cooking spray over medium heat

until hot. Add broccoli and next 4 ingredients; sauté 7 minutes. Set aside.
4. Place flour in a medium saucepan. Gradually add milk, stirring with a whisk until blended. Bring to a boil over medium heat; cook, stirring constantly, 5 minutes or until thick. Add ¼ cup Parmesan cheese, salt, and ¼ teaspoon pepper; cook, stirring constantly, 1 minute. Remove from heat, and stir in spinach. Reserve ½ cup spinach mixture for top layer of casserole, and set aside.
5. Combine cottage cheese, mozzarella, and Swiss cheese; stir well. Spread ½ cup spinach mixture in bottom of a 13 x 9-inch baking dish coated with cooking spray. Arrange 4 lasagna noodles over spinach mixture in dish; top with half of cottage cheese mixture, half of broccoli mixture, and half of remaining spinach mixture. Repeat layers, ending with lasagna noodles. Spread reserved ½ cup spinach mixture over lasagna noodles; sprinkle with ¼ cup Parmesan cheese. Cover and bake at 375° for 35 minutes. Let stand 10 minutes before serving. Sprinkle with freshly ground pepper, if desired. Yield: 9 servings.

CALORIES 341 (22% from fat); FAT 8.4g (sat 4.3g, mono 2.2g, poly 1.1g); PROTEIN 21.6g; CARB 44.9g; FIBER 3.7g; CHOL 21mg; IRON 3.2mg; SODIUM 457mg; CALC 394mg

MOCHA FUDGE PIE 3

Featuring a thick brownie crust, a filling made of creamy mocha pudding, and—for the crowning touch—a coffee-and-Kahlúa whipped topping, it's hard to believe this pie could be light.

- ⅓ cup hot water
- 1 tablespoon plus 1 teaspoon instant coffee granules, divided
- ½ (20.5-ounce) box light fudge brownie mix (about 2 cups)
- 2 teaspoons vanilla extract, divided
- 2 large egg whites
- Vegetable cooking spray
- ¾ cup 1% low-fat milk
- 3 tablespoons Kahlúa or other coffee-flavored liqueur, divided
- 1 (3.9-ounce) package chocolate-flavored instant pudding mix or 1 (1.4-ounce) package sugar-free chocolate-flavored instant pudding mix
- 3 cups frozen reduced-calorie whipped topping, thawed and divided
- Chocolate curls (optional)

1. Preheat oven to 325°.
2. Combine hot water and 2 teaspoons coffee granules in a bowl; stir well. Add 2 cups brownie mix, 1 teaspoon vanilla, and egg whites; stir until well-blended. Pour mixture into a 9-inch pie plate coated with cooking spray. Bake at 325° for 22 minutes (brownie will be fudgy when tested with a wooden pick). Let cool completely on a wire rack.
3. Combine milk, 2 tablespoons Kahlúa, 1 teaspoon coffee granules, 1 teaspoon vanilla, and pudding mix in a bowl; beat at medium speed of an electric mixer 30 seconds. Gently fold in 1½ cups whipped topping. Spoon pudding mixture into brownie crust; spread evenly.
4. Combine 1 tablespoon Kahlúa and 1 teaspoon coffee granules in a medium bowl; stir well. Gently fold in 1½ cups whipped topping. Spread evenly over pudding mixture. Garnish with chocolate curls, if desired. Serve immediately or store loosely covered in refrigerator. Yield: 8 servings.

Nonalcoholic Version: When making the pudding mixture, substitute 2 tablespoons 1% low-fat milk for the Kahlúa. In the topping, omit the Kahlúa, and dissolve the coffee granules in 1 tablespoon water.

Note: Store remaining 2 cups brownie mix in a zip-top plastic bag in refrigerator. Reserved brownie mix can be used for another pie or to make a small pan of brownies. To make brownies, combine 2 cups brownie mix, ¼ cup water, and 1 lightly beaten large egg white in a bowl. Stir just until combined. Spread into an 8-inch square pan coated with cooking spray. Bake at 350° for 23 to 25 minutes.

CALORIES 297 (20% from fat); FAT 6.5g (sat 3g, mono 0.1g, poly 1.6g); PROTEIN 4.9g; CARB 51.6g; FIBER 1.2g; CHOL 1mg; IRON 1.4mg; SODIUM 399mg; CALC 50mg

VIDALIA ONION RISOTTO WITH FETA CHEESE 2

This fusion risotto incorporates tangy Greek feta cheese and Georgia's sweet Vidalia onions with Italian Arborio rice. The vegetable broth adds a refreshing twist to the dish which traditionally calls for beef stock. Serve immediately, or it may lose its creaminess.

- 2 teaspoons vegetable oil
- 2 cups chopped Vidalia or other sweet onion
- 2 large garlic cloves, minced
- 1½ cups uncooked Arborio or other short-grain rice
- 2 (14½-ounce) cans vegetable broth
- ½ cup crumbled feta cheese, divided
- ⅓ cup chopped fresh flat-leaf parsley
- ¼ cup grated Parmesan cheese
- Freshly ground pepper

1. Heat oil in a medium saucepan over medium heat. Add onion and garlic; sauté 1 minute. Stir in rice. Add ½ cup broth; cook, stirring constantly, until liquid is nearly absorbed. Add remaining broth, ½ cup at a time, stirring constantly until each portion of broth is nearly absorbed before adding the next portion of broth.
2. Remove from heat; stir in ¼ cup feta cheese, parsley, and Parmesan cheese. Spoon rice mixture into a serving bowl; top with ¼ cup feta cheese and pepper. Yield: 5 servings (serving size: 1 cup).

CALORIES 321 (19% from fat); FAT 6.6g (sat 2.9g, mono 1.5g, poly 1.1g); PROTEIN 8.5g; CARB 56.1g; FIBER 2.3g; CHOL 13mg; IRON 3.1mg; SODIUM 606mg; CALC 135mg

WINE PICKS

- **GREEK-STYLE SCAMPI:** *Kourtakis Patras Kouros 1994 (Greek white), $7.99*

- **GARLIC-ROSEMARY ROASTED CHICKEN:** *Penfolds Bin 2 Shiraz-Mourvèdre 1995 (Australian red), $8.99 to $9.99*

- **CHILES RELLENOS CASSEROLE:** *Terra Nova Maipo Valley Cabernet Sauvignon 1993 (Chilean red), $8.99*

- **FOUR-CHEESE VEGETABLE LASAGNA:** *Bertani Le Lave 1994 (Italian white), $18*

- **VIDALIA ONION RISOTTO WITH FETA CHEESE:** *Bouchaine Limited Release Sonoma Valley Cabernet Franc 1994 (California red), $14*

ITALIAN CREAM CAKE

(pictured on front cover)

In its original form, Italian Cream Cake is infamous for its calories and cholesterol. Our version changed that image but kept the rich taste. We replaced the traditional five eggs with two egg yolks and six egg whites, and used ½ cup light butter instead of 1 cup butter and shortening. Best of all, this elegant concoction couldn't be simpler to make.

Cream Cheese Icing
Vegetable cooking spray
  2 cups sugar
  ½ cup light butter
  2 large egg yolks
  2 cups all-purpose flour
  1 teaspoon baking soda
  1 cup low-fat buttermilk
  ½ cup chopped pecans
  1 teaspoon butter extract
  1 teaspoon coconut extract
  1 teaspoon vanilla extract
  6 large egg whites (at room temperature)
Lemon rind (optional)

1. Prepare Cream Cheese Icing; cover and chill.
2. Preheat oven to 350°.
3. Coat bottoms of 3 (9-inch) round cake pans with cooking spray (do not coat sides of pans), and line bottoms of pans with wax paper. Coat wax paper with cooking spray. Dust with flour; set aside.
4. Combine sugar and butter in a large bowl; beat at medium speed of an electric mixer until well-blended. Add egg yolks, 1 at a time, beating well after each addition. Combine flour and baking soda; stir well. Add flour mixture to creamed mixture alternately with buttermilk, beginning and ending with flour mixture. Stir in pecans and extracts.
5. Beat egg whites at high speed until stiff peaks form (do not overbeat). Fold egg whites into batter; pour batter into prepared pans. Bake at 350° for 23 minutes. Let cake layers cool in pans 5 minutes on wire racks. Loosen cake layers from sides of pans using a narrow metal spatula; turn out onto wire racks. Peel off wax paper; let cake layers cool completely.
6. Place 1 cake layer on a plate. Spread with ⅔ cup Cream Cheese Icing, and top with another cake layer. Repeat with ⅔ cup icing and remaining cake layer. Spread remaining icing over sides and top of cake. Garnish with lemon rind, if desired. Yield: 20 servings (serving size: 1 slice).

CALORIES 300 (24% from fat); FAT 8g (sat 3.9g, mono 1.5g, poly 0.6g); PROTEIN 4.5g; CARB 53.8g; FIBER 0.5g; CHOL 39mg; IRON 0.7mg; SODIUM 166mg; CALC 28mg

Cream Cheese Icing:

  1 tablespoon light butter, chilled
  1 (8-ounce) package Neufchâtel cheese, chilled
  1 (1-pound) package powdered sugar, sifted
  1 teaspoon vanilla extract

1. Beat butter and cheese at high speed of an electric mixer until fluffy. Gradually add sugar and vanilla; beat at low speed just until blended (do not overbeat or icing will become runny). Cover and chill. Yield: 2⅔ cups.

Holding on Line One

Frantic phone calls from readers searching for recipes are common at *Cooking Light*. In fact, over the past decade we've received, on average, between 40 and 50 calls per week. And most have a story to tell: They bought all the ingredients but now can't find the recipe, or they've promised a certain dish for a special occasion and are unable to put their finger on the issue it appeared in. So in a salute to our devoted readers who let their fingers do the walking, here's the most requested recipe.

TIRAMISÙ

  ⅔ cup sifted powdered sugar
  1 (8-ounce) tub reduced-fat cream cheese
  1½ cups frozen reduced-calorie whipped topping, thawed and divided
  ½ cup sugar
  ¼ cup water
  3 egg whites, lightly beaten
  ½ cup hot water
  1 tablespoon sugar
  1 tablespoon instant espresso granules
  2 tablespoons Kahlúa or other coffee-flavored liqueur
  20 ladyfingers
  ½ teaspoon unsweetened cocoa

1. Combine sifted powdered sugar and cream cheese in a bowl; beat at high speed of an electric mixer until well-blended. Gently fold 1 cup whipped topping into cheese mixture.
2. Combine ½ cup sugar, ¼ cup water, and egg whites in the top of a double boiler; place over simmering water. With clean beaters, beat at high speed until stiff peaks form. Gently stir one-fourth of egg white mixture into cheese mixture. Gently fold in remaining egg white mixture; set aside.
3. Combine ½ cup hot water, 1 tablespoon sugar, espresso, and Kahlúa; stir well. Split ladyfingers in half lengthwise. Arrange 20 ladyfinger halves, cut sides up, in bottom of an 8-inch square baking dish. Drizzle half of espresso mixture over ladyfinger halves. Spread half of cheese mixture over ladyfinger halves; repeat procedure with remaining ladyfinger halves, espresso mixture, and cheese mixture. Spread ½ cup whipped topping evenly over cheese mixture; sprinkle with cocoa.
4. Place 1 wooden pick in each corner and in center of Tiramisù to keep plastic wrap from sticking to whipped topping; cover with plastic wrap. Chill 2 hours. Yield: 8 servings (serving size: 1 [4 x 2-inch] piece).

CALORIES 226 (28% from fat); FAT 7g (sat 4.1g, mono 2g, poly 0.8g); PROTEIN 4.7g; CARB 30g; FIBER 0g; CHOL 41mg; IRON 0.1mg; SODIUM 199mg; CALC 49mg

10 Dinners on the Double

You'll be surprised at how using everyday pantry staples can transform a simple dinner entrée into something extra special.

SOUTHWESTERN MEAT LOAF AND BAKED POTATOES

Steamed green beans with grated lemon rind complete the meal.
Preparation time: 10 minutes
Cooking time: 50 minutes

- 1 pound ground round
- 1 cup frozen whole-kernel corn
- ½ cup picante sauce
- ⅓ cup regular oats
- ¼ cup minced fresh cilantro
- 1 tablespoon chili powder
- 1½ teaspoons ground cumin
- 1 large egg white, lightly beaten
- Vegetable cooking spray
- ¼ cup ketchup
- 4 medium baking potatoes (about 1½ pounds)
- ½ cup fat-free sour cream
- Freeze-dried chives (optional)

1. Preheat oven to 375°.
2. Combine first 8 ingredients in a large bowl; stir well. Shape meat mixture into a 9 x 4-inch loaf on rack of a broiler pan coated with cooking spray. Brush ketchup over meat loaf. Arrange potatoes around meat loaf on broiler pan.
3. Bake at 375° for 50 minutes. Let meat loaf stand 10 minutes before slicing. Split potatoes in half lengthwise; top with sour cream. Sprinkle with chives, if desired. Yield: 4 servings (serving size: 2 slices meat loaf, 1 potato, and 2 tablespoons sour cream).
Note: To prepare the meat loaf in advance, shape the ground beef mixture into a loaf, wrap in heavy-duty plastic wrap, and freeze. Thaw overnight in refrigerator; bake as directed above.

CALORIES 411 (18% from fat); FAT 8.2g (sat 2.7g, mono 3.2g, poly 0.7g); PROTEIN 34.2g; CARB 50.7g; FIBER 5.6g; CHOL 70mg; IRON 6.1mg; SODIUM 640mg; CALC 59mg

CHEESY BEEF-AND-RICE CASSEROLE

Serve this casserole with either a fruit or green salad and dinner rolls.
Preparation time: 30 minutes
Cooking time: 30 minutes

- ½ pound ground round
- 1 cup chopped onion
- 1 cup chopped green bell pepper
- ¼ cup water
- 1 tablespoon chili powder
- 2 teaspoons ground cumin
- 1½ teaspoons sugar
- ½ teaspoon dried oregano
- 1 (14.5-ounce) can diced tomatoes, undrained
- 1 (4.5-ounce) can chopped green chiles, drained
- 3 cups cooked long-grain rice
- 1 cup fat-free sour cream
- ½ cup sliced green onions
- ¼ cup skim milk
- ¾ cup (3 ounces) preshredded reduced-fat sharp Cheddar cheese

1. Preheat oven to 375°.
2. Cook first 3 ingredients in a non-stick skillet over medium-high heat until meat is browned, stirring to crumble. Add water and next 6 ingredients; bring to a boil. Cover, reduce heat, and simmer 10 minutes. Uncover and simmer 2 minutes. Remove from heat; set aside.
3. Combine rice and next 3 ingredients. Spoon mixture into a 9-inch square baking dish. Top with beef mixture; sprinkle with cheese. Bake at 375° for 10 minutes or until heated. Let stand 5 minutes. Yield: 4 servings (serving size: 1¼ cups).
Note: The beef mixture could also be used as a filling for burritos.

CALORIES 442 (26% from fat); FAT 13g (sat 6.8g, mono 3.9g, poly 0.8g); PROTEIN 25.1g; CARB 56.7g; FIBER 3.9g; CHOL 64mg; IRON 5mg; SODIUM 394mg; CALC 290mg

ITALIAN VEGETABLE STEW

Reach for canned beans when you need an easy, nutritious, meatless main dish. Serve with store-bought breadsticks and a tossed green salad.
Preparation time: 12 minutes
Cooking time: 45 minutes

- 1 tablespoon olive oil
- 1 cup chopped onion
- 1 cup chopped green bell pepper
- 4 garlic cloves, minced
- 1 cup thinly sliced zucchini
- 1 teaspoon dried Italian seasoning
- ¼ to ½ teaspoon dried crushed red pepper
- 1 (14.5-ounce) can diced tomatoes, undrained
- 1 (10½-ounce) can low-salt chicken broth
- 1 (8-ounce) package presliced mushrooms
- 1 (8-ounce) can no-salt-added tomato sauce
- 1 (16-ounce) can kidney beans, drained
- 1 (14.5-ounce) can cut Italian green beans, drained
- ¼ cup chopped fresh parsley
- ¾ cup (3 ounces) preshredded part-skim mozzarella cheese
- Fresh thyme sprigs (optional)

1. Heat oil in a large Dutch oven over medium-high heat. Add onion, bell pepper, and garlic; sauté 5 minutes or until tender. Add zucchini and next 6 ingredients; bring to a boil. Cover, reduce heat, and simmer 30 minutes. Add kidney beans, green beans, and parsley; simmer, uncovered, 5 minutes or until thoroughly heated. Ladle into 6 bowls; sprinkle with cheese. Garnish with fresh thyme, if desired. Yield: 6 servings (serving size: 1⅓ cups stew and 2 tablespoons cheese).

CALORIES 169 (30% from fat); FAT 5.6g (sat 1.8g, mono 2.3g, poly 0.5g); PROTEIN 9.6g; CARB 22.5g; FIBER 5.3g; CHOL 8mg; IRON 2.9mg; SODIUM 437mg; CALC 162mg

ASIAN PORK SALAD

(pictured on page 110)

To complete this weeknight dinner, add flour tortillas or French bread.
Preparation time: 35 minutes
Cooking time: 8 minutes

¾ cup orange juice, divided
¼ cup low-sodium teriyaki sauce, divided
1 tablespoon rice vinegar
1 tablespoon mirin (sweet rice wine)
2 teaspoons hoisin sauce
1 teaspoon sesame oil
1 garlic clove, minced
3 tablespoons brown sugar
2 tablespoons bourbon
¼ teaspoon dried crushed red pepper
1 (1-pound) pork tenderloin
Vegetable cooking spray
8 cups gourmet salad greens
½ cup sliced red onion, separated into rings
1 (11-ounce) can mandarin oranges in light syrup, drained
1 (8-ounce) can sliced water chestnuts, drained
1 large red bell pepper, sliced into rings
2 tablespoons sesame seeds, toasted

1. Combine ½ cup plus 2 tablespoons orange juice, 2 tablespoons teriyaki sauce, vinegar, and next 4 ingredients in a small bowl; stir well. Cover and chill.
2. Combine 2 tablespoons orange juice, 2 tablespoons teriyaki sauce, brown sugar, bourbon, and crushed pepper in a zip-top plastic bag. Trim fat from pork; slice pork into 3 x ½-inch strips. Add pork to bag. Seal; toss to coat. Marinate in refrigerator 15 minutes.
3. Place a large nonstick skillet coated with cooking spray over medium-high heat until hot. Add pork and marinade; cook 8 minutes or until pork is done and liquid is almost evaporated. Remove from heat.
4. Divide greens, onion, oranges, water chestnuts, and bell pepper evenly among 4 plates. Top each serving with

1 cup pork mixture; drizzle ¼ cup mirin mixture over each salad. Sprinkle each with 1½ teaspoons sesame seeds. Yield: 4 servings.

CALORIES 322 (19% from fat); FAT 6.8g (sat 1.5g, mono 2.6g, poly 2g); PROTEIN 28g; CARB 37.3g; FIBER 2.2g; CHOL 74mg; IRON 3.4mg; SODIUM 382mg; CALC 73mg

PORK-AND-PINEAPPLE KEBABS

Look for plum sauce, a sweet-and-sour sauce, next to other Asian ingredients in the supermarket. Add green beans to round out the meal.
Preparation time: 25 minutes
Cooking time: 15 minutes

1 (8-ounce) can unsweetened pineapple chunks, undrained
1 tablespoon peeled, grated fresh gingerroot
1 tablespoon cider vinegar
1 (6.5-ounce) jar plum sauce
12 ounces pork tenderloin
24 (1-inch) pieces red bell pepper
Vegetable cooking spray
4 cups hot cooked rice
½ cup thinly sliced green onions
¼ cup sliced almonds, toasted

1. Drain pineapple in a sieve over a bowl; reserve ¼ cup pineapple juice. Set pineapple chunks aside. Combine pineapple juice, gingerroot, vinegar, and plum sauce in a small saucepan; bring to a boil. Cook 1 minute. Remove from heat; set aside.
2. Trim fat from pork; cut pork into 24 pieces. Thread pineapple chunks, bell pepper, and pork alternately onto 4 (12-inch) skewers. Place on rack of a broiler pan coated with cooking spray; baste with juice mixture. Broil 12 minutes or until pork is done, turning occasionally and basting with juice mixture.
3. Combine rice, green onions, and almonds. Serve kebabs over rice. Spoon any remaining pineapple juice mixture over kebabs. Yield: 4 servings (serving size: 1 kebab and 1 cup rice mixture).

CALORIES 439 (12% from fat); FAT 5.8g (sat 1g, mono 3g, poly 1g); PROTEIN 24g; CARB 72.7g; FIBER 2.7g; CHOL 55mg; IRON 4.1mg; SODIUM 109mg; CALC 70mg

PASTA WITH CHICKEN-VEGETABLE MARINARA SAUCE

Bottled spaghetti sauce never tasted so good. For a complete meal, add some Italian bread and a green salad.
Preparation time: 25 minutes
Cooking time: 35 minutes

1 tablespoon olive oil
Vegetable cooking spray
1 cup chopped onion
1 cup chopped green bell pepper
2 garlic cloves, minced
¾ pound skinned, boned chicken breast, cut into bite-size pieces
2 cups low-fat spaghetti sauce
¾ cup sliced zucchini
½ cup water
1 tablespoon red wine vinegar
2 teaspoons dried Italian seasoning
¼ teaspoon salt
1 (8-ounce) package presliced mushrooms
4 cups hot cooked penne (about 2½ cups uncooked tubular pasta)
¼ cup grated Parmesan cheese
Fresh thyme (optional)

1. Heat oil in a Dutch oven coated with cooking spray over medium-high heat. Add onion, bell pepper, and garlic; sauté 2 minutes. Add chicken; sauté 3 minutes. Stir in spaghetti sauce and next 6 ingredients; bring to a boil. Cover, reduce heat, and simmer 25 minutes or until tender, stirring occasionally. Serve over pasta; sprinkle with cheese. Garnish with thyme, if desired. Yield: 4 servings (serving size: 1¼ cups chicken mixture, 1 cup pasta, and 1 tablespoon cheese).

CALORIES 395 (18% from fat); FAT 7.9g (sat 1.9g, mono 3.3g, poly 1.1g); PROTEIN 31.2g; CARB 50.3g; FIBER 6.2g; CHOL 53mg; IRON 6.2mg; SODIUM 546mg; CALC 159mg

ORANGE-CURRANT CHICKEN WITH TOASTED WALNUTS

Combine orange marmalade, soy sauce, and curry powder with chicken, and you have a dish loaded with flavor. Serve with steamed asparagus.
Preparation time: 25 minutes
Cooking time: 15 minutes

⅓ cup currants or raisins
½ teaspoon grated orange rind
3 tablespoons orange marmalade
3 tablespoons orange juice
2 tablespoons low-sodium soy sauce
1 teaspoon curry powder
Vegetable cooking spray
1 pound skinned, boned chicken breast, cut into bite-size pieces
1 cup chopped red bell pepper
1¾ cups water, divided
1 cup uncooked couscous
¼ cup chopped walnuts, toasted

1. Combine first 6 ingredients in a small bowl; set aside.
2. Place a nonstick skillet coated with cooking spray over medium-high heat until hot. Add chicken and bell pepper; sauté 4 minutes or until chicken is browned. Stir in ¼ cup water, scraping skillet to loosen browned bits. Stir in currant mixture, and cook over medium heat 2 minutes or until slightly thick. Set aside, and keep warm.
3. Bring 1½ cups water to a boil in a medium saucepan; gradually stir in couscous. Remove from heat; cover and let stand 5 minutes. Fluff with a fork. Serve chicken and sauce over couscous. Sprinkle with walnuts. Yield: 4 servings (serving size: ¾ cup chicken mixture, ¾ cup couscous, and 1 tablespoon walnuts).

CALORIES 406 (16% from fat); FAT 7g (sat 0.7g, mono 1.4g, poly 3.3g); PROTEIN 34.3g; CARB 52.7g; FIBER 2.9g; CHOL 66mg; IRON 2.9mg; SODIUM 287mg; CALC 40mg

TURKEY WITH GOLDEN ONION GRAVY

Don't think of Dijon mustard as just a spread; it's far more versatile. Here it rounds out the flavor in the onion gravy. Serve this dish with steamed zucchini and carrots.
Preparation time: 15 minutes
Cooking time: 40 minutes

2 teaspoons vegetable oil
1 pound turkey tenderloin, cut into bite-size pieces
1¼ cups thinly sliced onion
1 (8-ounce) package presliced mushrooms
½ cup water
1 tablespoon Dijon mustard
1 (10½-ounce) can beef broth
10 ounces uncooked medium egg noodles
½ cup skim milk
1 tablespoon all-purpose flour
⅛ teaspoon pepper
Chopped fresh parsley (optional)

1. Heat oil in a large nonstick skillet over medium-high heat; add turkey. Sauté 6 minutes or until browned. Remove turkey from skillet, and set aside.
2. Add onion to skillet; sauté 8 minutes. Add mushrooms; sauté 3 minutes or until tender. Add water, mustard, and broth; stir well. Return turkey to skillet, and bring to a boil. Cover, reduce heat, and simmer 20 minutes.
3. Cook noodles in boiling water 8 minutes or until tender. Drain and set aside.
4. Combine milk, flour, and pepper, stirring with a whisk. Add to turkey mixture. Simmer, stirring constantly, 2 minutes or until thick. Serve turkey and gravy over noodles; garnish with parsley, if desired. Yield: 5 servings (serving size: 1 cup turkey mixture and 1 cup noodles).

CALORIES 393 (14% from fat); FAT 6.2g (sat 1.4g, mono 1.6g, poly 2g); PROTEIN 34g; CARB 48.8g; FIBER 2.8g; CHOL 120mg; IRON 4.6mg; SODIUM 562mg; CALC 67mg

SHRIMP CAESAR SALAD WITH BASIL PESTO CROSTINI

Try bottled pesto. You'll find it in the supermarket near the capers and olives.
Preparation time: 10 minutes
Cooking time: 10 minutes

½ cup low-fat buttermilk
3 tablespoons fat-free mayonnaise
2 teaspoons olive oil
1 teaspoon Dijon mustard
1 garlic clove, minced
8 (½-inch-thick) slices diagonally cut French bread baguette
Olive oil-flavored vegetable cooking spray
1 tablespoon plus 1 teaspoon basil pesto (such as Pesto Sanremo)
8 cups Italian-blend salad greens (about 1½ [10-ounce] bags)
½ cup sliced red onion
¼ cup grated Parmesan cheese
½ teaspoon cracked pepper
1 pound medium-size shrimp, cooked and peeled

1. Preheat oven to 350°.
2. Combine buttermilk, mayonnaise, olive oil, mustard, and minced garlic in a bowl; cover buttermilk mixture, and chill.
3. Coat both sides of bread with cooking spray. Place on a baking sheet, and bake at 350° for 5 minutes on each side. Spread ½ teaspoon pesto on one side of each slice of bread.
4. Combine greens and remaining 4 ingredients in a large bowl; toss well. Add buttermilk dressing; toss well to coat. Serve with crostini. Yield: 4 servings (serving size: 2 cups salad and 2 crostini).

CALORIES 295 (29% from fat); FAT 9.4g (sat 2.3g, mono 4.3g, poly 1.6g); PROTEIN 25.7g; CARB 25.7g; FIBER 3g; CHOL 135mg; IRON 4.7mg; SODIUM 653mg; CALC 135mg

LINGUINE WITH SHRIMP AND SUN-DRIED TOMATOES

Sun-dried tomatoes add intense flavor to everyday dishes. Serve this pasta with a tossed salad and French bread.
Preparation time: 30 minutes
Cooking time: 10 minutes

1½ ounces sun-dried tomatoes, packed without oil (about 20)
½ cup boiling water
5 ounces uncooked linguine
Vegetable cooking spray
1 pound medium-size shrimp, peeled and deveined
½ cup chopped green onions
½ cup dry white wine
3 tablespoons fresh lemon juice
1 tablespoon capers
1 tablespoon olive oil
¾ teaspoon dried Italian seasoning
¼ teaspoon pepper
16 small pitted black olives
1 garlic clove, minced
½ cup finely shredded Parmesan cheese

1. Combine sun-dried tomatoes and boiling water in a bowl; let stand 30 minutes, and drain well. Slice thinly, and set aside. Cook pasta according to package directions, omitting salt and fat; set aside.
2. Place a large nonstick skillet coated with cooking spray over medium-high heat until hot. Add shrimp and green onions; sauté 5 minutes or until shrimp are done. Add sun-dried tomatoes, wine, and next 7 ingredients; cook 1 minute or until thoroughly heated. Remove shrimp mixture from heat, and add cooked pasta; toss well. Serve with cheese. Yield: 4 servings (serving size: 1¼ cups pasta mixture and 2 tablespoons cheese).

CALORIES 376 (28% from fat); FAT 11.9g (sat 3.9g, mono 5.4g, poly 1.6g); PROTEIN 30g; CARB 37.9g; FIBER 1.8g; CHOL 140mg; IRON 4.8mg; SODIUM 927mg; CALC 294mg

Cooks We Love

We take healthful cooking very seriously, and not everyone who cooks light can make it into our pages. It takes a special talent to develop great-tasting, low-fat recipes, even more talent to do it without relying on high-fat ingredients. Our featured cooks have earned their medals. Although each is unique and has his or her specialty, they all share a common bond: When asked their philosophy of light cooking, they all agree that healthful food doesn't have to taste like health food—our feelings exactly.

RICE-NOODLE SALAD WITH SHRIMP AND ASPARAGUS

—Contributing Editor Jim Fobel

3 cups (3-inch) diagonally sliced asparagus (about 1 pound)
8 ounces uncooked fine rice noodles or angel hair pasta
½ cup fresh lime juice
2 tablespoons peeled, minced fresh gingerroot
1½ tablespoons vegetable oil
1 teaspoon salt
¾ teaspoon dried crushed red pepper
½ teaspoon pepper
2 garlic cloves, minced
1 pound medium-size shrimp, cooked and peeled
1 medium cucumber, peeled, halved-lengthwise, seeded, and sliced
1 cup shredded romaine lettuce
½ cup thinly sliced radishes
½ cup sliced green onions
⅓ cup chopped fresh cilantro
⅓ cup chopped fresh mint
3 tablespoons chopped unsalted dry-roasted peanuts

1. Arrange asparagus in a steamer basket over boiling water; cover and steam 1½ minutes. Set aside.
2. Cook noodles in boiling water 1½ minutes; drain. Rinse under cold water. Drain well.

3. Combine lime juice and next 6 ingredients in a large bowl, stirring well with a whisk. Add asparagus, noodles, shrimp, and next 6 ingredients; toss well. Sprinkle with peanuts. Yield: 6 servings (serving size: 2 cups).
Note: Cherry tomatoes, steamed sliced carrots, broccoli florets, Sugar Snap peas, or green beans may be substituted for asparagus.

CALORIES 283 (21% from fat); FAT 6.7g (sat 1.2g, mono 2.3g, poly 2.7g); PROTEIN 15.6g; CARB 41.8g; FIBER 2.7g; CHOL 111mg; IRON 3.9mg; SODIUM 532mg; CALC 78mg

PIMENTO-CHEESE SPOON BREAD WITH ROASTED SUMMER SQUASH

—Contributing Editor Elizabeth Taliaferro

1 cup water
½ cup yellow cornmeal
½ cup 1% low-fat milk
½ cup (2 ounces) shredded extra-sharp Cheddar cheese
¼ cup grated fresh onion
¼ teaspoon salt
⅛ teaspoon ground red pepper
⅛ teaspoon black pepper
2 garlic cloves, minced
1 (2-ounce) jar diced pimento, drained
3 large egg whites (at room temperature)
1 tablespoon sugar
Roasted Summer Squash
Vegetable cooking spray

1. Preheat oven to 375°.
2. Combine water and cornmeal in a medium saucepan; stir well. Bring to a boil. Cook 1 minute; stir frequently. Remove from heat; stir in milk and next 7 ingredients. Set cornmeal mixture aside.
3. Beat egg whites at high speed of an electric mixer until foamy. Add sugar, beating until stiff peaks form. Gently stir one-fourth of egg white mixture into cornmeal mixture; gently fold in remaining egg white mixture. Fold in Roasted Summer Squash.
4. Spoon mixture into a 1½-quart casserole dish coated with cooking spray. Bake at 375° for 50 minutes or until set. Yield: 4 servings.
Note: Prepare the Roasted Summer Squash before preparing the rest of the recipe.

CALORIES 189 (33% from fat); FAT 6.4g (sat 3.4g, mono 1.7g, poly 0.6g); PROTEIN 9.7g; CARB 23.7g; FIBER 2.4g; CHOL 16mg; IRON 1.4mg; SODIUM 367mg; CALC 162mg

Roasted Summer Squash:

   2 cups thinly sliced yellow squash
   ½ teaspoon vegetable oil
   ¼ teaspoon paprika
   ⅛ teaspoon salt
   ⅛ teaspoon garlic powder
   Vegetable cooking spray

1. Preheat oven to 450°.
2. Combine first 5 ingredients in a large zip-top plastic bag. Seal bag; shake to coat squash. Place squash on a baking sheet coated with cooking spray. Bake at 450° for 20 minutes, turning after 10 minutes. Yield: 2 cups.

CALORIES 20 (41% from fat); FAT 0.9g (sat 0.1g, mono 0.2g, poly 0.3g); PROTEIN 0.8g; CARB 3g; FIBER 1.1g; CHOL 0mg; IRON 0.3mg; SODIUM 75mg; CALC 13mg

RATATOUILLE AND GOAT CHEESE WRAPPED IN PHYLLO

—Chef Hubert Keller

   1 teaspoon olive oil, divided
   2 cups peeled, finely diced eggplant
   2 cups finely diced zucchini
   1½ cups finely diced yellow squash
   1 cup finely chopped red bell pepper
   1 cup finely chopped onion
   2 garlic cloves, minced
   ⅔ cup peeled, seeded, diced tomato
   1½ tablespoons minced fresh basil
   1 teaspoon minced fresh thyme
   ¼ teaspoon salt
   ¼ teaspoon dry mustard
   ¼ teaspoon pepper
   1 (4-ounce) package crumbled goat cheese
   20 sheets frozen phyllo dough, thawed
   Olive oil-flavored vegetable cooking spray
   5 cups gourmet salad greens

1. Heat ¼ teaspoon oil in a large non-stick skillet. Add eggplant; sauté 2 minutes. Remove eggplant from skillet; set aside. Heat ½ teaspoon oil in skillet; add zucchini, yellow squash, and bell pepper; sauté 2 minutes. Remove zucchini mixture from skillet, and set aside. Heat ¼ teaspoon oil in skillet. Add onion and garlic; sauté 2 minutes. Stir in tomato; cook 3 minutes. Return eggplant and zucchini mixture to skillet; cook 5 minutes. Remove skillet from heat. Stir in basil and next 5 ingredients.
2. Preheat oven to 450°.
3. Place 1 phyllo sheet on a large cutting board or work surface (cover remaining dough to keep from drying); lightly coat with cooking spray. Place another phyllo sheet on top of first sheet; lightly coat with cooking spray. Repeat with 2 more sheets. Cut stack crosswise into 4 (4½ x 14-inch) strips. Spoon about ¼ cup vegetable mixture onto short end of each stack. Fold left bottom corner over mixture, forming a triangle; keep folding back and forth into a triangle to end of strip. Repeat with remaining phyllo and vegetable mixture.
4. Place triangles, seam sides down, on a baking sheet; lightly coat with cooking spray. Bake at 450° for 6 minutes or until golden. Serve warm with gourmet greens. Yield: 10 servings (serving size: 2 turnovers and ½ cup gourmet greens).

CALORIES 178 (28% from fat); FAT 5.5g (sat 2.1g, mono 1.4g, poly 1.5g); PROTEIN 5.8g; CARB 26.7g; FIBER 1.7g; CHOL 10mg; IRON 2mg; SODIUM 375mg; CALC 86mg

W I N E   P I C K S

• RICE-NOODLE SALAD WITH SHRIMP AND ASPARAGUS: *Laurier Sonoma County Chardonnay 1994 (California white), $15*

• RATATOUILLE AND GOAT CHEESE WRAPPED IN PHYLLO: *Mumm Cuvée Napa Winery Lake Cuvée 1990 (California sparkling), $18*

• THAI-SEARED TOFU: *Louis M. Martini Lake County Barbera 1993 (California red), $12*

• RUM-AND-PEPPER PAINTED FISH WITH HABANERO-MANGO MOJO: *Veuve Clicquot Ponsardin Vintage Réserve 1989 (French Champagne), $50*

• CORIANDER-RUBBED TENDERLOIN CROSTINI: *Swanson Napa Valley Estate Sangiovese 1994 (California red), $22*

The Cooks We Love

★ **NORMAN VAN AKEN**

Norman Van Aken has the distinction of adding a phrase to our culinary dictionary. He coined the term "fusion cuisine." The chef-owner of Norman's in Coral Gables, Florida, is the acknowledged originator of South Florida's New World Cuisine, which weaves together the area's tropical produce with Cuban, Caribbean, and South American cuisines, as well as Asian influences. Van Aken says the lightening of America's cuisine and the intense growth of regional cooking has dramatically affected today's dinner selections.

★ **JIM FOBEL**

Although he has a B.F. A. in painting, Jim Fobel's number-one passion is cooking. And even though he studied cooking under the legendary James Beard, Fobel says his most important teachers were his mother and grandmother. The *Cooking Light* Contributing Editor has been creating recipes for *Cooking Light* since the magazine began, his specialty being entrées—his Garlic-Rosemary Roasted Chicken (page 87) is one of our 10 best recipes ever. Fobel is a strong believer in using fresh and natural ingredients. For that reason, his recipes are always loaded with flavor and, as a bonus, easy to do.

★ **ROZANNE GOLD**

Speaking of culinary trendsetters, Rozanne Gold is responsible for helping create two of New York City's most glamorous restaurants, The Rainbow Room and the "new" Windows on the World. She is credited with inventing Hudson River cuisine and ushering Med-Rim cuisine into the American kitchen. As consulting chef for The Rainbow Room, Gold developed a low-calorie, low-cholesterol concept called Evergreen, aimed at diners wanting to eat smarter. She's presently culinary director for the renowned consulting firm Joseph Baum & Michael Whiteman Co., creating highly visible food and restaurant projects all over the world.

★ **KEVIN GRAHAM**

Because he's dedicated to a healthful lifestyle, Kevin Graham commutes to and from his three restaurants in New Orleans on a bicycle—those restaurants being Graham's, his signature establishment; Graham's Cafe Creole; and his newest eating venture, Sapphire, which serves contemporary French food. For Graham, it seems no recipe is sacred when it comes to lightening it. At Graham's Cafe Creole, for example, he offers a fat-free seafood gumbo. Instead of a traditional roux for thickening, he uses a pureed bean mixture.

★ **JEANNE JONES**

You could easily dub Jeanne Jones the Queen of Light. For this prolific cookbook author with 30 books to her credit, the challenge of creating light, healthful recipes is her passion. Besides being one of our original contributors, Jones, of La Jolla, California, writes a syndicated newspaper column called "Cook It Light." "If food is properly balanced, no one should know it's light," she says. "It should be an extra gift that it's good for you. I try to create light recipes that not only meet all expectations in taste, texture, and temperature, but are also nutritious."

★ **HUBERT KELLER**

Hubert Keller is always making the lists of the 10 best chefs in America. The cuisine at his restaurant, Fleur de Lys, in San Francisco, reflects California's health-oriented life style. Though trained in France, Keller was inspired by San Francisco's abundant availability of fresh ingredients to explore a lighter, fresher way to prepare food—to the point of being one of the first chefs to develop a vegetarian menu in an upscale restaurant. He relies on fresh herbs, spices, reductions, pureed roasted garlic, fresh vegetables, and flavored oils and vinegars to thicken and flavor his dishes, adding a Mediterranean touch to traditional French cooking.

★ **GREG PATENT**

At age 19, *Cooking Light* Contributing Editor Greg Patent won second prize in the junior division of the Pillsbury Bake-Off with his recipe for Apricot Dessert Bars . . . not exactly light cooking. But that was 1958. Today, Patent possesses a magic flair for transforming even the heaviest of foods—especially baked goods, and *especially* cheesecakes—into healthful, uncompromisingly delicious recipes. "Light cooking is simply the way people should cook as long as taste and texture are not affected. If this can't be accomplished, then the food should just be limited," he says.

★ **STEVEN PETUSEVSKY**

Steven Petusevsky finds that vegetarian food can taste exciting, bold-flavored, and still be healthful. Petusevsky, who writes our Inspired Vegetarian column, incorporates this liberating philosophy in his homey-but-modern recipes, ranging from jazzy chiles rellenos to peasant lasagnas.

★ **ELIZABETH TALIAFERRO**

No cook has a longer history with our magazine than Contributing Editor Elizabeth Taliaferro. She tested recipes in our very first issue and has done the food styling for many *Cooking Light* covers. She's also worked as a home economist in the Test Kitchens at Oxmoor House, our company's book-publishing division. A resident of Birmingham, Alabama, Taliaferro has an amazing knack for being able to develop light, healthful recipes with flavors from around the world.

★ **CYNTHIA WALT**

Cynthia Walt believes that because Americans frequently eat on the run, they sacrifice the health factors and taste sensations that satisfy body and soul. Her remedy is a menu featuring organic, farm-raised ingredients and dishes that are often seasoned with fruits and spices. She is very creative in how she avoids and reduces fat in cooking by using intensely flavored broths, purees, and miso, and steaming many ingredients to avoid adding oil.

THAI-SEARED TOFU

—Contributing Editor Steven Petusevsky

½ cup chopped fresh basil
½ cup chopped fresh cilantro
½ cup low-sodium soy sauce
½ cup fresh lime juice
¼ cup chopped fresh mint
2 tablespoons molasses
1 tablespoon peeled, minced fresh gingerroot
1 tablespoon vegetable oil
2 teaspoons curry powder
½ teaspoon dried crushed red pepper
4 garlic cloves, minced
2 (10.5-ounce) packages reduced-fat firm tofu, drained
Vegetable cooking spray
6 cups hot cooked vermicelli (about 12 ounces uncooked pasta)

1. Combine first 11 ingredients in a medium bowl; stir with a whisk until blended. Cut each tofu cake crosswise into 4 slices. Place tofu slices in soy sauce mixture; cover and marinate in refrigerator at least 2 hours.
2. Coat a large nonstick skillet with cooking spray; place over medium-high heat until hot. Remove tofu slices from marinade, reserving marinade. Add tofu slices to skillet; cook 2 minutes on each side or until browned. Remove from skillet. Set aside, and keep warm.
3. Add reserved marinade to skillet; bring to a simmer over medium-high heat. Spoon pasta onto plates; top with tofu slices. Drizzle warm marinade over tofu and pasta. Yield: 4 servings (serving size: 1½ cups pasta, 2 tofu slices, and ½ cup sauce).

CALORIES 450 (14% from fat); FAT 7.1g (sat 1.1g, mono 1.7g, poly 3.2g); PROTEIN 19.7g; CARB 73.6g; FIBER 4.2g; CHOL 0mg; IRON 4.3mg; SODIUM 914mg; CALC 68mg

RUM-AND-PEPPER PAINTED FISH WITH HABANERO-MANGO MOJO

—Chef Norman Van Aken

2½ tablespoons black peppercorns
12 whole cloves
¾ cup white rum
½ cup sugar
½ cup low-sodium soy sauce
2½ tablespoons grated lemon rind
2 tablespoons fresh lemon juice
1 tablespoon vegetable oil
4 (6-ounce) grouper or other firm white fish fillets
Habanero-Mango Mojo
Black Bean-and-Fruit Salsa
Lime wedges (optional)

1. Heat a nonstick skillet over medium-high heat until hot. Add peppercorns and cloves; cook 1 minute. Place spice mixture in a spice or coffee grinder; process until finely ground. Place ground mixture in a saucepan. Add rum and next 4 ingredients; bring to a boil. Reduce heat; simmer, uncovered, 25 minutes or until reduced to ½ cup. Strain pepper "paint" through a fine sieve over a bowl; discard solids. Set pepper "paint" aside.
2. Preheat oven to 450°.
3. Wrap handle of skillet with aluminum foil; heat oil in skillet until hot. Brush pepper paint over one side of fish. Place fish, paint side down, in skillet, and sauté 3 minutes or until dark brown. Turn fish over, and place skillet in oven.
4. Bake 7 minutes or until fish flakes easily when tested with a fork. Serve fillets with Habanero-Mango Mojo and Black Bean-and-Fruit Salsa. Garnish with lime wedges, if desired. Yield: 4 servings (serving size: 5 ounces fish, ¼ cup mojo, and 1 cup salsa).
Note: Pepper paint may be refrigerated for up to 1 month.

CALORIES 581 (14% from fat); FAT 9.2g (sat 1.6g, mono 4g, poly 2.7g); PROTEIN 36.2g; CARB 55.1g; FIBER 3.7g; CHOL 63mg; IRON 2.9mg; SODIUM 945mg; CALC 91mg

Habanero-Mango Mojo:

1½ cups peeled, cubed ripe mango
¼ cup Chardonnay or other dry white wine
2 tablespoons orange juice
1 to 1½ teaspoons habanero pepper sauce

1. Combine all ingredients in a blender or food processor; cover and process until smooth. Yield: 1 cup (serving size: ¼ cup).

Black Bean-and-Fruit Salsa:

½ cup peeled, cubed ripe mango
1 cup peeled, diced papaya
½ cup cubed pineapple
½ cup diced red onion
½ cup canned black beans, rinsed and drained
½ to 1 teaspoon habanero pepper sauce
1 tablespoon minced fresh cilantro
1 tablespoon fresh lime juice
1 tablespoon extra-virgin olive oil
1 teaspoon ground cumin
½ teaspoon black pepper
1 garlic clove, minced

1. Combine all ingredients in a large bowl; toss gently to coat. Yield: 4 cups (serving size: 1 cup).

CALORIES 108 (33% from fat); FAT 3.9g (sat 0.5g, mono 2.6g, poly 0.4g); PROTEIN 2.7g; CARB 17.3g; FIBER 2.7g; CHOL 0mg; IRON 1.1mg; SODIUM 66mg; CALC 31mg

CORIANDER-RUBBED TENDERLOIN CROSTINI

—Chef Cynthia Walt

1 (18-ounce) beef tenderloin
    steak
2 tablespoons coarsely chopped
    green onions
2 tablespoons mirin (sweet rice
    wine)
2 tablespoons low-sodium soy
    sauce
2 teaspoons peeled, chopped
    fresh gingerroot
1 garlic clove, minced
¼ cup ground coriander
¼ cup coarsely ground pepper
Vegetable cooking spray
¼ cup chopped fresh parsley
¼ cup chopped fresh basil
¼ cup minced fresh cilantro
1 tablespoon balsamic vinegar
1 tablespoon extra-virgin olive oil
1 teaspoon low-sodium soy sauce
1 teaspoon coarsely ground
    pepper
1 garlic clove, minced
24 (¼-inch-thick) slices plum
    tomato
12 (1-inch-thick) slices diagonally
    cut Italian bread (each about
    1 ounce), toasted
Miso Mustard Sauce

1. Trim fat from beef. Combine tenderloin, green onions, and next 4 ingredients in a large zip-top plastic bag; seal. Marinate in refrigerator 3 hours, turning occasionally.
2. Preheat oven to 450°.
3. Combine coriander and ¼ cup pepper in a small bowl; set aside. Remove tenderloin from bag; pat dry with a paper towel. Discard marinade. Rub coriander mixture evenly over tenderloin. Place tenderloin on rack of a broiler pan coated with cooking spray. Insert meat thermometer into thickest portion of tenderloin. Bake at 450° for 20 minutes or until thermometer registers 145° (medium-rare) to 160° (medium). Place tenderloin on a platter; cover with aluminum foil. Let stand 10 minutes. Slice tenderloin diagonally across grain into 12 slices; set aside.

4. Combine parsley and next 7 ingredients in a large bowl. Add tomato slices; toss gently to coat. Place 2 tomato slices on each toast slice; top with 1 slice tenderloin and 1 tablespoon Miso Mustard Sauce. Yield: 12 servings.

CALORIES 199 (23% from fat); FAT 5.1g (sat 1.4g, mono 2.1g, poly 0.4g); PROTEIN 14.2g; CARB 23.5g; FIBER 2.3g; CHOL 27mg; IRON 3.2mg; SODIUM 495mg; CALC 73mg

Miso Mustard Sauce:

1 cup plain fat-free yogurt
¼ cup miso (soybean paste)
1 tablespoon wasabi powder
    (dried Japanese horseradish)
1 tablespoon Dijon mustard

1. Combine all ingredients in a small bowl; cover and chill. Yield: 1½ cups.
Note: Store remaining sauce in an airtight container in the refrigerator for up to 1 week.

GRILLED STRAWBERRIES WITH LEMON SORBET AND CRANBERRY SYRUP

—Chef Kevin Graham

2 cups sugar
2 cups water
1½ cups fresh lemon juice
1¼ cups sugar
5 cups cranberry juice cocktail
    (at room temperature)
½ cup fresh lemon juice (at room
    temperature)
48 medium strawberries
1 cup sifted powdered sugar
Vegetable cooking spray

1. Combine 2 cups sugar and water in a large heavy saucepan. Bring to a boil; cook 1 minute or until sugar dissolves. Add 1½ cups lemon juice; stir well. Pour mixture into the freezer can of an ice-cream freezer; freeze according to manufacturer's instructions. Spoon sorbet into a freezer-safe container; cover and freeze 8 hours or until firm.
2. Place 1¼ cups sugar in a Dutch oven. Place over medium heat; cook until sugar is golden (do not stir).

Carefully add cranberry juice and ½ cup lemon juice, stirring constantly (mixture will bubble vigorously); cook 35 minutes or until reduced to 2¼ cups. Cover and chill.
3. Prepare grill. Thread 3 strawberries onto each of 16 (6-inch) skewers. Dredge skewers in powdered sugar. Place skewers on grill rack coated with cooking spray; grill 2 minutes on each side or until thoroughly heated. Serve with sorbet and syrup. Yield: 16 servings (serving size: ¼ cup sorbet, 2 tablespoons syrup, and 3 strawberries).

CALORIES 255 (11% from fat); FAT 0.3g (sat 0g, mono 0g, poly 0.1g); PROTEIN 0.4g; CARB 65.9g; FIBER 1.2g; CHOL 0.3mg; IRON 0.3mg; SODIUM 4mg; CALC 11mg

CHOCOLATE ROULADE WITH RASPBERRIES

—Contributing Editor Greg Patent

Vegetable cooking spray
2 tablespoons dry breadcrumbs
4 large egg yolks
¾ cup sugar, divided
1 teaspoon vanilla extract
½ cup Dutch process cocoa
6 large egg whites (at room
    temperature)
⅛ teaspoon salt
2 tablespoons powdered sugar
2 cups frozen reduced-calorie
    whipped topping, thawed
3 tablespoons plus 1 teaspoon
    chocolate syrup
2½ cups raspberries

1. Preheat oven to 375°.
2. Coat a 15 x 10-inch jelly-roll pan with cooking spray; line bottom with wax paper. Coat wax paper with cooking spray. Dust with breadcrumbs, and set aside.
3. Beat egg yolks in a large bowl at high speed of an electric mixer for 4 minutes. Gradually add ¼ cup sugar, beating until thick and pale (about 2 minutes). Stir in vanilla. Gradually add cocoa; stir until well-blended. Beat egg whites with clean beaters at high speed until foamy; add salt. Gradually add ½ cup sugar, 1 tablespoon at a time,

beating until stiff peaks form. Gently stir one-fourth of egg white mixture into egg yolk mixture; gently fold in remaining egg white mixture.

4. Spoon batter into prepared pan, spreading evenly to sides of pan. Bake at 375° for 15 minutes or until cake springs back when touched lightly in center. Loosen cake from sides of pan; turn out onto a dishtowel dusted with powdered sugar; carefully peel off wax paper. Let cake cool 1 minute. Starting at narrow end, roll up cake and towel together. Place, seam side down, on a wire rack; let cool completely (about 1 hour).

5. Unroll cake carefully; remove towel. Spread whipped topping over cake, leaving a ½-inch margin around edges. Reroll cake; place, seam side down, on a platter. Cover and chill 1 hour. Cut cake into slices. Drizzle syrup on each of 10 plates. Place a cake slice on each; serve with raspberries. Yield: 10 servings (serving size: 1 [1-inch] slice, ¼ cup raspberries, and 1 teaspoon syrup).

CALORIES 181 (24% from fat); FAT 4.8g (sat 2.2g, mono 0.8g, poly 1g); PROTEIN 5.4g; CARB 29.5g; FIBER 1.9g; CHOL 87mg; IRON 1.3mg; SODIUM 91mg; CALC 36mg

PAVLOVA

—Cookbook Author Jeanne Jones

5 large egg whites (at room temperature)
¼ teaspoon salt
1 cup sugar
1 tablespoon plus 1 teaspoon cornstarch
½ teaspoon vanilla extract
½ teaspoon white vinegar
4 cups assorted fresh berries
2 tablespoons powdered sugar
1½ cups light vanilla ice cream, melted
1½ teaspoons Grand Marnier (orange-flavored liqueur) or ½ teaspoon extract of your choice
Fresh mint sprigs (optional)

1. Preheat oven to 275°.
2. Cover a large baking sheet with parchment paper. Draw a 10-inch circle on parchment paper. Turn parchment paper over. Secure with masking tape; set aside.
3. Beat egg whites at high speed of an electric mixer until foamy. Add salt, beating until stiff peaks form. Gradually add 1 cup sugar, 1 tablespoon at a time, beating until stiff peaks form (do not underbeat). Sprinkle cornstarch over egg white mixture; beat at low speed until well-blended. Stir in vanilla and vinegar.
4. Spoon egg white mixture onto drawn circle. Using the back of spoon, shape meringue into a "nest" with 2½-inch sides. Bake at 275° for 2 hours or until dry. Turn oven off; let meringue cool in closed oven at least 12 hours. Carefully remove meringue from paper; set aside.
5. Combine berries and powdered sugar; let stand 5 minutes. Combine ice cream and liqueur. Spoon fruit mixture onto meringue; drizzle sauce over top. Garnish with mint sprigs, if desired. Yield: 8 servings (serving size: 1 wedge, ½ cup fruit, and 1½ tablespoons sauce).

CALORIES 180 (7% from fat); FAT 1.3g (sat 0.7g, mono 0.3g, poly 0.2g); PROTEIN 3.5g; CARB 39.4g; FIBER 1.9g; CHOL 3mg; IRON 0.3mg; SODIUM 128mg; CALC 46mg

LEMON-ROSEMARY CUSTARD CAKES

—Chef Rozanne Gold

3 large egg whites (at room temperature)
¾ cup sugar, divided
2 tablespoons stick margarine, softened
¼ cup all-purpose flour
1 teaspoon grated lemon rind
¼ cup fresh lemon juice
1 teaspoon minced fresh rosemary
Dash of salt
1½ cups 1% low-fat milk
3 large egg yolks
Vegetable cooking spray
1 tablespoon sifted powdered sugar

1. Preheat oven to 350°.
2. Beat egg whites at medium-high speed of an electric mixer until foamy. Gradually add ¼ cup sugar, 1 tablespoon at a time, beating until stiff peaks form. Set aside.
3. Beat ½ cup sugar and margarine at medium speed until well-blended (about 5 minutes). Add flour and next 4 ingredients, beating well. Add milk and egg yolks; beat well. Gently stir one-fourth of egg white mixture into batter; gently fold in remaining egg white mixture. Spoon into 6 (6-ounce) custard cups coated with cooking spray. Place cups in a baking pan, and add hot water to pan to a depth of 1 inch. Bake at 350° for 45 minutes or until set. Remove cups from pan, and sprinkle with powdered sugar. Yield: 6 servings.

CALORIES 222 (29% from fat); FAT 7.2g (sat 2g, mono 2.9g, poly 1.6g); PROTEIN 5.9g; CARB 34.4g; FIBER 0.2g; CHOL 113mg; IRON 0.7mg; SODIUM 113mg; CALC 92mg

Food and Wine Shine

Kendall-Jackson's Brian Leonard loves playing matchmaker with garden-fresh food and fine wine.

Executive chef at Kendall-Jackson Vineyards in Santa Rosa, California, Brian Leonard has spent the past few years developing fresh, healthful dishes to pair with Kendall-Jackson wines.

Leonard feels that you need good, strong flavors to stand up to the complexities of wine. And he typically replaces fats and oils with a variety of herb-infused wine marinades, or garlic- and shallot-flavored wine reductions used as grilling glazes. He recommends that when pairing wines with food, you avoid using oils or fats in cooking as much as possible, especially strong-flavored extra-virgin olive oil. That's all you'll taste—oils coat the palate so you can't get the true taste of the food or the wine.

BAKED EGGPLANT STACKS WITH ROASTED-TOMATO SAUCE

  8 plum tomatoes (about 1 pound)
Vegetable cooking spray
1½ cups diced onion, divided
  ½ cup dry red wine
  1 teaspoon chopped fresh oregano
  ½ teaspoon freshly ground pepper
  ¼ teaspoon salt
  1 cup sliced onion
  ½ cup dry white wine
 20 garlic cloves, peeled (about 2 large heads)
  1 cup canned vegetable broth
  ¼ teaspoon salt
 18 (½-inch-thick) slices eggplant (about 2 medium)
  2 (10-ounce) packages frozen chopped spinach, thawed, drained, and squeezed dry
  4 ounces feta cheese, crumbled
Oregano sprigs (optional)

1. Preheat oven to 425°.
2. Place tomatoes in a shallow baking dish coated with cooking spray. Bake at 425° for 30 minutes. Set aside.
3. Heat a medium saucepan over medium-high heat. Add 1 cup diced onion; sauté 3 minutes. Stir in tomatoes, red wine, chopped oregano, pepper, and ¼ teaspoon salt; bring to a boil. Reduce heat; simmer 20 minutes. Place tomato mixture in a blender; cover and process until smooth. Set aside, and keep warm.
4. Place a saucepan coated with cooking spray over high heat. Add sliced onion; sauté 5 minutes. Add white wine and garlic. Bring to a boil; cook 5 minutes. Stir in broth; bring to a boil. Reduce heat; simmer 20 minutes. Place garlic mixture in blender; cover and process until smooth. Set aside, and keep warm.
5. Sprinkle ¼ teaspoon salt over eggplant. Place half of eggplant in a single layer on a baking sheet coated with cooking spray; broil 5 minutes on each side or until lightly browned. Repeat procedure with remaining eggplant; set aside.
6. Place a large nonstick skillet coated with cooking spray over medium-high heat. Add ½ cup diced onion; sauté 3 minutes. Add spinach; cook 10 minutes, stirring frequently. Remove from heat; stir in cheese.
7. Preheat oven to 425°.
8. Arrange 6 eggplant slices, 2 to 3 inches apart, on a baking sheet. Spread 2½ tablespoons spinach mixture over each slice. Top each with another eggplant slice, an additional 2½ tablespoons spinach mixture, and another eggplant slice. Bake at 425° for 15 minutes. Arrange 1 eggplant stack on each of 6 plates; spoon ⅓ cup tomato sauce and 2 tablespoons garlic sauce on each plate. Garnish with oregano sprigs, if desired. Yield: 6 servings.

CALORIES 158 (29% from fat); FAT 5.1g (sat 3g, mono 1g, poly 0.5g); PROTEIN 8.7g; CARB 23.8g; FIBER 6.8g; CHOL 17mg; IRON 3.6mg; SODIUM 662mg; CALC 279mg

Playing Favorites

So much has happened with vegetarian cuisine in the last 10 years. Not so long ago, if you wanted to eat meatless, you had to whisper this preference, or so it seemed.

Many articles have been published recently dealing with the subject of food as medicine. A large percentage of these studies confirm that a diet containing a sizable percentage of vegetables, fruits, grains, and soy-based foods offers plant-based natural chemicals that help our immune systems, strengthen our bodies, and improve our mental states. Best of all, we don't have to sacrifice flavor for all of those benefits.

COTTAGE CHEESE-AND-NOODLE PUDDING

A slimmed-down version of a traditional noodle kugel, this pudding can be served for brunch.

  5 cups cooked egg noodles
  2 cups 1% low-fat cottage cheese
  ½ cup packed brown sugar
  1 teaspoon salt
  ½ teaspoon ground cinnamon
  ½ teaspoon vanilla extract
  ¼ teaspoon pepper
  1 (8-ounce) carton vanilla low-fat yogurt
  4 ounces Neufchâtel cheese, cut into small pieces
  2 large egg whites, lightly beaten
  2 large eggs, lightly beaten
Vegetable cooking spray

1. Preheat oven to 375°.
2. Combine first 11 ingredients in a large bowl. Pour noodle mixture into a 13 x 9-inch baking dish coated with cooking spray.

3. Cover and bake at 375° for 45 minutes or until almost set. Uncover; bake 10 additional minutes or until lightly browned. Serve warm or at room temperature. Yield: 8 servings.

CALORIES 269 (23% from fat); FAT 6.8g (sat 3.4g, mono 2.1g, poly 0.6g); PROTEIN 16.3g; CARB 35.3g; FIBER 0.8g; CHOL 97mg; IRON 1.9mg; SODIUM 563mg; CALC 119mg

UDON NOODLES WITH ASIAN VEGETABLES AND PEANUT SAUCE

¼ cup plus 2 tablespoons water
¼ cup reduced-fat creamy peanut butter
2 tablespoons brown sugar
2 tablespoons low-sodium soy sauce
2 tablespoons rice vinegar
1½ teaspoons peeled, minced fresh gingerroot
1½ teaspoons dark sesame oil
½ teaspoon cornstarch
½ teaspoon chile paste with garlic (optional)
2 garlic cloves, minced
8 ounces uncooked udon noodles (thick, round fresh Japanese wheat noodles) or spaghetti
4 cups sliced bok choy
2 cups snow peas, halved crosswise
1 cup shredded carrot

1. Combine first 10 ingredients in a small saucepan; stir with a whisk until blended. Bring to a boil; cook, stirring constantly, 1 minute. Set aside.
2. Cook noodles in boiling water 8 minutes. Drain well. Combine noodles, peanut sauce, bok choy, snow peas, and carrot in a large bowl; toss well to coat. Yield: 4 servings (serving size: 2 cups).
Note: Chile paste with garlic and the udon noodles can be found with other ethnic foods in the supermarket or at an Asian market. The chile paste can be omitted if you prefer a not-so-hot sauce.

CALORIES 408 (20% from fat); FAT 9.1g (sat 1.5g, mono 3.7g, poly 3g); PROTEIN 14.6g; CARB 67.6g; FIBER 4.9g; CHOL 0mg; IRON 4.9mg; SODIUM 428mg; CALC 131mg

SPINACH-AND-MUSHROOM LASAGNA

(pictured on page 110)

This lasagna has more calcium per serving than an 8-ounce glass of milk.

1 (8-ounce) package uncooked lasagna noodles
1 teaspoon olive oil
7 cups sliced mushrooms (about 2 [8-ounce] packages)
3 cups sliced shiitake mushroom caps (about 2 [3½-ounce] packages)
½ teaspoon ground nutmeg
3 garlic cloves, minced
2 (15-ounce) containers light ricotta cheese
2 (10-ounce) packages frozen chopped spinach, thawed, drained, and squeezed dry
¼ cup grated Parmesan cheese
1 teaspoon dried Italian seasoning
1 teaspoon pepper
3 large egg whites
1 (25.5-ounce) bottle fat-free marinara sauce
Vegetable cooking spray
3 cups (12 ounces) shredded part-skim mozzarella cheese, divided
2 tablespoons grated Parmesan cheese

1. Cook lasagna noodles according to package directions, omitting salt and fat. Drain; set aside 9 noodles.
2. Heat oil in a nonstick skillet over medium heat. Add mushrooms; sauté 3 minutes. Add nutmeg and garlic; sauté 5 minutes. Set aside.
3. Combine ricotta and next 5 ingredients; set aside.
4. Preheat oven to 375°.
5. Spread ½ cup marinara sauce in bottom of a 13 x 9-inch baking dish coated with cooking spray. Arrange 3 lasagna noodles over sauce; top with half of ricotta cheese mixture, half of mushroom mixture, 1½ cups sauce, and 1 cup mozzarella cheese. Repeat layers, ending with noodles. Spread ½ cup sauce over noodles.

6. Cover and bake at 375° for 40 minutes. Uncover; sprinkle with 1 cup mozzarella cheese and Parmesan cheese. Bake 10 minutes. Let stand 10 minutes before serving. Yield: 9 servings.

CALORIES 392 (28% from fat); FAT 12.2g (sat 6.7g, mono 3.4g, poly 0.7g); PROTEIN 30g; CARB 38.6g; FIBER 5g; CHOL 38mg; IRON 3.8mg; SODIUM 617mg; CALC 494mg

ORZO-AND-PORTOBELLO CASSEROLE

¼ cup chopped sun-dried tomatoes, packed without oil
¼ cup boiling water
1 tablespoon olive oil
2 cups sliced leek
2 cups diced portobello mushroom caps
1 cup mushrooms, quartered
2 garlic cloves, minced
4 cups cooked orzo (about 2 cups uncooked rice-shaped pasta)
2 cups thinly sliced fennel bulb (about 1 large)
2 cups tomato juice
2 tablespoons minced fresh basil or 2 teaspoons dried basil
2 tablespoons balsamic vinegar
1 teaspoon paprika
⅛ teaspoon pepper
Vegetable cooking spray
1 cup (4 ounces) shredded provolone or part-skim mozzarella cheese
¼ cup grated Parmesan cheese

1. Preheat oven to 400°.
2. Combine tomatoes and boiling water in a bowl. Cover; let stand 10 minutes or until tomatoes are soft. Drain.
3. Heat oil in a nonstick skillet over medium heat. Add tomatoes, leek, mushrooms, and garlic; sauté 2 minutes. Combine mushroom mixture, orzo, and next 6 ingredients in a bowl; stir well. Spoon mixture into a 13 x 9-inch baking dish coated with cooking spray. Bake at 400° for 25 minutes. Sprinkle with cheeses; bake 5 additional minutes. Yield: 6 servings (serving size: 1⅓ cups).

CALORIES 381 (24% from fat); FAT 10g (sat 4.5g, mono 3.5g, poly 0.9g); PROTEIN 17g; CARB 57g; FIBER 2.7g; CHOL 16mg; IRON 4.8mg; SODIUM 624mg; CALC 277mg

EGGPLANT MANICOTTI WITH CREAMY PESTO FILLING

½ cup (2 ounces) shredded part-skim mozzarella cheese, divided
1 cup fresh basil leaves
½ cup fresh parsley leaves
½ cup spinach leaves
¼ cup pine nuts, toasted
¼ cup grated fresh Parmesan cheese
¼ cup tub fat-free cream cheese
¼ teaspoon salt
1 (15-ounce) container fat-free ricotta cheese
2 garlic cloves
1 (1½-pound) eggplant, cut lengthwise into 20 (⅛-inch-thick) slices
Vegetable cooking spray
2 cups low-fat spaghetti sauce, divided

1. Combine ¼ cup mozzarella cheese, basil, and next 8 ingredients in a food processor; process until smooth. Set pesto mixture aside.
2. Arrange half of eggplant in a single layer on a baking sheet coated with cooking spray. Broil 5 minutes or until lightly browned and very tender. Repeat procedure with remaining eggplant.
3. Preheat oven to 375°.
4. Spread 1 cup spaghetti sauce in bottom of a 13 x 9-inch baking dish coated with cooking spray. Place eggplant slices, browned sides down, on a smooth surface; spoon about 2 tablespoons pesto mixture in center of each slice (the amount will vary from 1 to 3 tablespoons depending on size of slices). Roll up, starting at short ends; place rolls, seam sides down, over sauce. Pour 1 cup spaghetti sauce over rolls.
5. Bake at 375° for 30 minutes. Top with ¼ cup mozzarella cheese; bake 10 additional minutes or until cheese is lightly browned. Yield: 4 servings (serving size: 5 rolls with sauce).
Note: Any leftover pesto mixture can be tossed with pasta.

CALORIES 282 (29% from fat); FAT 9.1g (sat 3.1g, mono 2.8g, poly 2.1g); PROTEIN 26.8g; CARB 31g; FIBER 5.4g; CHOL 24mg; IRON 2.7mg; SODIUM 760mg; CALC 451mg

SEVEN-LAYER TORTILLA PIE

(pictured on page 111)

1 tablespoon olive oil
1 cup chopped red bell pepper
¾ cup chopped green bell pepper
½ cup chopped red onion
½ cup seeded, chopped Anaheim chile or 1 (4.5-ounce) can chopped green chiles, drained
2 tablespoons minced fresh cilantro
1 teaspoon dried oregano
1 teaspoon chili powder
½ teaspoon ground cumin
2 cups no-salt-added tomato juice
2 (15-ounce) cans black beans, drained
2 (15-ounce) cans cannellini beans or other white beans, drained
1 cup (4 ounces) shredded reduced-fat Monterey Jack cheese
1 cup (4 ounces) shredded reduced-fat sharp Cheddar cheese
Vegetable cooking spray
7 (8-inch) flour tortillas

1. Heat oil in a large nonstick skillet over medium heat. Add red bell pepper and next 7 ingredients; sauté 5 minutes or until tender. Add tomato juice; cook 8 minutes or until reduced to 2½ cups.
2. Combine black beans and half of tomato juice mixture in a bowl. Stir cannellini beans into remaining tomato juice mixture. Set both aside.
3. Preheat oven to 325°.
4. Combine cheeses. Line a 9-inch pie plate with aluminum foil, allowing 6 inches of foil to extend over opposite edges of pie plate. Repeat procedure with another sheet of foil, extending foil over remaining edges of pie plate. Coat foil with cooking spray; place 1 tortilla in bottom of dish. Spread 1 cup cannellini bean mixture over tortilla; sprinkle with ¼ cup cheeses. Place 1 tortilla over cheeses, pressing gently. Spread 1 cup black bean mixture over tortilla; sprinkle with ¼ cup cheeses. Place 1 tortilla over cheeses, pressing gently. Repeat layers, ending with black bean mixture and cheeses.
5. Bring edges of foil to center; fold to seal. Bake at 325° for 40 minutes. Remove from oven; let stand, covered, 10 minutes. Remove foil packet from dish. Unwrap; slide onto a serving plate using a spatula. Cut pie into wedges. Yield: 8 servings (serving size: 1 wedge).

CALORIES 423 (23% from fat); FAT 11g (sat 4.1g, mono 2.5g, poly 1.9g); PROTEIN 24.5g; CARB 59.3g; FIBER 7.4g; CHOL 18mg; IRON 5mg; SODIUM 758mg; CALC 353mg

MEDITERRANEAN SALAD WITH ZESTY LEMON VINAIGRETTE

2 cups (2-inch) cut green beans
Zesty Lemon Vinaigrette
2 cups chopped tomatoes
1 (15-ounce) can no-salt-added chickpeas (garbanzo beans), rinsed and drained
1 (4-ounce) package crumbled feta cheese
1 (1¼-pound) eggplant, cut into 12 (¼-inch-thick) slices
Vegetable cooking spray
6 (¼-inch-thick) slices zucchini
6 red bell pepper rings
6 green bell pepper rings
2 cups thinly sliced fennel bulb (about 1 large)
4 cups gourmet salad greens
2 cups plain croutons

1. Arrange green beans in a steamer basket over boiling water; cover and steam 3 minutes or until tender. Rinse under cold water; drain well. Combine beans, ¼ cup Zesty Lemon Vinaigrette, and next 3 ingredients. Set aside.
2. Arrange eggplant slices in a single layer on a baking sheet coated with cooking spray. Brush eggplant with Zesty Lemon Vinaigrette. Broil 12 minutes or until lightly browned. Remove from baking sheet; let cool.
3. Arrange 2 eggplant slices, 1 zucchini slice, 1 each red and green pepper ring, and about ⅓ cup fennel slices

on each of 6 plates. Top each with ⅔ cup green bean mixture, ⅔ cup greens, and ⅓ cup croutons. Drizzle with remaining vinaigrette. Yield: 6 servings.

CALORIES 265 (29% from fat); FAT 8.5g (sat 3.3g, mono 2.9g, poly 1.1g); PROTEIN 11.7g; CARB 40g; FIBER 6g; CHOL 17mg; IRON 4.4mg; SODIUM 558mg; CALC 217mg

Zesty Lemon Vinaigrette:

- ½ cup lemon juice
- 2 tablespoons chopped fresh flat-leaf parsley
- 2 tablespoons water
- 1 tablespoon chopped fresh or 1 teaspoon dried oregano
- 1 tablespoon olive oil
- 1 tablespoon honey
- 1 tablespoon Dijon mustard
- 1 teaspoon salt
- ½ teaspoon fennel seeds, crushed
- ¼ teaspoon dried crushed red pepper
- 2 garlic cloves, minced

1. Combine all ingredients in a jar. Cover tightly; shake vigorously. Yield: 1 cup (serving size: 1 tablespoon).

CALORIES 16 (51% from fat); FAT 0.1g (sat 0.1g, mono 0.6g, poly 0.1g); PROTEIN 0.1g; CARB 2.1g; FIBER 0.1g; CHOL 0mg; IRON 0.1mg; SODIUM 102mg; CALC 5mg

COUSCOUS-AND-FETA CAKES

- 2½ cups water
- 1 cup uncooked couscous
- 1 tablespoon plus 1 teaspoon olive oil, divided
- 1 cup minced red onion
- 1 cup minced red bell pepper
- ½ cup minced green bell pepper
- 2 garlic cloves, minced
- 1 (4-ounce) package crumbled feta cheese
- ½ cup all-purpose flour
- ½ cup egg substitute
- 2 tablespoons minced fresh parsley
- ¼ teaspoon salt
- ¼ teaspoon white pepper

1. Bring water to a boil in a saucepan; stir in couscous. Remove from heat; cover and let stand 10 minutes. Fluff with a fork. Place 1 teaspoon oil in an electric skillet; heat to 375°. Add onion and next 3 ingredients; sauté 5 minutes. Combine couscous, onion mixture, cheese, and remaining 5 ingredients in a large bowl; stir well.
2. Place ½ teaspoon oil in skillet; heat to 375°. Place ⅓ cup couscous mixture for each of 4 portions into skillet, shaping each portion into a 3-inch cake in skillet. Cook 6 minutes or until golden, turning carefully after 3 minutes. Remove cakes, and keep warm. Repeat procedure with remaining oil and couscous mixture. Yield: 12 servings (serving size: 2 cakes).

CALORIES 242 (28% from fat); FAT 7.6g (sat 3.2g, mono 3.2g, poly 0.6g); PROTEIN 10g; CARB 34g; FIBER 2.4g; CHOL 16mg; IRON 2.2mg; SODIUM 344mg; CALC 112mg

GREEK RATATOUILLE

Begin cooking the rice first, so it'll be hot when you add the browned vegetables.

- 2 teaspoons olive oil, divided
- 1 cup chopped red onion
- 1 cup chopped red bell pepper
- 1 cup chopped green bell pepper
- 2 cups chopped zucchini
- 1¼ cups chopped yellow squash
- 3 cups small mushrooms, halved
- 3 garlic cloves, minced
- 3 cups hot cooked long-grain brown rice
- 1 tablespoon chopped fresh or 1 teaspoon dried oregano
- ½ teaspoon pepper
- ¼ teaspoon salt
- ¼ cup chopped fresh or 1 tablespoon dried basil
- 1 (4-ounce) package crumbled feta cheese

1. Heat 1 teaspoon oil in a large non-stick skillet over medium-high heat. Add onion and chopped peppers; cook 3 minutes or until lightly browned (do not stir). Remove onion mixture from skillet; place in a large bowl.
2. Heat ½ teaspoon oil in skillet. Add zucchini and squash; cook 3 minutes or until lightly browned (do not stir). Remove zucchini mixture from skillet, and place in bowl. Heat ½ teaspoon oil in skillet. Add mushrooms and garlic; cook 3 minutes or until lightly browned (do not stir). Return onion mixture and zucchini mixture to skillet. Stir in rice, oregano, ½ teaspoon pepper, and salt; cook just until heated. Remove from heat. Stir in basil and cheese. Yield: 4 servings (serving size: 2 cups).

CALORIES 322 (29% from fat); FAT 10.3g (sat 4.9g, mono 3.5g, poly 1.2g); PROTEIN 11.3g; CARB 48.4g; FIBER 5.9g; CHOL 25mg; IRON 2.9mg; SODIUM 478mg; CALC 201mg

PASTA WITH GARDEN BOLOGNESE SAUCE

Bolognese refers to a thick, robust tomato sauce enhanced with red wine. This one begins with a bottled pasta sauce.

- 2 teaspoons olive oil
- 2 cups shredded carrot
- 2 cups chopped onion
- 1 cup chopped celery
- 1 cup chopped red bell pepper
- 1 cup chopped green bell pepper
- 1¾ cups chopped portobello mushroom caps (about 1 large mushroom)
- 2 teaspoons dried oregano
- 3 garlic cloves, minced
- 1 cup dry red wine
- 1 (26-ounce) bottle fat-free marinara sauce
- 6 cups hot cooked ziti (about 3 cups uncooked short tubular pasta)
- 1½ cups (6 ounces) shredded part-skim mozzarella cheese

1. Heat oil in a large Dutch oven over medium-high heat. Add carrot and next 4 ingredients; sauté 10 minutes. Add mushroom, oregano, and garlic; sauté 2 minutes. Add wine and marinara sauce; bring to a boil. Reduce heat, and simmer 20 minutes. Serve over ziti, and sprinkle with cheese. Yield: 6 servings (serving size: 1 cup pasta, 1 cup sauce, and ¼ cup cheese).

CALORIES 388 (19% from fat); FAT 8g (sat 3.4g, mono 2.5g, poly 0.9g); PROTEIN 17.5g; CARB 63.1g; FIBER 7.9g; CHOL 16mg; IRON 3.6mg; SODIUM 210mg; CALC 240mg

Special Deliveries

Wait a minute, Mr. Postman! From all the reader recipes that you've brought us in 10 years, these are our 10 favorites.

WHITE CHILI

Cannellini beans, tomatillos, and lime juice lend a refreshing spin to this red meat-and-kidney bean classic.

—Pamela Hassell,
Boulder Creek, California

Vegetable cooking spray
1 tablespoon vegetable oil
1 pound skinned, boned chicken breast halves, chopped
½ cup chopped shallots
3 garlic cloves, minced
1 (14.5-ounce) can no-salt-added whole tomatoes, undrained and coarsely chopped
1 (14¼-ounce) can fat-free chicken broth
1 (11-ounce) can tomatillos, drained and coarsely chopped
1 (4.5-ounce) can chopped green chiles, undrained
½ teaspoon dried oregano
½ teaspoon coriander seeds, crushed
¼ teaspoon ground cumin
2 (16-ounce) cans cannellini beans or other white beans, drained
3 tablespoons lime juice
¼ teaspoon pepper
½ cup plus 1 tablespoon (about 4 ounces) shredded reduced-fat sharp Cheddar cheese

1. Coat a large saucepan with cooking spray. Add oil; place over medium-high heat until hot. Add chicken; sauté 3 minutes or until done. Remove chicken from pan; set aside.
2. Add shallots and garlic to pan; sauté 2 minutes or until tender. Stir in tomatoes and next 6 ingredients. Bring to a boil; reduce heat, and simmer 20 minutes. Add chicken and beans; cook 5 minutes or until thoroughly heated. Stir in lime juice and pepper. Ladle into bowls; top with cheese. Yield: 9 servings (serving size: 1 cup chili and 1 tablespoon cheese).

CALORIES 247 (23% from fat); FAT 6.2g (sat 2g, mono 1.7g, poly 1.7g); PROTEIN 23.3g; CARB 25.4g; FIBER 3.1g; CHOL 38mg; IRON 2.6mg; SODIUM 593mg; CALC 171mg

PENNSYLVANIA POT ROAST

This old-fashioned pot roast is the very essence of comfort food.

—Ann Nace, Perkasie, Pennsylvania

Vegetable cooking spray
1 (1½-pound) beef eye of round roast
¾ cup beef broth
1 cup chopped onion
½ cup canned crushed tomatoes with added puree, undrained
¼ cup diced carrot
¼ cup diced celery
¼ cup diced turnip
2 tablespoons chopped fresh parsley
¼ teaspoon dried thyme
4 black peppercorns
1 bay leaf

1. Place a large saucepan coated with cooking spray over medium-high heat until hot. Add roast, browning on all sides. Add broth and remaining 9 ingredients to pan; bring to a boil. Cover, reduce heat, and simmer 3 hours or until tender.
2. Slice roast; place on a serving platter. Set aside; keep warm. Increase heat to medium; cook broth mixture, uncovered, 10 minutes or until reduced to 1⅔ cups. Discard peppercorns and bay leaf. Serve sauce with roast. Serve with red potatoes. Yield: 5 servings (serving size: 3 ounces roast and ⅓ cup sauce).

CALORIES 217 (24% from fat); FAT 5.7g (sat 2g, mono 2.2g, poly 0.3g); PROTEIN 33.4g; CARB 6.1g; FIBER 1.2g; CHOL 85mg; IRON 3.4mg; SODIUM 356mg; CALC 28mg

NEW ENGLAND FISH CHOWDER

—Esther Pittello,
Chicopee, Massachusetts

2 tablespoons margarine
3 tablespoons shredded carrot
2 tablespoons diced celery
2 tablespoons minced fresh onion
2 tablespoons plus 1 teaspoon all-purpose flour
3½ cups skim milk, divided
2 cups peeled, diced baking potato
½ teaspoon salt
¼ teaspoon pepper
1 pound cod or other lean white fish fillets, cut into 1-inch pieces

1. Melt margarine in a saucepan over medium heat. Add carrot, celery, and onion; sauté 2 minutes. Stir in flour; gradually add 2½ cups milk, stirring constantly with a whisk. Add potato, salt, and pepper; bring to a boil. Reduce heat. Simmer, uncovered, 30 minutes; stir occasionally. Add fish and 1 cup milk; cook 10 additional minutes or until fish is done. Yield: 4 servings (serving size: 1½ cups).

CALORIES 299 (21% from fat); FAT 6.9g (sat 1.5g, mono 2.7g, poly 2.1g); PROTEIN 29.6g; CARB 28.3g; FIBER 1.6g; CHOL 53mg; IRON 1.3mg; SODIUM 541mg; CALC 297mg

PORK TENDERLOIN WITH ROSEMARY AND THYME

—Yvonne LaRocca Lewis, Germany

2 (½-pound) pork tenderloins
Vegetable cooking spray
2 tablespoons Dijon mustard
1 tablespoon honey
1 teaspoon chopped fresh rosemary
½ teaspoon chopped fresh thyme
¼ teaspoon pepper

1. Preheat oven to 350°.
2. Trim fat from pork; place on rack of a broiler pan coated with cooking spray. Combine mustard and remaining 4

ingredients in a bowl; brush over pork. Insert meat thermometer into thickest part of pork.

3. Bake at 350° for 50 minutes or until thermometer registers 160° (slightly pink), basting frequently with mustard mixture. Yield: 4 servings (serving size: 3 ounces pork).

CALORIES 176 (27% from fat); FAT 5g (sat 1.5g, mono 1.9g, poly 0.5g); PROTEIN 25.8g; CARB 5g; FIBER 0.1g; CHOL 83mg; IRON 1.5mg; SODIUM 283mg; CALC 11mg

CHICKEN AND RICE WITH CREAMY HERB SAUCE

Look for cream cheese with garlic and spices in the deli section of your supermarket; it comes in small tubs.
—*Juanita Syron, Gresham, Oregon*

¾ cup water
¼ cup dry white wine
1 teaspoon chicken-flavored bouillon granules
4 (4-ounce) skinned, boned chicken breast halves
1 tablespoon water
½ teaspoon cornstarch
½ (6-ounce) tub light cream cheese with garlic and spices
4 cups hot cooked long-grain rice
Chopped fresh parsley

1. Bring first 3 ingredients to a boil in a skillet; add chicken. Cover, reduce heat, and simmer 15 minutes, turning chicken after 8 minutes. Remove chicken from skillet. Set aside, and keep warm.
2. Bring cooking liquid to a boil; cook 5 minutes or until reduced to ⅔ cup. Combine 1 tablespoon water and cornstarch; add to skillet. Bring to a boil; cook, stirring constantly, 1 minute. Add cream cheese; cook, stirring constantly with a whisk, until well-blended. Serve chicken over rice; spoon sauce over chicken. Sprinkle with parsley. Yield: 4 servings (serving size: 1 chicken breast half, 1 cup rice, and 3 tablespoons sauce).

CALORIES 399 (12% from fat); FAT 5.5g (sat 2.6g, mono 0.3g, poly 0.4g); PROTEIN 32.7g; CARB 51.6g; FIBER 1g; CHOL 78mg; IRON 2.7mg; SODIUM 400mg; CALC 63mg

CORN BREAD DRESSING

—*Deborah McPherson, Odessa, Texas*

2 hard-cooked large eggs
McPherson Corn Bread
1 (12-ounce) can refrigerated fluffy buttermilk biscuits
1½ teaspoons rubbed sage
½ teaspoon pepper
5 cups low-salt chicken broth
⅔ cup chopped celery
⅔ cup chopped onion
2 large egg whites, lightly beaten
Vegetable cooking spray

1. Slice hard-cooked eggs in half lengthwise; carefully remove yolks. Chop egg whites; set aside. Reserve yolks for another use.
2. Crumble McPherson Corn Bread; set aside. Bake biscuits according to package directions; let cool. Tear 8 biscuits into small pieces; reserve remaining 2 biscuits for another use. Combine chopped egg whites, crumbled corn bread, torn biscuits, sage, and pepper in a large bowl.
3. Preheat oven to 400°.
4. Bring broth to a boil in a saucepan. Add celery and onion. Reduce heat; simmer, uncovered, 5 minutes. Add broth mixture to corn bread mixture; stir well. Add beaten egg whites; stir well. Spoon mixture into a 2-quart casserole coated with cooking spray. Bake, uncovered, at 400° for 45 minutes. Yield: 12 servings (serving size: ½ cup).

CALORIES 180 (19% from fat); FAT 3.8g (sat 0.9g, mono 1g, poly 0.9g); PROTEIN 7.1g; CARB 29.3g; FIBER 1.2g; CHOL 1mg; IRON 1.6mg; SODIUM 391mg; CALC 85mg

McPherson Corn Bread:

1 cup yellow cornmeal
1 cup all-purpose flour
1 tablespoon baking powder
½ teaspoon salt
1¼ cups skim milk
2 large egg whites, lightly beaten
Vegetable cooking spray

1. Preheat oven to 400°.
2. Combine first 4 ingredients in a bowl; stir well. Combine milk and egg

whites, and add to flour mixture, stirring just until moist.
3. Pour batter into a 9-inch square baking pan coated with cooking spray. Bake at 400° for 20 minutes or until a wooden pick inserted in center comes out clean. Remove from pan; let cool completely on a wire rack. Yield: 12 servings (serving size: 1 [3 x 2¼-inch] piece).

CALORIES 90 (4% from fat); FAT 0.4g (sat 0.1g, mono 0.1g, poly 0.1g); PROTEIN 3.4g; CARB 17.7g; FIBER 0.9g; CHOL 1mg; IRON 1mg; SODIUM 121mg; CALC 78mg

EASY REFRIGERATOR PICKLES

These pickles are crisp, refreshing, and both sweet and sour—everything a perfect pickle should be.
—*Alice Flake, Tacoma, Washington*

6 cups thinly sliced cucumber
2 cups thinly sliced onion
1½ cups white vinegar
1 cup sugar
½ teaspoon salt
½ teaspoon mustard seeds
½ teaspoon celery seeds
½ teaspoon ground turmeric

1. Place half of cucumber in a large glass bowl, and top with half of onion. Repeat procedure with remaining cucumber and onion.
2. Combine vinegar and remaining 5 ingredients in a saucepan; stir well. Bring to a boil; cook 1 minute. Pour over cucumber mixture; let cool. Cover and marinate in refrigerator 4 days. Yield: 7 cups (serving size: ¼ cup).
Note: Pickles can be stored in the refrigerator for up to 1 month.

CALORIES 23 (4% from fat); FAT 0.1g (sat 0g, mono 0g, poly 0g); PROTEIN 0.3g; CARB 5.8g; FIBER 0.5g; CHOL 0mg; IRON 0.1mg; SODIUM 22mg; CALC 7mg

MONKEY BREAD

Many of us at Cooking Light *found this ooey-gooey bread absolutely addictive. Sent to us by Rita M. Newton of Waukon, Iowa, it calls for frozen bread dough, which means no fooling around with yeast.*

  2 (1-pound) loaves frozen white bread dough
1¼ cups sugar, divided
 ¼ cup packed brown sugar
 ¼ cup 1% low-fat milk
  1 tablespoon reduced-calorie stick margarine
1¾ teaspoons ground cinnamon, divided
   Vegetable cooking spray

1. Thaw bread dough in refrigerator for 12 hours.
2. Combine 1 cup sugar, brown sugar, milk, margarine, and 1¼ teaspoons cinnamon in a small saucepan. Bring to a boil; cook 1 minute. Remove sugar syrup from heat; let cool 10 minutes.
3. Combine ¼ cup sugar and ½ teaspoon cinnamon in a shallow dish; stir well. Cut each loaf of dough into 24 equal portions. Shape each portion into a ball, and roll in cinnamon-sugar mixture; layer balls of dough in a 12-cup Bundt pan coated with cooking spray. Pour sugar syrup over dough; cover and let rise in a warm place (85°), free from drafts, 35 minutes or until doubled in bulk.
4. Preheat oven to 350°.
5. Uncover and bake at 350° for 25 minutes or until lightly browned. Immediately loosen edges of bread with a knife. Place a plate upside down on top of pan; invert onto plate. Remove pan; drizzle any remaining syrup over bread. Yield: 24 servings (serving size: 2 rolls).

CALORIES 201 (10% from fat); FAT 2.2g (sat 0.5g, mono 0.8g, poly 0.8g); PROTEIN 5.2g; CARB 40.1g; FIBER 0g; CHOL 0mg; IRON 1.4mg; SODIUM 302mg; CALC 41mg

ANZAC BISCUITS

Of Australian origin, these "biscuits" from Sandy Bennett of Waldport, Oregon, could possibly be the best cookies we've ever made. The cane syrup imparts a chewy, slightly sticky texture that gives them a wonderful richness.

  1 cup regular oats
  1 cup all-purpose flour
  1 cup packed brown sugar
 ½ cup shredded sweetened coconut
 ½ teaspoon baking soda
 ¼ cup stick margarine, melted
  3 tablespoons water
  2 tablespoons golden cane syrup (such as Lyle's) or light-colored corn syrup
   Vegetable cooking spray

1. Preheat oven to 325°.
2. Combine first 5 ingredients in a bowl; stir well. Add margarine, water, and syrup; stir well. Drop by level tablespoons, 2 inches apart, onto baking sheets coated with cooking spray. Bake at 325° for 12 minutes or until almost set. Remove from oven; let stand 2 to 3 minutes or until firm. Remove cookies from baking sheets. Place on wire racks; let cool completely. Yield: 2 dozen (serving size: 1 cookie).
Note: We found these cookies were much better when made with golden cane syrup such as Lyle's. Cane syrup is thicker and sweeter than corn syrup, and can be found in cans next to the jellies and syrups or in stores specializing in Caribbean and Creole goods.

CALORIES 98 (27% from fat); FAT 2.9g (sat 1g, mono 0.9g, poly 0.7g); PROTEIN 1.2g; CARB 17.3g; FIBER 0.6g; CHOL 0mg; IRON 0.6mg; SODIUM 59mg; CALC 11mg

GINGER COOKIES

(pictured on page 109)

Cookies can be one of the toughest foods to lighten, but it was absolutely no problem with this recipe from Elizabeth Graubard of Palm Harbor, Florida. Both their flavor and appearance rate a 10.

⅔ cup plus 3 tablespoons sugar, divided
 ¼ cup plus 2 tablespoons stick margarine, softened
 ¼ cup molasses
  1 large egg
  2 cups all-purpose flour
  2 teaspoons baking soda
  1 teaspoon ground ginger
  1 teaspoon ground cinnamon
 ½ teaspoon ground mace
   Vegetable cooking spray

1. Beat ⅔ cup sugar and margarine at medium speed of an electric mixer until well-blended. Add molasses and egg; beat well.
2. Combine flour and next 4 ingredients; gradually add to sugar mixture. Stir until well-blended. Divide in half. Wrap each portion in plastic wrap; freeze for 30 minutes.
3. Preheat oven to 350°.
4. Shape each portion of dough into 26 (1-inch) balls; roll in 3 tablespoons sugar. Place, 2 inches apart, on baking sheets coated with cooking spray. Bake at 350° for 12 minutes or until lightly browned. Remove from sheets; let cool on wire racks. Store in an airtight container. Yield: 52 cookies (serving size: 1 cookie).

CALORIES 46 (29% from fat); FAT 1.5g (sat 0.3g, mono 0.6g, poly 0.4g); PROTEIN 0.6g; CARB 7.7g; FIBER 0.1g; CHOL 4mg; IRON 0.3mg; SODIUM 49mg; CALC 13mg

They've Gotta Have It

Our food editors share the one Cooking Light *recipe they can't live without.*

LAMB-AND-BLACK BEAN CHILI

When I'm in the mood for chili, this is the recipe I turn to. The only ingredient I don't usually have on hand is the ground lamb, but you can use ground beef instead.

—Associate Food Editor Maureen Callahan

1½ pounds lean ground lamb
1 cup chopped onion
2 garlic cloves, minced
2 (14½-ounce) cans no-salt-added whole tomatoes, undrained and chopped
1 cup dry red wine
1 tablespoon chili powder
1½ teaspoons ground cumin
1½ teaspoons dried oregano
1 teaspoon sugar
¼ teaspoon salt
3 (15-ounce) cans black beans, drained
¼ teaspoon hot sauce
Cilantro sprigs (optional)

1. Combine first 3 ingredients in a Dutch oven; cook over medium heat until meat is browned, stirring to crumble. Drain in a colander; pat dry with paper towels. Wipe drippings from Dutch oven with a paper towel; return mixture to Dutch oven.
2. Add tomatoes and next 6 ingredients bring to a boil. Cover, reduce heat, and simmer 2 hours; stir occasionally. Stir in beans and hot sauce. Cover; simmer 30 minutes. Garnish with cilantro sprigs, if desired. Yield: 8 servings (serving size: 1 cup).

CALORIES 293 (22% from fat); FAT 7.2g (sat 2.4g, mono 2.8g, poly 0.8g); PROTEIN 28.5g; CARB 29.9g; FIBER 4.6g; CHOL 61mg; IRON 4.3mg; SODIUM 400mg; CALC 90mg

SCALLOPED POTATOES WITH CHEESE

This is an absolutely no-fail recipe—no matter how you change it. I use any type of cheese (Cheddar, Swiss, provolone), russet potatoes in place of red, and any kind of milk I have in the fridge. It's terrific with roasted chicken or pork.

—Senior Food Editor Jill Melton

1 garlic clove, halved
Butter-flavored vegetable cooking spray
6 medium-size red potatoes, peeled and cut into ⅛-inch-thick slices
2 tablespoons margarine, melted
½ teaspoon salt
⅛ teaspoon pepper
½ cup (2 ounces) shredded Gruyère cheese
1 cup skim milk

1. Preheat oven to 425°.
2. Rub an 11 x 7-inch baking dish with cut sides of garlic halves; discard garlic. Coat dish with cooking spray.
3. Arrange half of potato slices in dish; drizzle with 1 tablespoon margarine. Sprinkle with ¼ teaspoon salt and half of pepper; top with ¼ cup cheese. Repeat layers.
4. Bring milk to a boil over low heat in a small saucepan; pour over potato mixture. Bake, uncovered, at 425° for 40 minutes or until potatoes are tender. Yield: 7 servings (serving size: 1 cup).

CALORIES 228 (24% from fat); FAT 6.7g (sat 2.3g, mono 2.1g, poly 1.2g); PROTEIN 7.6g; CARB 36.6g; FIBER 3.2g; CHOL 10mg; IRON 1.4mg; SODIUM 262mg; CALC 142mg

HERBED BASMATI RICE

This is my staple at home. In fact, we have it so often my husband calls it "wife rice." I often use dried herbs in place of the fresh and add a few pine nuts, which I always have in the freezer.

—Food Editor Mary Creel

2 teaspoons margarine
1 garlic clove, minced
½ cup uncooked basmati rice
1 cup water
¼ teaspoon salt
2 tablespoons thinly sliced green onion tops
2 teaspoons minced fresh basil
1 teaspoon minced fresh thyme
2 tablespoons grated fresh Parmesan cheese
Thyme sprigs (optional)

1. Melt margarine in a small saucepan over medium heat. Add garlic; sauté 1 minute. Add rice; stir well. Add water and salt; bring to a boil. Cover, reduce heat, and simmer 20 minutes or until liquid is absorbed. Stir in green onions, basil, and minced thyme. Sprinkle with cheese; garnish with thyme sprigs, if desired. Yield: 4 servings (serving size: ½ cup).

CALORIES 115 (22% from fat); FAT 2.8g (sat 0.9g, mono 1.1g, poly 0.7g); PROTEIN 2.8g; CARB 19.2g; FIBER 0.3g; CHOL 2mg; IRON 1.5mg; SODIUM 217mg; CALC 52mg

CAVATAPPI WITH SPINACH, BEANS, AND ASIAGO CHEESE

For a simple dish, this contains many healthful ingredients, plus the flavors are complex. If you toss the spinach and Asiago cheese while the pasta is still warm, the spinach will wilt and the cheese will soften. When this happens, the flavors blend and become more pungent. This is peasant food at its best.

—Associate Food Editor Cynthia LaGrone

    8 cups coarsely chopped spinach
         leaves
    4 cups hot cooked cavatappi
         (about 6 ounces uncooked
         spiral-shaped pasta)
  ½ cup (2 ounces) shredded Asiago
         cheese
    2 tablespoons olive oil
  ¼ teaspoon salt
  ¼ teaspoon pepper
    2 garlic cloves, crushed
    1 (19-ounce) can cannellini
         beans or other white beans,
         drained
Freshly ground pepper (optional)

1. Combine first 8 ingredients in a large bowl; toss well. Sprinkle with freshly ground pepper, if desired. Yield: 4 servings (serving size: 2 cups).

CALORIES 401 (27% from fat); FAT 12g (sat 3.4g, mono 6.2g, poly 1.2g); PROTEIN 18.8g; CARB 54.7g; FIBER 6.7g; CHOL 10mg; IRON 6.4mg; SODIUM 464mg; CALC 306mg

Let Everyone Eat Cake!

For the first time in our history, we present a light chocolate layer cake. Our survey found chocolate is your favorite birthday cake—it's ours, too.

COOKING LIGHT'S ULTIMATE CHOCOLATE LAYER CAKE

(pictured on page 109)

Vegetable cooking spray
    2 cups sugar
  ½ cup plus 2 tablespoons light
         butter, softened
  ¾ cup egg substitute
    2 cups all-purpose flour
  ½ cup unsweetened cocoa
  ¾ teaspoon baking soda
  ¼ teaspoon salt
  ¾ cup low-fat sour cream
  ¾ cup boiling water
    1 teaspoon vanilla
         extract
Chocolate Frosting

1. Preheat oven to 350°.
2. Coat bottoms of 2 (8-inch) round cake pans with cooking spray (do not coat sides of pans); line bottoms of pans with wax paper. Coat wax paper with cooking spray; set aside.
3. Beat sugar and butter at medium speed of an electric mixer until well-blended. Gradually add egg substitute; beat well. Combine flour and next 3 ingredients in a bowl. With mixer running at low speed, add flour mixture to sugar mixture alternately with sour cream, beginning and ending with flour mixture. Gently stir in boiling water and vanilla.
4. Pour batter into prepared pans. Bake at 350° for 35 minutes or until cake springs back when touched in center. Loosen layers from sides of pans using a narrow metal spatula;

turn out onto wire racks. Peel off wax paper; let cool.
5. Place 1 cake layer on a plate; spread with ½ cup Chocolate Frosting. Top with other cake layer; spread remaining frosting over cake. Yield: 18 servings.

CALORIES 315 (22% from fat); FAT 7.8g (sat 4.9g, mono 1.3g, poly 0.2g); PROTEIN 4.8g; CARB 58.4g; FIBER 0.4g; CHOL 19mg; IRON 1.7mg; SODIUM 129mg; CALC 46mg

Chocolate Frosting:

(We've found that some cooks "pack" powdered sugar into a measuring cup rather than gently spooning it in. You may want to weigh your sugar for perfect results. You don't want to make this frosting ahead of time because it will dry out.)

    4 ounces tub light cream
         cheese, softened
    3 tablespoons skim milk
    3 (1-ounce) squares semisweet
         chocolate, melted
    3 cups sifted powdered sugar
         (about 10½ ounces)
  ¼ cup unsweetened cocoa
    1 teaspoon vanilla
         extract

1. Beat cheese and milk at high speed of an electric mixer until creamy. Add melted chocolate, and beat until well-blended.
2. Combine sugar and cocoa; gradually add sugar mixture to cheese mixture, beating at low speed until well-blended. Add vanilla; beat well for 1 minute until very creamy. Yield: 1¾ cups.

Ginger Cookies, page 106

Ultimate Chocolate Layer Cake, page 108

Asian Pork Salad, page 92

Spinach-and-Mushroom Lasagna, page 101

Seven-Layer Tortilla Pie, page 102

Peppered Salmon Fillet with Minted Tomato Salsa, page 115

Grilled Asian Beef Salad, page 116

Oven-Roasted Sweet Potatoes and Onions, page 115

The Top 10 Foods to Live By

Our national survey says you're eating more healthfully these days. To help you stay on course, we've chosen 10 of the most good-for-you foods, plus a flavorful recipe for each.

ORANGE-BANANA SHAKE

Ideal for breakfast or dessert, this shake is a delicious way to get your calcium and vitamin C.

    2 cups vanilla low-fat ice cream
    1½ cups orange juice
    1 (6-ounce) can pineapple juice
    1 medium-size ripe banana, cut
         into 4 pieces

1. Place all ingredients in a blender; cover and process until smooth. Serve immediately. Yield: 4 servings (serving size: 1 cup).

CALORIES 185 (15% from fat); FAT 3.1g (sat 1.8g, mono 0.8g, poly 0.2g); PROTEIN 3.6g; CARB 37.8g; FIBER 1.1g; CHOL 9mg; IRON 0.4mg; SODIUM 58mg; CALC 109mg

MANGO-BANANA FROZEN YOGURT

This creamy dessert is low in fat and high in calcium.

    1 cup sliced ripe banana
    ¾ cup peeled, chopped mango
    ⅓ cup orange juice
    3 tablespoons fresh lime juice
    1½ cups 2% low-fat milk
    ¾ cup sugar
    1 (16-ounce) carton vanilla
         low-fat yogurt

1. Combine first 4 ingredients in a blender; cover and process until smooth. Combine banana mixture, milk, sugar, and yogurt in a bowl; stirring with a whisk.
2. Pour mixture into the freezer can of an ice-cream freezer; freeze according to manufacturer's instructions. Spoon into a freezer-safe container; cover and freeze (ripen) at least 1 hour. Yield: 6 cups (serving size: ½ cup).

CALORIES 118 (8% from fat); FAT 1.1g (sat 0.7g, mono 0.3g, poly 0.1g); PROTEIN 3.1g; CARB 24.9g; FIBER 0.5g; CHOL 4mg; IRON 0.1mg; SODIUM 41mg; CALC 105mg

STRAWBERRY SPRING SALAD

Any salad greens can be used, but we liked the peppery taste of the Italian blend with the sweetness of the berries.

    3 tablespoons white wine vinegar
    3 tablespoons water
    1 tablespoon honey
    2 teaspoons extra-virgin olive oil
    ⅛ teaspoon salt
    ⅛ teaspoon pepper
    3 cups quartered strawberries
    1 (10-ounce) bag Italian-blend
         salad greens (about 6 cups)
    1 tablespoon plus 1 teaspoon
         toasted pine nuts

1. Combine first 6 ingredients, and stir well with a whisk.
2. Combine strawberries and greens. Add vinegar mixture; toss to coat. Sprinkle with pine nuts. Yield: 4 servings (serving size: 2 cups salad and 1 teaspoon nuts).

CALORIES 98 (41% from fat); FAT 4.5g (sat 0.6g, mono 2.4g, poly 1.2g); PROTEIN 4.5g; CARB 14.3g; FIBER 3.5g; CHOL 0mg; IRON 1mg; SODIUM 76mg; CALC 17mg

ORANGE JUICE Just one 6-ounce glass of orange juice provides at least 100% of the U.S. Recommended Dietary Allowance for vitamin C. But it's more than vitamin C that makes this fruit healthful—limonene increases the production of certain enzymes that may help the body get rid of possible carcinogens. Orange juice also contains beta carotene, folic acid, and potassium. And by eating an entire orange, you'll get some fiber.

YOGURT Yogurt is a nutrition powerhouse because of its high protein, calcium, phosphorus, and riboflavin content. Recently it's the live and active bacterial cultures that have gotten the attention. Active cultures help break down lactose, and some studies indicate that they may reduce vaginal yeast infections, lower cholesterol, and possibly combat cancer-causing compounds in the digestive tract. To ensure that your yogurt contains active cultures (because not all yogurts do), look for the "LAC" label signifying live and active cultures, or the phrase "contains active cultures" on the container.

STRAWBERRIES One of nature's sweetest fruits, strawberries are low in calories, packed with vitamin C, and a good source of fiber and potassium. Also, they contain folic acid, a vitamin that may not only help prevent birth defects such as spina bifida, but may also reduce cholesterol, thus lowering the chances of heart disease. Eight medium strawberries contain 50 calories and 3 grams of fiber, and provide 140% of the RDA for vitamin C and 20% of the RDA for folic acid.

DRIED APRICOTS Dried apricots may be one of the sweetest, most concentrated ways to meet these recommendations. Just ¼ cup of dried apricots equals a serving. And in this serving, you'll get 48% of the RDA for potassium, 80% of the RDA for beta carotene, and more than 5 grams of fiber—for just 130 calories.

LENTILS The Public Health Service recommends that women of childbearing age consume more folic acid. Most women don't get enough. By 1998, food producers will be required to add folic acid to bread, flour, pasta, rice, and other grain foods. In the meantime, hike your intake by eating more lentils. This no-soak member of the legume family has other impressive nutrition credentials as well. Containing just 100 calories, a half-cup of cooked lentils provides 4 grams of fiber. Lentils are virtually fat-free, low in sodium, a rich source of complex carbohydrates, and a good source of vegetable protein.

TOMATOES It used to be that tomatoes were praised only for their high vitamin C content. They are now also prized for their lycopene value. A powerful antioxidant, lycopene emerged a star after a Journal of the National Cancer Institute report stated that tomatoes, tomato sauce, and tomato juice "were significantly associated with lower prostate-cancer risk" for men. The report was so remarkable that women might also consider eating more tomatoes for their lycopene because it may decrease the risk of some cancers.

Tomatoes also supply about half the RDA for vitamin C and about 20% for beta carotene, and are a good source of potassium and fiber. Cooked tomatoes may have more lycopene activity than uncooked ones.

CUMIN PORK TENDERLOIN WITH DRIED-APRICOT CHUTNEY

2 tablespoons dark brown sugar
1 teaspoon ground cumin
1 teaspoon coarsely ground pepper
2 teaspoons cider vinegar
Dash of salt
1 (1-pound) pork tenderloin
Vegetable cooking spray
Dried-Apricot Chutney

1. Combine first 5 ingredients in a shallow dish. Stir well; set aside.
2. Trim fat from pork. Add pork to dish, turning to coat. Marinate in refrigerator 30 minutes, turning pork occasionally. Preheat oven to 400°. Remove pork from dish, discarding marinade. Place pork on rack of a broiler pan coated with cooking spray. Insert meat thermometer into thickest portion of pork. Bake at 400° for 25 minutes or until thermometer registers 160° (slightly pink). Cut pork into thin slices. Serve with Dried-Apricot Chutney. Yield: 4 servings (serving size: 3 ounces pork and ¼ cup chutney).

CALORIES 255 (17% from fat); FAT 4.7g (sat 1.5g, mono 2g, poly 0.6g); PROTEIN 26g; CARB 28.7g; FIBER 3.2g; CHOL 79mg; IRON 3.3mg; SODIUM 71mg; CALC 40mg

Dried-Apricot Chutney:

Just ¼ cup of this chutney contains 3 grams of fiber.

1 cup water, divided
1 cup coarsely chopped dried apricot
1 cup coarsely chopped onion
⅓ cup cider vinegar
⅓ cup raisins
1¼ teaspoons pumpkin-pie spice
1 teaspoon dry mustard
⅛ teaspoon dried crushed red pepper
1 cup peeled, coarsely chopped Golden Delicious apple

1. Combine ½ cup water, apricot, and next 6 ingredients in a medium saucepan, and stir well. Bring to a boil. Cover, reduce heat, and simmer 20 minutes, stirring occasionally. Add ½ cup water and apple; cover and cook 15 additional minutes or until apple is tender. Remove from heat; uncover and let stand 5 minutes before serving. Yield: 2½ cups (serving size: ¼ cup).
Note: Refrigerate remaining chutney in an airtight container for up to 1 week.

CALORIES 92 (3% from fat); FAT 0.3g (sat 0g, mono 0.1g, poly 0.1g); PROTEIN 1.4g; CARB 23.6g; FIBER 3g; CHOL 0mg; IRON 1.4mg; SODIUM 4mg; CALC 21mg

CURRIED LENTIL SOUP

You could say lentils are the dried bean of the '90s—they cook faster than other dried beans.

2 teaspoons olive oil
1 cup chopped onion
1¼ teaspoons curry powder
7 cups water
¾ cup lentils
2 tablespoons chopped fresh basil or 2 teaspoons dried basil
2 tablespoons balsamic vinegar
½ teaspoon salt
1 (14.5-ounce) can diced tomatoes, undrained
Fresh basil sprigs (optional)

1. Heat oil in a large Dutch oven over medium-high heat. Add onion; sauté 4 minutes. Add curry powder; sauté 1 minute. Add water and lentils; bring to a boil. Cover; reduce heat. Simmer 40 minutes or until lentils are tender.
2. Place 4 cups lentil mixture in a blender; cover and process until smooth. Return mixture to Dutch oven. Add chopped basil and next 3 ingredients; cook until thoroughly heated. Garnish with basil sprigs, if desired. Yield: 7 servings (serving size: 1 cup).
Note: We particularly liked this soup made with red lentils. However, they're smaller, cook in a much shorter time, and need less liquid, so adjust the recipe accordingly.

CALORIES 104 (15% from fat); FAT 1.7g (sat 0.2g, mono 1g, poly 0.2g); PROTEIN 6.7g; CARB 16.8g; FIBER 3.2g; CHOL 0mg; IRON 2.3mg; SODIUM 247mg; CALC 37mg

PEPPERED SALMON FILLET WITH MINTED TOMATO SALSA

(pictured on page 111)

4 cups chopped tomato
¼ cup finely chopped red onion
2 tablespoons chopped fresh mint
1 tablespoon chopped fresh basil
1 tablespoon seeded, finely chopped jalapeño pepper
1 tablespoon lemon juice
4 (6-ounce) salmon fillets (about 1½ inches thick)
Vegetable cooking spray
2 teaspoons Dijon mustard
1 teaspoon coarsely ground pepper
Fresh mint sprigs (optional)

1. Combine first 6 ingredients in a medium bowl.
2. Place salmon on rack of a broiler pan coated with cooking spray; spread each fillet with ½ teaspoon mustard. Sprinkle with ground pepper. Broil 10 minutes or until desired degree of doneness. Let stand 2 minutes. Serve with tomato salsa. Garnish with fresh mint sprigs, if desired. Yield: 4 servings (serving size: 5 ounces fish and ½ cup salsa).
Note: Salsa can be made ahead and refrigerated for up to 1 week.

CALORIES 314 (44% from fat); FAT 15.2g (sat 2.6g, mono 7.1g, poly 3.3g); PROTEIN 37.1g; CARB 5.4g; FIBER 1.4g; CHOL 115mg; IRON 1.3mg; SODIUM 170mg; CALC 18mg

OVEN-ROASTED SWEET POTATOES AND ONIONS

(pictured on page 112)

4 medium-size peeled sweet potatoes, peeled and cut into 2-inch pieces (about 2¼ pounds)
2 medium Vidalia or other sweet onions, cut into 1-inch pieces (about 1 pound)
2 tablespoons extra-virgin olive oil
¾ teaspoon garlic-pepper blend (such as Lawry's)
½ teaspoon salt

1. Preheat oven to 425°.
2. Combine all ingredients in a 13 x 9-inch baking dish, tossing to coat. Bake at 425° for 35 minutes or until tender, stirring occasionally. Yield: 6 servings (serving size: 1 cup).

CALORIES 247 (19% from fat); FAT 5.1g (sat 0.7g, mono 3.4g, poly 0.6g); PROTEIN 3.6g; CARB 47.8g; FIBER 6.5g; CHOL 0mg; IRON 1.2mg; SODIUM 255mg; CALC 53mg

TEX-MEX TOFU BURRITOS

Tofu, which has a nondescript taste on its own, acts like a sponge, soaking up the flavor of whatever it's cooked with. Here it absorbs the flavors of the cinnamon, cumin, and chili powder.

1 (10.5-ounce) package extra-firm light tofu, drained and cut into ½-inch cubes
1 teaspoon ground cumin
1 teaspoon chili powder
½ teaspoon ground cinnamon
2 teaspoons cider vinegar
2 teaspoons vegetable oil
1 cup sliced onion, separated into rings
1 cup (3 x ¼-inch) julienne-cut red bell pepper
1 cup (3 x ¼-inch) julienne-cut zucchini
½ cup corn, black bean, and roasted-red pepper salsa (such as Jardine's)
¼ teaspoon salt
4 (8-inch) fat-free flour tortillas
¼ cup sliced green onions
¼ cup low-fat sour cream
¼ cup (1 ounce) shredded reduced-fat Monterey Jack cheese

1. Place tofu in a shallow dish. Sprinkle with cumin, chili powder, cinnamon, and vinegar. Toss gently to coat; set aside.
2. Heat oil in a large nonstick skillet over medium heat. Add 1 cup onion; sauté 2 minutes. Add bell pepper and zucchini; sauté 4 minutes. Stir in tofu mixture, salsa, and salt; cook 2 minutes, stirring occasionally. Remove from heat.

3. Warm tortillas according to package directions. Spoon about ¾ cup tofu mixture down center of each tortilla. Top with 1 tablespoon each of green onions, sour cream, and cheese; roll up. Yield: 4 servings (serving size: 1 burrito).

CALORIES 231 (26% from fat); FAT 6.7g (sat 2.4g, mono 1.8g, poly 1.4g); PROTEIN 10.1g; CARB 31.8g; FIBER 1.6g; CHOL 10mg; IRON 1.2mg; SODIUM 794mg; CALC 99mg

TOFU Also known as soybean curd and bean curd, tofu is made from curdled soy milk, an iron-rich extraction from ground, cooked soybeans. Reports about the cholesterol-lowering effects of soy in a New England Journal of Medicine article propelled this already-recognized healthful food into a category all its own.

Staples in Chinese and Japanese cooking, soy foods are high in protein, low in saturated fat, cholesterol-free, lactose-free, and an excellent source of B vitamins and iron. They contain isoflavones, also known as phytoestrogens. These compounds may be important in fighting cancer and heart disease (by lowering LDL cholesterol levels), and may decrease menopausal symptoms. As little as 1 cup of soy milk or ½ cup tofu contains enough isoflavones to be effective. While we're featuring tofu for its versatility and broad appeal, there are a host of other soy products including soy flour, soy milk, soy oil, soy sauce, tempeh, and textured vegetable protein (miso).

SWEET POTATOES Packed with beta carotene, sweet potatoes are one of the most overlooked vegetables. Like soy, sweet potatoes contain phytoestrogens. For women, this could mean a reduced risk of cervical cancer. And more and more studies indicate a beneficial effect of phytoestrogens in reducing heart disease. One medium-size sweet potato contains about 130 calories, is a good source of vitamin C, and has more than six times the recommended amount of beta carotene. It contains almost 4 grams of fiber when eaten with the skin, and no fat or cholesterol.

OATS Found in more than 80% of American pantries, oats and oat bran were the health craze of the '80s; in 1997, they became the first products allowed to extol their benefits on food labels, thanks to the U.S. Food and Drug Administration. At first, oat bran's potential to lower cholesterol (due mainly to its soluble fiber content) made food manufacturers and consumers alike rush out and get as much as they could. Later research, however, questioned the effectiveness of the original study that caused the craze. Many studies later, it's believed that soluble fiber (also found in pears and apples) does lower cholesterol slightly, but only if cholesterol levels are high in the first place.

A more recent study on insoluble fiber (found in fruit, vegetables, and whole wheat) found that for each 10-gram increase in insoluble fiber in the daily diet, heart-disease risk declined by 29%.

FLANK STEAK Among cuts of beef, flank steak is one of the lowest-fat choices. A 3-ounce serving has just over 8 grams of total fat and 55 milligrams of cholesterol. For 176 calories, you'll get an assortment of minerals, including copper, iron, magnesium, and zinc.

Women who menstruate are more likely to be iron-deficient; their dietary intake of iron tends to be low as well. Both iron and zinc are more easily absorbed from animal sources than vegetable sources. Also, only animal foods provide vitamin B-12. Flank steak contributes almost 3 micrograms of this nutrient, essential for growth, per 3-ounce serving. (The RDA for adults is 2 micrograms.)

CARDAMOM-SCENTED OATMEAL-PEAR CRISP

1 cup quick-cooking oats
⅓ cup whole-wheat flour
½ cup packed dark brown sugar
1 teaspoon ground cinnamon
¼ cup plus 2 tablespoons chilled stick margarine, cut into small pieces
6 cups (1-inch pieces) peeled ripe Bartlett pears (about 2½ pounds)
½ cup dried cranberries
¼ cup packed dark brown sugar
¼ teaspoon ground cardamom
Vanilla low-fat frozen yogurt (optional)

1. Preheat oven to 375°.
2. Combine first 4 ingredients; cut in margarine with a pastry blender until mixture resembles coarse meal.
3. Combine pears, cranberries, ¼ cup brown sugar, and cardamom in a 13 x 9-inch baking dish; toss well. Sprinkle with oats mixture. Bake at 375° for 30 minutes or until pears are tender. Serve with vanilla frozen yogurt, if desired. Yield: 10 servings (serving size: ½ cup).

CALORIES 236 (30% from fat); FAT 7.9g (sat 1.4g, mono 3.2g, poly 2.4g); PROTEIN 2.6g; CARB 42g; FIBER 4.7g; CHOL 0mg; IRON 1.2mg; SODIUM 85mg; CALC 35mg

GRILLED ASIAN BEEF SALAD

(pictured on page 112)

1 (1-pound) lean flank steak
¼ teaspoon salt
⅛ teaspoon ground black pepper
Vegetable cooking spray
¼ cup seasoned rice vinegar
¼ cup fresh lime juice
1 tablespoon low-sodium soy sauce
1 teaspoon peeled, grated fresh gingerroot
⅛ teaspoon dried crushed red pepper
6 cups chopped romaine lettuce
1½ cups bean sprouts
½ cup red bell pepper strips

1. Trim fat from steak. Sprinkle both sides of steak with salt and black pepper. Prepare grill or broiler. Place steak on grill rack or rack of a broiler pan coated with cooking spray; cook 8 minutes on each side or until desired degree of doneness. Cut steak across grain into thin slices; cut slices into 2-inch pieces. Set aside.
2. Combine vinegar and next 4 ingredients in a small bowl. Combine steak, lettuce, bean sprouts, and bell pepper in a large bowl; toss well. Drizzle vinaigrette over salad; toss to coat. Yield: 4 servings (serving size: 2 cups).

CALORIES 245 (48% from fat); FAT 13.2g (sat 5.5g, mono 5.4g, poly 0.5g); PROTEIN 24.3g; CARB 7.2g; FIBER 2.1g; CHOL 60mg; IRON 3.6mg; SODIUM 325mg; CALC 43mg

WINE PICKS

- **CUMIN PORK TENDERLOIN WITH DRIED-APRICOT CHUTNEY:** *Kendall-Jackson Vintner's Reserve Merlot 1993 (California red), $18*

- **CURRIED LENTIL SOUP:** *Prince Michel Vineyards Rapidan River Vineyard Dry Riesling 1995 (Virginia white), $9.95*

- **PEPPERED SALMON FILLET WITH MINTED TOMATO SALSA:** *The Eyrie Vineyards Reserve Pinot Noir 1992 (Oregon red), $25.99*

- **TEX-MEX TOFU BURRITOS:** *Siglo Gran Reserva Rioja 1986 (Spanish red), $13; or Negra Modelo (Mexican beer)*

- **GRILLED ASIAN BEEF SALAD:** *Atlas Peak Cabernet Sauvignon 1993 (California red), $18*

The Low-Fat Lowdown

From marinating to making a slurry, here are the 10 best techniques for preparing light, healthful food—plus recipes to showcase them.

Cutting fat and calories from food doesn't mean losing flavor. Not since the invention of the food processor has there been a more revolutionary change in how we prepare food than we're undergoing today. Often these methods for cooking low-fat food are so basic that you wonder why more people weren't doing them sooner.

Over the last decade at *Cooking Light*, we've pioneered and perfected some important low-fat cooking techniques. Here are our our top 10, with a recipe to illustrate each one. Make them an everyday part of your life, and you'll forever change the way you eat.

ARM YOURSELF WITH A NON-STICK SKILLET AND A CAN OF COOKING SPRAY. For low-fat cooking, nonstick cookware and cooking spray are essential items. Specially designed surfaces allow you to sear, sauté, and pan-broil meats and vegetables with only a quick spritz of cooking spray.

PAN-SEARED SCALLOPS WITH WALNUTS AND SPICED CARROTS

1 teaspoon grated orange rind
½ cup fresh orange juice
1 tablespoon minced shallots
1 tablespoon olive oil
1 tablespoon honey
1 tablespoon Dijon mustard
1 garlic clove, minced
1½ pounds large sea scallops
1 tablespoon sugar
2 tablespoons coarsely chopped walnuts, toasted
1 tablespoon minced chives
Vegetable cooking spray
Spiced Carrots

1. Combine first 7 ingredients in a small bowl. Combine half of orange juice mixture and scallops in a large bowl, stirring to coat; set aside. Set aside remaining orange juice mixture.
2. Place sugar in a large nonstick skillet over medium heat; cook until sugar dissolves (do not stir). Add walnuts,

stirring until coated, and remove from heat. Spread walnuts in a single layer on wax paper, and let stand at room temperature until dry.
3. Drain scallops, and discard marinade. Press chives onto one side of marinated scallops.
4. Wash skillet, and dry. Coat skillet with cooking spray; place over medium-high heat until hot. Arrange scallops, chive sides down, in skillet; cook 2 minutes on each side. Remove scallops from skillet, and set aside. Add remaining orange juice mixture to skillet. Bring to a boil, and cook 2 minutes. Return scallops to skillet. Divide scallops and sauce evenly among 4 plates. Sprinkle each serving with walnuts. Serve with Spiced Carrots. Yield: 4 servings (serving size: 5 ounces scallops, 1½ teaspoons walnuts, and ½ cup carrots).

CALORIES 316 (28% from fat); FAT 8.5g (sat 1.1g, mono 3.1g, poly 3g); PROTEIN 30.8g; CARB 28.9g; FIBER 3.4g; CHOL 56mg; IRON 1.2mg; SODIUM 395mg; CALC 75mg

Spiced Carrots:

3½ cups (¼-inch-thick) sliced carrot
2 tablespoons sugar
2 tablespoons orange juice
1 tablespoon margarine
Dash of ground cinnamon

1. Place carrots in a medium saucepan; add water to cover. Bring to a boil. Cover; reduce heat. Simmer 20 minutes or until very tender. Drain. Place carrots in a large bowl; add sugar

and remaining ingredients. Mash to desired consistency. Yield: 4 servings (serving size: ½ cup).

CALORIES 94 (29% from fat); FAT 3g (sat 0.6g, mono 1.3g, poly 1g); PROTEIN 1g; CARB 16.9g; FIBER 3.1g; CHOL 0mg; IRON 0.5mg; SODIUM 67mg; CALC 28mg

MARINATE FOR FLAVOR AND TENDERNESS WITHOUT THE FAT. Leaner, more economical cuts of meat usually need tenderizing. The solution is marinating, which also adds flavor.

SAUCY FLANK STEAK SANDWICH

1 (1½-pound) lean flank steak
1 cup reduced-calorie ketchup
¼ cup red wine vinegar
2 tablespoons light-colored corn syrup
1 tablespoon prepared mustard
1 teaspoon Worcestershire sauce
1 teaspoon hot sauce
Vegetable cooking spray
8 (1½-ounce) hamburger buns
Ripe olives (optional)

1. Trim fat from steak. Combine steak, ketchup, and next 5 ingredients in a large zip-top plastic bag. Seal bag; marinate in refrigerator 8 hours, turning bag occasionally. Remove steak from bag, reserving marinade.
2. Prepare grill or broiler. Place steak on grill rack or rack of a broiler pan coated with cooking spray; cook 8 minutes on each side or until desired degree of doneness. Slice diagonally across grain into thin strips. Set aside; keep warm.
3. Pour reserved marinade through a sieve into a small microwave-safe bowl; cover with plastic wrap. Microwave at HIGH 5 minutes or until marinade boils. Divide steak evenly among bottom halves of buns; top each with 2 tablespoons marinade and top half of bun. Garnish with olives, if desired. Yield: 8 servings.

CALORIES 302 (32% from fat); FAT 10.8g (sat 4.1g, mono 4.2g, poly 0.6g); PROTEIN 19.4g; CARB 29.2g; FIBER 0g; CHOL 43mg; IRON 2.4mg; SODIUM 233mg; CALC 21mg

BLUEBERRY STREUSEL CAKE

1½ cups blueberries
¼ cup granulated sugar
⅓ cup vanilla wafer crumbs (about 8 cookies)
¼ cup packed brown sugar
1 tablespoon margarine, melted
1 teaspoon hot water
1½ cups all-purpose flour
⅓ cup granulated sugar
¾ teaspoon baking powder
¼ teaspoon baking soda
⅛ teaspoon salt
¾ cup plain low-fat yogurt
3 tablespoons vegetable oil
1 teaspoon vanilla extract
1 large egg
1 large egg white
Vegetable cooking spray

1. Preheat oven to 350°.
2. Combine blueberries and ¼ cup sugar in a bowl; gently mash with a potato masher until blueberries are crushed. Let stand 5 minutes.
3. Combine wafer crumbs and next 3 ingredients.
4. Combine flour and next 4 ingredients in a large bowl. Combine yogurt and next 4 ingredients; stir well with a whisk. Add to flour mixture, stirring until well-blended. Fold in blueberry mixture. Pour batter into a 9-inch round cake pan coated with cooking spray. Bake at 350° for 30 minutes. Sprinkle brown sugar mixture over cake; bake 10 additional minutes or until a wooden pick inserted in center comes out clean. Let cool on a wire rack. Yield: 8 servings (serving size: 1 wedge).

CALORIES 287 (28% from fat); FAT 8.8g (sat 2.3g, mono 2.3g, poly 2.8g); PROTEIN 5.2g; CARB 47.3g; FIBER 1.9g; CHOL 33mg; IRON 1.5mg; SODIUM 142mg; CALC 81mg

PORK LOIN WITH ROASTED ONION-APRICOT RICE

½ cup coarsely chopped dried apricots
½ cup dark rum
⅓ cup golden raisins
2 cups (½-inch) pieces Vidalia or other sweet onion
2 cups (½-inch) pieces red onion
1½ cups coarsely chopped boiling onion (about ½ pound)
1 tablespoon olive oil
¼ teaspoon salt
¼ teaspoon ground black pepper
1 (2-pound) lean boned center-cut pork loin roast
1 teaspoon cracked black pepper
¼ teaspoon salt
1 garlic clove, crushed
1 tablespoon brown sugar
1 tablespoon balsamic vinegar
1 garlic clove, crushed
3 cups hot cooked rice
2 tablespoons slivered almonds, toasted

1. Preheat oven to 450°.
2. Combine first 3 ingredients in a bowl; cover with plastic wrap and vent. Microwave at HIGH for 1½ minutes; set aside.
3. Combine Vidalia onions and next 5 ingredients in a 13 x 9-inch baking pan; stir well to coat. Bake at 450° for 30 minutes on bottom rack of oven.
4. Trim fat from roast; place on a rack in a shallow roasting pan. Combine cracked pepper, ¼ teaspoon salt, and 1 crushed garlic clove; rub over surface of roast. Insert a meat thermometer into thickest part of roast. Stir onions; place roast on next-to-bottom rack in oven. Bake onions and roast at 450° for 15 minutes. Reduce oven temperature to 350°. Bake an additional hour, stirring onions after 30 minutes. Stir apricot mixture into onions; continue baking onion mixture and roast 10 minutes or until thermometer registers 160°. Remove roast and onion mixture from oven. Cover roast loosely with aluminum foil; let stand 10 minutes. Stir brown sugar and remaining 4 ingredients into onion mixture. Yield: 6 servings (serving size: 3 ounces pork and 1 cup rice mixture).

CALORIES 525 (22% from fat); FAT 12.7g (sat 3.6g, mono 6.4g, poly 1.5g); PROTEIN 32.7g; CARB 55.4g; FIBER 4.5g; CHOL 79mg; IRON 3.3mg; SODIUM 294mg; CALC 69mg

CHICKEN-ARTICHOKE SPREAD

1 (14-ounce) can artichoke hearts, drained
Vegetable cooking spray
2 (4-ounce) skinned, boned chicken breast halves
½ cup minced green onions
3 small garlic cloves, minced
1 cup plain low-fat yogurt
2 tablespoons light mayonnaise
¼ cup grated fresh Parmesan cheese
2 teaspoons Worcestershire sauce
3 drops hot sauce
⅛ teaspoon paprika

1. Preheat oven to 350°.
2. Place artichoke hearts in food processor; process until finely chopped. Spoon into a bowl, and set aside.
3. Place a nonstick skillet coated with cooking spray over medium-high heat until hot. Add chicken; cook 4 minutes on each side or until chicken is done. Remove from skillet; let cool. Cut chicken into 1-inch pieces; set aside.
4. Coat skillet with cooking spray; add onions and garlic. Sauté 2 minutes or until tender. Place chicken and onion mixture in food processor; process until finely ground. Add yogurt and next 4 ingredients; pulse until well-blended. Stir chicken mixture into artichokes.
5. Spoon mixture into a 1-quart baking dish coated with cooking spray; sprinkle with paprika. Bake at 350° for 25 minutes or until heated. Serve spread warm or cold with French bread or crackers. Yield: 4 cups (serving size: ¼ cup).

CALORIES 45 (26% from fat); FAT 1.3g (sat 0.4g, mono 0.2g, poly 0.7g); PROTEIN 5.2g; CARB 3.3g; FIBER 0.1g; CHOL 11mg; IRON 0.4mg; SODIUM 102mg; CALC 55mg

---

USE A ROASTING PAN TO DRAIN FAT. A broiler rack and pan can be an extremely useful piece of low-fat cooking equipment. It's designed to let fat drip away from the meat as it cooks. For easy cleanup, coat the rack with cooking spray and line the bottom with aluminum foil.

PIZZA-STYLE MEAT LOAF

⅔ cup pizza sauce, divided
1½ pounds extra-lean ground round
¾ cup Italian-seasoned breadcrumbs
½ cup chopped onion
1 teaspoon dried Italian seasoning
1 teaspoon Worcestershire sauce
½ teaspoon ground red pepper
¼ teaspoon salt
¼ teaspoon black pepper
1 large egg white
2 (1-ounce) slices part-skim mozzarella cheese
½ cup diced red bell pepper
Vegetable cooking spray

1. Preheat oven to 350°.
2. Combine ⅓ cup sauce, meat, and next 8 ingredients; shape mixture into an 18 x 12-inch rectangle on wax paper. Arrange cheese over mixture; sprinkle with bell pepper, leaving a 1-inch border. Roll mixture up jelly-roll fashion starting at short side. Pinch ends to seal.
3. Place meat loaf on rack of a broiler pan coated with cooking spray. Bake at 350° for 1 hour. Brush ⅓ cup pizza sauce over meat loaf. Bake 5 additional minutes or until done; let stand 10 minutes before slicing. Yield: 6 servings (serving size: 1 slice).

CALORIES 291 (39% from fat); FAT 12.6g (sat 5.2g, mono 5.2g, poly 0.6g); PROTEIN 27.9g; CARB 15.4g; FIBER 0.9g; CHOL 75mg; IRON 4.4mg; SODIUM 671mg; CALC 96mg

---

USE HOMEMADE CHICKEN STOCK. Undeniably, the use of homemade chicken stock is the most underrated technique of all. It's a breeze to make and cheap, too. The flavor of homemade chicken stock far surpasses that of commercial versions. The secret to fat-free stock is to chill it overnight, and then skim the solidified fat from the top. Our homemade chicken stock is the basis for this classic Chinese soup.

SWEET-AND-SOUR CHICKEN SOUP

6 cups Low-Fat Chicken Stock
2 tablespoons rice vinegar
2 tablespoons low-sodium soy sauce
1 teaspoon peeled, minced fresh gingerroot
½ teaspoon bottled minced garlic
½ teaspoon salt
⅛ teaspoon ground white pepper
1 (3½-ounce) package shiitake mushrooms, stems removed and thinly sliced (about 1½ cups thinly sliced shiitake mushroom caps)
2 cups shredded cooked chicken
2 cups thinly sliced spinach leaves
1½ ounces somen (wheat noodles) or angel hair pasta, uncooked

1. Combine first 8 ingredients in a large Dutch oven; bring to a boil. Cover, reduce heat, and simmer 30 minutes. Stir in chicken, spinach, and noodles; cook 5 minutes. Yield: 6 servings (serving size: 1½ cups).

CALORIES 138 (23% from fat); FAT 3.5g (sat 0.9g, mono 1.3g, poly 0.7g); PROTEIN 17.4g; CARB 9.2g; FIBER 1.6g; CHOL 36mg; IRON 2.5mg; SODIUM 450mg; CALC 30mg

Low-Fat Chicken Stock:

1 (3-pound) chicken
4 quarts water
1 large onion, cut into 1-inch pieces
3 medium carrots, cut into 3-inch pieces (about ½ pound)
3 stalks celery, cut into 1-inch pieces
1 tablespoon black peppercorns
1 tablespoon dried thyme
2 bay leaves
1 large garlic clove

1. Remove and discard giblets and neck from chicken. Rinse under cold water; pat dry. Trim excess fat. Place chicken, 4 quarts water, and remaining ingredients in a large Dutch oven or stockpot; bring to a boil. Cover, reduce heat, and simmer 2 hours. Remove chicken; let cool. Remove and discard skin. Remove chicken from bones; shred with 2 forks to measure about 3 cups meat. Reserve meat. (Store chicken in an airtight container in refrigerator; reserve to use in soup or for other uses.) Strain stock through a paper towel-lined sieve into a large bowl; discard solids.
2. Cover and chill stock overnight. Skim solidified fat from surface of stock; discard. Yield: 10 cups.
Note: Stock may be frozen in airtight containers for up to 3 months.

TRIM THE FAT FROM MEAT AND CHICKEN. Many cuts of meat and poultry are well trimmed of fat, but not all—particularly the dark-meat portions of chicken. To remove all skin and fat from poultry, use a sharp knife or poultry shears.

THICKEN SOUPS, STEWS, AND SAUCES WITH A SLURRY OF FLOUR AND WATER IN PLACE OF CREAM. A slurry is a thin paste made from liquid (broth, milk, or water) and flour. When stirred into soups and stews and heated, it thickens and produces a velvety richness. A whisk is crucial in this technique to help disperse the flour and avoid lumps.

MASTER LOW-FAT WHITE SAUCE. A béchamel, or white sauce, is as versatile a sauce as there is. In our version, we use only a small amount of margarine and 1% low-fat milk. Steep the milk with onion and peppercorn for added flavor.

LEMON-GARLIC CHICKEN WITH BLOND BBQ SAUCE

4 chicken drumsticks (about 1 pound), skinned
4 chicken thighs (about 1 pound), skinned
⅓ cup fresh lemon juice
3 tablespoons Dijon mustard
¼ teaspoon garlic powder
2 tablespoons light mayonnaise
2 tablespoons barbecue sauce
1 teaspoon chili powder
¼ teaspoon paprika
¾ cup Italian-seasoned breadcrumbs
¼ cup grated Parmesan cheese
Vegetable cooking spray
Lemon wedges (optional)

1. Trim excess fat from chicken.
2. Combine lemon juice, mustard, and garlic powder in a large bowl; reserve 2 tablespoons. Set aside. Add chicken to lemon juice mixture in large bowl, turning to coat. Cover and marinate in refrigerator 30 minutes.
3. Combine reserved 2 tablespoons lemon juice mixture, mayonnaise, and next 3 ingredients. Cover and chill.
4. Preheat oven to 400°.
5. Combine breadcrumbs and cheese. Remove chicken from bowl. Discard marinade. Dredge chicken in breadcrumb mixture. Place chicken on rack of a broiler pan coated with cooking spray. Bake at 400° for 45 minutes or until golden and chicken is done. Serve with sauce, and garnish with lemon wedges, if desired. Yield: 4 servings (serving size: 1 drumstick, 1 thigh, and 2 tablespoons sauce).

CALORIES 301 (35% from fat); FAT 11.7g (sat3.3g, mono 3.4g, poly 2.7g); PROTEIN 27g; CARB 20.3g; FIBER 0.4g; CHOL 80mg; IRON 1.9mg; SODIUM 1,222mg; CALC 106mg

SPRING CHOWDER

1 tablespoon margarine
4 cups thinly sliced Vidalia or other sweet onion
1 cup chopped carrot
1 cup sliced celery
1 cup chopped extra-lean ham
3 cups chopped red potato (about 1¼ pounds)
1 (10½-ounce) can low-salt chicken broth
¼ cup all-purpose flour
2 cups 2% low-fat milk
¼ cup chopped fresh sage
½ teaspoon salt
¼ to ½ teaspoon pepper
⅛ teaspoon ground nutmeg
½ cup dry white wine
Sage sprigs (optional)

1. Melt margarine in a large Dutch oven over medium-high heat. Add onion, carrot, celery, and ham; sauté 10 minutes. Add potato and broth; bring to a boil. Cover, reduce heat, and simmer 45 minutes or until potato is tender.
2. Place flour in a bowl. Gradually add milk, stirring with a whisk until blended. Add milk mixture, chopped sage, salt, pepper, and nutmeg to soup; cook over medium-low heat 2 minutes. Add wine; cook 10 minutes or until thick. Garnish with sage sprigs, if desired. Yield: 8 servings (serving size: 1 cup).

CALORIES 179 (21% from fat); FAT 4.2g (sat 1.5g, mono 1.6g, poly 0.7g); PROTEIN 9g; CARB 27.1g; FIBER 3.2g; CHOL 14mg; IRON 1.8mg; SODIUM 444mg; CALC 121mg

POTATOES AU GRATIN

2½ cups 1% low-fat milk
1 tablespoon black peppercorns
1 (½-inch-thick) slice onion
1 garlic clove, crushed
1½ pounds peeled baking potato, cut into ¼-inch-thick slices (about 4 cups)
1 tablespoon stick margarine
2 tablespoons diced shallots
3 tablespoons all-purpose flour
½ cup (2 ounces) shredded reduced-fat, reduced-sodium Swiss cheese
¼ teaspoon salt
⅛ teaspoon ground black pepper
Vegetable cooking spray

1. Combine first 4 ingredients in a saucepan; bring to a boil. Remove from heat. Cover; let stand 10 minutes. Pour mixture through a sieve over a large bowl, reserving liquid; discard solids.
2. Preheat oven to 350°.
3. Place potato in a saucepan. Cover with water; bring to a boil. Reduce heat. Simmer 15 minutes or until tender; drain. Place in a bowl; set aside.
4. Melt margarine in a saucepan over medium heat. Add shallots; sauté 3 minutes or until soft. Stir in flour; gradually add reserved milk. Stir with a whisk until blended. Bring to a boil. Cook, stirring constantly, 1 minute or until slightly thickened. Remove from heat; stir in cheese, salt, and pepper. Pour milk mixture over potato; toss. Spoon potato mixture into an 11 x 7-inch baking dish coated with cooking spray. Bake at 350° for 20 minutes. Broil 5 minutes or until lightly browned. Yield: 4 servings (serving size: 1 cup).

CALORIES 282 (25% from fat); FAT 7.7g (sat 2.6g, mono 1.7g, poly 1.0g); PROTEIN 12.2g; CARB 40.5g; FIBER 2.6g; CHOL 11mg; IRON 0.8mg; SODIUM 272mg; CALC 285mg

MAY

Toss Your Troubles Away

When you're tired, hungry, and want dinner on the table, these one-dish pasta tosses do the trick. Throw in some of this, a little of that, and you'll have a spontaneous meal that's sure to excite the senses.

Pasta is of the moment; the Italians have known this for centuries. It needs to be prepared, cooked, tossed, and served in one unbroken sweep . . . *tempo presto*. Because pasta is so quick and easy, it's an instant tonic: Nothing can beat it for eating after work, when body and soul need rejuvenation. And few other foods have its ability to excite the senses, from the earthy feel and heady smell of the ingredients as you sauté them to the warm rush of steam rising from the cooked pasta after it lands in the colander. Although pasta is ideally a shared experience, it's also wonderful for eating all by yourself, especially if you need comforting.

TUNA NIÇOISE PASTA TOSS

2 cups small red potatoes, quartered (about 10 ounces)
2 cups (1-inch) cut green beans (about ½ pound)
3 tablespoons olive oil, divided
⅓ cup diced shallots
3 garlic cloves, minced
4 cups uncooked cavatappi (spiral-shaped pasta)
2 tablespoons minced fresh tarragon or 2 teaspoons dried tarragon
2 tablespoons coarse-grained mustard
1 tablespoon white wine vinegar
½ teaspoon salt
1 (9-ounce) can solid white tuna in water, drained
Freshly ground pepper

1. Place potatoes in a medium saucepan. Cover with water; bring to a boil. Reduce heat; simmer 7 minutes. Add beans; cook 3 additional minutes or until beans are crisp-tender. Drain.
2. Heat 1 tablespoon oil in saucepan over medium heat. Add shallots; sauté 3 minutes. Add potatoes, beans, and garlic; cook 3 minutes, stirring occasionally.
3. Cook pasta according to package directions, omitting salt and fat. Drain; set aside.
4. Combine 2 tablespoons oil, tarragon, and next 3 ingredients; stir well. Combine pasta, potato mixture, and tuna in a large bowl; toss well. Drizzle mustard mixture over pasta mixture, tossing gently to coat. Sprinkle with freshly ground pepper. Yield: 5 servings (serving size: 1½ cups).

CALORIES 366 (25% from fat); FAT 10.3g (sat 1.5g, mono 6.4g, poly 1.4g); PROTEIN 18.4g; CARB 50.1g; FIBER 3.4g; CHOL 15mg; IRON 4.1mg; SODIUM 467mg; CALC 69mg

ORZO "RISOTTO" WITH PROSCIUTTO

Orzo (small, rice-shaped pasta) mimics risotto's creamy texture in this dish.

2½ cups low-salt chicken broth
1 cup frozen petite green peas
1 tablespoon olive oil
3 cups chopped leek
¼ teaspoon salt
⅛ teaspoon pepper
1 cup uncooked orzo (rice-shaped pasta)
¼ cup (1 ounce) minced prosciutto or lean smoked ham
¼ cup grated fresh Parmesan cheese, divided
2 tablespoons minced fresh parsley

1. Bring broth to a boil in a small saucepan. Add peas; cook 3 minutes (do not drain). Set aside.
2. Heat oil in a large nonstick skillet over medium-high heat. Add leek, salt, and pepper; sauté 1 minute. Cover, reduce heat, and cook 10 minutes, stirring occasionally. Add broth mixture and orzo to skillet; bring to a boil. Reduce heat, and simmer, uncovered, 10 minutes. Stir in prosciutto, 2 tablespoons cheese, and parsley. Divide evenly among 4 shallow bowls; top each serving with 1½ teaspoons cheese. Yield: 4 servings (serving size: 1 cup).

CALORIES 379 (19% from fat); FAT 8g (sat 2g, mono 3.5g, poly 1g); PROTEIN 15.9g; CARB 60.1g; FIBER 2.4g; CHOL 9mg; IRON 5.3mg; SODIUM 478mg; CALC 151mg

PASTA ALFREDO WITH SWISS CHARD

1 pound Swiss chard
8 ounces uncooked penne (tubular-shaped pasta)
1 tablespoon olive oil
3 garlic cloves, minced
¾ cup part-skim ricotta cheese
¼ cup grated fresh Parmesan cheese, divided
½ teaspoon salt
⅛ teaspoon pepper

1. Remove and discard stems and center ribs from Swiss chard. Coarsely chop; set aside.

2. Cook pasta according to package directions, omitting salt and fat. Drain in a colander over a bowl, reserving ¾ cup cooking liquid; keep warm.

3. Heat oil in a large nonstick skillet over medium heat. Add garlic; sauté 30 seconds. Add Swiss chard; sauté 3 minutes or until wilted. Combine reserved cooking liquid, ricotta cheese, 2 tablespoons Parmesan cheese, salt, and pepper. Combine pasta, Swiss chard mixture, and ricotta cheese mixture; toss well. Sprinkle with 2 tablespoons Parmesan cheese. Serve immediately. Yield: 4 servings (serving size: 1½ cups).

CALORIES 357 (26% from fat); FAT 10.3g (sat 4.2g, mono 4.3g, poly 0.9g); PROTEIN 17.2g; CARB 49.2g; FIBER 2.2g; CHOL 20mg; IRON 4.1mg; SODIUM 680mg; CALC 284mg

VERMICELLI STIR-FRY WITH PEANUT SAUCE

You can substitute 1½ teaspoons olive oil and ¼ teaspoon dried crushed red pepper for the chili oil.

    8 ounces uncooked vermicelli
 1½ teaspoons dark sesame oil
 1½ cups cubed deli, lower-salt turkey breast (about 6 ounces)
   ⅓ cup thinly sliced green onions
 1½ teaspoons chili oil
    2 cups snow pea pods, diagonally halved crosswise
 1⅓ cups red bell pepper strips
    3 garlic cloves, minced
   ½ cup low-salt chicken broth
    3 tablespoons low-sodium soy sauce
    2 tablespoons reduced-fat peanut butter
    2 tablespoons chopped dry-roasted peanuts

1. Cook pasta according to package directions, omitting salt and fat; drain.

2. Heat sesame oil in a large nonstick skillet over medium heat. Add turkey and green onions; stir-fry 1 minute. Remove from skillet; keep warm.

3. Heat chili oil in skillet over medium-high heat. Add snow peas, bell pepper, and garlic; sauté 3 minutes. Combine broth, soy sauce, and peanut butter; stir well with a whisk. Add to skillet; cook 2 minutes, stirring frequently. Stir in turkey mixture; remove from heat.

4. Combine pasta and turkey mixture; toss well. Divide evenly among 4 shallow bowls; top each serving with 1½ teaspoons peanuts. Yield: 4 servings (serving size: 1½ cups).

CALORIES 405 (24% from fat); FAT 10.8g (sat 1.5g, mono 4.6g, poly 3g); PROTEIN 22.6g; CARB 59.7g; FIBER 4.4g; CHOL 15mg; IRON 5mg; SODIUM 648mg; CALC 56mg

VERMICELLI WITH SHRIMP AND ARUGULA

    8 ounces uncooked vermicelli
    2 tablespoons olive oil, divided
   ¼ teaspoon dried crushed red pepper
    4 garlic cloves, minced
   ¾ pound large shrimp, peeled and deveined
   ¾ cup clam juice
   ½ cup sliced green onions
   ¼ cup chopped fresh parsley
    2 tablespoons dry white wine
    1 teaspoon grated lemon rind
    2 tablespoons fresh lemon juice
   ¼ teaspoon salt
    4 cups torn arugula (about 10 ounces)

1. Cook pasta according to package directions, omitting salt and fat. Drain and keep warm.

2. Heat 1 tablespoon oil in a large nonstick skillet over medium-high heat. Add pepper and garlic; sauté 30 seconds. Add shrimp; sauté 3 minutes or until done. Stir in clam juice and next 6 ingredients. Combine pasta, shrimp mixture, arugula, and 1 tablespoon oil in a large bowl; toss well. Yield: 4 servings (serving size: 1½ cups).

Note: Substitute spinach for arugula, if desired.

CALORIES 374 (22% from fat); FAT 9.3g (sat 1.3g, mono 5.3g, poly 1.4g); PROTEIN 22.9g; CARB 48.8g; FIBER 1.9g; CHOL 97mg; IRON 4.3mg; SODIUM 367mg; CALC 193mg

THE PASTA PANTRY

Pastas are interchangeable as long as you use a variety that is similar to the size and shape specified in the recipe. Use any in the following categories.

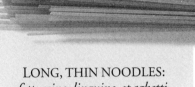

LONG, THIN NOODLES:
fettuccine, linguine, spaghetti, spaghettini, or vermicelli

TWISTED AND CURVE-SHAPED PASTA:
cavatappi, elbow macaroni, farfalle, fusilli, orecchiette, radiatore, rotelle, or seashell macaroni

TUBULAR-SHAPED PASTA:
mostaccioli, penne, rigatoni, or ziti

SMALL, TUBULAR- OR RICE-SHAPED PASTA:
orzo or tubetti

LINGUINE AND CHICKEN FLORENTINE

- 8 ounces uncooked linguine
- 1 tablespoon all-purpose flour
- ¼ teaspoon salt
- ¼ teaspoon pepper
- ½ pound skinned, boned chicken breast, cut into bite-size pieces
- 2 teaspoons olive oil
- ½ cup chopped onion
- 1 large garlic clove, minced
- 1 cup low-salt chicken broth
- ⅛ teaspoon ground nutmeg
- 8 cups torn spinach
- 1 cup (4 ounces) shredded reduced-fat, reduced-sodium Swiss cheese (such as Alpine Lace)
- ¼ cup chopped fresh basil

1. Cook pasta according to package directions, omitting salt and fat. Drain well; set aside.
2. Combine flour, salt, and pepper in a bowl; add chicken, tossing to coat. Heat oil in a large nonstick skillet over medium-high heat. Add chicken mixture, onion, and garlic; sauté 4 minutes. Add broth and nutmeg; bring to a simmer. Cook over medium-low heat 3 minutes or until chicken is done.
3. Combine pasta, spinach, cheese, and basil in a large bowl; toss well. Add chicken mixture, tossing gently. Yield: 4 servings (serving size: 1½ cups).

CALORIES 434 (22% from fat); FAT 10.7g (sat 4.7g, mono 2g, poly 0.9g); PROTEIN 32.7g; CARB 51.8g; FIBER 6.3g; CHOL 53mg; IRON 6.1mg; SODIUM 331mg; CALC 487mg

WINE PICKS

- *Bolla Amarone della Classico 1988 (Italian red), $18*
- *Bollini Reserve Special Selection Pinot Grigio 1994 (Italian white), $13*
- *Brolio Chianti Classico 1994 (Italian red), $10*
- *Napa Ridge North Coast Pinot Noir 1995 (California red), $10*

MENU SUGGESTION

PASTA CARBONARA WITH ASPARAGUS

Warm focaccia wedges

Broiled roma tomatoes*

*Halve tomatoes lengthwise. Combine ½ cup dry breadcrumbs, 1 tablespoon chopped fresh basil, 1 teaspoon olive oil, and 1 minced garlic clove. Sprinkle over tomato halves. Broil until golden.

PASTA CARBONARA WITH ASPARAGUS

- 2½ cups (1-inch) diagonally sliced, trimmed asparagus
- ¼ cup plus 2 tablespoons grated fresh Parmesan cheese, divided
- ¼ cup skim milk
- ¼ cup egg substitute
- 2 tablespoons chopped fresh chives
- ¼ teaspoon salt
- 8 ounces uncooked farfalle (bow-tie pasta)
- 2 bacon slices
- ¾ cup chopped onion
- 2 garlic cloves, minced
- Freshly ground pepper
- Chopped fresh chives (optional)

1. Arrange asparagus in a steamer basket over boiling water. Cover and steam 3 minutes or until crisp-tender. Drain; set aside.
2. Combine 2 tablespoons cheese, milk, and next 3 ingredients in a small bowl; set aside.
3. Cook pasta according to package directions, omitting salt and fat. Drain well; set aside.
4. Cook bacon in a nonstick skillet over medium-high heat until crisp. Crumble bacon; set aside. Add onion and garlic to bacon drippings in skillet; sauté 5 minutes or until tender. Remove from heat; stir in asparagus and bacon.
5. Combine pasta, milk mixture, and asparagus mixture in a large bowl; toss well. Divide mixture evenly among 4 shallow bowls; top each serving with 1

---

tablespoon cheese. Sprinkle with pepper; top with chives, if desired. Yield: 4 servings (serving size: 1½ cups).

CALORIES 321 (17% from fat); FAT 6.2g (sat 2.8g, mono 2g, poly 0.8g); PROTEIN 15.8g; CARB 50.8g; FIBER 3.8g; CHOL 10mg; IRON 3.4mg; SODIUM 437mg; CALC 188mg

ORECCHIETTE WITH BROCCOLI AND WHITE BEANS

If you don't have fresh rosemary, it can be omitted. Do not use dried rosemary, or it will overpower the recipe.

- 2 cups uncooked orecchiette (small, disk-shaped pasta) or small seashell macaroni
- 4 cups coarsely chopped broccoli (about ¾ pound)
- 1 tablespoon olive oil
- 1 cup red bell pepper strips
- 4 garlic cloves, minced
- ½ cup low-salt chicken broth
- ½ teaspoon salt
- 1 (15-ounce) can cannellini beans or other white beans, rinsed and drained
- 1 (4-inch) rosemary sprig
- ½ cup grated fresh Parmesan cheese, divided

1. Cook pasta according to package directions, omitting salt and fat. Drain well; set aside.
2. Arrange broccoli in a steamer basket over boiling water. Cover and steam 5 minutes or until crisp-tender. Set aside.
3. Heat oil in a large nonstick skillet over medium heat. Add bell pepper and garlic; sauté 2 minutes. Add chicken broth and next 3 ingredients; bring to a simmer. Cover and simmer 5 minutes. Discard rosemary.
4. Combine pasta, broccoli, bean mixture, and 2 tablespoons cheese in a large bowl; toss well. Divide evenly among 6 shallow bowls; top each serving with 1 tablespoon cheese. Yield: 6 servings (serving size: 1⅓ cups).

CALORIES 292 (19% from fat); FAT 6.2g (sat 2.1g, mono 2.5g, poly 1.2g); PROTEIN 14.4g; CARB 46.1g; FIBER 5.3g; CHOL 10mg; IRON 3.8mg; SODIUM 430mg; CALC 170mg

RIGATONI WITH BELL PEPPERS, OLIVES, AND FETA

(pictured on page 4)

Kalamata olives—dark purple, almond-shaped olives imported from Greece—are used in this Mediterranean-style recipe. Although black olives can be substituted for kalamatas, if desired, their flavor will not be as rich and fruity.

¼ cup chopped kalamata olives (about 16)
1 tablespoon chopped fresh oregano or 1 teaspoon dried oregano
¼ teaspoon salt
⅛ teaspoon dried crushed red pepper
2 teaspoons olive oil
2 cups thinly sliced onion
4 garlic cloves, minced
2 cups red bell pepper strips
2 cups green bell pepper strips
½ cup water
1 pound uncooked rigatoni
¾ cup crumbled feta cheese

1. Combine first 4 ingredients in a small bowl; set aside.
2. Heat oil in a large nonstick skillet over medium-high heat. Add onion; sauté 3 minutes or until tender. Add garlic; cook 1 minute. Stir in pepper strips. Cover, reduce heat, and cook 10 minutes. Add ½ cup water; cover and simmer 10 additional minutes or until peppers are tender. Stir in olive mixture; keep warm.
3. Cook pasta according to package directions, omitting salt and fat; drain.
4. Combine pasta and pepper mixture in a large bowl; toss well. Add feta cheese; toss gently to coat. Yield: 4 servings (serving size: 2 cups).

CALORIES 433 (20% from fat); FAT 9.7g (sat 3.9g, mono 3.4g, poly 1.4g); PROTEIN 14.9g; CARB 72.5g; FIBER 7g; CHOL 19mg; IRON 5.4mg; SODIUM 455mg; CALC 157mg

SPAGHETTI WITH CARAMELIZED ONIONS, MUSHROOMS, AND PANCETTA

(pictured on page 132)

Pancetta is Italian bacon that is cured with salt and spices but not smoked. Regular bacon or ham can be substituted for it.

8 ounces uncooked spaghetti
1 tablespoon olive oil
¼ cup chopped pancetta or bacon (about 1 ounce)
6 cups vertically sliced onion (about 3 large onions)
½ teaspoon salt, divided
¼ teaspoon pepper, divided
6 cups sliced mushrooms (about 1 pound)
2 teaspoons minced fresh oregano or ½ teaspoon dried oregano
¼ cup chopped fresh parsley, divided
3 garlic cloves, minced
½ cup low-salt chicken broth
Fresh oregano (optional)

1. Cook pasta according to package directions, omitting salt and fat. Drain well; set aside.
2. Heat oil in a large nonstick skillet over medium heat until hot. Add pancetta; sauté 3 minutes. Stir in onion, ¼ teaspoon salt, and ⅛ teaspoon pepper; cover and cook 15 minutes, stirring frequently. Uncover and cook 10 additional minutes, stirring frequently. Remove onion mixture from skillet; set aside.
3. Add mushrooms, ¼ teaspoon salt, and ⅛ teaspoon pepper to skillet; cook over medium-high heat 4 minutes. Add minced oregano and 2 tablespoons parsley; cook 1 minute. Add garlic; sauté 1 minute. Add onion mixture and broth; cook until thoroughly heated. Add mushroom mixture to pasta; toss to coat. Divide among 4 shallow bowls; sprinkle evenly with 2 tablespoons parsley. Garnish with oregano, if desired. Yield: 4 servings (serving size: 1½ cups).

CALORIES 383 (22% from fat); FAT 9.4g (sat 2.2g, mono 4.5g, poly 1.5g); PROTEIN 12.7g; CARB 64g; FIBER 6.3g; CHOL 5mg; IRON 4.7mg; SODIUM 367mg; CALC 72mg

PASTA PRIMAVERA

The bright green, feathery foliage on the fennel bulb is called fronds. The fronds are chopped up and added to this dish for a subtle licorice flavor.

2 cups diagonally sliced carrot
2 cups uncooked fusilli (twisted pasta)
1½ tablespoons olive oil
1 cup chopped fennel bulb
1½ cups thinly sliced leek (about 1 medium)
1 cup red bell pepper strips
¼ cup chopped fresh basil
2 tablespoons chopped fresh dillweed
2 tablespoons chopped fresh thyme
3 garlic cloves, minced
1 cup frozen green peas, thawed
½ cup dry vermouth
½ teaspoon salt
¾ cup grated Asiago cheese, divided
2 tablespoons chopped fennel fronds

1. Arrange carrot in a steamer basket over boiling water. Cover and steam 5 minutes or until crisp-tender. Set aside.
2. Cook pasta according to package directions, omitting salt and fat. Drain well, and set aside.
3. Heat oil in a large nonstick skillet over medium-high heat. Add 1 cup fennel; sauté 3 minutes. Add leek and next 5 ingredients; sauté 5 minutes. Add carrot, peas, vermouth, and salt. Cover, reduce heat, and simmer 2 minutes.
4. Combine pasta, vegetable mixture, cheese, and fennel fronds in a bowl, and toss well. Yield: 6 servings (serving size: 1⅓ cups).

CALORIES 294 (24% from fat); FAT 8g (sat 2.9g, mono 3.8g, poly 1.1g); PROTEIN 12.7g; CARB 42.8g; FIBER 3g; CHOL 10mg; IRON 3.7mg; SODIUM 477mg; CALC 358mg

PENNE WITH ROASTED VEGETABLES AND GOAT CHEESE

½ pound uncooked penne (tubular-shaped pasta)
2 cups (¼-inch-thick) sliced yellow squash
2 cups (¼-inch-thick) sliced zucchini
1 cup thinly sliced red onion, separated into rings
1 tablespoon olive oil
½ teaspoon salt
½ teaspoon pepper
4 plum tomatoes, quartered
1 garlic clove, minced
1½ tablespoons balsamic vinegar
1 cup goat cheese
3 tablespoons chopped fresh basil
1½ tablespoons chopped fresh thyme

1. Preheat oven to 475°.
2. Cook pasta according to package directions, omitting salt and fat. Drain and set aside.
3. Combine squash and next 7 ingredients in a large bowl; toss well to coat. Arrange vegetables in a single layer in a jelly-roll pan. Bake at 475° for 20 minutes or until browned, stirring after 10 minutes. Drizzle vinegar over vegetables; toss well.
4. Combine pasta, vegetable mixture, goat cheese, basil, and thyme in a large bowl; toss well. Yield: 4 servings (serving size: 1½ cups).

CALORIES 355 (27% from fat); FAT 10.7g (sat 4.9g, mono 4g, poly 1g); PROTEIN 13.4g; CARB 52.3g; FIBER 3.7g; CHOL 25mg; IRON 3.3mg; SODIUM 619mg; CALC 188mg

ISLAND HOPPING

Callaloo Calypso

From the Caribbean comes a zesty stew that will have your taste buds dancing.

Callaloo is a spicy soup from the Caribbean that has a swinging, Calypso-like attitude. Although it takes its name from the fleshy green leaves of the taro plant, the dish is now more commonly made with fresh or frozen spinach, collard greens, and/or kale. We've trimmed down the recipe by ditching the customary salt pork and substituting lean smoked pork chops. In the islands, callaloo is served over a creamy, polenta-like cornmeal pudding called fungi (FUN-jee), which we also have a recipe for. As a side dish, we've added mango slices sautéed in honey.

CALLALOO

5 cups water
1½ cups finely chopped onion
½ pound lean, boned, smoked center-cut loin pork chops, cut into ½-inch pieces
1 garlic clove, minced
4 cups chopped spinach
4 cups chopped collard greens
4 cups chopped kale
¼ cup white vinegar
2 tablespoons chopped fresh parsley
1 tablespoon hot pepper sauce
1 teaspoon dried thyme
½ teaspoon salt
1 (10-ounce) package frozen cut okra, thawed
Cornmeal Fungi

1. Combine first 4 ingredients in a large Dutch oven, and bring to a boil. Reduce heat, and simmer, uncovered, 30 minutes. Add spinach and next 8 ingredients; simmer 15 minutes or until vegetables are tender. Spoon Cornmeal Fungi evenly into 6 bowls, and

top with pork mixture. Yield: 6 servings (serving size: 1⅓ cups pork mixture and ½ cup Cornmeal Fungi).

CALORIES 248 (23% from fat); FAT 6.2g (sat 1.6g, mono 2.3g, poly 1.5g); PROTEIN 15.3g; CARB 36.1g; FIBER 5.3g; CHOL 23mg; IRON 4.6mg; SODIUM 529mg; CALC 217mg

Cornmeal Fungi:

1 cup yellow cornmeal
3 cups water
1 tablespoon margarine
½ teaspoon salt
¼ teaspoon pepper

1. Place cornmeal in a medium saucepan. Gradually add water, stirring constantly with a whisk. Bring to a boil; cook, stirring constantly, 1 minute. Stir in margarine, salt, and pepper; cook, stirring constantly, 2 additional minutes or until thick. Yield: 6 servings (serving size: ½ cup).

CALORIES 101 (21% from fat); FAT 2.3g (sat 0.4g, mono 0.9g, poly 0.8g); PROTEIN 2g; CARB 17.9g; FIBER 1.2g; CHOL 0mg; IRON 1mg; SODIUM 218mg; CALC 2mg

HONEYED MANGOES

3 tablespoons dark rum
2 tablespoons honey
½ teaspoon grated lime rind
1 tablespoon fresh lime juice
⅛ teaspoon ground cinnamon
5 cups peeled, sliced ripe mango (about 3 pounds)

1. Combine first 5 ingredients in a medium nonstick skillet, and cook over medium-high heat 1 minute, stirring occasionally. Add mango; cook 3 minutes, stirring occasionally. Divide mango evenly among 6 bowls; spoon remaining rum mixture over mango. Serve warm. Yield: 6 servings (serving size: ¾ cup).

CALORIES 112 (3% from fat); FAT 0.4g (sat 0.1g, mono 0.1g, poly 0.1g); PROTEIN 0.7g; CARB 29.5g; FIBER 2.1g; CHOL 0mg; IRON 0.2mg; SODIUM 3mg; CALC 15mg

There's No Place Like Maison

When chef Andrée Robert was in junior high school, she stunned her home economics class by preparing a rack of lamb. As awed as her teacher and seventh-grade classmates were, the ultimate compliment was still to come. "Papa said he would be proud to serve it in his restaurant," recalls Andrée—Papa being Lucien Robert of the family-run Maison Robert, one of Boston's most celebrated eating establishments.

Twenty-five years later finds Andrée serving not only rack of lamb but lots of other dishes at her father's restaurant. There's a difference, though: After taking over the cooking duties from Lucien in 1989, Andrée decided to take some risks—an especially bold move in a city as tradition-bound as Boston. Although Maison Robert has featured classic French cuisine since it opened in 1971, Andrée has made a concerted effort to prepare French food with less butter, fat, and calories. "Light and relaxed is the way I like to eat," Andrée says.

One of the first major showcases for her culinary innovations was a Mother's Day brunch that has since become an annual affair. "The brunch was her first solo effort and an immediate success," Lucien says. (And if you can't get reservations, *Cooking Light* features a sampling of her lightened Mother's Day dishes, all of which can be made easily at home.)

FENNEL, QUINOA, ORANGE, WALNUT, AND BASIL SALAD

"In this dish, the fresh orange and fennel marry really well with the flavor of the nutty quinoa, making for an interesting main-dish salad with many rich textures," Andrée says.

- 3 cups cooked quinoa (tiny, bead-shaped grain)
- 1 cup chopped fennel bulb
- 2 tablespoons minced shallots
- 1 teaspoon grated lemon rind
- 1 teaspoon grated orange rind
- ⅔ cup fresh orange juice
- 2 tablespoons fresh lemon juice
- ¼ cup chopped fresh basil
- 2 teaspoons olive oil
- ¼ teaspoon salt
- ⅛ teaspoon pepper
- 2 cups orange sections
- ¼ cup chopped walnuts, toasted

1. Combine first 3 ingredients in a large bowl; set aside. Combine lemon rind and next 7 ingredients in a small bowl; stir well. Pour over quinoa mixture; toss well.
2. Spoon 1 cup salad onto each of 4 plates. Arrange ½ cup orange sections around each salad; sprinkle each salad with 1 tablespoon walnuts. Yield: 4 servings.

CALORIES 380 (28% from fat); FAT 10.6g (sat 1g, mono 3.7g, poly 4.7g); PROTEIN 12.2g; CARB 62.9g; FIBER 13.3g; CHOL 0mg; IRON 7mg; SODIUM 189mg; CALC 114mg

---

WINE PICKS

- *Badger Mountain Columbia Valley Chardonnay 1995 (Washington state white), $9*
- *Bouvet Brut Nonvintage (French sparkling), $12*
- *Livingston Stanley's Selection Cabernet Sauvignon 1994 (California red), $20*
- *Mumm Carte Classique Extra Dry Champagne (French sparkling), $22*

DUCK SALAD WITH WILD RICE, PECANS, GRAPES, AND ORANGE DRESSING

"Because this dish uses boned duck breasts, it takes the fear out of cooking with duck," Andrée notes. "To make a complete meal, this main-dish salad only needs a loaf of crusty French bread and a glass of wine to round it out." If boneless duck breasts are unavailable, substitute 1 pound of pork tenderloin.

- Vegetable cooking spray
- 4 (4-ounce) skinned, boned duck breast halves
- 3½ cups cooked wild rice (about 1 cup uncooked rice)
- 1 cup sliced green onions
- 1 cup seedless green grapes, halved
- ¼ cup chopped pecans, toasted
- 1 tablespoon grated orange rind
- 1 cup fresh orange juice
- ⅓ cup sherry vinegar
- ¼ teaspoon salt
- ⅛ teaspoon pepper
- 7 red leaf lettuce leaves

1. Preheat oven to 450°.
2. Place a large nonstick skillet coated with cooking spray over medium-high heat until hot. Add duck; cook 2 minutes on each side or until lightly browned. Place duck in an 11 x 7-inch baking dish coated with cooking spray. Bake at 450° for 20 minutes or until done. Let cool. Cut into ¼-inch-wide strips. Combine duck, rice, and next 3 ingredients in a large bowl. Toss well; set aside.
3. Combine orange rind and next 4 ingredients in a small bowl; stir well. Pour orange juice mixture over duck mixture, and toss well. Serve salad on 7 lettuce-lined plates. Serve at room temperature. Yield: 7 servings (serving size: 1 cup).
Note: Have your butcher bone the duck breasts for you.

CALORIES 248 (30% from fat); FAT 8.3g (sat 2.1g, mono 3.4g, poly 1.5g); PROTEIN 14.5g; CARB 27.7g; FIBER 2.4g; CHOL 38mg; IRON 2.1mg; SODIUM 184mg; CALC 32mg

SALMON WRAPPED IN CABBAGE WITH CHIVES AND TOMATOES

"Because there are a lot of juices in this dish, I like serving it with a rice pilaf, which will absorb the flavors of the broth," says Andrée.

      4 large green cabbage leaves
      1 tablespoon margarine
      4 cups thinly sliced green
         cabbage
    ¾ cup thinly sliced onion
      1 cup low-salt chicken broth
      1 (8-ounce) bottle clam juice
      4 (6-ounce) salmon fillets
         (about 1 inch thick), skinned
    ¼ teaspoon salt
    ¼ teaspoon pepper
      1 cup coarsely chopped tomato
      1 tablespoon plus 1 teaspoon
         chopped fresh chives

1. Preheat oven to 400°.
2. Bring water to a boil in a medium saucepan. Add cabbage leaves; cook 30 seconds. Remove from water; set aside.
3. Melt margarine in a large nonstick skillet over medium-high heat. Add sliced cabbage and onion; sauté 5 minutes. Stir in broth and clam juice; cook over medium-high heat 15 minutes or until liquid evaporates.
4. Place 1 salmon fillet in center of each cabbage leaf. Sprinkle fillets with salt and pepper. Top each salmon fillet with ¼ cup onion mixture. Fold cabbage leaves over fillets. Place cabbage rolls, seam sides down, in an 11 x 7-inch baking dish.
5. Cover baking dish with aluminum foil. Bake at 400° for 25 minutes or until fish flakes easily when tested with a fork.
6. Arrange cabbage rolls on a platter. Sprinkle chopped tomato and chives over salmon packets. Yield: 4 servings (serving size: 1 cabbage roll, ¼ cup tomato, and 1 teaspoon chives).

CALORIES 362 (45% from fat); FAT 18.1g (sat 3.2g, mono 8.3g, poly 4.3g); PROTEIN 38.9g; CARB 10g; FIBER 3.4g; CHOL 115mg; IRON 1.9mg; SODIUM 431mg; CALC 72mg

LEMON CHIFFON CAKE WITH FRESH-FRUIT COMPOTE

"This is a very popular cake at Maison Robert," Andrée says. "It's not heavy, and it has a lot of flavor."

      1 cup sifted cake flour
    ½ cup granulated sugar
      1 teaspoon baking powder
    ¼ teaspoon salt
      2 tablespoons vegetable oil
      1 tablespoon grated lemon rind
    ¼ cup fresh lemon juice
      1 teaspoon vanilla extract
      2 large egg yolks
      6 large egg whites (at room
         temperature)
    ¼ teaspoon cream of tartar
      1 cup sliced strawberries
      1 cup blackberries
    ¼ cup brandy
      1 teaspoon granulated sugar
      1 tablespoon powdered sugar

1. Preheat oven to 350°.
2. Combine first 4 ingredients in a large bowl; stir well. Add oil and next 4 ingredients; beat mixture at medium speed of an electric mixer until smooth; set aside. Beat egg whites and cream of tartar at high speed of mixer until stiff peaks form, using clean, dry beaters. Gently stir one-fourth of egg white mixture into batter; gently fold in remaining egg white mixture. Spoon batter into an ungreased 10-inch tube pan, spreading evenly; break air pockets by cutting through batter with a knife. Bake at 350° for 25 minutes or until cake springs back when lightly touched. Invert pan; let cool for 40 minutes.
3. Combine berries, brandy, and 1 teaspoon granulated sugar in a medium bowl; stir gently. Let stand at room temperature for 30 minutes.
4. Loosen cake from sides of pan using a narrow metal spatula. Invert cake onto a plate, and sprinkle with powdered sugar. Serve fruit compote with cake. Yield: 8 servings (serving size: 1 slice and ¼ cup topping).

CALORIES 197 (23% from fat); FAT 5g (sat 1g, mono 1.5g, poly 2g); PROTEIN 4.6g; CARB 29.6g; FIBER 1.8g; CHOL 54mg; IRON 1.4mg; SODIUM 115mg; CALC 53mg

MERINGUE WITH PEACHES AND BLACKBERRIES

"At Maison Robert, we experiment a lot with meringues. Besides their being French, they're very versatile and low in fat. If you don't have peaches or blackberries, any seasonal fruit makes a fine substitution," Andrée suggests.

      6 large egg whites (at room
         temperature)
      1 cup sugar, divided
    ¼ cup ground toasted pecans
      6 cups peeled, sliced peaches
      3 cups raspberries
    ½ cup water
      1 tablespoon lemon juice
      2 cups blackberries

1. Preheat oven to 275°.
2. Cover a baking sheet with parchment paper. Draw 6 (4-inch) circles on paper. Turn paper over; secure with masking tape. Set aside.
3. Beat egg whites at high speed of an electric mixer until foamy. Gradually add ½ cup sugar, 1 tablespoon at a time, beating until stiff peaks form. (Do not underbeat.) Fold in pecans. Divide egg mixture evenly among 6 drawn circles. Using the back of a spoon, spread mixture into circles and form into shallow bowl shapes.
4. Bake at 275° for 2 hours or until dry. Turn oven off; let meringues cool in closed oven at least 12 hours. Carefully remove meringues from paper.
5. Combine peaches and ¼ cup sugar; stir well. Let stand 30 minutes. Combine ¼ cup sugar, raspberries, water, and lemon juice in a saucepan; bring to a boil. Remove from heat. Place raspberry mixture in a blender; cover and process until smooth. Strain pureed mixture through a sieve, discarding seeds. Let cool.
6. Spoon ¼ cup raspberry sauce onto each of 6 dessert plates, and top with meringues. Spoon ⅔ cup peach mixture and ⅓ cup blackberries in each meringue. Serve immediately. Yield: 6 servings.

CALORIES 307 (12% from fat); FAT 4g (sat 0.3g, mono 2.2g, poly 1.2g); PROTEIN 5.9g; CARB 66.9g; FIBER 11.1g; CHOL 0mg; IRON 0.9mg; SODIUM 53mg; CALC 42mg

Spicy Apple-Glazed Chick 'N' Grits Gorgonzola, page 148

Grilled Chicken Breasts on Mesclun, page 135

Shrimp-and-Orzo Salad, page 146

Banana Pudding, page 133

Spaghetti with Caramelized Onions,
Mushrooms, and Pancetta, page 125

Watercress-and-Sprout Salad, page 136

Top Banana Pudding

We've peeled back the fat and calories so you can have more than a heapin' helpin'.

No one knows the origin of banana pudding, but it has been a favorite Southern dessert for decades. Banana pudding's just something that everyone's grandmother and mother made, or makes. With its creamy filling, meringue peaks, and chewy crust, it just seems to say, "Dig in."

In this era of health-conscious eating, we're receiving more and more letters asking us for a lightened version. After finding a recipe that we felt was the most traditional, we proceeded with caution. We created a banana pudding that not only keeps the dessert's cool, sweet taste, but cuts the fat by a whopping three-fourths, to less than 3 grams per serving. The secret? We reduced the number of egg yolks from four to two, and used reduced-fat vanilla wafers and fat-free condensed milk. You'll never guess that this isn't the heavy version.

BEFORE & AFTER	
SERVING SIZE	
¾ cup	
CALORIES	
433	255
FAT	
12.7g	2.9g
PERCENT OF TOTAL CALORIES	
26%	10%
CHOLESTEROL	
79mg	51mg
SODIUM	
210mg	155mg

PEAK PERFORMANCE

Ever wonder how bakers get those "mile-high meringues" on cream pies and other desserts? Test Kitchens staffer Leigh Fran Jones shares her tips on getting stiff peaks.

◆ Egg whites will more than triple in volume when they're at room temperature. But because eggs are easier to separate right out of the refrigerator, do that first; then set the egg whites aside for about 30 minutes.

◆ Use a copper, stainless steel, or glass bowl. Plastic won't produce fluffy whites.

◆ Make sure the bowl is very clean. Any fat or grease will interfere with getting maximum volume.

◆ If you accidentally get some yolk (which contains fat) in the bowl, touch the yolk with a small piece of bread, and it will cling to the bread without removing any of the egg white.

◆ Start your electric mixer on high speed and beat the whites until they are foamy. Gradually add the sugar 1 tablespoon at a time to let the sugar dissolve before the egg whites reach their maximum volume.

◆ To determine when you've gotten stiff peaks, periodically check them by stopping the mixer and lifting the beaters out of the egg white mixture. A stiff peak will look shiny and glossy and stand straight up without curling over.

BANANA PUDDING

(pictured on page 131)

⅓ cup all-purpose flour
Dash of salt
2½ cups 1% low-fat milk
1 (14-ounce) can fat-free sweetened condensed milk
2 large egg yolks
2 teaspoons vanilla extract
3 cups sliced ripe banana
45 reduced-fat vanilla wafers
4 large egg whites (at room temperature)
¼ cup sugar

1. Preheat oven to 325°.
2. Combine flour and salt in a medium saucepan. Gradually add milks and egg yolks; stir well. Cook over medium heat, stirring constantly until thick, about 8 to 10 minutes. Remove from heat; stir in vanilla.
3. Arrange 1 cup banana slices in bottom of a 2-quart baking dish. Spoon one-third of pudding mixture over banana in dish. Arrange 15 wafers on top of pudding. Repeat layers twice, arranging the last 15 wafers around edge of dish. Push wafers into pudding.

4. Beat egg whites at high speed of an electric mixer until foamy. Gradually add sugar, 1 tablespoon at a time, beating until stiff peaks form. Spread meringue evenly over pudding, sealing to cookies around edge of dish. Bake at 325° for 25 minutes or until golden. Yield: 10 servings (serving size: ¾ cup).
Note: Banana Pudding may be a bit soupy when you first remove it from the oven. Let it cool at least 30 minutes before serving.

CALORIES 255 (10% from fat); FAT 2.9g (sat 1g, mono 0.9g, poly 0.2g); PROTEIN 7.9g; CARB 49.5g; FIBER 0.1g; CHOL 51mg; IRON 0.4mg; SODIUM 155mg; CALC 161mg

KEY POINTS

• Use bananas that are ripe but firm; they will be sweeter and will have more flavor.

• Don't be misled by the fact that the calories from fat in the before version are less than 30%. The reason is that the original is loaded with sugar, which raises the total calories and makes the percentage of calories from fat seem low in comparison—but it still packs 12.7 grams of fat.

The Bitter Truth

Once shunned for their bitterness, such exotic greens as arugula, radicchio, and curly endive are becoming supermarket standouts—in tune with today's healthful-living tastes.

Not so long ago, if you served a salad made with bitter greens and lettuces in place of iceberg, your guests might not have understood. Although arugula, endive, radicchio, sorrel, and watercress have always been popular in Europe, they're just being discovered here. Today, supermarkets across the country feature a year-round profusion of lettuces and greens that were once considered specialty items.

According to U.S. Department of Agriculture figures, consumption of these greens has increased nearly 40% since the advent of gourmet packaged salads. Of course, these lettuces and greens aren't just for salads, as our recipes demonstrate. They can stand up to spicy seasonings, aromatic herbs, and tangy dressings, hallmarks of contemporary cooking trends. They even hold their own in a soup or a risotto, for which we have recipes.

Then there's the health factor, which has also helped boost their appeal. People always knew that greens were good for them—they just didn't realize *how* good. According to a recent University of California-Berkeley *Wellness Newsletter*, radicchio and endive are nutritional champs, brimming with vitamin A and iron. As for versatility, in many cases these greens can be readily substituted for one another.

CURLY ENDIVE WITH BEANS, TOMATOES, AND CROUTONS

 2 (¾-ounce) slices French bread, cut into ¾-inch cubes
 1 small garlic clove, crushed
 ½ pound dried navy beans
 2 cups water
 1 bay leaf
18 cups chopped curly endive (about 1½ pounds)
2⅓ cups seeded, diced tomato
 ¼ cup minced fresh basil
 2 garlic cloves, minced
 ½ teaspoon salt
 ¼ teaspoon pepper
 2 teaspoons extra-virgin olive oil

1. Preheat oven to 350°.
2. Combine bread cubes and crushed garlic in a large zip-top plastic bag. Seal bag, and shake to coat bread cubes. Arrange bread cubes in a single layer on a baking sheet. Bake at 350° for 15 minutes or until toasted.
3. Sort and wash beans; place in a large Dutch oven. Cover beans with water to 2 inches above beans. Bring to a boil; cook 2 minutes. Remove from heat; cover and let stand 1 hour. Drain.
4. Add 2 cups water and bay leaf to navy beans in Dutch oven; bring to a boil. Cover, reduce heat, and simmer 1 hour. Discard bay leaf. Add endive; cover and cook 10 minutes, stirring occasionally. Stir in tomato and next 4 ingredients; cook, uncovered, 5 minutes.

Spoon bean mixture into a bowl. Drizzle with oil; top with croutons. Yield: 5 servings (serving size: 1 cup).
Note: Substitute 2½ cups drained canned beans, such as navy, cannellini, or other white beans, for dry beans. If using canned beans, omit step 3 and the simmering in step 4.

CALORIES 248 (12% from fat); FAT 3.3g (sat 0.6g, mono 1.5g, poly 0.8g); PROTEIN 14.2g; CARB 43.5g; FIBER 7.1g; CHOL 0mg; IRON 5mg; SODIUM 346mg; CALC 179mg

RISOTTO WITH ARUGULA AND TOASTED GARLIC

To make this recipe a main dish, you can add uncooked shrimp. Stir them in with the last ½ cup of broth. And so that the arugula retains its texture and sharp flavor, it's stirred into the rice at the last minute.

3½ cups low-salt chicken broth
 1 tablespoon olive oil
 3 garlic cloves, thinly sliced
1½ cups uncooked Arborio rice or other short-grain rice
 ½ cup chopped onion
 ½ cup dry white wine
 ¼ teaspoon salt
 ¼ teaspoon pepper
 4 cups trimmed arugula

1. Bring broth to a simmer in a small saucepan (do not boil). Keep broth warm over low heat.
2. Heat oil in a large saucepan over medium heat. Add garlic; sauté 3 minutes or until lightly browned. Remove garlic with a slotted spoon, and set aside. Add rice and onion to pan; sauté 5 minutes. Add wine, salt, and pepper; cook, stirring constantly, 1 minute or until wine is nearly absorbed. Add warm broth, ½ cup at a time, stirring constantly until each portion of broth is absorbed before adding the next (about 20 minutes total). Remove from heat; stir in garlic and arugula. Yield: 4 servings (serving size: 1 cup).

CALORIES 350 (14% from fat); FAT 5.5g (sat 0.9g, mono 3.1g, poly 0.6g); PROTEIN 8.6g; CARB 66.1g; FIBER 1.5g; CHOL 0mg; IRON 4.4mg; SODIUM 231mg; CALC 86mg

GRILLED ARUGULA-STUFFED SWORDFISH STEAKS

- 4 (6-ounce) swordfish steaks (about 1½ inches thick)
- ¼ cup dry white wine
- ¼ cup fresh lime juice
- ¼ cup low-sodium soy sauce
- 1 teaspoon Dijon mustard
- 1 teaspoon peeled, grated fresh gingerroot
- ½ teaspoon coarsely ground pepper
- ½ teaspoon dark sesame oil
- 1 garlic clove, minced
- ¼ teaspoon salt
- 4 cups trimmed arugula
- Vegetable cooking spray

1. Cut a horizontal slit through one side of each steak to form a deep pocket; set aside. Combine wine and next 7 ingredients in a large shallow dish; stir well. Add steaks, turning to coat. Cover and marinate in refrigerator 30 minutes.
2. Prepare grill. Remove steaks from marinade, reserving marinade. Sprinkle salt into pockets of steaks; set aside. Add arugula to marinade; toss well. Remove arugula from marinade; discard marinade. Stuff about ¾ cup arugula into each pocket; secure each pocket with a wooden pick.
3. Place swordfish steaks on grill rack coated with cooking spray, and grill 5 minutes on each side or until fish flakes easily when tested with a fork. Yield: 4 servings.

CALORIES 234 (29% from fat); FAT 7.6g (sat 2g, mono 2.7g, poly 1.8g); PROTEIN 35.3g; CARB 3.4g; FIBER 0g; CHOL 66mg; IRON 1.6mg; SODIUM 573mg; CALC 84mg

GRILLED CHICKEN BREASTS ON MESCLUN

(pictured on page 130)

- 4 (4-ounce) skinned, boned chicken breast halves
- 1 tablespoon ground cumin
- 1 teaspoon paprika
- ⅛ teaspoon salt
- ⅛ teaspoon ground red pepper
- ⅛ teaspoon black pepper
- 2 teaspoons vegetable oil
- Vegetable cooking spray
- 6 cups mesclun (gourmet salad greens)
- 3 tablespoons white wine vinegar
- 2 tablespoons orange marmalade
- 2 tablespoons low-sodium soy sauce
- 1 teaspoon dark sesame oil
- Lemon slices (optional)

1. Place each chicken breast half between 2 sheets of heavy-duty plastic wrap, and flatten to ¼-inch thickness using a meat mallet or rolling pin. Combine cumin and next 4 ingredients in a large zip-top plastic bag. Brush oil over chicken; add chicken to bag. Seal bag; shake to coat.
2. Prepare grill or broiler. Place chicken on grill rack or rack of a broiler pan coated with cooking spray; cook 3 minutes on each side or until chicken is done.
3. Place greens in a large bowl. Combine vinegar and next 3 ingredients; stir with a whisk until blended. Pour over greens; toss well. Place 1½ cups salad mixture on 4 plates. Arrange 1 chicken breast on top of each salad. Garnish with lemon slices, if desired. Yield: 4 servings.

CALORIES 226 (29% from fat); FAT 7.3g (sat 1.5g, mono 2.4g, poly 2.4g); PROTEIN 28.3g; CARB 12.5g; FIBER 1.4g; CHOL 72mg; IRON 2.8mg; SODIUM 347mg; CALC 64mg

ARUGULA: These clusters of dark green leaves resemble oak leaves and have a tangy, peppery flavor. Traditionally used almost exclusively in salads, arugula (also called rocket) can be added to rice dishes, pasta, or pizza. Other sharp-tasting greens such as watercress and dandelion can be substituted.

CURLY ENDIVE: This lettuce-like salad green grows in loose heads with an off-white, compact center and lacy, green-rimmed outer leaves that curl at the tips. It has a prickly texture and slightly bitter taste. Use in salads or stir into soups and bean dishes.

MESCLUN: This term applies to a mixture of salad greens such as arugula, dandelion, frisée, oak leaf, radicchio, and sorrel. It's often packaged as gourmet salad greens and is best eaten raw in salads. Thanks to mesclun, greens and lettuces that were once obscure to Americans are now commonly known and enjoyed.

RADICCHIO: This bitter-flavored member of the chicory family has burgundy-red leaves with white ribs. Most often used in salads, radicchio can also be grilled or roasted. If desired, other chicories such as escarole can be substituted.

SORREL: The sharp, sour flavor of this delicate green is almost too strong when raw but works well in small amounts in soups and sauces. The leaves are tender and smooth, and range from light to dark green. Spinach is a good substitute.

WATERCRESS: This member of the mustard family has small, crisp, dark green leaves with a sharp, peppery flavor and is best eaten raw. Choose leaves with deep color. Substitute with a pungent-flavored green such as arugula.

SORREL-AND-RICE SOUP

This soup can be served hot or cold. For a variation, substitute arugula, watercress, or spinach for sorrel.

> 3 (10½-ounce) cans low-salt chicken broth
> 1 cup chopped onion
> ½ cup uncooked long-grain rice
> 2 garlic cloves, minced
> 3 cups thinly sliced sorrel
> ¼ teaspoon salt
> ¼ teaspoon pepper
> 1½ cups plain low-fat yogurt
> Minced fresh parsley (optional)

1. Bring broth to a boil in a large saucepan. Add onion, rice, and garlic. Cover; reduce heat to low. Simmer 20 minutes or until rice is tender, stirring occasionally. Add sorrel, salt, and pepper; cook, uncovered, 1 minute or until sorrel wilts.
2. Place yogurt in a bowl. Gradually add ¾ cup broth mixture to yogurt, stirring constantly with a whisk. Stir yogurt mixture into remaining broth mixture in pan, and cook over low heat 1 minute or until thoroughly heated (do not boil). Ladle soup into bowls, and sprinkle with minced parsley, if desired. Yield: 5 servings (serving size: 1 cup).

CALORIES 157 (14% from fat); FAT 2.5g (sat 1g, mono 0.8g, poly 0.3g); PROTEIN 8.1g; CARB 26g; FIBER 2.2g; CHOL 4mg; IRON 2.7mg; SODIUM 253mg; CALC 173mg

WATERCRESS-AND-SPROUT SALAD

(pictured on page 132)

Pair this salad with grilled tuna for interesting textures, colors, and flavors.

> 2 tablespoons low-sodium soy sauce
> 1 tablespoon rice vinegar
> 1 tablespoon water
> 1 teaspoon sesame oil
> 4 cups trimmed watercress
> 1 cup bean sprouts
> 1 tablespoon sesame seeds, toasted

1. Combine first 4 ingredients in a medium bowl, and stir well with a whisk. Add watercress, sprouts, and sesame seeds; toss gently to coat. Serve immediately. Yield: 4 servings (serving size: 1 cup).

CALORIES 39 (55% from fat); FAT 2.4g (sat 0.4g, mono 0.9g, poly 1g); PROTEIN 2.3g; CARB 3.3g; FIBER 1.2g; CHOL 0mg; IRON 0.8mg; SODIUM 258mg; CALC 68mg

TRI-COLOR ITALIAN SALAD

This dish's unusual combination of ingredients provides bold taste sensations: sweet apple, bitter radicchio, tangy yogurt, pungent horseradish, and onion. Try it with grilled lamb or pork chops.

> 1 cup water
> ½ cup fresh or frozen green peas
> ¼ cup plain low-fat yogurt
> 1½ teaspoons prepared horseradish
> 1½ teaspoons white vinegar
> ⅛ teaspoon salt
> ⅛ teaspoon pepper
> 2 cups diced Red Delicious apple
> 2 cups torn radicchio
> ½ cup vertically sliced red onion
> ⅓ cup diced bottled roasted red bell pepper

1. Bring water to a boil in a small saucepan. Add peas; cook 1 minute. Drain and set aside.

2. Combine yogurt and next 4 ingredients in a large bowl. Add peas, apple, and remaining ingredients; toss well. Yield: 5 servings (serving size: 1 cup).

CALORIES 68 (8% from fat); FAT 0.6g (sat 0.2g, mono 0.1g, poly 0.1g); PROTEIN 2.6g; CARB 14.4g; FIBER 2.1g; CHOL 1mg; IRON 0.9mg; SODIUM 81mg; CALC 41mg

C A M P   C H O W

Geared for Camping

This handy fruit chew—a perfect fit in a fanny pack or backpack—is reminiscent of popular commercial dried-fruit snacks. It will keep at room temperature for about a week, or in the freezer for a few months.

APRICOT FRUIT SNACKS

> 3 cups chopped fresh apricots (about 1 pound)
> ½ cup sugar
> ¼ cup water
> Vegetable cooking spray

1. Preheat oven to 175° or lowest temperature on oven thermostat.
2. Combine apricots, sugar, and water in a large saucepan; bring to a boil. Cover and cook 5 minutes or until apricots are tender and sugar dissolves.
3. Place apricot mixture in a food processor, and process until smooth. Pour apricot puree into a 15 x 10-inch jelly-roll pan coated with cooking spray, spreading evenly. Place pan in oven, leaving door partially open. Bake at 175° for 8 hours or until dry and leathery (do not completely close door).
4. Peel leather off pan; let cool completely on a wire rack. Roll up leather; store in a zip-top plastic bag. Yield: 8 servings (serving size: ⅛ of roll or ¾ ounce).

CALORIES 76 (4% from fat); FAT 0.3g (sat 0g, mono 0g, poly 0.1g); PROTEIN 0.7g; CARB 18.8g; FIBER 1.2g; CHOL 0mg; IRON 0.3mg; SODIUM 1mg; CALC 8mg

Pocket Science

Stuffed chicken breasts never fail to impress. With our step-by-step instructions, we show you how to master this not-so-tricky technique.

If you want to truly impress people, serve stuffed chicken breasts. Your guests will definitely sit up and take notice, especially when they cut into the breast and discover a pocket filled with a wonderful blend of ingredients.

Although most people associate stuffed chicken breasts with fancy restaurants, they're not that difficult to do at home; all you really need are a sharp knife and a steady hand. Just follow our directions, and take your time. With practice, your stuffed chicken breasts will look more and more professional, as if you were a master chef.

An advantage of stuffed chicken breasts is that you can do much of the preparation ahead of time: You can prepare the boned breast for stuffing, then refrigerate until ready to stuff and cook. Or go ahead and stuff the breast before refrigerating. That means you don't have to wait to serve these elegant entrées to company—you can make them on a weeknight, impressing no one but yourself.

SPINACH-AND-BLUE CHEESE-STUFFED CHICKEN BREASTS

1	teaspoon vegetable oil, divided
1¼	cups finely chopped onion, divided
4	garlic cloves, minced
½	cup frozen chopped spinach, thawed, drained, and squeezed dry
2	tablespoons crumbled blue cheese
1	teaspoon Dijon mustard
4	(4-ounce) skinned, boned chicken breast halves
¼	teaspoon pepper
⅓	cup dry white wine
½	teaspoon dried thyme
1	cup low-salt chicken broth
2	tablespoons Dijon mustard

1. Heat ½ teaspoon oil in a large non-stick skillet over medium heat. Add ¼ cup onion; sauté 6 minutes or until tender. Add garlic, and sauté 1 minute. Add spinach, and sauté 3 minutes. Combine spinach mixture, cheese, and 1 teaspoon mustard in a small bowl. Stir well; set aside. Wipe skillet dry with a paper towel.
2. Cut a horizontal slit in thickest portion of each chicken breast half to form a pocket. Stuff about 2 tablespoons spinach mixture into each pocket. Sprinkle chicken with pepper.
3. Heat ½ teaspoon oil in skillet over medium-high heat. Add chicken, and cook 6 minutes on each side or until chicken is done. Remove chicken from skillet. Set aside, and keep warm. Add 1 cup chopped onion to skillet, and sauté 5 minutes. Add wine and thyme; cook 3 minutes or until reduced by half. Add broth and 2 tablespoons mustard; cook 4 minutes or until slightly thick, stirring occasionally. Return chicken to skillet; cover and simmer 2 minutes or until thoroughly heated. Serve sauce with chicken. Yield: 4 servings (serving size: 1 chicken breast half and 3 tablespoons sauce).

CALORIES 199 (21% from fat); FAT 4.7g (sat 1.3g, mono 1.4g, poly 1.1g); PROTEIN 29.2g; CARB 8.6g; FIBER 1.9g; CHOL 68mg; IRON 1.9mg; SODIUM 427mg; CALC 87mg

ARTICHOKE-AND-GOAT CHEESE-STUFFED CHICKEN BREASTS

1	(14-ounce) can artichoke bottoms
½	cup (2 ounces) crumbled goat or feta cheese
¼	cup chopped fresh chives, divided
1½	teaspoons chopped fresh thyme, divided
1½	teaspoons grated lemon rind, divided
8	(4-ounce) skinned, boned chicken breast halves
¼	teaspoon pepper
2	teaspoons olive oil, divided
1	teaspoon cornstarch
2	tablespoons lemon juice

1. Drain artichokes in a colander over a bowl, reserving liquid. Coarsely chop artichoke bottoms. Combine artichokes, cheese, 2 tablespoons chives, 1 teaspoon thyme, and 1 teaspoon lemon rind in a medium bowl; stir well.
2. Cut a horizontal slit in thickest portion of each chicken breast half to form a pocket. Stuff about ¼ cup artichoke mixture into each pocket. Sprinkle chicken with pepper.
3. Heat 1 teaspoon oil in a skillet over medium-high heat. Add 4 chicken breasts, and cook 6 minutes on each side or until chicken is done. Remove chicken from skillet. Set aside; keep warm. Repeat procedure with 1 teaspoon oil and remaining chicken breasts. Add reserved artichoke liquid, ½ teaspoon thyme, and ½ teaspoon lemon rind to skillet. Combine cornstarch and lemon juice; stir well. Add to skillet. Bring to a boil; cook, stirring constantly, 1 minute. Return chicken to skillet. Cover and simmer 2 minutes or until thoroughly heated. Spoon sauce over chicken. Top with 2 tablespoons chives. Yield: 8 servings (serving size: 1 chicken breast half and 1 tablespoon sauce).

CALORIES 181 (20% from fat); FAT 4.1g (sat 1.6g, mono 1.5g, poly 0.5g); PROTEIN 29g; CARB 6.7g; FIBER 0.1g; CHOL 72mg; IRON 1.5mg; SODIUM 347mg; CALC 73mg

HOW TO MAKE A POCKET

First, place chicken breast half on a cutting board, and trim all visible fat from chicken; then, follow these steps.

❶ *Insert the tip of a thin, sharp knife (such as a boning knife) into thickest side of the chicken breast. Make a 2-inch slit, cutting to, but not through, the opposite side of the breast.*

❷ *Holding the knife blade parallel to the cutting board, guide the blade around the inside of the breast, creating a pocket. Be careful not to cut through the sides of the breast.*

❸ *Using your fingers, stuff the breast, getting as much filling as you can into the pocket.*

MUSHROOM-STUFFED CHICKEN BREASTS WITH MADEIRA SAUCE

Sliced cheese is easier to fit into the pocket than shredded cheese; you can buy small amounts at the deli. Crimini mushrooms are dark brown and have a fuller flavor than button mushrooms.

- 1 teaspoon olive oil, divided
- 2 cups diced crimini or button mushrooms
- 1 large garlic clove, minced
- ¼ teaspoon pepper
- 4 (4-ounce) skinned, boned chicken breast halves
- 4 (½-ounce) slices Gouda or fontina cheese
- ¾ cup low-salt chicken broth
- ¼ cup Madeira or dry sherry
- 1 teaspoon cornstarch
- 1 teaspoon water
- Thyme sprigs (optional)

1. Heat ½ teaspoon oil in a large non-stick skillet over medium heat. Add diced mushrooms and garlic; sauté 3 minutes. Stir in pepper, and set aside.
2. Cut a horizontal slit in thickest portion of each chicken breast half to form a pocket. Stuff 2 tablespoons mushroom mixture and 1 slice cheese into each pocket.
3. Heat ½ teaspoon oil in skillet over medium-high heat. Add chicken; cook 6 minutes on each side or until chicken is done. Remove chicken from skillet. Set aside; keep warm.
4. Add broth and Madeira to skillet. Bring to a boil; cook 2 minutes or until reduced to ¾ cup. Combine cornstarch and water; add to skillet. Bring to a boil; cook, stirring constantly, 1 minute. Return chicken to skillet; cover and simmer 2 minutes or until thoroughly heated. Serve sauce with chicken. Garnish with thyme, if desired. Yield: 4 servings (serving size: 1 chicken breast half and 2 tablespoons sauce).

CALORIES 207 (30% from fat); FAT 6.9g (sat 3.1g, mono 2.3g, poly 0.6g); PROTEIN 31g; CARB 4.1g; FIBER 0.5g; CHOL 82mg; IRON 1.6mg; SODIUM 207mg; CALC 117mg

SHIITAKE-STUFFED CHICKEN BREASTS WITH TERIYAKI GLAZE

- 2 teaspoons dark sesame oil, divided
- 2 cups sliced shiitake mushroom caps (about 1 [3.75-ounce] package)
- 2 tablespoons minced green onions
- 1 tablespoon peeled, grated fresh gingerroot
- 3 tablespoons low-sodium teriyaki sauce, divided
- 4 (4-ounce) skinned, boned chicken breast halves
- ½ teaspoon grated orange rind
- ¼ cup fresh orange juice
- ¼ cup dry sherry
- 1 teaspoon honey
- Sliced green onions (optional)

1. Heat 1 teaspoon oil in a large non-stick skillet over medium heat. Add mushrooms, minced green onions, and gingerroot; sauté 3 minutes. Spoon into a small bowl, and stir in 1 tablespoon teriyaki sauce. Set aside.
2. Cut a horizontal slit in thickest portion of each chicken breast half to form a pocket. Stuff about 1½ tablespoons mushroom mixture into each pocket.
3. Heat 1 teaspoon oil in skillet over medium-high heat. Add chicken; cook 6 minutes on each side or until chicken is done. Remove chicken from skillet. Set aside; keep warm.
4. Add 2 tablespoons teriyaki sauce, orange rind, and next 3 ingredients to skillet; bring to a boil. Cook for 2 minutes or until reduced to ¼ cup. Spoon orange glaze over chicken. Garnish with sliced green onions, if desired. Yield: 4 servings (serving size: 1 chicken breast half and 1 tablespoon orange glaze).

CALORIES 180 (20% from fat); FAT 3.9g (sat 0.7g, mono 1.3g, poly 1.3g); PROTEIN 27.7g; CARB 7.7g; FIBER 0.7g; CHOL 66mg; IRON 1.4mg; SODIUM 269mg; CALC 22mg

ROASTED PEPPER-AND-CAPER-STUFFED CHICKEN BREASTS

1 (12-ounce) bottle roasted red bell peppers, drained and finely chopped
2 tablespoons capers
¼ teaspoon dried rosemary
¼ teaspoon dried thyme
1 garlic clove, minced
2 teaspoons olive oil, divided
4 (4-ounce) skinned, boned chicken breast halves
⅛ teaspoon salt
⅛ teaspoon pepper
2 tablespoons minced shallots
¼ cup dry white wine
1 (10½-ounce) can low-salt chicken broth
Chopped fresh parsley (optional)

1. Combine bell peppers, capers, rosemary, thyme, garlic, and 1 teaspoon oil in a small bowl; stir well.
2. Cut a horizontal slit through thickest portion of each chicken breast half to form a pocket. Stuff about ¼ cup bell pepper mixture into each pocket. Sprinkle salt and ⅛ teaspoon pepper over chicken.
3. Heat 1 teaspoon oil in a large nonstick skillet over medium-high heat. Add chicken, and sauté 6 minutes on each side or until chicken is done. Remove chicken from skillet. Set aside; keep warm.
4. Add shallots to skillet, and sauté 1 minute or until tender. Add wine and broth to skillet. Bring to a boil, and cook 5 minutes or until reduced to 1 cup. Return chicken to skillet; cover and simmer 2 minutes or until thoroughly heated. Serve sauce with chicken. Garnish with chopped parsley, if desired. Yield: 4 servings (serving size: 1 chicken breast half and ¼ cup sauce).

CALORIES 179 (23% from fat); FAT 4.5g (sat 0.8g, mono 2.2g, poly 0.6g); PROTEIN 27.9g; CARB 6g; FIBER 0.8g; CHOL 66mg; IRON 1.9mg; SODIUM 514mg; CALC 31mg

BRIE-AND-CARAMELIZED ONION-STUFFED CHICKEN BREASTS

Although this elegant dish is low on calories, the melted Brie-and-onion combination creates a rich-tasting, buttery consistency.

1 teaspoon olive oil, divided
1½ cups sliced onion
4 garlic cloves, thinly sliced
⅔ cup dry white wine, divided
2 ounces Brie or Camembert cheese, rind removed and cheese cut into small pieces (about 2 tablespoons)
⅛ teaspoon salt
⅛ teaspoon pepper
4 (4-ounce) skinned, boned chicken breast halves
2 tablespoons minced onion
1 tablespoon chopped fresh sage or ¾ teaspoon dried rubbed sage
2 garlic cloves, minced
1 (10½-ounce) can low-salt chicken broth
Sage sprigs (optional)

1. Heat ½ teaspoon oil in a nonstick skillet over medium heat. Add sliced onion; sauté 30 minutes or until golden. Add sliced garlic, and sauté 5 minutes. Stir in ⅓ cup wine; cook 5 minutes or until liquid almost evaporates. Spoon mixture into a bowl; let cool. Stir in Brie, salt, and pepper.
2. Cut a horizontal slit in thickest portion of each chicken breast half to form a pocket. Stuff about 1½ tablespoons onion mixture into each pocket.
3. Heat ½ teaspoon oil in skillet over medium-high heat. Add chicken, and cook 6 minutes on each side or until chicken is done. Remove chicken from skillet. Set aside; keep warm.
4. Add ⅓ cup wine, minced onion, chopped sage, and minced garlic to skillet. Cook over medium-high heat for 2 minutes. Stir in broth. Bring to a boil; cook 7 minutes or until reduced to ¾ cup. Return chicken to skillet; cover and simmer 2 minutes or until thoroughly heated. Serve sauce with chicken. Garnish with sage sprigs, if desired. Yield: 4 servings (serving size: 1 chicken breast half and 3 tablespoons sauce).

CALORIES 220 (29% from fat); FAT 7.1g (sat 3.2g, mono 2.5g, poly 0.7g); PROTEIN 30.8g; CARB 7.1g; FIBER 1g; CHOL 80mg; IRON 1.6mg; SODIUM 263mg; CALC 62mg

ITALIAN-STUFFED CHICKEN BREASTS

1 teaspoon olive oil, divided
¾ cup minced onion, divided
¼ cup (1 ounce) chopped prosciutto or lean smoked ham
1 tablespoon grated fresh Parmesan cheese
1 tablespoon dry breadcrumbs
1½ teaspoons minced fresh rosemary, divided
4 (4-ounce) skinned, boned chicken breast halves
1 cup low-salt chicken broth
¼ cup dry white wine
1 garlic clove, minced
Rosemary sprigs (optional)

1. Heat ½ teaspoon oil in a large nonstick skillet over medium heat. Add ½ cup onion, and sauté 4 minutes. Combine sautéed onion, prosciutto, cheese, breadcrumbs, and 1 teaspoon minced rosemary in a bowl. Stir well; set aside.
2. Cut a horizontal slit in thickest portion of each chicken breast half to form a pocket. Stuff about 3 tablespoons onion mixture into each pocket.
3. Heat ½ teaspoon oil in skillet over medium-high heat. Add chicken, and cook 6 minutes on each side or until chicken is done. Remove chicken from skillet. Set aside; keep warm. Add ¼ cup onion to skillet, and sauté 3 minutes. Add ½ teaspoon rosemary, broth, wine, and garlic; bring to a boil. Cook 5 minutes or until reduced to ¾ cup. Return chicken to skillet; cover and simmer 2 minutes or until thoroughly heated. Serve sauce with chicken. Garnish with rosemary sprigs, if desired. Yield: 4 servings (serving size: 1 chicken breast half and 3 tablespoons sauce).

CALORIES 183 (21% from fat); FAT 4.2g (sat 1.1g, mono 1.7g, poly 0.6g); PROTEIN 29.7g; CARB 5g; FIBER 0.7g; CHOL 71mg; IRON 1.5mg; SODIUM 244mg; CALC 49mg

CHICKEN BREASTS WITH CURRIED APPLE STUFFING

2 teaspoons vegetable oil, divided
¼ cup finely chopped onion
2 tablespoons finely chopped celery
1¾ cups peeled, chopped Granny Smith apple (about ¾ pound)
1¾ teaspoons curry powder, divided
¼ cup golden raisins
½ teaspoon minced garlic
1 (10½-ounce) can low-salt chicken broth, divided
4 (4-ounce) skinned, boned chicken breast halves
¾ cup apple juice
1 large garlic clove, minced
1 teaspoon cornstarch
1 teaspoon water

1. Heat 1 teaspoon oil in a nonstick skillet over medium-high heat. Add onion and celery; sauté 5 minutes or until tender. Add apple and 1 teaspoon curry powder; sauté 3 minutes or until apple is tender. Stir in raisins, ½ teaspoon minced garlic, and ⅓ cup broth; cook 4 minutes or until liquid almost evaporates. Spoon apple mixture into a small bowl; set aside.
2. Cut a horizontal slit through the thickest portion of each chicken breast half to form a pocket. Stuff about ¼ cup apple mixture into each pocket.
3. Heat 1 teaspoon oil in skillet over medium-high heat. Add chicken, and cook 6 minutes on each side or until done. Remove chicken from skillet; set aside.

4. Add ¾ teaspoon curry powder, remaining chicken broth, apple juice, and minced garlic clove to skillet. Bring to a boil; cook 5 minutes or until reduced to 1 cup.
5. Combine cornstarch and water; stir well. Add to broth mixture in skillet; stir with a whisk. Bring to a boil; cook, stirring constantly, 1 minute. Return chicken to skillet; cover and simmer 2 minutes or until heated. Serve sauce with chicken. Yield: 4 servings (serving size: 1 chicken breast half and ¼ cup sauce).

CALORIES 244 (17% from fat); FAT 4.6g (sat 1g, mono 1.3g, poly 1.6g); PROTEIN 27.7g; CARB 23.3g; FIBER 2.5g; CHOL 66mg; IRON 1.8mg; SODIUM 105mg; CALC 33mg

THE ENLIGHTENED CHEF

Florida's Alternative Cuisine

Chef Hubert Des Marais calls his cooking style "alternative cuisine"—a blend of the Deep South, the Caribbean, and South and Central America. His cooking technique (low in fat, sugar, salt, and cholesterol) has won accolades from an enthusiastic local following and treasured national culinary distinctions.

Des Marais is executive chef of the Four Seasons Resort's two restaurants in Palm Beach, Florida. The heart and soul of his kitchen is his secret garden, full of rare aromatic herbs and exotic flavorings, such as carambola, pineapple sage (named for its sweet, fruity scent), and piripiri hot peppers. Des Marais uses them all on a daily basis.

Des Marais feels that the preparation of his food counts not only on the flavors and textures of Florida's extraordinary fresh fish, vegetables, and fruits, but also on certain distinct seasoning combinations, such as sweet alongside a chile pepper or the essence of vanilla-pod scrapings along with spices like star anise and coriander seeds.

SKILLET-SEARED SALMON WITH CURRIED PINEAPPLE ESSENCE

*Hubert Des Marais garnishes this dish
with steamed whole bok choy leaves.*

1½ cups (1-inch) cubes fresh pineapple
½ cup rice vinegar
½ teaspoon curry powder
1 garlic clove, minced
1 teaspoon cracked pepper
6 (6-ounce) salmon fillets (1 inch thick)
1 teaspoon kosher salt
1 tablespoon ground cinnamon
1 tablespoon ground coriander
1 tablespoon black pepper
1 tablespoon ground allspice
1 tablespoon ground cardamom
1 tablespoon ground cloves
1 tablespoon ground ginger
1½ tablespoons vegetable oil

1. Combine first 4 ingredients in a saucepan. Bring to a boil; reduce heat, and simmer, uncovered, 5 minutes. Remove from heat; let cool slightly. Place pineapple mixture in a blender; cover and process until smooth. Stir in cracked pepper. Set pineapple essence aside.
2. Remove skin from salmon, and sprinkle salt evenly over fillets. Combine cinnamon and next 6 ingredients. Rub one side of each fillet with spice mixture.
3. Heat oil in a large nonstick skillet over medium-high heat until hot. Add salmon, spice side down, and cook 4 minutes on each side or until salmon flakes easily when tested with a fork. Serve with pineapple essence. Yield: 6 servings (serving size: 1 salmon fillet and 2 tablespoons pineapple essence).

CALORIES 308 (44% from fat); FAT 9.6g (sat 2.7g, mono 6.7g, poly 3.7g); PROTEIN 32.7g; CARB 9.6g; FIBER 1.8g; CHOL 102mg; IRON 2.1mg; SODIUM 280mg; CALC 53mg

A Beautiful Blendship

If you're searching for something light to serve with your coffee, we've got the goods. Seeing as how today's cups of joe come with pedigrees, we've created desserts that won't give your taste buds the runaround.

CHOCOLATE-OATMEAL HERMITS

⅓ cup packed brown sugar
¼ cup granulated sugar
¼ cup vegetable oil
2 teaspoons vanilla extract
2 large egg whites
1½ cups quick-cooking oats
¾ cup all-purpose flour
½ teaspoon baking powder
⅛ teaspoon salt
⅓ cup semisweet chocolate minichips
Vegetable cooking spray

1. Preheat oven to 375°.
2. Combine first 5 ingredients in a large bowl; beat at high speed of an electric mixer until well-blended. Combine oats, flour, baking powder, and salt; stir well. Add to sugar mixture, stirring just until oats mixture is moist. Stir in chocolate chips.
3. Drop dough by level tablespoons onto baking sheets coated with cooking spray. Bake at 375° for 10 minutes. Remove from baking sheets; let cool on wire racks. Yield: 2 dozen (serving size: 1 cookie).

CALORIES 84 (38% from fat); FAT 3.5g (sat 0.9g, mono 1g, poly 1.3g); PROTEIN 1.6g; CARB 11.8g; FIBER 0.7g; CHOL 0mg; IRON 0.5mg; SODIUM 30mg; CALC 12mg

STREUSEL-OAT SCONES

These are best served warm.

2 cups all-purpose flour
2 teaspoons baking powder
¼ teaspoon baking soda
¼ teaspoon salt
¼ cup sugar
¼ cup chilled stick margarine, cut into small pieces
¾ cup low-fat buttermilk
Vegetable cooking spray
¼ cup quick-cooking oats
¼ cup packed brown sugar
1 tablespoon margarine, melted
1 tablespoon all-purpose flour

1. Preheat oven to 450°.
2. Combine first 5 ingredients in a medium bowl; cut in ¼ cup margarine with a pastry blender or 2 knives until mixture resembles coarse meal. Add buttermilk, stirring just until flour mixture is moist. Turn dough out onto a baking sheet coated with cooking spray. Pat dough into an 8-inch circle; set aside.
3. Combine oats, brown sugar, 1 tablespoon margarine, and 1 tablespoon flour, forming a streusel. Gently pat streusel into surface of dough. Cut dough into 12 wedges (do not separate wedges). Bake at 450° for 15 minutes or until lightly browned. Serve warm. Yield: 1 dozen (serving size: 1 scone).

CALORIES 169 (29% from fat); FAT 5.4g (sat 1.2g, mono 2.2g, poly 1.6g); PROTEIN 3.1g; CARB 27.2g; FIBER 0.8g; CHOL 0mg; IRON 1.2mg; SODIUM 141mg; CALC 74mg

CINNAMON BISCOTTI

2½ cups all-purpose flour
¾ cup sugar
1½ teaspoons baking powder
1½ teaspoons ground cinnamon
¼ teaspoon salt
3 large eggs
2 tablespoons stick margarine, melted
2 teaspoons vanilla extract
Vegetable cooking spray
2 tablespoons sugar
½ teaspoon ground cinnamon

1. Preheat oven to 325°.
2. Combine first 5 ingredients in a large bowl; make a well in center of mixture. Combine eggs, margarine, and vanilla; stir with a whisk. Add to flour mixture, stirring just until moist.
3. Turn dough out onto a lightly floured surface, and knead lightly 10 times. Shape dough into a 16-inch-long roll. Place roll on a baking sheet coated with cooking spray; flatten to ¾-inch thickness. Combine 2 tablespoons sugar and ½ teaspoon cinnamon; sprinkle over dough.
4. Bake at 325° for 30 minutes. Remove roll from baking sheet; let cool 10 minutes on a wire rack. Cut roll diagonally into 24 (½-inch) slices. Place slices, cut sides down, on baking sheet. Bake at 325° for 10 minutes. Turn cookies over; bake 10 additional minutes (cookies will be slightly soft in center but will harden as they cool). Remove from baking sheet; let cool completely on a wire rack. Yield: 2 dozen (serving size: 1 cookie).

CALORIES 96 (17% from fat); FAT 1.8g (sat 0.4g, mono 0.7g, poly 0.4g); PROTEIN 2.2g; CARB 17.6g; FIBER 0.4g; CHOL 28mg; IRON 0.8mg; SODIUM 44mg; CALC 25mg

TRIPLE-LEMON MUFFINS

2 cups all-purpose flour
½ cup sugar
1 teaspoon baking powder
½ teaspoon baking soda
¼ teaspoon salt
3 tablespoons margarine, melted
1 teaspoon grated lemon rind
¼ cup fresh lemon juice, divided
2 large eggs
1 (8-ounce) carton lemon low-fat yogurt
Vegetable cooking spray
1½ tablespoons sugar

1. Preheat oven to 400°.
2. Combine first 5 ingredients in a medium bowl; make a well in center of mixture. Combine margarine, lemon rind, 2 tablespoons lemon juice, eggs, and yogurt; stir well with a whisk. Add to flour mixture, stirring just until moist.
3. Spoon batter into 12 muffin cups coated with cooking spray. Bake at 400° for 20 minutes or until golden.
4. Combine 2 tablespoons lemon juice and 1½ tablespoons sugar in a small saucepan; bring to a boil. Cook 2 minutes or until slightly thick. Brush lemon glaze over muffins; remove from pans. Yield: 1 dozen (serving size: 1 muffin).

CALORIES 181 (21% from fat); FAT 4.3g (sat 0.9g, mono 1.7g, poly 1.2g); PROTEIN 4g; CARB 31.5g; FIBER 0.6g; CHOL 37mg; IRON 1.1mg; SODIUM 158mg; CALC 56mg

DRIED-CRANBERRY MAZURKAS

Plain dried cranberries can be used instead of sweetened.

2½ cups sweetened dried cranberries (such as Craisins)
2 cups orange juice
2 tablespoons brown sugar
1 teaspoon minced orange rind
1 cup all-purpose flour
1 cup quick-cooking oats
½ cup packed brown sugar
½ cup chilled stick margarine, cut into pieces
Vegetable cooking spray

1. Preheat oven to 350°.
2. Combine first 4 ingredients in a saucepan. Bring to a simmer; cook over medium heat 13 minutes or until liquid is absorbed and mixture is thick. Spoon cranberry mixture into a blender or food processor; cover and process until smooth. Set aside.
3. Combine flour, oats, and ½ cup brown sugar; cut in margarine with a pastry blender or 2 knives until mixture resembles coarse meal. Reserve 1 cup flour mixture; set aside. Press remaining flour mixture into a 13 x 9-inch baking pan coated with cooking spray. Spread cranberry mixture evenly over flour mixture in pan. Sprinkle reserved 1 cup flour mixture over cranberry mixture.
4. Bake at 350° for 45 minutes or until browned. Cool in pan on a wire rack. Yield: 3 dozen (serving size: 1 bar).

CALORIES 93 (26% from fat); FAT 2.7g (sat 0.5g, mono 1.2g, poly 0.9g); PROTEIN 0.8g; CARB 16.6g; FIBER 0.8g; CHOL 0mg; IRON 0.3mg; SODIUM 31mg; CALC 7mg

ESPRESSO-SPICE CRUMB CAKE

1 cup boiling water
2 teaspoons instant espresso or 1 tablespoon plus 1 teaspoon instant coffee granules
3 cups all-purpose flour, divided
1½ teaspoons baking powder
½ teaspoon baking soda
½ teaspoon ground cinnamon
¼ teaspoon ground ginger
⅛ teaspoon ground nutmeg
¾ cup plus 2 tablespoons packed brown sugar, divided
¼ cup stick margarine, softened
¾ cup molasses
½ cup egg substitute
Vegetable cooking spray
¼ teaspoon ground cinnamon
1 tablespoon chilled stick margarine

1. Preheat oven to 350°.
2. Combine water and espresso; stir well. Set aside.
3. Combine 2¾ cups flour, baking powder, and next 4 ingredients; set aside.
4. Beat ¾ cup brown sugar and ¼ cup margarine at medium speed of an electric mixer until well-blended. Add molasses and egg substitute; beat well. Add flour mixture to sugar mixture alternately with coffee mixture, beginning and ending with flour mixture.
5. Pour batter into a 9-inch square cake pan coated with cooking spray. Combine ¼ cup flour, 2 tablespoons brown sugar, and ¼ teaspoon cinnamon; cut in 1 tablespoon margarine with a pastry blender or 2 knives until mixture resembles coarse meal, forming a streusel. Sprinkle streusel over batter. Bake at 350° for 50 minutes or until a wooden pick inserted in center comes out clean. Let cool in pan on a wire rack 10 minutes; remove from pan. Let cool completely on wire rack. Yield: 16 servings (serving size: 1 piece).

CALORIES 209 (17% from fat); FAT 3.9g (sat 0.7g, mono 1.6g, poly 1.2g); PROTEIN 3.3g; CARB 40.8g; FIBER 0.7g; CHOL 0mg; IRON 2.3mg; SODIUM 103mg; CALC 75mg

BLUEBERRY-BUTTERMILK CAKE

Almost any berry will work in place of the blueberries.

3½   cups all-purpose flour
1½   cups packed brown sugar
  1   teaspoon ground cinnamon
  ¼   teaspoon ground nutmeg
  ¼   teaspoon salt
  ½   cup plus 2 tablespoons chilled
       stick margarine, cut into
       small pieces and divided
1½   teaspoons baking powder
  ½   teaspoon baking soda
1½   cups low-fat buttermilk
  ½   cup egg substitute
  ½   cup apple butter
  1   teaspoon vanilla extract
  ½   teaspoon grated lemon rind
Vegetable cooking spray
  2   cups fresh blueberries

1. Preheat oven to 350°.
2. Combine first 5 ingredients in a large bowl; cut in ½ cup margarine with a pastry blender or 2 knives until mixture resembles coarse meal. Place 1 cup flour mixture in a small bowl; cut in 2 tablespoons margarine to form a streusel; set aside.
3. Add baking powder and baking soda to remaining flour mixture in large bowl; stir well. Combine buttermilk and next 4 ingredients. Pour buttermilk mixture over flour mixture; beat at low speed of an electric mixer until well-blended.
4. Pour batter into a 13 x 9-inch baking pan coated with cooking spray. Top batter with blueberries, and sprinkle with streusel. Bake at 350° for 50 minutes or until a wooden pick inserted in center of cake comes out clean. Let cake cool in pan on a wire rack. Yield: 16 servings (serving size: 1 piece).

CALORIES 259 (27% from fat); FAT 7.9g (sat 1.7g, mono 3.2g, poly 2.4g); PROTEIN 4.7g; CARB 42.9g; FIBER 1.6g; CHOL 0mg; IRON 1.8mg; SODIUM 189mg; CALC 78mg

CARAMELIZED ESPRESSO FRAPPÉ

  ½   cup boiling water
  1   teaspoon instant espresso or
       2 teaspoons instant coffee
       granules
  ¼   cup sugar
  ¼   cup water, divided
  1   cup skim milk
  ¼   cup hot cocoa mix
  1   cup crushed ice

1. Combine ½ cup boiling water and espresso; stir until coffee dissolves. Pour into an ice cube tray; freeze 4 hours or until firm.
2. Combine sugar and 2 tablespoons water in a small heavy saucepan over medium heat; cook until sugar dissolves. Continue cooking 5 additional minutes or until golden. Remove from heat; carefully stir in 2 tablespoons water with a whisk (mixture will bubble vigorously). Let cool.
3. Combine caramelized sugar, milk, and cocoa mix in a blender; cover and process until well-blended. With blender on, add coffee ice cubes, 1 at a time; process until smooth. Add crushed ice; process until smooth. Serve immediately. Yield: 2½ cups (serving size: ½ cup).

CALORIES 90 (4% from fat); FAT 0.4g (sat 0.1g, mono 0g, poly 0g); PROTEIN 2g; CARB 19.7g; FIBER 0g; CHOL 3mg; IRON 0mg; SODIUM 56mg; CALC 61mg

IN SEASON

Springtime Serenade

A salad made with the first vegetables of the season is the best and simplest way to put you back in touch with the earth.

To welcome spring, you need a salad, particularly one made with the season's first vegetables. After the staleness of winter's final days, salads refresh your spirit with their assortment of newly picked ingredients. Don't let spring's arrival pass without the celebratory crunch of fresh vegetables.

ASPARAGUS SALAD WITH CAESAR VINAIGRETTE

20   asparagus spears (about 1¼
       pounds)
  4   cups gourmet salad greens
  3   tablespoons tarragon vinegar
1½   teaspoons olive oil
  1   teaspoon water
  ½   teaspoon anchovy paste
  ⅛   teaspoon pepper
  1   garlic clove, minced
  ¼   cup garlic-flavored croutons
Chopped fresh parsley (optional)

1. Snap off tough ends of asparagus; remove scales with a knife or vegetable peeler, if desired. Arrange asparagus in a steamer basket over boiling water. Cover and steam 4 minutes or until crisp-tender. Rinse under cold water; drain well.
2. Arrange 1 cup greens on each of 4 plates; top each serving with 5 asparagus spears. Combine vinegar and next 5 ingredients in a small bowl; stir well with a whisk. Drizzle 1 tablespoon vinaigrette over each serving, and top each with 1 tablespoon croutons. Sprinkle with parsley, if desired. Yield: 4 servings.

CALORIES 70 (37% from fat); FAT 2.9g (sat 0.3g, mono 1.3g, poly 0.4g); PROTEIN 4.3g; CARB 8.9g; FIBER 1.6g; CHOL 0mg; IRON 1.2mg; SODIUM 102mg; CALC 28mg

CRUNCHY PEA SALAD

2¼ cups shelled green peas
1¼ cups diced cucumber
½ cup thinly sliced radishes
¼ cup thinly sliced green onions
2 tablespoons rice vinegar
1 tablespoon olive oil
1 tablespoon honey
½ teaspoon coarsely ground
    pepper
¼ teaspoon salt

1. Place peas in a steamer basket over boiling water. Cover and steam 6 minutes or until tender. Rinse under cold water; drain well.
2. Combine peas, cucumber, radishes, and green onions in a bowl. Combine vinegar and remaining 4 ingredients in a small bowl; stir with a whisk. Pour over vegetable mixture; toss well. Yield: 5 servings (serving size: 1 cup).

CALORIES 101 (28% from fat); FAT 3.1g (sat 0.4g, mono 2g, poly 0.4g); PROTEIN 4.2g; CARB 15.2g; FIBER 2.9g; CHOL 0mg; IRON 1.4mg; SODIUM 127mg; CALC 32mg

POTATO SALAD WITH PEAS

2 pounds red potatoes (about
    7 medium)
1 cup shelled green peas
3 tablespoons chopped fresh
    parsley
2 tablespoons chopped fresh
    chives
2 tablespoons chopped fresh
    basil
½ cup tarragon vinegar
1 tablespoon sugar
½ teaspoon salt
⅛ teaspoon cracked pepper
1 garlic clove, minced

1. Place potatoes in a large saucepan. Cover with water; bring to a boil. Reduce heat; simmer, partially covered, 25 minutes or until tender. Add peas; cook 1 minute. Drain; let cool slightly. Cut potatoes into ¼-inch slices.
2. Combine potatoes, peas, parsley, chives, and basil in a large bowl. Combine vinegar and remaining 4 ingredients in a small bowl, and stir with a whisk. Pour over potato mixture, tossing gently to coat. Yield: 6 servings (serving size: 1 cup).

CALORIES 152 (2% from fat); FAT 0.3g (sat 0.1g, mono 0g, poly 0.1g); PROTEIN 4.6g; CARB 33.2g; FIBER 3.4g; CHOL 0mg; IRON 1.6mg; SODIUM 209mg; CALC 23mg

HERBED PEA MEDLEY

2 cups shelled green peas
1 cup Sugar Snap peas, trimmed
    and halved crosswise
½ cup diced carrot
1 cup snow pea pods, halved
    crosswise
2 tablespoons chopped fresh
    parsley
1 tablespoon finely chopped
    fresh mint or 1 teaspoon
    dried mint
1 tablespoon margarine, melted
1 teaspoon grated orange rind
2 teaspoons lemon juice
½ teaspoon salt
¼ teaspoon pepper

1. Arrange first 3 ingredients in a steamer basket over boiling water. Cover and steam 4 minutes. Add snow peas. Cover; steam 2 additional minutes or until crisp-tender.
2. Combine parsley and remaining 6 ingredients in a large bowl; stir well. Add vegetable mixture; toss well. Yield: 4 servings (serving size: 1 cup).

CALORIES 123 (24% from fat); FAT 3.3g (sat 0.7g, mono 1.3g, poly 1.1g); PROTEIN 6.2g; CARB 18g; FIBER 4.9g; CHOL 0mg; IRON 2.8mg; SODIUM 339mg; CALC 59mg

TANGY LEEK SALAD

Select leeks with clean, white bottoms and crisp, fresh-looking green tops. Small to medium leeks, less than 1½ inches in diameter, are the most tender and have a mild, delicate flavor.

6 medium leeks
2 tablespoons red wine vinegar
2 teaspoons olive oil
½ teaspoon Dijon mustard
¼ teaspoon salt
⅛ teaspoon pepper
1 tablespoon capers
½ cup diced tomatoes
1 tablespoon chopped fresh basil

1. Remove roots, outer leaves, and tops from leeks, leaving 2 inches of each leek. Cut leeks into 2-inch pieces. Arrange leeks in a steamer basket over boiling water. Cover and steam 10 minutes or until tender. Rinse leeks under cold water; drain and chill. Combine vinegar and next 4 ingredients in a small bowl; stir with a whisk. Stir in capers. Divide leeks and tomato evenly among 4 small bowls. Spoon dressing over vegetables; sprinkle with basil. Yield: 4 servings.

CALORIES 141 (19% from fat); FAT 3.1g (sat 0.4g, mono 1.6g, poly 0.6g); PROTEIN 3.1g; CARB 27.9g; FIBER 2.6g; CHOL 0mg; IRON 4mg; SODIUM 372mg; CALC 112mg

Spring Salmon Dinner

Fresh salmon fillets get a lively kick from a spicy, herb-infused marinade. A colorful, citrus-chile salsa is included.

> ### MENU
> HERB-GRILLED SALMON
> WITH MANGO SALSA
>
> *Rice*
>
> *Gingersnap cookies*

HERB-GRILLED SALMON WITH MANGO SALSA

You can substitute 1 teaspoon vegetable oil and 1/8 teaspoon ground red pepper for the hot pepper oil.

4   (6-ounce) salmon fillets (about 1 inch thick)
1/4   cup chopped fresh cilantro
1/4   cup chopped fresh mint
1   teaspoon hot pepper oil (such as Crisco Savory Seasonings)
1/2   teaspoon salt
1/4   teaspoon pepper
Vegetable cooking spray
Mango Salsa
4   cups hot cooked rice

1. Combine first 4 ingredients in a large zip-top plastic bag. Seal; shake gently to coat. Marinate in refrigerator 20 minutes.
2. Remove salmon from bag; sprinkle with salt and pepper. Prepare grill. Place salmon on grill rack coated with cooking spray; cook 5 minutes on each side or until done. Serve with salsa and rice. Yield: 4 servings (serving size: 5 ounces salmon, 2/3 cup salsa, and 1 cup rice).
Note: Halibut or tuna can be substituted for salmon.

CALORIES 601 (25% from fat); FAT 16.4g (sat 2.9g, mono 7.4g, poly 3.8g); PROTEIN 41.2g; CARB 70.2g; FIBER 3g; CHOL 115mg; IRON 3mg; SODIUM 383mg; CALC 47mg

Mango Salsa:

This salsa is best when made ahead. The serrano chile adds just the right amount of "heat" to offset the sweetness of the pineapple, banana, and mango.

1   cup peeled, cubed ripe mango
1   cup sliced banana
1/4   cup chopped fresh mint
2   tablespoons fresh orange juice
1   teaspoon grated lime rind
1   tablespoon fresh lime juice
1   (8-ounce) can unsweetened pineapple chunks, drained
1   serrano chile, seeded and finely chopped

1. Combine all ingredients in a medium bowl. Stir well; cover and refrigerate. Yield: 2 2/3 cups (serving size: 2/3 cup).

CALORIES 79 (4% from fat); FAT 0.3g (sat 0.1g, mono 0.1g, poly 0.1g); PROTEIN 0.9g; CARB 20.4g; FIBER 2g; CHOL 0mg; IRON 0.4mg; SODIUM 2mg; CALC 15mg

> ### SHOPPING LIST
>
> 4 (6-ounce) salmon fillets
>
> 1 bunch fresh cilantro
>
> 2 bunches fresh mint
>
> hot pepper oil
>
> rice
>
> 1 ripe mango
>
> 1 banana
>
> 1 orange
>
> 1 lime
>
> 1 serrano chile
>
> 1 (8-ounce) can unsweetened pineapple chunks
>
> gingersnap cookies

Remember the Main

Steak, salmon, chicken, and shrimp go into these one-dish, main-course salads, all of which can be prepared and on the table in less than 45 minutes. Add some bread, and you have a complete meal.

STEAK AND BLACK-EYED PEA SALAD

Preparation time: 10 minutes
Cooking time: 10 minutes

1   (12-ounce) lean flank steak
1   tablespoon spicy brown mustard
1/2   teaspoon garlic powder
1/4   teaspoon pepper
Vegetable cooking spray
5   cups torn romaine lettuce
1   cup cherry tomatoes, halved
1   cup (1/4-inch-thick) sliced cucumber
1/2   cup sliced onion, separated into rings
1   (15.8-ounce) can black-eyed peas, rinsed and drained
3/4   cup fat-free Italian dressing

1. Preheat broiler. Trim fat from steak. Combine mustard, garlic powder, and pepper; spread over both sides of steak. Place steak on rack of a broiler pan coated with cooking spray; cook 5 minutes on each side or until desired degree of doneness. Cut steak diagonally across grain into thin slices.
2. Combine steak, lettuce, and next 4 ingredients in a bowl. Drizzle dressing over salad, and toss well. Yield: 4 servings (serving size: 2 cups).
Note: Substitute 1 (16-ounce) can cannellini beans for black-eyed peas, if desired.

CALORIES 323 (34% from fat); FAT 12.1g (sat 4.3g, mono 4.5g, poly 1.3g); PROTEIN 24.6g; CARB 29.1g; FIBER 4.7g; CHOL 45mg; IRON 4.8mg; SODIUM 679mg; CALC 76mg

CHICKEN, APPLE, AND SMOKED-GOUDA SALAD

Preparation time: 15 minutes
Cooking time: 10 minutes

¼   teaspoon pepper
⅛   teaspoon salt
¾   pound skinned, boned chicken
      breast halves
Vegetable cooking spray
8   cups torn prepackaged spinach
¾   cup chopped red bell pepper
½   cup thinly sliced celery
½   cup sliced red onion, separated
      into rings
1½ cups thinly sliced Red
      Delicious apple (about ½
      pound)
¾   cup fat-free honey mustard
      salad dressing
½   cup (2 ounces) shredded
      smoked Gouda or Jarlsberg
      cheese
¼   cup sliced almonds, toasted

1. Preheat broiler. Sprinkle pepper and salt over chicken. Place chicken on a broiler pan coated with cooking spray; broil 5 minutes on each side or until chicken is done. Cut chicken into ¼-inch-thick slices.
2. Combine chicken, spinach, and next 4 ingredients in a large bowl. Drizzle dressing over salad, and toss well. Sprinkle with cheese and almonds. Yield: 4 servings (serving size: 2½ cups).
Note: Substitute ready-to-eat roasted skinned, boned chicken breast (such as Tyson) for cooked chicken, if desired.

CALORIES 331 (27% from fat); FAT 10.1g (sat 3.6g, mono 3.9g, poly 1.5g); PROTEIN 29.8g; CARB 31.4g; FIBER 7.2g; CHOL 70mg; IRON 5mg; SODIUM 835mg; CALC 248mg

WARM CHICKEN-AND-ASPARAGUS SALAD

Preparation time: 15 minutes
Cooking time: 10 minutes

3   tablespoons water
2   tablespoons white wine vinegar
1   tablespoon olive oil
1   teaspoon Dijon mustard
¼   teaspoon coarsely ground
      pepper
⅛   teaspoon salt
2   cups (2-inch) diagonally
      sliced asparagus
2   teaspoons Dijon mustard
1   pound skinned, boned
      chicken breast halves
¼   teaspoon salt
⅛   teaspoon pepper
1   teaspoon olive oil
Vegetable cooking spray
⅓   cup thinly sliced green onions
1   (10-ounce) bag Italian-blend
      salad greens (about 6 cups)

1. Combine first 6 ingredients in a bowl. Stir well; set aside.
2. Arrange asparagus in a steamer basket over boiling water. Cover and steam 3 minutes or until crisp-tender; set aside.
3. Brush 2 teaspoons mustard over both sides of chicken; sprinkle chicken with ¼ teaspoon salt and ⅛ teaspoon pepper. Cut chicken across grain into thin slices. Heat 1 teaspoon oil in a large nonstick skillet coated with cooking spray over medium-high heat. Add chicken and green onions; sauté 6 minutes or until chicken is done. Add vinegar mixture to skillet, and cook, stirring constantly, 1 minute.
4. Arrange 1½ cups salad greens on each of 4 plates; top each with ½ cup asparagus. Divide chicken mixture evenly among salads. Yield: 4 servings.

CALORIES 208 (29% from fat); FAT 6.6g (sat 1.1g, mono 3.7g, poly 0.9g); PROTEIN 30g; CARB 6.8g; FIBER 2.6g; CHOL 66mg; IRON 2.6mg; SODIUM 421mg; CALC 68mg

SHRIMP-AND-ORZO SALAD

(pictured on page 130)

This recipe is even quicker to prepare if you use precooked shrimp.
Preparation time: 15 minutes
Cooking time: 10 minutes

⅓   cup red wine vinegar
1   teaspoon dried basil
1   teaspoon olive oil
½   teaspoon salt
½   teaspoon dried oregano
¼   teaspoon pepper
1   cup uncooked orzo (rice-
      shaped pasta)
2   cups seeded, diced tomato
1   cup frozen green peas, thawed
½   cup finely chopped purple
      onion
¼   cup chopped fresh parsley
1   pound medium shrimp,
      cooked and peeled
Boston lettuce leaves (optional)

1. Combine first 6 ingredients in a large bowl. Stir well; set aside.
2. Cook orzo according to package directions, omitting salt and fat. Drain orzo well.
3. Add orzo, tomato, and next 4 ingredients to vinegar mixture; toss well. Cover and chill. Serve in a lettuce-lined bowl, if desired. Yield: 4 servings (serving size: 1½ cups).

CALORIES 321 (11% from fat); FAT 3.8g (sat 0.6g, mono 1.2g, poly 1.2g); PROTEIN 26g; CARB 45.1g; FIBER 4.7g; CHOL 129mg; IRON 5.3mg; SODIUM 475mg; CALC 89mg

SALMON-AND-POTATO SALAD

This salad can also be made ahead and served chilled.
Preparation time: 15 minutes
Cooking time: 15 minutes

  2 tablespoons water
  ½ teaspoon grated lemon rind
  2 tablespoons fresh lemon juice
  2 tablespoons fat-free mayonnaise
  1 tablespoon capers
  ⅛ teaspoon salt
  ½ teaspoon pepper
  1 (1-pound) skinned salmon fillet
  8 small red potatoes, quartered
  2 (½-inch-thick) slices onion
Vegetable cooking spray
  ½ teaspoon dried dillweed
  ⅓ cup minced celery

1. Combine first 6 ingredients in a small bowl. Stir well; set aside.
2. Sprinkle pepper over salmon. Arrange salmon, potatoes, and onion in a steamer basket coated with cooking spray; sprinkle with dillweed. Place over boiling water. Cover and steam 15 minutes or until potatoes are tender and fish flakes easily when tested with a fork. Break salmon into chunks.
3. Combine salmon, potatoes, onion, and celery in a large bowl. Add mayonnaise mixture; toss gently to coat. Yield: 4 servings (serving size: 1 cup).

CALORIES 270 (30% from fat); FAT 8.9g (sat 1.6g, mono 4.1g, poly 2g); PROTEIN 24.3g; CARB 22.8g; FIBER 2.6g; CHOL 68mg; IRON 2.2mg; SODIUM 405mg; CALC 34mg

A Walk in the Park

Or, how to square your chair with exercise and a great breakfast.

In a recent column, I compared a healthful lifestyle to a nicely balanced chair: When all things are equal, it provides you with a comfortable perspective. The first "leg" of the chair was nutrition. This month, let's talk about exercise.

As the years have gone by, I've come to believe two things about exercise. First, I see it as breakfast for the brain. When you consider that your brain consumes more than 3 liters of oxygen daily, it needs a brisk tonic of fresh air for the day ahead. Second, the best exercise trains your body for what it needs to do. As you develop a personal exercise plan that will last the rest of your life, here are some points to remember.

• **Find an exercise program that matches what you like to do.** Everyone's different, and what works for one may bore another.

• **Consult a certified fitness professional.** This investment in your exercise plan is money well spent. Exercise physiologists and people involved in sports medicine who specialize in helping regular folks develop exercise plans can help you, so don't hesitate to call on them.

• **Stay comfortable . . . and stretch!**

• **Study modern exercise philosophy on strength and flexibility.** There are a number of old military-style calisthenics that have been proven to be not only useless, but also downright harmful. Many new techniques can put your muscles to better use and decrease your risk of injury.

After some reflection, exercise, stretching, and a hot shower, a good breakfast is next. And, as I said, everyone's different: I enjoy a bowl of hot cereal. My wife, Treena, meanwhile, switches back and forth between homemade muesli and her very own Square Eggs.

TREENA'S SQUARE EGGS

Olive oil-flavored vegetable cooking spray
  ⅔ cup egg substitute, divided
  1 slice (1 ounce) reduced-fat Swiss cheese, halved
  ½ teaspoon chipotle pepper sauce or hot sauce, divided
  ¼ teaspoon pepper, divided
  1 teaspoon bottled bacon-flavored chips
  2 teaspoons chopped fresh parsley

1. Place a nonstick skillet coated with cooking spray over medium-high heat until hot. Add ⅓ cup egg substitute, spreading over bottom of skillet (do not stir). Top with ½ slice cheese. Sprinkle with ¼ teaspoon pepper sauce and ⅛ teaspoon pepper. Loosen omelet with a spatula, and fold each side of omelet over the center, making a square. Slide omelet onto a plate. Set aside; keep warm. Repeat procedure with ⅓ cup egg substitute, ½ slice cheese, ¼ teaspoon pepper sauce, and ⅛ teaspoon pepper. Sprinkle each omelet with bacon chips and parsley. Serve immediately. Yield: 2 servings (serving size: 1 omelet).

CALORIES 92 (29% from fat); FAT 3g (sat 1.4g, mono 0.1g, poly 0.1g); PROTEIN 13.4g; CARB 2.2g; FIBER 0.1g; CHOL 9mg; IRON 1.7mg; SODIUM 172mg; CALC 196mg

With the Greatest of Cheese

We asked readers, instead of chefs, to create the recipes for this year's cheese contest. Our three winning cooks found uses for cheese that were light, unexpected, and on the money.

For this year's *Cooking Light* with Wisconsin Cheese Recipe Contest, we asked you, our readers, to create the recipes. And you did, by the wheel-full. When it came to choosing a grand-prize winner and a second-prize winner from our finalists, it was a long and difficult day in our Test Kitchens. Because of the high quality of the final recipes, we decided to honor two runners-up.

SPICY APPLE-GLAZED CHICK 'N' GRITS GORGONZOLA

(pictured on page 129)

I got the idea from a Southern dish called Shrimp and Grits. I love grits, but a lot of people find them bland. So I thought more people would eat grits if I balanced them with complementary flavors. For the contest I wanted to use a unique-flavored cheese, so I decided to try Gorgonzola. The recipe is extremely flavorful, so now people who aren't from the South can enjoy grits.

—Larry Elder, Charlotte, North Carolina
(Grand-Prize Winner)

4 (4-ounce) skinned, boned chicken breast halves
Vegetable cooking spray
¼ cup apple butter
¼ cup spicy brown mustard
¼ teaspoon salt
¼ teaspoon ground red pepper
⅛ teaspoon black pepper
Gorgonzola Cheese Grits
2 tablespoons chopped green onion tops
Fresh oregano (optional)

1. Preheat oven to 350°.
2. Place chicken breast halves between 2 sheets of heavy-duty plastic wrap; flatten to ½-inch thickness using a meat mallet or rolling pin. Place in a baking pan coated with cooking spray. Combine apple butter and next 4 ingredients; brush over chicken. Bake at 350° for 20 minutes. Cut chicken into ½-inch-thick slices.
3. Spoon Gorgonzola Cheese Grits into each of 4 shallow serving bowls. Top with chicken; sprinkle with green onions. Garnish with oregano, if desired. Yield: 4 servings (serving size: 1 cup grits, 1 chicken breast half, and 1½ teaspoons green onions).

CALORIES 371 (30% from fat); FAT 12.4g (sat 6.2g, mono 3.3g, poly 0.9g); PROTEIN 41.8g; CARB 21.5g; FIBER 1g; CHOL 94mg; IRON 6.8mg; SODIUM 1,209mg; CALC 190mg

Gorgonzola Cheese Grits:

2 (14¼-ounce) cans fat-free chicken broth
¾ cup uncooked quick-cooking grits
1 cup (4 ounces) crumbled Gorgonzola cheese
⅓ cup fat-free sour cream
¼ teaspoon ground nutmeg
¼ teaspoon freshly ground pepper

1. Bring broth to a boil in a saucepan; gradually add grits, stirring constantly. Reduce heat to low; cover and simmer 5 minutes or until thick, stirring occasionally. Remove from heat; stir in cheese and remaining ingredients. Yield: 4 cups (serving size 1 cup).

CALORIES 182 (41% from fat); FAT 8.3g (sat 5.3g, mono 2.2g, poly 0.2g); PROTEIN 14.4g; CARB 11.9g; FIBER 0.7g; CHOL 21mg; IRON 5.6mg; SODIUM 795mg; CALC 154mg

POLENTA WITH ROASTED RED PEPPERS AND FONTINA CHEESE

I'm a vegetarian, and invented this recipe from a meat dish that my grandmother used to make for me. My grandmother was a big polenta cooker. The dish was intended for my fiancé who was having a bad day at work. I cook it all the time as it's his favorite. Matter of fact, I'm using the contest prize money to pay for our wedding. The place where we're having the reception has agreed to include the recipe in the wedding menu.

—Sarah A. Soule, Tucson, Arizona
(Second-Place Winner)

3 large red bell peppers
1 (14.5-ounce) can whole tomatoes, undrained and chopped
Vegetable cooking spray
1 (16-ounce) tube polenta, cut crosswise into 12 slices
1¼ cups (5 ounces) shredded fontina cheese
Fresh basil (optional)

1. Preheat broiler. Cut peppers in half lengthwise; discard seeds and membranes. Place pepper halves, skin sides up, on an aluminum foil-lined baking sheet; flatten with hand. Broil 10 minutes or until blackened. Place in a zip-top plastic bag; seal. Let stand 15 minutes. Peel; cut into strips. Set aside.
2. Preheat oven to 350°. Drain tomatoes in sieve over bowl; reserve liquid. Set aside.
3. Place a large skillet over medium-low heat; add chopped tomatoes.

Cook 1 minute. Gradually add tomato liquid; simmer 1 minute. Add pepper strips; simmer 5 minutes. Remove from heat.

4. Spread ¼ cup pepper sauce in bottom of a 13 x 9-inch baking dish coated with cooking spray. Arrange polenta slices over pepper sauce; spread remaining pepper sauce over polenta. Sprinkle with cheese. Bake at 350° for 25 minutes. Garnish with basil, if desired. Yield: 6 servings.

CALORIES 187 (38% from fat); FAT 7.8g (sat 4.6g, mono 2.1g, poly 0.6g); PROTEIN 9.2g; CARB 20.2g; FIBER 3.4g; CHOL 27mg; IRON 2.4mg; SODIUM 622mg; CALC 151mg

CHEESY APPLE PIE IN A GLASS

Why pie in a dish? Because I like parfait-type desserts. I like their appealing look. I got the idea from my grandpa. He always ate a slice of longhorn cheese with the apple pies that my grandmother made. And cheese just goes well with apples. Mascarpone has a sweet taste, which is perfect for desserts.
—Joy Grimsley, Andover, Kansas
(Third-Place Winner)

4 cups peeled, thinly sliced Red Delicious apple (about 2 apples)
⅔ cup apple juice
¼ cup packed brown sugar
3 tablespoons raisins
1 teaspoon ground cinnamon
½ teaspoon ground nutmeg
½ teaspoon ground allspice, divided
1½ teaspoons vanilla extract
¼ teaspoon rum flavoring
3 ounces mascarpone cheese
¾ cup low-fat cinnamon crisp graham cracker crumbs (about 8 crackers), divided
1 cup vanilla fat-free frozen yogurt
Mascarpone cheese (optional)

1. Combine first 6 ingredients and ¼ teaspoon allspice in a medium saucepan. Cook over medium-low heat 20 minutes or until apples are tender and mixture is slightly thick. Remove mixture from heat; let cool. Stir in ¼ teaspoon allspice, vanilla, rum flavoring, and 3 ounces cheese.

2. Spoon ¼ cup mixture into each of 4 parfait glasses; sprinkle each with 1½ tablespoons crumbs. Top each with ¼ cup yogurt, ¼ cup apple mixture, and 1½ tablespoons crumbs. Garnish with additional cheese, if desired. Serve immediately. Yield: 4 servings.

CALORIES 339 (29% from fat); FAT 11.1g (sat 5.5g, mono 3g, poly 0.5g); PROTEIN 4.3g; CARB 57.8g; FIBER 3.8g; CHOL 19mg; IRON 1.2mg; SODIUM 124mg; CALC 144mg

INSPIRED VEGETARIAN

Don't Hold the Flavor

If you're still searching for the perfect veggie burger, then take a seat. We have three full-flavored variations that no one will beef about.

For people giving up or cutting back on meat, the hamburger presents a major stumbling block. Nothing is more American than a big, juicy burger with fries, after all. Unfortunately, we could not find a commercial veggie burger that suited our tastes; the ones we tested just didn't have the requisite flavor and texture. So we set out to develop our own. Now don't expect a Big Mac—what you're going to experience instead is a whole new '90s-style taste extravaganza.

At first glance, the recipes may seem long, but their ingredients are mostly spices. And because a burger wouldn't be a burger without fries on the side, we offer two low-fat variations (hold the grease). So the next time you crave a burger, you don't have to settle for the same old thing. We've got your order, hon: One veggie burger with fries, comin' up!

TEX-MEX BEAN BURGERS WITH TOMATO SALSA

1 cup chopped tomato
½ cup chopped red onion
¼ cup minced fresh cilantro
2 tablespoons seeded, minced jalapeño pepper
2 tablespoons fresh lime juice
2 (16-ounce) cans pinto beans, drained
1 tablespoon plus 1 teaspoon olive oil
⅔ cup minced fresh onion
4 garlic cloves, minced
2 tablespoons ground coriander
1 tablespoon plus 1 teaspoon all-purpose flour
1 tablespoon plus 1 teaspoon ground cumin
¼ teaspoon salt
½ teaspoon pepper
Vegetable cooking spray
¾ cup (3 ounces) shredded reduced-fat Monterey Jack cheese
6 (1½-ounce) hamburger buns

1. Combine first 5 ingredients in a bowl. Stir well; set salsa aside.

2. Place pinto beans in a bowl. Partially mash with a fork; set aside. Heat oil in a medium nonstick skillet over medium-high heat. Add onion and garlic; sauté 3 minutes or until tender. Add coriander, flour, cumin, salt, and pepper; cook, stirring constantly, 1 minute. Add onion mixture to beans, and stir well. Cut 6 (4-inch) squares of wax paper. Divide bean mixture into 6 equal portions, shaping into 3½-inch patties on wax paper squares.

3. Preheat broiler.

4. Invert patties onto a baking sheet coated with cooking spray; remove wax paper squares. Broil patties 4 minutes. Carefully turn patties over, and sprinkle with cheese. Broil 1 additional minute or until cheese melts. Place patties on bottom halves of buns; top each with ¼ cup salsa and top half of bun. Yield: 6 servings.

CALORIES 352 (21% from fat); FAT 8.2g (sat 2.7g, mono 3.2g, poly 1.3g); PROTEIN 16.7g; CARB 54g; FIBER 5g; CHOL 9mg; IRON 4.7mg; SODIUM 576mg; CALC 210mg

VEGETABLE BURGERS WITH INDIAN SEASONINGS

½ cup dried lentils
½ pound peeled, cubed red potatoes
¾ teaspoon salt
½ cup chopped carrot
½ cup chopped cauliflower
½ cup frozen petite green peas
1 tablespoon plus 2 teaspoons vegetable oil, divided
½ cup finely chopped onion
½ teaspoon ground cumin
½ teaspoon peeled, minced fresh gingerroot
¼ teaspoon mustard seeds
⅛ teaspoon ground red pepper
1 garlic clove, minced
1 tablespoon minced fresh cilantro
¼ cup uncooked farina
¼ cup egg substitute
½ cup dry breadcrumbs
3 (6-inch) pita bread rounds, cut in half

1. Combine lentils and potato in a saucepan. Cover with water; bring to a boil. Reduce heat; simmer 20 minutes or until tender. Drain. Combine lentil mixture and salt in a bowl; mash.
2. Arrange carrot, cauliflower, and peas in a steamer basket over boiling water. Cover and steam 3 minutes or until tender.
3. Heat 1 teaspoon oil in a nonstick skillet over medium heat until hot. Add onion; sauté 2 minutes. Add cumin and next 4 ingredients; sauté 1 minute. Remove from heat; stir in cilantro.
4. Add onion mixture, carrot mixture, and farina to lentil mixture; stir gently. With floured hands, divide mixture into 6 equal portions; shape into 4-inch patties. Dip patties in egg substitute; dredge in breadcrumbs. Heat 2 teaspoons oil in skillet over medium heat until hot. Add 3 patties; cook 2 minutes on each side or until browned. Remove from skillet. Repeat procedure with 2 teaspoons oil and 3 patties. Serve in pita bread halves. Yield: 6 servings.

CALORIES 255 (18% from fat); FAT 5.1g (sat 0.9g, mono 1.5g, poly 2.2g); PROTEIN 10.9g; CARB 41.5g; FIBER 4.2g; CHOL 1mg; IRON 5.7mg; SODIUM 518mg; CALC 94mg

TABBOULEH BURGERS

1 cup peeled, seeded, chopped cucumber
½ cup plain low-fat yogurt
1 tablespoon chopped fresh dillweed
1 tablespoon rice vinegar
⅛ teaspoon salt
¾ cup uncooked bulgur
½ cup boiling water
2 tablespoons fresh lemon juice
1 tablespoon plus 1 teaspoon olive oil, divided
¼ cup finely chopped green onions
2 tablespoons chopped pistachios
2 teaspoons ground cumin
2 teaspoons ground coriander
¼ teaspoon salt
¼ teaspoon ground red pepper
2 garlic cloves, minced
¼ cup chopped fresh parsley
1 (15-ounce) can chickpeas (garbanzo beans), drained
2 tablespoons all-purpose flour
2 large egg whites, lightly beaten
Vegetable cooking spray
6 (1½-ounce) hamburger buns

1. Combine first 5 ingredients in a small bowl; cover and chill.
2. Combine bulgur, boiling water, and lemon juice in a bowl. Let stand 30 minutes or until liquid is absorbed.
3. Heat 2 teaspoons oil in a nonstick skillet over medium heat. Add green onions and next 6 ingredients; sauté 1 minute or until onions are tender. Remove from heat; stir in parsley.
4. Place chickpeas in a food processor; process until ground. Add chickpeas and green onion mixture to bulgur mixture; toss well. Add flour and egg whites; stir well. Divide mixture into 6 equal portions; shape into 3-inch patties.
5. Heat 2 teaspoons oil in skillet coated with cooking spray. Place over medium heat until hot. Add patties; cook 3 minutes on each side or until browned. Place patties on bottom halves of buns; top each with ¼ cup cucumber sauce and top half of bun. Yield: 6 servings.

CALORIES 341 (21% from fat); FAT 8g (sat 0.9g, mono 3.7g, poly 7.9g); PROTEIN 13.7g; CARB 55.9g; FIBER 5.9g; CHOL 1mg; IRON 3.8mg; SODIUM 414mg; CALC 120mg

SWEET POTATO SHOESTRING FRIES

3 tablespoons orange juice
2 teaspoons vegetable oil
½ teaspoon ground ginger
¼ teaspoon salt
⅛ teaspoon ground red pepper
2 large sweet potatoes, peeled and cut into ⅛-inch strips (about 1½ pounds)
Vegetable cooking spray

1. Preheat oven to 400°.
2. Combine first 5 ingredients in a small saucepan; bring to a boil. Reduce heat; simmer 2 minutes or until slightly thick. Remove from heat; let cool.
3. Combine juice mixture and potato strips in a large bowl; toss well. Remove potato from bowl; discard juice mixture. Arrange potato strips in a single layer on a baking sheet coated with cooking spray. Bake at 400° for 30 minutes or until edges are crisp. Yield: 4 servings.

CALORIES 194 (8% from fat); FAT 1.8g (sat 0.3g, mono 0.4g, poly 0.8g); PROTEIN 2.9g; CARB 42.1g; FIBER 5.1g; CHOL 0mg; IRON 1mg; SODIUM 169mg; CALC 38mg

STEAK FRIES

5 medium-size red potatoes (about 1¾ pounds)
1 tablespoon olive oil
¼ teaspoon salt
¼ teaspoon pepper
⅛ teaspoon ground nutmeg
1 garlic clove, crushed

1. Preheat oven to 450°.
2. Peel potatoes; cut each potato lengthwise into 6 wedges. Pat potato wedges dry with paper towels; place in an 11 x 7-inch baking dish. Drizzle oil over potato. Sprinkle with salt, pepper, nutmeg, and garlic; toss well. Bake at 450° for 30 minutes or until tender, stirring occasionally. Yield: 6 servings (serving size: 5 wedges).

CALORIES 110 (20% from fat); FAT 2.4g (sat 0.5g, mono 0.7g, poly 1.1g); PROTEIN 2.4g; CARB 20.5g; FIBER 1.8g; CHOL 0mg; IRON 0.9mg; SODIUM 105mg; CALC 9mg

JUNE

Solving the Mysteries of the Pyramid

We've put the Food Guide Pyramid into action with these one-dish meals that you can create in no time.

Ever since the U.S. Department of Agriculture unveiled it in 1992, the Food Guide Pyramid has awed lots of people—particularly when they've tried to apply it to everyday eating. Once you take a closer look, though, you'll realize it's actually a good way to remember what makes for a smart diet.

The pyramid's foundation shows what foods you should eat the most of: breads, cereals, rice, and pasta—starchy foods that are good sources of complex carbohydrates. As the pyramid grows smaller, so do the numbers of servings of foods such as meats, fats, and sugars.

To help you apply that logic, we've constructed recipes that are practically scale models of the USDA pyramid. And talk about easy! These meals can be created in no time and can be served at room temperature or chilled. So try constructing your own pyramid from these blueprints. It may not give you immortality, but it will take the mystery out of how to eat your best.

ROTINI-VEGETABLE SALAD WITH PESTO DRESSING

1	large garlic clove, peeled
1	cup packed basil leaves
2	tablespoons grated fresh Parmesan cheese
¼	teaspoon salt
¼	teaspoon pepper
2	tablespoons water
2	tablespoons olive oil
3	cups cooked rotini (about 2 cups uncooked corkscrew pasta)
1½	cups diced zucchini
1½	cups halved cherry tomatoes
1	(15-ounce) can cannellini beans or other white beans, rinsed and drained

Fresh basil sprigs (optional)

1. Drop garlic through food chute with food processor on, and process until minced. Add basil leaves, cheese, salt, and pepper; process until finely minced. With food processor on, slowly pour water and oil through food chute; process until mixture is well-blended.
2. Combine rotini and next 3 ingredients in a large bowl; toss well. Add pesto mixture, tossing gently to coat. Garnish with basil sprigs, if desired. Yield: 4 servings (serving size: 1¾ cups).

CALORIES 365 (26% from fat); FAT 10.6g (sat 1.9g, mono 5.8g, poly 1.9g); PROTEIN 14.7g; CARB 54.9g; FIBER 6.2g; CHOL 2mg; IRON 4.6mg; SODIUM 359mg; CALC 134mg

PANZANELLA WITH BEANS

(pictured on page 167)

We've added garbanzo beans and feta cheese to this classic Italian salad. Once you add the bread cubes, serve immediately so that they'll be crispy.

3	tablespoons red wine vinegar
1½	tablespoons extra-virgin olive oil
¼	teaspoon salt
¼	teaspoon coarsely ground pepper
1	garlic clove, minced
2	cups chopped tomato (about 1 pound)
1	cup peeled, seeded, chopped cucumber
½	cup chopped green bell pepper
¼	cup chopped red onion
1	(15-ounce) can no-salt-added chickpeas (garbanzo beans), drained
4	cups (½-inch) sourdough bread cubes, toasted
½	cup chopped fresh parsley
¼	cup chopped fresh basil
½	cup crumbled feta cheese with basil and tomato

1. Combine first 5 ingredients in a large bowl. Add tomato and next 4 ingredients; toss to coat. Marinate at room temperature for up to 2 hours.
2. Add bread, parsley, and basil; toss. Sprinkle with cheese; serve immediately. Yield: 4 servings (serving size: 2 cups salad and 2 tablespoons feta cheese).

CALORIES 385 (27% from fat); FAT 11.7g (sat 3.3g, mono 5.2g, poly 2g); PROTEIN 15.9g; CARB 57g; FIBER 6.6g; CHOL 13mg; IRON 5.5mg; SODIUM 641mg; CALC 208mg

WINE PICKS

- *Boutari Red Naoussa 1993 (Greek red), $7.49*
- *Fontana Candida Frascati Superiore 1993 (Italian white), $9*
- *Murphy-Goode Alexander Valley Murphy Ranches Merlot 1993 (California red), $16*

BLACK BEAN-AND-BARLEY SALSA SALAD

2 cups water
1 cup uncooked quick-cooking barley
1 cup fresh or frozen whole-kernel corn
1 cup chopped tomato
½ cup minced fresh cilantro
⅓ cup diced red bell pepper
¼ cup finely chopped red onion
¼ cup minced green onions
1 (15-ounce) can no-salt-added black beans, rinsed and drained
¼ cup fresh lemon juice
1 teaspoon jalapeño hot sauce
1 teaspoon olive oil
¼ teaspoon salt
¼ teaspoon ground cumin
¼ teaspoon pepper

1. Bring 2 cups water to a boil in a medium saucepan. Add barley; cover, reduce heat, and simmer 8 minutes. Add corn (do not stir), and cover. Cook 6 minutes or until barley is tender. Remove barley mixture from heat; let stand, covered, 5 minutes.
2. Combine barley mixture, tomato, and next 5 ingredients in a large bowl. Combine lemon juice and remaining 5 ingredients. Pour lemon dressing over salad; toss gently to coat. Yield: 4 servings (serving size: 1½ cups).

CALORIES 330 (7% from fat); FAT 2.5g (sat 0.4g, mono 1g, poly 0.7g); PROTEIN 13g; CARB 68.5g; FIBER 13.2g; CHOL 0mg; IRON 3.9mg; SODIUM 176mg; CALC 62mg

FRUIT-AND-BULGUR SALAD

3 cups water
½ cup yellow split peas
¾ cup uncooked bulgur or cracked wheat
¾ cup boiling water
1 cup chopped Red Delicious apple
¼ cup dried cranberries
¼ cup pitted, chopped dates
¼ cup plain low-fat yogurt
2 tablespoons lemon juice
¼ teaspoon salt
¼ teaspoon curry powder
1 (11-ounce) can mandarin oranges in light syrup, drained
¼ cup plus 1 tablespoon chopped almonds, toasted

1. Bring 3 cups water and split peas to a boil in a saucepan. Reduce heat; cook, uncovered, 30 minutes or just until split peas are tender. Drain well.
2. Combine bulgur and ¾ cup boiling water in a large bowl. Cover and let stand 30 minutes. Add peas, apple, cranberries, and dates; stir well.
3. Combine yogurt and next 3 ingredients; add to bulgur mixture, stirring well. Gently stir in oranges. Top salad with toasted almonds. Yield: 5 servings (serving size: 1 cup salad and 1 tablespoon almonds).

CALORIES 275 (13% from fat); FAT 4.1g (sat 0.6g, mono 2.2g, poly 1g); PROTEIN 10.6g; CARB 53.3g; FIBER 8.4g; CHOL 1mg; IRON 2.6mg; SODIUM 140mg; CALC 84mg

MENU SUGGESTION

LEMONY SHRIMP-AND-COUSCOUS SALAD

Italian breadsticks*

Chocolate almond biscotti

*Roll out refrigerated breadstick dough; coat with cooking spray. Brush with 1 teaspoon olive oil; sprinkle with 2 teaspoons Italian seasoning. Shape and bake as directed.

LEMONY SHRIMP-AND-COUSCOUS SALAD

Although we call for raw, fresh shrimp, you can buy it cooked. Just skip the cooking step; use 1½ cups boiling water for the couscous.

1½ cups water
1 pound medium-size shrimp, peeled and deveined
1 cup uncooked couscous
1½ cups diced plum tomatoes
¼ cup thinly sliced green onions
¼ cup chopped fresh basil
¼ cup low-salt chicken broth
3 tablespoons fresh lemon juice
1 tablespoon olive oil
¼ teaspoon salt
¼ teaspoon pepper
½ cup grated fresh Parmesan cheese

1. Bring water to a boil in a medium saucepan. Add shrimp; cook 3 minutes. Drain shrimp in a colander over a bowl, reserving cooking liquid. Add couscous to reserved cooking liquid. Cover and let stand 5 minutes. Fluff with a fork.
2. Combine couscous, shrimp, tomatoes, green onions, and basil in a large bowl. Combine broth and next 4 ingredients. Pour dressing over salad; toss gently to coat. Sprinkle with cheese. Yield: 4 servings (serving size: 1 cup salad and 2 tablespoons cheese).

CALORIES 186 (26% from fat); FAT 5.3g (sat 1.8g, mono 2.2g, poly 0.6g); PROTEIN 16.2g; CARB 18.9g; FIBER 1.7g; CHOL 79mg; IRON 2.2mg; SODIUM 301mg; CALC 135mg

THE RIDDLE OF THE SERVING SIZE

When people consider the Food Guide Pyramid, their eyes sometimes glaze over at the thought of six to 11 servings of grains a day. But don't let the number of servings intimidate you. One serving can be quite reasonable, as shown at right.

A serving of grains equals:
- ½ cup cooked barley, bulgur, couscous, grits, oatmeal, pasta, polenta, quinoa, or rice
- 1 ounce dry cereal, such as 1 cup cornflakes
- 1 slice bread
- 1 tortilla
- ½ hamburger bun
- ½ bagel
- ½ English muffin

SOUTHWESTERN HAM-AND-RICE SALAD

This dish is like a deli salad. It calls for pantry staples, making it a quick-and-easy choice for weeknight meals.

    ¼ cup light mayonnaise
    1 tablespoon fresh lime juice
    ½ teaspoon chili powder
    ½ teaspoon dried oregano
    ¼ teaspoon ground cumin
    ⅛ teaspoon salt
    3 cups cooked long-grain
         brown rice
    1¼ cups diced lean ham
         (about 4 ounces)
    ½ cup diced celery
    ¼ cup diced red onion
    3 tablespoons chopped ripe olives

1. Combine first 6 ingredients in a small bowl. Combine rice and remaining 4 ingredients in a large bowl; stir in mayonnaise mixture. Yield: 4 servings (serving size: 1½ cups).

CALORIES 263 (26% from fat); FAT 7.6g (sat 1.6g, mono 1.7g, poly 3.4g); PROTEIN 10g; CARB 39g; FIBER 3.4g; CHOL 18mg; IRON 1.3mg; SODIUM 669mg; CALC 36mg

MEDITERRANEAN CHICKEN-AND-RICE SALAD

    3 tablespoons red wine vinegar
    1½ tablespoons extra-virgin olive
         oil
    ¼ teaspoon coarsely ground pepper
    1 garlic clove, minced
    3 cups cooked long-grain rice
    1½ cups diced cooked chicken
         breast (about 6 ounces)
    ½ cup drained diced bottled
         roasted red bell peppers
    ¼ cup medium pitted ripe olives,
         drained and halved
    ¼ cup chopped fresh chives
    ¼ cup chopped fresh basil
    ¼ cup chopped fresh oregano
    1 (14-ounce) can quartered
         artichoke hearts, drained

1. Combine first 4 ingredients in a small bowl. Set dressing aside.

2. Combine rice and remaining 7 ingredients in a large bowl. Add dressing; stir until well-blended. Yield: 4 servings (serving size: 2 cups).

CALORIES 360 (24% from fat); FAT 9.4g (sat 1.6g, mono 5.7g, poly 1.4g); PROTEIN 20.5g; CARB 49.9g; FIBER 4.1g; CHOL 36mg; IRON 5.6mg; SODIUM 421mg; CALC 156mg

FAST FOOD

No Bones about It

If it weren't for boned chicken breasts, we'd still be in the dark ages when it comes to quick-and-easy dinners. Trouble is, you can get pretty tired of the same old recipes. So we went to work to bring you some innovative ways to prepare them. These recipes do share some common themes, though: All of the chicken breasts are cooked in a skillet, served with a glaze, and prepared in no more than 30 minutes. And you'll find that spicy rubs, herbs, and citrus fruits perk up a boneless chicken breast.

So no matter how blasé your family has become toward boned chicken breasts, they'll love these, and about that there'll be no bones of contention.

CHICKEN WITH LEMON-CAPER SAUCE

(pictured on page 167)

Preparation time: 5 minutes
Cooking time: 15 minutes

    ¼ teaspoon salt, divided
    ¼ teaspoon pepper, divided
    4 (4-ounce) skinned, boned
         chicken breast halves
    1 tablespoon olive oil
    Vegetable cooking spray
    ⅓ cup extra-dry vermouth
    3 tablespoons fresh lemon juice
    1½ tablespoons capers
    1 tablespoon chopped fresh
         parsley

1. Sprinkle ⅛ teaspoon salt and ⅛ teaspoon pepper over chicken. Heat oil in a large nonstick skillet coated with cooking spray over medium-high heat. Add chicken; cook 6 minutes on each side or until done. Remove from skillet. Set aside; keep warm.

2. Add ⅛ teaspoon salt, ⅛ teaspoon pepper, vermouth, lemon juice, and capers to skillet, scraping skillet to loosen browned bits. Cook until reduced to ¼ cup (about 2 minutes). Stir in parsley. Spoon sauce over chicken. Yield: 4 servings.

CALORIES 163 (27% from fat); FAT 4.8g (sat 0.8g, mono 2.8g, poly 0.6g); PROTEIN 26.5g; CARB 2.1g; FIBER 0.1g; CHOL 66mg; IRON 1mg; SODIUM 474mg; CALC 17mg

HOT LICKS CHICKEN

The slightly sweet orange glaze tames some of the heat in the spicy rub. Serve this dish with roasted potato wedges and fresh broiled pineapple chunks.

Preparation time: 12 minutes
Cooking time: 13 minutes

    2 teaspoons poultry seasoning
    ½ teaspoon salt
    ½ teaspoon ground cumin
    ½ teaspoon ground coriander
    ¼ teaspoon ground allspice
    ¼ teaspoon ground red pepper
    ¼ teaspoon black pepper
    4 (4-ounce) skinned, boned
         chicken breast halves
    1 tablespoon olive oil
    Vegetable cooking spray
    ¼ cup water
    ¼ cup dry white wine
    1 tablespoon lemon juice
    ⅛ teaspoon salt
    1 tablespoon orange marmalade

1. Combine first 7 ingredients in a small bowl; stir well. Rub chicken with spice mixture; let stand 5 minutes.
2. Heat oil in a nonstick skillet coated with cooking spray over medium-high heat. Add chicken; cook 1 minute on each side or until lightly browned. Add water and wine to skillet; cover, reduce heat, and simmer 6 minutes or until

chicken is done. Remove chicken from skillet. Set aside; keep warm. Add lemon juice and ⅛ teaspoon salt to skillet. Bring to a boil; cook 4 minutes or until reduced to 3 tablespoons. Remove from heat; stir in marmalade. Spoon sauce over chicken. Yield: 4 servings.

CALORIES 174 (26% from fat); FAT 5.1g (sat 0.9g, mono 2.9g, poly 0.6g); PROTEIN 26.4g; CARB 4.6g; FIBER 0.2g; CHOL 66mg; IRON 1.3mg; SODIUM 445mg; CALC 27mg

HERBED CHICKEN PICCATA

Preparation time: 15 minutes
Cooking time: 12 minutes

    2 tablespoons dry breadcrumbs
    1 teaspoon dried basil
    1 teaspoon grated lemon rind
    ⅛ teaspoon pepper
    2 garlic cloves, minced
    4 (4-ounce) skinned, boned
        chicken breast halves
    Vegetable cooking spray
    1 teaspoon margarine
    8 thin lemon slices
    ¼ cup low-salt chicken broth
    2 tablespoons chopped fresh
        parsley
    2 tablespoons lemon juice

1. Combine first 5 ingredients in a shallow dish; set aside.
2. Place chicken between 2 sheets of heavy-duty plastic wrap; flatten to ¼-inch thickness, using a meat mallet or rolling pin. Lightly coat both sides of chicken breasts with cooking spray; dredge in breadcrumb mixture.
3. Melt margarine in a large nonstick skillet coated with cooking spray over medium-high heat. Add chicken; cook 4 minutes on each side or until done. Remove chicken from skillet. Set aside; keep warm. Add lemon slices to skillet; sauté 30 seconds. Add broth, parsley, and lemon juice; cook 1 minute. Spoon sauce over chicken. Yield: 4 servings.

CALORIES 160 (16% from fat); FAT 2.9g (sat 0.6g, mono 0.8g, poly 0.7g); PROTEIN 27.3g; CARB 6.9g; FIBER 0.4g; CHOL 66mg; IRON 1.4mg; SODIUM 115mg; CALC 46mg

---

MENU SUGGESTION

ORANGE-GINGER
CHICKEN

Lo mein noodles*

Asian cucumber salad*

*Slice chicken; arrange over cooked lo mein noodles. Sprinkle with chopped green onions.
*Combine ⅓ cup rice vinegar, 1 teaspoon sugar, ⅛ teaspoon red pepper flakes, and 1 tablespoon chopped cilantro; pour over 2 sliced cucumbers.

ORANGE-GINGER CHICKEN

Preparation time: 5 minutes
Cooking time: 15 minutes

    1 teaspoon dark sesame oil
    ½ teaspoon chili oil
    4 (4-ounce) skinned, boned
        chicken breast halves
    ½ cup orange marmalade
    3 tablespoons low-sodium soy
        sauce
    1 tablespoon peeled, minced
        fresh gingerroot
    1 tablespoon water
    2 garlic cloves, minced

1. Heat oils in a nonstick skillet over medium heat. Add chicken; cook 6 minutes on each side or until chicken is done. Add marmalade and remaining ingredients; cook 2 minutes or until thick and bubbly. Remove from heat. Yield: 4 servings.

CALORIES 247 (11% from fat); FAT 3.1g (sat 0.6g, mono 1.2g, poly 0.9g); PROTEIN 27.1g; CARB 28.3g; FIBER 0g; CHOL 66mg; IRON 1.2mg; SODIUM 547mg; CALC 33mg

---

The Shoelaces of Life

Feeling all tied up in knots? Pull up Kerr's chair for some solutions.

I don't know about you, but my life's pace seems to quicken every year. Sometimes I feel like a centipede wearing shoes—so many shoelaces, so little time.

Over the past few months, I've ruminated with you about what constitutes a well-balanced lifestyle. My metaphor for it has been a comfortable, sturdy chair, and so far, we've talked about the legs of food and exercise. Now let's consider a third chair leg: reflection. Some might call it stress management, but it's broader than that. We need ways to slow down, turn down the volume, and quietly reflect.

Perhaps these three suggestions can help you to balance your life's "chair."

1. Organize your workday so that more time—perhaps an hour—can be spent tying up loose ends, or letting go of things that aren't working.

2. Go to bed an hour earlier and rise an hour earlier to allow time for quiet reflection. The night before, set out tea or coffee, muffins, and marmalade as a comforting eye-opener.

3. Start a journal of what happens to you and how you feel about it. During your daily quiet time, jot down thoughts, review the previous day's entry, and make a special note of what you did with your feelings.

Now, here is a recipe (on page 156) I invented for my wife, Treena, who eats quite healthfully but still loves the rich, creamy taste of pasta dishes like this. Although I didn't invent it during my morning quiet time, it certainly deserves reflection!

CHICKEN ANTONINE CARÊME WITH PASTA

1 cup plain fat-free yogurt
1 (16-ounce) can one-third-less
    sodium chicken broth
½ teaspoon grated lemon rind
6 black peppercorns
2 whole cloves
1 bay leaf
4 (4-ounce) skinned, boned
    chicken breast halves
¼ teaspoon salt
¼ teaspoon pepper, divided
1 teaspoon olive oil
2 cups (¼-inch-thick) diagonally
    sliced celery
1 tablespoon cornstarch
2 tablespoons water
2 tablespoons fresh lemon juice
4 cups hot cooked angel hair
    (about 8 ounces uncooked
    pasta)
¼ cup grated fresh Parmesan
    cheese, divided
¼ cup chopped fresh parsley,
    divided

1. Place a colander in a medium bowl. Line colander with 4 layers of cheesecloth, extending cheesecloth over outside edges. Spoon yogurt into colander. Cover loosely with plastic wrap; refrigerate 12 hours. Spoon yogurt cheese into a bowl; discard liquid. Cover and refrigerate.
2. Combine broth and next 4 ingredients in a saucepan; bring to a boil. Reduce heat, and simmer, uncovered, until mixture is reduced to 1 cup (about 10 minutes). Strain mixture through a sieve over a bowl; discard solids. Set broth aside.
3. Sprinkle chicken with salt and ⅛ teaspoon pepper. Heat oil in a large nonstick skillet over medium-high heat. Place chicken in skillet; cook 3 minutes or until lightly browned. Add celery; turn chicken breasts over, nestling them into celery. Cover, reduce heat, and cook 5 minutes. Remove chicken and celery from skillet. Cut chicken into 1-inch pieces. Set chicken and celery aside; keep warm.
4. Add broth to skillet; cook over medium heat, scraping skillet to loosen browned bits. Combine cornstarch and water; stir into broth, and cook 30 seconds. Gradually add broth mixture to yogurt cheese, stirring constantly with a whisk. Stir in lemon juice.
5. Place hot pasta in a large bowl. Pour yogurt sauce over pasta. Add chicken and celery; toss gently to coat. Stir in 3 tablespoons Parmesan cheese, 3 tablespoons parsley, and ⅛ teaspoon pepper. Divide pasta mixture evenly among 4 plates. Sprinkle each serving with 1 tablespoon Parmesan cheese and 1 tablespoon parsley. Yield: 4 servings (serving size: 1¾ cups).

CALORIES 411 (12% from fat); FAT 5.4g (sat 1.9g, mono 1.9g, poly 0.9g); PROTEIN 38.5g; CARB 48g; FIBER 3.4g; CHOL 71mg; IRON 3.3mg; SODIUM 412mg; CALC 207mg

---

A LIGHT GUIDE TO ENJOYABLE EATING

Boosting the pleasure of eating may sound like an invitation to an around-the-clock pig-out, but food-friendly nutritionists say quite the opposite is true. Here are some secrets for indulging without overdoing.

• **THINK LEFTOVERS.** You can always have more of a good thing later. If you like what you're eating, save the rest and eat it tomorrow.
• **CHECK YOUR FUEL GAUGE.** If you pay attention to your stomach's signals, you'll know when to put your fork down.
• **EAT SENSUALLY.** You can make mealtimes more pleasurable by feeding all the senses. Buy a pretty little bunch of flowers, light a votive candle, and splurge on fresh herbs.
• **DON'T STARVE.** If you get too busy and forget to eat, you're more likely to wolf down whatever's handy instead of savoring a meal that you really like.
• **TAKE IT EASY.** Part of the enjoyment process is slowing down and finding the fun in eating—tasting different foods, experiencing the flavors, appreciating the social aspects.

The Science of Light

With only the atom of an idea, microbiologist Raji Jallepalli was able to open an India-inspired restaurant featuring light cuisine.

Before she became a master of fusion cuisine, chef Raji Jallepalli was a microbiologist. While dining at a restaurant in France in the early 1980s, her future was suddenly magnified before her, as if on a glass slide. "I remember thinking, 'This food could stand some lightening up,'" she says. "I also thought some assertive Indian flavors and bouquets would do it wonders." In 1989, Jallepalli traded in her lab coat for a chef's jacket, opening a restaurant in Memphis, Tennessee. Called Raji, it features healthful French-Indian fusion.

Her cuisine combines French techniques with the freshness that's associated with California cooking. To this culinary blend she adds exotic Indian spices such as fenugreek, cardamom, sandalwood, and cloves. But she adds them carefully. "Traditional Indian cooking uses spices by the handfuls," she says. "I use spices very delicately and very sparingly, more as perfumes. My food is complex in flavor, but it's not complicated."

Tempering and toasting spices in heavy nonstick pans "liberates" the flavor, or essence, locked within them, Jallepalli explains. "The range of flavors is extraordinary—light and perfumy; strong, dark, and smoky." She then uses coffee grinders, one marked "sweet" and one "hot," to grind the spices needed for her dishes. Plus she uses very little oil or butter and no cream in her cooking.

CRUSTILLANT OF CRAB WITH BLACKBERRY CHUTNEY

Fennel fronds are the bright green, feathery tops of fresh fennel.

- 1 teaspoon vegetable oil
- ¼ teaspoon mustard seeds
- ¼ teaspoon cumin seeds
- 1½ cups blackberries
- Dash of ground turmeric
- Dash of salt
- 1¼ cups (6 ounces) lump crabmeat, shell pieces removed
- 2 ounces goat cheese
- 1 teaspoon chopped fennel fronds
- 1 (16-ounce) package frozen phyllo dough, thawed
- Butter-flavored vegetable cooking spray
- Fennel fronds (optional)

1. Preheat oven to 500°.
2. Heat oil in a medium nonstick skillet over medium-high heat. Add seeds; sauté 30 seconds or until seeds begin to pop. Add blackberries, turmeric, and salt. Reduce heat; sauté 2 minutes or until berries are soft. Remove from heat; set aside.
3. Combine crabmeat, goat cheese, and chopped fennel fronds; shape mixture into 8 (1½-inch) balls. Unroll phyllo dough; remove parchment paper. Reroll phyllo. Cut about one-fourth of phyllo roll crosswise into very thin slices to yield 2 cups (it should look like shredded cabbage). Reserve remaining phyllo for another use; store in a zip-top plastic bag in refrigerator. Fluff phyllo with fingers to separate strands. Press each crab ball into phyllo; roll until coated. Gently place crab balls on a baking sheet coated with cooking spray. Spray each ball with cooking spray.
4. Bake at 500° for 3 minutes or until phyllo is golden. Serve with blackberry chutney. Garnish with fennel fronds, if desired. Yield: 4 servings (serving size: 2 crustillants and ⅓ cup chutney).

CALORIES 211 (32% from fat); FAT 7.5g (sat 2.8g, mono 1.7g, poly 2.4g); PROTEIN 13g; CARB 22.5g; FIBER 4g; CHOL 55mg; IRON 1.8mg; SODIUM 413mg; CALC 137mg

Put on a Healthy Face

We've picked summer's most nutrient-packed fruits, then created simple dessert recipes to show them off.

Even though there are no forbidden fruits, most people are not taking advantage of nature's dessert. The National Cancer Institute estimates that only one in three adults and one in five children get the recommended five servings of fruits and vegetables every day. There's no need to feel guilty or worried, though, because we're here to help you out. Setting out to determine which are summer's most nutrition-packed fruits, we came up with some unexpected winners.

Once we finished our list, we used the top five to create light desserts that require no cooking. This way, you can preserve nutrients and stay cool on a hot summer's night. Too, we kept the ingredient lists short because fresh fruit is so flavorful that it doesn't need a lot of embellishment. But as simple as these desserts are, they're special enough to serve to company. And if your kids want only chocolate for dessert, just serve our Strawberry-Apricot Caramel Sundae. We think they'll come around.

BRANDIED SUMMER FRUIT

This recipe uses all five of what we found to be summer's best-for-you fruits.

- 1½ cups sliced apricots
- 1 cup sliced strawberries
- 1 cup blackberries
- 1 cup peeled, cubed cantaloupe
- ½ cup raspberries
- ¼ cup apple juice
- ¼ cup brandy
- 2 tablespoons sugar
- Mint leaves (optional)

1. Combine first 8 ingredients in a medium bowl, and toss gently. Cover and chill 2 hours, stirring occasionally. Garnish fruit with mint leaves, if desired. Yield: 4 servings (serving size: 1 cup).

CALORIES 142 (4% from fat); FAT 0.7g (sat 0.1g, mono 0.1g, poly 0.3g); PROTEIN 1.6g; CARB 26.2g; FIBER 6.3g; CHOL 0mg; IRON 0.9mg; SODIUM 5mg; CALC 33mg

CANTALOUPE-BANANA SLUSH

- 2 cups coarsely chopped cantaloupe
- 2 cups sliced ripe banana (about 2 medium)
- 2 cups pineapple-orange-banana juice
- 1 tablespoon lime juice
- 1 tablespoon sugar

1. Arrange chopped cantaloupe and sliced banana in a single layer on a baking sheet; freeze until firm. Place frozen fruit in a food processor, and process until chunky. With processor on, slowly add pineapple-orange-banana juice, lime juice, and sugar; process until smooth. Serve immediately. Yield: 5 servings (serving size: 1 cup).

CALORIES 140 (3% from fat); FAT 0.5g (sat 0.2g, mono 0.1g, poly 0.1g); PROTEIN 2g; CARB 33.8g; FIBER 2.5g; CHOL 0mg; IRON 0.3mg; SODIUM 14mg; CALC 11mg

The recommendation is that you eat five servings of fruits and vegetables a day. Why? Research is focusing on substances such as vitamin C, beta carotene, and phytochemicals that can help prevent a variety of diseases. (What counts as one serving, by the way, is a medium piece of fruit or ½ cup of cut-up fruit. And fruit's benefits seem to be greatest when you eat the whole fruit rather than drink a glass of juice.)

APRICOTS   Rich in beta carotene, a potent antioxidant. The riper the fruit, the higher the beta carotene content. Apricots are high in soluble fiber, which works to help lower blood-cholesterol levels, and are a source of vitamin C and potassium. The highest vitamin C content is found next to the skin, so don't peel.

Shopping tips: Choose fruit that is orange-gold, smells sweet, and yields to soft pressure. Hard fruit tinged with green won't ripen fully.

Storage: Store-bought apricots usually need ripening, so place them in a paper bag at room temperature away from heat or direct sun. Adding a banana to the bag will hasten the process. Refrigerate once ripe. Don't rinse until ready to use.

BLACKBERRIES   Highest in fiber of all the berries. One cup of blackberries packs 40% more fiber than a bowl of shredded-wheat cereal. In addition, they contain flavonoids and are a good source of vitamin C.

Shopping tip: The blacker the berry, the riper and sweeter the fruit.

Storage: Refrigerate and use within two days. Don't rinse until just before use.

CANTALOUPE   The most nutritious of melons. One cup of cantaloupe contains 74 times the vitamin A of honeydew melon, more beta carotene than a small spinach salad, and almost as much vitamin C as an orange.

Shopping tips: Skip the thumping and shaking; look for sweet-smelling melons that have a thick netting and a golden (not green) undertone. The stem end should have a small indentation; a small crack is a sign of sweetness, but avoid fruit with mold. The blossom end should be slightly soft.

Storage: Melons don't ripen off the vine, but they do get juicier at room temperature. So leave them on the counter a few days, then refrigerate whole to preserve vitamin C. Rinse the exterior prior to cutting.

RASPBERRIES   The most expensive and fragile of all the berries, but also abundant in vitamin C and fiber. One cup of raspberries delivers half of the recommended daily dose of vitamin C and more fiber than two tablespoons of wheat bran. They're also a good source of tumor-fighting ellagic acid and lutein, a carotenoid-like beta carotene.

Shopping tip: Look for firm red berries that haven't leaked through the container bottom.

Storage: Refrigerate and use ASAP. Raspberries can turn mushy quickly.

STRAWBERRIES   Loaded with vitamin C. One cup of strawberries provides 140% of the Daily Value for vitamin C and more fiber than two slices of whole wheat bread. Strawberries also contain some potassium and are high in ellagic acid and flavonoids, phytochemicals which appear to deactivate potential carcinogens.

Shopping tips: Strawberries are grown in all 50 states, so buy local berries in season for the best flavor. Look for bright red berries with fresh, green caps. Berries don't ripen off the vine; white tips will stay hard and sour.

Storage: Remove overripe berries from the container, then refrigerate. Leave the stem caps attached until after rinsing so berries don't get waterlogged.

MELON-AND-RASPBERRY COMPOTE

    3 cups peeled, cubed cantaloupe
    1½ cups fresh raspberries
    ½ cup apple juice
    3 tablespoons fresh lime juice
    3 tablespoons honey
    Lime slices (optional)

1. Combine first 5 ingredients in a medium bowl, and toss gently. Cover and chill. Garnish compote with lime slices, if desired. Yield: 6 servings (serving size: ¾ cup).

CALORIES 87 (4% from fat); FAT 0.4g (sat 0.1g, mono 0.1g, poly 0.1g); PROTEIN 1.1g; CARB 22.1g; FIBER 3.3g; CHOL 0mg; IRON 0.5mg; SODIUM 8mg; CALC 18mg

MINT-AND-HONEY FRUIT CUP

    2 cups quartered strawberries
    1½ cups sliced apricots (about
       ½ pound)
    3 tablespoons honey
    1 tablespoon minced fresh mint

1. Combine all ingredients in a bowl; stir gently. Cover and chill. Yield: 4 servings (serving size: ¾ cup).

CALORIES 96 (4% from fat); FAT 0.5g (sat 0g, mono 0g, poly 0.3g); PROTEIN 1.1g; CARB 24.1g; FIBER 3g; CHOL 0mg; IRON 0.6mg; SODIUM 2mg; CALC 19mg

PEACH-AND-BLACKBERRY COMPOTE

    3 tablespoons honey
    3 tablespoons fresh lime juice
    1 teaspoon grated lime rind
    2 cups peeled, sliced peaches
    1 cup fresh blackberries

1. Combine first 3 ingredients in a bowl; stir well. Add peaches and blackberries; toss gently to coat. Cover and chill at least 1 hour. Yield: 4 servings (serving size: ¾ cup).

CALORIES 108 (2% from fat); FAT 0.2g (sat 0g, mono 0g, poly 0.1g); PROTEIN 0.9g; CARB 28.8g; FIBER 3g; CHOL 0mg; IRON 0.2mg; SODIUM 3mg; CALC 9mg

SLICED CANTALOUPE AND BLACKBERRIES WITH ALMOND CREAM

(pictured on page 168)

½ cup tub fat-free cream cheese, softened
2 tablespoons powdered sugar
1 tablespoon 1% low-fat milk
¼ teaspoon almond extract
½ (2½-pound) cantaloupe, peeled, seeded, and cut lengthwise into ¼-inch-thick slices
1 cup blackberries
1 tablespoon plus 1 teaspoon sliced almonds, toasted
Mint sprigs (optional)

1. Combine first 4 ingredients in a bowl; beat at high speed of an electric mixer until smooth. Arrange cantaloupe, berries, and cream cheese mixture evenly on 4 dessert plates. Sprinkle evenly with almonds. Garnish with mint sprigs, if desired. Yield: 4 servings.

CALORIES 97 (13% from fat); FAT 1.4g (sat 0.2g, mono 0.7g, poly 0.3g); PROTEIN 5.4g; CARB 15.9g; FIBER 3.7g; CHOL 5mg; IRON 0.4mg; SODIUM 179mg; CALC 109mg

STRAWBERRY-APRICOT CARAMEL SUNDAES

1 cup chopped apricots (about 6 ounces)
1 cup sliced strawberries
2 tablespoons orange juice
2 cups vanilla low-fat ice cream
¼ cup fat-free butterscotch-flavored sundae syrup
1 tablespoon plus 1 teaspoon chopped pistachios

1. Combine first 3 ingredients in a bowl, and stir well. Cover and chill 30 minutes. Spoon ice cream into stemmed glasses; top with fruit mixture and syrup. Sprinkle with pistachios. Yield: 4 servings (serving size: ½ cup ice cream, ½ cup fruit, 1 tablespoon syrup, and 1 teaspoon pistachios).

CALORIES 229 (28% from fat); FAT 7.2g (sat 2.3g, mono 3.6g, poly 0.8g); PROTEIN 5g; CARB 38.4g; FIBER 2.7g; CHOL 9mg; IRON 1mg; SODIUM 93mg; CALC 115mg

CELEBRATIONS

Tequila!

Now that summer's underway, the gods of festivity have officially proclaimed, "Let the margaritas flow!" That got us to thinking: There must be other culinary uses for tequila, the spicy, sharp-tasting Mexican liquor that's made from the sap of the agave plant. Its complex, full-bodied taste holds up to any flavor combination, so we developed recipes that meet its boldness head-on. They aren't for bland-loving folks, but for people who like their shrimp, chicken, pork, and veal with south-of-the-border flair.

You can use any grade of tequila, be it the *blanco,* which is colorless, or the aged-in-oak gold. And should you use mezcal (the one with the worm in the bottle), don't worry: The worm won't affect the fat or calorie count. So before margarita season ends and you find your tequila bottle running on empty, try adding a splash or two to these dishes.

GRILLED CHICKEN SALAD WITH TEQUILA-LIME MAYO

½ cup chopped onion
½ cup tequila
¼ cup fresh lime juice
1 tablespoon olive oil
1½ pounds skinned, boned chicken breast
Vegetable cooking spray
¾ cup fat-free mayonnaise
2 tablespoons pine nuts, toasted and chopped
1 tablespoon chopped fresh cilantro
2 tablespoons tequila
1 tablespoon plus 1 teaspoon fresh lime juice
¼ teaspoon salt
⅛ teaspoon ground red pepper
6 cups torn iceberg lettuce
2 medium tomatoes, each cut into 6 wedges

1. Combine first 5 ingredients in a large zip-top plastic bag. Seal bag; marinate in refrigerator 30 minutes, turning bag occasionally.
2. Prepare grill. Remove chicken from bag; discard marinade. Place chicken on grill rack coated with cooking spray; grill 5 minutes on each side or until done. Cut chicken into ½-inch pieces.
3. Combine mayonnaise and next 6 ingredients in a bowl; stir in chicken. Place 1 cup lettuce on each of 6 plates; top each with ⅔ cup chicken mixture and 2 tomato wedges. Yield: 6 servings.

CALORIES 234 (22% from fat); FAT 5.8g (sat 1.3g, mono 2.3g, poly 1.5g); PROTEIN 28.2g; CARB 10.6g; FIBER 1.3g; CHOL 72mg; IRON 1.7mg; SODIUM 452mg; CALC 29mg

MAHIMAHI WITH TEQUILA-TOMATO SALSA

If fresh tomatillos are unavailable, you can substitute drained canned tomatillos or increase the tomato to 1½ cups.

1 cup chopped tomato
½ cup peeled, chopped tomatillo
½ cup tequila
⅓ cup chopped green onions
¼ cup white wine vinegar
1 tablespoon olive oil
¼ teaspoon salt
⅛ teaspoon pepper
1 garlic clove, minced
6 (6-ounce) mahimahi or other firm white fish fillets (about 1 inch thick)
Vegetable cooking spray

1. Combine first 9 ingredients in a small bowl; stir well.
2. Prepare grill or broiler. Place fish on grill rack or rack of a broiler pan coated with cooking spray, and cook 5 minutes on each side or until fish flakes easily when tested with a fork. Serve with tomato salsa. Yield: 6 servings (serving size: 1 fillet and ⅓ cup salsa).

CALORIES 265 (22% from fat); FAT 6.4g (sat 0.9g, mono 3g, poly 1.5g); PROTEIN 36g; CARB 2.5g; FIBER 0.7g; CHOL 54mg; IRON 1.7mg; SODIUM 196mg; CALC 88mg

SPICY TEQUILA SHRIMP

- 1 teaspoon vegetable oil
- 1 cup vertically sliced onion
- ½ cup seeded, julienne-cut jalapeño pepper
- 5 garlic cloves, minced
- 1 pound large shrimp, peeled and deveined
- 1 tablespoon sherry vinegar
- ¼ teaspoon salt
- ½ cup tequila
- 3 cups seeded, chopped tomato
- ¼ cup chopped fresh cilantro
- 1 tablespoon fresh lime juice
- 6 cups hot cooked rice
- 1 medium-size ripe avocado, peeled and cut into 12 wedges

1. Heat oil in a nonstick skillet over medium heat. Add onion, pepper, and garlic; sauté 8 minutes. Add shrimp, vinegar, and salt; sauté 3 minutes.
2. Pour tequila into one side of skillet, and ignite tequila with a long match. Let flames die down. Add tomato and cilantro; cook 2 minutes or until thoroughly heated, stirring occasionally. Remove from heat; stir in lime juice. Spoon shrimp mixture over rice. Serve with avocado wedges. Yield: 6 servings (serving size: ¾ cup shrimp mixture, 1 cup rice, and 2 avocado wedges).

CALORIES 380 (18% from fat); FAT 7.5g (sat 1.2g, mono 3.6g, poly 1.6g); PROTEIN 17.6g; CARB 60.3g; FIBER 3.6g; CHOL 86mg; IRON 4.5mg; SODIUM 376mg; CALC 74mg

PORK CHOPS WITH MANGO-TEQUILA SALSA

- 2 tablespoons tequila
- 2 tablespoons jalapeño pepper jelly, melted
- 2 tablespoons fresh lime juice
- ¼ teaspoon salt
- ⅛ teaspoon pepper
- 4 (4-ounce) lean, boned center-cut loin pork chops (about ½ inch thick)
- Vegetable cooking spray
- Mango-Tequila Salsa

1. Combine first 6 ingredients in a large zip-top plastic bag. Seal bag;

marinate in refrigerator 8 hours, turning bag occasionally. Remove pork from bag, reserving marinade.
2. Prepare grill or broiler. Place pork on grill rack or rack of a broiler pan coated with cooking spray; cook 7 minutes on each side or until done, basting occasionally with reserved marinade. Serve with Mango-Tequila Salsa. Yield: 4 servings (serving size: 1 pork chop and ½ cup salsa).

CALORIES 341 (31% from fat); FAT 11.7g (sat 3.9g, mono 5.1g, poly 1.4g); PROTEIN 25.1g; CARB 23.8g; FIBER 1.8g; CHOL 77mg; IRON 1.4mg; SODIUM 358mg; CALC 19mg

Mango-Tequila Salsa:

- 2 cups peeled, diced mango
- ⅔ cup finely chopped red bell pepper
- 3 tablespoons tequila
- 2 tablespoons orange juice
- 1 tablespoon seeded, minced jalapeño pepper
- 2 teaspoons chopped fresh mint
- ¼ teaspoon salt

1. Combine all ingredients in a small bowl; stir well. Cover and chill. Yield: 2 cups (serving size: ½ cup).

CALORIES 90 (3% from fat); FAT 0.3g (sat 0.1g, mono 0.1g, poly 0.1g); PROTEIN 0.7g; CARB 16.4g; FIBER 1.7g; CHOL 0mg; IRON 0.5mg; SODIUM 149mg; CALC 11mg

TEQUILA PICCATA

- 2 tablespoons all-purpose flour
- ¼ teaspoon salt, divided
- ¼ teaspoon pepper, divided
- 8 (2-ounce) slices veal scaloppine (about 1 pound)
- 1 tablespoon olive oil, divided
- ¼ cup finely chopped shallots
- 2 garlic cloves, crushed
- ¼ cup tequila
- ¼ cup low-salt chicken broth
- 2 tablespoons fresh lemon juice
- 1 tablespoon capers
- 1 teaspoon minced fresh thyme or ¼ teaspoon dried thyme
- 2 cups hot cooked vermicelli (about 4 ounces uncooked pasta)

1. Combine flour, ⅛ teaspoon salt, and ⅛ teaspoon pepper in a shallow dish; stir well. Dredge veal in flour mixture; set aside.
2. Heat 1 teaspoon oil in a large non-stick skillet over medium-high heat. Add half of veal; cook 1½ minutes on each side or until browned. Remove veal from skillet. Set aside; keep warm. Repeat procedure with 1 teaspoon oil and remaining veal.
3. Heat 1 teaspoon oil in skillet over medium heat. Add shallots and garlic; sauté 1 minute. Add ⅛ teaspoon salt, ⅛ teaspoon pepper, tequila, and next 4 ingredients, scraping bottom of skillet with a wooden spoon to loosen browned bits. Bring to a boil; cook 2 minutes.
4. Place 2 veal slices and ½ cup pasta on each of 4 plates. Spoon 1½ tablespoons tequila mixture over each serving of veal. Yield: 4 servings.

CALORIES 285 (23% from fat); FAT 7.3g (sat 1.5g, mono 3.6g, poly 0.8g); PROTEIN 27.3g; CARB 26.1g; FIBER 1.4g; CHOL 94mg; IRON 2.4mg; SODIUM 419mg; CALC 31mg

MARINATED MUSHROOMS

These spicy, tequila-spiked mushrooms can be served on an antipasto platter or as a side dish with steak.

- ¼ cup tequila
- ¼ cup fresh lemon juice
- ½ teaspoon cracked pepper
- ¼ teaspoon salt
- ¼ teaspoon dried oregano
- 2 garlic cloves, halved
- 1 bay leaf
- 1 rosemary sprig
- 1 (8-ounce) package crimini mushrooms

1. Combine all ingredients in a bowl, and stir well. Cover and marinate mushrooms in refrigerator 8 hours. Discard garlic, bay leaf, and rosemary before serving. Yield: 6 servings (serving size: ½ cup).

CALORIES 35 (5% from fat); FAT 0.2g (sat 0g, mono 0g, poly 0.1g); PROTEIN 0.8g; CARB 2.8g; FIBER 0.5g; CHOL 0mg; IRON 0.6mg; SODIUM 99mg; CALC 4mg

STRAWBERRY-MARGARITA CRISP

For an elegant presentation, dip the rims of your glasses in water, then in sugar (either turbinado or granulated).

- 2 tablespoons graham cracker crumbs
- 9 crispy coconut macaroons (about ¼ pound)
- 2 tablespoons margarine, melted
- 4 cups medium strawberries
- ⅓ cup sugar
- ⅓ cup tequila
- 1 tablespoon cornstarch
- 1 tablespoon triple sec or other orange-flavored liqueur
- Vegetable cooking spray
- 1 tablespoon sliced almonds
- Sliced strawberries (optional)

1. Preheat oven to 350°.
2. Place graham cracker crumbs and macaroons in a food processor; process until macaroons are finely ground. With food processor on, slowly pour margarine through food chute, and process until well-blended.
3. Combine 4 cups strawberries and next 4 ingredients in a medium bowl; stir well. Spoon strawberry mixture into an 11 x 7-inch baking dish coated with cooking spray. Sprinkle with macaroon mixture and almonds. Bake at 350° for 25 minutes or until sauce is thickened and bubbly. Garnish with sliced strawberries, if desired. Yield: 6 servings.

CALORIES 252 (30% from fat); FAT 8.4g (sat 3.6g, mono 2.2g, poly 1.5g); PROTEIN 1.6g; CARB 36.3g; FIBER 3.1g; CHOL 0mg; IRON 0.7mg; SODIUM 71mg; CALC 21mg

IN SEASON

Lovable Cukes

Not just for salads, cucumbers are cool additions to everything from soup and sandwiches to spritzers.

There are foods that we take for granted—like cucumbers, for example. That doesn't mean we don't love them. But what have they done for us lately? Well, it's time for cucumbers to do some showing off, to demonstrate just how versatile they can be. Even though cucumbers have the reputation of being diet food, they can be so much more, as their subtle but distinct flavor lends itself to many possibilities. They're at their best when eaten uncooked, as they are in most of these recipes, adding some crunch and texture. To see just how far the cucumber envelope can be pushed, we even blended them into a refreshing spritzer. Now *that's* cool.

CUCUMBER-WHITE BEAN STUFFED TOMATOES

- 2 cups peeled, diced cucumber
- ⅓ cup finely chopped red onion
- 3 tablespoons finely chopped fresh basil
- 1 (19-ounce) can cannellini beans or other white beans, rinsed and drained
- 2 tablespoons tarragon vinegar or white wine vinegar
- 1 tablespoon extra-virgin olive oil
- ¼ teaspoon salt
- ⅛ teaspoon pepper
- 1 garlic clove, crushed
- 4 large tomatoes (about 2 pounds)
- 4 lettuce leaves
- 4 basil sprigs (optional)

1. Combine first 4 ingredients in a large bowl, and toss gently. Combine vinegar and next 4 ingredients in a small bowl; stir well with a whisk. Drizzle vinegar mixture over cucumber mixture, and toss gently to coat.
2. Core tomatoes; cut each tomato into 6 wedges, cutting to, but not through, bottom of tomato. Spread wedges slightly apart. Spoon ¾ cup cucumber mixture into center of each tomato. Serve on 4 lettuce-lined plates. Garnish with basil sprigs, if desired. Yield: 4 servings.

CALORIES 158 (26% from fat); FAT 4.5g (sat 0.6g, mono 2.6g, poly 0.6g); PROTEIN 6.5g; CARB 24.6g; FIBER 3.2g; CHOL 0mg; IRON 2.6mg; SODIUM 170mg; CALC 48mg

CUCUMBER SOUP WITH LEEKS AND CELERY

- 2 teaspoons margarine
- 2 cups peeled, cubed cucumber
- ¾ cup thinly sliced leek
- ½ cup diced celery
- 2 cups low-salt chicken broth
- 1½ cups peeled, diced baking potato
- 1 cup water
- ½ teaspoon salt
- ⅛ teaspoon pepper
- ⅓ cup diced cucumber
- ⅓ cup plain low-fat yogurt

1. Melt margarine in a large nonstick skillet over medium heat. Add 2 cups cucumber, leek, and celery; cover, reduce heat to low, and cook 10 minutes or until vegetables are tender, stirring occasionally. Add chicken broth, potato, 1 cup water, salt, and pepper; bring mixture to a boil. Cover, reduce heat, and simmer 10 minutes or until potato is tender.
2. Place cucumber mixture in a blender or food processor; cover and process until vegetables are finely chopped. Ladle soup into bowls; top each serving with 1 tablespoon diced cucumber and 1 tablespoon yogurt. Yield: 5 servings (serving size: 1 cup).

CALORIES 91 (25% from fat); FAT 2.5g (sat 0.7g, mono 1g, poly 0.7g); PROTEIN 3.4g; CARB 14.8g; FIBER 1.5g; CHOL 1mg; IRON 1.4mg; SODIUM 314mg; CALC 56mg

ROAST BEEF, CUCUMBER, AND TOMATO SANDWICHES

1 tablespoon sugar
2 tablespoons rice vinegar
Dash of ground red pepper
2 cups peeled, very thinly sliced cucumber
2 tablespoons thinly sliced green onions
3 tablespoons honey mustard
12 (1¼-ounce) slices rye bread
¾ pound very thinly sliced lean deli roast beef
12 (¼-inch-thick) slices tomato

1. Combine first 3 ingredients in a small bowl; stir well. Add cucumber and green onions; stir well. Cover and chill 2 hours.
2. Spread honey mustard evenly over 6 bread slices; top each with roast beef, about ¼ cup cucumber mixture, and 2 tomato slices. Top with remaining bread slices. Yield: 6 servings.

CALORIES 280 (14% from fat); FAT 4.3g (sat 1.4g, mono 1.7g, poly 0.6g); PROTEIN 19.3g; CARB 42.7g; FIBER 5.1g; CHOL 38mg; IRON 1.3mg; SODIUM 1,062mg; CALC 71mg

CUCUMBER PICKLE SPEARS

The longer these pickles marinate, the stronger their flavor becomes.

4 large pickling cucumbers (about 1 pound), each cut lengthwise into 6 spears
2 teaspoons salt
3 large dillweed sprigs
1 garlic clove, halved
1 cup white vinegar
1 cup water
¼ cup sugar

1. Place cucumber spears in a large bowl. Sprinkle with salt; toss gently to coat. Cover and chill 2 hours.
2. Drain cucumber spears in a colander. Rinse under cold water; drain well. Pack cucumber spears into a wide-mouth 1-quart jar. Add dillweed and garlic to jar; set aside.

3. Combine vinegar, water, and sugar in a small saucepan; bring to a boil, stirring until sugar dissolves. Pour hot liquid over cucumber spears. Cover jar with metal lid, and screw on band. Cool completely. Cover and marinate in refrigerator 5 days before serving. Yield: 24 spears (serving size: 1 spear).
Note: Pickles will last up to 6 weeks in the refrigerator.

CALORIES 13 (7% from fat); FAT 0.1g (sat 0g, mono 0g, poly 0.1g); PROTEIN 0.4g; CARB 3g; FIBER 0.6g; CHOL 0mg; IRON 0.2mg; SODIUM 99mg; CALC 10mg

CURRIED CUCUMBER DIP

Serve with fresh vegetables.

⅓ cup plain fat-free yogurt
⅓ cup fat-free sour cream
⅓ cup light mayonnaise
¾ teaspoon curry powder
¼ teaspoon ground cumin
¼ teaspoon salt
Dash of ground red pepper
¾ cup peeled, diced cucumber
¼ cup finely chopped radishes
2 tablespoons minced green onions

1. Combine first 7 ingredients in a medium bowl; stir with a whisk. Stir in cucumber, radishes, and green onions. Cover and chill. Yield: 1½ cups (serving size: 1 tablespoon).

CALORIES 14 (58% from fat); FAT 0.9g (sat 0.1g, mono 0.3g, poly 0.5g); PROTEIN 0.5g; CARB 1g; FIBER 0.1g; CHOL 1mg; IRON 0.1mg; SODIUM 54mg; CALC 8mg

CUCUMBER-LEMONADE SPRITZERS

¾ cup water
¼ cup plus 2 tablespoons brown sugar
1½ cups peeled, diced cucumber
⅓ cup fresh lemon juice
1 teaspoon peeled, minced fresh gingerroot
2 cups sparkling water, chilled
1 small cucumber, cut lengthwise into 4 spears (optional)

1. Combine ¾ cup water and sugar in a small saucepan. Bring to a boil; cook until sugar dissolves, stirring occasionally. Remove from heat; cool.
2. Place sugar mixture, diced cucumber, lemon juice, and gingerroot in a blender; cover and process until smooth. Cover and chill.
3. Combine cucumber mixture and sparkling water in a pitcher; stir gently with a whisk until blended. Serve over ice. Garnish each glass with a cucumber spear, if desired. Yield: 4 servings (serving size: 1 cup).

CALORIES 64 (1% from fat); FAT 0.1g (sat 0g, mono 0.1g, poly 0g); PROTEIN 0.4g; CARB 16.7g; FIBER 0.3g; CHOL 0mg; IRON 0.4mg; SODIUM 9mg; CALC 22mg

CUCUMBER TIPS

Buying: Generally, the smaller the cucumber, the smaller the seeds and the better the flavor.

Storing: Keep cucumbers away from apples and citrus fruit because these produce ethylene gas that can decay cucumbers. Store (unwashed) cucumbers unwrapped in the crisper bin of your refrigerator.

Where Opposites Attract

As East meets West in Australia, a vigorous cuisine emerges that juxtaposes several cultures. Becky Pate, our test kitchens director, went down under and brought back this report.

In Australia, Becky discovered an emerging, sophisticated cuisine that is a meeting of delicious opposites. More than ever before, Australia's eating habits reflect the influence of its converging cultures—European, Southeast Asian, and Aboriginal. In restaurants, you'll find a cuisine that combines the warm, rich heritage of Europe with the subtle blend of flavors and styling of the Far East. Here, Becky shares her favorites from some of Australia's most innovative restaurants.

PAN-SEARED TUNA WITH ONION-SOY VINAIGRETTE

This main-dish salad is from Melbourne's Chinois restaurant. Grating the onion brings out its pungency.

½ cup rice vinegar
¼ cup grated fresh onion
¼ cup low-sodium soy sauce
1 teaspoon vegetable oil
Dash of pepper
2 cups (2-inch) julienne-cut carrot
2 cups (2-inch) julienne-cut celery
2 cups (2-inch) julienne-cut cucumber
1 teaspoon vegetable oil
4 (6-ounce) tuna steaks
¼ teaspoon salt
¼ teaspoon coarsely ground pepper
Red onion slices (optional)
Celery leaves (optional)
Lemon slices (optional)

1. Combine first 5 ingredients in a small bowl. Stir well, and set aside. Combine carrot, celery, and cucumber in a bowl; toss well.
2. Brush 1 teaspoon oil over tuna; sprinkle with salt and pepper. Place a large nonstick skillet over medium-high heat until hot. Add tuna, and cook 3 minutes on each side or to desired degree of doneness. Remove from skillet, and cool. Cut tuna diagonally across grain into thin slices.
3. Arrange 1½ cups carrot mixture on each of 4 plates; top with tuna slices. Drizzle 2 tablespoons vinegar mixture over each serving. If desired, garnish with red onion slices, celery leaves, and lemon slices. Yield: 4 servings.

CALORIES 323 (30% from fat); FAT 10.9g (sat 2.6g, mono 3.4g, poly 3.7g); PROTEIN 41.2g; CARB 11.4g; FIBER 3.4g; CHOL 65mg; IRON 2.5mg; SODIUM 681mg; CALC 54mg

ROASTED TOMATO-AND-RED PEPPER SOUP

Jolley's Boathouse in Adelaide is a festive restaurant where fresh produce is highlighted.

1½ pounds red bell peppers
2 pounds tomatoes, halved and seeded
2 tablespoons olive oil
1 cup chopped onion
4 garlic cloves, minced
1½ cups tomato juice
1 tablespoon chopped fresh marjoram
½ teaspoon salt
¼ teaspoon pepper

1. Preheat broiler.
2. Cut peppers in half lengthwise; discard seeds and membranes. Place peppers and tomatoes, skin sides up, on an aluminum foil-lined baking sheet; flatten peppers with hand. Broil 15 minutes or until vegetables are blackened. Place peppers in a zip-top plastic bag; seal and let stand 10 minutes. Peel peppers and tomatoes; chop. Place half of chopped peppers and half of chopped tomatoes in a blender; cover and process until smooth. Set aside.
3. Heat olive oil in a saucepan over medium-low heat. Add onion and garlic; cover and cook 5 minutes. Add pureed vegetables, chopped peppers and tomatoes, tomato juice, and remaining 3 ingredients; cook mixture over medium heat until thoroughly heated. Yield: 5 servings (serving size: 1 cup).

CALORIES 126 (25% from fat); FAT 4g (sat 0.6g, mono 2.1g, poly 0g); PROTEIN 3.9g; CARB 22.7g; FIBER 5.6g; CHOL 0mg; IRON 3.4mg; SODIUM 521mg; CALC 42mg

STEAMED OYSTERS WITH CHILE, GINGER, AND CORIANDER

In the heart of downtown Melbourne is a little restaurant called Stella. It serves dishes like this one that are big on flavor.

12 oysters on the half shell, drained
2 tablespoons rice vinegar
2 tablespoons mirin (sweet rice wine)
12 small cilantro sprigs
12 thin slices peeled fresh gingerroot
1 small fresh red chile, halved lengthwise, seeded, and cut into 12 thin strips
¼ teaspoon Szechwan peppercorns, crushed

1. Arrange 6 oysters on the half shell in a steamer basket. Combine vinegar and mirin in a small bowl; stir well. Drizzle 1 teaspoon vinegar mixture over each oyster; top each with 1 cilantro sprig, 1 slice of gingerroot, and 1 strip of chile. Sprinkle half of crushed peppercorns over oysters. Steam, covered, 2 minutes or until edges of oysters curl. Repeat procedure with remaining oysters, vinegar mixture, cilantro, gingerroot, chile, and peppercorns. Serve warm. Yield: 4 servings (serving size: 3 oysters).

CALORIES 37 (27% from fat); FAT 3.1g (sat 0.3g, mono 0.1g, poly 0.3g); PROTEIN 3.1g; CARB 2.5g; FIBER 0.1g; CHOL 23mg; IRON 2.9mg; SODIUM 49mg; CALC 21mg

EMU FILLETS WITH QUANDONG-CHILE GLAZE

The Red Ochre Grill in Adelaide serves meats of the bush such as kangaroo and emu, and native produce like quandongs (desert peaches, for which dried peaches can be substituted). Beef tenderloin steaks can be substituted for emu.

- 4 (4-ounce) emu fillets
- ¾ cup dry red wine
- 2 rosemary sprigs
- 2 thyme sprigs
- 2 basil sprigs
- ½ cup water
- ¼ cup chopped dried quandongs or dried peaches
- 2 tablespoons sugar
- ½ cup port or other sweet red wine
- 1½ tablespoons red wine vinegar
- ½ cup beef consommé
- 1 tablespoon seeded, minced serrano chile
- Vegetable cooking spray
- 4 cups gourmet salad greens

1. Combine first 5 ingredients in a large zip-top plastic bag. Seal bag; marinate in refrigerator at least 12 hours, turning bag occasionally.
2. Combine ½ cup water, quandongs, and sugar in a small saucepan; bring to a boil. Reduce heat; simmer 4 minutes. Pour into a bowl; set aside.
3. Combine port and vinegar in pan. Bring to a boil over medium-high heat; cook 5 minutes. Return quandong mixture to pan. Stir in consommé and chile; cook 3 minutes or until reduced to ½ cup.
4. Prepare grill. Remove emu from bag, and discard marinade. Place emu on grill rack coated with cooking spray, and grill 7 minutes on each side or to desired degree of doneness. Serve emu over salad greens; drizzle with chile glaze. Yield: 4 servings (serving size: 1 emu fillet, 1 cup greens, and 2 tablespoons chile glaze).

CALORIES 253 (29% from fat); FAT 8.2g (sat 3.1g, mono 3.1g, poly 0.4g); PROTEIN 26.7g; CARB 15.2g; FIBER 1.8g; CHOL 77mg; IRON 4.4mg; SODIUM 263mg; CALC 33mg

BLACKBERRY-AND-VODKA SORBET WITH MIXED BERRIES

Across the bay from Sydney at Balmoral is the Bathers Pavilion. Formerly a bathhouse, it's been converted into a restaurant with a wonderful view of the water. This dessert uses superfine sugar because it's more finely granulated and dissolves almost instantly. If you don't have it, process granulated sugar in a food processor for about one minute.

- 5 cups blackberries
- 1 cup superfine sugar, divided
- ⅔ cup fresh lime juice, divided
- ¼ cup vodka
- ¼ cup fresh lemon juice
- 2 teaspoons Chambord (raspberry-flavored liqueur)
- 3 cups halved strawberries
- 3 cups blueberries
- ⅓ cup vodka

1. Place blackberries in a blender; cover and process until smooth. Press blackberry puree through a sieve into a bowl; discard seeds. Add ¾ cup sugar, ⅓ cup lime juice, ¼ cup vodka, lemon juice, and liqueur; stir well.
2. Pour blackberry mixture into freezer can of an ice cream freezer; freeze according to manufacturer's instructions. Spoon into a freezer-safe container; cover and freeze until firm.
3. Combine ¼ cup sugar, ⅓ cup lime juice, strawberries, blueberries, and ⅓ cup vodka in a large bowl; stir gently. Let stand 2 hours.
4. Spoon ¾ cup strawberry mixture into each of 8 glasses; top each with ½ cup sorbet. Yield: 8 servings.

CALORIES 242 (3% from fat); FAT 0.8g (sat 0g, mono 0.1g, poly 0.4g); PROTEIN 1.5g; CARB 51g; FIBER 10.5g; CHOL 0mg; IRON 0.8mg; SODIUM 5mg; CALC 43mg

FIGS POACHED WITH RED WINE AND TEA

In this intensely flavorful dessert from Bathers Pavilion, the combination of the strong black tea with the citrus and brandy reflects an Asian flair.

- ¾ cup brandy
- ¾ cup dry red wine
- ¾ cup honey
- 2 tablespoons grated orange rind
- 1 tablespoon grated lemon rind
- ⅔ cup fresh orange juice
- ⅓ cup fresh lemon juice
- ⅓ cup strong-brewed black tea
- 2 whole cloves
- 2 (3-inch) cinnamon sticks
- 1 (6-inch) vanilla bean, split lengthwise
- 1 (8-ounce) package dried figs or other dried fruits
- ¾ cup vanilla low-fat ice cream
- Lemon zest (optional)

1. Combine first 11 ingredients in a medium saucepan. Stir well; bring to a boil over medium heat. Reduce heat; simmer, uncovered, 30 minutes. Strain brandy mixture through a sieve into a bowl; discard solids. Return brandy mixture to pan. Add figs; bring to a boil. Reduce heat; simmer, uncovered, 1 hour or until figs are soft. Remove figs from pan, reserving brandy mixture. Let figs cool slightly; cut each fig in half.
2. Arrange 5 fig halves on each of 6 dessert dishes. Drizzle 1½ tablespoons brandy syrup over each serving; top with 2 tablespoons ice cream. Garnish with lemon zest, if desired. Yield: 6 servings.
Note: Step 1 can be done a day ahead; cover and chill, and bring back to room temperature before serving.

CALORIES 280 (5% from fat); FAT 1.6g (sat 0.8g, mono 0.4g, poly 0.3g); PROTEIN 2.6g; CARB 70.9g; FIBER 6.5g; CHOL 4mg; IRON 1.2mg; SODIUM 54mg; CALC 104mg

Frozen Mud Pie Sandwiches, page 175

Citrus Granita, page 181

Honey-Dijon Lamb Chops, page 181

Roasted Potato Wedges with Olive Tapenade, page 181

Chicken with Lemon-Caper Sauce, page 154

Panzanella with Beans, page 152

Café au Lait Granita, page 184

Sliced Cantaloupe and Blackberries with Almond Cream, page 159

Salade Niçoise, page 184

Asparagus Tart, page 192

Blueberry Crumble Pie, page 180

Pasta Puttanesca, page 188

Shrimp Fried Rice, page 203

Gingered Watermelon Compote, page 175

Caesar Potato Salad, page 173

*C*ool Comfort

When it comes to comfort foods, winter doesn't have exclusivity. Summer has its own, designed to keep you cool under the collar.

Although comfort foods are usually thought of as heavy winter fare, they're just as much a part of summer, in a lighter and more refreshing form: tuna salad, corn on the cob, and icy treats. These foods keep us cool and entice us to gather outdoors for barbecues, picnics, potlucks, family reunions, and beach parties.

Many of these recipes are '90s versions of the soothing, familiar summer dishes that we all grew up with. All are designed to be eaten when it's too darn hot to do most anything else. They require minimal work, which means you don't have to give up precious hammock time; most can even be made ahead in the morning. So this summer, don't let the humidity get you down. And if something else does . . . hey, we've got an ice-cream soda with your name on it.

SWEET ONION, TOMATO, AND CORN SALAD WITH BASIL

You can use dark balsamic vinegar in place of the white, though the salad won't look as pretty.

- 1 tablespoon chopped fresh basil
- 2 tablespoons white balsamic vinegar
- 2 teaspoons extra-virgin olive oil
- 1 teaspoon Dijon mustard
- ½ cup basil leaves
- 2 large tomatoes, thinly sliced
- ½ cup thinly sliced Vidalia or sweet onion
- 1 cup fresh white corn kernels (about 2 ears)

1. Combine first 4 ingredients in a bowl; stir well, and set aside.
2. Combine basil leaves and remaining 3 ingredients; toss well. Drizzle vinegar mixture over salads, and toss gently. Yield: 4 servings.

CALORIES 89 (32% from fat); FAT 3.2g (sat 0.4g, mono 1.9g, poly 0.6g); PROTEIN 2.3g; CARB 15.5g; FIBER 2.9g; CHOL 0mg; IRON 0.7mg; SODIUM 52mg; CALC 17mg

APPLE-CABBAGE SLAW

- 4 cups very thinly sliced cabbage
- 2 cups diced Fuji or Red Delicious apple (about 1 pound)
- ½ cup chopped green onions
- ¼ cup chopped fresh flat-leaf parsley
- ½ cup low-fat sour cream
- ¼ cup plain fat-free yogurt
- 2 tablespoons cider vinegar
- 2 tablespoons brown sugar
- ¼ teaspoon salt
- ⅛ teaspoon pepper
- 8 thin slices Fuji or Red Delicious apple
- ¼ cup lemon juice

1. Combine first 4 ingredients in a bowl; toss well. Combine sour cream and next 5 ingredients; add to cabbage mixture, stirring to coat.
2. Toss apple slices with lemon juice; drain apple slices. Place 1 cup cabbage mixture on each of 4 salad plates, and arrange 2 apple slices on each plate. Yield: 4 servings.

CALORIES 144 (25% from fat); FAT 4g (sat 2.3g, mono 1.1g, poly 0.3g); PROTEIN 3.1g; CARB 26.8g; FIBER 4.4g; CHOL 12mg; IRON 1.2mg; SODIUM 189mg; CALC 119mg

CAESAR POTATO SALAD

(pictured on page 172)

Store anchovy paste (which comes in a tube) in the refrigerator after opening.

- 1½ tablespoons extra-virgin olive oil
- 2 garlic cloves, minced
- 2 (1-inch) slices French bread
- 1½ pounds small red potatoes
- 3 tablespoons dry vermouth
- 2 tablespoons balsamic vinegar
- 1 tablespoon lemon juice
- 2 teaspoons Dijon mustard
- 2 teaspoons anchovy paste
- ¼ teaspoon salt
- ⅛ teaspoon pepper
- ¼ cup chopped green onions
- 3 tablespoons finely chopped fresh flat-leaf parsley
- 2 romaine lettuce leaves, cut crosswise into ¼-inch-wide strips
- ¼ cup grated fresh Parmesan cheese

1. Combine oil and garlic; let stand 30 minutes.
2. Preheat oven to 350°.
3. Brush 1½ teaspoons oil mixture over bread; cut into cubes. Place bread cubes in a single layer on a jelly-roll pan. Bake at 350° for 9 minutes or until toasted.
4. Arrange potatoes in a steamer basket over boiling water. Cover and steam 18 minutes or until tender. Let cool; cut into ¼-inch-thick slices. Combine potato slices and vermouth; toss gently to coat.
5. Combine remaining oil mixture, vinegar, and next 7 ingredients in a bowl. Pour over potato slices; toss gently to coat. Cover and chill.
6. Stir in lettuce. Sprinkle with croutons and cheese. Serve immediately. Yield: 6 servings (serving size: ⅔ cup).

CALORIES 176 (27% from fat); FAT 5.3g (sat 1.3g, mono 2.9g, poly 0.5g); PROTEIN 6.1g; CARB 24.9g; FIBER 3.1g; CHOL 3mg; IRON 2.3mg; SODIUM 497mg; CALC 97mg

MARINATED CUCUMBERS IN DILL

2½ cups peeled, thinly sliced English cucumber
¼ teaspoon salt
½ cup white wine vinegar
¼ cup sugar
3 tablespoons finely chopped fresh flat-leaf parsley
2 tablespoons water
1 tablespoon chopped fresh dillweed or ¾ teaspoon dried dillweed
¼ teaspoon white pepper

1. Place cucumber and salt in a bowl; add water to cover. Let stand 1 hour; rinse. Drain; blot dry with paper towels. Combine vinegar and remaining 5 ingredients in a bowl. Add cucumber; toss gently. Cover; chill at least 4 hours. Yield: 10 servings (serving size: ¼ cup).

CALORIES 27 (0% from fat); FAT 0g; PROTEIN 0.3g; CARB 6.3g; FIBER 0.2g; CHOL 0mg; IRON 0.2mg; SODIUM 63mg; CALC 9mg

---

SUMMER IS FOR PICNICS . . .

But take precautions against food poisoning—even if you're carrying only vegetable- and fruit-based dishes, which scientists have recently discovered may harbor harmful bacteria. You can keep your salads worry-free if you follow this simple advice.

◆ If possible, refrigerate fruits and vegetables overnight at 40° or lower before preparing them.
◆ Rinse whole fruits and vegetables in cold running water before eating, slicing, or packing them. In most (but not all) cases, the only place bacteria can live is on the surface of the food, unless it has been cut. Simple washing should eliminate any serious risk.
◆ Wash your hands before cutting vegetables and fruits (as well as other picnic foods), and use a clean knife and cutting board.
◆ Use a well-insulated cooler containing an ice pack, and keep it in the shade with the lid on.

LEMON-HERB GRILLED CHICKEN, CORN ON THE COB, AND ONIONS

Any combination of fresh herbs can be used in the marinade, including basil, parsley, or thyme.

½ cup dry vermouth or dry white wine
1 tablespoon chopped chives
1 tablespoon chopped fresh oregano
1 tablespoon chopped fresh rosemary
2 teaspoons grated lemon rind
3 tablespoons fresh lemon juice
2 tablespoons extra-virgin olive oil
1½ tablespoons Dijon mustard
⅛ teaspoon salt
⅛ teaspoon pepper
8 (½-inch-thick) slices red onion
4 (6-ounce) skinned chicken breast halves
4 ears corn with husks (about 2¼ pounds)
Vegetable cooking spray

1. Combine first 10 ingredients in a small bowl; stir well. Arrange onion in a single layer in a shallow dish. Add chicken; pour herb mixture over onion and chicken. Cover and marinate in refrigerator 1 hour.
2. Pull husks back from corn (do not remove). Remove silks. Pull husks back over corn, and tie tops with heavy string; set aside.
3. Prepare grill. Remove onion slices and chicken from dish, reserving marinade. Place chicken, bone sides up, on grill rack coated with cooking spray; grill 50 minutes or until chicken is done, turning and basting with reserved marinade every 10 minutes. Moisten corn with water; grill 10 minutes or until tender, turning corn after 5 minutes. Grill onion slices 6 minutes or until tender, turning and basting with reserved marinade after 3 minutes. Yield: 4 servings (serving size: 1 chicken breast half, 1 ear of corn, and 2 onion slices).

CALORIES 364 (29% from fat); FAT 11.9g (sat 2.1g, mono 6.5g, poly 1.8g); PROTEIN 33.7g; CARB 24.9g; FIBER 3.4g; CHOL 84mg; IRON 1.9mg; SODIUM 333mg; CALC 37mg

PICKLED SALMON AND SHRIMP

Serve this antipasto dish cold on a platter. Accompany it with an assortment of marinated vegetables, cheeses, olives, breads, and/or crackers.

1 tablespoon pickling spice, divided
½ teaspoon salt
1 large lemon, sliced
1 (1-pound) salmon fillet
36 small shrimp (about ½ pound), peeled
1 small red onion, thinly sliced and separated into rings
¾ cup white vinegar
¾ cup dry vermouth
¼ cup sugar
1 teaspoon capers
25 black peppercorns
1 bay leaf

1. Pour water into a large saucepan to a depth of 2 inches. Add 1½ teaspoons pickling spice, salt, and lemon; bring to a boil. Cover, reduce heat, and simmer 10 minutes. Add salmon and shrimp; simmer 7 minutes or until fish flakes easily when tested with a fork and shrimp are done. Drain fish mixture, discarding cooking liquid and lemon slices. Let cool.
2. Remove skin and bones from fish; break fish into bite-size pieces. Layer fish, shrimp, and onion rings in a 1-quart jar.
3. Combine 1½ teaspoons pickling spice, vinegar, and remaining 5 ingredients in a saucepan; bring to a boil. Reduce heat; simmer 1 minute or until sugar dissolves. Pour over fish mixture in jar. Cover and chill several hours or up to 5 days. Serve with salad greens, crackers, or vegetables on an antipasto platter. Yield: 8 servings (serving size: ½ cup).

CALORIES 156 (31% from fat); FAT 5.3g (sat 0.9g, mono 2.4g, poly 1.2g); PROTEIN 16.7g; CARB 10.7g; FIBER 0.2g; CHOL 71mg; IRON 0.9mg; SODIUM 210mg; CALC 26mg

TUNA-AND-ARTICHOKE
PASTA SALAD

2   teaspoons grated lemon rind
3   tablespoons fresh lemon juice
3   tablespoons extra-virgin olive
    oil
1   tablespoon peeled, minced
    fresh gingerroot
2   garlic cloves, minced
4   cups cooked elbow macaroni
    (about 8 ounces uncooked)
1   cup cherry tomatoes, halved
½   cup chopped green onions
⅓   cup chopped fresh flat-leaf
    parsley
1   (6-ounce) can albacore tuna in
    water, drained and flaked
1   (14-ounce) can quartered
    artichoke hearts, drained

1. Combine first 5 ingredients in a
large bowl. Add pasta and remaining
ingredients; toss gently to coat. Cover;
chill at least 1 hour. Yield: 8 servings
(serving size: 1 cup).

CALORIES 185 (29% from fat); FAT 6g (sat 0.9g, mono 3.9g,
poly 0.8g); PROTEIN 8.6g; CARB 24.9g; FIBER 1.6g;
CHOL 6mg; IRON 1.8mg; SODIUM 91mg; CALC 30mg

GINGERED WATERMELON
COMPOTE

(pictured on page 172)

¼   cup sugar
¼   cup water
2   teaspoons grated lime rind
¼   cup plus 2 tablespoons fresh
    lime juice
2   tablespoons peeled, chopped
    fresh gingerroot
2   tablespoons chopped fresh
    mint
8   cups (1-inch) watermelon balls
    (about a 5-pound watermelon)
2   cups (1-inch) honeydew melon
    balls (about a 3-pound
    honeydew melon)
2   cups (1-inch) cantaloupe balls
    (about a 3-pound cantaloupe)
Mint sprigs (optional)

1. Combine first 6 ingredients in a
small bowl; set aside.
2. Combine melon balls in a large
bowl; add lime juice mixture. Cover
and chill at least 1 hour. Garnish with
mint sprigs, if desired. Yield: 12 servings (serving size: 1 cup).

CALORIES 72 (8% from fat); FAT 0.6g (sat 0.3g, mono 0.1g,
poly 0g); PROTEIN 1.1g; CARB 17.5g; FIBER 1.2g;
CHOL 0mg; IRON 0.3mg; SODIUM 8mg; CALC 15mg

STRAWBERRY-
AMARETTI BOMBE

*This easy dessert is perfect for making
ahead and putting in the freezer.
You'll want to have it on hand when
an unexpected guest shows up.*

2   cups strawberry sorbet,
    softened
3   cups vanilla low-fat ice cream,
    softened
½   cup amaretti cookie crumbs
    (about 8 cookies) or reduced-
    fat vanilla wafer crumbs
2   tablespoons amaretto (almond-
    flavored liqueur)
½   (1-ounce) square bittersweet
    chocolate, coarsely grated
2   cups strawberries

1. Press sorbet into bottom and up
sides of a chilled 5-cup salad mold or
bowl. Freeze 1 hour or until firm.
2. Place ice cream in a bowl; fold in
cookie crumbs, amaretto, and chocolate. Spoon mixture into center of sorbet. Cover and freeze until firm.
3. Dip mold into hot water for a few
seconds. Place a plate upside down on
top of mold; invert bombe onto plate.
Serve with strawberries. Yield: 10 servings (serving size: 1 wedge).

CALORIES 123 (20% from fat); FAT 2.7g (sat 1.3g, mono 0.7g,
poly 0.2g); PROTEIN 2.1g; CARB 22.5g; FIBER 1.6g;
CHOL 6mg; IRON 0.3mg; SODIUM 36mg; CALC 64mg

FROZEN MUD PIE
SANDWICHES

(pictured on page 165)

*This version of an ice cream sandwich
has its own fudge sauce. These cool
sandwiches can be stored in the freezer
for up to 4 days. Chocolate or vanilla
frozen yogurt may be substituted for
coffee-flavored frozen yogurt.*

2   tablespoons sugar
2   tablespoons light-colored corn
    syrup
1½ tablespoons unsweetened cocoa
1   tablespoon 1% low-fat milk
1   teaspoon stick margarine
¼   teaspoon vanilla extract
1¼ cups coffee-flavored low-fat
    frozen yogurt, softened
20 chocolate wafer cookies

1. Combine first 4 ingredients in a
small heavy saucepan, and bring to a
boil over medium-low heat, stirring frequently with a whisk. Cook 2 minutes
or until thick, stirring frequently. Remove from heat; stir in margarine and
vanilla. Cover and chill thoroughly.
2. Spread 2 tablespoons yogurt onto
each of 10 cookies. Top each with about
1 teaspoon toffee syrup and 1 cookie;
press gently. Freeze at least 1 hour. Yield:
10 servings (serving size: 1 sandwich).

CALORIES 103 (30% from fat); FAT 3.4g (sat 1.1g, mono 1.1g,
poly 0.6g); PROTEIN 1.7g; CARB 16.7g; FIBER 0g;
CHOL 11mg; IRON 0.4mg; SODIUM 62mg; CALC 38mg

SUMMER-GIRL SODA

The All-American ice cream soda reappears with a new look and taste: fresh fruit, low-fat ice cream, and sherbet. You can substitute chopped fresh strawberries for the raspberries.

- ¾ cup raspberries
- ½ teaspoon sugar
- 1¼ cups vanilla low-fat ice cream, divided
- 1½ cups club soda, chilled and divided
- 1 cup raspberry sherbet
- 1 cup orange sherbet

1. Press raspberries through a sieve over a bowl; discard seeds. Combine raspberry pulp and sugar; stir well. Divide raspberry mixture evenly among 4 parfait glasses. Spoon 1 tablespoon ice cream into each glass; stir well. Stir 2 tablespoons club soda into each glass. Spoon ¼ cup ice cream, ¼ cup raspberry sherbet, and ¼ cup orange sherbet into each glass; add ¼ cup club soda to each glass. Serve immediately. Yield: 4 servings.

CALORIES 189 (16% from fat); FAT 3.3g (sat 1.7g, mono 0.8g, poly 0.2g); PROTEIN 2.8g; CARB 39g; FIBER 1.7g; CHOL 8mg; IRON 0.3mg; SODIUM 109mg; CALC 112mg

HEALTHY TRAVEL

Casting the Magic Wand

Fly-fishing is a contact sport of the first order. In no outdoor endeavor do you match wits with a natural element as consistently as you do when stalking a river.

Long regarded as an effete sport of the leisure class—up until the last two decades, anyway—fly-fishing is exploding in popularity. It tempts not just the occasional weekend fisherman looking for a new hobby, but also those finely tuned to the outdoors, people who want not merely to observe nature, but also to take it on firsthand, body to the river, hand crooked around the magic wand of a fly rod, wading a deep current, senses heightened to all that swims. No matter your reasons for treading the waters, you'll find this recipe captures the exhilaration of a fly-fishing adventure.

PAN-FRIED BROOK TROUT WITH GREENS

- 2 tablespoons all-purpose flour
- ¼ teaspoon salt
- ¼ teaspoon ground red pepper
- 8 (4-ounce) brook trout fillets
- Vegetable cooking spray
- 8 cups coarsely chopped spinach
- 1 cup thinly sliced iceberg lettuce
- ½ cup sliced green onions
- 2 tablespoons chopped fresh thyme or 2 teaspoons dried thyme
- 2 tablespoons chopped fresh oregano or 2 teaspoons dried oregano
- 2 tablespoons white vinegar
- ¼ teaspoon salt
- ⅛ teaspoon black pepper
- 4 lemon wedges

1. Combine first 3 ingredients in a shallow dish; stir well. Dredge trout fillets in flour mixture.
2. Heat a large cast-iron skillet coated with cooking spray over medium-high heat. Add 4 fillets; cook 3 minutes on each side or until fish flakes easily when tested with a fork. Remove from skillet. Set aside; keep warm. Repeat procedure with remaining fillets.
3. Coat skillet with cooking spray; add spinach and next 7 ingredients. Cook, stirring constantly, 1½ minutes or until spinach wilts.
4. Arrange ½ cup spinach mixture on each of 4 plates, and top each with 2 fillets. Serve with lemon wedges. Yield: 4 servings.

CALORIES 393 (37% from fat); FAT 16.1g (sat 2.8g, mono 5.5g, poly 5.6g); PROTEIN 51.4g; CARB 10.3g; FIBER 5.6g; CHOL 132mg; IRON 8.1mg; SODIUM 503mg; CALC 262mg

COOKING CLASS

Smoke Gets in Your Pies

To gear up for outdoor-cooking season, why not throw a pizza party where the guests cook their own pies on the grill?

Are your guests starting to find excuses to stay home? Is "Hey, come on over—we'll slap some burgers on the grill" not making it? Then let us suggest a backyard pizza party where guests make their own pies on the grill: light, thin-crusted pizzas that taste as if they were cooked in a smoky, wood-fired oven.

If you think grilling a pizza sounds difficult, we've got step-by-step instructions on page 178 that show you otherwise. Simplicity is the key to these highly flavored pies, which call for only a few topping ingredients used sparingly (of course, you can always do your own improvising).

To really save time, we have make-ahead instructions for the pizza dough, and because the crusts are thin, it takes only a few minutes to grill them. And considering the cooking method, these may be some of the best-tasting pizzas your guests have ever had—all in your backyard. No one will want an excuse to miss this party!

QUICK-AND-EASY PIZZA CRUST

We call for bread flour because it's higher in protein than all-purpose flour and makes a firmer, denser crust. You can, however, substitute all-purpose flour.

- 2 cups bread flour
- ½ teaspoon salt
- ½ teaspoon sugar
- 1 package quick-rise yeast
- ¾ cup warm water (120° to 130°)
- 1 tablespoon olive oil
- Vegetable cooking spray
- 2 tablespoons cornmeal

1. Combine first 4 ingredients in a large bowl; make a well in center of mixture. Combine water and oil; add to flour mixture. Stir until mixture forms a ball. Turn dough out onto a lightly floured surface; knead until smooth and elastic (about 10 minutes).
2. Place dough in a large bowl coated with cooking spray, turning to coat top. Cover and let rise in a warm place (85°), free from drafts, 45 minutes or until doubled in bulk. Punch dough down; divide in half. Cover and let dough rest 10 minutes.
3. Working with one portion at a time (cover remaining dough to keep from drying), roll each portion into a 10-inch circle on a lightly floured surface. Place dough on two baking sheets, each sprinkled with 1 tablespoon cornmeal. Yield: 2 (10-inch) pizza crusts (serving size: 1 crust).

CALORIES 603 (14% from fat); FAT 9.7g (sat 1.3g, mono 5.3g, poly 1.6g); PROTEIN 18.5g; CARB 108.5g; FIBER 1.4g; CHOL 0mg; IRON 7mg; SODIUM 589mg; CALC 24mg

Food Processor Variation:
Place first 4 ingredients in a food processor, and pulse 2 times or until well-blended. With processor on, slowly add water and oil through food chute; process until dough forms a ball. Process 1 additional minute. Turn out onto a lightly floured surface; knead 9 or 10 times. Proceed with step 2 in above recipe.

Bread Machine Variation:
Follow manufacturer's instructions for placing all ingredients except cooking spray and cornmeal into bread pan. Select dough cycle; start bread machine. Remove dough from machine at end of dough cycle (do not bake). Proceed with step 2 in above recipe.

PIZZA MARGHERITA

This classic pizza captures the colors of the Italian flag: red, white, and green.

  2 teaspoons olive oil
⅛ teaspoon salt
⅛ teaspoon pepper
¼ cup thinly sliced fresh basil
  2 tablespoons chopped fresh oregano
  2 (10-inch) Quick-and-Easy Pizza Crusts (page 176)
Vegetable cooking spray
  4 plum tomatoes, thinly sliced (about ½ pound)
  1 cup (4 ounces) shredded part-skim mozzarella cheese

1. Combine first 3 ingredients in a small bowl; set aside.
2. Combine basil and oregano in a small bowl; set aside.
3. Prepare grill. Place 1 crust on grill rack coated with cooking spray; grill 3 minutes or until puffy and golden. Turn crust, grill-mark side up; brush with half of oil mixture. Top with half of plum tomatoes, cheese, and herb mixture. Cook 4 to 5 minutes or until cheese melts and crust is lightly browned. Repeat with remaining crust and toppings. Yield: 6 servings (serving size: ⅓ pizza).

CALORIES 286 (26% from fat); FAT 8.3g (sat 2.6g, mono 3.8g, poly 1g); PROTEIN 11.7g; CARB 41.6g; FIBER 1.8g; CHOL 11mg; IRON 3.4mg; SODIUM 339mg; CALC 161mg

GRILLED AMERICAN PIZZA

  4 ounces turkey Italian sausage
  2 (10-inch) Quick-and-Easy Pizza Crusts (page 176)
Vegetable cooking spray
½ cup marinara sauce
  1 cup (4 ounces) shredded part-skim mozzarella cheese
½ cup thinly sliced mushrooms
½ cup vertically sliced onion
½ cup grated fresh Parmesan cheese

1. Remove casing from sausage. Cook sausage in a nonstick skillet over medium-high heat until browned; stir to crumble. Drain; pat dry with paper towels. Set aside.
2. Prepare grill. Place 1 crust on grill rack coated with cooking spray; grill 3 minutes or until puffy and golden. Turn crust, grill-mark side up; spread with ¼ cup marinara sauce. Top with half of sausage, mozzarella cheese, mushrooms, onion, and Parmesan cheese. Cover and grill pizza 4 to 5 minutes or until cheese melts and crust is lightly browned. Repeat with remaining crust and toppings. Yield: 6 servings (serving size: ⅓ pizza).

CALORIES 339 (31% from fat); FAT 11.5g (sat 4.6g, mono 2.7g, poly 0.9g); PROTEIN 17.8g; CARB 40.8g; FIBER 1.g; CHOL 29mg; IRON 3mg; SODIUM 678mg; CALC 252mg

GRILL DRILL

Because putting raw dough on a hot grill can be intimidating, we have some suggestions to help turn your fears into fun. Turn to page 178 for step-by-step photos.

• To make ahead, chill the rolled, uncooked crusts for up to 4 hours, or freeze the dough for up to 2 weeks. Make sure that the frozen dough is brought back to room temperature before rolling it out and grilling it.
• A little preparation goes a long way. Be sure you have all of your topping ingredients ready and nearby before you start to grill the pizza dough.
• To give your pizzas a more pronounced smoky flavor, soak a couple of handfuls of aromatic wood chips in water for about 30 minutes. Sprinkle them over the hot coals, and close the lid to your grill. Wait a few minutes before you place the pizza crusts on the grill rack.
• Coat the grill rack with cooking spray to prevent the pizza crusts from sticking.
• Don't fret when your crusts have irregular, puffy circles and grill marks. That's part of their rustic attraction.
• Some grills are large enough to cook both crusts at the same time.

STEP-BY-STEP FOR GRILLING PIZZA

With our pizza dough recipe, making your own crust is easier than you might imagine. And it's well worth it for the flavor and texture. By following these simple instructions, you'll be ready, able, and grilling in no time.

❶ *Roll each crust into a 10-inch circle.*

❷ *Place crust on a baking sheet sprinkled with cornmeal.*

❸ *Gently lift crust from the baking sheet to the grill.*

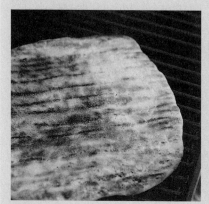

❹ *Turn crust, grill-mark side up, after about 3 minutes.*

❺ *Arrange toppings over crust, and grill until done.*

GRILLED VEGETABLE PIZZA WITH FETA AND SPINACH

Any flavor of feta cheese will work in this pizza. The tangy, fresh spinach mixture is a nice contrast to the grilled veggies and cheese.

3 tablespoons balsamic vinegar
1 garlic clove, crushed
1 (1¼-pound) eggplant, cut crosswise into ¼-inch-thick slices
½ teaspoon pepper
¼ teaspoon salt
Vegetable cooking spray
2 (10-inch) Quick-and-Easy Pizza Crusts (page 176)
2 teaspoons olive oil
2 cups chopped plum tomato (about 1 pound)
1 cup crumbled feta cheese with basil and tomato
2 tablespoons chopped fresh oregano or 1 teaspoon dried oregano
2 cups thinly sliced spinach leaves
2 tablespoons balsamic vinegar

1. Prepare grill. Combine 3 tablespoons vinegar and garlic; brush over both sides of eggplant slices. Sprinkle both sides of eggplant with pepper and salt; place on grill rack coated with cooking spray. Grill 2 minutes on each side or until tender. Remove from grill.
2. Place 1 crust on grill rack coated with cooking spray; grill 3 minutes or until puffy and golden. Turn crust, grill-mark side up; brush with half of oil. Arrange half of eggplant slices over crust, overlapping slightly. Top with half of tomato, cheese, and oregano. Cover and grill 3 to 4 minutes or until crust is lightly browned; remove from heat. Combine spinach and 2 tablespoons vinegar in a small bowl. Top pizza with half of spinach mixture. Repeat with remaining crust and toppings. Yield: 6 servings (serving size: ⅓ pizza).

CALORIES 309 (27% from fat); FAT 9.2g (sat 3.5g, mono 3.8g, poly 0.9g); PROTEIN 11.0g; CARB 47.1g; FIBER 3.5g; CHOL 17mg; IRON 4.1mg; SODIUM 794mg; CALC 166mg

GRILLED BARBECUED-CHICKEN PIZZA

⅔ cup barbecue sauce, divided
1 cup (about 6 ounces) roasted skinned, boned chicken breast (such as Tyson), chopped
2 (10-inch) Quick-and-Easy Pizza Crusts (page 176)
Vegetable cooking spray
½ cup (2 ounces) shredded smoked Gouda cheese
½ cup (2 ounces) shredded part-skim mozzarella cheese
¼ cup sliced green onions
¼ cup chopped fresh cilantro

1. Combine ¼ cup barbecue sauce and chicken in a bowl. Toss well.
2. Prepare grill. Place 1 crust on grill rack coated with cooking spray; grill 3 minutes or until puffy and golden. Turn crust, grill-mark side up; spread with 3 tablespoons barbecue sauce. Top with half of Gouda cheese, chicken, mozzarella cheese, and green onions. Cover; grill 3 to 4 minutes or until cheese melts and crust is lightly browned. Sprinkle with half of cilantro. Repeat with remaining crust and toppings. Yield: 6 servings (serving size: ⅓ pizza).

CALORIES 315 (24% from fat); FAT 8.4g (sat 3.3g, mono 3.1g, poly 0.8g); PROTEIN 17.7g; CARB 41.1g; FIBER 0.9g; CHOL 33mg; IRON 2.9mg; SODIUM 686mg; CALC 147mg

GRILLED MEDITERRANEAN CHICKEN PIZZA

2 teaspoons olive oil, divided
¼ teaspoon pepper
2 tablespoons chopped drained oil-packed sun-dried tomato halves
¼ cup chopped kalamata olives
2 teaspoons dried tarragon
2 teaspoons drained capers
½ cup dry white wine
2 cups (about 12 ounces) roasted skinned, boned chicken breast (such as Tyson), chopped
2 (10-inch) Quick-and-Easy Pizza Crusts (page 176)
Vegetable cooking spray

1. Combine 1½ teaspoons olive oil and ¼ teaspoon pepper in a small bowl; set aside.
2. Heat ½ teaspoon olive oil in a large nonstick skillet over medium-high heat. Add sun-dried tomato and next 3 ingredients; sauté 2 minutes or until thoroughly heated. Add wine, and simmer 1 minute or until liquid almost evaporates. Remove from heat, and stir in chicken. Set chicken mixture aside.
3. Prepare grill. Place 1 crust on grill rack coated with cooking spray; grill 3 minutes or until puffy and golden. Turn crust, grill-mark side up; brush with half of oil mixture. Top with half of chicken mixture. Cook 4 to 5 minutes or until crust is lightly browned. Repeat with remaining crust and toppings. Yield: 6 servings (serving size: ⅓ pizza).

CALORIES 300 (22% from fat); FAT 7.3g (sat 1.4g, mono 3.3g, poly 1.5g); PROTEIN 19.5g; CARB 38.3g; FIBER 0.8g; CHOL 35mg; IRON 2.9mg; SODIUM 662mg; CALC 22mg

GRILLED PIZZA BLANCA

2 (10-inch) Quick-and-Easy Pizza Crusts (page 176)
Vegetable cooking spray
1 teaspoon olive oil
½ cup grated fresh Parmesan cheese
1 (6-ounce) jar marinated artichoke hearts, drained and chopped
½ pound crabmeat, shell pieces removed

1. Prepare grill. Place 1 crust on grill rack coated with cooking spray; grill 3 minutes or until puffy and golden. Turn crust, grill-mark side up; brush with half of oil. Top with half of Parmesan, artichokes, and crabmeat. Cover and grill 3 to 4 minutes or until cheese melts and crust is lightly browned. Repeat with remaining crust and toppings. Yield: 6 servings (serving size: ⅓ pizza).

CALORIES 294 (22% from fat); FAT 7.2g (sat 2.2g, mono 3.1g, poly 0.9g); PROTEIN 17.9g; CARB 38.6g; FIBER 0.5g; CHOL 44mg; IRON 3mg; SODIUM 570mg; CALC 168mg

GOAT CHEESE-AND-GRILLED PEPPER PIZZA

Any combination of bell peppers can be used.

2 teaspoons olive oil
¼ teaspoon salt
¼ teaspoon pepper
1 cup yellow bell pepper rings
1 cup green bell pepper rings
1 cup red bell pepper rings
1 cup sliced red onion, separated into rings
Vegetable cooking spray
2 (10-inch) Quick-and-Easy Pizza Crusts (page 176)
½ cup crumbled herbed goat cheese, at room temperature

1. Combine first 3 ingredients in a small bowl; set aside.
2. Prepare grill. Place bell peppers and onion on grill rack coated with cooking spray; grill 10 to 12 minutes or until tender. Set aside.
3. Place 1 crust on grill rack coated with cooking spray; grill 3 minutes or until puffy and golden. Turn crust, grill-mark side up; brush with half of oil mixture. Top with half of grilled vegetables and goat cheese. Cover; grill 4 to 5 minutes or until cheese melts and crust is lightly browned. Repeat with remaining crust and toppings. Yield: 6 servings (serving size: ⅓ pizza).

CALORIES 267 (24% from fat); FAT 7.2g (sat 2.1g, mono 3.3g, poly 0.9g); PROTEIN 8.4g; CARB 42.2g; FIBER 2.1g; CHOL 8mg; IRON 3.4mg; SODIUM 402mg; CALC 63mg

WINE PICKS

• *Barone Ricasoli Chianti 1995 (Italian red), $7*
• *Isole e Olena Chianti Classico 1994 (Italian red), $14*
• *Markham Merlot Napa Valley 1994 (California red), $13.99*
• *Venezia Cabernet Sauvignon Alexander Valley 1994 (California red), $25*

Mood Indigo

The blues won't get you down with this jazzy Blueberry Crumble Pie. This combination of two desserts refuses to follow form, making its own sweet music.

You say you've got a case of the blues. Well, you don't need a case: Five cups will do just fine. We're talking blueberries here, as in Blueberry Crumble Pie, whose origins can be traced to the Deep South. Part pie, part crumble, the birth of the Blueberry Crumble Pie is what happens when two culinary classics meet.

Like the blues, this dessert doesn't always stick to form. Cut into it, and it loses its shape. The berries spill out of the shell and onto the serving plate. Although we tried adding tapioca to the recipe to help hold it together, it just wasn't the same. And because this is our lightened version of a heavier rendition, you won't get the blues after indulging yourself. So next time you go to the market, come home with the blues—fresh blueberries that is.

HOW WE DID IT

◆ Substituted low-fat sour cream for regular
◆ Used a reduced-fat graham-cracker crust instead of the traditional pastry crust
◆ Used brown sugar in place of white sugar and reduced the amount
◆ Added grated lemon rind for some extra zing

(pictured on page 170)

Don't worry when the pie doesn't hold its shape. The blueberries are supposed to spill out—that's the crumble.

5 cups fresh or frozen blueberries
1 (9-inch) reduced-fat graham-cracker crust
¾ cup packed brown sugar
3 tablespoons all-purpose flour
1½ teaspoons vanilla extract
¼ teaspoon grated lemon rind
1 (8-ounce) carton low-fat sour cream
¼ cup dry breadcrumbs
1 tablespoon granulated sugar
1 tablespoon margarine, melted

1. Preheat oven to 375°.
2. Place blueberries in crust; set aside.
3. Combine brown sugar and next 4 ingredients; spread over blueberries. Combine breadcrumbs, granulated sugar, and margarine; sprinkle over sour cream mixture. Bake at 375° for 40 minutes or until set and crumbs are lightly browned. Cool 1 hour on a wire rack. Yield: 8 servings.

CALORIES 312 (24% from fat); FAT 8.4g (sat 2.5g, mono 1.7g, poly 0.8g); PROTEIN 3.2g; CARB 56.5g; FIBER 4.3g; CHOL 11mg; IRON 1.3mg; SODIUM 166mg; CALC 61mg

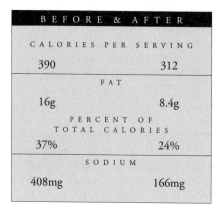

BEFORE & AFTER	
CALORIES PER SERVING	
390	312
FAT	
16g	8.4g
PERCENT OF TOTAL CALORIES	
37%	24%
SODIUM	
408mg	166mg

Introductory Spanish

This weekend, indulge in a romantic dinner from Spain. Our robust and flavorful menu features a sampling of tastes that showcase the country's rich culinary history.

VALENCIA ARTICHOKES

¼ cup low-fat sour cream
¼ cup plain low-fat yogurt
2 tablespoons orange juice
1 teaspoon chopped fresh dillweed
½ teaspoon honey
¼ teaspoon grated orange rind
2 medium artichokes (about 1¼ pounds)
1 teaspoon grated orange rind
⅛ teaspoon salt

1. Combine first 6 ingredients in a small bowl; stir well. Cover and chill.
2. Cut off stems of artichokes; remove bottom leaves. Trim about ½ inch from tops of artichokes. Place artichokes, stem ends down, in a large Dutch oven filled two-thirds with water. Add 1 teaspoon orange rind and salt; bring to a boil. Cover, reduce heat, and simmer 40 minutes or until a leaf near the center of each artichoke pulls out easily. Place artichokes in a large ice-filled bowl; cool. Place artichokes, stem sides up, on a rack to drain. Remove tough outer leaves and small inner leaves from artichokes; discard. Serve with yogurt dip. Yield: 2 servings (serving size: 2 tablespoons dip and 1 artichoke).
Note: Store remaining yogurt dip in refrigerator.

CALORIES 100 (21% from fat); FAT 2.3g (sat 1.3g, mono 0.6g, poly 0.2g); PROTEIN 4.6g; CARB 18.3g; FIBER 6.5g; CHOL 7mg; IRON 2.2mg; SODIUM 263mg; CALC 107mg

OYSTER BISQUE

1 teaspoon olive oil
¼ cup finely chopped carrot
¼ cup finely chopped celery
¼ cup finely chopped red bell
  pepper
1 tablespoon all-purpose flour
¾ cup evaporated skim milk
1 (12-ounce) container select
  oysters, drained
2 teaspoons chili sauce
1 teaspoon Worcestershire sauce
Dash of ground red pepper
¼ teaspoon paprika

1. Heat oil in a medium saucepan over medium-high heat. Add carrot, celery, and bell pepper; sauté 5 minutes or until tender. Combine flour and milk in a small bowl; stir with a whisk. Add to vegetable mixture in saucepan; cook over medium heat, stirring constantly, 3 minutes or until thick and bubbly. Add oysters; cook 2 minutes or until edges of oysters curl. Stir in chili sauce, Worcestershire sauce, and ground pepper. Sprinkle with paprika. Yield: 2 servings (serving size: 1 cup).

CALORIES 218 (25% from fat); FAT 6g (sat 1.3g, mono 2.1g, poly 1.3g); PROTEIN 17.7g; CARB 22.7g; FIBER 1.2g; CHOL 78mg; IRON 10mg; SODIUM 334mg; CALC 354mg

HONEY-DIJON LAMB CHOPS

(pictured on page 167)

2 tablespoons Dijon mustard
2 tablespoons fresh rosemary or
  2 teaspoons dried rosemary,
  crushed
2 tablespoons chopped fresh
  mint or 2 teaspoons dried
  mint flakes
1 tablespoon plus 1 teaspoon
  honey
½ teaspoon coarsely ground
  pepper
4 (4-ounce) lean lamb loin chops

1. Preheat broiler.
2. Combine first 5 ingredients in a small bowl, and stir well. Trim fat from lamb, and place chops on rack of a broiler pan. Broil 5 minutes on each side. Brush mustard mixture over chops. Broil chops 2 minutes on each side or to desired degree of doneness, basting occasionally with mustard mixture. Yield: 2 servings (serving size: 2 chops).

CALORIES 292 (36% from fat); FAT 11.4g (sat 3.7g, mono 4.5g, poly 0.7g); PROTEIN 31.5g; CARB 13.5g; FIBER 0.3g; CHOL 100mg; IRON 2.6mg; SODIUM 535mg; CALC 29mg

WINE PICKS

- *Carmen Cabernet Sauvignon Maipo Valley Reserve 1992 (Chilean red), $10*
- *Columbia Crest Sémillon-Chardonnay Columbia Valley 1995 (Washington state white), $7*
- *Freixenet Brut Rosé Cava Nonvintage (Spanish sparkling), $10*
- *Marqués de Cáceres Rioja 1992 (Spanish red), $12*
- *Torres Penedès Gran Viña Sol 1993 (Spanish white), $11*

ROASTED POTATO WEDGES WITH OLIVE TAPENADE

(pictured on page 167)

⅓ cup medium pitted ripe olives
1 tablespoon pine nuts
1 tablespoon water
1 teaspoon capers
1 teaspoon olive oil
1 garlic clove
2 medium baking potatoes, each
  cut into 8 wedges
2 teaspoons olive oil
1 tablespoon minced fresh parsley
1 tablespoon minced fresh thyme

1. Preheat oven to 400°.
2. Combine first 6 ingredients in a blender; cover and process until smooth. Place potato in a shallow 2-quart baking dish. Drizzle with 2 teaspoons oil; toss. Bake at 400° for 25 minutes or until tender, stirring occasionally. Add olive mixture; toss. Bake 5 minutes. Sprinkle with parsley and thyme. Yield: 2 servings (serving size: 8 potato wedges).

CALORIES 308 (27% from fat); FAT 9.2g (sat 1.5g, mono 5.1g, poly 2.5g); PROTEIN 5.7g; CARB 54.2g; FIBER 4.9g; CHOL 0mg; IRON 4.1mg; SODIUM 330mg; CALC 51mg

CITRUS GRANITA

(pictured on page 166)

1¼ cups water
⅓ cup sugar
¼ cup fresh lemon juice
¼ cup fresh orange juice

1. Combine all ingredients in a small saucepan. Bring to a boil; cook over medium-high heat, stirring constantly, 1 minute or until sugar dissolves. Remove from heat; cool. Pour into a 13 x 9-inch baking dish; cover and freeze at least 8 hours or until firm.
2. Remove from freezer; scrape entire mixture with tines of a fork until fluffy. Yield: 4 servings (serving size: 1 cup).

CALORIES 76 (0% from fat); FAT 0g; PROTEIN 0.2g; CARB 19.6g; FIBER 0g; CHOL 0mg; IRON 0mg; SODIUM 0mg; CALC 2mg

Joe Lando, Restaurant Man

The macho frontiersman on Dr. Quinn, Medicine Woman *prefers cooking on the range to riding it.*

Riding bareback, tossing tomahawks, and cuddling with your pet wolf: Nice work if you can get it, and Joe Lando has. The former chef for an Italian eatery in Los Angeles is currently riding the crest of fame opposite Jane Seymour on TV's *Dr. Quinn, Medicine Woman.*

As important as it is for Lando to stay fit for his role, he doesn't believe in giving up his favorite pastimes: cooking and eating. Moderation, he believes, is the answer.

At dinner Lando practices his culinary artistry. He keeps an array of flavorful ingredients such as lemons, garlic, spices, white and red wines, extra-virgin olive oil, flavored vinegars, and "lots of fresh herbs for my special, superintense marinades."

Lando recently opened a health-conscious fast-food restaurant in L.A.'s Brentwood section called The Daily Wrap. The restaurant has redefined burritos with fresh ethnic ingredients wrapped in a choice of flavored tortillas. You can span the globe with such wraps as Cajun, Caribbean Jerk, Mediterranean, Moroccan, Teriyaki, and Thai.

This veggie-filled favorite delights customers at Joe Lando's The Daily Wrap restaurant.

- ¾ cup chopped tomato
- 1 tablespoon diced red onion
- 1 tablespoon chopped fresh cilantro
- 1 teaspoon lime juice
- ⅛ teaspoon salt
- 1 garlic clove, minced
- 1 cup hot cooked jasmine or long-grain rice
- 2 tablespoons chopped fresh basil or 2 teaspoons dried basil
- 1 cup chopped red bell pepper
- ¾ cup diced zucchini
- ¾ cup diced yellow squash
- ¼ cup diced red onion
- 2 tablespoons balsamic vinegar
- 2 teaspoons olive oil
- 4 (8-inch) fat-free flour tortillas
- ¼ cup crumbled feta cheese

1. Preheat broiler.
2. Combine first 6 ingredients in a bowl, and set aside.
3. Combine rice and basil; set aside.
4. Arrange bell pepper and next 3 ingredients in a single layer on a baking sheet. Broil for 12 minutes or until vegetables are browned; spoon into a large bowl. Drizzle vinegar and oil over vegetables; toss to coat.
5. Warm tortillas according to package directions. Spoon ¼ cup rice mixture down center of each tortilla. Top each serving with ½ cup roasted vegetables, 2 tablespoons tomato mixture, and 1 tablespoon cheese; roll up. Yield: 4 servings.

CALORIES 231 (16% from fat); FAT 4.2g (sat 1.4g, mono 2g, poly 0.4g); PROTEIN 5.5g; CARB 43.7g; FIBER 2.1g; CHOL 6mg; IRON 1.5mg; SODIUM 499mg; CALC 60mg

Taking the Big out of the Big Easy

Some easy culinary tricks lighten this traditional Cajun-Creole dinner.

Of all of America's regional cuisines, few are as adventuresome as Louisiana's . . . or as heavy. Eat too many of those meals, and you can understand why New Orleans is called The Big Easy.

We've put a new spin on that tradition, however, with our dinner menu that combines traditional Cajun and Creole styles with the city's passion for Italian food. It's a kind of culinary magic that you can easily do in your kitchen. Take, for example, our Gulf of Mexico Gumbo: Instead of using a heavy, oil-based roux, we browned the flour in a cast-iron skillet to retain the dish's dark, nutty flavor. We've given our Pasta with Oysters and Tasso an updated twist by using angel hair pasta. Rather than sautéing the artichoke bottoms in butter, we steamed ours. And for a finishing touch, we made an icy granita out of *café au lait.*

The best part about all of this is that our Louisiana menu is every bit as tasty as its high-fat equivalent. If we keep this up, they'll soon be calling New Orleans The Light Easy.

CAJUN-CREOLE SEASONING

All the recipes in this menu except the dessert use this basic seasoning.

- 1 tablespoon salt
- ¾ teaspoon ground red pepper
- ½ teaspoon garlic powder
- ½ teaspoon black pepper

1. Combine all ingredients in a small bowl, and stir well. Yield: about 1½ tablespoons.

GULF OF MEXICO GUMBO

1 cup all-purpose flour
1 teaspoon vegetable oil
2 cups chopped onion
1 cup chopped green bell pepper
½ cup chopped celery
4 garlic cloves, minced
1 cup sliced okra
1 cup chopped tomato
1½ cups water
1 teaspoon Cajun-Creole Seasoning (page 182)
4 (8-ounce) bottles clam juice
2 bay leaves
½ pound skinned red snapper or other firm white fish fillet, cut into 1-inch pieces
¼ cup thinly sliced green onions
¾ pound crayfish, peeled
¼ pound medium-size shrimp, peeled and deveined
½ teaspoon hot sauce
4½ cups hot cooked long-grain rice

1. Place flour in a 9-inch cast-iron skillet; cook over medium heat, stirring constantly with a whisk, 20 minutes or until browned. (If flour browns too fast, remove it from heat, and stir until it cools down.) Remove from heat; set aside.
2. Heat oil in a large Dutch oven over medium heat. Add onion and next 3 ingredients; sauté 8 minutes or until vegetables are tender. Add okra and tomato; cover and cook 5 minutes, stirring occasionally. Add 1½ cups water and next 3 ingredients; bring to a boil. Gradually add browned flour, stirring with a whisk. Reduce heat; simmer, uncovered, for 45 minutes, stirring occasionally.
3. Add snapper; cook 5 minutes. Add green onions, crayfish, and shrimp; cook 10 minutes or until seafood is done. Stir in hot sauce; discard bay leaves. Serve gumbo over rice. Yield: 9 servings (serving size: 1 cup gumbo and ½ cup rice).
Note: One (8-ounce) container select oysters, undrained, can be substituted for crayfish, if desired.

CALORIES 254 (6% from fat); FAT 1.8g (sat 0.3g, mono 0.3g, poly 0.7g); PROTEIN 16.8g; CARB 41.8g; FIBER 2.4g; CHOL 59mg; IRON 3.1mg; SODIUM 447mg; CALC 73mg

PASTA WITH OYSTERS AND TASSO

Smoked pork chops can be substituted for the tasso in this dish.

1 (12-ounce) container select oysters, undrained
1 cup chopped green onions
1 cup evaporated skim milk
⅔ cup diced tasso
1 garlic clove, minced
2 tablespoons all-purpose flour
1 tablespoon chopped fresh parsley
⅛ teaspoon Cajun-Creole Seasoning (page 182)
6 cups hot cooked angel hair (about ¾ pound uncooked pasta)
Basil sprigs (optional)

1. Drain oysters, reserving ⅓ cup juice, and set both aside.
2. Combine green onions and next 3 ingredients in a saucepan; cook over medium-low heat 10 minutes, stirring occasionally.
3. Place flour in a small bowl. Add reserved oyster juice, stirring with a whisk until blended; add to milk mixture. Cook over medium heat, stirring constantly, 4 minutes or until thick. Add oysters, parsley, and Cajun-Creole Seasoning; cook 4 minutes or until edges of oysters curl. Combine oyster mixture and pasta in a large bowl; toss well. Garnish with basil sprigs, if desired. Yield: 7 servings (serving size: 1 cup).

Note: If you cannot find tasso you can substitute ⅔ cup diced smoked pork chops. If you would like to order tasso contact K-Paul's Louisiana Mail Order: 800/457-2857.

CALORIES 267 (11% from fat); FAT 3.4g (sat 0.9g, mono 0.8g, poly 0.8g); PROTEIN 14.6g; CARB 43.4g; FIBER 2.4g; CHOL 35mg; IRON 5.5mg; SODIUM 288mg; CALC 150mg

MARINATED ARTICHOKES AND MIRLITONS

Here, artichoke bottoms are steamed with gourdlike chayotes, which in Louisiana are known as mirlitons. Pattypan squash can be substituted for the mirlitons.

3 (8-ounce) mirlitons (chayotes)
1 (14-ounce) can artichoke bottoms, drained and sliced crosswise
½ cup white wine vinegar
¼ cup low-salt chicken broth
2 tablespoons chopped fresh basil
2 tablespoons chopped fresh parsley
1 tablespoon olive oil
½ teaspoon Cajun-Creole Seasoning (page 182)
2 garlic cloves, minced
1 (2-ounce) jar diced pimento, drained
Boston lettuce leaves (optional)

1. Peel mirlitons; cut in half lengthwise, and discard pits. Cut mirliton halves lengthwise into slices. Arrange mirliton slices and artichoke bottoms in a steamer basket over boiling water; cover and steam 40 minutes or until tender. Cool.
2. Combine vinegar and next 7 ingredients in a large bowl; stir with a whisk.
3. Add vegetables to vinegar mixture; toss well. Cover and marinate 1 hour, stirring occasionally. Spoon into a lettuce-lined bowl, if desired. Serve with a slotted spoon. Yield: 6 servings (serving size: 1 cup).

CALORIES 72 (35% from fat); FAT 2.8g (sat 0.3g, mono 1.7g, poly 0.2g); PROTEIN 2.2g; CARB 11.1g; FIBER 1.3g; CHOL 0mg; IRON 1.2mg; SODIUM 265mg; CALC 43mg

CAFÉ AU LAIT GRANITA

(pictured on page 168)

"Café au lait" is French for "coffee with milk," and granita is an Italian ice. When these French and Italian dishes get together, you have a new New Orleans dessert.

- **3 cups hot strong brewed coffee**
- **3 cups 1% low-fat milk**
- **½ cup sugar**

1. Combine brewed coffee, milk, and sugar in a pitcher; stir until sugar dissolves. Pour into ice cube trays; freeze 4 hours or until firm.
2. Let stand at room temperature 10 minutes. Place frozen cubes in a food processor; process until smooth. Spoon into chilled dishes; serve immediately. Yield: 2 quarts (serving size: 1 cup).

CALORIES 89 (10% from fat); FAT 1g (sat 0.6g, mono 0.3g, poly 0g); PROTEIN 3.1g; CARB 17.2g; FIBER 0g; CHOL 4mg; IRON 0.4mg; SODIUM 48mg; CALC 114mg

The Pleasure Principle

Eating the foods you love may be the best way to a healthier diet.

"Enjoy a variety of foods"—a seemingly harmless statement. But when an advisory committee considered making it part of the new federal Dietary Guidelines for Americans, some members balked. After an exhaustive debate, the group finally agreed on a revision. The carefully crafted result of all that debate? "*Eat* a variety of foods."

This small but significant change should come as no surprise. After all, the flood of diet and nutrition information would lead any reasonable person to assume that we're not supposed to actually *enjoy* our food. We're supposed to focus on fat tallies, and how our daily fare stacks up against The Pyramid, right . . . ?

What we seem to have forgotten is that food is one of greatest joys given to humankind—that is, for those who let themselves enjoy it.

CITRUS TIRAMISÙ

Even this lighter version of the classic Italian dessert is the essence of pleasure.

- **¼ cup sugar**
- **2 tablespoons cognac**
- **1 (8-ounce) tub fat-free cream cheese**
- **1 (3.5-ounce) carton mascarpone cheese**
- **1½ cups hot water**
- **1 tablespoon plus 2 teaspoons instant espresso coffee granules or 3 tablespoons plus 1 teaspoon instant coffee**
- **24 ladyfingers (2 [3-ounce] packages)**
- **1 cup orange sections, chopped (about 3 oranges)**
- **1 teaspoon unsweetened cocoa**
- **¼ cup candied orange peel or candied citron**

1. Place first 4 ingredients in food processor; process until smooth.
2. Combine hot water and espresso granules in a bowl. Split ladyfingers in half lengthwise. Quickly dip 12 ladyfinger halves, flat sides down, into espresso; arrange, dipped sides down, in the bottom of an 8-inch square baking dish. Dip 12 more ladyfinger halves, flat sides down, into espresso; arrange, dipped sides down, on top of first layer. Spread half of cheese mixture evenly over ladyfingers; top with half of oranges. Repeat procedure with remaining ladyfinger halves, espresso, cheese mixture, and oranges.
3. Cover with plastic wrap. Chill 8 hours. Sprinkle with cocoa; top with candied orange peel. Yield: 9 servings.
Note: Substitute 1½ cups very strong brewed coffee for espresso and 1½ cups water, if desired.

CALORIES 173 (31% from fat); FAT 6g (sat 2.9g, mono 1.5g, poly 1.4g); PROTEIN 5.2g; CARB 21.6g; FIBER 1.5g; CHOL 41mg; IRON 0.1mg; SODIUM 182mg; CALC 110mg

A Nice Touch

For a casual summertime meal, enjoy the flavors of the French Riviera with this cool, colorful salad.

Let's say you didn't know that Nice is a fashionable resort city on the French Riviera, famous for its cathedral, perfume, and flower market. You'd still know Nice by its most famous dish, the classic salade niçoise. In French, "a la niçoise" means "as prepared in Nice," identifying the cuisine found in and around that Mediterranean seaport. When it comes to salade niçoise, there are no absolutes; its ingredients can vary from cook to cook. The most familiar version, like the one we've prepared here, gets its taste from anchovies, black olives, eggs, green beans, lemon juice, tomatoes, tuna, and a garlic-basil vinaigrette. Served with French bread, this salad can serve as lunch or a light supper. It's perfect fare for the patio, terrace, or yacht.

SALADE NIÇOISE

(pictured on page 168)

- **3 tablespoons fresh lemon juice**
- **1 pound tuna steaks (about 2 [8-ounce] steaks)**
- **Freshly ground pepper**
- **Vegetable cooking spray**
- **10 small red potatoes (about 1 pound)**
- **½ pound green beans, trimmed**
- **4 cups torn romaine lettuce**
- **4 cups trimmed watercress (about 1 bunch)**
- **3 medium tomatoes, each cut into 6 wedges**
- **3 hard-cooked large eggs, quartered lengthwise**
- **1 small green bell pepper, cut into strips**
- **½ cup niçoise olives**
- **2 tablespoons capers**
- **6 canned anchovy fillets**
- **Garlic-Basil Vinaigrette**

1. Drizzle lemon juice over tuna; sprinkle with pepper. Marinate in refrigerator 15 minutes. Remove tuna from marinade; discard lemon juice. Prepare grill or broiler. Place tuna on grill rack or rack of a broiler pan coated with cooking spray; cook 4 minutes on each side or until medium-well done. Break tuna into chunks; set aside.

2. Arrange potatoes in a steamer basket over boiling water; cover and steam 3 minutes. Add green beans; steam, covered, 8 additional minutes or until vegetables are crisp-tender. Drain and let cool.

3. Combine lettuce and watercress on a large serving platter. Arrange tuna, potatoes, green beans, tomatoes, eggs, and bell pepper over greens. Top with olives, capers, and anchovy fillets. Drizzle Garlic-Basil Vinaigrette over salad. Yield: 6 servings.

CALORIES 295 (31% from fat); FAT 10.1g (sat 2.2g, mono 4.4g, poly 2.3g); PROTEIN 30g; CARB 22g; FIBER 4.5g; CHOL 64mg; IRON 4.4mg; SODIUM 458mg; CALC 127mg

Garlic-Basil Vinaigrette:

⅓ cup low-salt chicken broth
1½ tablespoons chopped fresh basil
1 tablespoon extra-virgin olive oil
1 tablespoon fresh lemon juice
1 tablespoon red wine vinegar
1 teaspoon Dijon mustard
3 garlic cloves, halved
Freshly ground pepper

1. Combine all ingredients in a blender; cover and process until smooth. Yield: 6 tablespoons (serving size: 1 tablespoon).

CALORIES 20 (81% from fat); FAT 1.8g (sat 0.2g, mono 1.3g, poly 0.2g); PROTEIN 0.2g; CARB 0.8g; FIBER 0g; CHOL 0mg; IRON 0.1mg; SODIUM 22mg; CALC 3mg

A Culinary Bridge to Cambodia

For Chef Leang Hong, owner of Galaxie Restaurant in Rhode Island, cooking is a way of staying connected to his lost homeland. Fresh, vibrant, and simple best describe these native dishes that are perfect for summer.

Hong explains that the appeal of Cambodian cooking is linked, ironically, to his country's scarred history. "It's a hybrid cuisine that combines some of the best traditions of the Chinese, Vietnamese, French, Thai, and Indian people who have invaded or influenced Cambodia through the centuries," he says.

Cambodians do have one distinguishing feature, however, with regard to their taste in food: a strong aversion to fat. Their favorite dishes are exceptionally lean, as you will discover for yourself as you prepare these recipes, for which Hong provided the blueprint. They're complex in flavor, but, as you will also see, they're quite simple to prepare.

CHAP CHAI (SEAFOOD-VEGETABLE SOUP)

Fish balls are available in the frozen-food section of most Asian markets.

1½ ounces dried wood ear mushrooms
2 cups boiling water
½ pound cleaned skinned squid
½ cup water
12 small clams in shells, scrubbed
1 teaspoon vegetable oil
2 large garlic cloves, minced
2 cups peeled, thinly sliced daikon radish (about ½ pound)
½ pound medium-size shrimp, peeled and deveined
6 (10½-ounce) cans low-salt chicken broth
1 (7-ounce) package fish balls or 7 ounces firm white fish cut into 1-inch pieces
3 cups thinly sliced napa (Chinese) cabbage
1 cup (1½-inch) julienne-cut green onions
¼ cup fish sauce
¼ teaspoon pepper

1. Combine mushrooms and 2 cups boiling water; cover and let stand 30 minutes or until soft. Drain mushrooms, and cut into ¼-inch-wide strips; set aside.

2. Cut squid into ¼-inch-thick rings; set aside.

3. Bring ½ cup water to a boil in a large Dutch oven. Add clams; cover and cook 3 minutes or until shells open. Discard any unopened shells. Remove clams with a slotted spoon; set aside. Pour cooking liquid into a bowl.

4. Heat oil in Dutch oven over medium-high heat. Add garlic, and sauté 2 minutes or until golden. Add reserved cooking liquid, daikon radish, shrimp, and broth. Bring to a boil; cook 2 minutes. Add fish balls; cook 1 minute. Add mushrooms, squid, clams, cabbage, and remaining ingredients; cook an additional minute. Yield: 13 servings (serving size: 1 cup).

Note: This soup is great the day it is made but will keep for up to 1 week in an airtight container in the refrigerator. Reheat slowly over low heat.

CALORIES 85 (24% from fat); FAT 2.3g (sat 0.5g, mono 0.6g, poly 0.7g); PROTEIN 11.6g; CARB 4.5g; FIBER 0.7g; CHOL 75mg; IRON 2mg; SODIUM 730mg; CALC 42mg

All of these ingredients can be found in Asian markets, though many are available at supermarkets as well. However, some of them may not be labeled consistently, so ask a clerk for help if necessary.

BEAN THREADS OR CELLOPHANE NOODLES: Made from the starch of green mung beans, they have a different texture from traditional noodles. They can also be found labeled as "transparent" or "shining noodles," "pea-stick noodles," or "mung bean sticks."

DAIKON: This is a large Asian radish, similar in appearance to a parsnip. Carrot can be substituted.

DRIED JELLIED FUNGUS: Available only in Asian stores, it's similar in appearance to dried wood ear mushrooms.

FINE RICE VERMICELLI: Unlike traditional vermicelli, these Asian noodles are wide and flat (similar in shape to fettuccine). You can find them labeled as "rice-stick noodles."

FISH SAUCE: Made from water, anchovies, and salt, it's very potent—a little goes a long way. It's also very high in sodium: 1 tablespoon contains the sodium of 1 teaspoon salt. Again, use sparingly.

OYSTER SAUCE: A concentrated sauce made from oysters, brine, and soy sauce. It's a commonly used Asian condiment.

RICE PAPER: This edible, translucent paper is similar to phyllo dough in texture. Rice paper can also be found labeled as "dried pastry flake."

UDON NOODLES: These thick Japanese noodles are similar to spaghetti. They come round or square and are typically made from either wheat or corn flour.

BANH BUNG (WARM NOODLE SALAD WITH BEEF)

Although traditional spaghetti has a different texture, it can be used in place of the fine rice vermicelli that's found in Asian markets.

1 (¾-pound) beef tenderloin
1 tablespoon oyster sauce
1 tablespoon low-sodium soy sauce
½ teaspoon sugar
3 quarts water
8 ounces uncooked fine rice vermicelli
½ cup light coconut milk
1 teaspoon vegetable oil
Vegetable cooking spray
1 cup thinly sliced yellow onion, separated into rings
4 cups fresh bean sprouts
2 cups peeled, julienne-cut cucumber
1 cup thinly sliced green cabbage
1 cup julienne-cut carrot
20 basil leaves
⅔ cup Lime-Vinegar Sauce (page 187)

1. Trim fat from beef. Cut across grain into thin slices; set aside.
2. Combine oyster sauce, soy sauce, and sugar. Stir well; set aside.
3. Bring 3 quarts water to a simmer in a large Dutch oven. Add rice vermicelli; simmer 2 minutes or just until tender. Drain and return vermicelli to Dutch oven. Add coconut milk; toss well. Set aside; keep warm.
4. Heat oil in a wok or large nonstick skillet coated with cooking spray over medium-high heat until hot. Add onion; stir-fry 2 minutes. Add beef; stir-fry 3 minutes. Add oyster sauce mixture; stir-fry 30 seconds. Remove from heat. Set aside; keep warm.
5. Combine bean sprouts and next 4 ingredients in a large bowl; toss gently. Spoon bean sprout mixture evenly into 4 large shallow bowls; top evenly with beef mixture and rice vermicelli mixture. Drizzle with Lime-Vinegar Sauce. Yield: 4 servings (serving size: 2 cups bean sprout mixture, ⅔ cup beef mixture, 1 cup rice vermicelli mixture,

and about 2½ tablespoons Lime-Vinegar Sauce).

Note: Substitute 8 ounces uncooked spaghetti for fine rice vermicelli, if desired. Cook in boiling water 10 minutes.

CALORIES 360 (34% from fat); FAT 13.7g (sat 4.7g, mono 4.8g, poly 2.6g); PROTEIN 27.1g; CARB 34.3g; FIBER 4.5g; CHOL 53mg; IRON 4.9mg; SODIUM 423mg; CALC 62mg

NIME CHOW (RAW SPRING ROLLS)

1 ounce uncooked bean threads (cellophane noodles)
2 cups hot water
12 (8-inch) round sheets rice paper
2 cups thinly sliced curly leaf lettuce
1 cup fresh bean sprouts
24 medium basil leaves
32 medium-size shrimp, cooked and peeled
1 cup Lime-Vinegar Sauce (page 187)
½ cup finely chopped unsalted, dry-roasted peanuts

1. Combine bean threads and 2 cups hot water in a bowl; let stand 10 minutes. Drain; cut into 2-inch lengths with scissors.
2. Add cold water to a large shallow dish to a depth of 1 inch. Cut 4 rice paper sheets in half, leaving remaining 8 sheets whole. Place 1 whole rice paper sheet and 1 half rice paper sheet in dish of water. Let stand 2 minutes or until soft. Remove sheets from water.
3. Place whole rice paper sheet on a flat surface; top with half sheet, lining up edges of sheets. Place ¼ cup lettuce over half sheet, leaving a ½-inch border around outer edge of half sheet. Arrange 1 tablespoon bean threads, 2 tablespoons bean sprouts, 3 basil leaves, and 4 shrimp over lettuce. Fold sides of rice paper sheets over filling; roll up jelly-roll fashion. Gently press seam to seal; place, seam side down, on a platter (cover to keep from drying). Repeat procedure with remaining rice paper sheets, lettuce, bean threads, bean sprouts, basil, and shrimp.
4. Cut each roll in half crosswise. Combine Lime-Vinegar Sauce and

peanuts in a small bowl; serve with rolls. Yield: 8 servings (serving size: 2 roll halves and 3 tablespoons sauce).

CALORIES 154 (18% from fat); FAT 3.1g (sat 0.5g, mono 1.2g, poly 1g); PROTEIN 14.5g; CARB 17.1g; FIBER 0.9g; CHOL 109mg; IRON 2mg; SODIUM 666mg; CALC 32mg

MAKING SPRING ROLLS

❶ *Place half sheet of rice paper on 1 whole sheet.*

❷ *Arrange filling over rice paper. Fold sides over filling, and roll up.*

NYOM
(WARM CHICKEN SALAD)

½ cup dried jellied fungus, cut into strips (about ½ ounce)
1 cup boiling water
2 (10½-ounce) cans low-salt chicken broth
4 ounces uncooked bean threads (cellophane noodles)
4 (4-ounce) skinned, boned chicken breast halves
3 cups thinly sliced green cabbage
2 cups fresh bean sprouts
1 cup (1½-inch) julienne-cut green onions
⅓ cup finely chopped unsalted, dry-roasted peanuts
3 tablespoons thinly sliced fresh basil
⅔ cup Lime-Vinegar Sauce (page 187)
¼ teaspoon ground red pepper

1. Combine fungus and 1 cup boiling water in a bowl; let stand 30 minutes. Drain.
2. Bring broth to a boil in a large saucepan. Add fungus; cook 1 minute. Add bean threads; cook 2 minutes or until tender. Remove fungus and bean threads with a slotted spoon; place in a bowl. Set aside.
3. Bring broth to a simmer. Add chicken; cover and cook 30 minutes or until chicken is done. Drain; cool slightly. Cut chicken across grain into thin slices.
4. Combine chicken, fungus, bean threads, cabbage, and next 4 ingredients in a large bowl; toss gently. Combine Lime-Vinegar Sauce and red pepper in a small bowl; stir well. Pour over chicken mixture; toss gently to coat. Serve immediately. Yield: 4 servings (serving size: 2 cups).

CALORIES 299 (30% from fat); FAT 11.8g (sat 2g, mono 5.3g, poly 3.5g); PROTEIN 33.9g; CARB 22.5g; FIBER 4.1g; CHOL 66mg; IRON 3.3mg; SODIUM 643mg; CALC 79mg

LORT CHA
(SHORT RICE NOODLES)

2 tablespoons low-sodium soy sauce
1 tablespoon oyster sauce
½ teaspoon sugar
1 pound uncooked udon noodles (thick, round fresh Japanese wheat noodles) or spaghetti
1½ teaspoons vegetable oil
Vegetable cooking spray
2 (4-ounce) lean, boned center-cut loin pork chops (about ¾ inch thick), cut into ¼-inch-wide strips
2 garlic cloves, minced
1 large egg, lightly beaten
1½ cups fresh bean sprouts
1½ cups thinly sliced green cabbage
1½ cups (1½-inch) julienne-cut green onions

1. Combine first 3 ingredients in a bowl. Stir well; set aside.
2. Cook noodles in boiling water 10 minutes (discard noodle seasoning packet). Drain; rinse under cold water.

3. Heat oil in a wok or large skillet coated with cooking spray over high heat until hot. Add pork and garlic; stir-fry 2 minutes. Add soy sauce mixture, and stir-fry 30 seconds. Add egg, and stir-fry 30 seconds. Add cooked noodles, bean sprouts, cabbage, and green onions; stir-fry 3 minutes or until vegetables wilt and udon noodles are thoroughly heated. Yield: 4 servings (serving size: 1½ cups).

CALORIES 326 (23% from fat); FAT 8.2g (sat 2.3g, mono 3g, poly 1.8g); PROTEIN 21.9g; CARB 40.4g; FIBER 3.8g; CHOL 91mg; IRON 3.4mg; SODIUM 411mg; CALC 65mg

LIME-VINEGAR SAUCE

This fat-free sauce is served with many Cambodian dishes. Sweet, salty, and sour, it gives everything from salads to noodles to soup a splash of intense flavor.

1 cup hot water
¼ cup sugar
½ teaspoon salt
2 tablespoons fresh lime juice
1 tablespoon white vinegar
1 tablespoon fish sauce
1 large garlic clove, minced

1. Combine first 3 ingredients in a small bowl; stir well. Cool completely. Stir in juice and remaining ingredients. Yield: 1¼ cups (serving size: 1 tablespoon).

CALORIES 11 (0% from fat); FAT 0g; PROTEIN 0g; CARB 2.7g; FIBER 0g; CHOL 0mg; IRON 0mg; SODIUM 162mg; CALC 1mg

W I N E 🍷 P I C K S

- *Bouchaine Dry Gewürztraminer 1995 (California white), $9*
- *Mirassou Family Selection Riesling 1996 (California white), $7.50*
- *Palmer White Riesling 1996 (New York state white), $9.99*
- *Sakonnet Fumé Vidal 1994 (Rhode Island white), $10*

Easy Italian Fare

In Italian, pasta puttanesca means "harlot's pasta." No one knows for sure how this zesty classic got its colorful name—only that its use of tomatoes, olives, and anchovy paste makes for an earthy dining experience.

For this easy meat, make the breadsticks first. They'll hold until the pasta and salad are finished. For the romaine salad: Combine romaine lettuce, prepackaged croutons, and red onion slices with a fat-free vinaigrette. Toss and serve.

MENU

PASTA PUTTANESCA

Romaine salad

FENNEL-AND-GARLIC BREADSTICKS

ANGEL FOOD CAKE AND MARINATED PEACHES

PASTA PUTTANESCA

(pictured on page 171)

Because the flavors are so intense, you won't need to add Parmesan cheese.

- 1 tablespoon extra-virgin olive oil
- 3 garlic cloves, minced
- 3½ cups diced plum tomato
- ¼ cup minced fresh flat-leaf parsley
- 3 tablespoons Spanish olives, halved
- 2 tablespoons minced fresh oregano or 2 teaspoons dried oregano
- 1½ tablespoons capers
- 2 teaspoons anchovy paste
- ⅛ to ¼ teaspoon dried crushed red pepper
- 4 cups hot cooked vermicelli (about 8 ounces uncooked pasta)
- Oregano sprigs (optional)

1. Heat oil in a nonstick skillet over low heat. Add garlic; sauté 5 minutes. Add tomato and next 6 ingredients. Bring to a boil. Reduce heat to medium; cook 10 minutes or until thick. Combine tomato mixture and pasta; toss well. Garnish with oregano sprigs, if desired. Yield: 4 servings (serving size: 1½ cups).

CALORIES 283 (19% from fat); FAT 6g (sat 0.8g, mono 3.2g, poly 1.1g); PROTEIN 9.3g; CARB 49.2g; FIBER 4.8g; CHOL 0mg; IRON 3.5mg; SODIUM 668mg; CALC 45mg

FENNEL-AND-GARLIC BREADSTICKS

- 1 teaspoon extra-virgin olive oil
- 1 teaspoon fennel seeds
- ¼ teaspoon coarsely ground pepper
- 2 garlic cloves, minced
- 1 (11-ounce) can refrigerated breadstick dough
- Olive-oil flavored vegetable cooking spray

1. Preheat oven to 350°.
2. Heat oil in a small nonstick skillet over medium heat. Add fennel seeds, pepper, and garlic; sauté 1 minute. Remove from heat, and set aside.
3. Unroll breadstick dough (do not separate into breadsticks). Beginning at center of dough, spread fennel seed mixture over half of short end of dough, pressing gently. Fold other half of dough over fennel seed mixture, pinching ends together to seal.
4. Cut dough along perforations to form 8 breadsticks. Twist each folded breadstick, and place on a baking sheet coated with cooking spray. Bake breadsticks at 350° for 18 minutes or until breadsticks are golden. Yield: 8 servings (serving size: 1 breadstick).

CALORIES 118 (24% from fat); FAT 3.2g (sat 0.6g, mono 1.3g, poly 0.9g); PROTEIN 3.1g; CARB 18.4g; FIBER 1.1g; CHOL 0mg; IRON 0.1mg; SODIUM 290mg; CALC 5mg

ANGEL FOOD CAKE AND MARINATED PEACHES

- 3 cups peeled, sliced fresh peaches
- ⅛ teaspoon ground nutmeg
- ⅛ teaspoon ground cinnamon
- ¼ cup peach schnapps
- 6 (1½-ounce) slices angel food cake

1. Combine first 4 ingredients in a bowl. Cover and marinate in refrigerator 30 minutes to 4 hours. Serve over cake. Yield: 6 servings (serving size: 1 slice cake and ½ cup peach mixture).

CALORIES 177 (2% from fat); FAT 0.4g (sat 0.1g, mono 0.1g, poly 0.2g); PROTEIN 3.1g; CARB 36.9g; FIBER 2g; CHOL 0mg; IRON 0.3mg; SODIUM 319mg; CALC 64mg

---

Crowning Glory

We have beef recipes fit for a king, including nachos made by a princess —the New York State Alternate Dairy Princess, Kirsten Rowe.

TEX-MEX NACHOS

—Kirsten Rowe, Ithaca, New York

- ¾ pound ground round
- ¼ cup sliced green onions
- ¾ cup taco sauce
- ¼ teaspoon garlic powder
- ⅛ teaspoon pepper
- 1 (15-ounce) can kidney beans, drained
- 1 (8¾-ounce) can no-salt-added whole-kernel corn, drained
- 2 ounces fat-free baked tortilla chips (about 2 cups)
- 3 cups shredded iceberg lettuce
- 1 cup chopped tomato
- 1 cup (4 ounces) shredded reduced-fat sharp Cheddar or Monterey Jack cheese
- ½ cup salsa
- ½ cup fat-free sour cream

1. Cook meat and green onions in a nonstick skillet over medium-high heat until browned, stirring to crumble. Drain well, and return meat mixture to skillet. Stir in taco sauce and next 4 ingredients; cook until thoroughly heated. For each serving, spoon 1 cup meat mixture over ½ cup chips; top with ¾ cup lettuce, ¼ cup tomato, ¼ cup cheese, 2 tablespoons salsa, and 2 tablespoons sour cream. Yield: 4 servings.

CALORIES 504 (22% from fat); FAT 12.5g (sat 5.3g, mono 3.9g, poly 0.7g); PROTEIN 39g; CARB 57.4g; FIBER 5.1g; CHOL 73mg; IRON 4.5mg; SODIUM 804mg; CALC 302mg

MEXICAN MEATBALL AND SALSA SOUP

—Julie DeMatteo, Clementon, New Jersey

 2 (6-inch) corn tortillas, cut into 20 (¼-inch-wide) strips
 ½ teaspoon vegetable oil
 ½ cup uncooked long-grain rice, divided
 1 pound ultra-lean ground beef
 1 tablespoon dried parsley flakes
 ½ teaspoon chili powder
 ½ teaspoon dried oregano
 ¼ teaspoon salt
 ¼ teaspoon pepper
 Vegetable cooking spray
 ½ cup chopped onion
 ½ cup thinly sliced celery
 ¼ cup thinly sliced carrot
 1 garlic clove, minced
 ⅔ cup salsa
 ½ cup water
 2 (10½-ounce) cans low-salt chicken broth
 ½ cup frozen whole-kernel corn
 ½ cup (2 ounces) shredded reduced-fat Monterey Jack cheese

1. Preheat oven to 400°.
2. Combine tortilla strips and oil; toss well to coat. Arrange in a single layer on a jelly-roll pan; bake at 400° for 10 minutes or until crisp and brown, stirring once. Set aside.
3. Combine ¼ cup rice, ground beef, and next 5 ingredients in a bowl; shape mixture into 24 (1-inch) meatballs. Place on a broiler pan; bake at 400° for 10 minutes.
4. Place a Dutch oven coated with cooking spray over medium-high heat. Add onion, celery, and carrot; sauté 4 minutes. Add garlic; sauté 1 minute. Add salsa, water, and broth; bring to a boil. Add ¼ cup rice and meatballs; cover, reduce heat, and simmer 20 minutes or until rice is tender and meatballs are done. Stir in corn; cook 1 minute or until thoroughly heated.
5. Spoon into bowls; sprinkle with cheese and tortilla strips. Yield: 4 servings (serving size: 1½ cups soup, 2 tablespoons cheese, and 5 tortilla strips).

CALORIES 368 (29% from fat); FAT 12g (sat 4.8g, mono 3.8g, poly 1.1g); PROTEIN 30.6g; CARB 37.7g; FIBER 3.3g; CHOL 81mg; IRON 2.8mg; SODIUM 679mg; CALC 181mg

MEATBALLS IN SAUCE

—Corinne Journeau, Queenston, Ontario, Canada

 2 pounds ground round
 1 cup fresh breadcrumbs
 ⅔ cup skim milk
 ½ cup minced fresh onion
 ¼ cup grated Parmesan cheese
 2 tablespoons Worcestershire sauce
 ½ teaspoon garlic powder
 ⅛ teaspoon pepper
 1 large egg, lightly beaten
 Vegetable cooking spray
 1 cup ketchup
 1 cup grape jelly

1. Preheat oven to 350°.
2. Combine first 9 ingredients in a bowl; shape mixture into 54 (1-inch) meatballs. Place half of meatballs on rack of a broiler pan coated with cooking spray; bake at 350° for 20 minutes or until done. Repeat procedure with remaining meatballs.
3. Combine ketchup and jelly in a large nonstick skillet. Bring to a boil over medium-high heat; cook until well-blended, stirring frequently. Add meatballs; cook until thoroughly heated. Serve hot. Yield: 4½ dozen (serving size: 3 meatballs and 1½ tablespoons sauce).

CALORIES 156 (19% from fat); FAT 3.3g (sat 1.2g, mono 1.2g, poly 0.3g); PROTEIN 13.8g; CARB 18.3g; FIBER 0.6g; CHOL 45mg; IRON 1.5mg; SODIUM 246mg; CALC 39mg

TEXAS SHEPHERD'S PIE

—Carol Reaves, San Antonio, Texas

 1½ pounds baking potatoes, peeled and cut into ¼-inch-thick slices
 ⅓ cup low-fat buttermilk
 ½ teaspoon salt, divided
 ½ teaspoon pepper, divided
 1 pound ground round
 ½ cup chopped onion
 ⅓ cup chopped celery
 ¼ cup shredded carrot
 ½ teaspoon fennel seeds
 1 teaspoon instant minced garlic
 1½ cups salsa
 Vegetable cooking spray
 ½ cup (2 ounces) shredded reduced-fat sharp Cheddar cheese

1. Preheat oven to 375°.
2. Place potato in a saucepan. Cover with water; bring to a boil. Reduce heat; simmer, uncovered, 10 minutes or until tender. Drain. Return potato to pan. Add buttermilk, ¼ teaspoon salt, and ¼ teaspoon pepper; beat at medium speed of an electric mixer until smooth.
3. Cook meat in a large nonstick skillet over medium-high heat until browned, stirring to crumble; drain. Return meat to skillet. Add ¼ teaspoon salt, ¼ teaspoon pepper, onion, and next 4 ingredients; cook over medium heat 5 minutes or until vegetables are crisp-tender, stirring frequently. Add salsa; simmer over medium-low heat 10 minutes. Spoon into an 8-inch square baking dish coated with cooking spray; spread potato mixture over meat mixture. Sprinkle with cheese. Bake, uncovered, at 375° for 20 minutes or until thoroughly heated. Yield: 4 servings.

CALORIES 434 (23% from fat); FAT 11.2g (sat 4.5g, mono 3.1g, poly 0.6g); PROTEIN 36g; CARB 46.5g; FIBER 5.3g; CHOL 82mg; IRON 4mg; SODIUM 729mg; CALC 224mg

Bushels and a Peck

Nothing rivals the taste of fresh corn, unless it's the memory of something even sweeter.

Corn has a rich and colorful history in North America. Although it originated in Mexico thousands of years ago, cultivation in our country probably began about 1,000 years ago.

FRESH CORN-AND-PASTA FRITTATA

1¼ cups egg substitute
¼ cup dry breadcrumbs
¼ cup (1 ounce) shredded provolone cheese
1 teaspoon olive oil
1 cup chopped green onions
1 cup presliced mushrooms
¾ cup fresh corn kernels (about 1 ear)
1 cup cooked angel hair pasta
¼ cup grated Parmesan cheese
Green onions (optional)

1. Preheat oven to 450°.
2. Combine first 3 ingredients in a small bowl. Stir well; set aside.
3. Wrap handle of a large nonstick skillet with aluminum foil. Heat olive oil in skillet over medium-high heat. Add chopped green onions, mushrooms, and corn; sauté 4 minutes or until soft. Add cooked pasta; toss until well-blended. Add egg substitute mixture; cook 2 minutes or until set around edges. Sprinkle with Parmesan cheese. Bake at 450° for 5 minutes or until center is set. Garnish with green onions, if desired. Yield: 2 servings.

CALORIES 416 (23% from fat); FAT 10.6g (sat 5g, mono 4g, poly 0.8g); PROTEIN 31.2g; CARB 50.4g; FIBER 4.8g; CHOL 18mg; IRON 6mg; SODIUM 664mg; CALC 368mg

CHEESE SOUFFLÉ WITH FRESH CORN

This quick-and-easy soufflé has a rich, creamy consistency due to the pureed fresh corn.

1½ cups fresh corn kernels (about 3 ears)
1 cup skim milk
½ cup all-purpose flour
½ cup fat-free cottage cheese
½ teaspoon salt
¼ teaspoon ground red pepper
⅛ teaspoon ground nutmeg
2 large egg yolks
1 cup (4 ounces) shredded reduced-fat extra-sharp Cheddar cheese
4 large egg whites (at room temperature)
½ teaspoon cream of tartar
Vegetable cooking spray

1. Preheat oven to 400°.
2. Place first 8 ingredients in a food processor, and process until blended, scraping sides of processor bowl once. Add Cheddar cheese; pulse 2 times or until well-blended. Spoon corn mixture into a large bowl.
3. Beat egg whites and cream of tartar at high speed of an electric mixer until stiff peaks form. Gently fold one-fourth of egg white mixture into corn mixture; gently fold in remaining egg white mixture. Pour into a 2½-quart soufflé dish coated with cooking spray.
4. Place soufflé in a 400° oven; immediately reduce oven temperature to 375°, and bake 45 minutes or until puffy and golden. Yield: 6 servings (serving size: 1 cup).

CALORIES 187 (29% from fat); FAT 6.1g (sat 2.8g, mono 1.8g, poly 0.6g); PROTEIN 14.9g; CARB 19.1g; FIBER 1.5g; CHOL 87mg; IRON 1mg; SODIUM 467mg; CALC 239mg

MENU SUGGESTION

CORN-AND-WILD RICE SALAD

Tomato sandwich*

Minted iced tea

*Cut 4 large tomatoes into 16 (¼-inch-thick) slices. Top each of 8 tomato slices with 1 ounce part-skim mozzarella and another tomato slice. Sprinkle with 1½ teaspoons chopped fresh basil.

CORN-AND-WILD RICE SALAD

1½ cups uncooked wild rice blend (such as Lundberg Farms)
2 cups fresh corn kernels (about 4 ears)
1 cup finely chopped celery
¾ cup shredded carrot
¾ cup dried cranberries or Craisins (about 3 ounces)
⅔ cup sunflower seeds or unsalted pumpkinseed kernels, toasted
½ cup finely chopped red onion
¼ cup raspberry vinegar
1 tablespoon olive oil
1 tablespoon low-sodium soy sauce
1 teaspoon grated orange peel
½ teaspoon pepper

1. Cook rice according to package directions, omitting salt and fat. Set aside; cool.
2. Combine rice, corn, and remaining ingredients in a bowl; stir well. Cover and chill. Yield: 8 servings (serving size: 1 cup).

CALORIES 270 (26% from fat); FAT 7.9g (sat 1.4g, mono 3.1g, poly 3g); PROTEIN 9.3g; CARB 45.3g; FIBER 4.6g; CHOL 0mg; IRON 3mg; SODIUM 78mg; CALC 31mg

JULY

Summer Baked in a Pie

What better way to capture summer's bounty of vegetables than to bake them in tarts and gratins? We've made it easy for you.

Besides showing off produce well, tarts and gratins are convenient ways to deal with summer's abundance. Baked, they last and continue to look good—and taste even better—for several days. You can serve them hot, warm, or at room temperature. They make marvelous do-ahead dishes, and, because they're so portable, are perfect picnic and lunchbox fare.

Savory tarts and gratins differ in that a gratin's crisp top is often a layer of cheese or breadcrumbs browned in an oven; a tart, meanwhile, is baked in a crust. The most familiar tart crusts are high in fat, but all around the Mediterranean you find easy-to-make savory crusts that don't rely on butter. A pizza crust is a good example, but this yeasted crust requires time. A more convenient crust is used widely in Greece for an array of vegetable *pittas* or pies.

GREEK BAKING-POWDER PIECRUST

This piecrust works for all the tarts in this story. Because the dough is moist and sticky like biscuit dough, it needs to be shaped into a ball and kneaded four or five times.

2¼ cups all-purpose flour
2 teaspoons baking powder
½ teaspoon salt
¾ cup water
3 tablespoons olive oil

1. Combine first 3 ingredients in a large bowl, and make a well in center of mixture. Add water and oil to flour mixture, stirring until well-blended.
2. Turn dough out onto a lightly floured surface; knead 4 or 5 times. Divide dough in half. Working with one half at a time, press each half gently into a 4-inch circle on heavy-duty plastic wrap, and cover dough with

additional plastic wrap. Chill for 15 minutes. Roll dough, still covered, into an 11-inch circle. Place dough in freezer 5 minutes or until plastic wrap can be easily removed. Yield: 2 (10-inch) crusts (serving size: ⅙ crust).
Note: Store dough up to 3 days in the refrigerator in a zip-top plastic bag.

CALORIES 116 (28% from fat); FAT 3.6g (sat 0.5g, mono 2.5g, poly 0.4g); PROTEIN 2.5g; CARB 18.1g; FIBER 0.6g; CHOL 0mg; IRON 1.2mg; SODIUM 98mg; CALC 49mg

---

NUTRITION NOTE

Some of these tarts are higher than 30% calories from fat. That's because the vegetables have so few calories to offset the fat in the eggs and cheese. But because the recipes in this story are all entrées, simply add some crusty French bread and a salad, and your complete meal will be under 30% calories from fat.

ASPARAGUS TART

(pictured on page 170)

For an elegant brunch entrée, arrange 2 ounces shredded smoked salmon in the prebaked crust.

1 (10-inch) Greek Baking-Powder Piecrust
Vegetable cooking spray
2 large eggs
2 large egg whites
1 pound fresh asparagus
¾ cup skim milk
¼ cup (1 ounce) shredded Gruyère or Swiss cheese
¼ cup finely grated fresh Parmesan cheese
¼ cup chopped fresh chives
2 tablespoons nonfat dry milk
1 teaspoon chopped fresh thyme or ¼ teaspoon dried thyme
¼ teaspoon salt
¼ teaspoon pepper

1. Preheat oven to 375°.
2. Press Greek Baking-Powder Piecrust into a 10-inch quiche dish coated with cooking spray. Combine eggs and egg whites in a bowl; beat well with a whisk. Brush 2 tablespoons egg mixture over crust; set remaining egg mixture aside. Bake crust at 375° for 7 minutes; cool on a wire rack.
3. Snap off tough ends of asparagus; remove scales with a knife or vegetable peeler, if desired. Cut asparagus into 5-inch pieces. Arrange asparagus in a steamer basket over boiling water. Cover and steam 5 minutes or until tender. Rinse under cold water. Drain well; set aside.
4. Add skim milk and remaining 7 ingredients to egg mixture in bowl; beat well. Pour egg mixture into crust. Arrange asparagus pieces in a spokelike design on top of egg mixture, alternating stems and tips. Bake at 375° for 35 minutes or until a knife inserted near center of tart comes out clean. Yield: 6 servings (serving size: 1 wedge).

CALORIES 226 (34% from fat); FAT 8.6g (sat 2.9g, mono 4.1g, poly 0.8g); PROTEIN 12.8g; CARB 25g; FIBER 2.3g; CHOL 81mg; IRON 2.2mg; SODIUM 370mg; CALC 257mg

GARLICKY TOMATO TART

(pictured on page 207)

1   (10-inch) Greek Baking-
     Powder Piecrust (page 192)
Vegetable cooking spray
2   large eggs
2   large egg whites
1   teaspoon olive oil
4   garlic cloves, minced
2   cups peeled, seeded, chopped
     tomato (about 1 pound)
1   tablespoon sun-dried tomato
     paste
½   teaspoon salt
⅛   teaspoon sugar
1   teaspoon chopped fresh thyme
1   tablespoon chopped fresh basil
⅛   teaspoon pepper
⅔   cup skim milk
2   tablespoons nonfat dry milk
2   large ripe tomatoes, cut into
     ¼-inch-thick slices
¼   cup (1 ounce) shredded
     Gruyère or Swiss cheese
¼   cup finely grated fresh
     Parmesan cheese

1. Preheat oven to 375°.
2. Press Greek Baking-Powder Piecrust into a 10-inch quiche dish
coated with cooking spray. Combine
eggs and egg whites in a bowl; beat
well with a whisk. Brush 2 tablespoons
egg mixture over crust; set remaining
mixture aside. Bake crust at 375° for 7
minutes; cool on a wire rack.
3. Heat oil in a nonstick skillet over
medium heat. Add garlic; sauté 30 seconds. Add 2 cups tomato and next 3
ingredients; sauté 15 minutes or until
thick (mixture will have a pasty consistency). Remove from heat; stir in
thyme, basil, and pepper. Add milks
to egg mixture in bowl; beat well. Stir
in tomato mixture. Arrange tomato
slices in bottom of crust; pour egg
mixture over tomato slices. Sprinkle
with cheeses. Bake at 375° for 45 minutes or until a knife inserted near center comes out clean. Yield: 6 servings
(serving size: 1 wedge).

CALORIES 245 (35% from fat); FAT 9.5g (sat 3g, mono 4.7g,
poly 1g); PROTEIN 12.2g; CARB 28.2g; FIBER 2.4g;
CHOL 84mg; IRON 2.2mg; SODIUM 477mg; CALC 248mg

ZUCCHINI, SWEET ONION, AND RED PEPPER TART

1   (10-inch) Greek Baking-
     Powder Piecrust (page 192)
Vegetable cooking spray
2   large eggs
2   large egg whites
1   cup chopped Vidalia or other
     sweet onion
2   cups diced red bell pepper
     (about 2 medium)
½   teaspoon salt, divided
4   cups chopped zucchini (about
     1 pound)
2   garlic cloves, minced
1   tablespoon water
1   teaspoon chopped fresh thyme
     or ¼ teaspoon dried thyme
½   cup skim milk
2   tablespoons nonfat dry milk
¼   cup (1 ounce) shredded
     Gruyère or Swiss cheese
¼   cup finely grated fresh
     Parmesan cheese

1. Preheat oven to 375°.
2. Press Greek Baking-Powder Piecrust into a 10-inch quiche dish
coated with cooking spray. Combine
eggs and egg whites in a bowl; beat
well with a whisk. Brush 2 tablespoons
egg mixture over crust; set remaining
mixture aside. Bake crust at 375° for 7
minutes; cool on a wire rack.
3. Place a large nonstick skillet coated
with cooking spray over medium heat
until hot. Add onion, bell pepper, and
¼ teaspoon salt; sauté 10 minutes or
until lightly browned. Add zucchini,
garlic, and water; sauté 10 minutes or
until vegetables are tender. Stir in
thyme. Spoon zucchini mixture into
prepared crust.
4. Add milks and ¼ teaspoon salt to
remaining egg mixture in bowl; beat
well. Pour egg mixture evenly over
zucchini mixture, and sprinkle with
cheeses. Bake at 375° for 45 minutes
or until a knife inserted near center
comes out clean. Yield: 6 servings
(serving size: 1 wedge).

CALORIES 242 (33% from fat); FAT 8.8g (sat 2.9g, mono 4.1g,
poly 0.9g); PROTEIN 12.5g; CARB 28.9g; FIBER 2.4g;
CHOL 84mg; IRON 2.6mg; SODIUM 466mg; CALC 251mg

SOUTHWESTERN CORN-AND-PEPPER GRATIN

1   teaspoon olive oil
1   cup chopped onion
1   cup diced green bell pepper
1   cup diced red bell pepper
¾   teaspoon salt, divided
½   teaspoon freshly ground
     pepper
2¾ cups fresh corn kernels (about
     4 ears), divided
2   tablespoons seeded, minced
     jalapeño pepper
1   teaspoon cumin seeds, crushed
     or ½ teaspoon ground cumin
¼   cup (1 ounce) shredded sharp
     Cheddar cheese
Vegetable cooking spray
¾   cup skim milk
¼   cup nonfat dry milk
1   tablespoon all-purpose flour
3   large eggs

1. Preheat oven to 425°.
2. Heat oil in a large nonstick skillet
over medium heat. Add onion, and
sauté 5 minutes or until tender. Add
bell peppers, ¼ teaspoon salt, and
freshly ground pepper; sauté 5 minutes. Add 2 cups corn, jalapeño pepper, and cumin; sauté 5 minutes or
until peppers are crisp-tender. Remove
from heat, and stir in cheese. Spoon
about ¾ cup bell pepper mixture into
each of 4 gratin dishes coated with
cooking spray.
3. Combine ¾ cup corn, ½ teaspoon
salt, skim milk, and remaining 3 ingredients in a blender; cover and process
until smooth. Pour about ½ cup egg
mixture over vegetable mixture in each
dish. Place dishes on a baking sheet.
Bake at 425° for 25 minutes or until
golden. Yield: 4 servings.
Note: This recipe can also be prepared
in a 2-quart baking dish. Bake at 425°
for 35 minutes or until golden.

CALORIES 279 (31% from fat); FAT 9.5g (sat 3.2g, mono 3.5g,
poly 1.5g); PROTEIN 15.9g; CARB 36.8g; FIBER 5.6g;
CHOL 176mg; IRON 2.8mg; SODIUM 617mg; CALC 243mg

EGGPLANT-PARMESAN GRATIN

Before you put the eggplant in the oven, use this simple trick so that the thicker part of it cooks as evenly as the edges: Make a lengthwise slit down the middle of the eggplant halves. To save time in making this gratin, simmer the tomato mixture while the eggplant bakes.

3   (1-pound) eggplants
Vegetable cooking spray
1   teaspoon olive oil
3   garlic cloves, minced
4   medium tomatoes, quartered
      (about 2 pounds)
¼   teaspoon sugar
¼   teaspoon salt
2   tablespoons chopped fresh
      basil or 2 teaspoons dried
      basil
½   teaspoon coarsely ground
      pepper
½   cup finely grated fresh
      Parmesan cheese
¼   cup dry breadcrumbs

1. Preheat oven to 475°.
2. Slice eggplants in half lengthwise. Working with each eggplant half, cut side up, make a 1-inch-deep slit lengthwise down the middle to within 1 inch of each end. Place eggplant halves, cut sides down, on a baking sheet coated with cooking spray. Bake at 475° for 35 minutes or until tender. Remove eggplant from oven; cool on baking sheet 10 minutes.
3. Reduce oven temperature to 425°. Peel eggplant halves; cut crosswise into ¼-inch-thick slices (pieces may fall apart).
4. Heat oil in a large nonstick skillet over medium heat. Add garlic, and sauté 30 seconds. Add tomato, sugar, and salt. Cook, uncovered, 30 minutes or until slightly thick, stirring frequently (mixture will have a pasty consistency). Stir in basil and pepper. Spoon tomato mixture into a food processor; process 1 minute or until smooth. Set aside.
5. Arrange one-third of eggplant slices in a 13 x 9-inch baking dish coated with cooking spray. Spoon half of tomato mixture evenly over eggplant slices. Repeat procedure with remaining eggplant slices and tomato mixture. Sprinkle with cheese and breadcrumbs. Bake at 425° for 45 minutes or until golden. Yield: 4 servings (serving size: 1 cup).

CALORIES 214 (26% from fat); FAT 6.1g (sat 2.7g, mono 2.1g, poly 0.6g); PROTEIN 10.9g; CARB 33.9g; FIBER 7.1g; CHOL 10mg; IRON 3.1mg; SODIUM 457mg; CALC 320mg

CREAMY ZUCCHINI-AND-RICE GRATIN

1   tablespoon olive oil, divided
1   cup chopped onion
7   cups finely chopped zucchini
      (about 2 pounds)
2   large garlic cloves, minced
¼   teaspoon salt
⅛   teaspoon pepper
1½ cups cooked Arborio or other
      short-grain rice (about ½ cup
      uncooked rice)
½   cup chopped fresh parsley
½   cup egg substitute
⅓   cup crumbled feta cheese
1   teaspoon fresh thyme or
      ¼ teaspoon dried thyme
Vegetable cooking spray
¼   cup fresh breadcrumbs

1. Preheat oven to 375°.
2. Heat 1 teaspoon oil in a large nonstick skillet over medium heat. Add onion; sauté 3 minutes or until tender. Add zucchini, garlic, salt, and pepper; sauté 10 minutes or until zucchini is tender. Spoon zucchini mixture into a large bowl using a slotted spoon; cool slightly.
3. Add rice and next 4 ingredients to zucchini mixture; stir well. Spoon zucchini mixture into a 2-quart baking dish coated with cooking spray. Sprinkle breadcrumbs evenly over top of zucchini mixture; drizzle with 2 teaspoons oil. Bake at 375° for 45 minutes or until set. Yield: 4 servings (serving size: 1 cup).

CALORIES 248 (30% from fat); FAT 8.3g (sat 3.4g, mono 3.5g, poly 0.6g); PROTEIN 11g; CARB 34g; FIBER 2.7g; CHOL 17mg; IRON 3.3mg; SODIUM 430mg; CALC 164mg

POTATO GRATIN WITH RED PEPPER LATTICE

3   medium-size red bell peppers
1   medium-size onion, peeled and
      cut in half
3   pounds Yukon gold or red
      potato, cut into ¼-inch slices
1   tablespoon chopped fresh
      rosemary or 1 teaspoon dried
      rosemary, crushed
¾   teaspoon salt
2   garlic cloves, minced
Vegetable cooking spray
3⅓ cups skim milk
½   teaspoon black pepper
2   large eggs, lightly beaten
¾   cup grated Asiago or Parmesan
      cheese

1. Preheat broiler.
2. Cut bell peppers in half lengthwise; discard seeds and membranes. Place pepper halves, skin sides up, on an aluminum foil-lined baking sheet; flatten with hand. Place onion halves, cut sides up, on baking sheet. Broil 15 minutes or until peppers are blackened. Place peppers in a zip-top plastic bag; seal. Let stand 15 minutes; peel. Cut onion into slivers, and set aside.
3. Preheat oven to 400°.
4. Cut 4 pepper halves into strips; set aside. Chop remaining pepper halves. Combine chopped peppers, onion, potato, and next 3 ingredients in a bowl; toss well.
5. Arrange potato mixture in a 13 x 9-inch baking dish coated with cooking spray. Combine milk, black pepper, and eggs; stir well. Pour milk mixture over potato mixture. Sprinkle with cheese. Cover and bake at 400° for 1 hour and 15 minutes. Uncover and arrange pepper strips on top in a lattice pattern. Bake 30 additional minutes. Yield: 9 servings (serving size: 1 cup).

CALORIES 220 (17% from fat); FAT 4.2g (sat 2.1g, mono 1.2g, poly 0.4g); PROTEIN 11.5g; CARB 35.2g; FIBER 3.2g; CHOL 57mg; IRON 1.9mg; SODIUM 419mg; CALC 250mg

CASSOULET GRATIN

Although this gratin has the elements of a cassoulet, its flavor is slightly reminiscent of baked beans.

    1   (16-ounce) package dried Great
            Northern beans
    1   medium-size onion, peeled
    1   whole clove
    8   cups water
    1   teaspoon salt
    2   garlic cloves
    1   bay leaf
    1   tablespoon olive oil
 1½   cups chopped onion
    4   garlic cloves, minced
   ¼   teaspoon sugar
    6   cups peeled, seeded, chopped
            tomato
    2   teaspoons chopped fresh thyme
            or ½ teaspoon dried thyme
   ½   teaspoon pepper
   ¼   cup thinly sliced fresh basil or
            1 tablespoon dried basil
        Vegetable cooking spray
   ½   cup fresh breadcrumbs
   ½   cup finely grated fresh
            Parmesan cheese

1. Sort and wash beans; place in a large Dutch oven. Cover with water to 2 inches above beans. Bring to a boil, and cook 2 minutes. Remove from heat; cover and let stand 1 hour. Drain. Wipe Dutch oven dry with a paper towel. Return beans to Dutch oven.
2. Stud peeled onion with whole clove. Add clove-studded onion, 8 cups water, and next 3 ingredients to beans. Bring to a boil; reduce heat, and simmer, uncovered, 45 minutes or until beans are tender. Drain beans in a colander over a bowl; reserve 2 cups cooking liquid. Discard clove-studded onion, garlic cloves, and bay leaf.
3. Preheat oven to 425°.
4. Heat oil in Dutch oven over medium-high heat. Add chopped onion; sauté 5 minutes. Add minced garlic and sugar; sauté 30 seconds. Reduce heat to medium. Add tomato; cook, uncovered, 10 minutes, stirring frequently. Stir in beans, reserved 2 cups cooking liquid, thyme, and pepper; simmer, uncovered, 20 minutes or

until mixture is thick, stirring occasionally. Stir in basil.
5. Spoon bean mixture into a 3-quart baking dish coated with cooking spray. Combine breadcrumbs and Parmesan cheese; sprinkle over top. Bake at 425° for 20 minutes or until browned. Yield: 9 servings (serving size: 1 cup).

CALORIES 254 (15% from fat); FAT 4.3g (sat 1.5g, mono 1.7g, poly 0.6g); PROTEIN 14.9g; CARB 41.4g; FIBER 7.3g; CHOL 4mg; IRON 3.5mg; SODIUM 263mg; CALC 181mg

---

What If . . . ?

If you don't have the nonfat dry milk called for in several of these recipes, don't worry; the recipe will still work without it. It's just that we found that 2 tablespoons of the dry milk, added to the liquid milk-and-egg mixture, makes for a creamier, richer custard.
If you don't have a 10-inch quiche dish, the tart recipes will work in a 10-inch deep-dish pie plate.
If you are a flour-scooper, your piecrust dough will be too stiff. So lightly spoon flour into the correct dry measuring cup, and level with a flat-edged spatula.

FAST FOOD

The Couscous Connection

You might think of couscous as a grain, but it's a light and airy pasta that subtly adopts the flavors it's served with.

Pour it from the box and the tiny, round shapes that pile up more closely resemble some ancient mystic grain than any kind of noodle, but couscous (KOOS-koos), is technically classified as a pasta. What's more, it's one of those perfect foods to keep on hand if you're short on time or patience.

ROSEMARY SWORDFISH ON VEGETABLE COUSCOUS

Preparation time: 15 minutes
Cooking time: 17 minutes

    1   tablespoon olive oil
    2   teaspoons minced fresh
            rosemary or ½ teaspoon dried
            rosemary, crushed
    1   garlic clove, crushed
    6   (6-ounce) swordfish steaks
   ½   cup diced carrot
   ½   cup diced zucchini
    3   tablespoons pitted, chopped
            kalamata olives
    2   tablespoons fresh lemon juice
   ¾   teaspoon ground cumin
   ¼   teaspoon ground cinnamon
   ⅛   teaspoon salt
   ⅛   teaspoon pepper
    1   (14¼-ounce) can no-salt-added
            chicken broth
    1   cup uncooked couscous
   ⅛   teaspoon salt
   ⅛   teaspoon pepper
        Vegetable cooking spray

1. Combine first 3 ingredients, and stir well. Rub swordfish steaks with oil mixture, and set aside.
2. Combine carrot and next 8 ingredients in a medium saucepan; bring to a boil. Reduce heat, and simmer, uncovered, 5 minutes or until vegetables are tender. Stir in couscous. Remove from heat; cover and let stand 5 minutes. Fluff with a fork.
3. Sprinkle both sides of swordfish steaks with ⅛ teaspoon salt and ⅛ teaspoon pepper. Place a large nonstick skillet coated with cooking spray over medium-high heat until hot. Add swordfish steaks; cook 4 minutes on each side or until done. Serve over couscous mixture. Yield: 6 servings (serving size: 5 ounces fish and ¾ cup couscous).

CALORIES 294 (28% from fat); FAT 12g (sat 2.8g, mono 5.5g, poly 2.3g); PROTEIN 46.7g; CARB 20.4g; FIBER 1.5g; CHOL 85mg; IRON 2.8mg; SODIUM 338mg; CALC 28mg

Greek Couscous

Preparation time: 20 minutes
Cooking time: 5 minutes

1½ cups water
1 cup uncooked couscous
½ teaspoon dried oregano
1½ cups diced plum tomatoes
1 cup peeled, diced cucumber
⅓ cup crumbled feta cheese
¼ cup small ripe olives, halved
3 tablespoons diced red onion
1 (15½-ounce) can chickpeas (garbanzo beans), drained
¼ cup water
3 tablespoons lemon juice
1½ tablespoons extra-virgin olive oil
¼ teaspoon salt
¼ teaspoon coarsely ground pepper

1. Bring 1½ cups water to a boil in a medium saucepan; stir in couscous and oregano. Remove from heat; cover and let stand 5 minutes. Fluff with a fork. Combine couscous, tomatoes, and next 5 ingredients in a bowl.
2. Combine ¼ cup water and remaining 4 ingredients; stir well with a whisk. Pour dressing over couscous mixture, tossing gently to coat. Yield: 4 servings (serving size: 1½ cups).

CALORIES 365 (29% from fat); FAT 11.9g (sat 3.1g, mono 6.1g, poly 1.8g); PROTEIN 13.9g; CARB 54g; FIBER 5.8g; CHOL 11mg; IRON 4mg; SODIUM 580mg; CALC 129mg

Shrimp Couscous with Mint

Preparation time: 15 minutes
Cooking time: 9 minutes

1½ cups water
1 cup uncooked couscous
½ pound medium-size shrimp, cooked and peeled
½ cup thinly sliced green onions
⅓ cup diced red bell pepper
2 tablespoons chopped fresh mint
1 (10-ounce) package frozen green peas, thawed
¼ cup low-salt chicken broth
3 tablespoons white wine vinegar
1½ tablespoons extra-virgin olive oil
½ teaspoon sugar
½ teaspoon salt
½ teaspoon coarsely ground pepper

1. Bring water to a boil in a medium saucepan; stir in couscous. Remove from heat; cover and let stand 5 minutes. Fluff with a fork. Combine couscous, shrimp, and next 4 ingredients in a bowl.
2. Combine broth and remaining 5 ingredients; stir well with a whisk. Pour dressing over couscous mixture, tossing gently to coat. Yield: 4 servings (serving size: 1½ cups).

CALORIES 286 (20% from fat); FAT 6.4g (sat 0.9g, mono 3.9g, poly 0.8g); PROTEIN 18.1g; CARB 39.3g; FIBER 5.4g; CHOL 83mg; IRON 3.8mg; SODIUM 483mg; CALC 51mg

Ham-and-Vegetable Couscous

Preparation time: 20 minutes
Cooking time: 5 minutes

1¾ cups water
½ teaspoon dried basil
1 cup uncooked couscous
1 cup chopped honey-baked ham
⅓ cup thinly sliced green onions
¼ cup grated Parmesan cheese
1 (15.25-ounce) can no-salt-added whole-kernel corn, drained
3 tablespoons water
2 tablespoons lemon juice
1 tablespoon extra-virgin olive oil
2 teaspoons Dijon mustard
¼ teaspoon salt
¼ teaspoon coarsely ground pepper

1. Bring 1¾ cups water and basil to a boil in a medium saucepan; stir in couscous. Remove from heat; cover and let stand 5 minutes. Fluff with a fork. Combine couscous, ham, and next 3 ingredients in a bowl.
2. Combine 3 tablespoons water and remaining 5 ingredients; stir well with a whisk. Pour dressing over couscous mixture, tossing gently to coat. Yield: 5 servings (serving size: 1¼ cups).

CALORIES 301 (25% from fat); FAT 8.2g (sat 2.1g, mono 3.8g, poly 0.6g); PROTEIN 16g; CARB 41g; FIBER 2.1g; CHOL 28mg; IRON 1.6mg; SODIUM 344mg; CALC 85mg

FLAVOR IT DIFFERENT

If you can boil water, you can pretty much master the art of cooking couscous. It needs so little attention; just add it to boiling water and it practically cooks itself. But don't think the fact that it's so quick means it has to be boring. Couscous is one of those foods that offers a wonderful blank culinary palette.

Although our recipes call for plain couscous, feel free to try them with any of the new flavored couscous products. We find the seasonings—ranging from roasted garlic to curry—are typically mild. You'll just be getting more salt and, in some cases, a tiny amount of fat.

Pasta Revisited

For those who love pasta, our readers present recipes ranging from a revved-up marinara sauce to an exotic salad toss.

Judith Ciampa Wright jazzes things up in her kitchen. Her husband is a musician, and he calls her cooking "jazz" because she likes to improvise with her recipes. Judy's husband, Joe, is a major reason for her new passion for healthful cooking. "Joe has high blood pressure, and if he gains weight, his blood pressure goes up. I encouraged Joe to see a nutritionist. That was the start of our healthy diet," says Judy. The health benefits are important, but Judy considers weight loss another advantage.

RED WINE-AND-ROSEMARY MARINARA

Marinara is one of my favorite things to jazz up. You can use the marinara for pasta, pizza sauce, or as a dip for breadsticks.

—Judith Ciampa Wright, Acton, Massachusetts

1 tablespoon olive oil
1 cup chopped onion
4 garlic cloves, minced
¾ cup dry red wine
2 tablespoons honey
2 teaspoons dried basil
1 teaspoon dried rosemary, crushed
½ teaspoon salt
¼ teaspoon dried crushed red pepper
1 (28-ounce) can crushed tomatoes, drained
1 (6-ounce) can no-salt-added tomato paste
5 cups hot cooked linguine (about 10 ounces uncooked pasta)

1. Heat oil in a large saucepan over medium heat. Add onion and garlic; sauté 3 minutes. Add wine and next 7 ingredients. Bring to a simmer; cook 20 minutes or until thick. Serve over linguine. Yield: 5 servings (serving size: 1 cup sauce and 1 cup pasta).

CALORIES 327 (11% from fat); FAT 4.1g (sat 0.5g, mono 2.1g, poly 0.6g); PROTEIN 10.2g; CARB 64.3g; FIBER 3.7g; CHOL 0mg; IRON 3.8mg; SODIUM 462mg; CALC 98mg

COUSCOUS SALAD

While visiting my husband's family in Paris, I asked my mother-in-law to prepare some authentic French recipes. I enjoyed this recipe in particular because it was naturally light. We love to take it on our summer picnics.

—Sue Costa, Peoria, Illinois

½ cup water
⅓ cup uncooked couscous
¼ cup red wine vinegar
2 tablespoons olive oil
1 tablespoon Dijon mustard
½ teaspoon dried parsley flakes
¼ teaspoon salt
¼ teaspoon pepper
⅛ teaspoon sugar
⅛ teaspoon garlic powder
1½ cups chopped green bell pepper
1¼ cups peeled, chopped cucumber
1 cup chopped onion
¼ cup raisins
1 (11-ounce) can extra-sweet whole-kernel corn, drained
1 (6-ounce) can albacore tuna in water, drained and flaked

1. Bring water to a boil in a medium saucepan; stir in couscous. Remove from heat; cover and let stand 5 minutes. Fluff with a fork. Spoon into a bowl; cover and chill.
2. Combine vinegar and next 7 ingredients in a large bowl; stir well with a whisk. Add couscous, bell pepper, and remaining ingredients, tossing well. Cover and chill. Yield: 7 servings (serving size: 1 cup).

CALORIES 151 (30% from fat); FAT 5g (sat 0.7g, mono 3g, poly 0.6g); PROTEIN 7.7g; CARB 19.9g; FIBER 2.8g; CHOL 8mg; IRON 0.9mg; SODIUM 338mg; CALC 14mg

SARAH'S PASTA WITH BLACK BEANS AND ARTICHOKE HEARTS

I modified this recipe from one of my favorite Cooking Light recipes by adding more convenience products. My family maintains a pretty active lifestyle, and to avoid eating out, we plan our meals ahead. We often have meals like this one that cook quickly when we're in a rush.

—Sarah Jacobs, Bloomington, Illinois

1 tablespoon olive oil
1 cup chopped onion
2 garlic cloves, minced
2 tablespoons minced fresh oregano or 2 teaspoons dried oregano
⅛ teaspoon dried crushed red pepper
⅛ teaspoon black pepper
1 (14½-ounce) can pasta-style tomatoes, undrained
1 (14.5-ounce) can no-salt-added whole tomatoes, undrained and chopped
1 (15-ounce) can no-salt-added black beans, drained
1 (4.5-ounce) jar sliced mushrooms, drained
3 cups hot cooked tricolor fusilli (about 6 ounces uncooked twisted pasta)
1 (14-ounce) can quartered artichoke hearts, drained
¼ cup grated fresh Romano cheese

1. Heat olive oil in a large skillet over medium heat. Add onion, and sauté 5 minutes. Add garlic, and sauté 1 minute. Stir in oregano and next 4 ingredients; cover, reduce heat, and simmer 10 minutes. Add black beans and mushrooms; cover and simmer 5 additional minutes.
2. Combine tomato mixture, hot pasta, artichokes, and grated Romano cheese in a large bowl; toss well. Serve warm. Yield: 7 servings (serving size: 1 cup).

CALORIES 234 (15% from fat); FAT 3.9g (sat 1.1g, mono 1.8g, poly 0.5g); PROTEIN 10.4g; CARB 41.6g; FIBER 4.1g; CHOL 4mg; IRON 2.9mg; SODIUM 350mg; CALC 116mg

THREE-CHEESE LASAGNA DIVAN

I wanted to find a dish that was healthy and would please a family with diverse tastes. And because I'm a working mom, I needed something that was quick to put together with staples we had on hand. This lasagna was a big hit with everyone.

—Alice George Rogers, Wilmore, Kentucky

2 cups chopped cooked chicken breast (about ¾ pound)
1 cup fat-free cottage cheese
¼ cup grated Parmesan cheese
¼ cup egg substitute
¼ cup chopped onion
¼ teaspoon garlic powder
1 (10¾-ounce) can condensed reduced-fat, reduced-sodium cream of mushroom soup, undiluted
1 (10-ounce) package frozen chopped broccoli, thawed and drained
Vegetable cooking spray
9 cooked lasagna noodles
9 (¾-ounce) slices reduced-fat American cheese, cut into small pieces
1 teaspoon paprika

1. Preheat oven to 350°.
2. Combine first 8 ingredients in a bowl, stirring well. Spread one-fourth of chicken mixture in bottom of an 11 x 7-inch baking dish coated with cooking spray. Arrange 3 noodles over chicken mixture. Top with one-fourth of chicken mixture, one-third of American cheese, and 3 noodles. Repeat layers, ending with cheese. Sprinkle with paprika. Cover and bake at 350° for 25 minutes or until thoroughly heated. Remove from oven; uncover and let stand 5 minutes before serving. Yield: 8 servings.

CALORIES 312 (22% from fat); FAT 7.5g (sat 3.4g, mono 2.2g, poly 1.2g); PROTEIN 29.8g; CARB 32.5g; FIBER 2.2g; CHOL 52mg; IRON 2.2mg; SODIUM 854mg; CALC 86mg

SUMMER PASTA SALAD WITH CHICKEN, MINT, AND DILL

When I make yogurt-based sauces, I try to add spices that will add a distinct flavor. A helpful hint for a prettier salad is to cut the chicken into strips and lay it over the vegetables. I also seed my tomatoes to give the salad a better appearance.

—Jennifer Detrick-Loucks, Denver, Colorado

1 (8-ounce) carton plain fat-free yogurt
1 tablespoon minced fresh dillweed or 1 teaspoon dried dillweed
1 tablespoon minced fresh mint or 1 teaspoon dried mint flakes
1 tablespoon coarse-grained mustard
1 tablespoon Worcestershire sauce
½ teaspoon pepper
¼ teaspoon salt
3 cups cooked fusilli (about 6 ounces uncooked twisted pasta)
2 cups skinned, cubed roasted chicken breast (about 8 ounces)
1 cup diced green bell pepper
1 cup diced tomato
½ cup thinly sliced green onions
1 (14-ounce) can quartered artichoke hearts, drained

1. Combine first 7 ingredients in a large bowl; stir well. Add pasta and remaining ingredients; toss gently to coat. Yield: 5 servings (serving size: 1½ cups).

CALORIES 281 (11% from fat); FAT 3.5g (sat 0.8g, mono 0.9g, poly 0.9g); PROTEIN 25g; CARB 37.6g; FIBER 2.6g; CHOL 44mg; IRON 3.3mg; SODIUM 314mg; CALC 148mg

INSPIRED VEGETARIAN

Port Authority

Of all the mushrooms, portobellos are the most satisfying and versatile. We have the recipes to prove it.

Once obscure, portobello mushrooms are becoming as commonplace in produce sections as the ubiquitous button mushroom. These saucer-shaped mushrooms range in size from 3 inches across to a gargantuan 10 inches. Portobellos are a fork-and-knife food: When grilled whole, they take on the texture of a steak; chopped, they add a ground beeflike character to sauces and chowders.

Portobellos must be handled differently than many species of mushrooms. Never wash or submerge them in water. The black gill structure acts like a sponge, absorbing water quickly. This not only makes it more difficult to brown or sear the mushroom, it also dilutes its intense earthy, musty flavor. To remove any loose dirt, merely wipe the surface of the mushroom with a damp paper towel.

TRIPLE MUSHROOM SALAD WITH WALNUTS

Olive oil-flavored vegetable cooking spray
1½ cups thinly sliced button mushrooms
1 cup sliced portobello mushroom caps
1 cup thinly sliced shiitake mushroom caps
2 tablespoons chopped fresh parsley
1 tablespoon minced shallots
3 garlic cloves, minced
¼ cup sherry vinegar
1 tablespoon low-sodium soy sauce
2 teaspoons honey
8 cups gourmet salad greens
2 tablespoons chopped walnuts, toasted

1. Place a large nonstick skillet coated with cooking spray over medium-high heat until hot. Add button mushrooms and next 5 ingredients; sauté 3 minutes or until mushrooms are tender. Combine vinegar, soy sauce, and honey; add to skillet. Remove from heat; spoon mushroom mixture over salad greens. Sprinkle with walnuts. Yield: 4 servings (serving size: 2 cups greens, ⅓ cup mushrooms, and 1½ teaspoons walnuts).

CALORIES 89 (29% from fat); FAT 2.9g (sat 0.2g, mono 0.5g, poly 1.7g); PROTEIN 3.9g; CARB 11.1g; FIBER 2.2g; CHOL 0mg; IRON 1.5mg; SODIUM 196mg; CALC 15mg

PARMESAN RISOTTO-STUFFED PORTOBELLOS

(pictured on page 206)

The spinach mixture makes a nice presentation for the stuffed mushrooms, but it may be omitted.

- 1 (14½-ounce) can vegetable broth
- 2 cups water
- 1 tablespoon olive oil, divided
- 1 cup minced fresh onion
- 1 cup minced celery
- 1 cup minced carrot
- 1 cup uncooked Arborio or other short-grain rice
- 1 cup dry white wine
- ½ cup grated Parmesan cheese
- ¼ cup minced green onions or chives
- 4 (5-ounce) portobello mushrooms (about 6 inches wide)
- ¼ cup (1 ounce) shredded part-skim mozzarella cheese
- ½ cup water
- 1 tablespoon chopped onion
- 3 garlic cloves, minced
- 1 (10-ounce) bag fresh spinach, trimmed

1. Bring broth and 2 cups water to a simmer in a medium saucepan (do not boil). Keep warm over low heat.
2. Heat 2 teaspoons oil in a large saucepan over medium-high heat. Add minced onion, celery, and carrot; sauté 1 minute. Add rice; sauté 5 minutes. Stir in wine; cook, stirring constantly, 5 minutes or until liquid is nearly absorbed. Add broth mixture, ½ cup at a time, stirring constantly until each portion of broth is absorbed before adding the next (about 20 minutes total). Remove from heat; stir in Parmesan cheese and green onions.
3. Preheat oven to 375°.
4. Remove stems from mushroom caps; discard. Place caps, gill sides up, in a 13 x 9-inch baking dish. Spoon 1¼ cups risotto mixture into each cap; top each with 1 tablespoon mozzarella cheese. Pour ½ cup water into dish. Bake at 375° for 30 minutes or until mushroom caps are tender.
5. Heat 1 teaspoon oil in a large Dutch oven over medium-high heat until hot. Add chopped onion and garlic; sauté 2 minutes or until tender. Add spinach, and sauté 2 minutes or until spinach is wilted. Arrange ½ cup spinach mixture on each of 4 plates. Remove stuffed mushrooms from baking dish with a slotted spoon; place on spinach mixture. Yield: 4 servings.

CALORIES 372 (23% from fat); FAT 9.6g (sat 3.3g, mono 3.8g, poly 0.9g); PROTEIN 15.9g; CARB 60.5g; FIBER 7.7g; CHOL 12mg; IRON 6.6mg; SODIUM 773mg; CALC 303mg

STACKED VEGETABLE PORTOBELLOS

- 4 small portobello mushrooms (about 12 ounces total)
- 1 tablespoon minced fresh parsley
- 1 tablespoon lemon juice
- 2 teaspoons olive oil
- 1 teaspoon dried Italian seasoning
- ¼ teaspoon pepper
- ¼ cup dry white wine
- 1 cup (¼-inch-thick) sliced zucchini
- 1 cup (¼-inch-thick) sliced yellow squash
- ½ cup (¼-inch-thick) sliced red onion
- 2 (¼-inch-thick) slices tomato
- ¼ cup crumbled goat cheese

A CAP FULL

To remove mushroom gills, hold cap in one hand, and gently scrape out with a spoon.

1. Remove stems from mushrooms; remove brown gills from the undersides of mushrooms using a spoon (see photo above).
2. Combine mushroom caps, parsley, and next 4 ingredients in a large zip-top plastic bag; seal bag. Marinate 30 minutes; remove mushrooms from bag, reserving marinade.
3. Preheat oven to 425°.
4. Place mushrooms and wine in a shallow baking dish. Bake at 425° for 10 minutes or until mushrooms are soft.
5. Place zucchini, yellow squash, and onion on a baking sheet; brush with reserved marinade. Bake at 425° for 10 minutes or until slightly soft.
6. Place 2 mushrooms, gill sides up, on a baking sheet; top evenly with baked vegetables. Top each with a tomato slice, 2 tablespoons cheese, and a mushroom, gill side down. Bake at 425° for 10 minutes or until thoroughly heated. Yield: 2 servings.

CALORIES 164 (47% from fat); FAT 8.6g (sat 2.9g, mono 4g, poly 0.9g); PROTEIN 7.8g; CARB 18.4g; FIBER 4.7g; CHOL 13mg; IRON 4.1mg; SODIUM 174mg; CALC 136mg

SELECTING PORTOBELLOS

When buying portobellos, look for those with a tight underside and lighter-colored gills. If the gill area appears very black and spread out, that's a sign of age. Two of our recipes work fine if you leave the gills in place, but in our Stacked Vegetable Portobellos, it's best to remove them. And don't discard the thick woody stems; they make excellent stock or broth flavorings.

Getting Your Z's

Although zucchini are most abundant in the summer, recipes for light zucchini bread aren't—so we've come up with one that tastes as rich as the high-fat version.

Virginia Rumbaugh of Hurricane, West Virginia, wrote and asked us to create a lighter version of her zucchini bread recipe. Here's what we did to the recipe to make it more healthful and tastier: First, we cut the fat in half by decreasing the amount of oil. Then, by increasing the amount of zucchini by a cup, we kept the bread moist. (Zucchini is 89% water.) In fact, to keep the cake from becoming gummy, our recipe calls for pressing the shredded zucchini on paper towels before adding it to the batter. To give the bread a fresh, zesty twist, we added grated lemon rind. So now when coworkers arrive at the office, arms laden with zucchini and that desperate do-your-part look on their faces, you can willingly oblige.

ZUCCHINI BREAD

3 cups shredded zucchini (about 3 medium)
4 cups all-purpose flour
1 cup plus 2 tablespoons granulated sugar, divided
½ cup chopped walnuts, toasted
¼ cup packed brown sugar
1 tablespoon plus 2 teaspoons baking powder
1 tablespoon grated lemon rind
1½ teaspoons ground cinnamon
½ teaspoon salt
¼ teaspoon ground nutmeg
1½ cups skim milk
¼ cup plus 2 tablespoons vegetable oil
2 teaspoons vanilla extract
2 large eggs
Vegetable cooking spray

1. Preheat oven to 350°.
2. Press shredded zucchini on several layers of paper towels. Cover with additional paper towels; set aside.
3. Combine flour, 1 cup granulated sugar, walnuts, and next 6 ingredients in a large bowl; make a well in center of mixture. Combine milk and next 3 ingredients in a bowl; stir with a whisk. Add zucchini; stir. Add to flour mixture; stir just until moist. Divide batter evenly between 2 (8 x 4-inch) loaf pans coated with cooking spray. Sprinkle each with 1 tablespoon granulated sugar. Bake at 350° for 1 hour and 10 minutes or until a wooden pick inserted in center comes out clean. Cool 5 minutes in pans on a wire rack; remove from pans. Cool completely on wire rack. Yield: 2 loaves (12 slices per loaf) (serving size: 1 slice).

CALORIES 183 (28% from fat); FAT 5.6g (sat 0.8g, mono 3g, poly 1.4g); PROTEIN 4g; CARB 29.6g; FIBER 0.8g; CHOL 19mg; IRON 1.4mg; SODIUM 64mg; CALC 89mg

BEFORE & AFTER	
SERVING SIZE	
1 slice	
CALORIES	
238	183
FAT	
13g	5.6g
PERCENT OF TOTAL CALORIES	
49%	28%
SODIUM	
213mg	64mg

Airport Options

Just in case there's nothing healthful or satisfying to eat on your next flight, these make-ahead sandwiches travel well—just be sure to keep them chilled in an insulated lunch bag.

TUNA ROLL-UPS

1 (6-ounce) can solid white tuna in water, drained and flaked
⅓ cup diced celery
2 tablespoons reduced-calorie spoonable salad dressing (such as Miracle Whip Light)
1 teaspoon lemon juice
¼ teaspoon dried dillweed
8 (¾-ounce) slices whole-wheat bread

1. Combine tuna and diced celery in a bowl; toss gently. Combine salad dressing, lemon juice, and dillweed, stirring well. Add dressing mixture to tuna mixture, tossing gently.
2. Trim crusts from bread; flatten each slice of bread to ⅛-inch thickness using a rolling pin. Spread 2 tablespoons tuna mixture evenly over each slice. Roll up; wrap in plastic wrap. Chill. Yield: 4 servings (serving size: 2 rolls).

CALORIES 143 (23% from fat); FAT 3.7g (sat 0.4g, mono 0.4g, poly 0.7g); PROTEIN 11.9g; CARB 16.2g; FIBER 1.3g; CHOL 17mg; IRON 1mg; SODIUM 344mg; CALC 37mg

Bill of Lights

*Create some culinary fireworks with these
low-fat recipes that explode with excitement.*

To assist you with the Fourth of July, we've put together our own Independence Day-themed recipes that can be mixed and matched for menus of your choice. Look what we have for you: substantial dishes, including desserts, that are not only healthful but exude the excitement of a fireworks display. Serve these revolutionary dishes to your friends and family, and see how proudly they'll hail you.

OUR AMERICAN HERO

(pictured on page 208)

Sliced fresh basil stirred into the mayonnaise gives it a fresh edge, while the arugula gives it a peppery bite.

- ½ cup light mayonnaise
- ¼ cup thinly sliced fresh basil
- ½ teaspoon coarsely ground pepper
- 1 (16-ounce) loaf Italian or French bread
- 1 pound thinly sliced lean deli roast beef
- 1 large tomato, cored and thinly sliced
- 1 cup thinly sliced red onion
- 1 large yellow bell pepper, seeded and thinly sliced into rings
- 1 cup trimmed arugula, watercress, or lettuce leaves
- ⅛ teaspoon salt
- ⅛ teaspoon pepper

1. Combine first 3 ingredients; chill 15 minutes.
2. Cut bread loaf in half horizontally. Spread mayonnaise mixture over bottom half of bread; top with roast beef, remaining 6 ingredients, and top half of bread. Cut loaf into 6 pieces. Yield: 6 servings.

CALORIES 400 (28% from fat); FAT 12.6g (sat 3.5g, mono 4.5g, poly 3.2g); PROTEIN 22.6g; CARB 48.5g; FIBER 3.2g; CHOL 7mg; IRON 4mg; SODIUM 1,104mg; CALC 29mg

CHOCOLATE-CHERRY BOMBE WITH CHERRY SAUCE

Frozen cherries can be used in place of fresh—just be sure to drain them well before adding to the sauce. You can omit the kirsch (and the flames), if desired.

- 2 cups cherry-vanilla fat-free frozen yogurt
- 2 cups chocolate fat-free frozen yogurt
- ½ cup sugar
- 1 tablespoon cornstarch
- 1 cup cranberry juice cocktail
- 1 cup pitted sweet cherries
- 3 tablespoons kirsch (cherry brandy)

1. Line a 1½-quart bowl with plastic wrap, allowing plastic wrap to extend over edge of bowl. Place bowl in freezer 10 minutes. Press cherry-vanilla yogurt into bottom and up sides of bowl; place in freezer 30 minutes or until firm. Spoon chocolate yogurt into center of bowl, pressing firmly. Cover with plastic wrap; freeze at least 4 hours.
2. Combine sugar and cornstarch in a small saucepan; stir in juice. Bring to a boil; cook 2 minutes or until sauce is thick and bubbly, stirring with a whisk. Stir in cherries.
3. Uncover and invert bombe onto a platter; remove plastic wrap. Add kirsch to cherry mixture (do not stir), and cook over low heat until warm. Ignite with a long match. Carefully pour over bombe; allow flames to die down. Serve immediately. Yield: 8 servings (serving size: 1 wedge).

CALORIES 192 (1% from fat); FAT 0.2g (sat 0g, mono 0.1g, poly 0.1g); PROTEIN 3.8g; CARB 42.6g; FIBER 0.4g; CHOL 0mg; IRON 0.1mg; SODIUM 59mg; CALC 111mg

SNAPPY ALMOND STARS

Measuring the flour accurately is critical in this recipe. Lightly spoon the flour into a dry measuring cup; then level it off. For optimal snap and crunch, roll the dough out as thin as possible. The thinner the cookie, the crisper the crunch.

- ½ cup packed dark brown sugar
- ¼ cup light butter
- 1 tablespoon cold water
- 1 cup plus 2 tablespoons all-purpose flour
- 2 tablespoons cornstarch
- ½ teaspoon ground cinnamon
- ⅛ teaspoon salt
- ¼ cup sliced almonds

1. Preheat oven to 375°.
2. Beat sugar and butter at medium speed of an electric mixer until well-blended (about 5 minutes). Add water, and beat well. Combine flour and next 3 ingredients. Add to sugar mixture; beat until well-blended. Gently press dough into a 4-inch disk; wrap in plastic wrap. Freeze 30 minutes.
3. Remove plastic wrap. Roll dough to a ¹⁄₁₆-inch thickness on a lightly floured surface; cut with a 2-inch star cutter. Place on a baking sheet; top with almonds. Bake at 375° for 8 minutes or until cookies are crisp and edges are browned. Cool cookies 30 seconds on baking sheet. Remove cookies from baking sheet, and cool on wire racks. Yield: 4 dozen (serving size: 1 cookie).

CALORIES 25 (29% from fat); FAT 0.8g (sat 0.4g, mono 0.2g, poly 0.1g); PROTEIN 0.4g; CARB 4.1g; FIBER 0.1g; CHOL 5mg; IRON 0.2mg; SODIUM 13mg; CALC 3mg

SUMMER FRUIT WITH SPARKLING CUSTARD SAUCE

Whisking the champagne into the custard sauce just before serving adds sparkle to this dessert. Substitute blueberries and peaches for the raspberries and nectarines, if desired.

```
1¼   cups 1% low-fat milk
 ½   cup sugar
 1   tablespoon cornstarch
 1   large egg, lightly beaten
 1   teaspoon vanilla extract
 ¾   cup brut champagne
1½   cups fresh raspberries
 3   medium nectarines, each cut
     into 8 wedges
```

1. Heat milk over medium-high heat in a heavy saucepan to 180° or until tiny bubbles form around edge (do not boil). Remove from heat.
2. Combine sugar and cornstarch in a medium heavy saucepan; add hot milk, stirring with a whisk. Cook over medium heat, stirring constantly until thick, about 4 minutes.
3. Gradually add hot milk mixture to egg in a bowl, stirring constantly with a whisk. Return milk mixture to pan. Cook over medium-low heat, stirring constantly, 6 minutes or until thickened. Remove from heat. Pour into a bowl; stir in vanilla. Cover surface with plastic wrap; chill.
4. To serve, stir champagne into chilled custard. Spoon sauce into stemmed glasses or small dishes; top with raspberries and nectarines. Yield: 6 servings (serving size: ⅓ cup custard sauce, ¼ cup berries, and 4 nectarine wedges).

CALORIES 185 (10% from fat); FAT 2g (sat 0.7g, mono 0.7g, poly 0.4g); PROTEIN 3.8g; CARB 34.4g; FIBER 4.2g; CHOL 39mg; IRON 0.7mg; SODIUM 38mg; CALC 79mg

ROMAN CANDLE BREADSTICKS

Use any combination of fresh herbs to make these quick-and-easy breadsticks.

```
 1   (11-ounce) can refrigerated soft
     breadstick dough
Olive oil-flavored vegetable
     cooking spray
 ¾   teaspoon paprika
 ¼   cup chopped fresh parsley
 ¼   cup chopped chives
```

1. Preheat oven to 350°.
2. Unroll dough (do not separate into strips). Stretch dough to 18 inches in length. Coat dough evenly with cooking spray. Sprinkle with paprika, parsley, and chives, pressing gently. Cut dough in half crosswise; cut dough along perforations to form 16 breadsticks. Twist each breadstick; place on a baking sheet.
3. Bake at 350° for 15 minutes or until browned. Yield: 16 servings (serving size: 1 breadstick).

CALORIES 56 (21% from fat); FAT 1.3g (sat 0.3g, mono 0g, poly 0g); PROTEIN 1.6g; CARB 9.2g; FIBER 0.6g CHOL 0mg; IRON 0.1mg; SODIUM 146mg; CALC 2mg

FIRE-AND-ICE MELON SOUP

Jalapeño pepper adds the "fire" to this chilled soup, though it can be omitted.

```
 6   cups peeled, cubed cantaloupe
     (about 1½ pounds)
 2   cups peeled, seeded, sliced
     cucumber
 ¼   cup honey
 ½   teaspoon grated lime rind
 3   tablespoons fresh lime juice
 1   teaspoon seeded, minced
     jalapeño pepper
 1   teaspoon ground cumin
 ½   teaspoon salt
 1   (16-ounce) carton plain
     fat-free yogurt
```

1. Combine cantaloupe and cucumber in a blender or food processor; cover and process until smooth. Pour half of cantaloupe mixture into a bowl. Add honey and next 3 ingredients to blender; cover and process until smooth. Add cumin, salt, and yogurt; cover and pulse until blended. Add to cantaloupe mixture in bowl. Stir well.
2. Cover and chill at least 1 hour or until thoroughly chilled. Yield: 6 servings (serving size: 1¼ cups).

CALORIES 151 (4% from fat); FAT 0.7g (sat 0.4g, mono 0.2g, poly 0.1g); PROTEIN 6.2g; CARB 33.2g; FIBER 2.1g; CHOL 2mg; IRON 0.8mg; SODIUM 271mg; CALC 181mg

BUFFALO CHICKEN SALAD WITH BLUE CHEESE-BUTTERMILK DRESSING

The popular flavors of Buffalo wings and blue cheese dip team up in this salad.

```
 1   tablespoon paprika
1½   tablespoons olive oil
 2   tablespoons hot sauce
 6   (4-ounce) skinned, boned
     chicken breast halves
 1   large carrot
 1   celery stalk
 3   cups cubed red potato
Vegetable cooking spray
 6   cups shredded romaine lettuce
 2   cups cherry tomato halves
Blue Cheese-Buttermilk Dressing
```

1. Combine first 3 ingredients in a large dish. Add chicken, turning to coat. Cover and marinate in refrigerator 30 minutes to 1 hour.
2. Cut carrot and celery lengthwise into 12 thin strips, using a vegetable peeler. Place strips in a bowl of ice water. Let stand 30 minutes.
3. Place potato in a saucepan; cover with water. Bring to a boil; cook 15 minutes or until tender. Drain; cool.
4. Prepare grill. Remove chicken from dish; discard marinade. Place chicken on grill rack coated with cooking spray; grill 5 minutes on each side or until chicken is done. Cut chicken diagonally across grain into thin slices.
5. Arrange lettuce on a large platter. Top with potato, carrot and celery

strips, chicken, and tomato halves. Serve with Blue Cheese-Buttermilk Dressing. Yield: 6 servings (serving size: 1 cup lettuce, 1 chicken breast half, and ¼ cup dressing).

CALORIES 317 (24% from fat); FAT 8.3g (sat 3.2g, mono 3g, poly 1.2g); PROTEIN 33.6g; CARB 26.6g; FIBER 4.1g; CHOL 80mg; IRON 2.7mg; SODIUM 473mg; CALC 172mg

Blue Cheese-Buttermilk Dressing:

½ cup low-fat buttermilk
½ cup plain fat-free yogurt
3 tablespoons white wine vinegar
1 teaspoon sugar
½ teaspoon salt
½ teaspoon coarsely ground pepper
½ cup thinly sliced green onions
½ cup crumbled blue cheese

1. Combine first 6 ingredients in a bowl; stir with a whisk until blended. Stir in onions and cheese. Yield: 1½ cups (serving size: ¼ cup).

CALORIES 61 (46% from fat); FAT 3.1g (sat 2g, mono 0.8g, poly 0.1g); PROTEIN 4g; CARB 4.1g; FIBER 0.2g; CHOL 7mg; IRON 0.2mg; SODIUM 354mg; CALC 120mg

FOR TWO

Shrimply Wonderful

Because these flavorful recipes don't call for a lot of shrimp, they're economical. And because the shrimp aren't deep-fried, they're healthful, too.

SHRIMP FRIED RICE

This is an excellent way to use cold, leftover rice. Oil coats the cold rice and prevents it from clumping.

2 tablespoons low-sodium soy sauce
⅛ teaspoon ground ginger
⅛ teaspoon ground red pepper
1 tablespoon vegetable oil, divided
¾ pound medium-size shrimp, peeled
1 cup frozen green peas, thawed
⅓ cup sliced green onions
1 (8-ounce) can sliced water chestnuts, drained
1 cup chilled cooked long-grain rice
2 tablespoons sliced almonds, toasted
1 tablespoon chopped fresh parsley

1. Combine first 3 ingredients; stir well. Set soy sauce mixture aside.
2. Heat 2 teaspoons oil in a large nonstick skillet over medium-high heat. Add shrimp; stir-fry 30 seconds. Add peas, onions, and water chestnuts; stir-fry 2 minutes. Add soy sauce mixture; stir well. Remove shrimp mixture from skillet; set aside.
3. Heat 1 teaspoon oil in skillet over medium-high heat. Add rice; stir-fry 2 minutes. Return shrimp mixture to skillet; stir-fry 1 minute or until thoroughly heated. Sprinkle shrimp mixture with almonds and parsley. Yield: 2 servings (serving size: 1½ cups).

CALORIES 449 (25% from fat); FAT 12.5g (sat 2g, mono 4.4g, poly 4.9g); PROTEIN 34.7g; CARB 49.1g; FIBER 5.4g; CHOL 194mg; IRON 6.6mg; SODIUM 764mg; CALC 129mg

SKILLET SHRIMP AND VEGETABLES

Vegetable cooking spray
1½ cups (¼-inch) peeled, cubed eggplant
1 cup green bell pepper pieces
1 cup cubed zucchini
1 cup coarsely chopped red onion
2 garlic cloves, peeled
2 teaspoons olive oil
¾ pound large shrimp, peeled
2 cups drained canned no-salt-added whole tomatoes, coarsely chopped
1 teaspoon dried thyme
⅛ teaspoon pepper
6 pitted ripe olives, quartered

1. Preheat broiler.
2. Line a broiler pan with aluminum foil; coat with cooking spray.
3. Place eggplant and next 4 ingredients on prepared broiler pan. Broil vegetables 5 minutes on each side or until lightly browned. Remove from heat. Crush garlic cloves; set eggplant mixture aside.
4. Heat oil in a large nonstick skillet over medium-high heat. Add shrimp; sauté 1 minute. Add eggplant mixture, tomatoes, thyme, and ⅛ teaspoon pepper. Reduce heat; cook 4 minutes or until thoroughly heated. Stir in olives. Yield: 2 servings (serving size: 2 cups).

CALORIES 319 (25% from fat); FAT 9g (sat 1.6g, mono 2.7g, poly 3.6g); PROTEIN 31.2g; CARB 30.9g; FIBER 4.6g; CHOL 194mg; IRON 7.1mg; SODIUM 627mg; CALC 226mg

---

STORING SHRIMP

Fresh uncooked shrimp is very perishable, so use it within two days of purchase. After bringing it home, rinse thoroughly under cold running water, and pat dry with paper towels. Cover shrimp loosely with wax paper so that air can circulate around it; store in the coolest part of the refrigerator, preferably on a bed of ice. Shrimp can be frozen, but it loses some of its texture after thawing.

SHRIMP JAMBALAYA

(pictured on page 206)

1 teaspoon olive oil
2 ounces turkey kielbasa,
    halved lengthwise and sliced
    (about ½ cup)
½ cup minced onion
½ cup diced green bell pepper
½ cup uncooked long-grain rice
⅛ teaspoon salt
⅛ teaspoon dried thyme
⅛ teaspoon black pepper
⅛ teaspoon ground red pepper
1 cup water
1 (10½-ounce) can low-salt
    chicken broth
1 (14.5-ounce) can diced
    tomatoes, undrained
½ pound medium-size shrimp,
    peeled
⅛ teaspoon hot sauce
1 tablespoon chopped fresh
    parsley

1. Heat oil in a medium saucepan over medium heat. Add kielbasa, onion, and bell pepper; sauté 5 minutes or until vegetables are tender. Add rice; sauté 2 minutes. Add salt and next 3 ingredients; sauté 1 minute.

2. Add water, broth, and tomatoes; bring to a boil. Cover, reduce heat, and simmer 15 minutes or until rice is tender.
3. Stir in shrimp and hot sauce; cover and cook 5 minutes or until shrimp are done. Remove from heat; stir in parsley. Yield: 2 servings (serving size: 2 cups).

CALORIES 420 (19% from fat); FAT 9g (sat 1.3g, mono 2.6g, poly 2g); PROTEIN 29.9g; CARB 55g; FIBER 2.8g; CHOL 150mg; IRON 7mg; SODIUM 860mg; CALC 143mg

WALDORF SHRIMP SALAD

2 cups water
1½ tablespoons fresh lemon juice,
    divided
½ pound medium-size shrimp,
    peeled
2 tablespoons coarsely chopped
    walnuts
1 cup diced Red Delicious
    apple
1 cup diced celery
3 tablespoons fat-free mayonnaise
2 teaspoons prepared
    horseradish
¼ teaspoon curry powder
⅛ teaspoon salt
Dash of pepper

1. Bring 2 cups water and 1 tablespoon lemon juice to a boil in a medium saucepan. Add shrimp; cook over high heat 3 minutes or until done. Drain in a colander over a bowl, reserving 1 tablespoon cooking liquid. Rinse shrimp under cold water; drain.
2. Heat a small nonstick skillet over medium heat. Add walnuts, and cook 2 minutes or until lightly toasted, stirring frequently. Combine shrimp, walnuts, apple, and celery in a bowl. Combine 1½ teaspoons lemon juice, reserved cooking liquid, mayonnaise, and remaining 4 ingredients in a bowl; stir well. Add mayonnaise mixture to shrimp mixture; toss well. Yield: 2 servings (serving size: 1½ cups).

CALORIES 206 (28% from fat); FAT 6.3g (sat 0.6g, mono 1.3g, poly 3.6g); PROTEIN 20.1g; CARB 18.9g; FIBER 3.5g; CHOL 129mg; IRON 2.9mg; SODIUM 611mg; CALC 86mg

YOU'RE SO VEIN

Is it really necessary to remove the black vein on the shrimp's back? The vein is harmless, so it's personal preference. But if you prefer to devein:

- Grasp the tail of the shrimp in one hand, and gently remove the shell.
- Pull off the tail (the tails should be removed for all of these recipes).
- At the tail end, pinch the vein and pull it out with your fingers—it should be fairly easy to grab. Or make a tiny slit along the back with a sharp paring knife, and lift the vein out with the tip of the knife. You don't need to buy one of those fancy deveining gadgets.

THE BIG SHRIMP

The good news is that shrimp, although higher in cholesterol than some other seafoods, are extremely low in fat, especially saturated fat. And that's what counts, because saturated fat in food can raise blood-cholesterol levels more than cholesterol in food. The amount of saturated fat in your diet should be less than 10% of the total calories (for women 25 to 50 years old, this is about 22 grams or less). Numbers talk, so you can see just how shrimp stacks up to other sources of protein.

3 ounces cooked	Calories	Cholesterol (mg)	Fat (g)	Saturated Fat (g)
Shrimp	84	166	0.9	0.3
Cheddar cheese (1 ounce)	114	30	9.4	6.0
Chicken, dark-meat	174	79	8.3	2.3
Crab	94	65	1.1	0.1
Egg (1)	77	221	5.2	1.6
Lobster	122	77	1.6	0.3
Pork loin	219	81	13.0	4.5
Sirloin steak	166	76	6.1	2.4

Glazed Pineapple Madagascar with St. Andrew's Glacé, page 210

Parmesan Risotto-Stuffed Portobellos, page 199

Shrimp Jambalaya, page 204

Garlicky Tomato Tart, page 193

*Jalapeño-Lime Marinade
on Grilled Shrimp Kebabs, page 220*

*Our American Hero,
page 201*

Roasted Pineapple-Carrot Salsa, page 216

Where Today's Specials are Tomorrow's Trends

At the CIA, student cooks are changing the way America dines out.

St. Andrew's Cafe is one of the reasons that the 51-year-old Culinary Institute of America (CIA), in Hyde Park, New York, is considered to be among America's premier cooking schools. One of four on-campus restaurants where students cook and serve, St. Andrew's is unique: It's devoted entirely to "contemporary cuisine," as it's called at the CIA. The menus feature gourmet-style foods that highlight fresh ingredients and minimize fats and oils.

TUSCAN BEAN SALAD

The basic components of the vinaigrette can be varied to suit your taste. Try, for example, red wine, balsamic, or rice vinegar instead of champagne vinegar; use vegetable or chicken broth in place of water; substitute other herbs, such as chives, tarragon, or basil, for the oregano.

St. Andrew's Champagne Vinaigrette
- 2 cups canned navy beans or other white beans, rinsed and drained
- ½ cup finely diced carrot
- ¼ cup finely diced celery
- ¼ cup finely diced red bell pepper
- ¼ cup finely diced yellow bell pepper
- ¼ cup minced green onions
- 2 tablespoons thinly sliced chives
- 2 tablespoons minced fresh parsley
- ⅛ teaspoon salt
- ⅛ teaspoon pepper

1. Prepare St. Andrew's Champagne Vinaigrette; cover and chill.
2. Combine beans and remaining 9 ingredients in a large bowl; add ½ cup St. Andrew's Champagne Vinaigrette, tossing until well-blended. Cover and chill. Yield: 4 servings (serving size: ¾ cup).

CALORIES 185 (29% from fat); FAT 6g (sat 0.8g, mono 3.3g, poly 1.3g); PROTEIN 7.8g; CARB 26.2g; FIBER 4g; CHOL 0mg; IRON 3mg; SODIUM 256mg; CALC 57mg

St. Andrew's Champagne Vinaigrette:

- ½ cup water
- 1 teaspoon cornstarch
- ¼ cup champagne vinegar or white wine vinegar
- 2 tablespoons olive oil
- ½ teaspoon dried oregano
- ½ teaspoon salt
- ⅛ teaspoon pepper

1. Combine water and cornstarch in a small saucepan, stirring with a whisk until cornstarch dissolves. Bring to a boil over medium-high heat; cook, stirring constantly, 1 minute. Remove from heat, and cool. Stir in vinegar and remaining ingredients. Cover and chill. Yield: ¾ cup plus 2 tablespoons (serving size: 1 tablespoon).

CALORIES 19 (90% from fat); FAT 1.9g (sat 0.3g, mono 1.4g, poly 0.2g); PROTEIN 0g; CARB 0.2g; FIBER 0g; CHOL 0mg; IRON 0mg; SODIUM 84mg; CALC 1mg

ST. ANDREW'S SALAD DRESSING

Pureeing the ricotta cheese gives it a consistency similar to sour cream. Serve with tossed greens, or use in place of mayonnaise in a potato or macaroni salad. This dressing is also thick enough to use as a vegetable dip.

- ½ cup part-skim ricotta cheese
- 1 cup plain low-fat yogurt
- ⅓ cup red wine vinegar
- ⅓ cup Dijon mustard
- ¼ cup drained capers, chopped
- 1½ tablespoons chopped fresh basil
- 1 tablespoon chopped fresh parsley
- 1 tablespoon minced shallots
- 2 garlic cloves, minced

1. Place ricotta cheese in a food processor, and process until smooth. Combine ricotta cheese, yogurt, and remaining ingredients in a medium bowl; stir until well-blended. Cover and chill. Yield: 3 cups (serving size: 1 tablespoon).

Note: Store salad dressing in an airtight container in refrigerator for up to 2 weeks.

CALORIES 10 (36% from fat); FAT 0.4g (sat 0.2g, mono 0.1g, poly 0g); PROTEIN 0.6g; CARB 0.7g; FIBER 0g; CHOL 1mg; IRON 0mg; SODIUM 112mg; CALC 16mg

SAUTÉED SALMON WITH ZUCCHINI NOODLES AND RED BELL PEPPER COULIS

These sautéed, julienne-cut zucchini strips are a lower-calorie alternative to pasta. A coulis is a thick puree or sauce.

Red Bell Pepper Coulis
4   medium zucchini
2   tablespoons fresh lime juice
1   teaspoon minced shallots
¼   teaspoon salt
⅛   teaspoon cracked pepper
1   garlic clove, minced
6   (6-ounce) salmon fillets
¼   cup all-purpose flour
1   tablespoon butter, divided
Chopped fresh parsley (optional)
Freshly ground pepper (optional)

1. Prepare Red Bell Pepper Coulis; set aside. Slice zucchini lengthwise into ¼-inch-thick strips, stopping at the inside part of the zucchini containing the seeds; discard seed portions. Cut strips lengthwise into long, thin "noodles;" set aside.
2. Combine lime juice and next 4 ingredients in a small bowl. Rub salmon with juice mixture. Dredge salmon in flour. Melt 2 teaspoons butter in a large nonstick skillet over medium-high heat. Add salmon; sauté 4 minutes on each side or until fish flakes easily when tested with a fork. Remove salmon fillets from skillet. Set aside, and keep warm.
3. Melt 1 teaspoon butter in skillet. Add zucchini noodles; sauté 4 minutes or until wilted, tossing gently.
4. Spoon Red Bell Pepper Coulis onto 6 serving plates. Top with zucchini noodles and salmon. If desired, garnish with chopped parsley and freshly ground pepper. Yield: 6 servings (serving size: 5 ounces salmon, ¾ cup zucchini, and 2½ tablespoons coulis).

CALORIES 376 (45% from fat); FAT 18.7g (sat 4g, mono 8.7g, poly 3.6g); PROTEIN 38.9g; CARB 12.3g; FIBER 1.8g; CHOL 121mg; IRON 2.5mg; SODIUM 318mg; CALC 32mg

Red Bell Pepper Coulis:

2   teaspoons olive oil
3   cups coarsely chopped red bell pepper
2   tablespoons minced shallots
1   tablespoon seeded, minced jalapeño pepper
2   garlic cloves, minced
¾   cup low-salt chicken broth
2   tablespoons balsamic vinegar
¼   teaspoon salt

1. Heat olive oil in a large nonstick skillet over medium-high heat. Add bell pepper and next 3 ingredients; sauté 2 minutes. Cover, reduce heat, and simmer 10 minutes or until tender. Add broth; simmer, uncovered, 15 minutes or until liquid is almost evaporated.
2. Place pepper mixture in a blender; cover and process until smooth. Strain puree through a sieve over a bowl; discard solids. Stir in vinegar and salt. Yield: 1 cup (serving size: 2½ tablespoons).

CALORIES 40 (45% from fat); FAT 2g (sat 0.3g, mono 1.1g, poly 0.3g); PROTEIN 1.1g; CARB 5.4g; FIBER 1.3g; CHOL 0mg; IRON 1.2mg; SODIUM 110mg; CALC 8mg

GLAZED PINEAPPLE MADAGASCAR WITH ST. ANDREW'S GLACÉ

(pictured on page 205)

St. Andrew's Glacé
4   (1-inch-thick) slices fresh pineapple
1   tablespoon drained brine-packed green peppercorns, crushed
1   tablespoon plus 1 teaspoon sugar
¾   cup fresh orange juice
1   tablespoon honey
¼   cup white rum

1. Prepare St. Andrew's Glacé.
2. Rub cut sides of pineapple with peppercorns; sprinkle sugar over one side of each pineapple slice. Place a large nonstick skillet over medium heat until hot. Add pineapple, sugar side down; sauté 5 minutes or until golden. Turn pineapple. Add orange juice, honey, and rum; bring to a boil.
3. Remove pineapple from skillet; set aside. Reduce heat, and simmer, uncovered, until juice mixture is reduced to ¼ cup or syrupy (about 10 minutes). Remove from heat.
4. Arrange pineapple on each of 4 plates. Drizzle orange syrup over slices; top with St. Andrew's Glacé. Yield: 4 servings (serving size: 1 slice pineapple, 1 tablespoon syrup, and ¼ cup glacé).

CALORIES 224 (8% from fat); FAT 2.2g (sat 1.4g, mono 0.6g, poly 0.1g); PROTEIN 4.5g; CARB 36.2g; FIBER 0.5g; CHOL 8mg; IRON 0.8mg; SODIUM 55mg; CALC 133mg

St. Andrew's Glacé:

1¾ cups part-skim ricotta cheese
2½ cups plain low-fat yogurt
1   cup maple syrup
1   tablespoon vanilla extract

1. Place ricotta cheese in a food processor, and process until smooth. Combine ricotta and remaining ingredients in a large bowl; stir well.
2. Pour mixture into freezer can of an ice cream freezer; freeze according to manufacturer's instructions. Spoon ice cream into a freezer-safe container; cover and freeze 1 hour or until firm. Yield: 5 cups (serving size: ¼ cup).
Note: You can change the flavor of this basic "ice cream" by adding 1½ cups pureed raspberries (or whatever fruit is in season) before freezing.

CALORIES 91 (22% from fat); FAT 2.2g (sat 1.4g, mono 0.6g, poly 0.1g); PROTEIN 3.9g; CARB 13.8g; FIBER 0g; CHOL 8mg; IRON 0.3mg; SODIUM 48mg; CALC 121mg

The Food of Friendship

Invite company for dinner, and listen to your friendship grow.

For the past few months, I've talked about "living within reason" in this column. I like to visualize my life in terms of a well-balanced chair, based on food, exercise, reflection, and friendship. If one leg is out of balance, it upsets the entire situation, doesn't it? I've found the last leg—that of friendship—to be a much more important element in my life than I presumed a decade ago.

The dining table is one of the last remaining gathering places in our culture, and there, I believe, friendship can be fostered. Invite your friends and family, cook and eat together, enjoy the pleasures of the table—and really listen. You'll rediscover the sense of renewal that friendship can bring.

And should you need inspiration for a cozy meal with friends, here's a recipe idea.

GRILLED FOCACCIA WITH PROSCIUTTO AND FENNEL

    2 cups thinly sliced fennel bulb
        (about 2 small bulbs)
Vegetable cooking spray
    1 (5.5-ounce) package
        (2 [6-inch]) focaccias
        (Italian flatbread)
1½ cups (6 ounces) preshredded
        fat-free mozzarella cheese
    1 tablespoon thinly sliced fresh
        sage
    3 ounces very thin slices
        prosciutto
    ⅛ teaspoon freshly ground
        black pepper
    1 teaspoon olive oil

1. Arrange fennel in a steamer basket over boiling water. Cover and steam 10 minutes or until tender. Place a nonstick skillet coated with cooking spray over medium-high heat until hot. Add fennel, and sauté 1 minute or until lightly browned.
2. Slice each focaccia in half horizontally. Sprinkle cheese over cut sides of 2 focaccia pieces. Sprinkle evenly with sage. Top with fennel and prosciutto; sprinkle with pepper. Top with remaining focaccia halves.
3. Brush each sandwich with ½ teaspoon oil. Place a large nonstick skillet coated with cooking spray over medium heat until hot. Add sandwiches, and cook 3 minutes on each side or until sandwiches are golden. Cut each sandwich into 3 wedges. Yield: 3 servings (serving size: 2 wedges).
Note: The combination of prepackaged focaccia, mozzarella, and prosciutto makes for a high-sodium sandwich. If you're watching the sodium in your diet, try substituting turkey for the prosciutto and a low-sodium cheese for the mozzarella.

CALORIES 303 (23% from fat); FAT 7.8g (sat 2.1g, mono 2.3g, poly 0.5g); PROTEIN 29g; CARB 31.2g; FIBER 2.3g; CHOL 27mg; IRON 2.1mg; SODIUM 1,251 mg; CALC 489mg

Red, White, and New

To help keep America's regional dishes off the endangered list, we've gathered one from each part of the country, then lightened them all for today's tastes.

All across America, you can get pretty much the same dishes nowadays, be they fajitas, spring rolls, or fettuccine Alfredo. As wonderful as our new food consciousness is, it can be a little scary, too. Are we losing our regional American cooking, recipes that define a particular area?

The issue is especially disconcerting if you go to a chain restaurant where they serve the same food in every city. As an antidote to such monotony, we decided to gather some of America's favorite indigenous dishes from across the land and lighten them for the health-oriented '90s. Here, then, is our salute to American classics—from recipe to shining recipe.

THE SOUTH

HONEY-PECAN CRUSTED CHICKEN

You would expect Southern fried chicken to be high in fat. Not our version, though—we baked the chicken instead of frying it, and we gave it a crisp, greaseless crust made from crushed cornflakes and chopped pecans.

    ¼ teaspoon salt
    ¼ teaspoon pepper
    4 (6-ounce) skinned chicken
        breast halves
    8 (4-ounce) chicken drumsticks,
        skinned
    ¼ cup honey
    2 tablespoons Dijon mustard
    ¾ teaspoon paprika
    ⅛ teaspoon garlic powder
1¼ cups finely crushed cornflakes
        (about 4 cups uncrushed
        cereal)
    ½ cup finely chopped pecans
Vegetable cooking spray

1. Preheat oven to 400°.
2. Sprinkle salt and pepper evenly over chicken; set aside. Combine honey and next 3 ingredients in a bowl. Combine cornflakes and pecans in a shallow dish; stir well. Brush both sides of chicken with honey mixture; dredge in cornflake mixture.
3. Place chicken pieces on a large baking sheet coated with cooking spray. Lightly coat chicken with cooking spray, and bake at 400° for 40 minutes or until done. Shield chicken with aluminum foil during last 10 minutes to prevent coating from getting too brown, if necessary. Yield: 8 servings.

CALORIES 270 (30% from fat); FAT 8.9g (sat 1.7g, mono 3.9g, poly 2.6g); PROTEIN 25g; CARB 21.4g; FIBER 0.5g; CHOL 71mg; IRON 2mg; SODIUM 416mg; CALC 15mg

CELERY MASHED POTATOES AND CHICKEN GRAVY

- 7 medium-size red potatoes, peeled and quartered (about 3¼ pounds)
- 2 tablespoons reduced-calorie stick margarine
- ½ cup chopped celery
- ½ cup chopped onion
- ⅓ cup 1% low-fat milk
- ¼ cup minced fresh parsley or 1 tablespoon dried parsley flakes
- ½ teaspoon salt
- ½ teaspoon poultry seasoning
- Chicken Gravy

1. Place potato in a large saucepan; cover with water. Bring to a boil. Reduce heat; simmer 20 minutes or until very tender. Drain and return to pan.
2. Melt margarine in a small skillet over medium-high heat; sauté celery and onion 8 minutes or until tender.
3. Add celery mixture, milk, parsley, salt, and seasoning to potato; beat at medium speed of an electric mixer until smooth. Serve with Chicken Gravy. Yield: 6 servings (serving size: 1 cup potatoes and 2½ tablespoons gravy).

CALORIES 208 (24% from fat); FAT 5.5g (sat 1g, mono 1.9g, poly 2.2g); PROTEIN 5.5g; CARB 36g; FIBER 4g; CHOL 1mg; IRON 3mg; SODIUM 361mg; CALC 53mg

Chicken Gravy:

- 2 tablespoons reduced-calorie stick margarine
- 2 tablespoons all-purpose flour
- ¼ teaspoon poultry seasoning
- ⅛ teaspoon salt
- ⅛ teaspoon paprika
- 1 cup low-salt chicken broth

1. Melt margarine in a small saucepan over medium heat; add flour and next 3 ingredients, stirring with a whisk. Gradually add broth, stirring until blended. Cook, stirring constantly, 2 minutes or until thick. Yield: 6 servings (serving size: 2½ tablespoons).

CALORIES 34 (71% from fat); FAT 2.7g (sat 0.4g, mono 0.9g, poly 1g); PROTEIN 0.7g; CARB 2.3g; FIBER 0.1g; CHOL 0mg; IRON 0.3mg; SODIUM 99mg; CALC 1mg

THE MID-ATLANTIC

ROASTED CORN-CHICKEN SOUP

This is a standard in Pennsylvania Dutch cooking. In our version, cheese-filled tortellini are used in place of traditional egg noodles.

- 6 cups water
- ¼ cup chopped fresh parsley or 1 tablespoon dried parsley flakes
- ½ teaspoon black peppercorns
- 3 pounds chicken pieces
- 5 (10½-ounce) cans low-salt chicken broth
- 3 medium carrots, quartered
- 3 medium parsnips, quartered
- 2 celery stalks, quartered
- 1 medium onion, quartered
- 4 whole cloves
- 3 garlic cloves
- 2 bay leaves
- 2 cups frozen whole-kernel corn, thawed
- Vegetable cooking spray
- ½ cup finely chopped celery
- ⅓ cup minced fresh parsley or 1 tablespoon dried parsley flakes
- ¾ teaspoon salt
- ½ teaspoon poultry seasoning
- ½ teaspoon pepper
- 1 (9-ounce) package fresh cheese tortellini, uncooked

1. Combine first 12 ingredients in a stockpot; bring to a boil. Reduce heat; simmer, uncovered, 40 minutes. Remove from heat. Remove chicken from stock; cool. Remove skin from chicken; remove chicken from bones. Discard skin and bones. Shred chicken into bite-size pieces; cover and chill.
2. Return stock to a boil. Reduce heat; simmer, uncovered, 1 hour. Strain stock through a sieve into a large bowl; discard solids. Cover and chill stock 8 hours. Skim solidified fat from surface; discard.
3. Preheat broiler. Place corn on a jelly-roll pan coated with cooking spray; broil 8 minutes or until corn is

light brown. Combine stock and chicken in stockpot; bring to a boil. Stir in corn, ½ cup celery, and remaining ingredients; bring to a boil. Reduce heat, and simmer, uncovered, 10 minutes. Yield: 7 servings (serving size: 2 cups).

CALORIES 278 (20% from fat); FAT 6.3g (sat 2.6g, mono 2.3g, poly 1.2g); PROTEIN 26g; CARB 29.1g; FIBER 1.5g; CHOL 70mg; IRON 2.1mg; SODIUM 525mg; CALC 19mg

NEW ENGLAND

NEW ENGLAND BOILED DINNER WITH HORSERADISH SAUCE

This updated dinner becomes a complete meal with a molded cranberry-orange salad, New England brown bread, and apple juice. These accompaniments round out the meal so that the percentage of calories from fat drops to less than 30%.

- 1 (3-pound) cured corned beef brisket
- 4 quarts water
- 1 teaspoon pickling spice
- 1 garlic clove, halved
- 2 cups trimmed Brussels sprouts (about 12 ounces)
- 12 small boiling onions
- 6 medium carrots, quartered
- 6 medium parsnips, quartered
- 1 large rutabaga, peeled and cut into 12 pieces (about 2¾ pounds)
- 1 tablespoon all-purpose flour
- 1 tablespoon sugar
- 1 tablespoon dry mustard
- 1 tablespoon cider vinegar
- 1 tablespoon prepared horseradish
- 2 teaspoons margarine

1. Trim fat from brisket. Place brisket in a large stockpot; add water, pickling spice, and garlic. Bring to a boil; cover, reduce heat, and simmer 1 hour. Add Brussels sprouts and next 4 ingredients; bring to a boil. Cover and simmer 1 hour or until brisket is tender. Remove vegetables and brisket from

pot; reserve 1 cup cooking liquid. Set vegetables aside; keep warm. Let brisket stand 5 minutes; cut into thin slices.

2. Combine flour, sugar, and mustard in a small saucepan; stir in vinegar until smooth. Gradually add reserved 1 cup cooking liquid, stirring with a whisk until blended. Bring to a boil over medium-high heat. Reduce heat; simmer, uncovered, 10 minutes. Remove from heat; add horseradish and margarine, stirring until blended. Serve horseradish sauce with brisket and vegetables. Yield: 6 servings (serving size: 3 ounces brisket, 2 onions, 4 pieces carrot, 4 pieces parsnip, 2 rutabaga pieces, ⅓ cup Brussels sprouts, and 2 tablespoons horseradish sauce).

CALORIES 423 (40% from fat); FAT 18.5g (sat 5.8g, mono 8.6g, poly 1.3g); PROTEIN 21.2g; CARB 45.9g; FIBER 7.3g; CHOL 83mg; IRON 4.1mg; SODIUM 1,162mg; CALC 177mg

THE MIDWEST

QUICK PASTIES WITH SWEET-AND-HOT KETCHUP

Pasties (PASS-tees) are individual meat-and-vegetable pies with a homemade sweet-hot ketchup. We've made one large loaf to save time, and used dough found in the refrigerator section of the grocery store to reduce the fat.

1 cup peeled, cubed baking
    potato
Vegetable cooking spray
1 cup chopped onion
1 pound ground round
2 teaspoons chili powder
2 teaspoons dried oregano
1 teaspoon sugar
½ teaspoon salt
¼ teaspoon ground cinnamon
¼ teaspoon ground nutmeg
¼ teaspoon ground ginger
2 tablespoons minced fresh
    parsley or 2 teaspoons dried
    parsley flakes
1 (10-ounce) can refrigerated
    pizza crust dough
Sweet-and-Hot Ketchup

1. Place potato in a saucepan; cover with water. Bring to a boil. Reduce heat, and simmer 15 minutes or until tender; drain. Set aside, and cool.
2. Preheat oven to 350°.
3. Place a large nonstick skillet coated with cooking spray over medium-high heat until hot. Add onion; sauté 4 minutes. Add meat, and cook until browned, stirring to crumble.
4. Combine chili powder and next 6 ingredients; stir into meat mixture. Remove from heat; add potatoes and parsley, stirring just until combined.
5. Unroll pizza crust dough onto a baking sheet coated with cooking spray; pat dough into a 14 x 10-inch rectangle. Spread meat mixture lengthwise over half of dough, leaving a 1-inch border. Fold remaining dough over meat mixture; tightly seal edges.
6. Bake loaf at 350° for 25 minutes or until golden. Let loaf stand 5 minutes. Cut loaf into 8 pieces, and serve with Sweet-and-Hot Ketchup. Yield: 8 servings (serving size: 1 piece pasty and 1 tablespoon ketchup).

CALORIES 232 (14% from fat); FAT 3.7g (sat 1.2g, mono 1.3g, poly 0.6g); PROTEIN 15g; CARB 31.7g; FIBER 1.3g; CHOL 32mg; IRON 1.8mg; SODIUM 533mg; CALC 22mg

Sweet-and-Hot Ketchup:

½ cup ketchup
2 tablespoons honey
¼ teaspoon hot sauce

1. Combine ketchup, honey, and hot sauce; stir well. Yield: ½ cup (serving size: 1 tablespoon).
Note: Recipe can easily be doubled; store in an airtight container in refrigerator. Serve as a condiment with roast beef, meat loaf, or hamburgers.

CALORIES 34 (0% from fat); FAT 0.1g (sat 0g, mono 0.1g, poly 0g); PROTEIN 0.4g; CARB 8.7g; FIBER 0.3g; CHOL 0mg; IRON 0.2mg; SODIUM 179mg; CALC 4mg

THE PACIFIC COAST

ZESTY SALMON WITH SPINACH FETTUCCINE

2 teaspoons grated lemon rind
¼ cup fresh lemon juice, divided
1 teaspoon olive oil
1 (12-ounce) skinned salmon
    fillet (½ inch thick), cut into
    ½-inch-wide strips
Vegetable cooking spray
1½ cups low-salt vegetable broth
1 tablespoon plus 1 teaspoon
    cornstarch
2 garlic cloves, minced
2 tablespoons low-fat sour cream
1 tablespoon plus 1 teaspoon
    reduced-calorie stick margarine
¼ cup chopped fresh parsley,
    divided
4 cups hot cooked spinach
    fettuccine (about 8 ounces
    uncooked pasta)
Lemon slices (optional)

1. Combine lemon rind, 2 tablespoons lemon juice, oil, and salmon in a large zip-top plastic bag. Seal bag; marinate in refrigerator 20 minutes.
2. Preheat broiler.
3. Remove salmon from bag; discard marinade. Place salmon on rack of a broiler pan coated with cooking spray; broil 6 minutes or until fish flakes easily when tested with a fork, turning after 3 minutes. Set aside; keep warm.
4. Combine broth, cornstarch, and garlic in a small saucepan. Bring to a boil over medium heat; cook, stirring constantly, 1 minute. Add 2 tablespoons lemon juice, sour cream, and margarine; cook, stirring constantly, 3 minutes or until thick. Remove from heat; stir in 2 tablespoons parsley.
5. Arrange pasta on a serving platter; top with salmon. Drizzle sauce over salmon. Sprinkle with 2 tablespoons parsley. Garnish with lemon slices, if desired. Yield: 4 servings (serving size: 1 cup pasta, 2 ounces fish, and ⅓ cup sauce).

CALORIES 408 (30% from fat); FAT 13.4g (sat 2.6g, mono 5.8g, poly 2.9g); PROTEIN 25.6g; CARB 45.4g; FIBER 2.5g; CHOL 61mg; IRON 2.6mg; SODIUM 463mg; CALC 33mg

VEGETARIAN TAMALE PIE

Our tamale is a meatless version that incorporates sun-dried tomatoes.

    ½ cup sun-dried tomato sprinkles
    ½ cup boiling water
    4 cups water
 1½ cups yellow cornmeal
    ¼ teaspoon salt
    1 cup (4 ounces) shredded
        Monterey Jack cheese with
        jalapeño peppers
 Vegetable cooking spray
    1 cup chopped onion
    2 teaspoons dried oregano
 1½ teaspoons chili powder
    1 (15-ounce) can black beans,
        rinsed and drained
    1 (16-ounce) can pinto beans,
        rinsed and drained
    1 (14¾-ounce) can no-salt-added
        cream-style corn
    1 (4.5-ounce) can chopped green
        chiles, drained
    ¼ cup plus 2 tablespoons low-fat
        sour cream

1. Combine tomato sprinkles and boiling water; let stand 20 minutes. Drain tomato sprinkles in a sieve over a bowl; set aside, reserving 1 tablespoon liquid.
2. Combine 4 cups water, cornmeal, and salt in a large saucepan; bring mixture to a boil. Cook over medium heat, stirring constantly with a whisk, 5 minutes or until mixture is thick. Stir in cheese. Pour half of cornmeal mixture into a 13 x 9-inch baking dish coated with cooking spray, and set aside.
3. Preheat oven to 400°.
4. Place a large nonstick skillet coated with cooking spray over medium-high heat until hot. Add onion, and sauté 5 minutes or until soft. Add tomato sprinkles, reserved tomato liquid, oregano, and next 5 ingredients; cook 1 minute. Spoon bean mixture evenly over cornmeal crust. Drop remaining cornmeal mixture by tablespoonfuls onto bean mixture.

5. Bake pie at 400° for 30 minutes or until set. Serve pie with sour cream. Yield: 6 servings. (serving size: 1 [4-inch] square and 1 tablespoon sour cream).

CALORIES 420 (20% from fat); FAT 9.4g (sat 5g, mono 2.5g, poly 1g); PROTEIN 18g; CARB 68.9g; FIBER 6.8g; CHOL 20mg; IRON 4.3mg; SODIUM 595mg; CALC 218mg

W I N E   P I C K S

- *Atlas Peak Consenso Cabernet Sauvignon 1993 (California red), $22*
- *Belvedere Alexander Valley Chardonnay 1995 (California white), $12*
- *Monteviña Refosco 1995 (California red), $8*
- *Villa Mt. Eden Grand Reserve Pinot Blanc, Bien Nacido Vineyard 1995 (California white), $20*

COOKING CLASS

Learning to Salsa

Although most people think of salsas as those chunky hot sauces that accompany Tex-Mex food, they can take many other forms, too. There's no law saying that salsas must be limited to the usual ingredients. And they don't even have to be hot. When you consider that salsa is the Spanish word for "sauce," be it cooked or uncooked, a whole world of possibilities unfolds.

Low in fat and calories, salsas are heaven-sent for light cooking. But what really makes a salsa "get up and salsa" is the use of fresh, peak-season ingredients such as mangoes, peaches, corn, and papaya. The other key to a successful salsa is how you cut the ingredients, and for that we have step-by-step instructions. Better begin practicing your salsa skills now.

MANGO-AND-ROASTED CORN SALSA

You can serve this colorful salsa with grilled chicken or pork.

 1½ cups fresh corn kernels
        (about 3 ears)
    1 teaspoon vegetable oil
 1½ cups peeled, diced mango
    ¼ cup fresh lemon juice
    2 tablespoons diced sweet onion
    2 tablespoons minced fresh mint
    2 tablespoons minced fresh cilantro
 1½ teaspoons peeled, grated fresh
        gingerroot
    ¼ teaspoon salt

1. Preheat oven to 400°.
2. Combine corn and oil, tossing well. Place on a baking sheet, spreading evenly. Bake at 400° for 15 minutes. Cool. Combine corn, mango, and remaining ingredients in a bowl; toss gently. Yield: 2½ cups (serving size: ¼ cup).

CALORIES 43 (17% from fat); FAT 0.8g (sat 0.1g, mono 0.2g, poly 0.4g); PROTEIN 0.9g; CARB 9.4g; FIBER 1.2g; CHOL 0mg; IRON 0.2mg; SODIUM 63mg; CALC 5mg

PEACH-GINGER SALSA

This salsa recipe can easily be doubled. It complements anything from tortilla chips to grilled chicken.

    1 cup peeled, cubed peaches
        (about 2 peaches)
    1 cup seeded, cubed tomato
        (about 3 tomatoes)
    ¼ cup sliced green onions
    2 teaspoons sugar
    2 teaspoons cider vinegar
    1 teaspoon peeled, minced
        fresh gingerroot
    ⅛ teaspoon salt
 Dash of freshly ground black pepper

1. Combine all ingredients; stir well. Cover and chill. Yield: 2 cups (serving size: ½ cup).

CALORIES 40 (5% from fat); FAT 0.2g (sat 0g, mono 0g, poly 0.1g); PROTEIN 0.8g; CARB 10g; FIBER 1.5g; CHOL 0mg; IRON 0.4mg; SODIUM 78mg; CALC 9mg

SALSA ROJA

*This traditional salsa is great paired
with grilled chicken and seafood, and,
of course, tortilla chips.*

    2   cups diced fresh plum tomatoes
    1½ cups diced red bell pepper
    1⅓ cups chopped onion
    2   large jalapeño peppers, seeded
        and diced
    1   (14.5-ounce) can plum
        tomatoes, undrained and
        chopped
    6   garlic cloves, minced
    ¾   cup chopped fresh cilantro
    ¼   cup chopped fresh parsley
    ¼   cup fresh lime juice
    2   tablespoons finely chopped
        fresh oregano
    2   tablespoons balsamic vinegar
    1   teaspoon ground cumin
    ¼   teaspoon salt
    ¼   teaspoon freshly ground
        pepper
    1   (5.5-ounce) can no-salt-added
        vegetable juice

1. Combine first 6 ingredients in a
large bowl, and toss gently. Combine
cilantro and remaining 8 ingredients
in a small bowl; stir well. Stir cilantro
mixture into tomato mixture. Chill.
Yield: 6 cups (serving size: ¼ cup).

CALORIES 18 (10% from fat); FAT 0.2g (sat 0g, mono 0g,
poly 0.1g); PROTEIN 0.7g; CARB 4g; FIBER 0.8g;
CHOL 0mg; IRON 0.8mg; SODIUM 57mg; CALC 20mg

SHARPEN YOUR SKILLS

How you cut your salsa ingredients can make all the difference. Cut them
too small, and you have mush; too large, and you have fruit salad. The trick is
to cut the ingredients small enough to disperse the flavors, yet large enough to
provide a refreshing crunch. To ensure that your salsas turn out right, follow
our instructions on how to chop, cube, dice, and mince.

Chop: *To cut into small,
irregular-size pieces. Use one
hand to grip the handle of a
chef's knife, and place the other
hand on the blunt edge of the
knife. Keep the knife tip on the
cutting surface while rapidly
lifting the handle up and down,
cutting through the food.*

Cube: *To cut food into ½-inch or
larger blocks. Use a chef's knife to
cut the food into slices of the desired
thickness, then cut the slices into
strips of the same thickness. Stack
the strips with the ends flush, and
cut crosswise into cubes.*

Dice: *To cut food into small
¼-inch cubes. Use a chef's knife to
cut the food into slices of desired
thickness, then cut the slices into
strips of the same thickness. Stack
the strips with the ends flush, and
cut crosswise into small cubes.*

Mince: *To chop into very small
pieces. Use your chef's knife in
the same rocking motion used
for chopping. Mincing herbs and
garlic helps release their flavor
throughout food.*

ROASTED FENNEL SALSA

This salsa complements a full-flavored fish such as grilled tuna or swordfish.

- 1 whole garlic head
- 2 medium fennel bulbs, thinly sliced
- Vegetable cooking spray
- 1 tablespoon olive oil
- ¼ teaspoon salt
- ¼ teaspoon freshly ground pepper
- ¼ teaspoon grated lemon rind
- 3 tablespoons fresh lemon juice
- ¼ teaspoon minced fresh rosemary

1. Preheat oven to 450°.
2. Remove white papery skin from garlic head (do not peel or separate cloves). Cut off, and discard top of garlic head; wrap in aluminum foil. Place garlic and fennel on a baking sheet coated with cooking spray. Brush fennel with oil; sprinkle with salt and pepper. Bake at 450° for 25 minutes or until lightly browned. Remove from oven; cool 10 minutes. Separate garlic cloves; squeeze to extract pulp. Discard skins. Chop fennel. Combine fennel, garlic, lemon rind, juice, and rosemary in a bowl. Serve warm or chilled. Yield: 2 cups (serving size: ¼ cup).

CALORIES 36 (48% from fat); FAT 1.9g (sat 0.2g, mono 1.3g, poly 0.2g); PROTEIN 1.1g; CARB 4.3g; FIBER 0.3g; CHOL 0mg; IRON 0.8mg; SODIUM 77mg; CALC 38mg

PAPAYA-BLACK BEAN SALSA

Look for a papaya that has part-yellow or completely yellow skin, and gives slightly when touched. The tropical flavors in this salsa go well with fish such as grouper, mahimahi, or snapper.

- 2 cups peeled, diced papaya
- 1 large red bell pepper, roasted, peeled, and diced
- ¾ cup sliced green onions
- ¼ cup fresh lime juice
- 3 tablespoons raspberry vinegar or white wine vinegar
- 3 tablespoons pineapple juice
- 2 tablespoons brown sugar
- ⅛ teaspoon salt
- ⅛ teaspoon ground red pepper
- 1 (15-ounce) can black beans, rinsed and drained

1. Combine all ingredients, and stir well. Cover and chill. Yield: 4 cups (serving size: ¼ cup).
Note: Unlike our other salsas, this salsa is best used within 1 to 2 days. After this, the enzymes in the papaya begin to soften the beans.

CALORIES 39 (5% from fat); FAT 0.2g (sat 0g, mono 0g, poly 0.1g); PROTEIN 1.6g; CARB 8.5g; FIBER 1.2g; CHOL 0mg; IRON 0.6mg; SODIUM 61mg; CALC 15mg

ROASTED PINEAPPLE-CARROT SALSA

(pictured on page 208)

Roasting the pineapple creates a rich depth of flavor. Serve with pork tenderloin or ham.

- 1 medium-size ripe pineapple
- 1 teaspoon dark sesame oil
- ⅛ teaspoon ground red pepper
- 1 (1-inch-thick) slice sweet onion
- 1 large jalapeño pepper, sliced lengthwise and seeded
- 2 tablespoons diced red bell pepper
- ½ cup chopped carrot
- 2 tablespoons fresh lime juice
- 2 tablespoons pineapple juice
- 1 tablespoon cider vinegar
- 1 teaspoon brown sugar
- 1 teaspoon peeled, grated fresh gingerroot
- ⅛ teaspoon ground allspice

1. Preheat oven to 450°.
2. Cut both ends off of pineapple using a large sharp knife, and cut pineapple pulp from rind. Cut pineapple pulp lengthwise into quarters. Remove core from quarters; discard core. Reserve 2 quarters for another use.
3. Combine oil and ground red pepper; brush over 2 pineapple quarters, onion slice, and jalapeño pepper. Place pineapple on a baking sheet, and bake at 450° for 15 minutes. Add onion; bake 10 minutes. Add jalapeño pepper; bake 10 additional minutes or until pineapple, onion, and jalapeño are lightly browned. Remove from oven, and let cool. Dice pineapple, onion, and jalapeño; combine with bell pepper in a bowl.
4. Cook carrot in boiling water 4 minutes or until crisp-tender.
5. Combine carrot, lime juice, and remaining 5 ingredients. Add to pineapple mixture; stir well. Yield: 2½ cups (serving size: ¼ cup).

CALORIES 20 (27% from fat); FAT 0.6g (sat 0.1g, mono 0.2g, poly 0.2g); PROTEIN 0.2g; CARB 4.1g; FIBER 0.5g; CHOL 0mg; IRON 0.2mg; SODIUM 3mg; CALC 5mg

The RPM Solution

Rubs, pastes, and marinades are the answer to the dinner rut. These spirited herb-and-spice applications can help you instantly create meals to remember.

After a hard day at work, who has the energy to chop, dice, fold, or mix? When you're too weary to whisk or too sleepy to sauté, we've got the solution: RPMs (rubs, pastes, and marinades).

You can create complex taste sensations by applying these simple herb-and-spice mixtures to fish, fowl, pork, beef, or vegetables. You can even make them in advance, so when dinnertime rolls around, preparation is minimal. Best of all, the ingredients for these sassy RPMs are as close as your spice rack. So whenever you want to serve a flavor-kicking dish, think RPMs. After all, you're never too pooped to enjoy a terrific meal.

RUBS

Rubs are merely dry mixtures of herbs and spices. Many rub recipes call for whole spices to be crushed; to do this, a mortar and pestle are the tools of choice. But for an alternative method, place whole spices in a plastic bag, and pound with a rolling pin or meat mallet. You can store the dry rubs indefinitely in an airtight container in a cool, dry place.

Although how much rub you use is up to your taste buds, a general rule is 3 tablespoons to cover 1 pound of food. When using rubs, make sure you're applying them to food that is completely dry. The most effective way to apply a rub is to place the mixture in a zip-top bag, then put the food inside and shake. To create a crisp coating while bringing out the flavors of the spices in the rub, sauté the coated foods in a little oil.

ALSATIAN RUB

2 tablespoons plus 1 teaspoon salt-free lemon pepper
1½ tablespoons instant minced onion
1 teaspoon caraway seeds, crushed
½ teaspoon garlic powder
½ teaspoon sugar
¼ teaspoon white pepper
½ teaspoon salt

1. Combine all ingredients. Yield: ¼ cup (serving size: 1 tablespoon).

CALORIES 22 (8% from fat); FAT 0.2g (sat 0.1g, mono 0.1g, poly 0g); PROTEIN 0.8g; CARB 5.2g; FIBER 1.1g; CHOL 0mg; IRON 1.3mg; SODIUM 299mg; CALC 26mg

---

ASIAN RUB

2 tablespoons sesame seeds, toasted
2 teaspoons ground turmeric
1 teaspoon ground coriander
½ teaspoon salt
½ teaspoon onion powder
¼ teaspoon ground cumin
⅛ teaspoon ground cinnamon

1. Combine all ingredients. Yield: ¼ cup (serving size: 1 tablespoon).

CALORIES 32 (68% from fat); FAT 2.4g (sat 0.4g, mono 0.9g, poly 1g); PROTEIN 1g; CARB 2.2g; FIBER 0.3g; CHOL 0mg; IRON 1.3mg; SODIUM 295mg; CALC 51mg

---

MEDITERRANEAN RUB

2 tablespoons fennel seeds, crushed
1 tablespoon freeze-dried chives
1 tablespoon mustard seeds, crushed
1 teaspoon lemon pepper
¼ teaspoon garlic powder
¼ teaspoon salt

1. Combine all ingredients. Yield: ¼ cup (serving size: 1 tablespoon).

CALORIES 25 (47% from fat); FAT 1.3g (sat 0.1g, mono 0.9g, poly 0.2g); PROTEIN 1.3g; CARB 3g; FIBER 0.8g; CHOL 0mg; IRON 1mg; SODIUM 150mg; CALC 52mg

FOR ROASTED POTATO WEDGES: Combine 2 tablespoons Mediterranean Rub, 1 tablespoon oil, and 1 pound quartered small red-skinned potatoes. Bake at 400° for 40 minutes or until tender.

SPICY BAYOU RUB

2 tablespoons paprika
2 teaspoons garlic powder
1½ teaspoons dried thyme
1 teaspoon ground red pepper
¾ teaspoon dried oregano
½ teaspoon salt
½ teaspoon ground black pepper
¼ teaspoon ground nutmeg

1. Combine all ingredients. Yield: ¼ cup (serving size: 1 tablespoon).

CALORIES 20 (32% from fat); FAT 0.7g (sat 0.2g, mono 0.1g, poly 0.4g); PROTEIN 0.9g; CARB 4g; FIBER 1.1g; CHOL 0mg; IRON 1.7mg; SODIUM 295mg; CALC 24mg

FIRE-AND-SPICE RUB

2 tablespoons cracked black pepper
2 tablespoons grated Parmesan cheese
2 teaspoons dried basil
2 teaspoons dried rosemary
2 teaspoons dried thyme
¼ teaspoon garlic powder
¼ teaspoon salt

1. Combine all ingredients. Yield: ⅓ cup (serving size: 1 tablespoon).

CALORIES 20 (12% from fat); FAT 0.8g (sat 0.4g, mono 0.2g, poly 0.1g); PROTEIN 1.3g; CARB 2.7g; FIBER 0.9g; CHOL 2mg; IRON 1.8mg; SODIUM 156mg; CALC 64mg

PASTES

Pastes are similar to rubs, but they get their consistency from the addition of a liquid, such as honey, juice, oil, or vinegar. When using pastes, a general rule is ¼ cup of paste to cover 1 pound of food. Don't be timid when applying a paste; it needs to be rubbed in so that the flavors penetrate the food.

For maximum flavor, chill foods for 30 minutes to an hour after rubbing. Broiling is best for these foods because it caramelizes any sugars in the paste, resulting in deep, rich flavors; this cooking method also helps prevent the paste from coming off the food. Pastes will keep in the refrigerator in an airtight container for up to one week.

SWEET CURRY PASTE

If you don't have mango chutney, it can be omitted. Simply increase the orange marmalade to ¾ cup.

½ cup mango chutney
¼ cup orange marmalade
1 tablespoon dark sesame oil
½ teaspoon ground red pepper
½ teaspoon curry powder
¼ teaspoon salt

1. Combine all ingredients, and stir well with a whisk. Yield: ⅔ cup (serving size: 1 tablespoon).

CALORIES 65 (20% from fat); FAT 1.4g (sat 0.2g, mono 0.6g, poly 0.6g); PROTEIN 0.2g; CARB 13.8g; FIBER 0.1g; CHOL 0mg; IRON 0.2mg; SODIUM 90mg; CALC 8mg

SWEET CURRY PASTE FOR PORK LOIN: Rub ⅔ cup Sweet Curry Paste over a 3-pound pork loin roast. Marinate in refrigerator 1 hour. Bake at 325° for 1 hour or until meat thermometer registers 160°.

SWEET FENNEL PASTE

⅔ cup coarsely chopped fennel bulb
⅓ cup applesauce
1 teaspoon dried oregano
1 teaspoon fennel seeds
2 teaspoons vegetable oil
1 teaspoon prepared horseradish
¼ teaspoon salt
¼ teaspoon pepper
⅛ teaspoon garlic powder

1. Place all ingredients in a blender; cover and process until mixture is almost smooth. Yield: ¾ cup (serving size: 1 tablespoon).

CALORIES 12 (60% from fat); FAT 0.8g (sat 0.1g, mono 0.2g, poly 0.4g); PROTEIN 0.2g; CARB 1.3g; FIBER 0.2g; CHOL 0mg; IRON 0.2mg; SODIUM 50mg; CALC 10mg

MIDDLE EASTERN ORANGE PASTE

Curry paste, which comes in a jar, can be found at Indian and Asian markets and specialty grocery stores. It's a combination of oil and spices such as chile pepper, coriander, cumin, and turmeric, and is often used in lieu of curry powder in curried dishes.

2 tablespoons tahini (sesame-seed paste)
1 tablespoon curry paste (such as Patak's Original)
1 tablespoon honey
2½ teaspoons grated orange rind
1 teaspoon dried thyme
1 teaspoon orange juice
¼ teaspoon pepper
¼ teaspoon salt
2 garlic cloves, minced

1. Combine all ingredients, and stir well with a whisk. Yield: ⅓ cup (serving size: 1 tablespoon).

CALORIES 54 (55% from fat); FAT 3.3g (sat 0.4g, mono 1.2g, poly 1.3g); PROTEIN 1.2g; CARB 6.1g; FIBER 0.7g; CHOL 0mg; IRON 1mg; SODIUM 203mg; CALC 36mg

SPICED CHILE PASTE

Cooking pasilla chiles in a dry skillet releases their oils, making them more flavorful and aromatic. Dried pasilla chiles can be found in the produce section of most supermarkets.

  2 dried pasilla chiles (about ½ ounce)
 ¼ cup cider vinegar
  1 tablespoon olive oil
  1 tablespoon plus 1 teaspoon ground cumin
  2 teaspoons ground cinnamon
  1 teaspoon chili powder
 ½ teaspoon salt

1. Remove stems and seeds from chiles. Tear chiles into large pieces; place in a small skillet over medium heat. Cook 6 minutes or until thoroughly heated, shaking skillet frequently. Remove chiles from skillet.
2. Combine chiles and hot water to cover in a bowl; cover and let stand 20 minutes or until soft. Drain well. Combine softened chiles, vinegar, and remaining ingredients in a blender; cover and process until smooth. Yield: ¼ cup plus 1 tablespoon (serving size: 1 tablespoon).

CALORIES 37 (78% from fat); FAT 3.2g (sat 0.4g, mono 2.2g, poly 0.3g); PROTEIN 0.4g; CARB 2.7g; FIBER 0.6g; CHOL 0mg; IRON 1.6mg; SODIUM 243mg; CALC 29mg

HOW DO YOU LIKE IT?

- **ADVENTUROUS** Middle Eastern Orange Paste, Sweet Fennel Paste.

- **BIG AND BOLD** Browned Garlic-and-Burgundy Marinade, Ginger-Molasses Marinade.

- **HOT, HOT, HOT** Fire-and-Spice Rub, Jalapeño-Lime Marinade, Spiced Chile Paste, Spicy Bayou Rub.

- **MELLOW** French Twist Paste, Zesty Dijon Marinade.

- **SWEET** Ginger-Molasses Marinade.

- **VERSATILE** Lemon-Herb Marinade, Zesty Dijon Marinade.

MENU

Mediterranean Tuna Salad*

ROASTED FENNEL SALSA
(page 216)

Sliced French bread

Lemon sorbet with fresh blueberries

*Rub ½ cup French Twist Paste on 1 pound fresh tuna steaks. Broil or grill to desired degree of doneness; cut into strips. Place tuna strips on bed of mixed baby greens. Top with Roasted Fennel Salsa.

FRENCH TWIST PASTE

  1 tablespoon olive oil
1½ cups minced shallots or sweet onion
  3 garlic cloves, minced
 ¼ cup Dijon mustard
  1 teaspoon dried rosemary, crushed
  1 tablespoon plus 1 teaspoon balsamic vinegar
 ¼ teaspoon pepper

1. Heat oil in a nonstick skillet over medium heat. Add shallots and garlic; sauté 3 minutes or until tender. Remove from heat; cool. Stir in mustard and remaining ingredients. Yield: ¾ cup (serving size: 1 tablespoon).

CALORIES 32 (42% from fat); FAT 1.5g (sat 0.2g, mono 1g, poly 0.1g); PROTEIN 0.6g; CARB 4g; FIBER 0.2g; CHOL 0mg; IRON 0.3mg; SODIUM 151mg; CALC 10mg

---

WHAT GOES WITH WHAT

Although there are no rules for applying RPMs, it's safe to say that bolder flavors go best with beef, pork, or lamb, while milder flavors best complement chicken and fish. We found the following flavor combinations particularly good.

- **BEEF** • Asian Rub, Browned Garlic-and-Burgundy Marinade (the boldest of the lot), Mediterranean Rub, Spiced Chile Paste.

- **CHICKEN** • *White meat*—Asian Rub, French Twist Paste, Lemon-Herb Marinade, Mediterranean Rub, Sweet Fennel Paste, Zesty Dijon Marinade. *Dark meat*—Ginger-Molasses Marinade, Middle Eastern Orange Paste, Spiced Chile Paste.

- **HALIBUT** (or any mild, firm white fish) • Asian Rub, Fire-and-Spice Rub, French Twist Paste, Lemon-Herb Marinade, Spicy Bayou Rub.

- **LAMB** • Fire-and-Spice Rub, Lemon-Herb Marinade, Spiced Chile Paste, Sweet Curry Paste, Zesty Dijon Marinade.

- **PORK** • Alsatian Rub, Asian Rub, Fire-and-Spice Rub, Ginger-Molasses Marinade, Middle Eastern Orange Paste, Spiced Chile Paste, Sweet Curry Paste.

- **POTATOES** • Mediterranean Rub.

- **SALMON** • Ginger-Molasses Marinade, Lemon-Herb Marinade, Spicy Bayou Rub, Sweet Curry Paste.

- **SCALLOPS** • Asian Rub, Middle Eastern Orange Paste, Spiced Chile Paste, Spicy Bayou Rub.

- **SHRIMP** • Fire-and-Spice Rub, Jalapeño-Lime Marinade, Spicy Bayou Rub.

MARINADES

A marinade is a seasoned liquid in which food is soaked to absorb flavor. Marinades are the mildest of the RPMs. If you discover you're going to have more marinade than you need, store the unused portion in the refrigerator in an airtight container for up to a week. Generally speaking, the longer you marinate food, the stronger it will taste. As a rule, ⅔ to 1 cup of marinade will flavor and tenderize 1 to 1½ pounds of food. Simply mix the marinade in a zip-top plastic bag, toss your food inside, and chill.

Marinated foods lend themselves particularly well to grilling or broiling because you can baste the food frequently with the remaining marinade. Just remember, if you're going to use leftover marinade as a sauce, you will need to bring it to a boil first—this will kill any harmful bacteria left over from marinating raw meat or fish.

JALAPEÑO-LIME MARINADE

½ cup frozen orange juice
    concentrate, thawed
1 teaspoon grated lime rind
¼ cup fresh lime juice
¼ cup honey
2 teaspoons ground cumin
¼ teaspoon salt
3 garlic cloves, minced
2 jalapeño peppers, seeded and
    finely chopped

1. Combine all ingredients. Yield: 1⅓ cups (serving size: 1 tablespoon).

CALORIES 26 (3% from fat); FAT 0.1g (sat 0g, mono 0.1g, poly 0g); PROTEIN 0.3g; CARB 6.5g; FIBER 0.1g; CHOL 0mg; IRON 0.2mg; SODIUM 29mg; CALC 6mg

FOR GRILLED SHRIMP KEBABS (pictured on page 208): Butterfly 2 pounds large, peeled shrimp. Marinate shrimp in 1⅓ cups Jalapeño-Lime Marinade 30 minutes. Thread on skewers; grill, basting with remaining marinade.

GINGER-MOLASSES MARINADE

½ cup low-sodium soy sauce
¼ cup molasses
1 tablespoon olive oil
1 teaspoon ground ginger

1. Combine all ingredients, and stir well. Yield: ¾ cup (serving size: 1 tablespoon).

CALORIES 48 (32% from fat); FAT 1.7g (sat 0.2g, mono 1.3g, poly 0.1g); PROTEIN 0g; CARB 7g; FIBER 0g; CHOL 0mg; IRON 0.5mg; SODIUM 393mg; CALC 21mg

FOR GRILLED CHICKEN BREASTS: Marinate 4 skinned, boned chicken breast halves in ¾ cup Ginger-Molasses Marinade. Grill; slice and serve over mixed greens.

ZESTY DIJON MARINADE

1 cup balsamic vinegar
½ cup Dijon mustard
¼ cup olive oil
½ teaspoon freshly ground
    pepper
¼ teaspoon salt
2 garlic cloves, crushed

1. Combine all ingredients, and stir well. Yield: 1½ cups (serving size: 1 tablespoon).

CALORIES 28 (84% from fat); FAT 2.6g (sat 0.3g, mono 1.8g, poly 0.2g); PROTEIN 0g; CARB 0.8g; FIBER 0g; CHOL 0mg; IRON 0mg; SODIUM 173mg; CALC 1mg

BROWNED GARLIC-AND-BURGUNDY MARINADE

2 teaspoons olive oil
Vegetable cooking spray
3 garlic cloves, thinly sliced
¾ cup dry red wine
3 tablespoons low-sodium soy
    sauce
1 teaspoon dried tarragon

1. Heat olive oil in a small nonstick skillet coated with cooking spray over medium-high heat until hot. Add garlic, and sauté 5 minutes or until brown. Remove from heat; stir in wine, soy sauce, and tarragon. Yield: 1 cup (serving size: 1 tablespoon).

CALORIES 15 (36% from fat); FAT 0.6g (sat 0.1g, mono 0.4g, poly 0.1g); PROTEIN 0.1g; CARB 0.2g; FIBER 0g; CHOL 0mg; IRON 0.1mg; SODIUM 74mg; CALC 2mg

LEMON-HERB MARINADE

2 teaspoons grated lemon rind
⅔ cup fresh lemon juice
¼ cup chopped fresh basil
¼ cup chopped fresh mint
¼ cup white wine vinegar
2 tablespoons chopped fresh
    oregano
1½ tablespoons olive oil
¼ teaspoon salt
2 garlic cloves, crushed

1. Combine all ingredients, and stir well. Yield: 1¼ cups (serving size: 1 tablespoon).

CALORIES 12 (75% from fat); FAT 1g (sat 0.1g, mono 0.8g, poly 0.1g); PROTEIN 0.1g; CARB 1.1g; FIBER 0g; CHOL 0mg; IRON 0.1mg; SODIUM 30mg; CALC 5mg

NOT TO WORRY

You may be surprised to see that several of the dry rubs contain more than 30% fat, yet have no added fat at all. This is because spices contain small amounts of natural oils. But when these dry rubs, as well as the marinades and pastes (which also contain some oil), are used in a recipe, the fat percentage totals less than 30% per serving—as is the case when the Mediterranean Rub is combined with potatoes.

AUGUST

All This and a Heavenly Cheesecake, Too

At our 10th-birthday blowout, there was something for everyone, including you: The 10 best entries from our Cooking Light/Kraft Foods *Recipe of the Decade Contest. And the $20,000 winner is . . .*

BROWNIE CHEESECAKE TORTE

(pictured on page 244)

The judges liked the way Priscilla added moisture and extra taste with pureed carrots and that she didn't use the predictable prunes or applesauce.

—Priscilla Yee, Concord, California

- 1 (15.1-ounce) package low-fat fudge brownie mix (such as SnackWells)
- 2 teaspoons instant coffee granules
- ½ teaspoon ground cinnamon
- 1 (4-ounce) jar carrot baby food
- Vegetable cooking spray
- ½ cup plus 2 tablespoons sugar, divided
- 1 tablespoon plus 1 teaspoon all-purpose flour
- 1 teaspoon vanilla extract
- 1 (8-ounce) block ⅓-less-fat cream cheese (Neufchâtel), softened
- 1 (8-ounce) block fat-free cream cheese, softened
- 2 large egg whites
- 3 tablespoons skim milk, divided
- 2 tablespoons unsweetened cocoa
- Chocolate syrup (optional)
- Fresh raspberries (optional)

1. Preheat oven to 425°.
2. Combine first 4 ingredients in a bowl. Firmly press mixture into bottom and 1 inch up sides of a 9-inch springform pan coated with cooking spray. Set aside.
3. Combine ½ cup sugar, flour, vanilla, and cheeses; beat at medium speed of an electric mixer until well-blended. Add egg whites and 2 tablespoons milk; beat well. Combine ½ cup batter, 1 tablespoon milk, 2 tablespoons sugar, and cocoa in a small bowl; stir well. Spoon remaining batter alternately with cocoa mixture into prepared crust. Swirl together using the tip of a knife.
4. Bake at 425° for 10 minutes. Reduce oven temperature to 250° (do not remove torte from oven); bake 45 minutes or until almost set. Cool completely on a wire rack. If desired, garnish with chocolate syrup and fresh raspberries. Yield: 12 servings (serving size: 1 wedge).

CALORIES 277 (24% from fat); FAT 7.5g (sat 3.8g, mono 2.3g, poly 0.9g); PROTEIN 7.9g; CARB 44.1g; FIBER 1.3g; CHOL 18mg; IRON 1.6mg; SODIUM 338mg; CALC 76mg

BLUSHING TIRAMISÙ

—Nadine Grant, Torrance, California

- 6 cups (1-inch) cubes angel food cake (about 1 [10-ounce] cake)
- 2 (0.78-ounce) packages instant vanilla-flavored cappuccino mix (such as Maxwell House)
- 1 cup hot water
- 1 (8-ounce) block ⅓-less-fat cream cheese (Neufchâtel), softened
- ½ cup packed brown sugar
- 1 teaspoon vanilla extract
- ½ teaspoon ground cinnamon
- 1 (8-ounce) container frozen reduced-calorie whipped topping, thawed
- 1 tablespoon unsweetened cocoa
- Raspberry Puree
- Fresh raspberries (optional)

1. Place cake cubes in a single layer in a 13 x 9-inch baking dish. Combine cappuccino mix and hot water in a small bowl; pour over cake cubes.
2. Combine cheese and next 3 ingredients in a large bowl. Beat at high speed of an electric mixer 2 minutes or until fluffy; fold in whipped topping. Spread cheese mixture over cake cubes. Sift cocoa over cheese mixture. Cover and chill 1 hour. Serve with Raspberry Puree. Garnish with fresh raspberries, if desired. Yield: 12 servings (serving size: 1 [3-inch] square and 2 tablespoons sauce).

CALORIES 218 (30% from fat); FAT 7.3g (sat 4.6g, mono 1.3g, poly 1g); PROTEIN 4.4g; CARB 34.7g; FIBER 1.7g; CHOL 15mg; IRON 0.5mg; SODIUM 223mg; CALC 66mg

Raspberry Puree:

- 1 (10-ounce) package frozen raspberries in light syrup, thawed and undrained
- 2 tablespoons lemon juice

1. Place raspberries and lemon juice in a food processor; process until mixture is smooth. Yield: 1½ cups (serving size: 2 tablespoons).

CALORIES 25 (0% from fat); FAT 0g; PROTEIN 0.2g; CARB 6.4g; FIBER 1.7g; CHOL 0mg; IRON 0.2mg; SODIUM 0mg; CALC 4mg

MALAY CHICKEN SALAD WITH CURRIED GINGER DRESSING

—Connie Emerson, Reno, Nevada

1   cup uncooked instant rice
¼   cup all-purpose flour
¼   teaspoon ground cumin
¼   teaspoon ground coriander
½   pound skinned, boned chicken,
       cut into bite-size pieces
2   tablespoons vegetable oil
4   cups torn Boston lettuce
1½ cups cubed pineapple
1½ cups peeled, cubed papaya
       or mango
1   cup seedless red grapes, halved
Curried Ginger Dressing
½   cup chopped fresh cilantro

1. Cook rice according to package directions, and cool.
2. Combine flour and next 3 ingredients in a large zip-top plastic bag; seal and shake to coat.
3. Heat oil in a large nonstick skillet over medium-high heat. Add chicken, and sauté 8 minutes or until done. Set aside.
4. Divide lettuce, rice, pineapple, papaya, grape halves, and chicken evenly among 4 serving plates. Top each serving with Curried Ginger Dressing, and sprinkle with cilantro. Yield: 4 servings (serving size: 1 serving salad and ¼ cup dressing).

CALORIES 494 (28% from fat); FAT 15.2g (sat 2.9g, mono 5.5g, poly 5.6g); PROTEIN 21.3g; CARB 73.8g; FIBER 3.2g; CHOL 36mg; IRON 3mg; SODIUM 385mg; CALC 62mg

Curried Ginger Dressing:

¼   cup fat-free mayonnaise
¼   cup reduced-fat peanut butter
¼   cup thawed orange juice
       concentrate, undiluted
¼   cup honey
½   teaspoon ground ginger
½   teaspoon curry powder

1. Combine all ingredients in a bowl. Yield: 1 cup (serving size: ¼ cup).

CALORIES 201 (27% from fat); FAT 6.1g (sat 1.2g, mono 2.9g, poly 1.8g); PROTEIN 4.6g; CARB 35.6g; FIBER 0.2g; CHOL 0mg; IRON 0.6mg; SODIUM 342mg; CALC 8mg

WILD-MUSHROOM CANNELLONI WITH BASIL ALFREDO SAUCE

—Edwina Gadsby, Great Falls, Montana

12   uncooked cannelloni shells
1   teaspoon margarine
Butter-flavored vegetable cooking
       spray
1   tablespoon minced shallots
1   garlic clove, minced
1   pound coarsely chopped
       assorted fresh wild
       mushrooms
1   cup sliced green onions
1   cup chopped bottled roasted
       red bell peppers, drained
2   tablespoons balsamic vinegar
3   tablespoons chopped fresh
       flat-leaf parsley
1   teaspoon chopped fresh
       oregano or ¼ teaspoon dried
       oregano
1   teaspoon chopped fresh thyme
       or ¼ teaspoon dried thyme
1   cup (4 ounces) shredded
       part-skim mozzarella cheese
1   (10-ounce) container light
       Alfredo sauce
2   tablespoons chopped fresh
       basil or 2 teaspoons dried
       basil
2   cups diced plum tomato
       (about ½ pound)
2   tablespoons grated Parmesan
       cheese
Flat-leaf parsley sprigs (optional)

1. Preheat oven to 325 °.
2. Cook pasta according to package directions. Drain and rinse under cold water. Drain well; set aside.
3. Melt margarine in a large nonstick skillet coated with cooking spray over medium-high heat. Add shallots and garlic; sauté 1 minute. Add mushrooms, and cook 5 minutes or until liquid almost evaporates. Add green onions, bell peppers, and vinegar; sauté 2 minutes. Remove mushroom mixture from heat; stir in chopped parsley, oregano, and thyme. Cool. Stir in mozzarella cheese.
4. Spoon about ⅓ cup mushroom mixture into each cannelloni shell.

Arrange stuffed shells in a 13 x 9-inch baking dish coated with cooking spray. Combine Alfredo sauce and basil; pour over shells. Cover with aluminum foil; bake at 325° for 20 minutes or until thoroughly heated. Sprinkle tomato and Parmesan cheese over shells. Garnish with parsley sprigs, if desired. Yield: 6 servings (serving size: 2 stuffed cannelloni plus sauce).
Note: The 1-pound assorted fresh wild mushrooms may include chanterelle, crimini, oyster, porcini, portobello, and/or shiitake mushrooms.

CALORIES 396 (25% from fat); FAT 11g (sat 5.9g, mono 2.1g, poly 1.5g); PROTEIN 16.9g; CARB 57g; FIBER 2.5g; CHOL 29mg; IRON 1.8mg; SODIUM 519mg; CALC 195mg

GRAND MARNIER ICE CREAM

—Cynthia Hoogendoorn, Poughkeepsie, New York

1¼   cups egg substitute (at room
       temperature)
½   cup sugar
½   cup water
2   tablespoons grated orange rind
¼   cup Grand Marnier (orange-
       flavored liqueur)
1   (8-ounce) container frozen
       reduced-calorie whipped
       topping, thawed
Orange rind strips (optional)

1. Place egg substitute in a large bowl. Beat at high speed of an electric mixer for 2 minutes; set aside.
2. Combine sugar, water, and grated rind in a saucepan. Bring to a boil over medium-high heat; cook for 4 minutes. Immediately pour sugar mixture over egg substitute; beat at high speed 2 minutes or until mixture cools. Fold in liqueur and thawed whipped topping.
3. Spoon liqueur mixture into a 13 x 9-inch baking dish; cover and freeze until mixture is firm. Garnish with orange rind strips, if desired. Yield: 10 servings (serving size: ½ cup).

CALORIES 121 (22% from fat); FAT 3g (sat 2.1g, mono 0g, poly 0.9g); PROTEIN 3.7g; CARB 17.7g; FIBER 0g; CHOL 0mg; IRON 0.6mg; SODIUM 61mg; CALC 28mg

BAJA-SPICED CHICKEN SALAD WITH CHUTNEY DRESSING

(pictured on page 242)

—Julie DeMatteo, Clementon, New Jersey

- 1 cup dry breadcrumbs
- ½ teaspoon curry powder
- ½ teaspoon ground ginger
- ½ teaspoon salt
- ½ teaspoon ground cumin
- ¼ teaspoon ground red pepper
- ¼ teaspoon ground allspice
- 2 teaspoons water
- 2 large egg whites, lightly beaten
- 4 (4-ounce) skinned, boned chicken breast halves
- ¼ cup all-purpose flour
- 1 teaspoon olive oil
- ¼ cup plus 2 tablespoons fat-free peppercorn ranch dressing
- ¼ cup mango chutney
- 2 tablespoons water
- 1½ teaspoons curry powder
- ¼ teaspoon ground ginger
- 2 teaspoons olive oil
- Vegetable cooking spray
- 2 Granny Smith apples
- 2 teaspoons lemon juice
- 1 (10-ounce) package Italian-blend salad greens (about 6 cups)
- 1 cup trimmed watercress (about 1 small bunch)
- ½ cup golden raisins
- ¼ cup walnut halves, toasted
- 1 teaspoon coarsely ground black pepper

1. Combine first 7 ingredients in a shallow dish. Combine 2 teaspoons water and egg whites. Coat chicken with flour. Dip chicken in egg white mixture; dredge in breadcrumb mixture. Cover and marinate in refrigerator 30 minutes.

2. Combine 1 teaspoon oil and next 5 ingredients in a food processor; process until smooth.

3. Heat 2 teaspoons oil in a nonstick skillet coated with cooking spray over medium heat until hot. Lightly coat chicken with cooking spray on both sides. Place chicken in skillet, and cook 5 minutes on each side or until done; cut into ½-inch slices.

4. Cut each apple into 16 wedges; toss with lemon juice. Place 1½ cups greens and ¼ cup watercress on each of 4 serving plates. Top each with 8 apple wedges, 3 ounces chicken, 2 tablespoons raisins, and 1 tablespoon walnuts. Sprinkle with ¼ teaspoon black pepper; drizzle 2 tablespoons dressing mixture over each salad. Yield: 4 servings.

CALORIES 553 (21% from fat); FAT 13.1g (sat 2g, mono 5.2g, poly 4.5g); PROTEIN 37.5g; CARB 73g; FIBER 6.7g; CHOL 72mg; IRON 5.2mg; SODIUM 876mg; CALC 146mg

FAJITA SALAD WITH CREAMY CILANTRO-LIME SAUCE

—Louis F. deLaunay, Grapevine, Texas

- 1 tablespoon olive oil
- 1 teaspoon ground cumin
- 1 teaspoon paprika
- 1 teaspoon chili powder
- ½ teaspoon salt
- ¼ teaspoon black pepper
- 1 pound skinned, boned chicken breast, cut into thin strips
- Vegetable cooking spray
- 6 cups shredded romaine lettuce
- 1⅓ cups thinly sliced green bell pepper rings
- 1 cup sliced red onion, separated into rings
- ½ cup (2 ounces) shredded reduced-fat Monterey Jack cheese
- 2 tablespoons sliced ripe olives
- 1 (15-ounce) can pinto beans, rinsed and drained
- 1 medium tomato, cut into 8 wedges
- Creamy Cilantro-Lime Sauce

1. Combine first 6 ingredients in a bowl. Add chicken; toss to coat. Coat a large nonstick skillet with cooking spray; place over medium heat until hot. Add chicken mixture; sauté 8 minutes or until chicken is done.

2. Divide lettuce and next 6 ingredients among 4 bowls; top with chicken mixture. Serve with Creamy Cilantro-Lime Sauce. Yield: 4 servings (serving size: 1 serving salad, 3 ounces chicken, and ⅓ cup sauce).

CALORIES 427 (46% from fat); FAT 21.9g (sat 6g, mono 6.8g, poly 6g); PROTEIN 40.7g; CARB 17.3g; FIBER 6.6g; CHOL 101mg; IRON 5.4mg; SODIUM 1,061mg; CALC 360mg

Creamy Cilantro-Lime Sauce:

- ½ cup fat-free sour cream
- ½ cup light mayonnaise
- ⅓ cup skim milk
- 3 tablespoons lime juice
- 2 tablespoons chopped fresh cilantro
- 1 tablespoon balsamic vinegar
- 2 large garlic cloves, minced

1. Combine all ingredients; stir well with a whisk. Cover and chill. Yield: 1⅓ cups (serving size: ⅓ cup).

CALORIES 113 (65% from fat); FAT 8.1g (sat 1.2g, mono 2.4g, poly 4.2g); PROTEIN 3.2g; CARB 6.6g; FIBER 0.1g; CHOL 10mg; IRON 0.2mg; SODIUM 254mg; CALC 32mg

CHICKEN WITH PECAN-PARSLEY CREAM

—Julie Fox, Annapolis, Maryland

- 3 tablespoons all-purpose flour
- ½ teaspoon freshly ground pepper
- ¼ teaspoon salt
- 4 (4-ounce) skinned, boned chicken breast halves
- 1 tablespoon olive oil
- ¼ cup finely chopped pecans
- 1 cup low-salt chicken broth
- ⅓ cup sweet Marsala
- ⅓ cup grated Parmesan cheese
- 4 ounces block-style fat-free cream cheese, cut into pieces
- ⅓ cup finely chopped fresh parsley
- 1 garlic clove, minced
- 3 cups hot cooked instant rice
- 2 tablespoons grated Parmesan cheese
- ¼ cup pecan pieces
- Parsley sprigs (optional)

1. Combine first 3 ingredients in a shallow dish; dredge chicken in flour mixture. Heat oil in a large nonstick

skillet over medium-high heat. Add chicken; cook 4 minutes on each side or until done. Remove chicken from skillet. Set aside; keep warm.

2. Place chopped pecans in skillet, and cook 3 minutes or until lightly browned. Add chicken broth and next 3 ingredients, stirring with a whisk until cheeses melt. Remove from heat. Stir in chopped parsley and garlic.

3. Spoon ¾ cup rice onto each of 4 serving plates, and drizzle each with 3 tablespoons sauce. Top each serving with a chicken breast half, and spoon 3 tablespoons sauce over chicken. Sprinkle each serving with 1½ teaspoons Parmesan cheese and 1 tablespoon pecan pieces. Garnish with parsley sprigs, if desired. Yield: 4 servings.

CALORIES 533 (28% from fat); FAT 16.6g (sat 3.9g, mono 8.5g, poly 2.5g); PROTEIN 40.9g; CARB 47.1g; FIBER 1.9g; CHOL 81mg; IRON 3.6mg; SODIUM 656mg; CALC 303mg

MEXICALI CRAB CAKES

(pictured on page 243)

—Susan Driscoll,
Upper Darby, Pennsylvania

1½ tablespoons stick margarine
¼ cup finely chopped celery
¼ cup finely chopped red bell pepper
1½ teaspoons seeded, chopped jalapeño pepper
¼ cup light mayonnaise
1 teaspoon chopped fresh cilantro or parsley
1 teaspoon Dijon mustard
½ teaspoon garlic salt
¼ teaspoon pepper
1 large egg, lightly beaten
½ cup fresh breadcrumbs
¼ cup chopped green onions
1 pound lump crabmeat, shell pieces removed
1 (8¾-ounce) can no-salt-added whole-kernel corn, drained
1 cup finely crushed cornflakes
Vegetable cooking spray
1¼ cups cocktail sauce or medium-hot salsa
Cilantro sprigs (optional)

1. Preheat oven to 450°.

2. Melt margarine in a large nonstick skillet over medium heat. Add celery, bell pepper, and jalapeño; sauté 3 minutes or until tender. Cool.

3. Combine mayonnaise and next 5 ingredients in a large bowl. Add celery mixture, breadcrumbs, and next 3 ingredients; stir well. Divide crabmeat mixture into 10 equal portions, shaping each into a ½-inch-thick patty. Dredge patties in cornflakes.

4. Place patties on a baking sheet coated with cooking spray. Bake at 450° for 15 minutes; turn patties over, and bake 10 additional minutes or until golden. Serve crab cakes with cocktail sauce. Garnish with cilantro sprigs, if desired. Yield: 5 servings (serving size: 2 crab cakes and ¼ cup sauce).

CALORIES 308 (30% from fat); FAT 10.2g (sat 1.9g, mono 3.2g, poly 3.6g); PROTEIN 23.2g; CARB 30.9g; FIBER 1.1g; CHOL 139mg; IRON 2.3mg; SODIUM 1,634mg; CALC 126mg

SPICED STUFFED PORK TENDERLOIN WITH MANGO-CHILE SAUCE

—Gloria Bradley, Naperville, Illinois

¾ cup low-salt chicken broth
¼ cup uncooked orzo (rice-shaped pasta)
2 tablespoons chopped bottled roasted red bell peppers, drained
1 tablespoon chopped green onions
1 tablespoon grated Parmesan cheese
1 (1¼-pound) pork tenderloin
1 (0.7-ounce) package Italian salad dressing mix (such as Good Seasons)
1 tablespoon brown sugar
Vegetable cooking spray
Mango-Chile Sauce
Lime slices (optional)
Flat-leaf parsley sprigs (optional)

1. Preheat oven to 350°.

2. Bring broth to a boil in a small saucepan. Add orzo, and cook 7 minutes or until liquid is absorbed.

Remove from heat; stir in bell peppers, green onions, and cheese.

3. Trim fat from pork; slice pork lengthwise, cutting to, but not through, other side. Open halves, laying pork flat. Place plastic wrap over pork; flatten to an even thickness using a meat mallet or rolling pin. Spread orzo mixture over pork, leaving a ½-inch margin around edges. Roll up pork, jelly-roll fashion, starting with short side. Secure at 2-inch intervals with heavy string. Combine salad dressing mix and sugar; rub over pork roll. Place pork on rack of a broiler pan coated with cooking spray; insert a meat thermometer into thickest part of pork.

4. Bake at 350° for 45 minutes or until thermometer registers 160° (slightly pink). Cover with aluminum foil; let stand 15 minutes before slicing.

5. Cut pork roll into 8 slices, and serve with Mango-Chile Sauce. If desired, garnish with lime slices and parsley. Yield: 4 servings (serving size: 2 pork slices and ⅓ cup sauce).

CALORIES 313 (19% from fat); FAT 6.7g (sat 2.2g, mono 2.6g, poly 0.8g); PROTEIN 37.2g; CARB 24g; FIBER 1.1g; CHOL 105mg; IRON 2.8mg; SODIUM 711mg; CALC 38mg

Mango-Chile Sauce:

¾ cup low-salt chicken broth
⅔ cup peeled, chopped ripe mango
⅓ cup peeled, chopped peach or nectarine
1 tablespoon fresh lime juice
1 tablespoon brown sugar
1 teaspoon chopped canned chipotle chile in adobo sauce
¼ cup fat-free sour cream

1. Combine first 5 ingredients in a saucepan; cook over medium heat 10 minutes or until thick, stirring occasionally. Stir in chile. Pour mixture into a blender; cover and process until smooth. Add sour cream, and process until smooth. Yield: 1⅓ cups (serving size: ⅓ cup).

CALORIES 50 (7% from fat); FAT 0.4g (sat 0.1g, mono 0.1g, poly 0.1g); PROTEIN 1.7g; CARB 10.4g; FIBER 0.7g; CHOL 0mg; IRON 0.3mg; SODIUM 31mg; CALC 6mg

The Seat of the Matter

Take measure of your life so that you'll be sitting pretty.

Over the past few months, we've explored a series of simple lifestyle ideas that are analogous to a commonplace dining chair. The "legs" we've discussed are food, exercise, personal reflection, and friendship—a balanced lifestyle requires all four. Now it's time for the "seat," which I'll call self-awareness.

The seat is where I need some measurements to meet my individual specifications—just like day-to-day eating must meet my nutritional needs, not someone else's. What is right for me? I like to divide the search for personal moderation into two areas: the physical and the emotional. You may discover you have risk factors in both areas. Some risks you can overcome on your own. Others may take a little help from professionals.

So, where do we go from here in developing that comfortable, sturdy seat of our chair called self-awareness?

• Ask for extended time with your physician to discuss your recent laboratory results and to create a 12-month plan with reasonable goals.

• If necessary, visit a professional counselor to discuss emotional issues that may be in the way of your achieving the sense of well-being you deserve.

In the meantime, here's a recipe to help you enjoy your journey.

WHITE BEAN-AND-GREEN CHILE QUESADILLAS

- 1 (8-ounce) carton plain low-fat yogurt
- 1 cup canned Great Northern beans, rinsed and drained
- ½ teaspoon ground cumin
- 8 (8-inch) flour tortillas
- 1 tablespoon plus 1 teaspoon chopped pickled jalapeño peppers
- ½ cup canned chopped green chiles
- ¼ cup canned black beans, rinsed and drained
- 8 (⅛-inch-thick) slices tomato
- ¾ cup (3 ounces) shredded reduced-fat sharp Cheddar cheese
- 1 tablespoon plus 1 teaspoon minced fresh cilantro
- Vegetable cooking spray

1. Spoon yogurt onto several layers of heavy-duty paper towels; spread to ½-inch thickness. Cover with additional paper towels; let stand 5 minutes. Scrape yogurt cheese into a bowl using a rubber spatula; cover and refrigerate.
2. Combine Great Northern beans and cumin in a small bowl. Place ¼ cup bean mixture on each of 4 tortillas; mash with a fork to within ½-inch of the edges. Sprinkle each portion with 1 teaspoon jalapeño; top each with 2 tablespoons chiles and 1 tablespoon black beans. Arrange 2 tomato slices on each portion; top with 3 tablespoons cheese, 1 teaspoon cilantro, and remaining tortillas.
3. Place a large nonstick skillet coated with cooking spray over medium-high heat until hot. Add 1 quesadilla; cook 3 minutes on each side or until golden. Remove quesadilla from skillet. Set aside; keep warm. Repeat procedure with remaining quesadillas. Cut each quesadilla into 4 wedges. Serve warm with yogurt cheese. Yield: 4 servings (serving size: 1 quesadilla and 1 tablespoon yogurt cheese).

CALORIES 498 (22% from fat); FAT 12.2g (sat 4.1g, mono 4.1g, poly 2.9g); PROTEIN 23.6g; CARB 74.2g; FIBER 6g; CHOL 18mg; IRON 5.1mg; SODIUM 826mg; CALC 457mg

Take Cover

There's nothing old-fashioned about covered-dish meals, except their taste. In today's hurried times, casseroles are more relevant than ever.

Covered dishes offer a convenient way to experience the joy of sharing food with our family and friends with the least amount of culinary stress. For the most part, the preparation can be done earlier in the day.

Covered-dish entrées make easy dinners because they normally contain ingredients that offer substantial value both nutritionally and tastewise. Except for the Cabbage-Rice Casserole, which is a side dish, all of these casseroles can be entrées. If you accompany them with a loaf of warm, crusty bread and a green salad, dinner is ready. With one dish to clean up, what could be better?

CABBAGE-RICE CASSEROLE

- 2 teaspoons olive oil
- 6 cups finely chopped cabbage
- 1 cup diced onion
- 3 cups water
- 1 cup chopped tomato
- 2 tablespoons brown sugar
- 2 tablespoons cider vinegar
- ¼ teaspoon salt
- 1 cup uncooked white basmati rice
- ¼ cup currants

1. Preheat oven to 350°.
2. Heat oil in a large nonstick skillet over medium heat. Add cabbage and onion; sauté 1 minute. Add water and next 4 ingredients; bring to boil. Add rice and currants; spoon into an 11 x 7-inch baking dish. Cover; bake at 350° for 50 minutes or until rice is tender. Yield: 6 servings (serving size: 1 cup).

CALORIES 174 (10% from fat); FAT 2g (sat 0.3g, mono 1.2g, poly 0.3g); PROTEIN 3.7g; CARB 36.1g; FIBER 3.1g; CHOL 0mg; IRON 2.1mg; SODIUM 117mg; CALC 53mg

CHEESY EGGPLANT-ORZO CASSEROLE

Try dolloping the ricotta cheese on top of the eggplant instead of mixing it with the tomato sauce. It's like eating little pillows of cheese.

- 2 tablespoons chopped sun-dried tomatoes, packed without oil
- ½ cup boiling water
- 1 tablespoon olive oil
- 6 cups peeled, diced eggplant (about 1¼ pounds)
- 1½ cups diced onion
- 1 cup diced red bell pepper
- 4 garlic cloves, minced
- 1 cup diced tomato
- 3 cups cooked orzo (about 1½ cups uncooked rice-shaped pasta)
- 1½ cups fat-free ricotta cheese
- 1 cup tomato juice
- ½ cup chopped fresh basil
- 1 (8-ounce) can no-salt-added tomato sauce
- 1 cup dry breadcrumbs
- ½ cup grated Parmesan cheese
- ⅓ cup pine nuts

1. Preheat oven to 350°.
2. Combine sun-dried tomatoes and boiling water in a small bowl; cover and let stand 10 minutes or until soft. Drain and set aside.
3. Heat oil in a large nonstick skillet over medium-high heat. Add eggplant and next 3 ingredients; sauté 5 minutes. Add diced tomato, and cook 2 minutes. Add sun-dried tomatoes, orzo, and next 4 ingredients; stir well. Spoon orzo mixture into a 13 x 9-inch baking dish. Combine breadcrumbs, Parmesan cheese, and pine nuts; sprinkle over orzo mixture. Cover and bake at 350° for 30 minutes or until thoroughly heated. Uncover and bake 10 additional minutes or until lightly browned. Yield: 8 servings (serving size: 1½ cups).

CALORIES 353 (27% from fat); FAT 10.3g (sat 2.6g, mono 4.2g, poly 3.1g); PROTEIN 17.9g; CARB 51.3g; FIBER 3.8g; CHOL 11mg; IRON 3mg; SODIUM 345mg; CALC 224mg

GARDEN PASTITSIO

In this traditional Greek casserole, the soy protein in the tempeh replaces beef or lamb. Tempeh can be found at health-food stores or Oriental markets.

- 2 teaspoons olive oil
- 2 cups diced onion
- 1 cup diced celery
- 2 teaspoons chopped fresh oregano or ¾ teaspoon dried oregano
- 3 garlic cloves, minced
- 1 (8-ounce) package tempeh, crumbled
- 2 teaspoons cornstarch
- 1 tablespoon water
- 5 cups 1% low-fat milk
- 1 tablespoon fresh lemon juice
- 1½ teaspoons chopped fresh dillweed or ½ teaspoon dried dillweed
- ½ teaspoon salt
- ¼ teaspoon ground white pepper
- 8 cups hot cooked elbow macaroni (about 1 pound uncooked)
- 2 (4-ounce) packages crumbled feta cheese, divided
- 1 (10-ounce) package frozen chopped spinach, thawed, drained, and squeezed dry

Vegetable cooking spray

1. Preheat oven to 375°.
2. Heat oil in a Dutch oven over medium heat. Add onion and next 4 ingredients; sauté 5 minutes. Combine cornstarch and water, stirring well. Add cornstarch mixture and milk to Dutch oven; bring to a boil. Reduce heat, and simmer 20 minutes, stirring occasionally. Stir in lemon juice, dillweed, salt, pepper, macaroni, 4 ounces feta, and spinach. Spoon mixture into a 13 x 9-inch baking dish coated with cooking spray; sprinkle with 4 ounces feta. Bake at 375° for 30 minutes or until lightly browned. Yield: 8 servings (serving size: 1½ cups).

CALORIES 428 (25% from fat); FAT 12.1g (sat 5.9g, mono 3.2g, poly 2g); PROTEIN 22.5g; CARB 58.2g; FIBER 4.4g; CHOL 31mg; IRON 3.8mg; SODIUM 583mg; CALC 423mg

CHILI-CHEESE CASSEROLE FOR A CROWD

The ingredients in this dish are reminiscent of mole, the Mexican sauce made from onion, garlic, chiles, and chocolate. The chipotle chiles can be omitted.

- 2 teaspoons olive oil
- 2 cups chopped onion
- 1 cup chopped green bell pepper
- 1 cup chopped red bell pepper
- 1½ tablespoons chili powder
- 1 tablespoon dried oregano
- 1 tablespoon unsweetened cocoa
- 1 teaspoon ground cumin
- 6 garlic cloves, minced
- 2 cups water
- 1½ cups uncooked bulgur or cracked wheat
- 2 tablespoons minced fresh cilantro
- 1 (16-ounce) can pinto beans, drained
- 1 (15-ounce) can black beans, drained
- 1 (14½-ounce) can no-salt-added diced tomatoes, undrained
- 1 (14½-ounce) can vegetable broth
- 2 drained canned chipotle chiles in adobo sauce, minced
- 2 cups (8 ounces) shredded reduced-fat Monterey Jack cheese, divided
- 2 cups baked tortilla chips

1. Preheat oven to 375°.
2. Heat oil in a Dutch oven over medium-high heat. Add onion and next 7 ingredients; sauté 5 minutes. Add water and next 7 ingredients; bring to a boil. Reduce heat; simmer, uncovered, 10 minutes, stirring occasionally.
3. Spoon half of bean mixture into a 13 x 9-inch baking dish; sprinkle with 1 cup cheese. Top with remaining bean mixture. Cover and bake at 375° for 40 minutes. Uncover; sprinkle with 1 cup cheese. Bake 10 additional minutes. Press chips into casserole. Yield: 12 servings (serving size: 1½ cups).

CALORIES 237 (21% from fat); FAT 5.5g (sat 2.4g, mono 0.7g, poly 0.6g); PROTEIN 13.4g; CARB 36.2g; FIBER 7.4g; CHOL 12mg; IRON 2.5mg; SODIUM 459mg; CALC 198mg

SMASHED POTATO-AND-BROCCOLI CASSEROLE

While most potato casseroles are served as side dishes, this one has enough protein to be served as a main dish.

- 2 pounds baking potatoes, halved
- 1 cup chopped broccoli
- ½ cup diced onion
- ½ cup part-skim ricotta cheese
- 1½ teaspoons chopped fresh dillweed or ½ teaspoon dried dillweed
- ½ teaspoon salt
- ⅛ teaspoon ground red pepper
- 1 (8-ounce) container fat-free sour cream
- Vegetable cooking spray
- ¾ cup (3 ounces) shredded reduced-fat sharp Cheddar cheese

1. Preheat oven to 375°.
2. Place potatoes in a saucepan; cover with water. Bring to a boil. Reduce heat; simmer 20 minutes or until tender. Drain potatoes in a colander over a bowl, reserving 1 cup cooking liquid. Return potatoes and liquid to pan; mash with a potato masher until slightly chunky.
3. Add broccoli and next 6 ingredients to pan; stir well. Spoon potato mixture into an 11 x 7-inch baking dish coated with cooking spray; bake at 375° for 35 minutes. Sprinkle with cheese; bake 5 additional minutes or until cheese melts. Yield: 6 servings (serving size: 1 cup).

CALORIES 292 (17% from fat); FAT 5.6g (sat 3.2g, mono 1.5g, poly 0.3g); PROTEIN 14.9g; CARB 45.5g; FIBER 3.9g; CHOL 19mg; IRON 2.5mg; SODIUM 405mg; CALC 257mg

RATATOUILLE BAKE

- 2 teaspoons olive oil
- 2 cups peeled, diced eggplant
- 2 cups sliced zucchini
- 1½ cups diced onion
- 1 cup diced red bell pepper
- ½ cup sliced celery
- 1 tablespoon paprika
- 2 teaspoons dried oregano
- 2 teaspoons dried basil
- ½ teaspoon dried crushed red pepper
- 1½ cups uncooked long-grain rice
- 1 (14.5-ounce) can no-salt-added whole tomatoes, undrained and chopped
- 1 (14½-ounce) can vegetable broth
- 1½ cups crumbled feta cheese
- 1 (15½-ounce) can chickpeas (garbanzo beans), drained

1. Preheat oven to 375°.
2. Heat oil in a Dutch oven over medium-high heat. Add eggplant and next 8 ingredients; sauté 1 minute.
3. Add rice; sauté 3 minutes. Stir in tomatoes and broth; bring to a boil. Add cheese and chickpeas; stir well. Spoon rice mixture into a 13 x 9-inch baking dish. Cover and bake at 375° for 40 minutes or until rice is tender. Yield: 9 servings (serving size: 1 cup).

CALORIES 284 (22% from fat); FAT 6.8g (sat 3.2g, mono 2g, poly 0.9g); PROTEIN 10.5g; CARB 46.4g; FIBER 3.5g; CHOL 17mg; IRON 3.8mg; SODIUM 519mg; CALC 171mg

QUICK & EASY WEEKNIGHTS

Touch of Asia

This Asian-inspired salad is paired with refrigerated biscuits infused with orange marmalade and chives.

SPINACH SALAD WITH SESAME PORK

- 1 pound pork tenderloin
- 1 tablespoon dark sesame oil, divided
- ¼ cup chopped green onions
- 2 tablespoons low-sodium soy sauce
- 1 tablespoon honey
- 1 teaspoon ground ginger
- ½ teaspoon freshly ground pepper
- 2 garlic cloves, minced
- Vegetable cooking spray
- 1 tablespoon rice vinegar or white vinegar
- 1 tablespoon water
- 8 cups torn spinach (about 6 ounces)
- 1 (2-ounce) jar diced pimento, drained
- 2 tablespoons coarsely grated Gruyère cheese or aged Swiss cheese
- 2 tablespoons sesame seeds, toasted

1. Trim fat from pork; slice into thin strips. Combine 1 teaspoon oil, green onions, and next 5 ingredients; rub evenly over pork. Place pork on rack of a broiler pan coated with cooking spray; broil 4 minutes on each side or to desired degree of doneness.
2. Combine 2 teaspoons oil, vinegar, and water in a small bowl; stir with a whisk. Add vinaigrette to spinach; toss. Place 2 cups spinach on each of 4 plates; arrange pork over spinach. Top each serving with 1 tablespoon pimento, 1½ teaspoons cheese, and 1½ teaspoons sesame seeds. Yield: 4 servings.

CALORIES 266 (39% from fat); FAT 11.5g (sat 3g, mono 4.4g, poly 3.2g); PROTEIN 29.9g; CARB 11.3g; FIBER 4.9g; CHOL 83mg; IRON 5.4mg; SODIUM 356mg; CALC 208mg

ORANGE-CHIVE BUBBLE BUNS

¼ cup orange marmalade (at room temperature)
1 teaspoon freeze-dried chives
1 (4.5-ounce) can refrigerated buttermilk biscuits
Vegetable cooking spray

1. Preheat oven to 400°.
2. Combine marmalade and chives. Separate biscuits; cut each into 4 pieces. Add biscuit pieces to marmalade mixture; toss. Place 6 biscuit pieces in each of 4 muffin cups coated with cooking spray. Bake at 400° for 13 minutes or until golden. Remove from cups; serve warm. Yield: 4 servings (serving size: 1 bun).

CALORIES 125 (9% from fat); FAT 1.2g (sat 0.3g, mono 0.6g, poly 0.1g); PROTEIN 2.1g; CARB 27.8g; FIBER 0.5g; CHOL 0mg; IRON 0.9mg; SODIUM 281mg; CALC 8mg

GLOBETROTTING

Beyond Casablanca

Inspired by the different flavors and spices used in Morocco's exotic, low-fat dishes, we've brought back recipes that you can make at home.

A typical Morrocan meal begins with small dishes set in the center of the round table. These dishes are filled with savory foods—combinations of cooked vegetables in marinades served at room temperature and called "salads" (appetizers to us).

The salads may be followed by a tagine, a stew made with lamb, chicken, or fish and a cook's own selection of ingredients such as onions, olives, tangy preserved lemon, prunes, or nuts. A tagine is served in the center of the table in a heavy terra cotta dish (also called a tagine) with a conical lid. Dessert may consist of almond-and-honey pastries and, as always, fresh fruit.

CUMIN-SCENTED CARROT "SALAD"

3 cups coarsely shredded carrot
1 teaspoon ground cumin
3 tablespoons fresh lemon juice
1 tablespoon extra-virgin olive oil
1 tablespoon water
¼ teaspoon salt
⅛ teaspoon pepper
2 garlic cloves, crushed
¼ cup finely chopped fresh parsley

1. Place carrot in a steamer basket over boiling water. Cover and steam 3 minutes or until crisp-tender. Rinse under cold water, and drain well. Spoon into a medium bowl.
2. Place a small skillet over medium-low heat. Add cumin; cook, stirring constantly, 20 seconds. Remove from heat. Add lemon juice and next 5 ingredients; stir with a whisk until blended. Add lemon juice mixture and parsley to carrot; toss well. Cover and chill. Yield: 6 servings (serving size: ½ cup).

CALORIES 49 (44% from fat); FAT 2.4g (sat 0.3g, mono 1.7g, poly 0.3g); PROTEIN 0.8g; CARB 6.9g; FIBER 1.9g; CHOL 0mg; IRON 0.7mg; SODIUM 119mg; CALC 24mg

PUREED TOMATO-AND-ALMOND "SALAD"

This salad is like a tomato salsa. Serve it with pita bread chips.

¼ cup slivered almonds, toasted
½ teaspoon vegetable oil
½ cup finely chopped onion
1 garlic clove, crushed
½ teaspoon ground cinnamon
½ teaspoon ground ginger
⅛ teaspoon saffron threads, crushed
1 (28-ounce) can plum tomatoes, undrained
1 tablespoon finely chopped fresh parsley

1. Place almonds in a food processor; process until ground. Set aside.

2. Heat oil in a medium nonstick skillet over medium heat. Add onion and garlic; sauté 6 minutes or until golden. Add cinnamon, ginger, and saffron; stir until well-blended.
3. Place tomatoes in food processor; process until smooth. Add tomatoes to skillet; cook, uncovered, until reduced to 2½ cups. Add ground almonds; stir until well-blended. Spread tomato mixture in a thin layer over a serving plate; sprinkle with parsley. Yield: 2½ cups (serving size: ¼ cup).

CALORIES 36 (43% from fat); FAT 1.7g (sat 0.1g, mono 0.9g, poly 0.4g); PROTEIN 1.4g; CARB 4.9g; FIBER 1g; CHOL 0mg; IRON 0.7mg; SODIUM 130mg; CALC 31mg

MIXED HERB "SALAD"

This dish, composed of wilted spinach, herbs, and olives, is more of a vegetable side dish than a salad.

16 cups torn spinach (about ¾ pound)
1½ teaspoons olive oil
½ cup finely chopped fresh parsley
⅓ cup finely chopped fresh cilantro
1 garlic clove, minced
1 tablespoon chopped black olives
¼ teaspoon grated lemon rind
1 teaspoon lemon juice
¼ teaspoon salt
⅛ teaspoon ground red pepper

1. Steam half of spinach in a Dutch oven, covered, 2 minutes or until spinach wilts. Place steamed spinach in a medium bowl; repeat procedure with remaining spinach. Wipe Dutch oven with paper towels.
2. Add oil to Dutch oven; place over medium heat until hot. Add parsley, cilantro, and garlic; sauté 1 minute. Remove from heat; stir in spinach, olives, and remaining ingredients. Serve warm. Yield: 4 servings (serving size: ½ cup).

CALORIES 73 (35% from fat); FAT 2.8g (sat 0.4g, mono 1.5g, poly 0.5g); PROTEIN 6.9g; CARB 9.2g; FIBER 9.6g; CHOL 0mg; IRON 6.9mg; SODIUM 349mg; CALC 243mg

ROASTED EGGPLANT "SALAD"

(pictured on page 242)

Serve this dish warm with pita bread.

1 medium eggplant, cut into
   1-inch cubes (about ¾
   pound)
1 cup (1-inch) pieces green
   bell pepper
1 cup (1-inch) pieces red
   bell pepper
1 large Vidalia or other sweet
   onion, cut into 8 wedges
1 garlic clove, chopped
1 tablespoon olive oil
¼ teaspoon salt
⅛ teaspoon black pepper
1 teaspoon ground cumin
2 tablespoons red wine vinegar
¼ teaspoon ground red pepper
1 tablespoon finely chopped
   fresh parsley

1. Preheat oven to 400°.
2. Combine first 5 ingredients in a shallow roasting pan. Drizzle oil over vegetables. Sprinkle with salt and black pepper; toss well. Bake at 400° for 45 minutes or until tender, stirring occasionally. Spoon mixture into a bowl.
3. Place a small skillet over medium-low heat. Add cumin; cook, stirring constantly, 20 seconds. Add cumin, vinegar, and ground red pepper to eggplant mixture; toss well. Sprinkle with parsley. Yield: 8 servings (serving size: ½ cup).

CALORIES 48 (38% from fat); FAT 2g (sat 0.3g, mono 1.3g, poly 0.3g); PROTEIN 1.2g; CARB 7.6g; FIBER 1.8g; CHOL 0mg; IRON 1mg; SODIUM 78mg; CALC 28mg

CHICKEN TAGINE

This traditional Moroccan stew is seasoned with pungent herbs and spices.

¼ cup chopped fresh parsley
¼ cup chopped fresh cilantro
1 teaspoon ground cumin
1 teaspoon ground turmeric
4 garlic cloves, minced
2 chicken breast halves (about
   ¾ pound), skinned
2 chicken drumsticks (about
   ½ pound), skinned
2 chicken thighs (about
   ½ pound), skinned
½ cup low-salt chicken broth
¼ cup chopped green olives
1 tablespoon grated lemon
   rind
1½ teaspoons fresh lemon juice
¼ teaspoon salt
1 (14½-ounce) can plum
   tomatoes, undrained and
   chopped
4 cups hot cooked couscous
Fresh cilantro sprigs (optional)

1. Preheat oven to 400°.
2. Combine first 5 ingredients in a small bowl; rub over chicken. Place chicken pieces in a 13 x 9-inch baking dish; add broth and next 5 ingredients. Cover and bake at 400° for 1 hour or until chicken is done. Serve over couscous. Garnish with cilantro sprigs, if desired. Yield: 4 servings (serving size: 4 ounces chicken, ½ cup tomato sauce, and 1 cup couscous).

CALORIES 375 (12% from fat); FAT 5.1g (sat 1g, mono 1.7g, poly 1.1g); PROTEIN 34.8g; CARB 47.9g; FIBER 3.4g; CHOL 84mg; IRON 4.3mg; SODIUM 501mg; CALC 71mg

HONEY-BAKED FIGS

12 dried figs
⅓ cup honey
2 tablespoons slivered almonds,
   toasted

1. Place dried figs in a medium saucepan. Add water to cover, and bring to a boil. Cover, reduce heat, and simmer 20 minutes. Remove pan from heat; uncover and let stand 20 minutes.
2. Preheat oven to 325°.
3. Drain figs well, and place figs in a 1½-quart baking dish; drizzle with honey. Bake at 325° for 25 minutes or until thoroughly heated, stirring occasionally. Sprinkle with almonds. Serve warm. Yield: 4 servings (serving size: 3 figs).

CALORIES 253 (10% from fat); FAT 2.8g (sat 0.3g, mono 1.5g, poly 0.8g); PROTEIN 2.6g; CARB 60.8g; FIBER 10g; CHOL 0mg; IRON 1.5mg; SODIUM 8mg; CALC 93mg

MOROCCAN MINT TEA

8 cups boiling water
2 regular-size tea bags
2 cups mint sprigs
⅓ cup sugar

1. Pour boiling water over tea bags. Cover and let stand 5 minutes. Remove tea bags; discard. Add mint and sugar; stir well. Discard mint. Serve hot or cold. Yield: 2 quarts (serving size: 1 cup).

CALORIES 32 (0% from fat); FAT 0g; PROTEIN 0g; CARB 8.3g; FIBER 0g; CHOL 0mg; IRON 0mg; SODIUM 0mg; CALC 0mg

Seafood That Can Take the Heat

Fire up the coals: Grilling seafood is easy if you know which kinds to buy.

If putting a tuna steak or halibut fillet on the grill sounds a little intimidating, then fear not. Grilling seafood is no more difficult than grilling steak or chicken. If you know which kind to use, and how to prepare the rack and fire, grilling seafood is practically foolproof.

The most important thing to know when grilling seafood is what kind to use. You want fish that has a thick, firm, meaty texture, so that it won't fall apart while cooking.

GRILLED-SHRIMP SALAD WITH SMOKY TOMATO VINAIGRETTE

4   (1-inch-thick) slices day-old French bread or other firm white bread, cut into 1-inch cubes
1   large tomato, cut into 1-inch-thick slices (about 12 ounces)
1   tablespoon plus 1 teaspoon olive oil, divided
½   teaspoon salt, divided
½   teaspoon freshly ground pepper, divided
3   tablespoons coarsely chopped fresh parsley
2   tablespoons fresh lemon juice
1   tablespoon canned chipotle chile in adobo sauce
1   tablespoon water
2   teaspoons ground coriander
1   garlic clove, chopped
48   large shrimp, peeled and deveined (about 2 pounds)
Vegetable cooking spray
9½   cups torn romaine lettuce
¾   cup peeled, cubed avocado
½   cup sliced red onion

1. Preheat oven to 350°.
2. Place bread cubes in a single layer on a baking sheet. Bake at 350° for 12 minutes or until bread is toasted. Set aside.
3. Brush tomato slices with 1 teaspoon olive oil; sprinkle with ¼ teaspoon salt and ¼ teaspoon pepper. Place tomato slices on an aluminum foil-lined baking sheet. Broil 10 minutes on each side or until tomato is blackened. Combine tomato, 1 tablespoon olive oil, ¼ teaspoon salt, ¼ teaspoon pepper, parsley, and next 5 ingredients in a food processor; process until blended. Divide vinaigrette in half. Set aside.
4. Thread shrimp onto 6 (12-inch) skewers, and brush with half of vinaigrette. Prepare grill. Place kebabs on grill rack coated with cooking spray, and grill 4 minutes on each side or until shrimp are done. Remove shrimp from skewers. Combine remaining vinaigrette, bread cubes, shrimp, lettuce, avocado, and onion in a large bowl; toss gently. Yield: 6 servings (serving size: 2½ cups).

CALORIES 257 (30% from fat); FAT 8.7g (sat 1.4g, mono 4.5g, poly 1.7g); PROTEIN 27g; CARB 17.4g; FIBER 3g; CHOL 173mg; IRON 4.7mg; SODIUM 495mg; CALC 112mg

SEAFOOD GLOSSARY

Because of their textures, the following fish and shellfish are particularly suitable for the rigors of the grill.

GROUPER: This white-meat fish is sold in fillets and steaks. If you can't find grouper, you can use sea bass or mahimahi.

HALIBUT: The meat of this fish is white and mild-flavored, and comes in steaks and fillets. Although it's a firm fish, it's a tad more delicate than the other fish in this story. So be gentle when turning it on the grill.

SALMON: With a range of flavor from rich to mild, salmon can take on a char and still keep its distinct taste. Salmon's pink meat comes in steaks and fillets.

SCALLOPS: This bivalve is usually classified into two groups: bay scallops and sea scallops. The larger sea scallops are best for grilling because, like shrimp, they have a meatier texture and can be easily skewered. They cook fast, though, so keep a close eye on them.

SHRIMP: Large shrimp are best for grilling. They can be easily skewered, and they cook quickly.

SWORDFISH: This mild but distinctive-tasting fish has a firm, meaty texture. Its natural oil content keeps it moist while grilling. You can usually find it sold as steaks.

TUNA: If you're new to grilling fish, fresh tuna is a good starter. It cooks like a beefsteak, and its deep-red meat almost never sticks to the grill.

GRILLED HOT MUSSELS WITH LEMON AND PARSLEY

Serve this dish immediately off the grill as an appetizer.

- ½ cup dry white wine
- 2 tablespoons olive oil
- 1 tablespoon dried crushed red pepper
- 36 mussels, scrubbed and debearded
- 2 lemons, halved
- ¼ cup coarsely chopped fresh parsley
- ½ teaspoon freshly ground black pepper
- ¼ teaspoon salt

1. Combine first 3 ingredients in a shallow 2-quart baking dish.
2. Prepare grill. Place baking dish on one side of grill rack; arrange mussels on other side of grill rack. Cover and grill mussels 10 minutes or until shells open. Remove mussels from grill rack, and place in baking dish, stirring to coat with wine mixture. Discard any unopened shells.
3. Arrange mussels on a platter. Squeeze lemon over mussels. Sprinkle with fresh parsley, black pepper, and salt. Yield: 4 servings (serving size: 9 mussels).

CALORIES 171 (36% from fat); FAT 6.9g (sat 1.1g, mono 3.2g, poly 1.2g); PROTEIN 17.9g; CARB 12.6g; FIBER 0.8g; CHOL 40mg; IRON 5.6mg; SODIUM 419mg; CALC 67mg

GRILLED BARBECUED OYSTERS

- ½ cup hot sauce
- ¼ cup Worcestershire sauce
- 2 tablespoons lemon juice
- 1 tablespoon olive oil
- ¼ teaspoon salt
- ¼ teaspoon cracked black pepper
- 4 garlic cloves, minced
- 4 dozen oysters in the shell, scrubbed
- ¼ cup chopped fresh flat-leaf parsley
- 8 lemon wedges

1. Combine first 7 ingredients in a saucepan. Prepare grill. Place pan containing barbecue sauce on grill rack. Place oysters on rack; grill 5 minutes or until a few oysters begin to open. Remove oysters from heat. Open with an oyster knife, leaving on the half shell.
2. Sprinkle oysters with parsley, and drizzle with barbecue sauce. Serve with lemon wedges. Yield: 4 servings (serving size: 1 dozen oysters).

CALORIES 118 (44% from fat); FAT 5.8g (sat 1.1g, mono 2.8g, poly 1.2g); PROTEIN 7.3g; CARB 8.2g; FIBER 0.5g; CHOL 47mg; IRON 6.7mg; SODIUM 571mg; CALC 83mg

CHILE-RUBBED GRILLED-SCALLOP SALAD

- ½ cup fresh lime juice
- 3 tablespoons sugar
- 2 tablespoons finely chopped unsalted, dry-roasted peanuts
- 2 tablespoons fish sauce
- 1 tablespoon peeled, minced fresh gingerroot
- 3 garlic cloves, minced
- 2 tablespoons seeded, finely chopped serrano chile
- 1 tablespoon freshly cracked black pepper
- 1½ pounds sea scallops
- Vegetable cooking spray
- 8 cups coarsely chopped napa (Chinese) cabbage
- 2 cups red bell pepper strips
- ½ cup finely chopped fresh basil
- ½ cup minced fresh cilantro
- ⅓ cup finely chopped fresh mint

1. Combine first 6 ingredients in a small bowl; stir well. Set aside. Combine chile and cracked pepper; rub chile mixture onto scallops. Thread scallops evenly onto each of 4 (12-inch) skewers. Prepare grill. Place kebabs on grill rack coated with cooking spray, and grill 4 minutes on each side or until done. Remove from heat; cool slightly.
2. Place cabbage and remaining 4 ingredients in a large bowl; add lime juice mixture, tossing to coat. Divide cabbage mixture evenly among 4 plates. Top each with 1 kebab. Yield: 4 servings (serving size: 5 ounces scallops, 2 cups cabbage mixture, and about ¼ cup dressing).

CALORIES 267 (15% from fat); FAT 4.4g (sat 0.6g, mono 1.3g, poly 1.5g); PROTEIN 33.2g; CARB 25.9g; FIBER 3.5g; CHOL 56mg; IRON 3.4mg; SODIUM 1,403mg; CALC 230mg

GRILLED GROUPER WITH APRICOT-GINGER RELISH

If you can't find quality apricots for this easy-to-prepare dish, substitute peaches.

- 2 cups diced fresh apricots (about 6 medium)
- ½ cup diced red bell pepper
- ⅓ cup rice wine vinegar
- ¼ cup minced green onions
- 2 tablespoons sugar
- 2 tablespoons peeled, minced fresh gingerroot
- ½ teaspoon freshly ground pepper
- ¼ teaspoon salt
- ¼ teaspoon hot sauce
- 1 tablespoon chile paste with garlic
- 4 (6-ounce) grouper fillets (½ inch thick)
- Vegetable cooking spray

1. Combine first 9 ingredients in a small bowl; stir well. Let stand 1 hour.
2. Rub chile paste over both sides of grouper fillets. Prepare grill.
3. Place grouper fillets on grill rack coated with cooking spray; grill 6 minutes on each side or until fish flakes

easily when tested with a fork. Serve grouper fillets with apricot-ginger relish. Yield: 4 servings (serving size: 1 fillet and ½ cup relish).

CALORIES 234 (9% from fat); FAT 2.4g (sat 0.5g, mono 0.5g, poly 0.7g); PROTEIN 34.5g; CARB 17.3g; FIBER 2.2g; CHOL 63mg; IRON 2.4mg; SODIUM 342mg; CALC 64mg

PEPPERED HALIBUT, GREEN BEANS, AND OLIVE SALAD

Served with a loaf of crusty French bread, this lively salad makes the perfect summertime dinner.

¼ cup chopped fresh basil
¼ cup fat-free chicken broth
¼ cup balsamic vinegar
2 tablespoons water
2 teaspoons olive oil
½ teaspoon black pepper
¼ teaspoon salt
2 garlic cloves, minced
½ pound green beans, trimmed
4 (6-ounce) halibut steaks (about 1 inch thick)
Olive oil-flavored vegetable cooking spray
3 tablespoons freshly cracked mixed peppercorns
½ teaspoon salt
8 cups torn red leaf lettuce
2 tablespoons fresh lemon juice
2 medium tomatoes, each cut into 8 wedges
¼ cup chopped ripe Greek olives

1. Combine first 8 ingredients in a small bowl; cover and chill vinaigrette. Wash beans, and trim ends; remove strings. Place beans in a large saucepan of boiling water. Cook 2 minutes; drain. Rinse under cold water; drain well. Set aside.
2. Coat halibut with cooking spray; rub peppercorns and salt over both sides of steaks. Prepare grill. Place halibut on grill rack coated with cooking spray; grill 3 minutes on each side or until fish flakes easily when tested with a fork. Remove from heat; cool slightly. Break halibut into pieces; discard skin and bones.

3. Place lettuce in a large bowl; add lemon juice, tossing to coat. Divide lettuce mixture evenly among 4 plates. Arrange green beans, halibut, and tomato wedges evenly on plates; sprinkle each serving with chopped olives. Drizzle vinaigrette over salads. Yield: 4 servings.

CALORIES 274 (26% from fat); FAT 7.8g (sat 1.1g, mono 3.6g, poly 2.1g); PROTEIN 38.3g; CARB 13.5g; FIBER 4.1g; CHOL 80mg; IRON 4.7mg; SODIUM 620mg; CALC 168mg

GRILLED TUNA SKEWERS WITH TOMATO-BLACK OLIVE RELISH

The slightly acidic flavor of the relish contrasts nicely with the rich taste of the grilled tuna. Serve this dish with an assortment of grilled vegetables and saffron rice.

⅓ cup chopped fresh oregano
2 tablespoons ground cumin
1 tablespoon dried crushed red pepper
½ teaspoon salt
¼ teaspoon freshly ground pepper
4 large garlic cloves, minced
1½ pounds tuna steaks (about 1 inch thick), cut into 32 (1-inch) pieces
3 small red onions, each cut into 8 (1-inch) pieces
3 lemons, each cut into 8 wedges
Vegetable cooking spray
Tomato-Black Olive Relish

1. Combine first 7 ingredients in a large zip-top plastic bag. Seal bag, and shake well. Remove tuna from bag; thread 4 tuna pieces, 3 red onion pieces, and 3 lemon wedges onto each of 8 (12-inch) skewers.
2. Prepare grill. Place skewers on grill rack coated with cooking spray; grill 4 minutes on each side or until tuna is medium-rare or desired degree of doneness. Serve with Tomato-Black Olive Relish. Yield: 4 servings (serving size: 2 skewers and ⅔ cup relish).

CALORIES 381 (33% from fat); FAT 13.8g (sat 2.9g, mono 5.2g, poly 3.9g); PROTEIN 44g; CARB 27.8g; FIBER 4.5g; CHOL 65mg; IRON 8.2mg; SODIUM 532mg; CALC 222mg

Tomato-Black Olive Relish:

2 cups finely diced tomato
½ cup finely diced red onion
¼ cup chopped ripe olives
2 tablespoons fresh lemon juice
1 tablespoon plus 1 teaspoon chopped fresh oregano or 1 teaspoon dried oregano
2 teaspoons olive oil
⅛ teaspoon salt
⅛ teaspoon freshly ground pepper
2 large garlic cloves, minced

1. Combine all ingredients in a medium bowl, and stir well. Cover and chill 1 hour. Yield: 2⅔ cups (serving size: ⅔ cup).

CALORIES 72 (45% from fat); FAT 3.6g (sat 0.5g, mono 2.4g, poly 0.5g); PROTEIN 1.6g; CARB 10.2g; FIBER 2.4g; CHOL 0mg; IRON 1.1mg; SODIUM 157mg; CALC 34mg

GREAT GRILLING

◆ To avoid overcooking seafood, go with a medium-hot fire rather than a really hot one.

◆ Start checking the fish several minutes before you think it's done either by testing for flakiness with a fork or by making a small slit in the thickest part of the fish with a sharp knife. Cooked fish will be firm to the touch and opaque; undercooked fish will appear shiny and semi-translucent.

◆ When you grill seafood, it's particularly important that the rack be very clean. Any residue on the rack could interfere with the seafood's delicate flavor; a clean rack also helps prevent sticking.

◆ Lightly spray the grill rack with cooking spray before placing it over the coals.

◆ Always place seafood on a hot grill rack and leave it there for several minutes before you try to move it. This way, a sear will develop between the fish and the grill rack, which will further help prevent sticking.

GRILLED SALMON WITH NECTARINE-RED ONION RELISH

(pictured on page 241)

2½ cups coarsely chopped nectarines (about 3 medium)
1 cup coarsely chopped red bell pepper
1 cup coarsely chopped red onion
¼ cup thinly sliced fresh basil
¼ cup white wine vinegar
½ teaspoon grated orange rind
¼ cup fresh orange juice
2 tablespoons seeded, minced jalapeño pepper
2 tablespoons fresh lime juice
2 teaspoons sugar
2 garlic cloves, minced
¼ teaspoon salt, divided
½ teaspoon freshly ground pepper
4 (6-ounce) salmon fillets
Vegetable cooking spray

1. Combine first 11 ingredients and ⅛ teaspoon salt in a medium bowl; stir well. Let stand 2 hours.
2. Sprinkle pepper and ⅛ teaspoon salt over salmon fillets. Prepare grill. Place fillets on grill rack coated with cooking spray, and grill 5 minutes on each side or until fish flakes easily when tested with a fork. Serve immediately with nectarine-red onion relish. Yield: 4 servings (serving size: 1 fillet and 1 cup relish).

CALORIES 380 (36% from fat); FAT 15.4g (sat 2.6g, mono 7.2g, poly 3.5g); PROTEIN 38.1g; CARB 21.6g; FIBER 3.5g; CHOL 115mg; IRON 1.6mg; SODIUM 236mg; CALC 36mg

W I N E   P I C K S

- *Randall Bridge Chardonnay 1996 (Australian white), $4.99*
- *Simi Rosé of Cabernet Sauvignon 1996 (California rosé), $9*
- *Sutter Home California Gewürztraminer 1994 (California white), $5.95*

GRILLED SESAME-GINGER SWORDFISH ON WATERCRESS

Getting a good sear on the swordfish will give it a deep, grilled taste that will stand up to the Asian flavors of the salad.

2 teaspoons anise seeds, crushed
2 teaspoons ground ginger
2 teaspoons white pepper
½ teaspoon freshly ground black pepper
¼ teaspoon salt
½ teaspoon olive oil
4 (6-ounce) swordfish steaks (about 1 inch thick)
4 cups trimmed watercress or spinach (about 2 bunches)
½ cup thinly sliced red onion
¼ cup rice wine vinegar
2 tablespoons low-sodium soy sauce
1 tablespoon peeled, minced fresh gingerroot
1 tablespoon dark sesame oil
2 teaspoons water
1 teaspoon sugar
¼ teaspoon freshly ground black pepper
1 tablespoon plus 1 teaspoon sesame seeds, toasted

1. Combine first 5 ingredients in a small bowl.
2. Brush olive oil evenly over steaks. Rub anise seed mixture over both sides of steaks. Prepare grill. Place steaks on grill rack; grill 5 minutes on each side or until fish flakes easily when tested with a fork. Set aside.
3. Combine watercress and onion in a large bowl. Combine vinegar and next 6 ingredients in a jar. Cover tightly, and shake vigorously. Pour over watercress mixture, and toss gently. Arrange watercress mixture on a platter, and top with steaks. Sprinkle steaks with toasted sesame seeds. Yield: 4 servings (serving size: 1 cup watercress mixture, 5 ounces swordfish, and 1 teaspoon sesame seeds).

CALORIES 281 (40% from fat); FAT 12.4g (sat 2.6g, mono 5g, poly 3.7g); PROTEIN 34.3g; CARB 6.1g; FIBER 1.6g; CHOL 64mg; IRON 2.7mg; SODIUM 504mg; CALC 94mg

WELL-BODY ALMANAC

Berry, Berry Good for You

Blueberries hit their peak in summer, so enjoy them while they last. Not only are they one of summer's most luscious treats, they also pack a powerful antioxidant punch. Blueberries topped a list of 40 fruits, juices, and vegetables tested by Tufts University researchers to determine which of them were best at scavenging free radicals—particles that can damage cells and may lead to serious illnesses like heart disease and cancer. Concord grape juice, strawberries, kale, and spinach also fared well. Most nutrition researchers agree that eating plenty of these and other brightly colored fruits and vegetables might help you enjoy a healthier old age.

UPSIDE-DOWN BERRY CAKES

¼ cup all-purpose flour
¼ cup sugar
½ teaspoon baking powder
Dash of salt
¼ cup skim milk
1 tablespoon plus 1 teaspoon reduced-calorie stick margarine, melted
Vegetable cooking spray
1 cup fresh blueberries

1. Preheat oven to 375°.
2. Combine first 4 ingredients in a small bowl; stir well. Add milk and margarine, stirring just until flour mixture is moist. Divide batter evenly between 2 (10-ounce) custard cups coated with cooking spray. Top each with ½ cup blueberries.
3. Bake at 375° for 35 minutes or until lightly browned and fruit topping is bubbly. Yield: 2 servings.

CALORIES 237 (17% from fat); FAT 4.5g (sat 0.7g, mono 1.5g, poly 1.8g); PROTEIN 3.1g; CARB 47.9g; FIBER 3.7g; CHOL 1mg; IRON 0.9mg; SODIUM 126mg; CALC 90mg

Sibling Rivalry

Although related, red and green tomatoes have very different personalities. The red is sweet and sophisticated; the green is tart and sassy and not to be ignored. To promote family harmony, we've come up with recipes for both.

GREEN-TOMATO SALSA WITH THAI SPICES

4   green tomatoes (about 2 pounds)
1   large red onion
¼   cup minced fresh cilantro
2   tablespoons fresh lime juice
2   tablespoons fish sauce
1   tablespoon rice vinegar
2   teaspoons seeded, minced serrano chile
2   teaspoons peeled, minced fresh gingerroot
2   teaspoons ground coriander
2   teaspoons vegetable oil
1   teaspoon sesame oil
1   cup chopped green onions
1   cup julienne-cut yellow bell pepper

1. Cut tomatoes and red onion in half vertically. Cut each half horizontally into thin slices.
2. Combine cilantro and next 8 ingredients in a large bowl; stir well. Add tomatoes, red and green onions, and bell pepper; toss well. Let stand 1 hour. Yield: 8 servings (serving size: 1 cup).
Note: Fish sauce is a salty condiment that can be found in Asian markets, specialty shops, and some supermarkets.

CALORIES 51 (39% from fat); FAT 2.2g (sat 0.3g, mono 0.6g, poly 0.9g); PROTEIN 1.6g; CARB 8g; FIBER 2g; CHOL 0mg; IRON 1mg; SODIUM 528mg; CALC 28mg

TOMATO-CORN SALSA

(pictured on page 243)

4   ears corn
Vegetable cooking spray
1   cup (½-inch-thick) slices red onion
¼   cup lime juice
1   teaspoon ground coriander
½   teaspoon ground cumin
½   teaspoon ground red pepper
¼   teaspoon salt
1   garlic clove, minced
2½ cups chopped red tomato
¾   cup sliced green onions

1. Prepare grill. Place corn on grill rack coated with cooking spray; grill 15 minutes or until corn is lightly browned, turning every 5 minutes. Cool. Cut kernels from ears of corn to measure 2½ cups. Grill onion slices 2 minutes on each side. Cool. Chop onion slices to equal ¾ cup.
2. Combine lime juice and next 5 ingredients in a large bowl; stir well. Add corn kernels, chopped onion, tomato, and green onions; stir well. Serve at room temperature or chilled with fat-free baked tortilla chips. Yield: 4 cups (serving size: ¼ cup).

CALORIES 33 (11% from fat); FAT 0.4g (sat 0.1g, mono 0.1g, poly 0.2g); PROTEIN 1.1g; CARB 7.5g; FIBER 1.3g; CHOL 0mg; IRON 0.4mg; SODIUM 44mg; CALC 8mg

TOMATO-AND-CANNELLINI BEAN SALAD

Watercress gives a peppery bite to this salad, but spinach works fine also. The dressing can be made ahead of time and tossed with the salad just before serving.

⅔   cup boiling water
½   ounce sun-dried tomato halves, packed without oil (about 10)
¼   cup rice vinegar
1   tablespoon vegetable oil
2   teaspoons molasses
2   teaspoons low-sodium soy sauce
6   cups trimmed watercress or chopped fresh spinach
1   cup chopped green onions
6   plum tomatoes, each cut into 6 wedges (about 1 pound)
1   (16-ounce) can cannellini beans or other white beans, rinsed and drained

1. Combine boiling water and sun-dried tomatoes in a bowl; let stand 10 minutes or until soft. Place sun-dried tomato mixture, vinegar, oil, molasses, and soy sauce in a blender; cover and process until well-blended. Cool.
2. Combine watercress and remaining 3 ingredients in a large bowl. Pour tomato vinaigrette over watercress mixture; toss gently. Yield: 4 servings (serving size: 2½ cups).

CALORIES 214 (25% from fat); FAT 5.9g (sat 0.8g, mono 3g, poly 1.4g); PROTEIN 9.8g; CARB 34.8g; FIBER 6.5g; CHOL 0mg; IRON 3.5mg; SODIUM 348mg; CALC 134mg

HOW TO KEEP A TOMATO

As a rule, red tomatoes are best if kept out of the refrigerator. Cold temperatures are the kiss of death to their flavor. However, green tomatoes will ripen if kept out. So if you want them to stay green, the refrigerator is the place for them.

ROASTED TOMATO-GARLIC SAUCE

This easy, versatile sauce is good served with pasta or over fish, or used in any recipe calling for marinara sauce. Make it chunky or smooth, whatever your preference. And don't panic about the 25 cloves of garlic; roasting mellows their flavor.

    1 cup chopped onion
    1 tablespoon vegetable oil
   25 garlic cloves, peeled (about
       3 heads)
    5 large red tomatoes, each cut
       into 8 wedges (about 3
       pounds)
   ½   cup water
    1 tablespoon balsamic vinegar
   ½   teaspoon salt

1. Preheat oven to 450°.
2. Combine first 4 ingredients in a 13 x 9-inch baking dish. Bake at 450° for 20 minutes.
3. Combine tomato mixture, water, vinegar, and salt in a large saucepan; bring to a boil. Cook over high heat 10 minutes. Place mixture in a blender or food processor; cover and process until desired consistency. Yield: 5 cups (serving size: ½ cup).

CALORIES 49 (31% from fat); FAT 1.7g (sat 0.3g, mono 0.5g, poly 0.8g); PROTEIN 1.5g; CARB 8.3g; FIBER 1.6g; CHOL 0mg; IRON 0.6mg; SODIUM 127mg; CALC 22mg

MARINATED TOMATO-BASIL SALAD

   32 (½-inch-thick) slices red
       tomato (about 8 tomatoes or
       4¼ pounds)
    1 cup thinly sliced red onion,
       separated into rings
   ½   cup chopped fresh basil
   ½   cup rice vinegar
    1 tablespoon olive oil
    1 teaspoon sugar
   ½   teaspoon salt

1. Arrange tomato slices and onion in a 13 x 9-inch dish. Combine basil and remaining 4 ingredients; stir well

with a whisk. Pour over tomatoes and onion. Cover and chill at least 2 hours. Yield: 8 servings (serving size: 4 tomato slices).

CALORIES 35 (49% from fat); FAT 1.9g (sat 0.3g, mono 1.3g, poly 0.2g); PROTEIN 0.7g; CARB 4.7g; FIBER 1g; CHOL 0mg; IRON 0.4mg; SODIUM 152mg; CALC 10mg

GREEN TOMATO-AND-LEMON CHUTNEY

Serve this tangy chutney over grilled salmon.

   ¾   cup thinly sliced lemon (about
       2 medium)
   ½   cup sugar
    2 tablespoons water
    1 teaspoon vegetable oil
   ½   cup thinly sliced red onion
   ½   teaspoon minced serrano chile
    3 garlic cloves, minced
    4 cups thinly sliced green tomato
       (about 1½ pounds)
    1 tablespoon curry powder
   ¼   teaspoon salt
   ⅛   teaspoon pepper

1. Combine first 3 ingredients in a glass bowl; stir well. Cover and chill at least 8 hours. Drain lemon slices, and set aside.
2. Heat oil in a large saucepan over medium-high heat. Add onion, chile, and garlic; sauté 4 minutes. Add tomato and curry powder; sauté 5 minutes. Remove from heat. Stir in lemon slices, salt, and pepper. Yield: 3 cups (serving size: ½ cup).
Note: Marinating the lemon slices for 8 hours in a sugar solution helps to extract the bitter flavor from the rind; the rind absorbs the sugar and becomes sweet.

CALORIES 58 (12% from fat); FAT 0.8g (sat 0.1g, mono 0.2g, poly 0.3g); PROTEIN 1.1g; CARB 14.1g; FIBER 1.1g; CHOL 0mg; IRON 0.6mg; SODIUM 57mg; CALC 23mg

---

SEARCHING FOR GREEN TOMATOES

Ask the produce manager at your grocery store for green tomatoes. Supermarkets often have some because 90% of all tomatoes are picked and shipped in the firm, green stage so they won't bruise so easily. Then they're placed in rooms where ethylene gas (the gas all fruits release as they ripen) is piped in to encourage the ripening process. The leftover green tomatoes are often thrown away.

SWEET-AND-SOUR SHIITAKES WITH GREEN TOMATOES

    2 tablespoons rice vinegar
    2 tablespoons low-sodium
       soy sauce
    1 tablespoon brown sugar
   1½ teaspoons dark sesame oil
   ½   teaspoon ground ginger
   ⅛   teaspoon ground red pepper
       Vegetable cooking spray
    2 cups sliced fresh shiitake
       mushroom caps
    4 medium-size green tomatoes,
       peeled and cut into ½-inch-
       thick wedges
    1 medium-size red onion, cut
       into 8 wedges

1. Combine first 6 ingredients. Place a wok or large nonstick skillet coated with cooking spray over medium-high heat until hot. Add mushrooms; stir-fry 2 minutes. Remove from wok; set aside. Coat wok with cooking spray. Add tomatoes; stir-fry 3 minutes. Remove from wok; set aside. Coat wok with cooking spray. Add onion; stir-fry 2 minutes. Return mushrooms and tomatoes to wok. Add vinegar mixture. Bring to a boil; cook, stirring constantly, 30 seconds. Yield: 4 servings (serving size: 1½ cups).

CALORIES 81 (30% from fat); FAT 2.7g (sat 0.3g, mono 0.7g, poly 0.9g); PROTEIN 2.6g; CARB 13.4g; FIBER 2.7g; CHOL 0mg; IRON 1.3mg; SODIUM 214mg; CALC 27mg

H☀T

A Culinary Heat Wave

South Florida's sunny new cuisine is a spicy mixture of Hispanic and Caribbean cooking that's now hotter than Miami Beach.

You can hardly pick up a food or travel magazine today without reading about South Florida's superstar chefs. These innovative chefs have developed a dynamic fusion cuisine based on tropical ingredients, Caribbean cooking techniques, and cross-cultural ingredient combinations. The food is big-flavored: Garlic, cumin, oregano, cilantro, and lime juice are cooking cornerstones. This emphasis on flavor over fat makes sense in a state where bathing suits are seen as everyday wear. Call it a culinary heat wave—with no end in sight.

PINEAPPLE GAZPACHO

½ cup coarsely chopped yellow bell pepper
¼ cup pineapple juice
¼ cup chopped onion
2 teaspoons rice vinegar
½ teaspoon habanero pepper sauce
⅛ teaspoon salt
⅛ teaspoon pepper
1 (1½-pound) peeled, cored pineapple, cut into chunks
1 medium cucumber, peeled, seeded, and quartered
1 tablespoon brown sugar
¼ cup peeled, seeded, and finely diced cucumber
¼ cup finely diced red bell pepper
¼ cup finely diced green bell pepper
¼ cup chopped fresh cilantro

1. Place first 9 ingredients in a blender or food processor; cover and process until minced. Pour into a bowl; stir in sugar. Cover and chill.
2. Spoon soup into bowls. Combine diced cucumber and remaining 3 ingredients, tossing gently. Top each serving with 3 tablespoons cucumber mixture. Yield: 4 servings (serving size: 1 cup).
Note: You can substitute any hot sauce for habanero pepper sauce.

CALORIES 119 (8% from fat); FAT 1g (sat 0.1g, mono 0.1g, poly 0.4g); PROTEIN 1.5g; CARB 29.1g; FIBER 4g; CHOL 0mg; IRON 1.5mg; SODIUM 90mg; CALC 36mg

SHRIMP ENCHILADO

1 tablespoon olive oil
1½ cups diced onion
¾ cup diced red bell pepper
¾ cup diced green bell pepper
¾ teaspoon dried oregano
¾ teaspoon ground cumin
5 garlic cloves, minced
1 (6-ounce) can tomato paste
1¾ cups dry white wine
1 bay leaf
1½ pounds large shrimp, peeled and deveined
¾ teaspoon salt
⅛ teaspoon pepper
6 cups hot cooked rice
3 tablespoons finely chopped fresh cilantro

1. Heat oil in a large nonstick skillet over medium heat. Add onion and next 5 ingredients; sauté 5 minutes or until tender. Stir in tomato paste; cook 1 minute. Stir in wine and bay leaf; bring to a boil. Reduce heat; simmer, uncovered, 5 minutes.
2. Add shrimp to skillet; cover and cook over medium-low heat 5 minutes or until shrimp are done. Remove from heat, and discard bay leaf. Stir in salt and ⅛ teaspoon pepper. Serve shrimp mixture over rice, and sprinkle with cilantro. Yield: 6 servings (serving size: 1 cup shrimp mixture and 1 cup rice).

CALORIES 397 (10% from fat); FAT 4.6g (sat 0.7g, mono 2g, poly 1g); PROTEIN 24.6g; CARB 63.6g; FIBER 3.8g; CHOL 136mg; IRON 6.1mg; SODIUM 454mg; CALC 108mg

BLACK-EYED PEA SALAD

This colorful salad can also be served as a topping for Adobo Tuna (page 238) or as a salsa with chips.

2 tablespoons red wine vinegar
1 tablespoon olive oil
⅛ teaspoon salt
⅛ teaspoon pepper
2½ cups drained canned black-eyed peas, rinsed
¾ cup diced celery
¼ cup chopped fresh cilantro
¼ cup diced red bell pepper
¼ cup diced green bell pepper
¼ cup diced red onion

1. Combine first 4 ingredients in a medium bowl; stir well. Add black-eyed peas and remaining ingredients; stir well. Cover and chill at least 1 hour. Stir before serving. Yield: 4 servings (serving size: 1 cup).

CALORIES 160 (25% from fat); FAT 4.4g (sat 0.7g, mono 2.5g, poly 0.7g); PROTEIN 7.7g; CARB 23.7g; FIBER 1g; CHOL 0mg; IRON 2.1mg; SODIUM 542mg; CALC 48mg

GINGER-MANGO GELATO

2 cups peeled, diced mango
2 tablespoons fresh lime juice
2 teaspoons minced crystallized ginger
1½ cups water
¾ cup sugar
Fresh mint sprigs (optional)

1. Place first 3 ingredients in a blender or food processor; cover and process until smooth. Combine water and sugar in a saucepan. Bring to a boil; cook, stirring constantly, 1 minute. Remove from heat; stir in mango mixture. Cool to room temperature.
2. Pour mixture into freezer can of an ice-cream freezer, and freeze according to manufacturer's instructions. Garnish with mint sprigs, if desired. Yield: 6 servings (serving size: ½ cup).

CALORIES 136 (1% from fat); FAT 0.2g (sat 0g, mono 0.1g, poly 0g); PROTEIN 0.3g; CARB 35.3g; FIBER 0.8g; CHOL 0mg; IRON 0.2mg; SODIUM 2mg; CALC 8mg

TROPICAL FRUIT NAPOLEONS

½ cup fat-free sour cream
⅓ cup sifted powdered sugar
⅓ cup tub-style light cream cheese
¼ cup soft tofu
½ teaspoon grated lemon rind
2 tablespoons dry breadcrumbs
2 tablespoons granulated sugar
¼ teaspoon ground cinnamon
5 sheets frozen phyllo dough, thawed
2 tablespoons reduced-calorie stick margarine, melted
Vegetable cooking spray
½ cup diced carambola (star fruit)
½ cup peeled, diced papaya
½ cup peeled, diced banana
1 tablespoon powdered sugar

1. Combine first 5 ingredients in a bowl; beat at medium speed of an electric mixer until smooth. Cover and chill.
2. Combine breadcrumbs, granulated sugar, and cinnamon in a bowl.
3. Preheat oven to 375°.
4. Place 1 phyllo sheet on a large cutting board or work surface; lightly brush with margarine. Sprinkle with 1 tablespoon breadcrumb mixture. Repeat layers with remaining phyllo, margarine, and breadcrumb mixture, ending with phyllo. Gently press phyllo layers together. Lightly coat top phyllo sheet with cooking spray. Cut 12 (3-inch) circles through phyllo layers, using a sharp round cookie cutter. Carefully place layered circles on a baking sheet coated with cooking spray; discard remaining phyllo scraps. Coat bottom of another baking sheet with cooking spray; place baking sheet, coated side down, on top of layered phyllo circles. Bake at 375° for 12 minutes or until crisp. Remove top baking sheet; place phyllo stacks on a wire rack. Cool completely.
5. Combine carambola, papaya, and banana; stir gently. Place 1 phyllo stack on each of 4 plates. Spread about 1 tablespoon sour cream mixture on top of each stack; top each with about 3 tablespoons papaya mixture and 1 tablespoon sour cream mixture. For each serving, repeat layers with remaining phyllo stacks, sour cream mixture, and papaya mixture, ending with phyllo stacks. Sprinkle 1 tablespoon powdered sugar over napoleons. Yield: 4 servings.

CALORIES 290 (29% from fat); FAT 9.5g (sat 2.8g, mono 3.1g, poly 2.8g); PROTEIN 7.5g; CARB 44.3g; FIBER 1.3g; CHOL 11mg; IRON 1.4mg; SODIUM 326mg; CALC 59mg

ADOBO TUNA

This variation of adobo sauce—a marinade made from chiles, herbs, and vinegar—uses garlic, cumin, and lime juice.

⅓ cup fresh lime juice
½ teaspoon dried oregano
½ teaspoon ground cumin
¼ teaspoon salt
4 garlic cloves, minced
4 (6-ounce) tuna steaks (about ½ inch thick)
1 teaspoon olive oil
1 teaspoon cracked pepper
Vegetable cooking spray
Lime slices (optional)

1. Combine first 5 ingredients in a large shallow dish; add fish, turning to coat. Cover and marinate in refrigerator 1 hour, turning fish occasionally.
2. Preheat broiler. Remove fish from dish, discarding marinade. Brush oil over fish; sprinkle with pepper. Place fish on rack of a broiler pan coated with cooking spray; broil 4 minutes or until medium-rare (do not turn). Garnish with lime slices, if desired. Yield: 4 servings (serving size: 1 steak).

CALORIES 250 (33% from fat); FAT 9.3g (sat 2.2g, mono 3.5g, poly 2.5g); PROTEIN 38.3g; CARB 1.1g; FIBER 0.2g; CHOL 63mg; IRON 1.9mg; SODIUM 123mg; CALC 6mg

FOR TWO

The Way We Stir

A large skillet is a must for these one-dish stir-fry meals.

TURKEY SCALOPPINE WITH APRICOT-GINGER SAUCE

½ pound turkey tenderloin, cut into 3 x ½-inch-wide strips
2 tablespoons all-purpose flour
¼ teaspoon salt
¼ teaspoon pepper
2 teaspoons vegetable oil
Vegetable cooking spray
1 cup green bell pepper strips
2 tablespoons minced shallots
1 teaspoon peeled, minced fresh gingerroot
⅔ cup apricot nectar
⅔ cup low-salt chicken broth
1 tablespoon chopped dried apricots
1 tablespoon currants
2 teaspoons brown sugar
2 teaspoons balsamic vinegar

1. Combine first 4 ingredients in a large zip-top plastic bag; seal and shake to coat. Heat oil in a large nonstick skillet coated with cooking spray over medium-high heat until hot. Add turkey mixture; stir-fry 3 minutes or until lightly browned. Remove from skillet; keep warm. Wipe skillet with paper towels.
2. Coat skillet with cooking spray; place over medium-high heat. Add bell pepper, shallots, and gingerroot; stir-fry 1½ minutes. Add nectar and remaining 5 ingredients; bring to a boil. Cook over medium heat 3 minutes or until slightly thick. Add turkey; cook 1 minute or until thoroughly heated. Yield: 2 servings (serving size: 1¼ cups).

CALORIES 311 (22% from fat); FAT 7.5g (sat 1.5g, mono 1.7g, poly 2.8g); PROTEIN 29.6g; CARB 31.3g; FIBER 2.3g; CHOL 68mg; IRON 3.7mg; SODIUM 398mg; CALC 36mg

SAUTÉED SCALLOPS AND MUSHROOMS WITH PINE NUTS

½ pound sea scallops, halved crosswise
⅛ teaspoon salt
⅛ teaspoon pepper
Vegetable cooking spray
1 tablespoon stick margarine
2 cups sliced mushrooms
2 tablespoons pine nuts, toasted
2 tablespoons minced shallots
1 garlic clove, minced
⅓ cup dry white wine
2 tablespoons fresh lemon juice
2 cups hot cooked angel hair (about 4 ounces uncooked pasta)

1. Sprinkle scallops with salt and pepper. Coat a nonstick skillet with cooking spray; add margarine, and place over medium-high heat until margarine melts. Add scallops, mushrooms, and pine nuts; stir-fry 2 minutes or until scallops are done. Remove from skillet.
2. Add shallots and garlic to skillet; stir-fry 30 seconds. Stir in wine and lemon juice. Bring to a boil; cook 2 minutes. Add scallop mixture; cook 30 seconds or until thoroughly heated. Serve over pasta. Yield: 2 servings (serving size: 1 cup scallop mixture and 1 cup pasta).

CALORIES 436 (27% from fat); FAT 13.2g (sat 2.2g, mono 4.6g, poly 4.7g); PROTEIN 30.1g; CARB 51.1g; FIBER 3.6g; CHOL 37mg; IRON 4.4mg; SODIUM 399mg; CALC 56mg

SHRIMP AND PAPAYA WITH FRESH HERBS

¾ pound large shrimp, peeled and deveined
1 tablespoon fresh lemon juice
⅛ teaspoon salt
⅛ teaspoon pepper
Vegetable cooking spray
1 tablespoon stick margarine
¼ cup minced shallots
½ cup peeled, diced papaya
1 tablespoon chopped fresh basil
1 tablespoon chopped fresh chives
⅓ cup dry white wine
½ teaspoon Worcestershire sauce

1. Combine first 4 ingredients. Coat a large nonstick skillet with cooking spray; add margarine, and place over medium-high heat until margarine melts. Add shrimp mixture; sauté 3 minutes. Remove from skillet.
2. Add shallots to skillet; stir-fry 1 minute. Add papaya, basil, and chives; stir-fry 30 seconds. Stir in wine and Worcestershire sauce. Bring to a boil; cook 2 minutes, stirring occasionally. Return shrimp to skillet; stir-fry 30 seconds or until thoroughly heated. Yield: 2 servings (serving size: 1 cup).

CALORIES 268 (30% from fat); FAT 9g (sat 1.7g, mono 3g, poly 3g); PROTEIN 35.5g; CARB 10g; FIBER 0.8g; CHOL 259mg; IRON 4.6mg; SODIUM 478mg; CALC 115mg

VEAL PAPRIKASH

¼ cup low-fat sour cream (at room temperature)
1 teaspoon Hungarian sweet paprika
1 teaspoon vegetable oil
Vegetable cooking spray
1 cup vertically sliced onion
1 (8-ounce) package presliced mushrooms
1 garlic clove, minced
½ pound lean veal cutlets (about ¼ inch thick), cut into 3 x ½-inch-wide strips
¼ cup dry white wine
¼ teaspoon salt
¼ teaspoon dried thyme
⅛ teaspoon pepper
2 cups hot cooked egg noodles
Chopped chives (optional)

1. Combine sour cream and paprika in a small bowl. Stir well; set aside.
2. Heat oil in a nonstick skillet coated with cooking spray over medium-high heat until hot. Add onion, mushrooms, and garlic; stir-fry 3 minutes or until tender. Remove from skillet. Wipe skillet with paper towels.
3. Coat skillet with cooking spray; place over medium-high heat. Add veal; stir-fry 2 minutes. Add wine and next 3 ingredients; cook over medium heat 3 minutes or until liquid evaporates. Remove from heat.
4. Add sour cream mixture and mushroom mixture to skillet; stir. Cook over low heat 1 minute or until thoroughly heated; stir. Serve over noodles. Sprinkle with chives, if desired. Yield: 2 servings (serving size: 1 cup veal mixture and 1 cup noodles).

CALORIES 462 (24% from fat); FAT 12.5g (sat 4.2g, mono 3.5g, poly 2.6g); PROTEIN 34.8g; CARB 53g; FIBER 6.4g; CHOL 158mg; IRON 5.8mg; SODIUM 423mg; CALC 96mg

BEEF, PEPPER, AND SHIITAKE MUSHROOM STIR-FRY

1 teaspoon olive oil, divided
Vegetable cooking spray
6 ounces beef tenderloin, cut into ½-inch strips
½ cup sliced shallots
½ cup green bell pepper, cut into ¼-inch-wide strips
½ cup red bell pepper, cut into ¼-inch-wide strips
½ cup yellow bell pepper, cut into ¼-inch-wide strips
3 garlic cloves, minced
2 cups sliced shiitake mushroom caps (about 1 [3.5-ounce] package)
¼ cup dry white wine
½ cup no-salt-added beef broth
1 tablespoon chopped fresh basil
¼ teaspoon salt
¼ teaspoon pepper
1½ cups hot cooked rice

1. Heat ½ teaspoon oil in a nonstick skillet coated with cooking spray over medium-high heat until hot. Add beef; stir-fry 2 minutes. Remove from skillet; set aside. Wipe skillet with a paper towel.
2. Heat ½ teaspoon oil in skillet. Add shallots, bell pepper, and garlic; stir-fry 1 minute. Add mushrooms; stir-fry 2 minutes. Stir in wine; cook 1 minute. Add broth; reduce heat, and simmer 3 minutes. Add beef; cook 1 minute. Stir in basil, salt, and ¼ teaspoon pepper. Serve with rice. Yield: 2 servings (serving size: 1 cup beef mixture and ¾ cup rice).

CALORIES 406 (20% from fat); FAT 9.2g (sat 2.7g, mono 3.8g, poly 0.9g); PROTEIN 24.7g; CARB 55.8g; FIBER 4g; CHOL 53mg; IRON 6.8mg; SODIUM 355mg; CALC 60mg

PORK-AND-APPLE STIR-FRY

Vegetable cooking spray
8   ounces lean, boned pork loin, cut into ½-inch pieces
¼   teaspoon salt
¼   teaspoon coarsely ground pepper
2   tablespoons sugar
2   tablespoons cider vinegar
⅓   cup dry white wine
⅓   cup fat-free chicken broth
1   cup red bell pepper strips
1   cup peeled, thinly sliced Granny Smith apple
1   teaspoon peeled, grated fresh gingerroot
1   cup (1-inch) sliced green onions
1   teaspoon cornstarch
1   teaspoon water
1½ cups hot cooked rice

1. Place a large nonstick skillet coated with cooking spray over medium-high heat until hot. Add pork; sauté 5 minutes or until done, browning on all sides. Remove pork from skillet; sprinkle with salt and ground pepper.
2. Add sugar and vinegar to skillet; cook 1 minute. Add wine and chicken broth; cook 30 seconds. Add bell pepper, apple, and gingerroot; stir-fry 3 minutes. Add green onions, and stir-fry 2 minutes or until apple is tender. Combine cornstarch and water in a small bowl; add to skillet. Bring to a boil. Cook, stirring constantly, 1 minute. Return pork to skillet, and cook until thoroughly heated. Serve

with rice. Yield: 2 servings (serving size: 1 cup pork mixture and ¾ cup rice).

CALORIES 472 (18% from fat); FAT 9.5g (sat 3.1g, mono 3.9g, poly 1.1g); PROTEIN 29.3g; CARB 67.3g; FIBER 4.5g; CHOL 68mg; IRON 4.1mg; SODIUM 408mg; CALC 72mg

CHICKEN SAUSAGE WITH VEGETABLES AND PASTA

Vegetable cooking spray
2   (3-ounce) fully cooked chicken sausages, cut diagonally into ¼-inch-thick slices
2   cups vertically sliced onion
2   cups seeded, chopped tomato
2   garlic cloves, minced
1   tablespoon all-purpose flour
1   cup water
⅛   teaspoon salt
⅛   teaspoon pepper
1   cup broccoli florets
1   cup (2 x ¼-inch) julienne-cut red bell pepper
1   cup (2 x ¼-inch) julienne-cut yellow bell pepper
2   cups hot cooked penne (about 4 ounces uncooked tubular-shaped pasta)
2   teaspoons minced fresh basil

1. Place a large nonstick skillet coated with cooking spray over medium-high heat until hot. Add sausage; stir-fry 4 minutes or until browned. Remove from skillet. Set aside; keep warm. Wipe skillet with paper towels.
2. Coat skillet with cooking spray, and place over medium-high heat. Add onion; stir-fry 3 minutes. Add tomato and garlic; stir-fry 5 minutes. Sprinkle with flour, stirring to coat. Add water, salt, and ⅛ teaspoon pepper; bring to a boil. Cover, reduce heat, and simmer over medium-low heat 10 minutes, stirring occasionally. Add broccoli and bell peppers; cook 10 minutes or until vegetables are tender and sauce is thick. Stir in sausage and pasta. Sprinkle with basil. Yield: 2 servings (serving size: 2½ cups).

CALORIES 539 (29% from fat); FAT 17.6g (sat 6.6g, mono 7.4g, poly 1.6g); PROTEIN 24g; CARB 71g; FIBER 9.8g; CHOL 75mg; IRON 4.9mg; SODIUM 630mg; CALC 77mg

CHICKEN-LINGUINE PRIMAVERA

½   pound skinned, boned chicken breast, cut into bite-size pieces
⅓   cup all-purpose flour
⅛   teaspoon salt
⅛   teaspoon pepper
1   tablespoon olive oil
Vegetable cooking spray
1   cup broccoli florets
1   cup sliced yellow squash
⅓   cup diagonally sliced carrot
2   garlic cloves, minced
2   tablespoons chopped fresh basil
8   cherry tomatoes, halved
½   cup no-salt-added chicken broth
⅓   cup dry white wine
2   cups hot cooked linguine (about 4 ounces uncooked pasta)
¼   cup grated fresh Parmesan cheese

1. Dredge chicken in flour. Sprinkle with salt and pepper.
2. Heat oil in a large nonstick skillet coated with cooking spray over medium heat until hot. Add chicken; stir-fry 4 minutes or until browned. Add broccoli and next 3 ingredients; stir-fry 2 minutes. Stir in basil and tomatoes. Spoon mixture into a large bowl; set aside.
3. Add broth and wine to skillet, scraping bottom of skillet to loosen browned bits; bring to a boil. Add broth mixture and pasta to chicken mixture; toss. Sprinkle with cheese. Yield: 2 servings (serving size: 1¼ cups chicken mixture and 2 tablespoons cheese).

CALORIES 459 (27% from fat); FAT 13.7g (sat 3.8g, mono 6.5g, poly 1.5g); PROTEIN 39.7g; CARB 43.7g; FIBER 5.3g; CHOL 75mg; IRON 4mg; SODIUM 510mg; CALC 242mg

Macaroni Salad, page 248

Grilled Salmon with Nectarine-Red Onion Relish, page 234

Baja-Spiced Chicken Salad with Chutney Dressing, page 224

Roasted Eggplant "Salad," page 230

Tomato-Corn Salsa, page 235

Mexicali Crab Cakes, page 225

Brownie Cheesecake Torte, page 222

In a Crust

As the long, hot summer moves slowly along, you'll find cooling relief with these icebox pies.

Like a sultry breeze off the bayou or a sudden cloudburst, we bring you relief from the hot days of summer. Our soothing deliverance comes in the form of frozen fruit pies that you keep in the freezer, ready to serve whenever you feel the summer droops coming on.

CHOCOLATE CHIP-CHERRY PIE

40 reduced-calorie chocolate wafers
 2 tablespoons sugar
 2 tablespoons stick margarine, melted
 1 large egg white
Vegetable cooking spray
 4 cups vanilla low-fat frozen yogurt
 1 cup pitted, chopped sweet cherries
 ½ cup semisweet chocolate minichips
 ½ cup black cherry preserves, melted

1. Preheat oven to 350°.
2. Place cookies in a food processor; process until crumbly. Add sugar, margarine, and egg white; pulse 5 times or just until moist. Press crumb mixture evenly into a 9-inch pie plate coated with cooking spray. Bake at 350° for 8 minutes; cool on a wire rack 15 minutes. Freeze piecrust 30 minutes.
3. Place an extra-large bowl in freezer. Remove yogurt from freezer; let stand at room temperature while crust is cooling.
4. Spoon yogurt into chilled extra-large bowl. Stir cherries and minichips into yogurt; freeze 30 minutes or just until set but not solid.
5. Spread preserves over bottom of prepared crust. Spoon yogurt mixture evenly over preserves; freeze until set. Cover with plastic wrap; freeze 6 hours or until firm.
6. Place pie in refrigerator 30 minutes before serving to soften. Yield: 9 servings (serving size: 1 wedge).

CALORIES 288 (30% from fat); FAT 9.7g (sat 3.8g, mono 3g, poly 2.3g); PROTEIN 4g; CARB 50.3g; FIBER 0.6g; CHOL 8mg; IRON 1mg; SODIUM 165mg; CALC 90mg

STRAWBERRY-SWIRL FROZEN PIE

40 reduced-calorie vanilla wafers
 2 tablespoons sugar
 2 tablespoons stick margarine, melted
 1 large egg white
Vegetable cooking spray
 3 cups strawberry low-fat frozen yogurt
 1½ cups sliced strawberries
 3 tablespoons sugar
 1 cup frozen reduced-calorie whipped topping, thawed

1. Preheat oven to 350°.
2. Place cookies in a food processor; process until crumbly. Add 2 tablespoons sugar, margarine, and egg white; pulse 5 times or just until moist. Press crumb mixture evenly into a 9-inch pie plate coated with cooking spray. Bake at 350° for 8 minutes; cool on a wire rack 15 minutes. Freeze piecrust 30 minutes.
3. Place an extra-large bowl in freezer. Remove yogurt from freezer; let stand at room temperature while crust is cooling.
4. Combine strawberries and 3 tablespoons sugar in a large bowl; stir well. Let stand 20 minutes or until juicy. Wipe out food processor bowl with a paper towel. Add sugared strawberries, and process just until finely chopped.
5. Spoon yogurt into chilled extra-large bowl; fold in strawberry mixture until well-blended. Freeze 30 minutes or just until set but not solid.
6. Spoon yogurt mixture into prepared crust; freeze until set. Cover with plastic wrap; freeze 6 hours or until firm.
7. Place pie in refrigerator 30 minutes before serving to soften. Serve with whipped topping. Yield: 8 servings (serving size: 1 wedge and 2 tablespoons topping).

CALORIES 237 (29% from fat); FAT 7.7g (sat 2.7g, mono 2.1g, poly 2.4g); PROTEIN 4.2g; CARB 40.6g; FIBER 1.7g; CHOL 7mg; IRON 0.2mg; SODIUM 157mg; CALC 80mg

BETWEEN A ROCK AND A SOFT PLACE

Frozen pies can be a little tricky in terms of their texture—you don't want your pies as hard as a rock, nor do you want "pie soup." Because low-fat ice creams and frozen yogurts have less butterfat and a higher water content, they melt quickly. Our Test Kitchens staff did numerous retests of ways to achieve the best consistency. We found that these techniques will help you make a pie that's creamy and soft.

• While the piecrust is cooling, take the frozen yogurt or ice cream out of the freezer and let it soften. This makes it easier to fold in the other ingredients for the filling.

• Freeze the piecrust 30 minutes. The ice cream or yogurt mixture won't melt as it would if you put it into a piecrust at room temperature.

• It's best to partially refreeze the filling before spooning it into the pie shell. To do this, combine the slightly softened frozen yogurt or ice cream and other ingredients specified in the recipe in a chilled extra-large bowl. Put the bowl back in the freezer for about 30 to 45 minutes to let it set back up. Don't let the mixture freeze solid, or the consistency will be too hard to spoon into the piecrust.

• Place the filled piecrust back in the freezer until set; then cover with plastic wrap.

• Take the pie out of the freezer, and let it stand in the refrigerator about 30 minutes before serving. This step will make it easier to cut the pie into wedges.

FROZEN LEMONADE PIE WITH BLUEBERRY SAUCE

44 oatmeal crunch graham
     crackers (11 full cracker
     sheets)
2 tablespoons sugar
1 tablespoon stick margarine,
     melted
1 large egg white
Vegetable cooking spray
4 cups vanilla low-fat frozen
     yogurt
½ cup thawed lemonade
     concentrate, undiluted
Blueberry Sauce

1. Preheat oven to 350°.
2. Place crackers in a food processor; process until crumbly. Add sugar, margarine, and egg white; pulse 5 times or just until moist. Press crumb mixture evenly into a 9-inch pie plate coated with cooking spray. Bake at 350° for 8 minutes, and cool on a wire rack 15 minutes. Freeze piecrust 30 minutes.
3. Place an extra-large bowl in freezer. Remove yogurt from freezer; let stand at room temperature while crust is cooling.
4. Spoon yogurt into chilled extra-large bowl. Fold lemonade concentrate into yogurt; freeze 30 minutes or just until set but not solid.
5. Spoon yogurt mixture into prepared crust; freeze until set. Cover with plastic wrap; freeze 6 hours or until firm.
6. Place pie in refrigerator 30 minutes before serving to soften. Serve pie with Blueberry Sauce. Yield: 8 servings (serving size: 1 wedge and 3 tablespoons sauce).

CALORIES 260 (18% from fat); FAT 5.2g (sat 2.1g, mono 1.2g, poly 1.7g); PROTEIN 4.7g; CARB 50.3g; FIBER 1.6g; CHOL 9mg; IRON 0.8mg; SODIUM 153mg; CALC 104mg

Blueberry Sauce:

¾ cup water
¼ cup sugar
2¼ teaspoons cornstarch
1½ cups blueberries

1. Combine first 3 ingredients in a small heavy saucepan; stir with a whisk. Bring to a boil; cook, stirring constantly, 1 minute or until thick. Add blueberries; cook 2 minutes or until bubbly. Yield: 1½ cups (serving size: 3 tablespoons).

CALORIES 38 (2% from fat); FAT 0.1g (sat 0g, mono 0.1g, poly 0g); PROTEIN 0.2g; CARB 9.6g; FIBER 1.1g; CHOL 0mg; IRON 0mg; SODIUM 2mg; CALC 2mg

PLUM-BERRY SWIRL ICE-CREAM PIE

1½ cups coarsely chopped plums
3 tablespoons sugar
1 tablespoon water
40 low-fat honey graham crackers
     (10 full cracker sheets)
2 tablespoons sugar
2 tablespoons stick margarine,
     melted
1 large egg white
Vegetable cooking spray
4 cups vanilla low-fat ice cream
1 cup wild berry sorbet
1 cup frozen reduced-calorie
     whipped topping,
     thawed

1. Combine first 3 ingredients in a small saucepan; stir well. Cover and cook over low heat 15 minutes or until plums are tender, stirring occasionally. Spoon plum mixture into a blender; cover and pulse 3 times. Cool to room temperature.
2. Preheat oven to 350°.
3. Place crackers in a food processor; process until crumbly. Add 2 tablespoons sugar, melted margarine, and egg white; pulse 5 times or just until moist. Press crumb mixture evenly into a 9-inch pie plate coated with cooking spray. Bake at 350° for 8 minutes; cool on a wire rack 15 minutes. Freeze piecrust 30 minutes.
4. Place an extra-large bowl in freezer. Remove ice cream from freezer; let stand at room temperature while crust is cooling.
5. Spoon ice cream into chilled extra-large bowl. Fold plum mixture and sorbet into ice cream to create a marbled effect; freeze 45 minutes or just until set but not solid.
6. Spoon ice-cream mixture into prepared crust; freeze until set. Cover with plastic wrap; freeze 6 hours or until firm.
7. Place pie in refrigerator 30 minutes before serving to soften. Serve pie with whipped topping. Yield: 8 servings (serving size: 1 wedge and 2 tablespoons whipped topping).

CALORIES 283 (26% from fat); FAT 8.1g (sat 3.3g, mono 2.6g, poly 1.7g); PROTEIN 4.7g; CARB 50.3g; FIBER 2.2g; CHOL 9mg; IRON 0.8mg; SODIUM 218mg; CALC 115mg

PEACH MELBA PIE

40 reduced-calorie vanilla wafers
2 tablespoons stick margarine,
     melted
1 large egg white
Vegetable cooking spray
4 cups vanilla low-fat frozen
     yogurt
1½ cups peeled, thinly sliced
     peaches
3 tablespoons sugar
2 teaspoons lemon juice
Raspberry Sauce

1. Preheat oven to 350°.
2. Place cookies in a food processor; process until crumbly. Add margarine and egg white; pulse 5 times or just until moist. Press crumb mixture evenly into a 9-inch pie plate coated with cooking spray. Bake at 350° for 8 minutes, and cool on a wire rack 15 minutes. Freeze piecrust 30 minutes.
3. Place an extra-large bowl in freezer. Remove yogurt from freezer, and let stand at room temperature while crust is cooling.
4. Wipe out food processor bowl with a paper towel; add peaches, sugar, and lemon juice. Process until smooth. Spoon yogurt into chilled extra-large bowl. Fold in peach mixture until well-blended; freeze 30 minutes or just until set but not solid.
5. Spoon yogurt mixture into prepared crust; freeze until set. Cover with plastic wrap; freeze 6 hours or until firm.
6. Place pie in refrigerator 30 minutes before serving to soften. Serve pie with

Raspberry Sauce. Yield: 8 servings (serving size: 1 wedge and 3 tablespoons sauce).

CALORIES 301 (21% from fat); FAT 7.2g (sat 2.3g, mono 2.1g, poly 2.2g); PROTEIN 5.1g; CARB 58.1g; FIBER 4.1g; CHOL 9mg; IRON 0.3mg; SODIUM 166mg; CALC 103mg

Raspberry Sauce:

- ½ **cup seedless raspberry jam**
- 1 **tablespoon lemon juice**
- 2½ **cups fresh raspberries**

1. Melt jam over low heat in a small saucepan; stir in lemon juice. Combine jam mixture and raspberries in a bowl; stir gently to combine. Serve warm or at room temperature. Yield: 1½ cups (serving size: 3 tablespoons).

CALORIES 62 (3% from fat); FAT 0.2g (sat 0g, mono 0g, poly 0.1g); PROTEIN 0.4g; CARB 35.8g; FIBER 2.6g; CHOL 0mg; IRON 0.2mg; SODIUM 6mg; CALC 9mg

FROZEN STRAWBERRY DAIQUIRI PIE

Substitute apple juice or white grape juice for rum, if desired.

- 40 **graham crackers (10 full cracker sheets)**
- 2 **tablespoons sugar**
- 2 **tablespoons stick margarine, melted**
- 1 **large egg white**
- **Vegetable cooking spray**
- 4 **cups vanilla low-fat frozen yogurt**
- ⅓ **cup frozen strawberry daiquiri concentrate, undiluted**
- 3 **tablespoons white rum**
- **Strawberry-Rum Sauce**

1. Preheat oven to 350°.
2. Place crackers in a food processor; process until crumbly. Add sugar, margarine, and egg white; pulse 5 times or just until moist. Press crumb mixture evenly into a 9-inch pie plate coated with cooking spray. Bake at 350° for 8 minutes, and cool on a wire rack 15 minutes. Freeze piecrust 30 minutes.
3. Place an extra-large bowl in freezer. Remove frozen yogurt and daiquiri

concentrate from freezer; let stand at room temperature while crust is cooling.
4. Spoon yogurt into chilled extra-large bowl. Gently fold concentrate and rum into yogurt. Freeze 45 minutes or just until set but not solid.
5. Spoon yogurt mixture into prepared crust; freeze until set. Cover with plastic wrap; freeze 6 hours or until firm.
6. Place pie in refrigerator 30 minutes before serving to soften. Serve pie with Strawberry-Rum Sauce. Yield: 8 servings (serving size: 1 wedge and 3 tablespoons sauce).

CALORIES 257 (23% from fat); FAT 6.5g (sat 2.2g, mono 1.0g, poly 2g); PROTEIN 4.4g; CARB 39.7g; FIBER 1.2g; CHOL 9mg; IRON 0.8mg; SODIUM 177mg; CALC 104mg

Strawberry-Rum Sauce:

- 2½ **cups quartered strawberries**
- 2 **tablespoons sugar**
- 2 **tablespoons white rum**
- 1 **teaspoon grated lime rind**

1. Combine first 3 ingredients in a small bowl; stir gently. Let stand 20 minutes. Place half of strawberry mixture and lime rind in a blender; cover and process until smooth. Add to remaining strawberry mixture; stir well. Cover and chill. Yield: 1½ cups (serving size: 3 tablespoons).

CALORIES 37 (5% from fat); FAT 0.2g (sat 0g, mono 0g, poly 0.1g); PROTEIN 0.3g; CARB 6.4g; FIBER 1.2g; CHOL 0mg; IRON 0.2mg; SODIUM 1mg; CALC 7mg

TROPICAL SUNDAE PIE

- 1½ **cups diced fresh pineapple**
- ¼ **cup sugar**
- 3 **tablespoons white rum**
- 24 **gingersnaps**
- 1 **tablespoon stick margarine, melted**
- 1 **large egg white**
- **Vegetable cooking spray**
- 4 **cups vanilla low-fat frozen yogurt**
- 2 **tablespoons sliced almonds, toasted**
- 2 **tablespoons flaked sweetened coconut, toasted**
- **Fresh pineapple chunks (optional)**

1. Combine diced fresh pineapple and sugar in a small saucepan; bring to a boil. Cook over medium heat 10 minutes or until reduced to 1 cup. Remove from heat, and stir in rum. Set aside, and cool completely.
2. Preheat oven to 350°.
3. Place gingersnaps in a food processor; process until crumbly. Add margarine and egg white; pulse 5 times or just until moist. Press crumb mixture evenly into a 9-inch pie plate coated with cooking spray. Bake at 350° for 7 minutes; cool on a wire rack 15 minutes. Freeze piecrust 30 minutes.
4. Place an extra-large bowl in freezer. Remove yogurt from freezer; let stand at room temperature while crust is cooling.
5. Spoon yogurt into chilled extra-large bowl; fold in pineapple mixture. Freeze 30 minutes or just until set but not solid.
6. Spoon yogurt mixture into prepared crust. Sprinkle mixture with almonds and coconut; freeze until set. Cover with plastic wrap, and freeze 6 hours or until firm.
7. Place pie in refrigerator 30 minutes before serving to soften. Garnish with pineapple chunks, if desired. Yield: 8 servings (serving size: 1 wedge).

CALORIES 281 (29% from fat); FAT 8.7g (sat 3.1g, mono 2.9g, poly 2.2g); PROTEIN 5.1g; CARB 43.2g; FIBER 0.7g; CHOL 18mg; IRON 1.4mg; SODIUM 91mg; CALC 139mg

Hey, Macaroni!

*What could be simpler than doing the
macaroni (salad, that is)? The hard
part is getting rid of the fat and calories. And we've done that for you.*

Macaroni salad is one of those summertime staples that turns up at picnics, barbecues, and the corner deli.
But when we looked over Paula
Hampton's recipe for My Very Best
Macaroni Salad, we liked her twist on
the usual. Chock-full of a wide array of
vegetables and little bits of ham and
cheese, this salad was dressed a little
more stylishly than usual. Trouble
is, more than half of the calories came
from fat. "Help," said Hampton. And
we did. When the high-fat salad and
the remodeled version stood side-by-
side in our Test Kitchens, our taste-
testers had trouble telling the
difference. Now that's the right way to
do the macaroni.

BEFORE & AFTER	
SERVING SIZE	
1 cup	
CALORIES	
324	229
FAT	
19.4g	7.5g
PERCENT OF TOTAL CALORIES	
54%	29%
CHOLESTEROL	
70mg	15mg

HOW WE DID IT

- Switched to light versions of
  mayonnaise and sour cream
- Used reduced-fat sharp Cheddar
  cheese and lean ham

MENU SUGGESTION
Barbecued chicken*
MACARONI SALAD
Watermelon wedges

*Process ⅓ cup raspberry jam, ⅓ cup
ketchup, 2 tablespoons mustard, and
1 teaspoon cider vinegar in a blender.
Grill 4 chicken leg quarters 10 minutes
on each side. Brush with sauce; cook
15 additional minutes or until done,
basting frequently.

MACARONI SALAD

(pictured on page 241)

- ⅔ cup low-fat sour cream
- ⅓ cup light mayonnaise
- 2 tablespoons chopped fresh
  parsley
- 2 tablespoons sweet pickle relish
- 1 tablespoon spicy brown
  mustard
- ¼ teaspoon white pepper
- 4 cups cooked elbow macaroni
  (about 8 ounces uncooked
  pasta)
- 1 cup sliced green onions
- 1 cup frozen green peas, thawed
- ¾ cup (3 ounces) diced reduced-
  fat sharp Cheddar cheese
- ½ cup diced carrot
- ½ cup diced green bell pepper
- ½ cup sliced celery
- ½ cup diced lean ham (about 2
  ounces)

1. Combine first 6 ingredients in a
large bowl; stir well. Add macaroni
and remaining ingredients; toss well to
coat. Cover and chill. Yield: 8 servings
(serving size: 1 cup).

CALORIES 229 (29% from fat); FAT 7.5g (sat 0.7g, mono 0.3g,
poly 2g); PROTEIN 9.9g; CARB 28.8g; FIBER 1.9g;
CHOL 15mg; IRON 1.8mg; SODIUM 203mg; CALC 123mg

SEPTEMBER

Fahrenheit 451

Roasting food at very high temperatures isn't just for big hunks of meat. It also does wonders for vegetables and fruits, making them sweeter and meltingly soft.

When you think of roasting food in the oven, the usual suspects come to mind—pot roast, chicken, ham, turkey, and leg of lamb. But we have a few roasting surprises for you. As it turns out, roasting may be the simplest, boldest method of cooking fruits and vegetables. The high heat 400° to 500°—locks in flavors while caramelizing outer layers. With little enhancement, a metamorphosis occurs: Unadorned vegetables become beautifully glazed side dishes, and plain fruits become full-blown desserts.

MENU SUGGESTION

French toast*

ROASTED SUMMER-FRUIT SALAD

*Dip 6 (1-inch-thick) diagonally cut French bread slices in a mixture of ¾ cup beaten egg substitute, ¼ cup skim milk, and 1 teaspoon vanilla. Cook in a nonstick skillet coated with butter-flavored cooking spray until browned.

ROASTED SPICED PLUMS

These go well over low-fat ice cream or pound cake.

    4 plums, halved
    Vegetable cooking spray
    ½ cup orange juice
    ¼ cup packed brown sugar
    ½ teaspoon ground cinnamon
    ⅛ teaspoon freshly grated nutmeg
    ⅛ teaspoon ground cumin
    ⅛ teaspoon ground cardamom
    1 tablespoon slivered almonds, toasted

1. Preheat oven to 450°.
2. Place plum halves, cut sides up, in an 11 x 7-inch baking dish coated with cooking spray. Combine orange juice and next 5 ingredients. Drizzle orange juice mixture over plums. Bake at 450° for 20 minutes. Top with almonds. Yield: 4 servings (serving size: 2 plum halves and ¾ teaspoon almonds).

CALORIES 96 (13% from fat); FAT 1.4g (sat 0.1g, mono 0.8g, poly 0.3g); PROTEIN 1.1g; CARB 21.4g; FIBER 1.7g; CHOL 0mg; IRON 0.5mg; SODIUM 4mg; CALC 22mg

ROASTED PINEAPPLE WITH CILANTRO

You can top this dish with frozen yogurt.

    1 large pineapple, peeled and cored
    2 tablespoons pineapple juice
    1 tablespoon chopped fresh cilantro
    1 tablespoon honey
    ½ teaspoon ground ginger
    ⅛ teaspoon ground cloves

1. Preheat oven to 425°.
2. Cut pineapple into 10 wedges; place wedges on a jelly-roll pan. Combine pineapple juice and remaining 4 ingredients in a bowl; stir with a whisk. Drizzle juice mixture over pineapple. Bake at 425° for 20 minutes; broil for 2 minutes or until pineapple is browned. Yield: 5 servings (serving size: 2 pineapple wedges).

CALORIES 40 (5% from fat); FAT 0.2g (sat 0g, mono 0g, poly 0.1g); PROTEIN 0.2g; CARB 10.2g; FIBER 0.7g; CHOL 0mg; IRON 0.3mg; SODIUM 1mg; CALC 6mg

ROASTED SUMMER-FRUIT SALAD

Serve this unusual salad for brunch or as a side dish with pork or ham.

    1½ cups peeled, sliced papaya
    1½ cups peeled, sliced peaches or nectarines
    ¾ cup peeled, cubed ripe mango
    1 tablespoon fresh lime juice
    1 tablespoon margarine, melted
    1 teaspoon sugar
    ¼ cup plus 2 tablespoons balsamic vinegar

1. Preheat oven to 475°.
2. Place fruit in an 11 x 7-inch baking dish. Combine lime juice and margarine. Drizzle over fruit; sprinkle with sugar. Bake at 475° for 10 minutes.
3. Bring vinegar to a boil in a small saucepan; cook 3 minutes or until vinegar is reduced to 1½ tablespoons. Drizzle vinegar reduction over roasted fruit, and toss gently. Yield: 6 servings (serving size: ½ cup).

CALORIES 66 (27% from fat); FAT 2g (sat 0.4g, mono 0.9g, poly 0.6g); PROTEIN 0.6g; CARB 12.8g; FIBER 1.6g; CHOL 0mg; IRON 0.2mg; SODIUM 24mg; CALC 14mg

ROASTED BANANAS WITH BROWN SUGAR-WALNUT GLAZE

(pictured on page 261)

⅓ cup packed brown sugar
¼ cup fresh lemon juice
2 tablespoons reduced-calorie margarine, melted
¼ teaspoon ground cinnamon
4 large firm ripe bananas (about 1½ pounds)
Vegetable cooking spray
¼ cup chopped walnuts, toasted
1½ cups vanilla low-fat frozen yogurt

1. Preheat oven to 450°.
2. Combine first 4 ingredients in a bowl, and set aside.
3. Cut bananas in half lengthwise. Place banana halves, cut sides up, on a jelly-roll pan coated with cooking spray. Bake at 450° for 4 minutes. Drizzle sugar mixture evenly over banana halves; sprinkle with walnuts. Bake 3 additional minutes. Cut each banana piece into thirds crosswise. Serve bananas with frozen yogurt; drizzle with any remaining sugar mixture. Yield: 6 servings (serving size: 4 banana pieces and ¼ cup frozen yogurt).

CALORIES 237 (27% from fat); FAT 7g (sat 1.5g, mono 1.7g, poly 3.1g); PROTEIN 3.9g; CARB 44.5g; FIBER 3.7g; CHOL 5mg; IRON 0.7mg; SODIUM 58mg; CALC 66mg

ROASTED SWEET POTATO WEDGES

2 (8-ounce) sweet potatoes, peeled
1 teaspoon olive oil
½ teaspoon curry powder
¼ teaspoon salt
¼ teaspoon ground cumin
⅛ teaspoon ground cloves
⅛ teaspoon pepper

1. Preheat oven to 425°.
2. Cut sweet potatoes in half lengthwise; cut each half lengthwise into 6 wedges. Combine sweet potatoes, oil, and remaining ingredients in a bowl; toss gently to coat. Place wedges in a single layer on a baking sheet; bake at 425° for 25 minutes or until very tender. Yield: 4 servings (serving size: 6 wedges).

CALORIES 101 (13% from fat); FAT 1.5g (sat 0.2g, mono 0.9g, poly 0.2g); PROTEIN 1.5g; CARB 20.9g; FIBER 2.7g; CHOL 0mg; IRON 0.7mg; SODIUM 158mg; CALC 22mg

TOMATO-STUFFED ROASTED EGGPLANT WITH FETA

2 medium eggplants, cut in half lengthwise (about 2 pounds)
1¼ cups (¼-inch-thick) slices plum tomato (about 4 tomatoes)
1 tablespoon olive oil
1 tablespoon chopped fresh rosemary
1 tablespoon chopped fresh basil
¼ teaspoon salt
⅛ teaspoon pepper
2 garlic cloves, minced
¼ cup crumbled feta cheese
Basil sprigs (optional)

1. Preheat oven to 500°.
2. Cut each eggplant half lengthwise into ¼-inch-thick slices, starting 1 inch from stem end. Place eggplant halves on a baking sheet. Gently press slices open; place tomato slices between eggplant slices. Brush oil over eggplant; sprinkle with rosemary and next 4 ingredients. Bake at 500° for 15 minutes; sprinkle with cheese. Bake 4 additional minutes or until cheese begins to brown. Garnish with basil sprigs, if desired. Yield: 8 servings.

CALORIES 112 (43% from fat); FAT 5.4g (sat 1.6g, mono 3g, poly 0.4g); PROTEIN 3.6g; CARB 15g; FIBER 3.6g; CHOL 6mg; IRON 1.4mg; SODIUM 238mg; CALC 110mg

BALSAMIC ROASTED ONIONS

3 large sweet onions (about 1¾ pounds)
Vegetable cooking spray
¼ cup balsamic vinegar
1 tablespoon olive oil
1 teaspoon dried thyme
½ teaspoon dried basil
¼ teaspoon salt
⅛ teaspoon pepper

1. Preheat oven to 450°.
2. Peel onions, leaving roots intact; cut each onion into 6 wedges.
3. Place onion wedges in an 11 x 7-inch baking dish coated with cooking spray. Combine vinegar and remaining 5 ingredients; pour over onion wedges, tossing gently to coat. Cover; bake at 450° for 25 minutes. Uncover; bake 45 minutes or until tender. Yield: 6 servings (serving size: 1 cup).

CALORIES 72 (33% from fat); FAT 2.6g (sat 0.4g, mono 1.7g, poly 0.3g); PROTEIN 1.6g; CARB 11.8g; FIBER 2.5g; CHOL 0mg; IRON 0.7mg; SODIUM 102mg; CALC 33mg

ROASTED FENNEL

2 medium fennel bulbs
2 cups cubed red potato
1 cup red bell pepper strips
1 small red onion, cut into 8 wedges
1 tablespoon olive oil
½ teaspoon dried basil
½ teaspoon dried marjoram
¼ teaspoon salt
⅛ teaspoon pepper

1. Preheat oven to 425°.
2. Trim tough leaves from fennel; remove and discard stalks. Cut bulbs into quarters lengthwise; discard cores. Cut bulbs into 1-inch pieces to measure 4 cups. Combine fennel, potato, and remaining ingredients. Arrange in a single layer on a jelly-roll pan. Bake at 425° for 50 minutes or until tender, stirring once. Yield: 4 servings (serving size: 1 cup).

CALORIES 132 (27% from fat); FAT 3.9g (sat 0.5g, mono 2.5g, poly 0.4g); PROTEIN 4.5g; CARB 21.9g; FIBER 2.3g; CHOL 0mg; IRON 3.6mg; SODIUM 161mg; CALC 105mg

The Beef Goes On

These satisfying, no-fuss recipes come together in a flash on a busy weekday.

When you have recipes for minestrone, chili, and lasagna, you're talking stick-to-the-ribs food. But when you're caught in rush-hour traffic, you don't think of these dishes as meals you can throw together in a hurry when you get home. Now, with our shortcuts, you can change the way you think about them.

LINGUINE WITH SPICY BEEF AND ARTICHOKES

Preparation time: 17 minutes
Cooking time: 22 minutes

½ **pound ground round**
2 **cups low-fat vegetable primavera spaghetti sauce**
1 **cup water**
2 **tablespoons tomato paste**
½ **teaspoon dried crushed red pepper**
3 **garlic cloves, crushed**
1 **(14-ounce) can quartered artichoke hearts, drained**
5 **cups hot cooked linguine (about 10 ounces uncooked pasta)**

1. Cook ground round in a large nonstick skillet over medium-high heat until browned, stirring to crumble. Drain well, and return meat to skillet. Add spaghetti sauce and next 4 ingredients, stirring well. Bring to a boil; reduce heat, and simmer, uncovered, 10 minutes. Stir in artichokes; cover and simmer 2 minutes. Serve meat mixture over linguine. Yield: 5 servings (serving size: 1 cup pasta and 1 cup sauce).

CALORIES 345 (10% from fat); FAT 3.8g (sat 1.1g, mono 1.3g, poly 0.6g); PROTEIN 20.6g; CARB 56.9g; FIBER 1.7g; CHOL 28mg; IRON 4.5mg; SODIUM 505mg; CALC 65mg

LAZY LASAGNA

Lasagna typically takes longer to put together than it does to cook. Precooked noodles and prepackaged convenience products, however, make this a zip to prepare.
Preparation time: 15 minutes
Cooking time: 35 minutes

1 **pound ground round**
1 **(26-ounce) jar low-fat spaghetti sauce**
1 **(16-ounce) carton fat-free cottage cheese**
2 **tablespoons grated Parmesan cheese**
Vegetable cooking spray
1 **(8-ounce) package precooked lasagna noodles**
1 **cup (4 ounces) preshredded reduced-fat mild Cheddar cheese, divided**
Chopped fresh parsley (optional)

1. Preheat oven to 350°.
2. Cook ground round in a large nonstick skillet over medium-high heat until browned, stirring to crumble. Drain well, and return meat to skillet. Add sauce; bring to a boil. Reduce heat, and simmer 5 minutes. Combine cottage cheese and Parmesan cheese in a bowl.
3. Spread ½ cup meat mixture in bottom of a 13 x 9-inch baking dish coated with cooking spray. Arrange 4 noodles over meat mixture; top with half of cottage cheese mixture, 1 cup meat mixture, and ⅓ cup Cheddar cheese. Repeat layers, ending with noodles. Spread remaining meat mixture over noodles. Cover and bake at 350° for 30 minutes. Uncover; sprinkle with ⅓ cup Cheddar cheese, and bake 5 additional minutes or until cheese melts. Let stand 10 minutes before serving. Garnish with parsley, if desired. Yield: 9 servings.

CALORIES 275 (20% from fat); FAT 6.2g (sat 2.8g, mono 2.1g, poly 0.4g); PROTEIN 28.1g; CARB 26.1g; FIBER 1.9g; CHOL 43mg; IRON 2.8mg; SODIUM 584mg; CALC 181mg

FRENCH-STYLE BEEF AND BOW TIES

Preparation time: 20 minutes
Cooking time: 12 minutes

¼ **cup red wine vinegar**
3 **tablespoons no-salt-added beef broth**
1½ **tablespoons extra-virgin olive oil**
1 **tablespoon honey mustard**
½ **teaspoon pepper**
¼ **teaspoon salt**
3 **cups hot cooked farfalle (about 6 ounces uncooked bow tie pasta)**
2 **cups diced zucchini**
2 **cups chopped plum tomato**
⅓ **cup chopped fresh parsley**
4 **ounces sliced lean deli roast beef, cut into ½-inch-wide strips**

1. Combine first 6 ingredients, stirring with a wire whisk. Combine pasta and remaining 4 ingredients in a large bowl; add dressing, tossing to coat. Yield: 4 servings (serving size: 2 cups).

CALORIES 268 (30% from fat); FAT 8.9g (sat 1.6g, mono 4.8g, poly 0.9g); PROTEIN 12.3g; CARB 35.9g; FIBER 3.6g; CHOL 23mg; IRON 3.4mg; SODIUM 436mg; CALC 34mg

FUSILLI WITH CURRIED BEEF AND CAULIFLOWER

Preparation time: 15 minutes
Cooking time: 25 minutes

1 **cup no-salt-added beef broth**
½ **cup plain fat-free yogurt**
1 **tablespoon cornstarch**
2 **teaspoons curry powder**
½ **teaspoon salt**
¼ **teaspoon pepper**
2 **teaspoons olive oil**
½ **pound lean, boned sirloin steak, cut into ½-inch cubes**
Vegetable cooking spray
4 **cups small cauliflower florets**
½ **cup water**
1 **cup frozen green peas, thawed**
4 **cups hot cooked fusilli (about 8 ounces uncooked twisted pasta)**

1. Combine first 6 ingredients in a small bowl; stir well with a whisk. Set aside.

2. Heat oil in a large nonstick skillet over medium-high heat. Add steak cubes, and sauté 5 minutes or until browned. Remove from skillet, and set aside. Wipe skillet dry with paper towels. Coat skillet with cooking spray; place over medium heat until hot. Add cauliflower; sauté 3 minutes. Add water; cover, reduce heat, and simmer 4 minutes. Return meat to skillet; stir in broth mixture and peas. Bring to a boil; cook 2 minutes, stirring gently. Serve over pasta. Yield: 4 servings (serving size: 1 cup pasta and 1 cup meat mixture).

CALORIES 389 (16% from fat); FAT 6.8g (sat 2g, mono 3.2g, poly 0.8g); PROTEIN 25.3g; CARB 54.9g; FIBER 5g; CHOL 38mg; IRON 4.8mg; SODIUM 419mg; CALC 106mg

FOUR-LAYER CHILI WITH BEANS

Preparation time : 15 minutes
Cooking time: 30 minutes

¾ pound ground round
2 garlic cloves, minced
2 teaspoons chili powder
1 teaspoon ground cinnamon
¾ teaspoon ground cumin
2 cups water
¾ teaspoon salt
¼ teaspoon pepper
2 (14.5-ounce) cans no-salt-added stewed tomatoes, undrained
1 (15-ounce) can kidney beans, drained
4½ cups hot cooked vermicelli (about 9 ounces uncooked pasta)
¼ cup plus 2 tablespoons diced onion
¼ cup plus 2 tablespoons (1½ ounces) shredded reduced-fat sharp Cheddar cheese

1. Cook ground round and garlic in a Dutch oven over medium-high heat until meat is browned, stirring to crumble. Drain well, and return meat mixture to Dutch oven. Add chili powder, cinnamon, and cumin; cook 1 minute. Add water and next 4 ingredients; bring to a boil. Reduce heat, and simmer 20 minutes. Serve chili over pasta; top with onion and cheese. Yield: 6 servings (serving size: ¾ cup pasta, 1 cup chili, 1 tablespoon onion, and 1 tablespoon cheese).

CALORIES 352 (12% from fat); FAT 4.8g (sat 1.8g, mono 1.5g, poly 0.7g); PROTEIN 25.8g; CARB 51.6g; FIBER 3.9g; CHOL 37mg; IRON 5.3mg; SODIUM 497mg; CALC 138mg

THAI BEEF-AND-NOODLE SALAD

You can find plum sauce in the Asian-foods section of most supermarkets near the soy sauce and other Asian condiments.
Preparation time: 20 minutes
Cooking time: 15 minutes

1 (9-ounce) package frozen French-cut green beans, thawed
4 cups hot cooked linguine (about 8 ounces uncooked pasta)
4 ounces sliced deli roast beef, cut into 1-inch-wide strips
¼ cup chopped fresh cilantro
¼ cup plum sauce
2 tablespoons lime juice
1 tablespoon low-sodium soy sauce
½ teaspoon pepper
¼ teaspoon salt

1. Arrange beans in a steamer basket over boiling water. Cover and steam 5 minutes or until crisp-tender. Rinse beans under cold water; drain. Combine beans, pasta, beef, and cilantro in a large bowl.

2. Combine plum sauce and remaining 4 ingredients in a small bowl. Add plum sauce mixture to pasta mixture, and toss to coat. Serve salad at room temperature or chilled. Yield: 4 servings (serving size: 1½ cups).

CALORIES 176 (15% from fat); FAT 2.9g (sat 0.9g, mono 0.9g, poly 0.3g); PROTEIN 9.7g; CARB 28.4g; FIBER 3g; CHOL 23mg; IRON 2.4mg; SODIUM 838mg; CALC 46mg

HEARTY BEEF, PASTA, AND SPINACH MINESTRONE

Preparation time: 5 minutes
Cooking time: 40 minutes

½ pound ground round
6 cups water
1 (14.5-ounce) can no-salt-added stewed tomatoes, undrained and chopped
1 (4.4-ounce) package minestrone soup mix (such as Lipton's Kettle Creations)
½ cup uncooked ditalini (very short tubular-shaped pasta)
1 (10-ounce) package frozen chopped spinach, thawed, drained, and squeezed dry

1. Cook ground round in a large Dutch oven over medium heat until browned, stirring to crumble. Drain well, and return meat to Dutch oven. Stir in water, tomato, and soup mix; bring to a boil. Reduce heat, and simmer, uncovered, 10 minutes, stirring occasionally. Stir in pasta and spinach; simmer for 7 minutes or until pasta is tender. Yield: 4 servings (serving size: 2 cups).

CALORIES 281 (12% from fat); FAT 3.7g (sat 0.9g, mono 1.0g, poly 0.3g); PROTEIN 22g; CARB 40.4g; FIBER 5.6g; CHOL 32mg; IRON 4.9mg; SODIUM 851mg; CALC 129mg

Heroic Sandwiches

To build a better sandwich, don't hold the veggies.

Sandwiches can be wraps—ingredients rolled into a tortilla or other similar bread; they can be grilled on French bread; or they may even be panini or little Italian appetizer morsels. These selections will have you opening wide.

HUMMUS CLUB SANDWICHES

(pictured on page 261)

3 tablespoons plain fat-free yogurt
2 tablespoons water
1 tablespoon lemon juice
1 tablespoon tahini (sesame-seed paste)
½ teaspoon ground cumin
¼ teaspoon salt
2 garlic cloves, peeled
1 (15½-ounce) can chickpeas (garbanzo beans), drained
12 (1-ounce) slices whole-wheat bread
2 cups shredded Bibb lettuce
8 (¼-inch-thick) slices tomato
4 (¼-inch-thick) slices red onion
1 cup (⅛-inch-thick) slices cucumber
4 cups alfalfa sprouts (4 ounces)

1. Combine first 8 ingredients in a food processor; process until smooth.
2. Spread 2 tablespoons chickpea mixture over 1 bread slice; top with ½ cup lettuce, 2 tomato slices, 1 onion slice, 1 bread slice, ¼ cup cucumber, 1 cup sprouts, and 1 bread slice. Cut sandwich diagonally into quarters; secure with wooden picks. Repeat with remaining ingredients. Yield: 4 sandwiches.

CALORIES 382 (16% from fat); FAT 6.8g (sat 1g, mono 1.8g, poly 3g); PROTEIN 18.8g; CARB 67.7g; FIBER 7.7g; CHOL 3mg; IRON 5mg; SODIUM 757mg; CALC 180mg

GREEK-SALAD PITAS

1 cup peeled, seeded, diced cucumber
1 cup diced red bell pepper
1 cup diced green bell pepper
½ cup crumbled feta cheese
¼ cup diced red onion
¼ cup chopped pepperoncini peppers
¼ cup kalamata olives, pitted and chopped
2 tablespoons lemon juice
2 teaspoons dried oregano
1 teaspoon extra-virgin olive oil
¼ teaspoon ground white pepper
4 (6-inch) pita bread rounds, cut in half
8 curly leaf lettuce leaves

1. Combine first 11 ingredients in a large bowl; toss gently. Line each pita half with a lettuce leaf; fill with ½ cup salad mixture. Yield: 4 servings (serving size: 2 stuffed pita halves).

CALORIES 211 (30% from fat); FAT 7g (sat 2.9g, mono 2.7g, poly 1.1g); PROTEIN 7.3g; CARB 31g; FIBER 3.3g; CHOL 14mg; IRON 3.3mg; SODIUM 580mg; CALC 142mg

SHANGHAI TOFU BURGERS WITH CHINESE SLAW

The Chinese Slaw can also be served as a side salad.

½ cup minced green onions
¼ cup pineapple juice
1 tablespoon low-sodium tamari or soy sauce
2 teaspoons peeled, minced fresh gingerroot
2 teaspoons sesame seeds, toasted
1½ teaspoons dark sesame oil
1 teaspoon chile paste with garlic
2 garlic cloves, minced
1 pound firm tofu, drained
Vegetable cooking spray
8 (1½-ounce) hamburger buns
Chinese Slaw
½ cup Roasted Red Bell Pepper Sauce (page 255)

1. Combine first 8 ingredients in a shallow dish. Cut tofu lengthwise into 8 (½-inch-thick) slices. Add tofu to dish, and spoon green onion mixture over tofu. Cover and marinate in refrigerator at least 1 hour, turning tofu occasionally.
2. Preheat oven to 425°.
3. Place tofu on a baking sheet coated with cooking spray. Bake at 425° for 20 minutes or until lightly browned. Place 1 tofu slice on bottom half of a bun; top with ½ cup Chinese Slaw. Drizzle with 1 tablespoon Roasted Red Bell Pepper Sauce; cover with top half of bun. Repeat procedure with remaining ingredients. Yield: 8 sandwiches.

CALORIES 217 (29% from fat); FAT 7g (sat 1.1g, mono 2.2g, poly 3.2g); PROTEIN 9.7g; CARB 29.6g; FIBER 2.6g; CHOL 1mg; IRON 5.1mg; SODIUM 443mg; CALC 160mg

Chinese Slaw:

4 cups shredded green cabbage
¾ cup diagonally sliced green onions
½ cup shredded carrot
½ cup thinly sliced red bell pepper
2 tablespoons low-sodium tamari or soy sauce
1 tablespoon sesame seeds, toasted
1 tablespoon peeled, grated fresh gingerroot
1 tablespoon mirin (sweet rice wine)
1 tablespoon rice vinegar
1½ teaspoons dark sesame oil
2 teaspoons sugar

1. Combine all ingredients in a large bowl. Let stand at least 15 minutes. Yield: 8 servings (serving size: ½ cup).

CALORIES 34 (44% from fat); FAT 1.6g (sat 0.2g, mono 0.6g, poly 0.7g); PROTEIN 1g; CARB 4.1g; FIBER 1g; CHOL 0mg; IRON 0.7mg; SODIUM 125mg; CALC 58mg

GRILLED PORTOBELLO CLUB

2 tablespoons balsamic vinegar
2 tablespoons lemon juice
2 tablespoons water
1 teaspoon extra-virgin olive oil
2 teaspoons dried Italian seasoning
1 teaspoon minced fresh rosemary
½ teaspoon pepper
2 garlic cloves, minced
4 (4-inch) portobello mushroom caps
Vegetable cooking spray
¼ cup Roasted Red Bell Pepper Sauce
4 (2-ounce) Kaiser rolls or onion buns
4 (½-ounce) slices provolone cheese
2 romaine lettuce leaves, halved
4 (¼-inch-thick) slices tomato

1. Combine first 9 ingredients in a large zip-top plastic bag; seal and marinate 30 minutes. Remove mushrooms from bag, reserving marinade.
2. Prepare grill or broiler. Place mushrooms on grill rack or rack of a broiler pan coated with cooking spray; grill or broil 6 minutes on each side or until browned, basting occasionally with reserved marinade. Spread 1½ teaspoons Roasted Red Bell Pepper Sauce over cut sides of 1 roll. Place 1 mushroom cap on bottom half of roll; top with 1 cheese slice, 1 lettuce leaf half, 1 tomato slice, and roll top. Repeat procedure with remaining ingredients. Yield: 4 sandwiches.

CALORIES 274 (30% from fat); FAT 9g (sat 2.7g, mono 1.4g, poly 0.9g); PROTEIN 11.4g; CARB 38.7g; FIBER 1.9g; CHOL 10mg; IRON 4.8mg; SODIUM 542mg; CALC 157mg

ROASTED RED BELL PEPPER SAUCE

This versatile sauce is used in both Grilled Portobello Club and Shanghai Tofu Burgers.

1 cup bottled roasted red bell peppers
½ cup tomato juice
2 tablespoons chopped sun-dried tomatoes, packed without oil (about 1 ounce)
2 tablespoons balsamic vinegar
2 tablespoons tomato paste
½ teaspoon pepper
2 garlic cloves

1. Combine all ingredients in a blender or food processor; cover and process until smooth. Yield: 1½ cups (serving size: 1 tablespoon).
Note: Store pepper sauce in an airtight container in refrigerator for up to 2 weeks.

CALORIES 5 (20% from fat); FAT 0.1g (sat 0g, mono 0g, poly 0.1g); PROTEIN 0.2g; CARB 1.2g; FIBER 0.1g; CHOL 0mg; IRON 0.2mg; SODIUM 40mg; CALC 2mg

EGGLESS EGG-SALAD SANDWICH

1 pound firm tofu, drained
½ cup diced celery
½ cup diced red onion
¼ cup shredded carrot
1 tablespoon miso (soybean paste)
1 teaspoon ground turmeric
1 teaspoon curry powder
2 teaspoons Dijon mustard
½ teaspoon salt
10 (1-ounce) slices pumpernickel bread
15 (⅛-inch-thick) slices cucumber
5 Bibb lettuce leaves
10 (⅛-inch-thick) slices large tomato

1. Combine first 9 ingredients in a bowl; beat at medium speed of an electric mixer until combined (mixture will not be smooth). Spread ⅔ cup tofu mixture evenly over 1 bread slice; top with 3 cucumber slices, 1 lettuce leaf, 2 tomato slices, and 1 bread slice. Repeat procedure with remaining ingredients. Yield: 5 sandwiches.

CALORIES 242 (21% from fat); FAT 5.6g (sat 0.8g, mono1.1g, poly 3g); PROTEIN 13.9g; CARB 38g; FIBER 6.1g; CHOL 1mg; IRON 7mg; SODIUM 765mg; CALC 165mg

GARDEN GRILLED CHEESE

To flatten the sandwiches as they cook, place another skillet on top of them.

2 tablespoons plus 2 teaspoons Dijon mustard
8 (1-ounce) slices sourdough bread
1 cup (4 ounces) shredded reduced-fat sharp Cheddar cheese
½ cup drained canned artichoke hearts, sliced
1⅓ cups sliced bottled roasted red bell peppers
Vegetable cooking spray

1. Spread 2 teaspoons mustard on 1 bread slice; top with ¼ cup cheese, 2 tablespoons artichokes, ⅓ cup bell peppers, and 1 bread slice. Repeat procedure with remaining mustard, bread, cheese, artichokes, and bell peppers.
2. Heat a large nonstick skillet coated with cooking spray over medium heat until hot. Add sandwiches; cook 2 minutes on each side or until golden. Yield: 4 sandwiches.

CALORIES 264 (26% from fat); FAT 7.6g (sat 3.2g, mono1.5g, poly 0.3g); PROTEIN 14.8g; CARB 34.7g; FIBER 0.9g; CHOL 19mg; IRON 2.9mg; SODIUM 951mg; CALC 321mg

PROVENÇALE HERO

- 2 tablespoons water
- 2 tablespoons lemon juice
- 2 tablespoons balsamic vinegar
- 1 tablespoon minced fresh rosemary or 1 teaspoon dried rosemary
- 2 teaspoons dried Italian seasoning
- 2 teaspoons olive oil
- ½ teaspoon pepper
- 2 garlic cloves, minced
- 2 cups (1-inch) peeled, cubed eggplant (about 1 medium)
- 1½ cups (1-inch) cubed yellow squash (about 2 small)
- 1 cup (1-inch) pieces red bell pepper (about 1 large)
- ¾ cup (1-inch) cubed zucchini (about 1 small)
- 1 cup (1-inch) cubed tomato (about 1 large)
- 1 (16-ounce) loaf French bread, cut in half lengthwise
- 6 (1-ounce) slices part-skim mozzarella cheese

1. Preheat oven to 425°.
2. Combine first 8 ingredients in a large bowl; stir with a whisk. Add eggplant and next 3 ingredients; toss gently. Place vegetable mixture in a jelly-roll pan. Bake at 425° for 20 minutes or until vegetables are tender, stirring occasionally.
3. Combine roasted vegetables and tomato; toss gently. Arrange vegetable mixture on bottom half of loaf; top with cheese slices and top half of loaf. Place loaf on a jelly-roll pan, and bake at 425° for 5 minutes or until cheese melts. Cut loaf crosswise into 6 pieces. Yield: 6 sandwiches.

CALORIES 339 (21% from fat); FAT 8g (sat 3.6g, mono 3.2g, poly 1.2g); PROTEIN 15.3g; CARB 50.5g; FIBER 3.8g; CHOL 19mg; IRON 3.3mg; SODIUM 577mg; CALC 257mg

---

Show Me the Cookie

Audry Jagels from St. Louis, Missouri, puts us to the test by asking us to lighten her Oatmeal-Spice Cookies, a family favorite for 30 years.

BEFORE & AFTER	
SERVING SIZE	
1 cookie	
CALORIES	
106	79
FAT	
5.3g	2.1g
PERCENT OF TOTAL CALORIES	
45%	24%

OATMEAL-SPICE COOKIES

Generous amounts of cinnamon, nutmeg, and ginger give this cookie its spicy kick. If you prefer a milder flavor, you can cut the amount of spices in half.

- 1½ cups all-purpose flour
- 1 teaspoon baking soda
- 1 teaspoon ground cinnamon
- 1 teaspoon ground nutmeg
- ½ teaspoon salt
- ½ teaspoon ground ginger
- 1 cup packed brown sugar
- ½ cup granulated sugar
- ½ cup stick margarine, softened
- 3 tablespoons light-colored corn syrup
- 1½ teaspoons vanilla extract
- 2 large egg whites
- 1 large egg
- 3 cups quick-cooking oats
- 1⅓ cups raisins
- Vegetable cooking spray

1. Preheat oven to 350°.
2. Combine first 6 ingredients in a small bowl. Combine brown sugar and next 6 ingredients in a large bowl; beat at medium speed of an electric mixer until well-blended. Stir in oats and raisins; let stand 5 minutes. Stir in flour mixture.
3. Drop dough by level tablespoonfuls 2 inches apart onto baking sheets coated with cooking spray. Bake at 350° for 10 minutes or until lightly browned. Remove cookies from baking sheets, and cool on wire racks. Yield: 4½ dozen (serving size: 1 cookie).
Note: Store cookies in an airtight container for up to 1 week.

CALORIES 79 (24% from fat); FAT 2.1g (sat 0.4g, mono 0.9g, poly 0.7g); PROTEIN 1.5g; CARB 13.9g; FIBER 0.8g; CHOL 4mg; IRON 0.5mg; SODIUM 71mg; CALC 9mg

---

BAKING KNOW-HOW

- When measuring flour, stir the flour in its storage container, and then lightly scoop it into a measuring cup, leveling it off with a flat spatula. (Don't pack it down.)

- If the spices and leavening ingredients (baking powder and baking soda) are lumpy when you measure them, put them in a small metal sieve, and sift them into the flour. Otherwise, they may create yellowish spots and bitter pockets in the cookie.

- Bake cookies in a preheated oven on the middle rack, where air circulation is best and heat distribution is even.

Journey to a French Farmhouse

While living in France, Susan Herrmann Loomis goes in search of recipes from farmhouse cooks. In their kitchens, she discovers a simple, robust cuisine that fits perfectly into our own lifestyles.

French-style farmhouse food reflects the seasons, is ultimately satisfying, and offers the best possible flavors because it's in its prime. Its basis consists of vegetables, poultry, a regular infusion of fish, and wonderful bread. Meat is often only used as a seasoning or as a small element of a meal, for it's a valuable commodity that a farmer would often rather sell than eat.

Though this cuisine is simple, it has the depth and layering of flavor found in the finest French restaurants for which it provides inspiration. Why? The French farm cook understands her ingredients, encourages their flavor, then gets out of the way.

The French eat seasonal ingredients, take the time to prepare and savor them, and rarely eat between meals—valuable lessons and a key to healthful living.

French farm cooks are therefore worth emulating. We may not all be able to step outside the back door into the garden and choose our supper, but we can all follow the seasons and buy from local farmers and farmers' markets. That's the first step, and perhaps the most important, in making food as healthful and delicious as that prepared on a French farm.

MENU

PORK BRAISED IN MILK
WITH APPLES

Parslied potatoes

SEMOLINA PUDDING
CAKE

PORK BRAISED IN MILK WITH APPLES

Braising the pork in milk makes it tender; browning it in oil and butter contributes an extralush layer of flavor. This recipe serves six, so you may have leftover cooked pork for making sandwiches.

1	(3¼-pound) lean, boned pork loin roast
2	teaspoons olive oil
2	teaspoons butter
3	cups thinly sliced onion, separated into rings
4	cups 2% low-fat milk
2	bay leaves
1	teaspoon dried thyme
½	teaspoon salt
¼	teaspoon pepper
2	garlic cloves, minced
2½	pounds cooking apples, cut into 1-inch pieces
3	tablespoons water

1. Trim fat from pork. Heat oil and butter in a large Dutch oven over medium-high heat. Add pork, and cook 6 minutes, browning on all sides. Remove pork from Dutch oven. Set aside, and keep warm. Add onion to Dutch oven, and sauté over medium heat 7 minutes or until browned. Set aside.

2. While onion cooks, combine milk and bay leaves in a large heavy saucepan. Cook over medium-high heat to 180° or until tiny bubbles form around edge (do not boil). Remove from heat.

3. Rub pork with dried thyme and next 3 ingredients; insert meat thermometer into thickest portion of pork. Return pork to Dutch oven; add milk mixture. Cover; bring to a simmer over medium heat. Reduce heat to low; cook 1 hour and 15 minutes or until meat thermometer registers 160° (slightly pink), turning once. (Do not boil.) Discard bay leaves. Remove pork from Dutch oven, reserving 2¼ cups braising liquid. Discard remaining braising liquid.

4. While pork cooks, combine apples and water in a large saucepan. Cover; cook over medium heat 15 minutes or until tender, stirring occasionally. Partially mash apples with a fork.

5. Thinly slice pork; serve with reserved braising liquid and apples. Yield: 6 servings (serving size: 3 ounces pork, about ⅓ cup braising liquid, and ½ cup cooked apples).

CALORIES 328 (22% from fat); FAT 7.9g (sat 3.1g, mono 3.3g, poly 0.8g); PROTEIN 27.6g; CARB 38.2g; FIBER 7.0g; CHOL 84mg; IRON 2.3mg; SODIUM 307mg; CALC 139mg

SEMOLINA PUDDING CAKE

This cake is a cross between a pudding cake and a soufflé. Look for semolina flour next to the flour and sugar in the supermarket. And don't worry about testing this cake for doneness. Instead, trust the time and temperature so you don't overcook it. If you insert a toothpick into the cake, the center will always be soft.

    1 cup sugar, divided
Vegetable cooking spray
    4 cups skim milk
    1 (3-inch) piece vanilla bean,
         split lengthwise, or
         1 tablespoon vanilla extract
    ¾ cup plus 1 tablespoon semolina
         flour (pasta flour)
Dash of salt
    3 large eggs, lightly beaten
    ¼ teaspoon ground nutmeg

1. Place ½ cup sugar in a small heavy saucepan over medium heat, and cook until sugar is golden (about 5 minutes). Immediately pour sugar syrup into a 1½-quart soufflé dish coated with cooking spray, tipping quickly until syrup coats bottom of dish.
2. Combine milk and ½ cup sugar in a large heavy saucepan; stir well. Scrape seeds from vanilla bean; add seeds and bean to milk mixture. Cook over medium-high heat to 180° or until tiny bubbles form around edge (do not boil). Remove from heat (add extract at this point if using in place of vanilla bean); cover and let stand 10 minutes. Discard bean.
3. Preheat oven to 375°.
4. Place milk mixture over medium heat. Gradually add flour and salt, stirring constantly with a whisk. Cook, stirring constantly, 12 minutes or until mixture is thick and bubbly. Gradually add hot milk mixture to eggs, stirring constantly with a whisk; stir in nutmeg. Spoon mixture into prepared dish.
5. Bake at 375° for 45 minutes or until puffy and almost set. (Cake will be slightly "jiggly" in center.) Cool in dish 5 minutes. (Cake will deflate slightly upon standing.) Loosen cake from sides of dish using a narrow metal spatula. Place a plate upside down on top of cake; invert onto plate. Serve warm or chilled. Yield: 8 servings.

CALORIES 238 (10% from fat); FAT 2.6g (sat 1g, mono 1.1g, poly 0.4g); PROTEIN 8.8g; CARB 44.5g; FIBER 0.6g; CHOL 85mg; IRON 0.4mg; SODIUM 92mg; CALC 160mg

---

> ### MENU
> #### VEGETABLE POTAGE
> #### CHICKEN WITH GARLIC CROUTONS
> #### PROVENÇALE POTATO RAGOÛT WITH GREEN OLIVES
> #### PEACHES IN RED WINE

VEGETABLE POTAGE

This soup can be served chunky or pureed. Always simple and fresh, it varies according to the season. If you can't find all of the following vegetables, just use whatever you have on hand.

    5 cups water
    2 cups peeled, chopped celeriac
 1½ cups sliced carrots
 1¼ cups diced onion
    1 cup peeled, diced potato
    1 cup chopped Granny Smith
         apple (1 large apple)
    1 cup sliced leek
    ½ cup peeled, chopped Jerusalem
         artichoke
    ¾ teaspoon salt
    3 thyme sprigs
    2 garlic cloves
    2 bay leaves

1. Combine all ingredients in a Dutch oven; bring to a boil. Cover, reduce heat, and simmer 40 minutes or until vegetables are tender. Discard thyme and bay leaves. Place vegetable mixture in a blender in 2 batches; cover and process until smooth. Yield: 7 servings (serving size: 1 cup).

CALORIES 90 (4% from fat); FAT 0.4g (sat 0.1g, mono 0.1g, poly 0.2g); PROTEIN 2.2g; CARB 21.2g; FIBER 3.3g; CHOL 0mg; IRON 1.4mg; SODIUM 309mg; CALC 47mg

---

CHICKEN WITH GARLIC CROUTONS

(pictured on page 261)

  12 ounces French bread, cut into
         2-inch cubes
    1 (4-pound) roasting chicken
    ½ teaspoon salt
    ¼ teaspoon coarsely ground
         pepper
    1 navel orange, halved
    2 bay leaves
Vegetable cooking spray
    4 garlic cloves, minced
Thyme sprigs (optional)

1. Preheat oven to 450°.
2. Place bread cubes on a baking sheet. Bake at 450° for 5 minutes.
3. Remove and discard giblets and neck from chicken. Rinse under cold water; pat dry. Trim excess fat. Sprinkle salt and pepper over chicken. Squeeze orange over a bowl to extract juice. Place 1 orange half, bay leaves, and 3 tablespoons orange juice in neck cavity. Lift wing tips up and over back; tuck under chicken. Place chicken, breast side up, on rack of a broiler pan coated with cooking spray. Pierce skin several times with a meat fork. Insert meat thermometer into meaty part of thigh, making sure not to touch bone.
4. Bake chicken at 450° for 50 minutes or until thermometer registers 180°. Place croutons around chicken; bake 10 additional minutes. Remove chicken from pan, reserving pan drippings. Cover chicken loosely with aluminum foil; let stand 10 minutes. Discard skin. Arrange croutons on a jelly-roll pan. Drizzle pan drippings and garlic over croutons; stir to coat. Bake at 450° for 5 minutes or until crisp. Garnish with thyme sprigs, if desired. Yield: 6 servings (serving size: 3 ounces chicken and 1 cup croutons).

CALORIES 353 (31% from fat); FAT 12g (sat 2.6g, mono 6.1g, poly 2.3g); PROTEIN 29.9g; CARB 33g; FIBER 1.4g; CHOL 77mg; IRON 2.3mg; SODIUM 500mg; CALC 42mg

PROVENÇALE POTATO RAGOÛT WITH GREEN OLIVES

A ragoût (ra-GOO) is a well-seasoned stewlike dish; this one, unlike most, is meatless. When cooked, the potatoes should be so soft that they fall apart; this helps thicken the dish.

1½ tablespoons olive oil
1½ cups thinly sliced onion
3½ cups seeded, coarsely chopped tomato
4 cups peeled, cubed baking potato (about 2 pounds)
1½ cups water
¼ teaspoon salt
¼ teaspoon pepper
6 thyme sprigs
3 garlic cloves, crushed
3 bay leaves
½ cup sliced green olives

1. Heat oil in a large nonstick skillet over medium-high heat. Add onion, and sauté 10 minutes or until soft.
2. Add tomato; cook 10 minutes or until liquid almost evaporates, stirring frequently. Add potato and next 6 ingredients; bring to boil. Cover, reduce heat, and simmer 40 minutes or until potato is tender, stirring occasionally.
3. Stir in olives; cook 5 minutes. Discard thyme and bay leaves. Yield: 6 servings (serving size: about ¾ cup).

CALORIES 188 (29% from fat); FAT 6.1g (sat 0.9g, mono 4.2g, poly 0.9g); PROTEIN 4.2g; CARB 31.9g; FIBER 4.7g; CHOL 0mg; IRON 2.1mg; SODIUM 255mg; CALC 37mg

WINE PICKS

- PORK BRAISED IN MILK WITH APPLES: *Domaine Tempier Bandol Rouge 1994, (French red), $20*

- CHICKEN WITH GARLIC CROUTONS: *A. Rafanelli Zinfandel 1995 (California red), $18 and/or Ridge Lytton Springs Zinfandel 1995, (California red), $22.50*

PEACHES IN RED WINE

(pictured on page 262)

Leaving the peels on the peaches helps them retain their shape and texture and cuts down on preparation time. Wash the fuzz off the peel before using.

¼ cup sugar
¼ cup orange rind strips (about 1 orange)
¼ cup lemon rind strips (about 2 large lemons)
⅛ teaspoon ground cardamom
7 whole cloves
4 black peppercorns
1 (3-inch) cinnamon stick
1 (750-milliliter) bottle dry red wine (such as Côtes du Rhône)
6 cups fresh sliced peaches (about 2¼ pounds)

1. Combine first 8 ingredients in a large saucepan. Bring to a boil over medium-high heat; cook 10 minutes or until wine mixture is reduced to 1½ cups. Cool to room temperature.
2. Strain mixture through a sieve over a bowl; discard solids. Combine wine mixture and peaches in a bowl; cover and chill 4 hours, stirring occasionally. Yield: 6 servings (serving size: 1 cup).

CALORIES 112 (2% from fat); FAT 0.2g (sat 0g, mono 0.1g, poly 0.1g); PROTEIN 1.4g; CARB 28.9g; FIBER 2.7g; CHOL 0mg; IRON 0.7mg; SODIUM 10mg; CALC 18mg

PEAR CLAFOUTI

The keys to a successful clafouti (cla-foo-TEE) are minimal use of flour and a hot oven. This recipe can replace the dessert in either menu.

Vegetable cooking spray
1 teaspoon all-purpose flour
2 cups peeled, cubed pear
¾ cup all-purpose flour
¼ teaspoon salt
⅛ teaspoon nutmeg
2 cups 1% low-fat milk, divided
3 large eggs, lightly beaten
½ cup sugar
½ teaspoon vanilla extract

1. Preheat oven to 375°.
2. Coat a 10-inch deep-dish pie plate with cooking spray, and dust plate with 1 teaspoon flour. Arrange pear cubes in bottom of prepared dish.
3. Combine ¾ cup flour, salt, and nutmeg in a bowl. Gradually add 1 cup milk, stirring with a whisk until well-blended. Add 1 cup milk, eggs, sugar, and vanilla extract, stirring until smooth. Pour batter over pear cubes. Bake mixture at 375° for 35 minutes or until set. Yield: 6 servings (serving size: 1 wedge).

CALORIES 230 (15% from fat); FAT 3.9g (sat 1.3g, mono 1g, poly 0.5g); PROTEIN 7.7g; CARB 41.1g; FIBER 1.8g; CHOL 113mg; IRON 1.3mg; SODIUM 171mg; CALC 121mg

THE KERR PACKAGE

Sharing a Piece of the Pie

I hope the metaphor I've used in this column during the past few months—that of a simple dining chair—has helped you. I started with four legs of food, exercise, friendship, and reflection, and fit those legs into a seat representing healthy self-awareness. With this support, we can enjoy life with balance and perspective. Isn't that what good health is all about?

Let's call the final part of the chair "personal values." While this is a highly individual matter, I feel that personal values must be related to one's surrounding community. It's been said, "The common good is the good we do in common."

My wife, Treena, and I have made choices about the way we eat that have given us a great deal of joy by sharing in the "common good." We trimmed back our food budget and set the savings aside each month. We added 50% to our household budget and sent 50% to help support two Ecuadorean children who might not have made it without outside help. We decreased . . . and they increased. It was a good we did in common. Many of you will have ideas for sharing your bounty with others.

Here's a dish that Treena and I have often enjoyed. I hope it helps you in your quest to "live within reason."

TUNA KEBABS

½ teaspoon dark sesame oil
1 teaspoon peeled, grated fresh gingerroot
1 garlic clove, minced
¼ cup dry white wine
2 tablespoons low-sodium tamari or soy sauce
1 teaspoon brown sugar
1 teaspoon Shanghai Coastline Spice Mix
2 tablespoons peanut butter
4 (6-ounce) tuna steaks (about 1 inch thick)
1 (14-ounce) can artichoke hearts (8- to 10-count), drained and halved
Vegetable cooking spray
Shanghai Spinach Rice

1. Heat oil in a small saucepan over medium-high heat. Add gingerroot and garlic; sauté 2 minutes. Stir in wine and next 3 ingredients; remove from heat. Stir in peanut butter. Set aside; keep warm.
2. Prepare grill. Cut tuna steaks into 20 (1-inch) pieces. Thread tuna and artichokes alternately onto 4 (12-inch) skewers. Place kebabs on a grill rack coated with cooking spray; grill 3 minutes or to desired degree of doneness, turning and basting with peanut sauce. Serve with Shanghai Spinach Rice. Yield: 4 servings (serving size: 5 ounces tuna and 1¼ cups rice).

CALORIES 577 (21% from fat); FAT 13.8g (sat 3.1g, mono 4.7g, poly 4.5g); PROTEIN 49g; CARB 59.3g; FIBER 1.9g; CHOL 65mg; IRON 5.9mg; SODIUM 521mg; CALC 66mg

Shanghai Spinach Rice:

2⅔ cups water
1⅓ cups uncooked long-grain rice
1 cup chopped spinach leaves
½ teaspoon Shanghai Coastline Spice Mix
¼ teaspoon salt

1. Bring water to a boil in a medium saucepan. Add rice; cover, reduce heat, and simmer 20 minutes or until liquid is absorbed. Stir in spinach, spice mix, and salt. Yield: 4 servings (serving size: 1¼ cups).

CALORIES 229 (2% from fat); FAT 0.5g (sat 0.1g, mono 0.1g, poly 0.1g); PROTEIN 4.8g; CARB 49.9g; FIBER 1.3g; CHOL 0mg; IRON 3.1mg; SODIUM 161mg; CALC 32mg

Shanghai Coastline Spice Mix:

¼ cup plus 3 tablespoons dried crushed red pepper
2¾ teaspoons ground ginger
2¾ teaspoons aniseed

1. Combine all ingredients in a spice or coffee grinder, and process until finely ground. Store spice mix in an airtight container for up to 6 months. Yield: ½ cup.

MIND SET

Quick Fixes to Avoid

When you're in a slump, the last thing to do is reach for a candy bar, a shot glass, a smoke, or a latte. That's because sugar, alcohol, nicotine, and caffeine are more likely to make you feel worse, at least in the long run. Help avert a stress-related bad mood with this complex-carbo-loaded breakfast.

BUCKWHEAT-CINNAMON PANCAKES

½ cup all-purpose flour
½ cup buckwheat flour
1 tablespoon sugar
2 teaspoons baking powder
¾ teaspoon ground cinnamon
¼ teaspoon salt
1 cup skim milk
1 tablespoon vegetable oil
1 large egg
3 tablespoons maple syrup
Fresh berries (optional)

1. Combine first 6 ingredients in a large bowl; stir well. Combine milk, oil, and egg; stir well. Add to flour mixture, stirring until smooth.
2. Spoon about ¼ cup batter for each pancake onto a hot nonstick griddle or skillet. Turn pancakes when tops are covered with bubbles and edges look cooked. Drizzle with maple syrup. Garnish with fresh berries, if desired. Yield: 3 servings (serving size: 3 pancakes).

CALORIES 308 (21% from fat); FAT 7.3g (sat 1.6g, mono 2.2g, poly 2.6g); PROTEIN 9.6g; CARB 52.9g; FIBER 0.6g; CHOL 242mg; IRON 2.8mg; SODIUM 262mg; CALC 321mg

HEALTHY TRAVEL

Island Flavors

For a taste of Hawaii at home, enjoy this rich-tasting, low-fat fruit smoothie.

TROPICAL PARADISE

1½ cups pineapple-orange juice
1 cup sliced banana (about 1 medium)
1 cup ice cubes
¾ cup diced pineapple
½ cup vanilla fat-free frozen yogurt
1 tablespoon flaked sweetened coconut

1. Combine all ingredients in a blender; cover and process until smooth. Serve immediately. Yield: 4 cups (serving size: 1 cup).

CALORIES 125 (3% from fat); FAT 0.9g (sat 0.5g, mono 0.1g, poly 0.1g); PROTEIN 1.7g; CARB 29.6g; FIBER 1.6g; CHOL 0mg; IRON 0.4mg; SODIUM 21mg; CALC 45mg

Hummus Club Sandwiches, page 254

Roasted Bananas with Brown Sugar-Walnut Glaze, page 251

Chicken with Garlic Croutons, page 258

Peaches in Red Wine, page 259

Banana-Spice Muffins, page 273

Chicken Saté, page 278

Linguine with Two Sauces, page 276

Chickpea, Bulgur, and
Tomato Pilaf, page 266

Caesar Chicken-Pasta Salad, page 269

Cranberry-Apple Tart, page 280

$\mathcal{A}$ Toast to the Green and Gold

With so many olive oils crowding the shelves, how do you know which is best to buy? We sort out the confusion and provide recipes to showcase the oil's golden flavor.

A little more than a decade ago, olive oil was an exotic ingredient to most Americans. Today, however, olive oil is rapidly becoming a staple in households nationwide. But many of us aren't sure whether to opt for the 3-liter tin at the supermarket or the boutique bottle. Most consumers choose something in between: They don't buy the cheapest or the most expensive, settling instead on a midpriced oil, like a blended extra-virgin in a big bottle, and then using it for everything. But that strategy may actually be giving you the least taste for your money.

Olive oil is used for two very different purposes: as a fat for cooking and as a condiment to add flavor to a dish. If you use the same midrange oil for both purposes, you're paying too much for cooking fat and aren't getting enough flavor as a condiment. When you heat olive oil, it loses much of its taste, so it's a waste to use an extra-virgin oil that way. Besides, less-expensive "pure" grade oil is actually better to cook with because it's refined, with no olive particles at the bottom of the bottle that can burn at high heat.

When you're using olive oil for its flavor—tossing it with roasted vegetables or adding it to pasta—a higher-priced extra-virgin oil will usually produce a much better result than a midpriced one. It's worth it to splurge on a really good-flavored oil for the intense taste.

Because good olive oil is intensely flavored, a little goes a long way. And even though olive oil is more healthful than saturated fats, it isn't any less fattening.

SANTA BARBARA PASTA SALAD

This salad can be stored in the refrigerator for up to a week.

  1 (16-ounce) package frozen baby lima beans
  3 cups cooked orecchiette (about 1¾ cups uncooked pasta)
1½ cups diced red bell pepper
  1 cup finely chopped onion
  1 cup peeled, chopped tomatillos (about 4 large)
  1 cup fresh corn kernels (about 3 ears)
  ⅓ cup minced fresh cilantro
  2 tablespoons white wine vinegar
  2 tablespoons extra-virgin olive oil
  ¾ teaspoon salt
  1 (4.5-ounce) can chopped green chiles

1. Cook beans in boiling water 18 minutes or until tender. Drain well.

2. Combine beans, pasta, and remaining ingredients in a bowl. Serve salad at room temperature or chilled. Yield: 10 servings (serving size: 1 cup).

CALORIES 159 (20% from fat); FAT 3.6g (sat 0.5g, mono 2.1g, poly 0.7g); PROTEIN 6.2g; CARB 27g; FIBER 3g; CHOL 0mg; IRON 2.3mg; SODIUM 248mg; CALC 30mg

VEGETABLE PIZZA WITH FETA CHEESE

We cooked the vegetables in a flavorful citrus-vermouth mixture, but you can skip the procedure and use plain steamed or sautéed vegetables. A strong extra-virgin olive oil is drizzled over the pizza at the very end.

  ½ cup dry vermouth
1½ teaspoons grated lemon rind
  3 tablespoons fresh lemon juice
  2 tablespoons chopped red onion
  ½ teaspoon salt
  ¼ teaspoon dried thyme
  6 black peppercorns
  1 cup sliced zucchini
  1 cup sliced yellow squash
  ½ cup chopped red bell pepper
  3 cups sliced cremini mushrooms (about ½ pound)
  1 (1-pound) Italian cheese-flavored pizza crust (such as Boboli)
  ¾ cup crumbled feta cheese
  1 tablespoon chopped fresh parsley
  1 tablespoon extra-virgin olive oil

1. Preheat oven to 375°.
2. Combine first 7 ingredients in a large saucepan; bring to a boil. Add zucchini, squash, and bell pepper; reduce heat, and simmer 4 minutes. Add mushrooms; simmer 2 minutes. Drain well; discard liquid and peppercorns.
3. Place pizza crust on a baking sheet. Sprinkle with half of feta cheese; top with vegetable mixture. Sprinkle with remaining feta cheese and parsley. Bake at 375° for 10 minutes or until thoroughly heated (cheese will not melt). Drizzle with olive oil. Yield: 6 servings (serving size: 1 wedge).

CALORIES 296 (29% from fat); FAT 9.5g (sat 3.8g, mono 4g, poly 1.3g); PROTEIN 12.8g; CARB 39.4g; FIBER 2.6g; CHOL 19mg; IRON 3mg; SODIUM 657mg; CALC 165mg

GREEN BEANS WITH LEMON AND BROWNED GARLIC

¾ cup water
1 pound green beans, trimmed
2½ teaspoons olive oil
3 garlic cloves, minced
3 tablespoons fresh lemon juice
⅛ teaspoon salt
⅛ teaspoon pepper

1. Bring water to a boil in a nonstick skillet. Add beans, and cook 3 minutes; drain. Set aside. Heat oil in skillet over medium-high heat. Add beans and garlic; sauté 1 minute. Add lemon juice, salt, and pepper; sauté 1 minute. Yield: 4 servings (serving size: 1 cup).

CALORIES 66 (40% from fat); FAT 2.9g (sat 0.4g, mono 2g, poly 0.3g); PROTEIN 2.3g; CARB 9.9g; FIBER 2.4g; CHOL 0mg; IRON 1.2mg; SODIUM 78mg; CALC 47mg

CHICKPEA, BULGUR, AND TOMATO PILAF

(pictured on page 263)

1 cup uncooked bulgur
1 cup boiling water
1 cup diced plum tomato
1 cup diagonally sliced green onions
½ cup chopped flat-leaf parsley
1½ teaspoons grated lemon rind
¼ cup fresh lemon juice
3 tablespoons extra-virgin olive oil
½ teaspoon salt
⅛ teaspoon hot sauce
Dash of pepper
1 (15-ounce) can chickpeas (garbanzo beans), drained
3 (6-inch) pita bread rounds, each cut into 4 wedges

1. Combine bulgur and water in a bowl. Cover; let stand 30 minutes. Add tomato and next 9 ingredients; stir well. Cover; chill. Serve with pita bread wedges. Yield: 5 servings (serving size: 1 cup salad and 2 pita wedges).

CALORIES 336 (29% from fat); FAT 10.8g (sat 1.5g, mono 6.7g, poly 1.8g); PROTEIN 11.2g; CARB 55.2g; FIBER 8.7g; CHOL 1mg; IRON 3.7mg; SODIUM 472mg; CALC 79mg

LINGUINE WITH ROASTED TOMATOES AND GARLIC

2 pounds cherry tomatoes
2 tablespoons extra-virgin olive oil, divided
½ teaspoon salt, divided
¼ teaspoon pepper
5 large unpeeled garlic cloves
4 cups hot cooked linguine (about 8 ounces uncooked pasta)
¼ cup chopped fresh parsley
2 tablespoons chopped fresh basil

1. Preheat oven to 450°.
2. Combine cherry tomatoes, 1 tablespoon oil, ¼ teaspoon salt, pepper, and garlic in a 13 x 9-inch baking dish; toss gently. Bake at 450° for 45 minutes or until garlic is browned, stirring occasionally. (Tomato skins will pop.) Squeeze garlic cloves to extract garlic pulp; mash pulp, and discard skins. Add garlic pulp to tomato mixture, stirring gently.
3. Combine tomato mixture, 1 tablespoon oil, ¼ teaspoon salt, pasta, parsley, and basil in a large bowl; toss gently. Yield: 4 servings (serving size: 1 cup).

CALORIES 312 (26% from fat); FAT 8.5g (sat 1.1g, mono 5.2g, poly 1.3g); PROTEIN 9g; CARB 51.8g; FIBER 5.4g; CHOL 0mg; IRON 3.3mg; SODIUM 318mg; CALC 36mg

ROASTED-EGGPLANT DIP WITH FOCACCIA

1 (1-pound) eggplant
2 tablespoons extra-virgin olive oil
2 tablespoons sherry vinegar
½ teaspoon salt
½ teaspoon dried marjoram
⅛ teaspoon pepper
2 garlic cloves, minced
1 cup finely chopped onion
1 cup finely chopped tomato
2 tablespoons chopped fresh parsley
1 (12.5-ounce) package focaccia (Italian flatbread), cut in 12 wedges

1. Preheat oven to 425°.
2. Place eggplant on a baking sheet; bake at 425° for 45 minutes or until tender. Cool. Peel eggplant, and finely chop to measure 1 cup. Reserve any remaining eggplant for another use.
3. Combine oil and next 5 ingredients in a medium bowl. Add chopped eggplant, onion, tomato, and parsley; stir well. Cover and chill. Serve with focaccia. Yield: 12 servings (serving size: ¼ cup dip and 1 wedge focaccia).

CALORIES 234 (27% from fat); FAT 7.1g (sat 1.4g, mono 4.3g, poly 1.0g); PROTEIN 7.3g; CARB 37g; FIBER 4.4g; CHOL 0mg; IRON 0.8mg; SODIUM 531mg; CALC 76mg

BRUSCHETTA POMODORO

Pomodoro *is Italian for "tomato."*

2 cups minced plum tomato (about ¾ pound)
1½ teaspoons capers
2 tablespoons chopped kalamata olives
1 tablespoon chopped red onion
1 tablespoon chopped fresh basil
1 tablespoon extra-virgin olive oil
¼ teaspoon salt
¼ teaspoon balsamic vinegar
⅛ teaspoon pepper
10 (½-inch-thick) slices diagonally cut French bread baguette, toasted

1. Combine all ingredients except French bread; cover and let stand 30 minutes. Drain tomato mixture. Top each bread slice with 1 tablespoon tomato mixture. Yield: 10 servings.

CALORIES 95 (20% from fat); FAT 2.6g (sat 0.4g, mono 1.4g, poly 0.5g); PROTEIN 2.2g; CARB 15.8g; FIBER 1.1g; CHOL 1mg; IRON 0.8mg; SODIUM 255mg; CALC 15mg

GREEK MEATBALLS WITH LEMON-HERB ORZO

1   tablespoon plus ½ teaspoon extra-virgin olive oil, divided
1   cup minced onion
1   cup Italian-seasoned breadcrumbs
¼   cup chopped fresh parsley
½   teaspoon chopped fresh oregano
⅛   teaspoon pepper
½   cup water
¼   cup grated carrot
¼   teaspoon salt
½   pound lean ground lamb
4   garlic cloves, minced
1   large egg, lightly beaten
Vegetable cooking spray
Lemon-Herb Orzo

1. Preheat oven to 425°.
2. Heat 1 teaspoon oil in a large non-stick skillet over medium-high heat. Add onion; sauté 3 minutes. Combine onion, breadcrumbs, and next 9 ingredients. Shape into 30 (1½-inch) meatballs; place on rack of a broiler pan coated with cooking spray. Bake at 425° for 20 minutes or until done.
3. Combine Lemon-Herb Orzo and meatballs in a large bowl. Drizzle each serving with ½ teaspoon olive oil. Yield: 5 servings (serving size: 6 meatballs and 1 cup orzo).

CALORIES 478 (18% from fat); FAT 9.4g (sat 2.4g, mono 4.3g, poly 1.1g); PROTEIN 24.4g; CARB 72.9g; FIBER 2.9g; CHOL 77mg; IRON 4.9mg; SODIUM 806mg; CALC 71mg

Lemon-Herb Orzo:

5   cups hot cooked orzo (about 2½ cups uncooked rice-shaped pasta)
¼   cup chopped fresh parsley
2   tablespoons fresh lemon juice
½   teaspoon chopped fresh oregano
⅛   teaspoon pepper

1. Combine all ingredients in a large bowl, and toss well. Yield: 5 servings (serving size: 1 cup).

CALORIES 255 (4% from fat); FAT 1.1g (sat 0.2g, mono 0.1g, poly 0.5g); PROTEIN 8.8g; CARB 51.6g; FIBER 1.8g; CHOL 0mg; IRON 2.8mg; SODIUM 7mg; CALC 17mg

SPICY CRUSTED SWORDFISH WITH CITRUS-WALNUT SAUCE

2   tablespoons Italian-seasoned breadcrumbs
½   teaspoon ground cinnamon
½   teaspoon ground ginger
½   teaspoon pepper
¼   teaspoon salt
¼   teaspoon ground cumin
1   tablespoon extra-virgin olive oil, divided
4   (6-ounce) swordfish steaks (about 1 inch thick)
1   cup water
⅔   cup uncooked couscous
½   teaspoon grated lemon rind
1   tablespoon fresh lemon juice
¼   teaspoon salt
1   tablespoon chopped fresh mint
½   cup currants or raisins
1   teaspoon grated orange rind
½   cup fresh orange juice
2   tablespoons coarsely chopped toasted walnuts
1   tablespoon honey
Cherry tomatoes (optional)

1. Combine first 6 ingredients in a bowl. Stir in 1 teaspoon oil. Rub spice mixture over both sides of swordfish. Cover and chill 30 minutes.
2. Bring water to a boil in a medium saucepan; gradually stir in couscous. Remove from heat; cover and let stand 5 minutes. Fluff with a fork. Stir in lemon rind, lemon juice, ¼ teaspoon salt, and mint. Set aside; keep warm.
3. Combine 1 teaspoon oil, currants, and next 4 ingredients in a small saucepan. Bring to a simmer. Set aside, and keep warm.
4. Heat 1 teaspoon oil in a large non-stick skillet over medium-high heat. Add swordfish, and cook 5 minutes on each side or until fish flakes easily when tested with a fork. Serve with couscous, and drizzle with sauce. Garnish with cherry tomatoes, if desired. Yield: 4 servings (serving size: 5 ounces swordfish, ½ cup couscous, and ¼ cup sauce).

CALORIES 399 (28% from fat); FAT 12.5g (sat 2.5g, mono 5.5g, poly 3.3g); PROTEIN 36.5g; CARB 36g; FIBER 1.9g; CHOL 64mg; IRON 2.6mg; SODIUM 544mg; CALC 33mg

START THE PRESSES: AN OLIVE-OIL GLOSSARY

Europeans have strict standards for labeling olive oil. In the United States, these standards are not as explicit but are generally observed.

• COLD-PRESSED. All good condiment olive oils are cold-pressed, meaning the oils are extracted using methods in which the temperature isn't raised. The oil may be filtered but not refined in any heat process.

• EXTRA-VIRGIN oil comes from whole, unblemished olives pressed within a day after harvest. Less than 1% of the oil can be made up of free oleic acid, which can make the oil taste sharp. Most extra-virgin oils in the United States are blends of different grades of oils with a predictable flavor profile. Like wine, extra-virgin oils that come from a single location have a characteristic fragrance, taste, and color depending on the variety of olive, growing conditions, and soil.

• VIRGIN is rarely sold in the United States. Its standards are the same as for extra-virgin oil, except that its free oleic acid can be up to 3%, which means that the quality is good, but not equal to extra-virgin.

• PURE is a blend of refined and extra-virgin olive oils. Usually the extra-virgin oil is added at the end of the process—from 5% to 30% of the total—to provide a color and taste profile that will be acceptable to the consumer.

• LIGHT olive oils actually have no fewer calories than regular ones—the term applies to color and taste. These are mostly refined oils that have little or no extra-virgin oil added for taste. As a result, they are bland.

size: 2 chicken thighs and about 1 cup potato mixture).

CALORIES 349 (29% from fat); FAT 11.4g (sat 2.4g, mono 5.4g, poly 2.3g); PROTEIN 36.9g; CARB 25.9g; FIBER 3g; CHOL 141mg; IRON 4mg; SODIUM 539mg; CALC 69mg

MENU SUGGESTION

SKILLET-ROASTED LEMON
CHICKEN WITH
POTATOES

French bread

*Minted orange compote**

*Toss peeled, sliced oranges with orange liqueur and chopped fresh mint.

SKILLET-ROASTED LEMON CHICKEN WITH POTATOES

1   tablespoon extra-virgin olive oil, divided
1   large lemon, sliced
½   teaspoon grated lemon rind
1   tablespoon fresh lemon juice
½   teaspoon salt, divided
¼   teaspoon pepper, divided
4   garlic cloves, minced
8   (3-ounce) skinned, boned chicken thighs
1   teaspoon chopped fresh rosemary or ¼ teaspoon dried rosemary
10   cherry tomatoes
10   kalamata olives
8   small red potatoes, quartered (about 1 pound)
2   garlic cloves, minced
Rosemary sprig (optional)

1. Preheat oven to 450°.
2. Coat a 10-inch cast-iron skillet with 1 teaspoon oil. Arrange lemon slices in a single layer in bottom of skillet.
3. Combine 1 teaspoon oil, lemon rind, lemon juice, ¼ teaspoon salt, ⅛ teaspoon pepper, and 4 garlic cloves in a large bowl. Add chicken, and toss to coat. Arrange chicken in a single layer on top of lemon slices.
4. Combine 1 teaspoon olive oil, ¼ teaspoon salt, ⅛ teaspoon pepper, chopped rosemary, and next 4 ingredients in a bowl; toss to coat. Arrange potato mixture over chicken. Bake at 450° for 1 hour or until chicken is done. Garnish with a rosemary sprig, if desired. Yield: 4 servings (serving

ROSEMARY CHICKEN WITH TWO-CORN POLENTA

½   cup yellow cornmeal
½   teaspoon salt, divided
2   cups water
½   cup fresh corn kernels (about 1 ear) or frozen whole-kernel corn, thawed
4   (4-ounce) skinned, boned chicken breast halves
1   tablespoon chopped fresh rosemary
⅛   teaspoon pepper
1   tablespoon plus 1 teaspoon extra-virgin olive oil, divided
Rosemary sprigs (optional)

1. Place cornmeal and ¼ teaspoon salt in a large saucepan. Gradually add water, stirring constantly with a whisk. Bring to a boil. Reduce heat to medium, and cook 10 minutes, stirring frequently. Stir in corn kernels. Set aside, and keep warm.
2. Place each chicken breast half between 2 sheets of heavy-duty plastic wrap; flatten to ¼-inch thickness using a meat mallet or rolling pin. Sprinkle with ¼ teaspoon salt, chopped rosemary, and pepper.
3. Heat 2 teaspoons oil in a large nonstick skillet over medium-high heat. Add chicken, and cook 3 minutes on each side or until done.
4. Arrange a chicken breast half and ½ cup polenta on each of 4 plates; drizzle ½ teaspoon oil over each serving of polenta. Garnish with rosemary sprigs, if desired. Yield: 4 servings.

CALORIES 261 (28% from fat); FAT 8.1g (sat 1.5g, mono 4.5g, poly 1.3g); PROTEIN 28.5g; CARB 17.3g; FIBER 1.6g; CHOL 72mg; IRON 1.8mg; SODIUM 359mg; CALC 18mg

BASIL-PARSLEY SAUCE

This sauce can be used for artichokes as an alternative to melted butter.

1   cup fat-free chicken broth
2   tablespoons cornstarch
2   large egg yolks, lightly beaten
¾   cup minced fresh parsley
½   cup chopped fresh basil
2   tablespoons extra-virgin olive oil
1   tablespoon Dijon mustard
1   tablespoon finely chopped lemon rind
1   garlic clove, minced

1. Combine broth and cornstarch in a small saucepan. Bring to a boil, and cook, stirring constantly, 1 minute. Gradually add hot broth mixture to egg yolks, stirring constantly with a whisk. Return broth mixture to pan; cook over medium-low heat 15 minutes or until thermometer registers 160°. Pour into a bowl; stir in parsley and remaining ingredients. Cover and chill. Serve with steamed fresh vegetables such as artichokes, carrots, or potatoes, if desired. Yield: 1⅓ cups (serving size: 1 tablespoon).

CALORIES 29 (59% from fat); FAT 1.9g (sat 0.3g, mono 1.2g, poly 0.2g); PROTEIN 0.7g; CARB 1.1g; FIBER 0.1g; CHOL 21mg; IRON 0.2mg; SODIUM 31mg; CALC 9mg

ROSEMARY-LEMON CAKE WITH CURRANTS

1   cup all-purpose flour
1   teaspoon fresh rosemary
1   teaspoon baking powder
¼   teaspoon baking soda
⅛   teaspoon salt
½   cup sugar
3   tablespoons olive oil
⅓   cup plain fat-free yogurt
½   teaspoon vanilla extract
¼   teaspoon almond extract
1   large egg
1   large egg white
2   teaspoons grated lemon rind
¼   cup currants or raisins
Vegetable cooking spray
2   tablespoons sugar
3   tablespoons lemon juice

1. Preheat oven to 350°.
2. Combine first 5 ingredients in a bowl; set aside. Combine ½ cup sugar and oil in a large bowl; beat at high speed of an electric mixer 2 minutes. Add yogurt and next 4 ingredients; beat 1 minute. Add flour mixture; beat at low speed until well-blended. Fold in grated lemon rind and currants.
3. Pour batter into a 9-inch springform pan coated with cooking spray. Bake at 350° for 25 minutes or until cake is golden and springs back when touched lightly in center. Remove from oven. Pierce cake with a fork. Combine 2 tablespoons sugar and lemon juice; spoon over cake. Cool on a wire rack. Yield: 8 servings.

CALORIES 192 (28% from fat); FAT 6g (sat 0.9g, mono 4g, poly 0.8g); PROTEIN 3.4g; CARB 31.8g; FIBER 0.7g; CHOL 27mg; IRON 0.9mg; SODIUM 84mg; CALC 51mg

SHERRY VINAIGRETTE WITH CURRANTS

Serve this vinaigrette with mixed greens.

  ⅓ cup sherry vinegar
  ⅓ cup water
  ¼ cup currants
  2 tablespoons extra-virgin olive oil
  2 teaspoons Dijon mustard
  ½ teaspoon sugar
  ½ teaspoon kosher salt
  ⅛ teaspoon freshly ground pepper
  4 garlic cloves, crushed

1. Combine all ingredients in a jar. Cover tightly, and shake vigorously. Yield: 1 cup (serving size: 1 tablespoon).

CALORIES 23 (68% from fat); FAT 1.8g (sat 0.3g, mono 0.5g, poly 0.8g); PROTEIN 0.1g; CARB 0.9g; FIBER 0.1g; CHOL 0mg; IRON 0mg; SODIUM 121mg; CALC 2mg

QUICK & EASY WEEKNIGHTS

O Mighty Caesar

Already loaded with late summer's bounty of tomatoes and basil, this salad can be embellished with almost anything you like.

> **MENU**
>
> CAESAR CHICKEN-PASTA SALAD
>
> OVEN-ROASTED ASPARAGUS WITH THYME
>
> About 424 calories and 12 grams of fat (26% calories from fat)

CAESAR CHICKEN-PASTA SALAD

(pictured on page 262)

While this salad can be enjoyed the way it is, you can include or substitute different kinds of chicken, turkey, cheese, salad dressing, or herbs.
Preparation time: 10 minutes
Cooking time: 10 minutes

  3 cups (about 12 ounces) skinned, shredded roasted chicken breast (such as Tyson's)
  3 cups cooked penne (about 6 ounces uncooked tubular-shaped pasta)
  2 cups thinly sliced romaine lettuce
  1½ cups halved cherry tomatoes
  ½ cup thinly sliced fresh basil
  ½ cup chopped green onions
  ⅓ cup fat-free Caesar dressing
  ¼ cup chopped fresh parsley
  1 (4-ounce) package crumbled feta cheese
  1 garlic clove, minced

1. Combine all ingredients in a large bowl; toss well to coat. Yield: 4 servings (serving size: 2 cups).
Note: To lower the sodium in this dish, use plain cooked chicken in place of the commercial roasted variety, which is fairly high in sodium.

CALORIES 362 (22% from fat); FAT 8.8g (sat 5.2g, mono 1.4g, poly 0.6g); PROTEIN 19.4g; CARB 40.4g; FIBER 3.5g; CHOL 78mg; IRON 2.6mg; SODIUM 951mg; CALC 206mg

OVEN-ROASTED ASPARAGUS WITH THYME

Select a bundle of firm, bright green asparagus spears that are approximately the same size and thickness to ensure even cooking.
Preparation time: 10 minutes
Cooking time: 20 minutes

  1½ pounds asparagus spears
  1 large garlic clove, halved
  2 teaspoons olive oil
  ½ teaspoon salt
  ¼ teaspoon dried thyme
  ¼ teaspoon freshly ground pepper

1. Preheat oven to 400°.
2. Snap off tough ends of asparagus; remove scales with a knife or vegetable peeler, if desired. Set aside.
3. Rub cut sides of garlic over a 13 x 9-inch baking dish; place garlic in dish. Add asparagus; drizzle with oil. Sprinkle asparagus with salt, thyme, and pepper; toss gently. Bake at 400° for 20 minutes, stirring once. Yield: 4 servings.

CALORIES 62 (38% from fat); FAT 2.6g (sat 0.4g, mono 1.7g, poly 0.4g); PROTEIN 4g; CARB 8.3g; FIBER 3.7g; CHOL 0mg; IRON 1.8mg; SODIUM 297mg; CALC 42mg

All in the Family

From French-inspired biscotti to Tex-Mex fajitas, our readers share some of their families' favorites.

SOFT SPICE BISCOTTI

I don't bake them a second time, so they are nice and chewy, not hard and dry like most biscotti. You can dip them or eat them by themselves.

—Priscilla M. Bleifer, Dedham, Massachusetts

1 cup granulated sugar
1 cup packed dark brown sugar
½ cup sliced almonds
⅓ cup vegetable oil
2 teaspoons ground cinnamon
1 teaspoon ground cloves
2 teaspoons water
2 large egg whites
1 large egg
2½ cups all-purpose flour
2 teaspoons baking powder
Vegetable cooking spray

1. Preheat oven to 375°.
2. Combine first 9 ingredients in a large bowl; beat at low speed of an electric mixer 1 minute. Combine flour and baking powder; gradually add flour mixture to sugar mixture, beating until well-blended (dough will be soft). Turn dough out onto a lightly floured surface; shape dough into 3 (6 x 4-inch) rectangles. Place rectangles on a baking sheet coated with cooking spray; flatten to ¾-inch thickness. Bake at 375° for 25 minutes. Remove rectangles from baking sheet; cool 10 minutes on a wire rack.
3. Cut each rectangle diagonally into ¾-inch slices. Yield: 2 dozen.

CALORIES 98 (28% from fat); FAT 3g (sat 0.5g, mono 1.1g, poly 1.2g); PROTEIN 1.5g; CARB 16.6g; FIBER 0.4g; CHOL 6mg; IRON 1mg; SODIUM 7mg; CALC 26mg

SMOKE'S CHILI

This recipe is not mine from the 'ground up.' I started using it about 10 years ago and fine-tuned it to my liking. I find chili is an individual food taste that's always in the mouth of the beholder.

—Smokey Jordan, Charlottesville, Virginia

2 teaspoons vegetable oil, divided
3½ pounds lean, boned chuck roast, cut into ½-inch pieces
3 cups chopped green bell pepper
1½ cups chopped onion
¼ to ½ teaspoon dried crushed red pepper
1 garlic clove, minced
2 tablespoons chili powder
1¼ teaspoons ground cumin
1 tablespoon brown sugar
1½ teaspoons dried oregano
½ teaspoon salt
1 (28-ounce) can whole tomatoes, undrained and chopped
1 (12-ounce) can tomato paste
1 (12-ounce) bottle beer
2 (15-ounce) cans kidney beans, drained
¾ cup low-fat sour cream
¾ cup (3 ounces) shredded reduced-fat Monterey Jack cheese

1. Heat ½ teaspoon oil in a large Dutch oven over medium-high heat; add half of meat. Cook 10 minutes or until browned; remove from heat, and drain. Repeat procedure with ½ teaspoon oil and remaining meat; set aside.
2. Heat 1 teaspoon oil in Dutch oven over medium heat. Add bell pepper and next 3 ingredients; sauté 8 minutes or until vegetables are tender. Add chili powder and cumin; cook, stirring constantly, 1 minute. Add meat, sugar, and next 5 ingredients; bring to a boil. Cover, reduce heat, and simmer 45 minutes. Add beans; simmer, uncovered, 40 additional minutes or until meat is tender. Serve with sour cream and cheese. Yield: 12 servings (serving size: 1 cup chili, 1 tablespoon sour cream, and 1 tablespoon cheese).

Note: To freeze, cool chili, and place in an airtight freezer container or a heavy-duty, zip-top plastic bag. Freeze chili up to 3 months.

CALORIES 330 (29% from fat); FAT 10.8g (sat 4.3g, mono 3.2g, poly 1.1g); PROTEIN 38.2g; CARB 20g; FIBER 3.4g; CHOL 94mg; IRON 5.5mg; SODIUM 527mg; CALC 133mg

ITALIAN TURKEY BURGERS

My husband likes food packed with flavor, and the Italian spices make these turkey burgers one of his favorites.

—Nancy Alexandroff, Oak Park, Illinois

4 (1½-ounce) Italian rolls, split lengthwise
Olive oil-flavored vegetable cooking spray
1 garlic clove, halved
1 pound ground turkey
½ cup low-fat spaghetti sauce
⅓ cup finely chopped onion
¼ cup Italian-seasoned breadcrumbs
¼ cup grated fresh Parmesan cheese
1 tablespoon chopped fresh parsley
2 (1-ounce) slices part-skim mozzarella cheese, cut in half

1. Preheat broiler.
2. Place rolls, cut sides up, on rack of a broiler pan coated with cooking spray. Lightly coat cut sides of rolls with cooking spray. Broil 2 minutes or until lightly toasted. Rub garlic evenly over cut sides of rolls. Set aside, and keep warm.
3. Combine turkey and next 5 ingredients. Divide mixture into 4 equal portions, shaping into ½-inch-thick patties. Place on broiler pan; broil 7 minutes on each side or until done. Place burgers on bottom halves of rolls; top each burger with ½ cheese slice. Broil 1 minute or until cheese melts. Cover with tops of rolls. Yield: 4 servings.

CALORIES 372 (22% from fat); FAT 9g (sat 4.1g, mono 2.1g, poly 1.3g); PROTEIN 36.6g; CARB 33.8g; FIBER 2g; CHOL 78mg; IRON 3.2mg; SODIUM 785mg; CALC 225mg

MARINATED BALSAMIC BEAN SALAD

This is great at lunch or as a side dish on hot summer nights. It keeps well for quite a long time in the fridge.

—Susan Morreal, San Diego, California

1   cup frozen whole-kernel corn
1   cup frozen cut green beans
1   (16-ounce) can kidney beans
1   (15-ounce) can chickpeas
       (garbanzo beans)
1   (15-ounce) can black beans
1   cup diced red onion
½   cup balsamic vinegar
¼   cup water
2   tablespoons Dijon mustard
1   tablespoon dried basil
1   tablespoon olive oil
1   teaspoon sugar
1   teaspoon dried thyme
¼   teaspoon salt
¼   teaspoon ground white
       pepper
2   garlic cloves, minced

1. Combine first 5 ingredients in a colander; rinse and drain. Combine onion and remaining 10 ingredients in a bowl; add bean mixture, and toss gently to coat. Cover and marinate in refrigerator at least 4 hours, stirring occasionally. Serve with a slotted spoon. Yield: 7 servings (serving size: 1 cup).

CALORIES 214 (16% from fat); FAT 3.8g (sat 0.5g, mono 1.7g, poly 0.8g); PROTEIN 10.6g; CARB 37g; FIBER 6.4g; CHOL 0mg; IRON 3.5mg; SODIUM 526mg; CALC 74mg

CHICKEN-TORTILLA SOUP

My family loves this recipe. It's a big hit every time I serve it. I hope you enjoy it as much as we do.

—Leigh Anne Henry, Jacksonville, Florida

1   teaspoon olive oil
1   cup chopped onion
2   garlic cloves, minced
2   cups shredded cooked chicken
       breast (about 10 ounces)
1   cup frozen whole-kernel corn
¼   cup dry white wine
1   tablespoon seeded, chopped
       jalapeño pepper
1   teaspoon ground cumin
1   teaspoon Worcestershire sauce
½   teaspoon chili powder
2   (14¼-ounce) cans no-salt-
       added chicken broth
1   (14.5-ounce) can peeled, diced
       tomatoes (such as Del Monte
       Fresh Cut), undrained
1   (10¾-ounce) can condensed
       reduced-fat, reduced-sodium
       tomato soup (such as
       Campbell's Healthy Request),
       undiluted
1   cup crushed unsalted baked
       tortilla chips (about 16)
½   cup fat-free sour cream

1. Heat oil in a Dutch oven over medium-high heat. Add onion and garlic; sauté 2 minutes. Stir in chicken and next 9 ingredients; bring to a boil. Reduce heat, and simmer 1 hour. Ladle soup into bowls; top with tortilla chips and sour cream. Yield: 8 servings (serving size: 1 cup soup, 2 tablespoons chips, and 1 tablespoon sour cream).

CALORIES 185 (18% from fat); FAT 3.7g (sat 0.8g, mono 1.4g, poly 0.7g); PROTEIN 15.3g; CARB 22.2g; FIBER 2g; CHOL 30mg; IRON 1.1mg; SODIUM 409mg; CALC 32mg

HEART-SMART FAJITAS

My husband is not big on leftovers. So because I'm cooking for two, I try to use recipes in which the portions are easily controllable, like these fajitas. We love greens, so I serve these fajitas with a fresh garden salad.

—Ginny Jannack, West Palm Beach, Florida

1   (1-pound) lean flank steak
8   (8-inch) fat-free flour tortillas
Vegetable cooking spray
2   large tomatoes, cut into
       ½-inch-thick wedges
2   medium onions, cut into
       ½-inch-thick wedges
3   tablespoons commercial taco
       seasoning (¾ envelope)
2   small garlic cloves, minced
½   cup chopped tomato
½   cup shredded iceberg lettuce
½   cup chopped onion
½   cup (2 ounces) shredded
       reduced-fat sharp Cheddar
       cheese
½   cup fat-free sour cream
½   cup salsa

1. Trim fat from steak. Slice steak diagonally across grain into thin strips.
2. Heat tortillas according to package directions. Set aside; keep warm.
3. Heat a large nonstick skillet coated with cooking spray over medium-high heat. Add steak; sauté 2 minutes or until browned. Add tomato wedges, onions, seasoning, and garlic; stir well. Bring to a boil. Cover, reduce heat, and simmer 10 minutes, stirring occasionally. Divide steak mixture evenly among tortillas; roll up. Top each fajita with 1 tablespoon chopped tomato and 1 tablespoon each of remaining ingredients. Yield: 8 servings (serving size: 1 fajita).

CALORIES 263 (21% from fat); FAT 6.1g (sat 2.7g, mono 2.2g, poly 0.4g); PROTEIN 17.9g; CARB 34.1g; FIBER 2g; CHOL 33mg; IRON 1.7mg; SODIUM 589mg; CALC 87mg

A Stirring Discovery

Coming up with a light muffin that has plenty of taste and just the right texture is a challenge. But that's just what we did, thanks to the addition of ricotta cheese.

Throughout history, there has never been much news from the muffin front . . . until now. The discovery of a new baking technique has the muffin world clamoring: Light ricotta cheese is the latest headline-maker. Although it's certainly not new, ricotta isn't something typically added to muffins.

When you work ricotta into the muffin mix, the creamy cheese acts as a tenderizer by adding just enough moisture. And because its rich taste is amazingly subtle, it doesn't overwhelm the other flavors. In the rather dull history of muffin-making, a significant event has occurred—and a very tender one at that.

MENU SUGGESTION

*Citrus pork tenderloin**

Green beans with lemon zest

CARROT-SWEET POTATO MUFFINS

*Brush 1 pound pork tenderloin with ½ cup orange marmalade and ¼ cup low-sodium soy sauce. Grill.

CARROT-SWEET POTATO MUFFINS

2¾ cups all-purpose flour
½ cup granulated sugar
½ cup packed brown sugar
1 tablespoon baking powder
1 teaspoon baking soda
1 teaspoon salt
1 teaspoon ground cinnamon
½ teaspoon ground allspice
1¼ cups coarsely shredded carrot
¾ cup 2% low-fat milk
½ cup low-fat buttermilk
⅓ cup light ricotta cheese
½ cup mashed cooked sweet potato
¼ cup vegetable oil
1 tablespoon vanilla extract
1 large egg white
1 large egg
Vegetable cooking spray

1. Preheat oven to 400°.
2. Combine first 8 ingredients in a large bowl. Stir in carrot; make a well in center of mixture. Combine milk and next 7 ingredients; stir well with a whisk. Add to flour mixture, stirring just until moist. Spoon batter into 18 muffin cups coated with cooking spray.

---

3. Bake at 400° for 20 minutes or until done. Remove from pans immediately, and cool on a wire rack. Yield: 1½ dozen (serving size: 1 muffin).

CALORIES 168 (21% from fat); FAT 4.0g (sat 0.9g, mono 1.1g, poly 1.6g); PROTEIN 3.7g; CARB 29.2g; FIBER 0.9g; CHOL 14mg; IRON 1.3mg; SODIUM 224mg; CALC 85mg

CINNAMON-APPLE MUFFINS

2⅓ cups all-purpose flour
1 cup sugar
1 tablespoon baking powder
2 teaspoons ground cinnamon
1 teaspoon baking soda
½ teaspoon salt
1½ cups peeled, finely chopped Granny Smith apple
1 cup low-fat buttermilk
⅓ cup 2% low-fat milk
⅓ cup light ricotta cheese
3 tablespoons vegetable oil
1 tablespoon vanilla extract
2 large egg whites
1 large egg
Vegetable cooking spray
3 tablespoons sugar
2 teaspoons ground cinnamon

1. Preheat oven to 400°.
2. Combine first 6 ingredients in a large bowl. Stir in apple; make a well in center of mixture. Combine buttermilk and next 6 ingredients; stir well with a whisk. Add to flour mixture, stirring just until moist. Spoon batter into 18 muffin cups coated with cooking spray.
3. Combine 3 tablespoons sugar and 2 teaspoons cinnamon; sprinkle evenly over batter. Bake at 400° for 18 minutes or until done. Remove from pans immediately; cool on a wire rack. Yield: 1½ dozen (serving size: 1 muffin).

CALORIES 153 (19% from fat); FAT 3.2g (sat 0.7g, mono 0.9g, poly 1.2g); PROTEIN 3.4g; CARB 27.6g; FIBER 0.8g; CHOL 13mg; IRON 1.0mg; SODIUM 133mg; CALC 67mg

BANANA-SPICE MUFFINS

(pictured on page 262)

2½ cups all-purpose flour
⅓ cup granulated sugar
⅓ cup packed brown sugar
1 tablespoon baking powder
1 teaspoon baking soda
½ teaspoon salt
1 teaspoon ground allspice
1 teaspoon ground ginger
1 cup mashed ripe banana (about 2 small)
⅔ cup 2% low-fat milk
⅓ cup low-fat buttermilk
⅓ cup light ricotta cheese
2 tablespoons vegetable oil
1 tablespoon vanilla extract
1 large egg white
1 large egg
Vegetable cooking spray

1. Preheat oven to 400°.
2. Combine first 8 ingredients in a large bowl; make a well in center of mixture. Combine banana and next 7 ingredients. Add to flour mixture, stirring just until moist. Spoon batter into 18 muffin cups coated with cooking spray.
3. Bake at 400° for 18 minutes or until done. Remove from pans immediately, and cool on a wire rack. Yield: 1½ dozen (serving size: 1 muffin).

CALORIES 125 (17% from fat); FAT 2.4g (sat 0.8g, mono 0.7g, poly 0.9g); PROTEIN 3.2g; CARB 22.6g; FIBER 0.8g; CHOL 13mg; IRON 1mg; SODIUM 194mg; CALC 59mg

---

MUFFIN "MUSTS"

◆ The less muffin batter is stirred, the better. Overstirring results in muffins that are tough with undesirable tunnels inside.

◆ If all the cups aren't used when filling the muffin pan with batter, pour water into the empty cups to keep the pan from buckling.

◆ Muffins are best when eaten the day they are made, but they freeze well, too. Cover them tightly, and freeze for up to one month.

MOLASSES-PRUNE MUFFINS

2½ cups all-purpose flour
1 cup quick-cooking oats
¾ cup sugar
¼ cup toasted wheat germ
1 tablespoon baking powder
1 teaspoon ground cinnamon
½ teaspoon baking soda
½ teaspoon salt
1 cup finely chopped pitted prunes
1 cup low-fat buttermilk
½ cup light ricotta cheese
3 tablespoons vegetable oil
2 tablespoons molasses
1 tablespoon vanilla extract
2 large eggs
Vegetable cooking spray

1. Preheat oven to 400°.
2. Combine first 8 ingredients in a bowl. Stir in prunes; make a well in center of mixture. Combine buttermilk and next 5 ingredients; stir well with a whisk. Add to flour mixture, stirring just until moist. Spoon into 18 muffin cups coated with cooking spray.
3. Bake at 400° for 18 minutes or until done. Remove from pans immediately, and cool on a wire rack. Yield: 1½ dozen (serving size: 1 muffin).

CALORIES 190 (19% from fat); FAT 4g (sat 1g, mono 1.1g, poly 1.5g); PROTEIN 5g; CARB 34.2g; FIBER 1.9g; CHOL 25mg; IRON 1.7mg; SODIUM 121mg; CALC 89mg

---

PEAR-OATMEAL MUFFINS

2½ cups all-purpose flour
¾ cup sugar
½ cup quick-cooking oats
1 tablespoon baking powder
1 teaspoon baking soda
½ teaspoon salt
¼ teaspoon ground cardamom
¼ teaspoon ground allspice
2 cups chopped ripe pear
¾ cup low-fat buttermilk
⅓ cup light ricotta cheese
¼ cup vegetable oil
1 tablespoon vanilla extract
1 large egg white
1 large egg
Vegetable cooking spray
½ cup quick-cooking oats

1. Preheat oven to 400°.
2. Combine first 8 ingredients in a large bowl. Stir in pear; make a well in center of mixture. Combine buttermilk and next 5 ingredients; stir well with a whisk. Add to flour mixture, stirring just until moist. Spoon batter into 18 muffin cups coated with cooking spray; sprinkle ½ cup oats evenly over batter.
3. Bake at 400° for 18 minutes or until done. Remove from pans immediately, and cool on a wire rack. Yield: 1½ dozen (serving size: 1 muffin).

CALORIES 166 (23% from fat); FAT 4.2g (sat 0.9g, mono 1.2g, poly 1.7g); PROTEIN 3.9g; CARB 28.4g; FIBER 1.4g; CHOL 13mg; IRON 1.2mg; SODIUM 150mg; CALC 71mg

---

TOUGH MUFFINS

Some readers try to trim fat even further in our recipes by making their own adjustments and substitutions. Out of curiosity, we tested some of these changes to see how they might affect the texture of our new muffin formula. Here's what we found.

◆ **Fat-free ricotta cheese instead of light ricotta cheese:** It made the muffins tough.

◆ **Egg substitute instead of eggs:** It yielded muffins nowhere near as tender as the original recipe's, but they were acceptable.

◆ **Applesauce instead of oil:** Again, not as tender; these tasted best when eaten hot.

◆ **"Mock" buttermilk (lemon juice and milk):** It made the muffins tough.

Substitutes aside, the most common reason for tough muffins is too much flour. This is generally caused by "scooping" instead of "spooning." To accurately measure flour, stir it with a fork to aerate; then lightly spoon it into a dry measuring cup, leveling the top with a flat edge.

CRANBERRY-CITRUS MUFFINS

Turbinado sugar, with its coarse texture and mild molasses flavor, helps make the topping for these muffins extra-special. But granulated sugar also works well.

2½ cups all-purpose flour
1½ cups fresh or frozen cranberries
1 cup granulated sugar
1 tablespoon baking powder
1 teaspoon baking soda
½ teaspoon salt
¾ cup 2% low-fat milk
⅓ cup light ricotta cheese
1 tablespoon grated orange rind
½ cup orange juice
1 tablespoon grated lemon rind
2 tablespoons vegetable oil
1 tablespoon vanilla extract
2 large egg whites
1 large egg
Vegetable cooking spray
¼ cup plus 2 tablespoons turbinado or granulated sugar

1. Preheat oven to 400°.
2. Combine first 6 ingredients in a medium bowl; make a well in center of mixture. Combine milk and next 8 ingredients; stir well with a whisk. Add to flour mixture, stirring just until moist. Spoon batter into 18 muffin cups coated with cooking spray. Sprinkle turbinado sugar evenly over batter.
3. Bake at 400° for 18 minutes or until done. Remove from pans immediately, and cool on a wire rack. Yield: 1½ dozen (serving size: 1 muffin).

CALORIES 159 (14% from fat); FAT 2.4g (sat 0.6g, mono 0.7g, poly 0.9g); PROTEIN 3.4g; CARB 31.4g; FIBER 0.6g; CHOL 14mg; IRON 1mg; SODIUM 153mg; CALC 69mg

BLUEBERRY-ALMOND STREUSEL MUFFINS

2½ cups all-purpose flour
1 cup granulated sugar
1 tablespoon baking powder
1 teaspoon baking soda
½ teaspoon salt
¾ cup 2% low-fat milk
½ cup low-fat buttermilk
⅓ cup light ricotta cheese
2 tablespoons vegetable oil
1 tablespoon vanilla extract
1 teaspoon almond extract
3 large egg whites
1⅓ cups blueberries
Vegetable cooking spray
¼ cup all-purpose flour
½ cup finely chopped almonds
1 tablespoon brown sugar
1 tablespoon reduced-calorie stick margarine, melted

1. Preheat oven to 400°.
2. Combine first 5 ingredients in a large bowl; make a well in center of mixture. Combine milk and next 6 ingredients; stir well with a whisk. Add to flour mixture, stirring just until moist. Gently stir in blueberries. Spoon batter into 18 muffin cups coated with cooking spray.
3. Combine ¼ cup flour and remaining 3 ingredients; sprinkle evenly over batter. Bake at 400° for 18 minutes or until done. Remove from pans immediately, and cool on a wire rack. Yield: 1½ dozen (serving size: 1 muffin).

CALORIES 171 (24% from fat); FAT 4.5g (sat 0.8g, mono 1.8g, poly 1.2g); PROTEIN 4g; CARB 28.8g; FIBER 1.4g; CHOL 1mg; IRON 1.1mg; SODIUM 139mg; CALC 69mg

COOKING CLASS

Gathering Mushrooms

When it comes to mushrooms, supermarkets aren't just pushing buttons—from the plethora of exotic fungi available, we have recipes and what you need to know.

It wasn't so long ago that if you wanted to cook with anything other than a button mushroom, you had to go foraging. But now you only have to stroll to the produce section of any supermarket, where you're likely to find a wide variety of cultivated mushrooms with glamorous and exotic-sounding names like portobello, cremino, enoki, or shiitake.

By no means should you be intimidated by the unfamiliar names or shapes of this new crop of mushrooms. They're simple to cook with and well worth getting to know. Although each has its own unique flavor and texture, you can easily mix and match them to make new and different combinations. With so many kinds of mushrooms available, you'll have a great time discovering their uses.

CITRUS SALAD WITH SHIITAKE AND ENOKI MUSHROOMS

¼ cup rice vinegar
3 tablespoons orange juice
2 tablespoons light teriyaki sauce
1 tablespoon dark sesame oil
2 teaspoons peeled, minced fresh gingerroot
1 garlic clove, minced
2 cups orange sections
1½ cups thinly sliced cucumber
1½ cups sliced shiitake mushroom caps (about 1 [3½-ounce] package)
½ cup thinly sliced radishes
4 cups sliced romaine lettuce
1 (3-ounce) package enoki mushrooms

1. Combine first 6 ingredients in a bowl, and stir well. Stir in orange sections and next 3 ingredients; let stand 5 minutes.
2. Arrange 1 cup lettuce on each of 4 salad plates; spoon 1 cup orange mixture over each serving. Divide enoki mushrooms evenly among salads. Yield: 4 servings.

CALORIES 115 (31% from fat); FAT 4g (sat 0.6g, mono 1.4g, poly 1.6g); PROTEIN 3.6g; CARB 19.1g; FIBER 5.9g; CHOL 0mg; IRON 1.6mg; SODIUM 141mg; CALC 73mg

DUXELLES OF MUSHROOMS

A combination of finely chopped mushrooms, shallots, and onions, duxelles (dook-SEHL) is traditionally cooked in butter until it forms a thick paste. Our version has the same texture and intense flavor as the original, but without the fat. Try it spread on pizza or sandwiches, as a topping for broiled sole, or stirred into mashed potatoes.

  1 (8-ounce) package button mushrooms
 ½ cup minced onion
Butter-flavored vegetable cooking spray
  2 teaspoons minced shallots
 ½ teaspoon salt
 ⅛ teaspoon pepper
 ⅛ teaspoon nutmeg

1. Place mushrooms in a food processor, and process until finely chopped, scraping down sides of processor bowl occasionally.
2. Place mushrooms and onion in a nonstick skillet coated with cooking spray over medium-high heat; cook 3 minutes or until onion is tender. Add shallots and remaining ingredients. Cook, stirring constantly, 2 minutes. Yield: 1 cup (serving size: ¼ cup).

CALORIES 26 (17% from fat); FAT 0.5g (sat 0.1g, mono 0g, poly 0.1g); PROTEIN 1.5g; CARB 4.8g; FIBER 1.2g; CHOL 0mg; IRON 0.8mg; SODIUM 296mg; CALC 8mg

CRAB-STUFFED PORTOBELLOS

Serve as an appetizer or as a light lunch on a bed of gourmet salad greens.

  8 (4-inch) portobello mushrooms
  1 (8-ounce) block fat-free cream cheese, softened
 ½ cup finely chopped green onions
 ¼ cup light mayonnaise
  1 teaspoon lemon juice
 ½ teaspoon Old Bay seasoning
Dash of ground red pepper
  1 pound crabmeat, shell pieces removed
  1 cup quartered cherry tomatoes (about 12)
 ½ cup (2 ounces) shredded reduced-fat, reduced-sodium Swiss cheese (such as Alpine Lace)
 ½ cup dry breadcrumbs

1. Preheat oven to 425°.
2. Remove brown gills from undersides of mushrooms, using a spoon; discard gills. Remove and discard stems. Set mushroom caps aside.
3. Beat cream cheese at medium speed of an electric mixer until smooth. Add green onions and next 4 ingredients; beat well. Stir in crabmeat, tomatoes, and Swiss cheese. Spoon mixture evenly into mushroom caps. Sprinkle each cap with 1 tablespoon breadcrumbs; place on a baking sheet. Bake at 425° for 15 minutes or until tops are lightly browned. Yield: 8 servings (serving size: 1 stuffed mushroom).

CALORIES 175 (27% from fat); FAT 5.3g (sat 1.3g, mono 0.3g, poly 2g); PROTEIN 20.5g; CARB 11g; FIBER 1.6g; CHOL 69mg; IRON 2mg; SODIUM 593mg; CALC 249mg

MUSHROOM PRIMER

BUTTON: These familiar mushrooms have something of a split personality. Raw, they possess an almost nutty flavor and crisp texture. When they're sautéed or cooked in stews and sauces, their flavor concentrates and deepens to become earthy and rich. When buying buttons, look for the whitest ones (they darken with age).

CREMINO: A darker, richer-flavored cousin of the common button mushroom, the cremino (kray-MEE-no; plural, cremini) has a firm texture that stands up well to cooking. It complements both button and portobello mushrooms, as all three are part of the same family.

ENOKI: The tiny white strands of the enoki (en-OH-kee) mushroom have a delicate flavor and soft texture that tend to get lost in cooked dishes. Enoki are best raw; use them as a garnish or in salads. Or cook them quickly—1 to 2 minutes at most—for a stir-fry.

OYSTER: This mushroom derives its seafaring name from its graceful shell-like shape and its mild, slightly briny flavor. It's best when stir-fried, sautéed, or braised to bring out its distinct flavor and velvety texture.

PORTOBELLO: Surprisingly, these meaty-flavored mushrooms are actually button mushrooms that have been left to grow an extra few days. Portobellos are good candidates for stuffing, grilling, roasting, or broiling. The Italian-sounding name belies the fact that these large (up to 6 inches in diameter), dark-brown mushrooms are grown in America.

SHIITAKE: A staple in Asian cooking, shiitakes (shee-TAH-kays) can be recognized by their delicate caramel coloring and rich, smoky flavor. Eat them raw or cooked, but discard the stems because they are typically stringy and tough.

LINGUINE WITH TWO SAUCES

(pictured on page 263)

Prepare the tomato sauce first. As it simmers, make the mushroom sauce. While cremini mushrooms add a richer flavor than buttons, either will work.

    2   teaspoons olive oil
    2   garlic cloves, minced
    1   tablespoon chopped fresh basil
    ¾   teaspoon pepper, divided
    ½   teaspoon salt, divided
    2   (14.5-ounce) cans Italian-style
        diced tomatoes, undrained
  Vegetable cooking spray
    4   cups sliced cremini or button
        mushrooms (about 12 ounces)
    ½   cup all-purpose flour
    2   cups 1% low-fat milk
    1   cup (4 ounces) shredded
        reduced-fat, reduced-sodium
        Swiss cheese (such as Alpine
        Lace)
    ½   cup dry white wine
    8   cups hot cooked linguine
        (about 1 pound uncooked
        pasta)
    ¼   cup grated fresh Parmesan
        cheese
  Fresh oregano sprigs (optional)

1. Preheat oven to 350°.
2. Heat oil in a nonstick skillet over medium heat. Add garlic; sauté 30 seconds. Add basil, ¼ teaspoon pepper, ¼ teaspoon salt, and tomatoes; cook over low heat 20 minutes, stirring occasionally. Set tomato sauce aside.
3. Place a large saucepan coated with cooking spray over medium-high heat until hot. Add mushrooms; cook 5 minutes. Remove from pan; set aside. Add flour to pan. Gradually add milk, stirring with a whisk until blended. Place flour mixture over medium heat; cook, stirring constantly, until thick (about 3 minutes). Stir in Swiss cheese, wine, ½ teaspoon pepper, and ¼ teaspoon salt. Cook, stirring constantly, until cheese melts (about 1 minute). Remove from heat; stir in mushrooms.
4. Combine linguine and mushroom sauce in a large bowl. Spoon linguine mixture into a 13 x 9-inch baking dish coated with cooking spray. Spread tomato sauce evenly over linguine mixture; sprinkle with Parmesan cheese. Cover and bake at 350° for 20 minutes. Uncover and bake 5 additional minutes. Garnish with oregano sprigs, if desired. Yield: 8 servings (serving size: 1¼ cups).

CALORIES 349 (19% from fat); FAT 7.2g (sat 3.4g, mono 1.4g, poly 0.6g); PROTEIN 16.3g; CARB 54.8g; FIBER 3.2g; CHOL 15mg; IRON 3.3mg; SODIUM 527mg; CALC 172mg

SAUTÉ OF CHICKEN, LEEKS, AND MUSHROOMS

    2   small leeks, trimmed
    4   chicken thighs (about ¾
        pound), skinned
    ½   teaspoon salt
    ½   teaspoon pepper
    1   teaspoon margarine
    ½   cup dry white wine
    ½   cup low-salt chicken broth
    3   cups sliced shiitake mushroom
        caps (about 2 [3½-ounce]
        packages)
    ¼   cup evaporated skim milk
    ½   teaspoon dried tarragon
    4   cups hot cooked brown
        rice

1. Remove roots, outer leaves, and tops from leeks. Rinse leeks under cold running water; cut into 2-inch julienne strips to measure 1 cup.
2. Sprinkle chicken with salt and pepper. Melt margarine in a nonstick skillet over medium heat. Add chicken; cook 4 minutes on each side or until browned. Add leeks; cook 3 minutes or until soft. Add wine and broth; bring to a boil. Cover, reduce heat, and simmer 10 minutes or until chicken is done, turning chicken once. Remove chicken from skillet; set aside, and keep warm.
3. Add mushrooms to leek mixture in skillet; cook over high heat 1 minute. Add milk and tarragon; reduce heat, and simmer, uncovered, 3 minutes or until sauce is thick. Serve chicken and sauce over brown rice. Yield: 4 servings (serving size: 1 chicken thigh, 1 cup rice, and ½ cup sauce).

CALORIES 352 (14% from fat); FAT 5.6g (sat 1.3g, mono 1.9g, poly 1.7g); PROTEIN 20.8g; CARB 54.2g; FIBER 4.4g; CHOL 55mg; IRON 3mg; SODIUM 400mg; CALC 98mg

WILD-MUSHROOM SPOON BREAD

Serve with roasted chicken or pork.

    2   teaspoons vegetable oil
    1   cup chopped onion
    1½ teaspoons minced fresh thyme
    2   garlic cloves, minced
    2   cups sliced shiitake mushroom
        caps
    2   cups sliced cremini mushrooms
    2   cups water
    ¾   teaspoon salt
    1   cup cornmeal
    1   cup 1% low-fat milk
    2   large egg yolks, lightly beaten
    4   large egg whites (at room
        temperature)
  Vegetable cooking spray

1. Preheat oven to 400°.
2. Heat oil in a large nonstick skillet over medium-high heat. Add onion, thyme, and garlic; sauté 3 minutes or until tender. Spoon onion mixture into a bowl; set aside. Add mushrooms to skillet. Cover and cook over low heat 8 minutes or until liquid nearly evaporates, stirring occasionally.
3. Combine water and salt in a saucepan; bring to a boil. Gradually add cornmeal, stirring constantly with a whisk. Cook, stirring constantly, 2 minutes. Remove from heat; stir in onion mixture, mushrooms, milk, and egg yolks.
4. Beat egg whites at high speed of an electric mixer until stiff peaks form. Gently fold egg whites into cornmeal mixture. Pour into a 2-quart soufflé dish coated with cooking spray. Bake at 400° for 40 minutes or until puffy and set. Serve immediately. Yield: 6 servings (serving size: 1 cup).

CALORIES 171 (23% from fat); FAT 4.4g (sat 1.2g, mono 1.3g, poly 1.2g); PROTEIN 7.9g; CARB 25.1g; FIBER 2.4g; CHOL 74mg; IRON 1.9mg; SODIUM 355mg; CALC 71mg

CREAMY POTATO-MUSHROOM SOUP

2 bacon slices
4 cups chopped cremini mushrooms
½ cup chopped shallots
3½ cups cubed Yukon Gold or baking potato
1 (14½-ounce) can fat-free chicken broth
2 cups 1% low-fat milk
2 tablespoons sherry
½ teaspoon salt
¼ teaspoon pepper

1. Cook bacon in a Dutch oven over medium heat until crisp. Remove bacon from Dutch oven; crumble and set aside. Add mushrooms and shallots to bacon drippings in Dutch oven; sauté 5 minutes or until mushrooms are soft. Remove from Dutch oven; set aside.
2. Add potato and broth to Dutch oven; bring to a boil. Cover, reduce heat, and simmer 12 minutes or until potato is very tender. Transfer potato mixture to a food processor; process until smooth. Return to Dutch oven. Add mushroom mixture, milk, and remaining 3 ingredients; cook over low heat 10 minutes or until thoroughly heated. Ladle soup into bowls; top with crumbled bacon. Yield: 4 servings (serving size: 1½ cups).

CALORIES 236 (13% from fat); FAT 3.5g (sat 1.5g, mono 1.2g, poly 0.4g); PROTEIN 13.2g; CARB 39.4g; FIBER 3.3g; CHOL 9mg; IRON 2.4mg; SODIUM 521mg; CALC 172mg

MUSHROOM-LOVER'S PIZZA

Almost any combination of mushrooms can be used to top this pizza.

1 (10-ounce) can refrigerated pizza crust dough
1 tablespoon cornmeal
1¼ cups sliced oyster mushroom caps (about 3.75 ounces)
1¼ cups sliced cremini mushrooms
¼ cup thinly sliced shallots
1 teaspoon dried Italian seasoning
¼ teaspoon pepper
¼ cup grated fresh Parmesan cheese
¼ cup (1 ounce) shredded fontina cheese or Swiss cheese

1. Preheat oven to 500°.
2. Roll dough into a 13 x 9-inch rectangle; place on a baking sheet sprinkled with cornmeal. Arrange mushrooms and shallots over dough. Sprinkle with Italian seasoning and pepper; top with cheeses. Bake at 500° for 10 minutes or until crust is golden. Yield: 6 servings.

CALORIES 160 (23% from fat); FAT 4.5g (sat 2.1g, mono 1.3g, poly 0.7g); PROTEIN 4.9g; CARB 25.3g; FIBER 0.6g; CHOL 11mg; IRON 0.8mg; SODIUM 249mg; CALC 85mg

GLOBETROTTING

In Search of Exotic Discoveries

Cookbook author Marie Simmons and writer Eileen Stukane traveled halfway around the world to reach Malaysia. This haunting land is a melting pot of Malays, Chinese, Indians, and ethnic tribes. As everyone has blended to form one exotic nation, so have they created a spicy, multicultural cuisine.

BEEF RENDANG
Malaysian-Style Beef Stew

We simmered the meat in beef broth rather than high-fat coconut milk; however, just before serving, we added a small amount of coconut milk for flavoring. (Be sure to use unsweetened canned light coconut milk, instead of the sweetened type popular in making fruit drinks.)

1 pound lean, boned sirloin steak
2 teaspoons vegetable oil
Vegetable cooking spray
⅓ cup chopped shallots
1 tablespoon peeled, grated fresh gingerroot
1 tablespoon peeled, minced fresh lemon grass
½ teaspoon dried crushed red pepper
3 garlic cloves, minced
2 (14¼-ounce) cans fat-free beef broth, divided
½ cup unsweetened light coconut milk
⅛ teaspoon salt
4 cups hot cooked rice
1 tablespoon plus 1 teaspoon chopped fresh cilantro

1. Trim fat from steak; cut steak into ½-inch cubes. Heat oil in a large non-stick skillet over high heat. Add steak; cook 4 minutes or until steak loses its pink color. Drain well, and set aside. Wipe drippings from skillet with a paper towel.
2. Place skillet coated with cooking spray over medium-high heat until hot. Add shallots and next 4 ingredients; sauté 1 minute. Return steak to skillet. Stir in 2 cups broth; bring to a boil. Cover, reduce heat, and simmer 45 minutes. Stir in remaining broth; cover and simmer 45 additional minutes or until steak is tender. Remove from heat; stir in coconut milk and salt. Serve over rice, and sprinkle with fresh cilantro. Yield: 4 servings (serving size: ⅓ cup meat mixture and 1 cup rice).

CALORIES 506 (28% from fat); FAT 15.8g (sat 9g, mono 3.5g, poly 1.4g); PROTEIN 30.5g; CARB 56.4g; FIBER 1.3g; CHOL 73mg; IRON 5.4mg; SODIUM 141mg; CALC 47mg

CURRIED VEGETABLES

- 1 cup diagonally sliced carrot
- 1¼ cups peeled, cubed baking potato (about ½ pound)
- 2 cups cauliflower florets
- 2 cups (1-inch) diagonally sliced green beans
- 1½ teaspoons vegetable oil
- ½ cup coarsely chopped onion
- 1 tablespoon peeled, grated fresh gingerroot
- 1 garlic clove, minced
- 1 tablespoon curry powder
- ½ cup no-salt-added chicken broth
- 1 cup plain low-fat yogurt
- ½ teaspoon salt
- ⅛ teaspoon pepper
- 6 cups hot cooked rice
- ¼ cup chopped unsalted cashews
- ¼ cup coarsely chopped fresh cilantro

1. Layer first 4 ingredients in a steamer basket over boiling water. Cover and steam 10 minutes or until vegetables are tender.
2. Heat oil in a large skillet over medium-high heat. Add onion, and sauté until golden. Add gingerroot and garlic; sauté 1 minute. Add curry powder, and stir well. Add broth, and bring to a boil. Remove from heat.
3. Combine yogurt, salt, and pepper in a small bowl. Gradually add about half of hot broth mixture to yogurt mixture, stirring constantly with a whisk. Stir yogurt mixture into remaining broth mixture in skillet. Add steamed vegetables to skillet, tossing gently. Serve vegetable mixture over rice; sprinkle with cashews and cilantro. Yield: 6 servings (serving size: 1 cup vegetable mixture, 1 cup rice, 2 teaspoons cashews, and 2 teaspoons cilantro).

CALORIES 359 (13% from fat); FAT 5.1g (sat 1.2g, mono 2.2g, poly 1.1g); PROTEIN 9.6g; CARB 69.1g; FIBER 4.7g; CHOL 2mg; IRON 3.4mg; SODIUM 252mg; CALC 137mg

PANSOH
Chicken with Lemon Grass and Ginger

You may substitute ½ teaspoon grated lemon zest for each tablespoon of lemon grass.

- 1 pound skinned, boned chicken breasts, cut into 1-inch pieces
- ½ pound skinned, boned chicken thighs, cut into 1-inch pieces
- ⅔ cup chopped shallots
- ½ cup chopped fresh cilantro
- ¼ cup peeled, chopped fresh gingerroot
- 3 tablespoons peeled, finely chopped fresh lemon grass
- ½ teaspoon salt
- ⅛ teaspoon pepper
- 1 pound okra pods
- 6 cups hot cooked long-grain rice

1. Preheat oven to 325°.
2. Combine first 8 ingredients in a large bowl; stir well. Cut 1 (20-inch-long) sheet of aluminum foil; place chicken mixture on half of foil sheet. Spread into a single layer, leaving a 1-inch margin around edges of foil. Fold other half of foil sheet over chicken mixture. Bring edges of foil together, and fold several times to form a sealed packet. Place foil packet on a baking sheet. Bake at 325° for 45 minutes.
3. Arrange okra in a steamer basket over boiling water. Cover and steam 10 minutes or until crisp-tender.
4. Remove chicken mixture from oven, and let stand 5 minutes. For each serving, spoon ⅔ cup chicken mixture and juices over 1 cup rice; top with ½ cup okra. Yield: 6 servings.

CALORIES 399 (6% from fat); FAT 2.8g (sat 0.7g, mono 0.7g, poly 0.6g); PROTEIN 31.2g; CARB 59.7g; FIBER 2.1g; CHOL 75mg; IRON 3.9mg; SODIUM 288mg; CALC 111mg

CHICKEN SATÉ

(pictured on page 263)

Tamarind concentrate is available as a paste or pulp, usually in a sticky, semidry block. Steep it in boiling water to extract the tart, flavorful juice; the remaining fibrous part should be discarded. You can use 1 tablespoon dark molasses and 1 tablespoon lime juice as a substitute.

- ⅓ cup unsalted, dry-roasted peanuts
- 2 cups water
- 2 tablespoons tamarind concentrate
- 1 tablespoon vegetable oil
- ¼ cup chopped shallots
- 2 tablespoons peeled, finely chopped fresh lemon grass
- ½ teaspoon dried crushed red pepper
- 1 garlic clove, chopped
- 3 tablespoons sugar
- ½ teaspoon salt
- 1 pound skinned, boned chicken breast halves
- Vegetable cooking spray
- 1 cup hot cooked rice
- ½ cup chopped cucumber
- 1 tablespoon plus 1 teaspoon chopped fresh cilantro
- Fresh pineapple (optional)

1. Place peanuts in a food processor; process until ground. Spoon into a bowl; set aside.
2. Combine water and tamarind concentrate in a saucepan; stir well. Bring to a boil; cook, stirring constantly, 1 minute. Remove from heat; let stand 20 minutes. Strain mixture through a sieve over a bowl, and discard pulp.
3. Heat oil in a saucepan over medium heat. Add shallots and next 3 ingredients; sauté 1 minute or until shallots are tender. Stir in ground peanuts, tamarind mixture, sugar, and salt. Bring to a boil; cook 17 minutes or until mixture is reduced by half. Strain sauce through a sieve over a bowl; discard solids.
4. Place each chicken breast half between 2 sheets of heavy-duty plastic wrap; flatten to ⅛-inch thickness using a meat mallet. Remove plastic wrap;

cut chicken into ¾-inch-wide strips. Combine 3 tablespoons tamarind sauce and chicken strips in a heavy-duty, zip-top plastic bag. Seal; marinate in refrigerator 1 hour. Remove chicken from bag; discard marinade.

5. Loosely thread chicken strips onto 8 (8-inch) skewers. Prepare grill or broiler. Place skewers on a grill rack or rack of a broiler pan coated with cooking spray; cook 5 minutes on each side or until done. Serve skewers with rice and remaining tamarind sauce. Top each with cucumber and cilantro. Garnish with pineapple, if desired. Yield: 4 servings (serving size: 2 skewers, ¼ cup sauce, ¼ cup rice, 2 tablespoons cucumber, and 1 teaspoon cilantro).

CALORIES 361 (32% from fat); FAT 12.7g (sat 2.3g, mono 5g, poly 4.5g); PROTEIN 31.3g; CARB 30.5g; FIBER 1.9g; CHOL 72mg; IRON 1.9mg; SODIUM 362mg; CALC 42mg

STIR-FRIED NOODLES WITH SHRIMP

2 cups snow peas, trimmed
1 tablespoon plus 1 teaspoon vegetable oil, divided
1 large egg, lightly beaten
1 large egg white, lightly beaten
½ cup minced shallots
1 tablespoon peeled, minced fresh gingerroot
1 garlic clove, minced
1½ pounds large shrimp, peeled and deveined
½ teaspoon dried crushed red pepper
5 cups hot cooked linguine (about 10 ounces uncooked pasta)
2 cups fresh bean sprouts
¼ cup low-sodium soy sauce
¼ cup diagonally sliced green onions

1. Arrange snow peas in a steamer basket over boiling water. Cover and steam 3 minutes or until crisp-tender.
2. Heat 1 teaspoon oil in a large Dutch oven over medium heat. Add egg and egg white; cook, stirring constantly, until egg is done. Remove from Dutch oven; set aside.

3. Heat 1 tablespoon oil in Dutch oven over medium heat. Add shallots, gingerroot, and garlic; sauté 3 minutes or until shallots begin to brown. Add shrimp and red pepper; sauté 4 minutes or until shrimp is done. Add pasta, and toss well. Add snow peas, egg, bean sprouts, and soy sauce; cook until thoroughly heated. Remove from heat; sprinkle with green onions. Yield: 6 servings (serving size: 2 cups).

CALORIES 375 (16% from fat); FAT 6.8g (sat 1.3g, mono 1.6g, poly 2.7g); PROTEIN 33.1g; CARB 42.9g; FIBER 3.8g; CHOL 209mg; IRON 6.1mg; SODIUM 455mg; CALC 106mg

WON TON MEE

Won ton wrappers are available fresh or frozen in many supermarkets.

¾ pound pork tenderloin
1 teaspoon peeled, grated fresh gingerroot
½ teaspoon sugar
1 garlic clove, crushed
1 tablespoon low-sodium soy sauce
2 teaspoons vegetable oil
1 tablespoon minced canned water chestnuts
1 tablespoon thinly sliced green onions
1 teaspoon peeled, grated fresh gingerroot
1 teaspoon low-sodium soy sauce
¼ teaspoon dark sesame oil
1 garlic clove, crushed
1 large egg white, lightly beaten
12 won ton wrappers
8 cups water
5½ cups low-salt chicken broth
2 (¼-inch-thick) slices peeled fresh gingerroot
1 garlic clove, crushed
2 cups thinly sliced napa (Chinese) cabbage
1⅓ cups hot cooked whole-wheat spaghetti
¼ cup diagonally sliced green onions
1 tablespoon plus 1 teaspoon low-sodium soy sauce
2 teaspoons oyster sauce
1 teaspoon dark sesame oil

1. Trim fat from pork. Combine 1 teaspoon gingerroot, sugar, and 1 garlic clove in a small bowl. Rub pork with gingerroot mixture. Drizzle 1 tablespoon soy sauce over pork.
2. Heat vegetable oil in a nonstick skillet over medium-high heat. Add pork, and cook 2 minutes on each side or until browned. Cover; reduce heat to medium-low. Cook 20 minutes or until meat thermometer registers 160° (slightly pink), turning after 10 minutes. Remove from skillet; cool.
3. Finely chop 1½ ounces pork to yield ¼ cup, and set aside. Cut remaining pork crosswise into 12 slices; set aside.
4. Combine ¼ cup chopped pork, water chestnuts, and next 6 ingredients in a small bowl, stirring well.
5. Working with 1 won ton wrapper at a time (cover remaining wrappers to keep them from drying), spoon 1 teaspoon of chopped pork mixture into center of each wrapper. Moisten edges of dough with water, and bring 2 opposite corners to center, pinching points to seal. Bring remaining 2 corners to center, pinching points to seal. Pinch 4 edges together to seal.
6. Bring 8 cups water to a boil in a large saucepan. Add won tons, and cook 5 minutes. Drain and set aside.
7. Combine broth, gingerroot slices, and 1 garlic clove in saucepan; bring to a boil. Cover, reduce heat, and simmer 20 minutes. Stir in cabbage, and cook 1 minute.
8. Ladle 1½ cups broth mixture into each of 4 bowls. Add 3 won tons, 3 slices pork, and ⅓ cup spaghetti to each bowl. Top each serving with 1 tablespoon green onions, 1 teaspoon soy sauce, ½ teaspoon oyster sauce, and ¼ teaspoon sesame oil. Yield: 4 servings.

CALORIES 329 (24% from fat); FAT 8.7g (sat 2g, mono 3.1g, poly 2.5g); PROTEIN 28.1g; CARB 35.2g; FIBER 0.9g; CHOL 57mg; IRON 4.6mg; SODIUM 850mg; CALC 50mg

Sweet Pilgrimage

Because the colonists were so inventive, their classic New England desserts are still a hit.

We're inclined to think of New Englanders as bearers of a tradition in cookery that's historically rich, but a trifle stodgy and unimaginative: baked beans, Thanksgiving turkey, the boiled dinner. The truth is that even as far back as the Pilgrim days, New England cooks have been endlessly resourceful and inventive. And that's especially true at the end of the meal, when the dessert trolley rolls around. Here we highlight seven of their most famous sweets—each a new comfort dessert.

MAPLE RICE PUDDING

For our low-fat version of this pudding, we used short-grain Arborio rice to create a richer, creamier texture.

    4   cups 2% low-fat milk
    ⅔   cup Arborio rice or other
          short-grain rice
    ⅔   cup maple syrup
    ¼   cup raisins
    1   teaspoon vanilla extract
    ¼   teaspoon salt
    ¼   teaspoon ground cinnamon
    ¼   teaspoon ground nutmeg

1. Combine first 4 ingredients in a medium saucepan; bring mixture to a boil over medium heat, stirring frequently. Reduce heat to low; cook 50 minutes or until rice is tender and mixture is creamy, stirring occasionally. Remove from heat; stir in vanilla, salt, cinnamon, and nutmeg. Yield: 8 servings.

CALORIES 206 (11% from fat); FAT 2.5g (sat 1.5g, mono 0.7g, poly 0.1g); PROTEIN 5.3g; CARB 40.6g; FIBER 0.5g; CHOL 10mg; IRON 1.2mg; SODIUM 137mg; CALC 170mg

CRANBERRY-APPLE TART

(pictured on page 264)

Native Americans introduced Pilgrims to the cranberry. Colonial cooks paired the tart find with apples to make what has become a familiar fall pie.

    1   cup sugar
    2   tablespoons all-purpose flour
    1   teaspoon grated orange rind
    ⅛   teaspoon ground cinnamon
    ⅓   cup water
    4   cups diced Golden Delicious
            apple
    1½   cups fresh or frozen cranberries
    1½   cups all-purpose flour,
            divided
    7½   tablespoons ice water
    1½   teaspoons sugar
    ½   teaspoon salt
    4½   tablespoons vegetable
            shortening
    Vegetable cooking spray

1. Preheat oven to 425°.
2. Combine first 5 ingredients in a large saucepan. Stir in apple and cranberries; bring to a boil. Reduce heat, and simmer 15 minutes or until cranberries pop, stirring occasionally. Remove from heat; cool.
3. Combine ¼ cup flour and ice water, stirring with a whisk until well-blended. Combine 1¼ cups flour, 1½ teaspoons sugar, and salt in a bowl; cut in shortening with a pastry blender or 2 knives until mixture resembles coarse meal.
4. Add ice water mixture; stir with a fork until flour mixture is moist. Gently press two-thirds of flour mixture into a 4-inch circle on heavy-duty plastic wrap; cover with additional plastic wrap. Repeat procedure with remaining flour mixture. Roll larger portion of dough, still covered, into an 11-inch circle. Roll smaller portion of dough, still covered, into a 9-inch circle. Chill both portions of dough 10 minutes or until plastic can be easily removed.
5. Working with larger portion of dough, remove top sheet of plastic; fit dough, uncovered side down, into a 9-inch round removable-bottom tart pan coated with cooking spray. Remove remaining sheet of plastic. Fold edges of pastry under; press up sides of pan. Spoon cranberry mixture into crust.
6. Working with smaller portion of dough, remove top sheet of plastic. Cut dough into ½-inch-wide strips. Gently remove dough strips from bottom sheet of plastic; arrange in a lattice design over cranberry mixture. Seal dough strips to edge of crust. Place tart on a baking sheet.
7. Bake at 425° for 40 minutes or until crust is browned and filling is bubbly. Cool tart on a wire rack. Yield: 8 servings.

CALORIES 287 (20% from fat); FAT 6.5g (sat 1.8g, mono 2.3g, poly 2.2g); PROTEIN 2.8g; CARB 55.9g; FIBER 2.6g; CHOL 0mg; IRON 1.3mg; SODIUM 147mg; CALC 10mg

BOSTON CREAM PIE

This dessert isn't a pie at all; it consists of two layers of sponge cake with a custard filling. It was Boston's Parker House hotel that crowned this "pie" with its now familiar chocolate topping. (In the more traditional version, powdered sugar is dusted on top.)

Vanilla Pastry Cream
Vegetable cooking spray
  2 teaspoons cake flour
  ½ cup sugar
3½ tablespoons stick margarine
  1 teaspoon vanilla extract
  1 large egg yolk
1½ cups sifted cake flour
1½ teaspoons baking powder
  ½ teaspoon salt
  ¾ cup skim milk
  2 large egg whites
  3 tablespoons sugar
Chocolate Glaze

1. Prepare Vanilla Pastry Cream.
2. Preheat oven to 350°.
3. Coat bottom of a 9-inch round cake pan with cooking spray. Dust with 2 teaspoons flour; set aside.
4. Beat ½ cup sugar and margarine in a medium bowl at medium speed of an electric mixer until well-blended (about 5 minutes). Add vanilla and egg yolk; beat well. Sift together 1½ cups flour, baking powder, and salt. Add flour mixture to creamed mixture alternately with milk, beginning and ending with flour mixture.
5. Beat egg whites at high speed of mixer until foamy, using clean, dry beaters. Gradually add 3 tablespoons sugar, beating mixture until stiff peaks form. Gently stir one-fourth of egg white mixture into batter. Gently fold in remaining egg white mixture. Pour into prepared pan. Bake at 350° for 35 minutes or until a wooden pick inserted in center comes out clean. Cool in pan 10 minutes on a wire rack; remove from pan. Cool completely on wire rack.
6. Split cake in half horizontally using a serrated knife; place bottom layer, cut side up, on a serving plate. Spread Vanilla Pastry Cream evenly over bottom layer; top with remaining cake layer. Spread Chocolate Glaze evenly over top. Chill 1 hour or until glaze is set. Yield: 10 servings.

CALORIES 269 (26% from fat); FAT 7.7g (sat 2.6g, mono 3g, poly 1.5g); PROTEIN 5.4g; CARB 45.2g; FIBER 0.1g; CHOL 48mg; IRON 1.7mg; SODIUM 214mg; CALC 124mg

Vanilla Pastry Cream:

  1 large egg, lightly beaten
  ⅓ cup sugar
2½ tablespoons cornstarch
1¼ cups 2% low-fat milk
1½ teaspoons vanilla extract

1. Place egg in a bowl, and set aside. Combine sugar and cornstarch in a saucepan. Gradually add milk to saucepan, stirring with a whisk until blended. Bring to a boil over medium heat; cook, stirring constantly, 1 minute. Remove from heat. Gradually stir one-fourth of hot milk mixture into egg; add to remaining milk mixture, stirring constantly. Cook over medium heat, stirring constantly, 1 minute or until thick. Remove from heat; stir in vanilla. Pour mixture into a bowl; place plastic wrap on surface, and chill. Yield: 1½ cups.

Chocolate Glaze:

  2 ounces semisweet chocolate, coarsely chopped
3½ tablespoons water
2½ tablespoons fat-free sweetened condensed milk

1. Combine all ingredients in a medium glass bowl; microwave at HIGH 1 minute or until almost melted. Stir until smooth. Yield: ¼ cup.

MARLBOROUGH PIE

This rich pie can be made with shredded apples or applesauce.

  1 cup all-purpose flour, divided
3½ tablespoons ice water
  1 teaspoon sugar
  ¼ teaspoon salt
  3 tablespoons vegetable shortening
Vegetable cooking spray
  2 cups sweetened applesauce
  ½ cup sugar
  ½ cup evaporated skim milk
  2 tablespoons reduced-calorie stick margarine, melted
  2 tablespoons lemon juice
  2 tablespoons cream sherry
  ½ teaspoon ground cinnamon
  ¼ teaspoon ground nutmeg
  2 large eggs

1. Preheat oven to 400°.
2. Combine ¼ cup flour and ice water, stirring with a whisk until well-blended. Combine ¾ cup flour, 1 teaspoon sugar, and salt in a bowl; cut in shortening with a pastry blender or 2 knives until mixture resembles coarse meal. Add ice water mixture; mix with a fork until flour mixture is moist. Gently press mixture into a 4-inch circle on heavy-duty plastic wrap; cover with additional plastic wrap. Roll dough, still covered, into an 11-inch circle; chill for 10 minutes or until plastic can be easily removed.
3. Remove top sheet of plastic wrap; fit dough, uncovered side down, into a 9-inch pie plate coated with cooking spray. Remove remaining sheet of plastic wrap. Fold edges under, and flute. Pierce bottom and sides of dough with a fork. Bake at 400° for 8 minutes; cool on a wire rack.
4. Combine applesauce and remaining 8 ingredients in a bowl, stirring well with a whisk. Pour into prepared crust; bake at 400° for 10 minutes. Reduce oven temperature to 325°; bake 55 additional minutes or until filling is set. Cool completely on a wire rack. Yield: 8 servings.

CALORIES 245 (28% from fat); FAT 7.5g (sat 2g, mono 2.8g, poly 2.2g); PROTEIN 4.6g; CARB 40.2g; FIBER 1.2g; CHOL 56mg; IRON 1.3mg; SODIUM 138mg; CALC 60mg

UPSIDE-DOWN PINEAPPLE-SPICE CAKE

1 tablespoon plus 1 teaspoon
   stick margarine
⅓ cup orange juice
¼ cup packed brown sugar
7 (½-inch) slices fresh pineapple
¼ cup stick margarine, softened
½ cup granulated sugar
¼ cup honey
1 large egg
1¼ cups sifted cake flour
1½ teaspoons ground cinnamon
1 teaspoon baking powder
½ teaspoon baking soda
½ teaspoon salt
½ teaspoon ground nutmeg
¼ cup skim milk
2 teaspoons grated orange rind
1¼ teaspoons vanilla extract

1. Preheat oven to 350°.
2. Melt 1 tablespoon plus 1 teaspoon margarine in a 10-inch cast-iron or heavy skillet. Add orange juice and brown sugar; bring to a boil, stirring constantly. Remove from heat. Arrange pineapple slices in a single layer over brown sugar mixture; set aside.
3. Beat ¼ cup margarine and next 3 ingredients at medium speed of an electric mixer until thick and fluffy. Combine flour and next 5 ingredients in a large bowl. Add flour mixture to creamed mixture alternately with milk, beginning and ending with flour mixture; beat well after each addition. Stir in rind and vanilla. Pour batter over pineapple slices.
4. Bake at 350° for 35 minutes or until a wooden pick inserted in center comes out clean. Cool in skillet 5 minutes on a wire rack. Loosen cake from sides of skillet using a narrow metal spatula. Invert onto a cake plate, and cut into wedges. Serve warm. Yield: 10 servings (serving size: 1 wedge).

CALORIES 278 (28% from fat); FAT 8.5g (sat 2.2g, mono 3.5g, poly 2.3g); PROTEIN 2.7g; CARB 48.9g; FIBER 0.1g; CHOL 30mg; IRON 1.9mg; SODIUM 332mg; CALC 64mg

CHOCOLATE-POTATO TWEED CAKE

3 large egg whites
⅛ teaspoon cream of tartar
1½ cups sugar, divided
⅓ cup stick margarine, softened
1 cup peeled, cooked, mashed
   red potato
1 large egg
2¼ cups all-purpose flour
½ cup unsweetened cocoa
1½ teaspoons baking powder
1 teaspoon salt
1 teaspoon ground cinnamon
½ teaspoon baking soda
¼ teaspoon ground cloves
¼ teaspoon ground nutmeg
½ cup 1% low-fat milk
1 teaspoon vanilla extract
Vegetable cooking spray
1 teaspoon sifted unsweetened
   cocoa
¾ cup frozen reduced-calorie
   whipped topping, thawed

1. Preheat oven to 350°.
2. Beat egg whites and cream of tartar at high speed of an electric mixer until foamy. Gradually add ¼ cup sugar, 1 tablespoon at a time; beat until stiff peaks form. Set aside.
3. Beat 1¼ cups sugar and margarine in a large bowl at medium speed until well-blended (about 5 minutes). Add mashed potatoes and 1 egg; beat well. Combine flour and next 7 ingredients. Add flour mixture to potato mixture alternately with milk, beginning and ending with flour mixture. Fold egg white mixture and vanilla into batter; pour batter into a 12-cup Bundt pan coated with cooking spray.
4. Bake at 350° for 45 minutes or until a wooden pick inserted in center comes out clean. Cool in pan 10 minutes; remove from pan. Cool completely on a wire rack. Cut into 12 slices. Sprinkle with cocoa; dollop each serving with 1 tablespoon whipped topping. Yield: 12 servings.

CALORIES 289 (22% from fat); FAT 7g (sat 1.9g, mono 2.5g, poly 1.9g); PROTEIN 6g; CARB 50.9g; FIBER 1.1g; CHOL 19mg; IRON 2.3mg; SODIUM 338mg; CALC 69mg

SPICED PEARS IN RED WINE

If you can't find Seckels (they're in season August through December), five or six full-size Bosc pears can be substituted. Look for crystallized ginger and star anise in the spice section at Asian markets, supermarkets, or specialty-food shops.

2 tablespoons lemon juice
10 Seckel pears (about 2¾
   pounds), peeled
1 (750-milliliter) bottle Merlot
   or other red wine
½ cup sugar
5 (3 x 1-inch) orange rind
   strips
½ cup orange juice
2 (3-inch) cinnamon sticks
1 star anise (optional)
5 teaspoons chopped crystallized
   ginger

1. Sprinkle lemon juice over pears; drain.
2. Combine wine and next 4 ingredients in a large non-aluminum Dutch oven. Add star anise, if desired; bring to a boil. Reduce heat, and cook, covered, 10 minutes. Add pears; simmer 10 minutes or until tender, turning pears occasionally. Remove pears from wine mixture using a slotted spoon. Place in a shallow bowl; set aside.
3. Bring wine mixture to a boil over high heat; cook 10 minutes or until reduced to about 2 cups. Discard solids. Spoon wine mixture over pears; sprinkle with ginger. Yield: 10 servings (serving size: 1 pear, 3 tablespoons wine sauce, and ½ teaspoon ginger).

CALORIES 146 (4% from fat); FAT 0.7g (sat 0g, mono 0.1g, poly 0.2g); PROTEIN 0.9g; CARB 37.5g; FIBER 4.3g; CHOL 0mg; IRON 0.7mg; SODIUM 6mg; CALC 25mg

OCTOBER

Nobody Does It Bitter

Americans are catching on to just how many boldly flavorful olives there are in the world.

Able to grow in difficult soil, the olive tree offers shade, beauty, and sustenance—no wonder its branches are an age-old symbol of peace. But the truth is, olives are hot, and not just because of their healthful oil: They fit right in with the mature food tastes and light-cooking preferences of today. The intense, sophisticated flavors of olives give recipes a powerful zing, and a little goes a long way. And although olives are fairly high in fat, it's monounsaturated, the kind that helps lower cholesterol.

Native to Asia Minor and the Mediterranean, each variety is as different as the country it's grown in, be it France, Greece, Italy, Lebanon, Morocco, or Spain. When we last counted, there were some 30 different kinds of olives sold commercially, available in shades of green, gold, purple, and black.

For the following recipes, we have created Mediterranean-style dishes that any olive can feel perfectly at home in. Although each recipe calls for a specific type of olive, don't be afraid to experiment with different kinds.

PROVENÇALE PIZZA

1 package dry yeast
½ cup warm water (105° to 115°)
2 teaspoons olive oil, divided
1⅓ cups all-purpose flour
¼ teaspoon salt
Vegetable cooking spray
4 cups finely chopped onion
½ cup sliced bottled roasted red bell peppers
1 teaspoon minced fresh thyme or ¼ teaspoon dried thyme
2 garlic cloves, minced
¼ cup dry white wine
1 teaspoon cornmeal
8 pitted oil-cured olives, halved
¼ cup grated fresh Parmesan cheese

1. Sprinkle yeast over warm water in a small bowl, and let stand 5 minutes.

Stir in 1 teaspoon oil. Place flour and salt in a food processor; pulse 2 times or until blended. With processor on, slowly add yeast mixture through food chute; process until mixture forms a ball. Turn dough out onto a lightly floured surface, and knead lightly 4 or 5 times.
2. Place dough in a large bowl coated with cooking spray, turning to coat top. Cover and let rise in a warm place (85°), free from drafts, for 40 minutes or until doubled in bulk.
3. Heat 1 teaspoon oil in a large non-stick skillet over medium-high heat until hot. Add onion, and sauté 15 minutes or until onion is golden. Add bell pepper, thyme, and garlic; reduce heat to medium-low, and cook 5 minutes, stirring frequently. Stir in wine, and simmer 5 minutes or until wine evaporates.

4. Preheat oven to 450°.
5. Punch dough down; roll dough into a 10½-inch circle on a lightly floured surface. Place dough on a large baking sheet sprinkled with cornmeal. Top with onion mixture and olives. Sprinkle with cheese. Bake at 450° for 20 minutes or until crust is golden. Yield: 4 servings (serving size: 1 wedge).

CALORIES 316 (17% from fat); FAT 5.9g (sat 1.8g, mono 3g, poly 0.8g); PROTEIN 10.9g; CARB 56.1g; FIBER 5.2g; CHOL 5mg; IRON 4.3mg; SODIUM 367mg; CALC 142mg

HUMMUS PITAS WITH FETA-OLIVE SALSA

1 (15-ounce) can no-salt-added chickpeas (garbanzo beans)
1 tablespoon tahini (sesame seed paste)
1 garlic clove, peeled
Dash of dried crushed red pepper
3 tablespoons fresh lemon juice
1 cup chopped tomato
¾ cup seeded, chopped English cucumber
¼ cup chopped green onions
¼ cup chopped pitted kalamata olives
¼ cup crumbled feta cheese
2 tablespoons minced fresh cilantro
1 tablespoon minced fresh mint
4 (6-inch) pita bread rounds, halved

1. Drain chickpeas in a colander over a bowl, reserving 1 tablespoon liquid. Combine chickpeas, tahini, garlic, and red pepper in a food processor; process until smooth, scraping sides of processor bowl once. Add lemon juice and reserved chickpea liquid; process until smooth. Spoon mixture into a bowl.
2. Combine tomato and next 6 ingredients in a bowl. Spoon ¼ cup hummus mixture into each pita half; top with ¼ cup feta-olive salsa. Yield: 4 servings (serving size: 2 stuffed pita halves).

CALORIES 299 (22% from fat); FAT 7.3g (sat 2g, mono 2.3g, poly 2.4g); PROTEIN 12.7g; CARB 47.7g; FIBER 4.9g; CHOL 8mg; IRON 4.1mg; SODIUM 337mg; CALC 135mg

PENNE PUTTANESCA

2 (14.5-ounce) cans no-salt-added whole tomatoes, undrained and chopped
Vegetable cooking spray
1 cup chopped green onions
4 canned anchovy fillets, drained and finely chopped or 2 teaspoons anchovy paste
½ cup dry white wine
¼ cup chopped pitted niçoise olives
2 tablespoons capers
2 teaspoons dried marjoram
¼ teaspoon pepper
4 garlic cloves, minced
5 cups hot cooked penne (about 12 ounces uncooked tubular-shaped pasta)
¼ cup plus 1 tablespoon grated Parmesan cheese

1. Drain tomatoes in a colander over a bowl; reserve ½ cup juice. Set aside.
2. Place a large nonstick skillet coated with cooking spray over medium-low heat. Add onions and anchovies; sauté 3 minutes or until tender. Add tomatoes, reserved juice, wine, and next 5 ingredients; cook over medium heat 8 minutes or until reduced to 2½ cups. For each serving, spoon ½ cup tomato mixture over 1 cup pasta; sprinkle with 1 tablespoon cheese. Yield: 5 servings.

CALORIES 229 (15% from fat); FAT 3.9g (sat 1.5g, mono 1.2g, poly 0.5g); PROTEIN 10g; CARB 39.2g; FIBER 2.5g; CHOL 5mg; IRON 2.9mg; SODIUM 742mg; CALC 168mg

CHICKEN SALAD WITH OLIVES, FENNEL, AND ORANGE

1 large orange
2 cups shredded ready-to-eat roasted skinned, boned chicken breasts (about 2 breasts)
1 cup thinly sliced fennel bulb (about 1 medium bulb)
1½ tablespoons minced fennel fronds
1½ tablespoons white wine vinegar
1 tablespoon minced shallots
½ teaspoon sugar
½ teaspoon extra-virgin olive oil
6 oil-cured olives, pitted and thinly sliced

1. Peel orange; cut in half lengthwise. Cut halves crosswise into slices. Combine orange, chicken, and remaining ingredients in a large bowl; toss well. Yield: 3 servings (serving size: 1 cup). *Note:* We recommend serving this salad the same day it's made.

CALORIES 138 (20% from fat); FAT 3.1g (sat 0.9g, mono 1.2g, poly 0.2g); PROTEIN 8.8g; CARB 9.2g; FIBER 2.4g; CHOL 47mg; IRON 1.2mg; SODIUM 461mg; CALC 59mg

WHY NOT TAKE OLIVE ME?

Of the olive varieties available today, we chose the following, which you can find in most supermarkets.

KALAMATA: This smooth, dark-purple olive comes from Greece. Sometimes spelled "calamata," it has a pleasing aftertaste.

MANZANILLA: These are traditional green cocktail olives. They have a crisp flesh and smoky flavor. (Black Mission olives can be substituted in recipes.)

NIÇOISE: These small, dark-brown or purple olives have a sharp and slightly sour flavor. Because the pits are large for the size of the olive, there isn't much fruit left after they're pitted.

OIL-CURED: Oil-cured are jet-black and very wrinkled. They're the most bitter of all.

SPANISH OMELETS

(pictured on page 298)

1½ cups sliced potato
½ cup chopped onion
½ cup chopped red bell pepper
1 garlic clove, minced
¼ cup sliced pitted manzanilla (or green) olives
1 tablespoon minced fresh oregano or 1 teaspoon dried oregano
½ cup (2 ounces) shredded part-skim mozzarella cheese
8 large egg whites
4 large eggs
¼ teaspoon salt
⅛ teaspoon pepper
½ teaspoon olive oil, divided
Vegetable cooking spray

1. Place potato in a saucepan; cover with water. Bring to a boil; reduce heat, and simmer 15 minutes or until tender. Drain and let cool. Dice potato, and set aside.
2. Heat a medium nonstick skillet over medium heat. Add onion, bell pepper, and garlic; sauté 8 minutes. Add potato, olives, and oregano; cook 1 minute or until thoroughly heated. Remove from heat; stir in cheese.
3. Combine egg whites and next 3 ingredients in a bowl; stir well with a whisk.
4. Heat ¼ teaspoon olive oil in a small nonstick skillet coated with cooking spray over medium-high heat; add half of egg mixture. Carefully lift edges of omelet with a spatula; allow uncooked portion to flow underneath cooked portion. Cook 3 minutes; flip omelet. Spoon 1 cup potato mixture onto half of omelet. Carefully loosen with a spatula; fold in half. Cook 1 additional minute on each side. Slide onto a plate. Repeat procedure with cooking spray, ¼ teaspoon olive oil, egg mixture, and potato mixture. Yield: 4 servings (serving size: ½ omelet). *Note:* Substitute 2 cups egg substitute for 8 egg whites and 4 eggs, if desired.

CALORIES 213 (38% from fat); FAT 9.1g (sat 3.3g, mono 3.5g, poly 1g); PROTEIN 18.1g; CARB 14.5g; FIBER 1.7g; CHOL 229mg; IRON 2mg; SODIUM 462mg; CALC 157mg

CHICKEN WITH OLIVES AND RAISINS

To round off this dish, serve it with couscous.

- ⅔ cup dry white wine
- ½ cup raisins
- ½ chopped pitted manzanilla (or green) olives
- ¼ cup balsamic vinegar
- 2 tablespoons minced fresh oregano or 2 teaspoons dried oregano
- 4 garlic cloves, minced
- 4 (4-ounce) skinned, boned chicken breast halves
- 1 teaspoon olive oil
- ¾ cup minced shallots
- 1 cup low-salt chicken broth

1. Combine first 7 ingredients in a large zip-top plastic bag; seal bag, and shake to coat. Marinate in refrigerator for 1 to 2 hours. Remove chicken from bag, reserving marinade.
2. Heat oil in a large nonstick skillet over medium-high heat. Add chicken; sauté 3 minutes on each side. Remove from skillet. Set aside; keep warm. Reduce heat to medium. Add shallots; sauté 3 minutes. Add reserved marinade and broth; simmer 3 minutes. Return chicken to skillet; cook 2 minutes or until thoroughly heated. Yield: 4 servings (serving size: 1 chicken breast half and ½ cup sauce).

CALORIES 266 (21% from fat); FAT 6.1g (sat 1.4g, mono 3g, poly 1g); PROTEIN 30.6g; CARB 23.1g; FIBER 1.7g; CHOL 77mg; IRON 3.2mg; SODIUM 248mg; CALC 70mg

FOR TWO

Core of the Matter

Apples are not just for pies and desserts. As proof, here are recipes using apples in savory dishes.

WARM SPINACH SALAD WITH CHICKEN AND APPLES

- 2 (4-ounce) skinned, boned chicken breast halves
- ⅛ teaspoon salt
- Vegetable cooking spray
- 1 cup chopped Red Delicious apple
- 1 tablespoon lemon juice
- 1 tablespoon cornstarch
- ½ cup low-salt chicken broth
- 3 tablespoons apple jelly
- 1 tablespoon apple juice
- 1 tablespoon olive oil
- 1 teaspoon cider vinegar
- ⅛ teaspoon salt
- 1 small garlic clove, minced
- 6 cups fresh spinach leaves
- 1 cup chopped radicchio
- ¼ cup grated fresh Parmesan cheese

1. Sprinkle chicken with ⅛ teaspoon salt. Place a nonstick skillet coated with cooking spray over medium-high heat. Add chicken; cook 4 minutes on each side or until done. Slice into thin strips. Set aside; keep warm. Toss apple with lemon juice; set aside.
2. Combine cornstarch and broth in a bowl; add to skillet. Bring to a boil. Cook, stirring constantly, 1 minute. Reduce heat to medium. Add jelly and next 5 ingredients; stir with a whisk. Add spinach and radicchio; cook 2 minutes or until spinach slightly wilts. Divide spinach mixture between 2 plates. Top with chicken and apple; sprinkle with cheese. Yield: 2 servings (serving size: 1 chicken breast half, 1 cup spinach mixture, ½ cup apple, and 2 tablespoons cheese).

Note: If radicchio is not available, increase spinach to 7 cups.

CALORIES 425 (25% from fat); FAT 13.3g (sat 3.8g, mono 6.4g, poly 1.3g); PROTEIN 37.7g; CARB 41.8g; FIBER 9.8g; CHOL 75mg; IRON 6.8mg; SODIUM 779mg; CALC 383mg

CURRIED SWEET POTATO-APPLE PILAF

- 1½ teaspoons olive oil
- ¼ cup chopped green onions
- 1 garlic clove, minced
- ½ cup uncooked long-grain rice
- 1 cup water
- ⅔ cup peeled, diced sweet potato
- 1 cup peeled, cubed Granny Smith apple
- ¼ cup frozen green peas
- 2 tablespoons currants
- ¾ teaspoon curry powder
- ½ teaspoon ground cumin
- ¼ teaspoon salt

1. Heat oil in a saucepan over medium-high heat. Add onions and garlic; sauté 1 minute. Stir in rice; sauté 1 minute. Add water and potato; bring to a boil. Cover, reduce heat, and simmer 15 minutes or until liquid is almost absorbed. Stir in apple and remaining ingredients. Cover; simmer 3 minutes or until heated. Yield: 2 servings (serving size: 1¼ cups).

CALORIES 307 (13% from fat); FAT 4.3g (sat 0.6g, mono 2.7g, poly 0.5g); PROTEIN 5.7g; CARB 61.6g; FIBER 4.4g; CHOL 0mg; IRON 3.5mg; SODIUM 326mg; CALC 53mg

TURKEY CUTLETS WITH APPLE CHUTNEY

- 1¼ cups chopped Granny Smith apple (about 8 ounces)
- 1 cup diced tomato
- ¾ cup thinly sliced onion
- 3 tablespoons brown sugar
- 2 tablespoons cider vinegar
- ⅛ teaspoon ground cloves
- ⅛ teaspoon ground ginger
- 4 (2-ounce) turkey cutlets
- ⅛ teaspoon salt
- Dash of white pepper
- 1 teaspoon oil
- Vegetable cooking spray

1. Combine first 7 ingredients in a saucepan; bring to a boil. Cover, reduce heat, and simmer 45 minutes, stirring occasionally. Remove from heat; let stand 10 minutes. Cover; chill.
2. Sprinkle turkey with salt and pepper. Heat oil in a nonstick skillet coated with cooking spray over medium-high heat. Add turkey; cook 2 minutes on each side or until done. Serve turkey with apple chutney. Yield: 2 servings (serving size: 3 ounces turkey and ¼ cup chutney).
Note: Refrigerate remaining chutney in an airtight container for up to 2 weeks.

CALORIES 203 (20% from fat); FAT 4.6g (sat 1g, mono 1g, poly 1.6g); PROTEIN 27.2g; CARB 12.6g; FIBER 1.7g; CHOL 68mg; IRON 1.7mg; SODIUM 217mg; CALC 25mg

Everyone into the Kitchen

Letting your kids help make dinner can teach them, and you, many things.

Cooking with your children can be a true joy. And it's more than an exercise in making dinner or baking cookies. It's a form of communication—an opportunity to let the parent-child guard down and talk about the day in school.

There are many other lessons to be learned from cooking with our offspring. Improved hand-eye coordination, for example, can be a side benefit of learning to roll burritos or egg rolls. You can also teach kids about counting, color composition, shapes, and especially the importance of cleaning up after oneself. Above all, these kitchen experiences should be fun and without pressure.

All of these recipes are kids' favorites. Depending on their age, your children should be able to prepare these recipes with minimal supervision. They are all recipes that the whole family will enjoy.

OPEN-FACED APPLE-CHEESE BAGELS

Vegetable cooking spray
1 medium Granny Smith apple, cut into 16 wedges
1 teaspoon brown sugar
¼ cup tub-style light cream cheese, softened
2 (3-ounce) plain bagels, split and toasted (such as Lender's Big and Crusty)
¼ cup (1 ounce) shredded reduced-fat sharp Cheddar cheese
2 (¾-ounce) slices lean Canadian bacon, coarsely chopped
2 tablespoons chopped green onions

1. Preheat oven to 425°.
2. Place a nonstick skillet coated with cooking spray over medium-high heat until hot. Add apple and sugar; sauté 3 minutes. Remove from heat.
3. Spread 1 tablespoon cream cheese over each bagel half; top each with 4 apple wedges. Sprinkle cheese and bacon evenly over apple. Bake at 425° for 8 minutes. Remove from oven; sprinkle with green onions. Yield: 2 servings (serving size: 2 bagel halves).

CALORIES 424 (23% from fat); FAT 10.8g (sat 5g, mono 1.6g, poly 1.0g); PROTEIN 20.6g; CARB 60.6g; FIBER 4.1g; CHOL 36mg; IRON 3.6mg; SODIUM 1,016mg; CALC 239mg

GARDEN-VEGGIE PRIMAVERA

1 tablespoon olive oil
½ cup sliced carrot
½ cup sliced celery
½ cup broccoli florets
½ cup red bell pepper rings
1 garlic clove, minced
½ cup tomato juice
¼ cup chopped fresh basil
½ cup frozen green peas
¼ teaspoon salt
⅛ teaspoon pepper
2 cups hot cooked farfalle (about 1½ cups uncooked bow tie pasta)
2 tablespoons grated fresh Parmesan cheese

1. Heat oil in a large nonstick skillet over medium heat until hot. Add carrot and next 4 ingredients; sauté 3 minutes. Stir in tomato juice and basil; simmer 3 minutes. Add peas, salt, and ⅛ teaspoon pepper; cook 2 minutes. Add pasta; toss well. Sprinkle with cheese. Yield: 4 servings (serving size: 1 cup).

CALORIES 175 (25% from fat); FAT 4.9g (sat 1.1g, mono 2.8g, poly 0.6g); PROTEIN 6.4g; CARB 26.4g; FIBER 2.4g; CHOL 2mg; IRON 1.8mg; SODIUM 357mg; CALC 75mg

NOODLE-AND-CHEESE PUDDING

1 cup 1% low-fat cottage cheese
1 cup vanilla low-fat yogurt
½ cup packed brown sugar
½ cup tub-style light cream cheese
½ teaspoon salt
½ teaspoon ground cinnamon
½ teaspoon pepper
½ teaspoon vanilla extract
2 large eggs, lightly beaten
2 large egg whites, lightly beaten
4 cups cooked medium egg noodles (about 8 ounces uncooked)
Vegetable cooking spray

1. Preheat oven to 375°.
2. Combine first 10 ingredients in a large bowl. Add noodles; toss gently to coat. Spoon noodle mixture into a 13 x 9-inch baking dish coated with cooking spray. Cover and bake at 375° for 1 hour. Serve warm or at room temperature. Yield: 9 servings.

CALORIES 230 (19% from fat); FAT 4.9g (sat 2.2g, mono 1.7g, poly 0.5g); PROTEIN 11.2g; CARB 34.9g; FIBER 1.6g; CHOL 82mg; IRON 1.7mg; SODIUM 355mg; CALC 102mg

SABRINA'S GARDEN BOLOGNESE

½ cup chopped sun-dried tomatoes, packed without water
½ cup boiling water
2 teaspoons olive oil
1 cup diced onion
1 cup diced zucchini
1 cup sliced mushrooms
½ cup diced green bell pepper
½ cup diced red bell pepper
2 garlic cloves, minced
1 (25.5-ounce) jar fat-free pasta sauce
3 tablespoons minced fresh basil or 1 tablespoon dried basil
4 cups hot cooked linguine (about 8 ounces uncooked pasta)

1. Combine sun-dried tomatoes and boiling water in a bowl; let stand 30 minutes. Drain tomatoes; chop.
2. Heat oil in a Dutch oven over medium-high heat. Add sun-dried tomatoes, onion, and next 5 ingredients; sauté 3 minutes. Stir in pasta sauce. Bring to a boil; reduce heat, and simmer 20 minutes. Stir in basil. Serve with linguine. Yield: 4 servings (serving size: 1 cup sauce and 1 cup pasta).

CALORIES 354 (10% from fat); FAT 4g (sat 0.6g, mono 1.9g, poly 0.9g); PROTEIN 11.9g; CARB 69.7g; FIBER 4g; CHOL 0mg; IRON 2.9mg; SODIUM 557mg; CALC 47mg

NOODLE FRITTATA

2 teaspoons vegetable oil
1 cup chopped broccoli florets
½ cup diced carrot
½ cup frozen green peas, thawed
1 cup hot cooked angel hair (about 2 ounces uncooked pasta)
4 large eggs, lightly beaten
2 large egg whites, lightly beaten
⅛ teaspoon salt
⅛ teaspoon pepper
½ cup (2 ounces) shredded reduced-fat extra-sharp Cheddar cheese
1 cup low-fat vegetable primavera spaghetti sauce

1. Heat oil in a large nonstick skillet over medium heat. Add broccoli, carrot, and peas; sauté 8 minutes. Stir in pasta; sauté 1 minute. Combine 4 eggs and next 3 ingredients in a large bowl; stir with a whisk. Stir egg mixture into vegetable mixture in skillet, and cook 5 minutes. Top with cheese.
2. Preheat broiler. Wrap handle of skillet with aluminum foil; broil frittata 1½ minutes. Serve with spaghetti sauce. Yield: 4 servings (serving size: 1 wedge and ¼ cup sauce).

CALORIES 253 (39% from fat); FAT 11g (sat 3.7g, mono 3.4g, poly 2g); PROTEIN 16.8g; CARB 20.8g; FIBER 1.6g; CHOL 230mg; IRON 1.9mg; SODIUM 489mg; CALC 175mg

THREE-BEAN TACOS

1 teaspoon olive oil
1 cup diced onion
½ cup diced red bell pepper
½ cup diced green bell pepper
1 tablespoon chili powder
2 teaspoons dried oregano
1 teaspoon ground cumin
1 garlic clove, minced
1 cup canned chickpeas (garbanzo beans), rinsed and drained
½ cup canned black beans, rinsed and drained
½ cup canned pinto beans, rinsed and drained
1 (8-ounce) can no-salt-added tomato sauce
12 taco shells
¾ cup shredded iceberg lettuce
¾ cup diced tomato
½ cup (2 ounces) finely shredded reduced-fat sharp Cheddar cheese
½ cup salsa

1. Heat oil in a large nonstick skillet over medium-high heat until hot. Add onion and next 6 ingredients; sauté 2 minutes. Add chickpeas, beans, and tomato sauce. Bring to a boil; reduce heat, and simmer 20 minutes or until thick.
2. Prepare taco shells according to package directions. Spoon ¼ cup bean mixture into each taco shell. Top each with 1 tablespoon lettuce, 1 tablespoon tomato, 2 teaspoons cheese, and 2 teaspoons salsa. Yield: 12 servings (serving size: 1 taco).

CALORIES 140 (34% from fat); FAT 5.3g (sat 1.2g, mono 0.8g, poly 1.4g); PROTEIN 5.3g; CARB 18.7g; FIBER 2.8g; CHOL 3mg; IRON 1.6mg; SODIUM 185mg; CALC 82mg

CRISPY ZUCCHINI COINS

½ cup Italian-seasoned breadcrumbs
3 tablespoons grated Parmesan cheese
¼ teaspoon pepper
3 cups thinly sliced zucchini (about 1 pound)
2 egg whites, lightly beaten
Vegetable cooking spray

1. Preheat oven to 450°.
2. Combine first 3 ingredients in a shallow bowl, stirring well.
3. Dip zucchini slices in egg whites; dredge in breadcrumb mixture. Place zucchini in a single layer on a baking sheet coated with cooking spray. Bake at 450° for 20 minutes. Turn zucchini over; bake 15 additional minutes or until outside is crispy and browned. Yield: 4 servings (serving size: about ⅔ cup).

CALORIES 94 (17% from fat); FAT 1.8g (sat 0.9g, mono 0.3g, poly 0.1g); PROTEIN 6.5g; CARB 13.6g; FIBER 0.6g; CHOL 3mg; IRON 1mg; SODIUM 498mg; CALC 83mg

COCOA-PEANUT BUTTER BANANA BITES

4 small firm ripe bananas (about 1 pound)
½ cup crispy wheat cereal squares, crushed
1 tablespoon smooth peanut butter
1 tablespoon honey
1 teaspoon unsweetened cocoa

1. Cut bananas in half lengthwise.
2. Combine cereal and remaining 3 ingredients; stir well. Spread 1 tablespoon cereal mixture over cut sides of 4 banana halves; top with remaining

halves. Cut each banana crosswise into 6 pieces. Serve immediately. Yield: 8 servings (serving size: 3 pieces).

CALORIES 84 (15% from fat); FAT 1.4g (sat 0.3g, mono 0.5g, poly 0.4g); PROTEIN 1.5g; CARB 18.3g; FIBER 2g; CHOL 0mg; IRON 0.7mg; SODIUM 30mg; CALC 6mg

TUTTI-FRUTTI SMOOTHIE

This creamy drink is ideal for breakfast, an after-school snack, or dessert.

  1   cup sliced ripe banana
       (about 1 medium)
  1   cup orange juice
  ¾   cup peeled, sliced peaches
  ¾   cup sliced strawberries
  1   tablespoon honey

1. Combine all ingredients in a blender; cover and process until smooth. Serve immediately. Yield: 3 cups (serving size: 1 cup).

CALORIES 134 (3% from fat); FAT 0.5g (sat 0.1g, mono 0.1g, poly 0.1g); PROTEIN 1.6g; CARB 33.8g; FIBER 3.3g; CHOL 0mg; IRON 0.5mg; SODIUM 2mg; CALC 18mg

FAST FOOD

Now You're Really Sizzlin'

If you want to sear in flavor when you cook seafood, sautéing is the quickest way to go.

Sautéing seafood is one of the fastest ways to get dinner on the table, and one of the most flavorful. That's because the intense heat sears the surface of fish and shellfish, locking in the juices. The high temperatures also help produce a rich, deep crust. In these five simple recipes, we've built even more depth into the flavor of the seafood by adding spices, salsas, and sauces.

CITRUS SCALLOPS

Preparation time: 20 minutes
Cooking time: 4 minutes

  1½ pounds sea scallops
  2   tablespoons lemon juice
  1   tablespoon chopped fresh
       parsley
  1   teaspoon grated orange rind
  ½   teaspoon salt
  ⅛   teaspoon pepper
  2   garlic cloves, minced
  1   tablespoon olive oil
  1   tablespoon chopped fresh
       parsley

1. Combine first 7 ingredients in a large bowl, stirring well to coat. Chill 5 minutes.
2. Heat oil in a large nonstick skillet over medium-high heat. Add scallop mixture; sauté 4 minutes or until scallops are done. Top with 1 tablespoon parsley. Yield: 4 servings (serving size: 5 ounces scallops).

CALORIES 184 (26% from fat); FAT 5.3g (sat 0.6g, mono 2.6g, poly 0.7g); PROTEIN 28.7g; CARB 5.3g; FIBER 0g; CHOL 56mg; IRON 0.6mg; SODIUM 362mg; CALC 45mg

CAJUN SHRIMP

Try serving these spicy shrimp with easy-to-make cheese grits. Simply stir shredded cheese into plain cooked grits.
Preparation time: 10 minutes
Cooking time: 4 minutes

  1½ pounds large shrimp, peeled
       and deveined
  1   teaspoon paprika
  ¾   teaspoon dried thyme
  ¾   teaspoon dried oregano
  ¼   teaspoon garlic powder
  ¼   teaspoon salt
  ¼   teaspoon black pepper
  ¼   to ½ teaspoon ground red
       pepper
  1   tablespoon vegetable oil

1. Combine first 8 ingredients in a large zip-top plastic bag; seal bag, and shake to coat. Heat oil in a large nonstick skillet over medium-high heat

until hot. Add shrimp; sauté 4 minutes or until shrimp are done. Yield: 4 servings (serving size: 5 ounces shrimp).

CALORIES 185 (29% from fat); FAT 6g (sat 1.1g, mono 1.4g, poly 2.7g); PROTEIN 29g; CARB 2.2g; FIBER 0.3g; CHOL 215mg; IRON 4.1mg; SODIUM 357mg; CALC 85mg

SALMON WITH CORN-AND-TOMATO SALSA

Preparation time: 20 minutes
Cooking time: 11 minutes

  1   cup diced plum tomatoes
  ¼   cup minced red onion
  2   tablespoons chopped fresh
       cilantro
  2   tablespoons white wine vinegar
  2   tablespoons fresh lime juice
  ⅛   teaspoon salt
  1   jalapeño pepper, seeded and
       minced
Vegetable cooking spray
  1   cup frozen whole-kernel corn,
       thawed
  4   (6-ounce) salmon fillets
  ¼   teaspoon salt
  ¼   teaspoon pepper
  2   tablespoons honey
Lime wedges (optional)
Cilantro sprigs (optional)

1. Combine first 7 ingredients in a bowl; set aside.
2. Place a large nonstick skillet coated with cooking spray over medium-high heat until hot. Add corn; cook 2 minutes, stirring occasionally. Add corn to tomato mixture; stir well.
3. Sprinkle salmon with ¼ teaspoon salt and ¼ teaspoon pepper; drizzle with honey. Coat skillet with cooking spray; place over medium-high heat until hot. Add salmon; cook 5 minutes on each side or until fish flakes easily when tested with a fork. Serve salmon with salsa. If desired, garnish with lime wedges and cilantro sprigs. Yield: 4 servings (serving size: 1 salmon fillet and ½ cup salsa).

CALORIES 374 (37% from fat); FAT 15.2g (sat 2.6g, mono 7.1g, poly 3.4g); PROTEIN 38g; CARB 21.4g; FIBER 2g; CHOL 115mg; IRON 1.4mg; SODIUM 312mg; CALC 20mg

HALIBUT FILLETS WITH TERIYAKI SAUCE

Sesame pasta-and-vegetable salad*

*Combine 2 cups cooked vermicelli, ½ cup thinly sliced zucchini, ½ cup sliced carrots, and ¼ cup chopped green onions in a bowl. Toss with 2 tablespoons low-sodium teriyaki sauce and 1 tablespoon dark sesame oil.

HALIBUT FILLETS WITH TERIYAKI SAUCE

Another white fish, such as grouper or haddock, can be substituted for the halibut.
Preparation time: 5 minutes
Cooking time: 10 minutes

- ½ cup pineapple juice
- 3 tablespoons low-sodium teriyaki sauce
- 1 tablespoon honey
- ¾ teaspoon cornstarch
- ¼ teaspoon garlic powder
- ⅛ teaspoon ground red pepper
- 2 tablespoons seasoned breadcrumbs
- 4 (6-ounce) halibut fillets, skinned (about 1 inch thick)
- 1 tablespoon vegetable oil

1. Combine first 6 ingredients in a small bowl; stir well with a whisk.
2. Combine breadcrumbs and halibut in a large zip-top plastic bag. Seal and shake to coat.
3. Heat oil in a large nonstick skillet over medium heat. Add fillets; cook 4 minutes on each side or until halibut flakes easily when tested with a fork. Remove halibut from skillet; set aside, and keep warm.
4. Add teriyaki mixture to skillet. Bring to a boil; cook, stirring constantly, 1 minute. Pour over halibut. Yield: 4 servings (serving size: 1 halibut fillet and 2 tablespoons sauce).

CALORIES 280 (24% from fat); FAT 7.4g (sat 1.2g, mono 2.1g, poly 3.1g); PROTEIN 36.9g; CARB 14.1g; FIBER 0.1g; CHOL 80mg; IRON 1.9mg; SODIUM 304mg; CALC 96mg

SWORDFISH WITH OLIVES AND CAPERS

Preparation time: 15 minutes
Cooking time: 19 minutes

- ⅓ cup dry white wine
- 1½ teaspoons capers
- ¼ teaspoon salt
- ⅛ teaspoon dried crushed red pepper
- 12 pimento-stuffed olives, halved
- 2 garlic cloves, minced
- 1 (14.5-ounce) can no-salt-added diced tomatoes, undrained
- ¼ teaspoon salt
- 4 (6-ounce) swordfish steaks (about 1½ inches thick)
- 1 teaspoon olive oil
- Olive oil-flavored vegetable cooking spray
- 1 cup thinly sliced onion
- 2 cups cooked linguine (about 4 ounces uncooked pasta)

1. Combine first 7 ingredients in a medium bowl; set aside.
2. Sprinkle ¼ teaspoon salt over swordfish. Heat oil in a large nonstick skillet coated with cooking spray over medium-high heat until hot. Add swordfish; cook 4 minutes on each side or until swordfish flakes easily when tested with a fork. Remove swordfish from skillet; set aside, and keep warm.
3. Coat skillet with cooking spray; place over medium-high heat until hot. Add onion; sauté 4 minutes or until lightly browned. Add tomato mixture; bring to a boil. Cover, reduce heat, and simmer 5 minutes.
4. Return swordfish steaks to skillet, nestling them in tomato mixture. Cover and simmer 1 minute or until sauce thickens. Place ½ cup linguine on each plate; top each with a swordfish steak and ½ cup sauce. Yield: 4 servings.

CALORIES 353 (23% from fat); FAT 9.6g (sat 2.3g, mono 4.4g, poly 2.0g); PROTEIN 38g; CARB 26.9g; FIBER 1.6g; CHOL 66mg; IRON 3mg; SODIUM 722mg; CALC 55mg

QUICK & EASY WEEKNIGHTS

Simple Continental Fare

By tossing together a few simple ingredients, you can create a light continental meal: Tuscan bean soup with a tangy romaine salad. Add Italian bread and a glass of wine to complete this perfect picture.

MENU

TOMATO-AND-WHITE BEAN SOUP

ROMAINE SALAD WITH TANGY LEMON-DIJON DRESSING

Toasted Italian bread

About 435 calories and 11.5 grams of fat (24% calories from fat)

TOMATO-AND-WHITE BEAN SOUP

You can substitute navy beans for the cannellini beans, if preferred.

- 2 teaspoons olive oil
- 1 cup chopped onion
- 3 garlic cloves, crushed
- 2 (14.5-ounce) cans no-salt-added whole tomatoes, undrained and chopped
- 2 (16-ounce) cans cannellini or other white beans, drained
- 1 (14½-ounce) can fat-free chicken broth
- 1 tablespoon chopped fresh parsley
- ¾ teaspoon dried oregano
- ¼ teaspoon pepper
- ¼ cup grated Parmesan cheese

1. Heat oil in a large saucepan over medium heat. Add onion and garlic; sauté 4 minutes or until tender. Add

tomatoes and next 5 ingredients; bring to a boil. Reduce heat, and simmer, uncovered, 10 minutes. Ladle into bowls, and sprinkle with cheese. Yield: 4 servings (serving size: 2 cups soup and 1 tablespoon cheese).

CALORIES 297 (22% from fat); FAT 7.2g (sat 1.7g, mono 2.9g, poly 1.8g); PROTEIN 18.2g; CARB 42.0g; FIBER 5.7g; CHOL 4mg; IRON 4.2mg; SODIUM 451mg; CALC 154mg

Digging Those New Potatoes

Sweet and buttery in flavor, blue-, yellow-, and gold-skinned potatoes are enjoying a '90s revival.

ROMAINE SALAD WITH TANGY LEMON-DIJON DRESSING

¼ cup water
3 tablespoons Dijon mustard
2 tablespoons fresh lemon juice
2 teaspoons olive oil
¼ teaspoon salt
¼ teaspoon pepper
2 garlic cloves, minced
8 cups torn romaine lettuce
¼ cup finely chopped red onion
¼ cup plus 2 tablespoons plain croutons
Cracked pepper (optional)

1. Combine first 7 ingredients in a small bowl, stirring with a whisk until well-blended. Combine lettuce and onion in a bowl. Drizzle dressing over salad; toss well. Top with croutons. Sprinkle with cracked pepper, if desired. Yield: 4 servings (serving size: 1½ cups salad and 1½ tablespoons croutons).

CALORIES 82 (44% from fat); FAT 4.0g (sat 0.5g, mono 1.9g, poly 0.6g); PROTEIN 2.8g; CARB 9.3g; FIBER 2.2g; CHOL 0mg; IRON 1.6mg; SODIUM 524mg; CALC 46mg

Supermarket choices that were once limited to brown- or red-skinned potatoes are now blooming and svelte. Tasty newcomers with blue, yellow, and even gold skins are headed for America's dining tables. And instead of concealing them with goop, we're now celebrating their natural attributes.

Trendsetting "new" potatoes such as Yukon golds, Peruvian blues, yellow Finns, and fingerlings may be hot additions to our food scene, but they're old hat to the international set, says Stephen Love, a potato-variety development specialist at the University of Idaho. "Most of the world has always eaten blue, yellow, and gold potatoes as part of their normal diets. They're categorized as folk varieties and aren't really new."

Like all potatoes, these new specialty strains have high vitamin C and potassium contents, but research conducted at the University of Idaho has uncovered significantly higher variations in their concentrations of natural sugars.

If you're interested in trying these upscale potatoes, the best place to find them in their fingerling or more common rounded shapes continues to be farmers' markets. But you can also look for them in the produce departments of natural-foods markets, specialty-foods shops, and major supermarket chains.

FINGERLING POTATOES WITH OREGANO PESTO

Any kind of potato will work in place of the fingerlings. Just cut the potatoes up into 2-inch chunks.

2 cups torn spinach leaves
2 cups fresh parsley leaves
1 cup fresh oregano leaves
2 tablespoons grated fresh Parmesan cheese
2 tablespoons sliced almonds, toasted
1 tablespoon lemon juice
¼ teaspoon salt
2 large garlic cloves, peeled
2 tablespoons olive oil
16 fingerling potatoes (about 1½ pounds)

1. Preheat oven to 425°.
2. Combine first 8 ingredients in a food processor; process until smooth. With food processor on, slowly add oil through food chute; process until well-blended.
3. Place potatoes on a jelly-roll pan. Bake at 425° for 20 minutes or until potatoes are tender, stirring occasionally. Place potatoes in a large bowl, and add ⅓ cup pesto, tossing gently to coat. Yield: 4 servings (serving size: 4 potatoes).
Note: Store remaining pesto in an airtight container in refrigerator for up to 1 week.

CALORIES 188 (25% from fat); FAT 5.3g (sat 0.9g, mono 3.4g, poly 0.6g); PROTEIN 5.9g; CARB 31.2g; FIBER 4.9g; CHOL 1mg; IRON 4.1mg; SODIUM 135mg; CALC 96mg

ROASTED-GARLIC MASHED POTATOES

1 whole garlic head
1 tablespoon olive oil
1 pound peeled Yukon Gold or red potatoes, quartered
3 cups water
½ cup 1% low-fat milk
¼ teaspoon salt
¼ teaspoon pepper

1. Preheat oven to 375°.
2. Remove white papery skin from garlic head (do not peel or separate cloves). Rub oil over garlic head; wrap in aluminum foil. Bake at 375° for 1 hour; cool 10 minutes. Separate cloves; squeeze to extract garlic pulp. Set aside. Discard skins.
3. Place potatoes and water in a saucepan. Bring to a boil; cook 15 minutes or until very tender. Drain. Heat milk in pan over medium heat until hot (do not boil). Add potatoes, salt, and pepper; beat at medium speed of an electric mixer until potato mixture is smooth. Add garlic pulp; stir well. Yield: 5 servings (serving size: ½ cup).

CALORIES 105 (27% from fat); FAT 3.1g (sat 0.5g, mono 2.1g, poly 0.3g); PROTEIN 3.9g; CARB 16.6g; FIBER 1.8g; CHOL 1mg; IRON 3.2mg; SODIUM 140mg; CALC 79mg

Variations:

Mashed Potatoes with Sage: Omit garlic; stir in 2 tablespoons minced fresh sage to beaten potato mixture.
Chive-and-Goat Cheese Potatoes: Omit garlic; stir in ½ cup crumbled goat cheese and 3 tablespoons minced chives to beaten potato mixture.

PROVENÇALE POTATO GRATIN

1¼ pounds yellow Finnish or red potatoes, cut into ⅛-inch-thick slices
Vegetable cooking spray
3 plum tomatoes, cut into ⅛-inch-thick slices (about 1 cup), divided
1 cup thinly sliced red onion, separated into rings and divided
3 tablespoons chopped fresh basil, divided
¼ teaspoon salt
¼ teaspoon pepper
2 tablespoons thinly sliced ripe olives
½ cup low-salt chicken broth or water
2 teaspoons olive oil
½ cup grated Asiago cheese

1. Preheat oven to 400°. Arrange one-third of potato slices in bottom of an 8-inch baking dish or a 2-quart casserole coated with cooking spray. Top potatoes with ⅓ cup tomato slices, ⅓ cup onion slices, 1 tablespoon basil, ¼ teaspoon salt, and ¼ teaspoon pepper. Repeat layers except for salt and pepper; sprinkle sliced ripe olives over the top layer.
2. Combine broth and oil; drizzle over potato mixture. Cover with aluminum foil, and bake at 400° for 40 minutes. Uncover; bake 25 minutes or until potatoes are tender. Sprinkle potatoes with cheese, and bake for 3 minutes or until cheese melts. Yield: 4 servings (serving size: 1 cup).
Note: This recipe can also be prepared in 4 individual gratin dishes. The baking time will be the same.

CALORIES 240 (27% from fat); FAT 7.2g (sat 2.8g, mono 3.1g, poly 0.6g); PROTEIN 9.2g; CARB 36.5g; FIBER 4g; CHOL 10mg; IRON 1.4mg; SODIUM 435mg; CALC 193mg

ROASTED VARIEGATED POTATOES WITH GARLIC AND ROSEMARY

Blanching the potatoes and garlic before roasting decreases the cooking time significantly.

1 whole garlic head
4 fingerling potatoes (about ½ pound)
4 yellow Finnish potatoes (about ½ pound)
4 small red or blue potatoes (about ½ pound)
1 tablespoon chopped fresh rosemary
1 tablespoon olive oil
¼ teaspoon salt
¼ teaspoon pepper
Rosemary sprigs (optional)

1. Preheat oven to 425°.
2. Remove white papery skin from garlic head (do not peel or separate cloves). Place potatoes and garlic in a saucepan. Cover with water; bring to a boil. Drain immediately; pat dry.
3. Combine chopped rosemary and next 3 ingredients in a large bowl; add potatoes, tossing to coat. Arrange potatoes and garlic on a jelly-roll pan. Bake at 425° for 30 minutes or until tender, stirring occasionally. Separate garlic head into cloves, and discard skins. Serve with potatoes. Garnish with

rosemary sprigs, if desired. Yield: 4 servings (serving size: 3 potatoes).

CALORIES 181 (18% from fat); FAT 3.7g (sat 0.5g, mono 2.5g, poly 0.4g); PROTEIN 4.8g; CARB 33.8g; FIBER 3.4g; CHOL 0mg; IRON 2.6mg; SODIUM 161mg; CALC 55mg

CHICKEN AND POTATOES NIÇOISE

Niçoise is a French word meaning "as prepared in Nice." In this variation on salade Niçoise, we substituted chicken for tuna and tossed the potatoes with a garlicky vinaigrette.

  3 cups thinly sliced yellow Finnish potatoes or red potatoes (about 1 pound)
  ¼ cup dry white wine
  2 cups (2-inch) cut green beans (about ½ pound)
  ¼ cup minced shallots, divided
  2 tablespoons Dijon mustard, divided
  ½ teaspoon dried tarragon
  4 (4-ounce) skinned, boned chicken breast halves
Vegetable cooking spray
  3 tablespoons white wine vinegar
  2 tablespoons olive oil
  1 tablespoon anchovy paste
  3 garlic cloves, minced
  4 curly leaf lettuce leaves
  8 cherry tomatoes, halved
  1 tablespoon chopped green onions

1. Arrange potatoes in a steamer basket over boiling water. Cover and steam 15 minutes or until tender; cool slightly. Place potatoes in a bowl; add wine, stirring gently to coat. Arrange green beans in steamer basket over boiling water. Cover and steam 6 minutes or until crisp-tender. Rinse under cold water; drain and set aside.
2. Preheat broiler. Combine 2 tablespoons shallots, 1 tablespoon mustard, and tarragon in a small bowl. Brush shallot mixture over both sides of chicken.
3. Place chicken on a broiler pan coated with cooking spray; broil 6 minutes on each side or until chicken

is done. Cool slightly; cut chicken into ½-inch-wide strips. Set aside.
4. Combine 2 tablespoons shallots, 1 tablespoon mustard, vinegar, and next 3 ingredients in a large bowl. Add potatoes and green beans; toss gently to coat.
5. Spoon 1¼ cups potato salad onto each of 4 lettuce-lined plates; top each evenly with chicken strips and tomato halves. Sprinkle with green onions. Yield: 4 servings.

CALORIES 353 (29% from fat); FAT 11.3g (sat 1.9g, mono 6.3g, poly 1.4g); PROTEIN 31.8g; CARB 27.8g; FIBER 3.9g; CHOL 72mg; IRON 3.4mg; SODIUM 820mg; CALC 65mg

CHICKEN WITH POTATOES, GREEN BEANS, AND SUN-DRIED TOMATOES

Any kind of potato will work in place of the fingerlings.

  ¾ ounce sun-dried tomatoes, packed without oil (about 9)
  1 cup boiling water
  8 fingerling potatoes (about 12 ounces)
  2 cups (1½-inch) cut green beans (about 8 ounces)
  2 tablespoons all-purpose flour
  ¼ teaspoon salt
  ⅛ teaspoon pepper
  4 (4-ounce) skinned, boned chicken breast halves, cut into 1-inch strips
  1 tablespoon olive oil
  ¼ cup chopped shallots
  2 garlic cloves, minced
  ¼ cup dry white wine
  8 (¼-inch-thick) slices lemon (about 2 lemons)
  12 kalamata olives

1. Combine sun-dried tomatoes and boiling water in a bowl; let stand 30 minutes. Drain tomatoes; cut into thin strips, and set aside.
2. Arrange potatoes in a steamer basket over boiling water. Cover and steam 5 minutes. Add green beans to basket; steam, covered, 5 additional minutes or until potatoes are tender. Drain vegetables; set aside.

3. Place flour, salt, and pepper in a zip-top plastic bag; add chicken. Seal and shake to coat. Remove chicken from bag, shaking off excess flour.
4. Heat oil in a large nonstick skillet over medium-high heat. Add shallots and garlic; sauté 1 minute. Add chicken; sauté 3 minutes on each side. Stir in wine, scraping skillet to loosen browned bits. Add sun-dried tomatoes, lemon slices, and olives; cover and cook 2 minutes. Remove chicken mixture from skillet; set aside, and keep warm. Add potatoes and green beans to skillet; cook, uncovered, until thoroughly heated. Yield: 4 servings (serving size: 3 ounces chicken, 2 potatoes, and ½ cup green beans).

CALORIES 291 (20% from fat); FAT 6.5g (sat 1.2g, mono 3.8g, poly 1g); PROTEIN 31g; CARB 31.5g; FIBER 3.2g; CHOL 66mg; IRON 3.5mg; SODIUM 432mg; CALC 96mg

W I N E   P I C K S

• PROVENÇALE POTATO GRATIN *and* ROASTED VARIEGATED POTATOES WITH GARLIC AND ROSEMARY: *E. Guigal Côtes du Rhône 1992 (French red), $11 or Château de Beaucastel 1994 (French red), $45*

POTATO-WATERCRESS SOUP

This soup can also be served chilled.

- 2 teaspoons olive oil
- 1 cup finely chopped onion
- 3 garlic cloves, minced
- 3 cups peeled, cubed Yukon gold potatoes or baking potatoes
- 3 cups low-salt chicken broth
- 2 cups water
- ½ teaspoon salt
- ¼ teaspoon pepper
- ½ cup plain fat-free yogurt
- ¾ cup trimmed, minced watercress or thinly sliced spinach leaves
- ¼ cup (1 ounce) grated Gruyère cheese or Swiss cheese

1. Heat olive oil in a large saucepan over medium-high heat. Add onion and garlic; sauté 4 minutes or until onion is tender. Stir in potatoes and next 4 ingredients; bring to a boil. Cover, reduce heat, and simmer 30 minutes or until potatoes are tender.
2. Place potato mixture in a blender; cover and process until smooth. Add yogurt; process just until blended. Add watercress and cheese, stirring until cheese melts. Yield: 7 servings (serving size: 1 cup).

CALORIES 120 (26% from fat); FAT 3.4g (sat 1.2g, mono 1.6g, poly 0.3g); PROTEIN 4.7g; CARB 18.3g; FIBER 1.6g; CHOL 5mg; IRON 0.8mg; SODIUM 233mg; CALC 91mg

---

HOLIDAYS AND DESSERTS

Sweet Remembrances

Low-fat Jewish treats? Isn't that an oxymoron? Not with these lightened holiday desserts.

HONEY CAKE

Traditionally served the first night of Rosh Hashanah (the Jewish New Year), this cake expresses hope that the year to come will be sweet. You can make it two to three days ahead of time and store it in a zip-top plastic bag; the flavor actually improves over time.

Vegetable cooking spray
- 1 tablespoon dry breadcrumbs
- ¼ cup hot water
- 2 teaspoons instant espresso granules or 1 tablespoon plus 1 teaspoon instant coffee granules
- ½ cup sugar
- 2 large eggs
- ½ cup honey
- 3 tablespoons stick margarine, melted
- 1¾ cups all-purpose flour
- 1 teaspoon baking powder
- 1 teaspoon ground cinnamon
- ¼ teaspoon salt
- ½ cup chopped walnuts
- ½ cup golden raisins

1. Preheat oven to 325°.
2. Coat an 8 x 4-inch loaf pan with cooking spray; dust with breadcrumbs.
3. Combine water and espresso.
4. Combine sugar and eggs in a medium bowl; stir well with a whisk. Add honey and margarine; stir well. Combine flour and next 3 ingredients. Add half of flour mixture to sugar mixture; stir well. Add espresso mixture; stir well. Add remaining flour mixture, and stir just until flour mixture is moist. Stir in walnuts and raisins.

5. Spoon cake batter into prepared loaf pan; bake at 325° for 1 hour and 20 minutes or until a wooden pick inserted in center of cake comes out clean. Cool cake in pan 10 minutes on a wire rack, and remove from pan. Cool cake completely on wire rack. Yield: 12 servings (serving size: 1 slice).

CALORIES 236 (26% from fat); FAT 7g (sat 1.1g, mono 2.3g, poly 3g); PROTEIN 4.7g; CARB 40.9g; FIBER 1.3g; CHOL 37mg; IRON 1.5mg; SODIUM 100mg; CALC 42mg

CINNAMON-APPLE CAKE

This cake is usually served at Hanukkah (Festival of Lights). The cream cheese in the batter gives the cake lots of moisture. Because it's so tender, use a serrated knife for cutting.

- 1¾ cups sugar, divided
- ½ cup stick margarine, softened
- 1 teaspoon vanilla extract
- 6 ounces block-style fat-free cream cheese, softened (about ¾ cup)
- 2 large eggs
- 1½ cups all-purpose flour
- 1½ teaspoons baking powder
- ¼ teaspoon salt
- 2 teaspoons ground cinnamon
- 3 cups peeled, chopped Rome apple (about 2 large)

Vegetable cooking spray

1. Preheat oven to 350°.
2. Beat 1½ cups sugar, margarine, vanilla, and cream cheese at medium speed of an electric mixer until well-blended (about 4 minutes). Add eggs, 1 at a time, beating well after each addition. Combine flour, baking powder, and salt; add to creamed mixture, beating at low speed until blended.
3. Combine ¼ cup sugar and cinnamon. Combine 2 tablespoons cinnamon mixture and apple in a bowl; stir apple mixture into batter. Pour batter into an 8-inch springform pan coated with cooking spray, and sprinkle with remaining cinnamon mixture.
4. Bake at 350° for 1 hour and 15 minutes or until cake pulls away from sides of pan. Cool cake completely on

a wire rack, and cut, using a serrated knife. Yield: 12 servings.

Note: You can also make this cake in a 9-inch square cake pan or a 9-inch springform pan; just reduce the cooking time by 5 minutes.

CALORIES 281 (28% from fat); FAT 8.7g (sat 1.8g, mono 3.7g, poly 2.6g); PROTEIN 4.8g; CARB 46.3g; FIBER 1.2g; CHOL 39mg; IRON 1.1mg; SODIUM 234mg; CALC 89mg

HAMANTASCHEN

Begin preparing these Purim favorites the day ahead so the dough and filling can chill overnight.

⅔ cup sugar
¼ cup plus 2 tablespoons stick
     margarine
1 teaspoon vanilla extract
2 ounces block-style fat-free
     cream cheese (about ¼ cup)
1 large egg
2 cups all-purpose flour
1½ teaspoons baking powder
¼ teaspoon salt
12 ounces dried figs (about 2
     cups)
3 tablespoons sugar
3 tablespoons boiling water
1 tablespoon light-colored
     corn syrup
1 tablespoon lemon juice
Vegetable cooking spray

1. Combine first 4 ingredients in a large bowl; beat at medium speed of an electric mixer 2 minutes or until light and fluffy. Add egg; beat at high speed 1 minute or until smooth. Combine flour, baking powder, and salt; add to sugar mixture, beating at low speed just until flour mixture is moist. Divide dough in half. Gently shape each into a ball; wrap dough in plastic wrap. Chill 8 hours or overnight.
2. Place figs in a food processor, and pulse 6 times or until chopped. With processor on, slowly add 3 tablespoons sugar and next 3 ingredients through food chute; process until smooth, scraping sides of processor bowl twice. Spoon fig mixture into a bowl; cover and chill 8 hours or overnight.

3. Shape each ball of dough into a 10-inch log, using plastic wrap to support dough. Remove plastic wrap; cut each log into 10 (1-inch) slices. Quickly shape slices into 20 balls; place on a tray lined with wax paper. Chill 30 minutes.
4. Preheat oven to 400°.
5. Place each ball of dough between 2 sheets of wax paper; flatten to a 3½-inch circle. Spoon 1 level tablespoon fig mixture into the center of each circle. With floured hands, fold dough over filling to form a triangle; pinch edges together to seal. Place triangles 2 inches apart on baking sheets coated with cooking spray; bake at 400° for 10 minutes or until lightly browned. Remove from baking sheets; cool on a wire rack. Yield: 20 pastries.

CALORIES 163 (22% from fat); FAT 4g (sat 0.8g, mono 1.7g, poly 1.3g); PROTEIN 2.6g; CARB 30.3g; FIBER 3.2g; CHOL 12mg; IRON 1mg; SODIUM 93mg; CALC 57mg

CHALLAH BREAD PUDDING

This dessert is traditionally made from leftover challah, but you can also use any other egg-rich bread to give the pudding its dense, rich texture.

2½ cups 2% low-fat milk
½ cup dried tart cherries
½ cup golden raisins
½ cup fat-free sweetened
     condensed milk
2 teaspoons vanilla extract
1 teaspoon ground cinnamon
½ teaspoon freshly grated nutmeg
¼ teaspoon salt
3 large eggs, lightly beaten
8 cups (1-inch) cubes challah
     or other egg bread (about
     ½ loaf)
Vegetable cooking spray
2 tablespoons sugar

1. Combine first 9 ingredients in a large bowl. Add challah cubes, tossing to coat. Let challah mixture stand 30 minutes, stirring occasionally.
2. Preheat oven to 325°.
3. Coat an 11 x 7-inch baking dish with cooking spray. Spoon challah

mixture into dish; sprinkle with sugar. Bake at 325° for 55 minutes or until pudding is set. Let stand 15 minutes before serving. Yield: 12 servings.

CALORIES 235 (22% from fat); FAT 5.7g (sat 1.7g, mono 1.7g, poly 1.6g); PROTEIN 7.3g; CARB 38.6g; FIBER 1.4g; CHOL 78mg; IRON 1.6mg; SODIUM 276mg; CALC 89mg

CHOCOLATE-PINE NUT MERINGUE SMOOCHES

(pictured on page 300)

These are traditionally served at Passover, when flourless desserts are the rule. The meringue can be very sensitive to humidity, so it's best not to make them on a damp day.

4 large egg whites (at room
     temperature)
⅛ teaspoon salt
¼ teaspoon cream of tartar
1 cup sugar
1 teaspoon vanilla extract
⅓ cup pine nuts, toasted
2 ounces bittersweet chocolate,
     finely chopped

1. Preheat oven to 250°.
2. Beat egg whites and salt at medium speed of an electric mixer until foamy. Add cream of tartar; beat until soft peaks form. Gradually add sugar, 2 tablespoons at a time, beating at medium-high speed until stiff peaks form. Add vanilla; beat well. Fold in pine nuts and chocolate.
3. Cover a baking sheet with parchment paper. Spoon egg white mixture into 16 mounds on prepared baking sheet. Bake at 250° for 1 hour or until dry to touch. (Meringues are done when the surface is dry and they can be removed from paper without sticking to fingers.) Turn oven off; partially open oven door. Leave meringues in oven 30 minutes. Remove from oven; carefully remove meringues from paper. Store meringues in an airtight container up to 3 days. Yield: 16 servings.

CALORIES 87 (28% from fat); FAT 2.7g (sat 0.9g, mono 1g, poly 0.8g); PROTEIN 1.8g; CARB 15.3g; FIBER 0.1g; CHOL 0mg; IRON 0.4mg; SODIUM 32mg; CALC 3mg

HARVEST-FESTIVAL FRUIT STRUDELS

Although these are connected to Sukkoth (the end of the growing season), you can make them any time of the year because dried fruits and fresh apples are always available.

½ cup sugar
½ cup port or other sweet red wine
1 tablespoon grated orange rind
⅓ cup fresh orange juice
2 (8-ounce) packages dried mixed fruit, diced
1 (3-inch) cinnamon stick
5⅓ cups diced cooking apple (about 2 pounds)
¼ cup stick margarine
1 tablespoon plus 1 teaspoon vegetable oil
½ cup dry breadcrumbs
½ teaspoon freshly grated nutmeg
16 sheets frozen phyllo dough, thawed
Vegetable cooking spray

1. Combine first 6 ingredients in a saucepan; bring to a boil, stirring occasionally. Cover, reduce heat, and simmer 35 minutes or until liquid is absorbed, stirring occasionally. Remove from heat; stir in apple. Cool, uncovered, and discard cinnamon stick.
2. Combine margarine and oil in a small saucepan; cook over low heat until margarine melts, stirring well. Combine breadcrumbs and nutmeg in a small bowl.
3. Preheat oven to 350°.
4. Place 1 phyllo sheet on a large cutting board or work surface (cover remaining dough to keep from drying), and lightly brush with margarine mixture. Sprinkle 1½ teaspoons breadcrumb mixture lengthwise down the 4-inch center section of phyllo. Spoon ⅓ cup fruit mixture onto breadcrumb mixture about 2 inches from one short end, spreading fruit mixture to form a 4 x 2-inch rectangle. Fold one long side of phyllo over filling; repeat with other long side, overlapping phyllo.
5. Starting at short edge with filling, roll up phyllo jelly-roll fashion. (Do not roll tightly, or strudel may split.) Place strudel, seam side down, on a baking sheet coated with cooking spray. Lightly coat strudel with cooking spray. Repeat procedure with remaining phyllo, margarine mixture, breadcrumb mixture, and fruit mixture. Bake at 350° for 30 minutes or until strudels are golden. Serve warm or at room temperature. Yield: 16 servings.

CALORIES 233 (22% from fat); FAT 5.7g (sat 1g, mono 2g, poly 2.3g); PROTEIN 2.4g; CARB 45g; FIBER 1.3g; CHOL 0mg; IRON 1.8mg; SODIUM 161mg; CALC 25mg

CHEESE BLINTZES

(pictured on page 298)

Served anytime except the Sabbath, these are especially good for Shavuoth, when dairy products are the typical fare. You can make these blintzes ahead for dessert or brunch. Refrigerate the filled blintzes, then sauté them just before you're ready to serve.

1 cup fat-free cottage cheese
4 ounces tub-style light cream cheese (about ½ cup)
¼ cup granulated sugar
1 teaspoon vanilla extract
1 cup all-purpose flour
1½ cups skim milk
1½ tablespoons vegetable oil
1½ teaspoons vanilla extract
¼ teaspoon salt
3 large eggs
Vegetable cooking spray
2 cups blueberries or other fresh berries
2 teaspoons powdered sugar

1. Place cottage cheese in a blender or food processor; cover and process until smooth, scraping sides of container once. Add cream cheese, sugar, and 1 teaspoon vanilla; process until smooth. Pour mixture into a bowl; cover and chill.
2. Place flour in a medium bowl. Combine milk and next 4 ingredients; add to flour, stirring with a whisk until almost smooth. Cover and chill 2 hours.
3. Place a 10-inch crêpe pan or nonstick skillet coated with cooking spray over medium-high heat until hot. Remove pan from heat. Pour 3 tablespoons batter into pan; quickly tilt pan in all directions so batter covers pan with a thin film. Cook about 1 minute.
4. Carefully lift edge of crêpe with a spatula to test for doneness. The crêpe is ready to turn when it can be shaken loose from the pan and the underside is lightly browned. Turn crêpe over; cook 30 seconds on other side. Place crêpe on a towel; cool. Repeat procedure with remaining batter. Stack crêpes between single sheets of wax paper or paper towels to prevent sticking.
5. Spoon 3 tablespoons cheese mixture in center of each crêpe; fold sides and ends of crêpe over filling to form a rectangle. Place filled crêpes, seam sides down, on a baking sheet lined with plastic wrap. (Blintzes may be covered and chilled at this point.)
6. Place a large nonstick skillet coated with cooking spray over medium heat until hot. Place 4 blintzes, seam sides down, in skillet; cook 2 minutes or until lightly browned. Turn blintzes over; cook for 2 minutes. Repeat procedure with remaining blintzes. Serve warm with blueberries, and sprinkle with powdered sugar. Yield: 8 servings (serving size: 1 blintz and ¼ cup blueberries).

CALORIES 176 (29% from fat); FAT 5.7g (sat 2.2g, mono 1g, poly 1.2g); PROTEIN 9.1g; CARB 22.1g; FIBER 1.9g; CHOL 63mg; IRON 0.7mg; SODIUM 256mg; CALC 82mg

KOSHER DEFINED

"Kosher" means "fit to eat," and the Jewish dietary laws, or kashruth, stretch back thousands of years. Even though the prescriptions are specific, there is room for interpretation in many cases. For this reason, we don't make any claims for the kosherness of these dessert recipes in any religious sense. What we do claim, however, is that they satisfy the general guidelines for the holidays in question, and they can be eaten all year.

Sesame Beef Stir-Fry (page 315)

Spicy Bistro Steak Subs (page 312)

Spanish Omelet (page 285)

Cheese Blintz (page 296)

Savory Broiled Quail (page 310)

Venison-Vegetable Chili (page 311)

Weinkraut with Apples (page 307)

Honey-Mustard Game Hens (page 307)

Chocolate-Pine Nut Meringue Smooches (page 295)

COOKING CLASS

A Pumpkin in Your Pantry

Cooking with fresh pumpkin is easy. And as for taste, freshness adds a whole new depth of flavor.

Pick up a pumpkin and take it home. You'll find this creamy, sweet fruit is a breeze to prepare and absolutely delicious. Try the familiar Halloween variety: Cut the pumpkin into pieces and use a big, sharp knife to cut off the skin. Then toss the raw cubes with fall vegetables, salt, pepper, a dash of olive oil, and a sprinkling of vermouth, then roast the mixture in a 400° oven until tender. The result will be delicious, and the gorgeous, bright-orange pumpkin flesh adds a splash of color—as well as a healthful dose of beta carotene—to a favorite fall dish.

You can prepare fresh pumpkin every way imaginable, including throwing the whole thing, stem and all, in the oven and baking it until tender. (Talk about the lazy approach!) Basically, a whole fresh pumpkin works just as well in recipes as winter squash, but pumpkin has a mildly distinctive and appealing flavor. So for wonderful flavor and beautiful color in the fall, give fresh pumpkin first consideration.

CREAMY PUMPKIN SOUP

Sprinkle with toasted croutons, if desired.

- 2 teaspoons stick margarine
- 1 cup chopped onion
- ¾ teaspoon dried rubbed sage
- ½ teaspoon curry powder
- ¼ teaspoon ground nutmeg
- 3 tablespoons all-purpose flour
- 3 (10½-ounce) cans low-salt chicken broth
- 1 tablespoon tomato paste
- ¼ teaspoon salt
- 3 cups peeled, cubed fresh pumpkin (about 1 pound)
- 1 cup peeled, chopped McIntosh or other sweet cooking apple
- ½ cup evaporated skim milk
- Sage sprigs (optional)

1. Melt margarine in a Dutch oven over medium heat. Add onion; sauté 3 minutes. Add rubbed sage, curry powder, and nutmeg; cook 30 seconds. Stir in flour; cook 30 seconds. Add broth, tomato paste, and salt, stirring well with a whisk. Stir in pumpkin and apple; bring to a boil. Cover, reduce heat, and simmer 25 minutes or until pumpkin is tender, stirring occasionally. Remove from heat; cool slightly.
2. Place mixture in a blender or food processor; cover and process until smooth. Return mixture to Dutch oven; add milk. Cook until thoroughly heated. Garnish with sage sprigs, if desired. Yield: 5 servings (serving size: 1 cup).

CALORIES 122 (23% from fat); FAT 3.1g (sat 0.8g, mono 1.2g, poly 0.7g); PROTEIN 5.5g; CARB 19.9g; FIBER 2.3g; CHOL 1mg; IRON 2mg; SODIUM 228mg; CALC 102mg

SCALLOPED PUMPKIN AND SPINACH

- 6 cups peeled, cubed fresh pumpkin (about 2 pounds)
- Vegetable cooking spray
- 1½ cups thinly sliced onion
- ¼ cup all-purpose flour
- 2 cups low-salt chicken broth
- ½ teaspoon salt
- ¼ teaspoon ground nutmeg
- ¼ teaspoon pepper
- ¾ cup (3 ounces) shredded reduced-fat Swiss cheese, divided
- 1 (10-ounce) package frozen chopped spinach, thawed, drained, and squeezed dry

1. Preheat oven to 375°.
2. Cook pumpkin in boiling water 8 minutes or until tender. Drain.
3. Place a large nonstick skillet coated with cooking spray over medium heat; add onion, and sauté 7 minutes or until golden. Remove from skillet.
4. Add flour to skillet. Gradually add broth, stirring with a whisk until blended. Cook over medium heat, stirring constantly, until thick and bubbly (about 6 minutes). Remove from heat; stir in salt, nutmeg, and pepper.
5. Combine pumpkin, onion, ¼ cup cheese, and spinach; spoon into a 6-cup gratin dish coated with cooking spray. Pour sauce over pumpkin mixture. Sprinkle with ½ cup cheese. Bake at 375° for 30 minutes or until bubbly. Broil 3 minutes or until cheese is golden. Let stand 5 minutes. Yield: 4 servings (serving size: 1 cup).

CALORIES 189 (25% from fat); FAT 5.3g (sat 2.5g, mono 1.8g, poly 0.4g); PROTEIN 13.5g; CARB 25.6g; FIBER 5.2g; CHOL 13mg; IRON 4.0mg; SODIUM 421mg; CALC 377mg

WHAT TO LOOK FOR

Unlike most fruit (pumpkin is a fruit—it's part of the melon family), when you choose a pumpkin, look for tough skin. Give it the fingernail test: If you can make a mark with gentle pressure from your nail, the pumpkin isn't ready for cooking.

One final note: No matter how proud your children are of the pumpkin they chose for their jack-o'-lantern, don't give in to the temptation to cook a carved pumpkin. The cut surface is an ideal breeding ground for bacteria.

SMASHED POTATOES AND PUMPKIN

3 cups peeled, cubed fresh pumpkin (about 1 pound)
3 cups peeled, diced yellow Finnish potatoes or baking potatoes (about 1 pound)
1 cup 1% low-fat milk
1 (10½-ounce) can low-salt chicken broth
2 garlic cloves, sliced
1 bay leaf
½ cup low-fat sour cream
2 teaspoons lemon juice
¼ teaspoon salt
⅛ teaspoon white pepper
⅛ teaspoon ground nutmeg

1. Combine first 6 ingredients in a Dutch oven; bring to a boil. Cover, reduce heat, and simmer 20 minutes or until liquid is absorbed, stirring occasionally. Remove from heat; discard bay leaf.

2. Mash pumpkin mixture with a potato masher. Stir in sour cream and remaining ingredients. Yield: 6 servings (serving size: 1 cup).

CALORIES 136 (23% from fat); FAT 3.4g (sat 2.0g, mono 1.0g, poly 0.2g); PROTEIN 4.4g; CARB 23.4g; FIBER 1.8g; CHOL 10mg; IRON 1.0mg; SODIUM 148mg; CALC 92mg

PUMPKIN GNOCCHI GRATIN

Gnocchi (NYOH-kee) is the Italian word for "dumplings." This pumpkin gnocchi and sauce can be prepared up to 3 hours in advance. Slightly reheat the gratin sauce before assembling the dish.

1 tablespoon stick margarine
2 tablespoons all-purpose flour
2 tablespoons dry white wine
1 (10½-ounce) can low-salt chicken broth
⅛ teaspoon salt
1¾ cups all-purpose flour
1 cup fresh or canned pumpkin puree
½ teaspoon salt
¼ teaspoon ground nutmeg
3½ quarts water
Vegetable cooking spray
⅓ cup grated Parmesan cheese
¼ teaspoon paprika
¼ teaspoon cracked pepper

1. Melt margarine in a medium nonstick saucepan over medium heat. Stir in 2 tablespoons flour; cook 30 seconds. Add wine and broth; bring to a boil. Reduce heat; simmer 3 minutes or until thick. Stir in ⅛ teaspoon salt. Remove mixture from heat; set aside, and keep warm.

2. Combine 1¾ cups flour and next 3 ingredients in a large bowl. Stir well to form a smooth dough (dough will be slightly sticky). Turn dough out onto a lightly floured surface. Shape dough into a 12 x 3-inch-long roll. Cut roll lengthwise into 6 (½-inch-wide) strips; cut each strip into 12 (1-inch) pieces. Press each piece of dough with a lightly floured fork. Place gnocchi on a lightly floured baking sheet.

3. Preheat oven to 450°.

4. Bring water to a boil in a large Dutch oven. Add half of gnocchi; cook 3 minutes or until done. Remove gnocchi with a slotted spoon; place in a colander. Repeat procedure with remaining gnocchi.

5. Place gnocchi in a 13 x 9-inch baking dish coated with cooking spray; spoon sauce evenly over gnocchi. Sprinkle with cheese, paprika, and pepper. Bake at 450° for 15 minutes or until thoroughly heated. Serve warm. Yield 6 servings (serving size: ½ cup).

CALORIES 202 (18% from fat); FAT 4.1g (sat 1.4g, mono 1.4g, poly 0.8g); PROTEIN 7g; CARB 34.2g; FIBER 1.7g; CHOL 3mg; IRON 2.6mg; SODIUM 365mg; CALC 80mg

MAPLE-PUMPKIN SAUTÉ

Serve this fall-inspired side dish in place of sweet potatoes to complement entrées such as baked ham or roast turkey.

4 cups peeled, cubed fresh pumpkin (about 1½ pounds)
1½ cups chopped Red Delicious apple
½ cup finely chopped onion
⅓ cup raisins
Vegetable cooking spray
3 tablespoons maple syrup
¼ teaspoon salt
⅛ teaspoon ground ginger

1. Combine first 4 ingredients in a large nonstick skillet coated with cooking spray; cover and cook over medium-high heat 20 minutes or until tender, stirring occasionally. Stir in syrup, salt, and ginger. Yield: 4 servings (serving size: 1 cup).

CALORIES 137 (3% from fat); FAT 0.4g (sat 0.1g, mono 0g, poly 0.1g); PROTEIN 1.9g; CARB 35.1g; FIBER 3.6g; CHOL 0mg; IRON 1.5mg; SODIUM 151mg; CALC 47mg

PUMPKIN RISOTTO WITH PROSCIUTTO

2 cups peeled, cubed fresh
    pumpkin (about 1 pound)
3 cups low-salt chicken broth
Vegetable cooking spray
2 cups finely chopped onion
1 large garlic clove, minced
1 cup uncooked Arborio rice or
    other short-grain rice
¼ cup dry white wine
2 tablespoons grated Romano
    cheese or Parmesan cheese
2 tablespoons minced fresh
    parsley
¼ teaspoon salt
¼ teaspoon white pepper
1 ounce very thinly sliced
    prosciutto or lean ham,
    chopped (about ¼ cup)

1. Arrange pumpkin in a steamer basket over boiling water. Cover and steam 15 minutes or until tender; set aside.
2. Bring broth to a simmer in a saucepan (do not boil). Keep warm over low heat.
3. Coat a large saucepan with cooking spray; place over medium heat until hot. Add onion and garlic; sauté 5 minutes. Add rice; sauté 1 minute. Add wine; cook, stirring constantly, 1 minute or until liquid is nearly absorbed. Add warm broth, ½ cup at a time, stirring constantly until each portion of broth is absorbed before adding the next (about 18 minutes total). Stir in pumpkin; cook 2 minutes or until thoroughly heated. Remove from heat; stir in cheese and remaining ingredients. Serve immediately. Yield: 6 servings (serving size: ⅔ cup).

CALORIES 187 (11% from fat); FAT 2.3g (sat 0.8g, mono 0.8g, poly 0.3g); PROTEIN 6.3g; CARB 35.6g; FIBER 2g; CHOL 5mg; IRON 2.6mg; SODIUM 240mg; CALC 50mg

PUMPKIN-SPICE BUNDT CAKE

The rum glaze will seep into the cake if it's spooned over the cake while it is still warm.

3¼ cups all-purpose flour
1 tablespoon baking powder
2½ teaspoons ground cinnamon
1 teaspoon baking soda
1 teaspoon ground nutmeg
¼ teaspoon salt
1½ cups fresh or canned pumpkin
    puree
½ cup applesauce
1½ cups granulated sugar
½ cup stick margarine, softened
3 large egg whites
2 teaspoons vanilla extract
Vegetable cooking spray
3 tablespoons dark or light
    brown sugar
1 tablespoon dark rum
1 teaspoon skim milk
3 tablespoons powdered sugar

1. Preheat oven to 350°.
2. Combine first 6 ingredients; set flour mixture aside. Combine pumpkin and applesauce; set aside.
3. Beat granulated sugar and margarine in a large bowl at medium speed of an electric mixer until well-blended (about 5 minutes). Add egg whites and vanilla, beating well. Add flour mixture to sugar mixture alternately with pumpkin mixture, beginning and ending with flour mixture. Pour batter into a 12-cup Bundt pan coated with cooking spray. Bake at 350° for 50 minutes or until a wooden pick inserted in center comes out clean. Cool in pan 10 minutes; remove from pan.
4. Combine brown sugar, rum, and milk in a small saucepan; cook over low heat until brown sugar dissolves. Remove from heat; add powdered sugar, stirring with a whisk. Spoon glaze over warm cake. Yield: 16 servings (serving size: 1 slice).

CALORIES 248 (22% from fat); FAT 6.1g (sat 1.2g, mono 2.6g, poly 1.9g); PROTEIN 3.7g; CARB 44.8g; FIBER 1.2g; CHOL 0mg; IRON 1.7mg; SODIUM 194mg; CALC 70mg

WHEN YOU NEED FRESH RAW CUBED PUMPKIN

❶ *Cut straight down one side of stem with a large, heavy knife.*

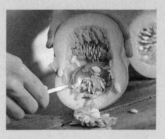

❷ *Clean out halves, spooning out the seeds and stringy pulp.*

❸ *Place pumpkin half, cut side down, on a cutting board. Using a downward motion with the knife, remove the peel in small sections.*

❹ *Cut peeled pumpkin into wedges, then hold wedges firmly while cutting into cubes. Proceed with recipe.*

WHEN YOU NEED FRESH PUMPKIN PUREE

Use this simple method when you want the pulp mashed or pureed, keeping in mind that 3 pounds of fresh pumpkin yields 3 cups of mashed cooked pumpkin. Fresh cooked pumpkin puree will keep in a sealed container in the refrigerator for about 5 days, or in the freezer for up to 6 months.

❶ *Place whole, uncut pumpkin on an aluminum foil-lined baking sheet. Bake at 350° for 1½ hours or until tender, turning baking sheet occasionally. Remove from oven, and cool.*

❷ *Next, peel the pumpkin. After you've baked the pumpkin and allowed it to cool thoroughly, you should be able to remove the peel with little effort.*

❸ *To clean the pumpkin, remove the seeds and stringy pulp with a large spoon. Then process the flesh in a food processor or by hand (using a potato masher) until smooth.*

GINGERSNAP PUMPKIN PIE

Serve this pie with a dollop of light whipped topping, if desired.

1¾ cups gingersnap crumbs (about 43 cookies, finely crushed)
2½ tablespoons reduced-calorie stick margarine, melted
2 tablespoons granulated sugar
Vegetable cooking spray
1½ cups fresh or canned pumpkin puree
¾ cup packed brown sugar
1 tablespoon cornstarch
1 teaspoon ground cinnamon
1 teaspoon vanilla extract
¼ teaspoon salt
¼ teaspoon ground nutmeg
2 large egg whites
1 large egg
1 (12-ounce) can evaporated skim milk

1. Preheat oven to 325°.
2. Combine first 3 ingredients in a bowl; toss with a fork until moist. Press into bottom and up sides of a 9-inch pie plate coated with cooking spray. Bake at 325° for 5 minutes; cool on a wire rack.
3. Combine pumpkin and remaining 9 ingredients in a bowl. Pour into prepared crust. Bake at 325° for 1 hour or until a knife inserted in center comes out clean. Cool on a wire rack. Yield: 10 servings (serving size: 1 wedge).

CALORIES 295 (25% from fat); FAT 8.2g (sat 2.0g, mono 3.4g, poly 2.1g); PROTEIN 6.6g; CARB 50g; FIBER 0.6g; CHOL 36mg; IRON 3 mg; SODIUM 195mg; CALC 189mg

HEALTH WATCH

The Key to B

B vitamins are taking center stage for your heart's health.

Most people get plenty of B_{12}—found in cheese, other milk products, meat, and fish—but they tend to run low on B_6 and folate. Here's a folate-rich recipe that makes getting your Bs a simple matter.

SPINACH LASAGNA

Vegetable cooking spray
1 cup chopped onion
1 cup sliced mushrooms
3 ounces ⅓-less-fat cream cheese (Neufchâtel) (about ⅓ cup)
1 (12-ounce) container 1% low-fat cottage cheese
⅓ cup low-fat sour cream
½ cup grated Parmesan cheese
2 large eggs
2 (10-ounce) packages frozen chopped spinach, thawed, drained, and squeezed dry
12 cooked lasagna noodles
1 (27.5-ounce) jar low-fat chunky mushroom pasta sauce
1 cup (4 ounces) shredded part-skim mozzarella cheese
¼ cup grated Parmesan cheese
½ cup (2 ounces) shredded sharp Cheddar cheese

1. Preheat oven to 350°.
2. Heat a medium nonstick skillet coated with cooking spray over medium-high heat. Add onion and mushrooms; sauté 5 minutes or until tender.
3. Beat cream cheese at medium speed of an electric mixer until smooth; add cottage cheese and next 3 ingredients, beating well. Add onion mixture and spinach; beat well.
4. Spread ½ cup spinach mixture in bottom of a 13 x 9-inch baking dish coated with cooking spray. Arrange 3 noodles over spinach mixture; top with 1 cup spinach mixture, ¾ cup pasta sauce, ¼ cup mozzarella cheese, and 1 tablespoon Parmesan cheese. Repeat layers, ending with Parmesan cheese.
5. Cover and bake at 350° for 50 minutes. Sprinkle with Cheddar cheese; bake, uncovered, 10 additional minutes. Let stand 10 minutes before serving. Yield: 8 servings.

CALORIES 413 (29% from fat); FAT 13.3g (sat 7.5g, mono 3.7g, poly 0.9g); PROTEIN 26.7g; CARB 47.9g; FIBER 5.3g; CHOL 90mg; IRON 4.2mg; SODIUM 834mg; CALC 400mg

Great Cooks, Good Sports

These chefs prove that you can be passionate about eating and staying in shape.

It may not seem that a bodybuilder, a ballerina, and a boxer would have a lot in common, but don't let looks deceive. When they're not lifting weights, twirling on pointe, or punching the speed bag, chefs Jim Shiebler, Patricia Williams, and Louis Lanza can be found in their respective restaurant kitchens creating light, high-flavor food.

"PUMP IT UP" GRILLED CHICKEN WITH PAPAYA-JALAPEÑO COULIS

Coulis is a French term referring to a thick puree or sauce.

—Recipe by Jim Shiebler
Chef saucier, Ritz-Carlton, Marina del Rey, near Los Angeles

- 1½ cups peeled, cubed papaya
- 2 tablespoons lime juice
- 1 tablespoon water
- ¼ cup chopped fresh cilantro
- 2 teaspoons seeded, minced red jalapeño pepper
- ¼ teaspoon salt, divided
- ¼ teaspoon pepper, divided
- 1 tablespoon lime juice
- 4 (4-ounce) skinned, boned chicken breast halves
- 16 (¼-inch-thick) slices red potato (about ¼ pound)
- Vegetable cooking spray
- 4 (¼-inch-thick slices) radicchio
- 8 green onions

1. Place first 3 ingredients in a blender; cover and process until smooth. Pour into a bowl; stir in cilantro, jalapeño, ⅛ teaspoon salt, and ⅛ teaspoon pepper. Set coulis aside.
2. Drizzle 1 tablespoon lime juice over chicken. Sprinkle ⅛ teaspoon salt and ⅛ teaspoon pepper over chicken breast halves and potato.
3. Prepare grill. Place chicken breast halves on grill rack coated with cooking spray; grill 10 minutes. Turn chicken; continue to cook. Place potato slices on grill rack; grill 5 minutes. Turn potato slices. Place radicchio and green onions on grill rack; grill 3 minutes, turning after 1½ minutes. Remove chicken, potatoes, radicchio, and green onions from grill. Serve with papaya coulis. Yield: 4 servings (serving size: 1 chicken breast half, 4 potato slices, 1 radicchio slice, 2 green onions, and ¼ cup papaya coulis).

CALORIES 224 (15% from fat); FAT 3.7g (sat 0.9g, mono 1.1g, poly 0.7g); PROTEIN 29.7g; CARB 18.6g; FIBER 2.4g; CHOL 72mg; IRON 2mg; SODIUM 245mg; CALC 79mg

KICKIN' ASIAN CHICKEN SALAD

Wasabi is the Japanese version of horseradish. It comes in powder form and is available in Asian groceries and some supermarkets. It's green and very fiery. If you prefer, though, you can substitute prepared horseradish.

—Recipe by Louis Lanza
Chef-owner, Josephina, and Josie's, in Manhattan's Upper West Side

- 1 tablespoon prepared wasabi powder (dried Japanese horseradish)
- 2 tablespoons honey
- 2 tablespoons red wine vinegar
- 1 tablespoon chopped shallots
- ½ teaspoon dark sesame oil
- ¼ teaspoon salt
- ¼ teaspoon pepper
- 1 ounce firm tofu
- ¾ pound beets
- ¾ pound sweet potato
- 1 cup shiitake mushrooms
- 6 cups gourmet salad greens
- ¾ pound ready-to-eat roasted skinned, boned chicken breasts, shredded (such as Tyson)

1. Preheat oven to 400°.
2. Place first 8 ingredients in a blender; cover and process until smooth. Set aside.
3. Leave root and 1 inch of stem on beets; scrub with a brush. Place beets and sweet potato in a shallow baking dish. Bake at 400° for 45 minutes. Add mushrooms; bake 15 additional minutes. Cool to touch. Peel beets and potato; cut into ½-inch cubes. Thinly slice mushrooms.
4. Combine beets, sweet potato, sliced mushrooms, salad greens, and chicken. Drizzle dressing over salad; toss well. Serve immediately. Yield: 4 servings (serving size: 2 cups).

CALORIES 337 (15% from fat); FAT 5.6g (sat 1.3g, mono 1.7g, poly 1.6g); PROTEIN 31.2g; CARB 41.4g; FIBER 4.2g; CHOL 72mg; IRON 3.1mg; SODIUM 366mg; CALC 60mg

- "PUMP IT UP" GRILLED CHICKEN WITH PAPAYA-JALAPEÑO COULIS: *Georges Duboeuf Régnié Cru Beaujolais 1996 (French red), $8*

- GISELLE'S ANGEL FOOD CAKE: *Bonny Doon Framboise Infusion of Raspberries (nonvintage), $10*

GISELLE'S ANGEL FOOD CAKE

Superfine sugar is very finely granulated and can be found in a box next to regular sugar in the supermarket. If you prefer regular granulated sugar, pulse it two or three times in your food processor before using.

—*Recipe by Patricia Williams Chef, City Wine & Cigar Company in New York's Tribeca district*

1⅓ cups superfine sugar, divided
1 cup all-purpose flour
10 large egg whites (at room temperature)
1 teaspoon cream of tartar
Dash of salt
1½ teaspoons vanilla extract
1 teaspoon fresh lemon juice
⅛ teaspoon almond extract
Seasonal berries (optional)

1. Preheat oven to 350°.
2. Sift together ⅓ cup sugar and flour; set flour mixture aside.
3. Beat egg whites at medium speed of an electric mixer in a large bowl until foamy. Add cream of tartar and salt; beat until soft peaks form. Add 1 cup sugar, 2 tablespoons at a time, beating until stiff peaks form. Sift flour mixture over egg white mixture, ¼ cup at a time; fold in. Fold in vanilla, lemon juice, and almond extract.
4. Spoon cake batter into a 10-inch tube pan, spreading evenly. Break large air pockets by cutting through cake batter with a knife. Bake at 350° for 40 minutes or until cake springs back when lightly touched. Invert pan; cool cake for 40 minutes. Loosen cake from sides of pan using a narrow metal spatula. Invert cake onto a serving plate. Garnish with fresh berries, if desired. Yield: 6 servings.

CALORIES 279 (1% from fat); FAT 0.2g (sat 0g, mono 0g, poly 0.1g); PROTEIN 7.8g; CARB 61.3g; FIBER 0.6g; CHOL 0mg; IRON 1mg; SODIUM 93mg; CALC 7mg

LIGHTEN UP

The Spice of Life

A Pennsylvania family's tradition, applesauce spice cake, needed a low-fat makeover.

For more than 40 years, Faith Murphy of Butler, New Jersey, has toted her favorite applesauce spice cake to potlucks, picnics, and family gatherings. Our challenge was to lighten up this family favorite, yet remain faithful to the flavor. By the time we finished, the fat in Faith's applesauce spice cake had dropped from 15 grams per serving to just a shade over 5 grams. Best of all, it's just as big a hit with her fans, the apples of her eye.

BEFORE & AFTER	
SERVING SIZE	
1 slice	
CALORIES	
331	244
FAT	
15g	5.3g
PERCENT OF TOTAL CALORIES	
41%	20%

APPLESAUCE SPICE CAKE WITH CREAM CHEESE ICING

1½ cups packed brown sugar
½ cup chilled light butter
1½ cups chunky applesauce
¼ cup apple butter
2 large egg whites
1 large egg
3 cups all-purpose flour
2 teaspoons baking soda
1 teaspoon ground cinnamon
½ teaspoon ground nutmeg
¼ teaspoon salt
1 cup raisins
Vegetable cooking spray
Cream Cheese Icing
¼ cup chopped pecans, toasted

1. Preheat oven to 350°.
2. Beat sugar and butter at medium speed of an electric mixer until well-blended (about 5 minutes). Add applesauce and next 3 ingredients; beat well. Add flour and next 4 ingredients; beat well. Stir in raisins. Pour batter into a 13 x 9-inch baking pan coated with cooking spray. Bake at 350° for 45 minutes or until a wooden pick inserted in center comes out clean. Cool completely on a wire rack.
3. Spread Cream Cheese Icing over cake, and sprinkle with pecans. Yield: 20 servings (serving size: 1 slice).

CALORIES 244 (20% from fat); FAT 5.3g (sat 2.7g, mono 0.8g, poly 0.4g); PROTEIN 4g; CARB 47g; FIBER 1.3g; CHOL 24mg; IRON 1.4mg; SODIUM 224mg; CALC 23mg

Cream Cheese Icing:

1½ teaspoons chilled light butter
½ (8-ounce) block ⅓-less-fat cream cheese (Neufchâtel), chilled
2 cups sifted powdered sugar
1 teaspoon vanilla extract

1. Beat butter and cream cheese at high speed of an electric mixer until fluffy. Add sugar; beat at low speed until well-blended. Add vanilla; beat well. Yield: 1 cup.

German Light

In Hamburg, you'll discover that German food can be both light and versatile.

You may assume that Germans live on sausages, sauerkraut, and dark beer. At first, light German food sounds like a contradiction. But with the fish markets, the trendy restaurants, and the bakeries of northern Germany, German cooking has lightened up. Over the past decade, German eating in general has changed. There are foods like barley and cabbage that seem heavy, but now Germans make light, healthy, good-tasting food out of these ingredients.

If you crave big, satisfying flavors this fall and winter, give these German recipes a try. Though ingredients like bacon may seem to disqualify some of these recipes as light cooking in the puristic sense, these dishes are well-balanced. While German food will never be dainty or delicate, the Germans do have a lot to teach us about cooking healthful food.

WEINKRAUT WITH APPLES

(pictured on page 300)

You'll almost never catch Germans eating sauerkraut out of the can. This sweet-and-sour version is one of the many ways that sauerkraut can be turned into a delicious side dish. At Landhaus Scherrer, Hamburg's best restaurant, they serve weinkraut topped with grilled quail; we suggest serving this with Honey-Mustard Game Hens.

7½ cups refrigerated sauerkraut, drained
2 bacon slices, cut into 1-inch pieces
2⅓ cups coarsely chopped onion
4 cups peeled, coarsely chopped Braeburn or other cooking apple (about 1¼ pounds)
1 cup low-salt chicken broth
½ teaspoon pepper
2 bay leaves
1 (750-milliliter) bottle Riesling or other dry white wine
1 teaspoon caraway seeds (optional)

1. Place sauerkraut in a colander; rinse under cold water. Drain well, pressing sauerkraut with back of a spoon to remove as much water as possible.

2. Cook bacon in a large Dutch oven over medium-high heat for 3 minutes. Add onion; sauté 5 minutes. Add apple; cook 5 minutes or until tender, stirring occasionally. Stir in sauerkraut, broth, and next 3 ingredients; add caraway seeds, if desired. Bring mixture to a boil; reduce heat, and simmer 2 hours or until liquid evaporates and mixture is tender, stirring occasionally. Discard bay leaves before serving. Yield: 8 servings (serving size: 1 cup).

CALORIES 115 (10% from fat); FAT 1.3g (sat 0.4g, mono 0.4g, poly 0.2g); PROTEIN 2.4g; CARB 21.4g; FIBER 2.4g; CHOL 2mg; IRON 0.7mg; SODIUM 1,012mg; CALC 20mg

HONEY-MUSTARD GAME HENS

(pictured on page 300)

3 (1½-pound) Cornish hens
½ teaspoon salt
½ teaspoon pepper
¼ cup coarse-grained mustard
2 tablespoons Riesling or other dry white wine
1 tablespoon honey
½ teaspoon pepper
¼ teaspoon ground mace
¼ teaspoon ground cloves
Vegetable cooking spray
Rosemary sprigs (optional)

1. Remove and discard giblets and necks from hens. Rinse hens under cold water; pat dry. Remove skin; trim excess fat. Split hens in half lengthwise. Sprinkle salt and ½ teaspoon pepper over hen halves; set aside.
2. Combine mustard and next 5 ingredients in a small bowl; set aside.
3. Prepare grill or broiler. Place hen halves, meaty sides up, on grill rack or rack of a broiler pan coated with cooking spray; cook 15 minutes on each side or until juices run clear, basting occasionally with mustard mixture. Garnish with rosemary sprigs, if desired. Yield: 6 servings.

CALORIES 202 (34% from fat); FAT 7.6g (sat 1.9g, mono 2.5g, poly 1.6g); PROTEIN 27.4g; CARB 3.9g; FIBER 0.1g; CHOL 82mg; IRON 1.3mg; SODIUM 372mg; CALC 18mg

HERRING SANDWICHES

2 (2½-ounce) hoagie rolls or submarine rolls
1 teaspoon coarse-grained mustard
1 (8-ounce) jar herring in wine sauce, drained
8 (¼-inch-thick) slices cucumber
2 (½-inch-thick) slices tomato
2 (¼-inch-thick) slices onion

1. Cut rolls in half horizontally. Spread mustard over cut sides of rolls. Divide herring evenly between roll bottoms; top with cucumber, tomato, onion, and roll tops. Serve immediately. Yield: 2 servings.

CALORIES 417 (26% from fat); FAT 12g (sat 1.8g, mono 5.5g, poly 2.3g); PROTEIN 21.3g; CARB 56.4g; FIBER 0.9g; CHOL 45mg; IRON 3.3mg; SODIUM 1,221mg; CALC 27mg

BROILED SALMON ON WEINKRAUT WITH JUNIPER BERRIES

Fish and sauerkraut sounds like a strange combination, but in fact, it's astonishingly good. In Germany, you'd be more likely to find fried cod on top of the sauerkraut, but broiled salmon is a delicious substitute. Serve this dish with rye bread or boiled potatoes.

7½ cups refrigerated sauerkraut, drained
 2 bacon slices, cut into 1-inch pieces
 2 cups coarsely chopped onion
1½ tablespoons juniper berries
 ½ teaspoon pepper
 3 bay leaves
 1 (750-milliliter) bottle Riesling or other dry white wine
 1 (8-ounce) bottle clam juice
 7 (6-ounce) salmon steaks (1 inch thick)
    Vegetable cooking spray

1. Place sauerkraut in a colander; rinse under cold water. Drain well, pressing sauerkraut with back of a spoon to remove as much water as possible.
2. Cook bacon in a large Dutch oven over medium-high heat for 3 minutes. Add onion; sauté 5 minutes. Stir in sauerkraut, juniper berries, and next 4 ingredients. Bring to a boil; reduce heat, and simmer 45 minutes or until liquid evaporates and mixture is tender. Discard bay leaves.
3. Preheat broiler. Place salmon steaks on rack of a broiler pan coated with cooking spray, and broil 3 minutes on each side or until fish flakes easily when tested with a fork. Serve with sauerkraut mixture. Yield: 7 servings (serving size: 1 salmon steak and 1 cup sauerkraut mixture).

CALORIES 297 (32% from fat); FAT 10.4g (sat 1.8g, mono 3.5g, poly 3.9g); PROTEIN 32.7g; CARB 14.1g; FIBER 0.9g; CHOL 83mg; IRON 1.8mg; SODIUM 1,613mg; CALC 42mg

HAMBURG FISH SOUP

This hearty fish soup came from a street fair in Hamburg. The juniper berries give it an herbal sweetness that is distinctively German. The shrimp are the tiny North Sea variety that are available here in cans.

 2 (1½-pound) whole flounder, cleaned
 6 cups water
 2 teaspoons black peppercorns
 ¼ cup chopped fresh dillweed
 1 cup chopped fresh parsley
 2 tablespoons vegetable oil
 2 cups thinly sliced leek (about 2 medium)
1½ cups finely chopped onion
 2 tablespoons all-purpose flour
 2 cups peeled, diced red potatoes
 1 cup sliced carrot
1½ tablespoons juniper berries
 1 teaspoon salt
 1 teaspoon pepper
 6 bay leaves
 1 cup Riesling or other dry white wine
 ¼ cup finely chopped fresh parsley
 2 tablespoons balsamic vinegar
 1 teaspoon coarse-grained mustard
 1 (7-ounce) can tiny peeled shrimp, drained
    Slivered leek (optional)

1. Cut flounder into fillets, reserving bones. Remove skin from fillets, and discard. Cut fillets into 2-inch pieces; cover and chill.
2. Combine fish bones, water, and next 3 ingredients in a large Dutch oven; bring to a boil. Cover, reduce heat, and simmer 30 minutes. Drain mixture in a sieve over a bowl, reserving broth. Discard solids.
3. Heat oil in Dutch oven over medium heat. Add sliced leek and onion; sauté 10 minutes or until tender. Sprinkle flour over leek mixture; cook, stirring constantly, 1 minute. Gradually add reserved broth, stirring until well-blended. Add potatoes and next 5 ingredients; cook 25 minutes or until vegetables are tender. Add fish, wine, and next 3 ingredients; cook over low heat 5 minutes or until fish flakes easily when tested with a fork. Discard bay leaves. Ladle soup into bowls; top with shrimp. Garnish with slivered leek, if desired. Yield: 11 servings (serving size: 1 cup soup and about 1 tablespoon shrimp).
Note: Juniper berries can be found in the spice section of most supermarkets. Your fishmonger will be happy to fillet the flounder for you.

CALORIES 114 (26% from fat); FAT 4.3g (sat 0.8g, mono 1.2g, poly 2g); PROTEIN 6.3g; CARB 12.4g; FIBER 1.6g; CHOL 22mg; IRON 1.3mg; SODIUM 274mg; CALC 35mg

IN SEASON

Game Time

Wild pheasant, venison, duck, and quail were our ancestors' original entrées. Now that they're farm-raised, it's easy to enjoy these meats that are big on flavor, but lower in fat and calories.

Wild game doesn't even have to be wild anymore. From a number of excellent mail-order suppliers, you can order farm-raised pheasants, quail, venison, boar, and even moose and caribou.

Whether you buy your game or hunt it, less is more in its preparation and cooking. Overmarinating kills the distinctive flavors—and those flavors are the best reasons for eating game. If you want something that tastes like chicken, eat chicken.

Armed with that knowledge and the recipes that follow, throw on an apron and pour yourself a glass of sturdy wine. You don't need many sides to go along with game—a salad, a simple polenta, some robust grilled vegetables—so you are free to concentrate on the main course. Now take your time. No food deserves it more than the original food.

ROAST DUCKLING WITH SWEET-AND-SOUR CABBAGE

1   (4-pound) cleaned domestic duckling (fresh or frozen and thawed)
1½ teaspoons salt, divided
¾   teaspoon pepper, divided
½   teaspoon ground coriander
½   teaspoon ground allspice
4   cups rock salt
12 chestnuts
1   teaspoon vegetable oil
½   cup minced onion
3   cups shredded red cabbage
1   cup peeled, chopped Golden Delicious apple
2   tablespoons brown sugar
2   tablespoons red wine vinegar
1   bay leaf
¼   cup low-salt chicken broth
1   teaspoon juniper berries, crushed

1. Preheat oven to 450°.
2. Remove giblets and neck from duckling; reserve for another use. Rinse duckling under cold water; pat dry. Trim excess fat. Starting at neck cavity, loosen skin from breast and drumsticks by inserting fingers and pushing hand between skin and meat.
3. Combine ½ teaspoon salt, ½ teaspoon pepper, coriander, and allspice. Sprinkle mixture under skin. Tie ends of legs together with string. Lift wing tips up and over back; tuck under duckling.
4. Spread rock salt in bottom of a shallow roasting pan. Place duckling, breast side up, on salt. Pierce skin several times with a fork. Insert meat thermometer into meaty part of thigh, making sure not to touch bone. Bake at 450° for 50 minutes or until thermometer registers 180°. Cover loosely with aluminum foil; let stand 10 minutes. Discard skin.
5. Meanwhile, soak chestnuts in a bowl of water for 30 minutes. Drain. Cut a slit in shell on rounded side of each nut. (Make sure slit goes all the way through shell. If not, it will explode.) Arrange nuts in a single layer on a microwave-safe plate. Microwave at HIGH 2 minutes. Cool 5 minutes; peel and chop nuts.
6. Heat oil in a saucepan over medium heat. Add onion; sauté 3 minutes. Add cabbage and next 4 ingredients; cover, reduce heat to low, and cook 5 minutes. Stir in nuts, broth, berries, 1 teaspoon salt, and ¼ teaspoon pepper; cook, uncovered, 10 minutes, stirring occasionally. Discard bay leaf. Serve cabbage mixture with duckling. Yield: 4 servings (serving size: 3 ounces duckling and ¾ cup cabbage mixture).
Note: If bottled peeled chestnuts are used, omit step 5 and just chop the nuts.

CALORIES 294 (36% from fat); FAT 11.6g (sat 3.9g, mono 3.7g, poly 2.1g); PROTEIN 21.8g; CARB 25.7g; FIBER 5.2g; CHOL 76mg; IRON 3.3mg; SODIUM 948mg; CALC 66mg

SIMPLE ROAST DUCKLING

1   (4-pound) cleaned domestic duckling (fresh or frozen and thawed)
1½ tablespoons five-spice powder
1   teaspoon salt
4   cups rock salt

1. Preheat oven to 500°.
2. Remove giblets and neck from duckling; reserve for another use. Rinse duckling under cold water; pat dry. Trim excess fat. Starting at neck cavity, loosen skin from breast and drumsticks by inserting fingers and pushing hand between skin and meat.
3. Combine five-spice powder and 1 teaspoon salt. Sprinkle spice mixture under loosened skin; rub into body cavity. Tie ends of legs together with string. Lift wing tips up and over back; tuck under duckling.
4. Spread rock salt in bottom of a shallow roasting pan. Place duckling, breast side up, on rock salt. Pierce skin several times with a meat fork. Insert a meat thermometer into meaty part of thigh, making sure not to touch bone. Bake at 500° for 45 minutes or until thermometer registers 180°. Cover loosely with aluminum foil; let stand 10 minutes. Discard skin. Yield: 4 servings (serving size: 3 ounces).

CALORIES 178 (48% from fat); FAT 9.5g (sat 3.6g, mono 3.2g, poly 1.2g); PROTEIN 20.1g; CARB 2g; FIBER 0.6g; CHOL 76mg; IRON 3.3mg; SODIUM 642mg; CALC 45mg

PHEASANT SALAD

¼   teaspoon ground allspice
¼   teaspoon pepper
⅛   teaspoon salt
1   (1-pound) whole pheasant breast with skin attached
Vegetable cooking spray
12 cups gourmet salad greens
1   cup thinly sliced red cabbage
2   tablespoons raspberry-flavored vinegar
3   tablespoons water
1½ teaspoons vegetable oil
¼   teaspoon salt
⅛   teaspoon pepper
3   tablespoons dried cranberries
1   tablespoon skinned, coarsely chopped hazelnuts, toasted

1. Preheat oven to 400°.
2. Combine first 3 ingredients; rub over pheasant beneath skin (skin should be loose). Place breast, skin side up, on rack of a broiler pan coated with cooking spray. Lightly coat pheasant breast with cooking spray. Insert meat thermometer into meat, making sure not to touch bone; bake at 400° for 45 minutes or until thermometer registers 180°. Let stand 10 minutes. Discard skin; thinly slice breast, and set aside.
3. Combine salad greens and cabbage in a bowl. Combine vinegar and next 4 ingredients, stirring well with a whisk. Reserve 1 tablespoon vinaigrette; set aside. Pour remaining vinaigrette over greens mixture, tossing gently. Arrange 2 cups greens mixture on each of 3 salad plates. Divide pheasant evenly among salads; sprinkle each with 1 tablespoon cranberries and 1 teaspoon hazelnuts. Drizzle reserved vinaigrette over salads. Yield: 3 servings.
Note: To get a 1-pound pheasant breast, have your butcher portion a 2¼-pound pheasant; reserve remaining pieces for another use.

CALORIES 260 (29% from fat); FAT 8.3g (sat 1.9g, mono 3.3g, poly 2.2g); PROTEIN 32.2g; CARB 14.8g; FIBER 5.1g; CHOL 72mg; IRON 3.9mg; SODIUM 350mg; CALC 109mg

SAVORY BROILED QUAIL

(pictured on page 299)

3 tablespoons low-sodium soy
  sauce
3 tablespoons sherry
1½ teaspoons dark sesame oil
4 (4-ounce) semiboned quail
Vegetable cooking spray
¼ teaspoon cornstarch

1. Combine first 3 ingredients in a large zip-top plastic bag; add quail. Seal and marinate in refrigerator 2 hours, turning bag occasionally. Remove quail from bag; reserve marinade.

2. Preheat broiler.
3. Place quail on rack of a broiler pan coated with cooking spray; broil 5 minutes on each side or until done, basting frequently with reserved marinade. Combine pan drippings, reserved marinade, and cornstarch in a microwave-safe bowl; microwave at HIGH for 1½ minutes or until mixture boils. Remove skin from quail and discard. Serve sauce with quail. Yield: 2 servings (serving size: 2 quail and 2 tablespoons sauce).

Note: Semiboned quail have had the breast bones removed, leaving only the bones in the wings and leg-thigh sections. Some butchers insert wire loops into the breasts to help keep their shape; these should be removed before cooking.

CALORIES 200 (40% from fat); FAT 8.9g (sat 2.0g, mono 2.8g, poly 2.8g); PROTEIN 24.6g; CARB 1.8g; FIBER 0g; CHOL 78mg; IRON 5mg; SODIUM 643mg; CALC 17mg

DUCK PÂTÉ

1 tablespoon reduced-calorie
  margarine
½ cup chopped onion
1¼ ounces duck liver (reserved
  from a 4-pound duckling)
½ cup port or other sweet red
  wine
½ cup coarsely chopped cooked
  duck meat (reserved from a
  4-pound roasted duckling)
2 tablespoons fat-free sour cream
1 teaspoon fresh thyme leaves
½ teaspoon salt
¼ teaspoon ground allspice
¼ teaspoon pepper
1 tablespoon chopped pistachios
16 fat-free saltine crackers

1. Melt margarine in a small nonstick skillet over medium-high heat. Add onion and liver; cook 1 minute. Add wine; bring to a boil. Cover, reduce heat, and cook 2 minutes. Remove from heat; cool slightly.
2. Place liver mixture, duck meat, and next 5 ingredients in a food processor; process until smooth, scraping sides of processor bowl occasionally. Spoon mixture into a small bowl; cover and chill. Sprinkle with pistachios just before serving. Serve with crackers. Yield: 16 servings (serving size: 1 tablespoon pâté and 1 cracker).

CALORIES 43 (29% from fat); FAT 1.4g (sat 0.3g, mono 0.5g, poly 0.6g); PROTEIN 2.5g; CARB 5.1g; FIBER 0.2g; CHOL 16mg; IRON 1.3mg; SODIUM 119mg; CALC 5mg

MUSTARD-AND-HERB CRUSTED RACK OF VENISON

1 (3-pound) rack of venison
  (with 8 ribs)
Vegetable cooking spray
3 tablespoons Dijon mustard
3 tablespoons honey
2 teaspoons minced fresh
  thyme
1 teaspoon minced fresh
  rosemary
¼ teaspoon salt
¼ teaspoon pepper
2 garlic cloves, crushed
1 cup fresh breadcrumbs
1 tablespoon chopped fresh
  flat-leaf parsley
Rosemary sprigs (optional)

1. Preheat oven to 400°.
2. Place venison, meat side up, on rack of a broiler pan coated with cooking spray. Insert meat thermometer into thickest portion of venison, making sure not to touch bone. Wrap bones with aluminum foil.
3. Combine mustard and next 6 ingredients; spread over venison. Bake at 400° for 20 minutes or until meat thermometer registers 120°.
4. Remove venison from oven. Combine breadcrumbs and parsley. Carefully pat breadcrumb mixture into mustard mixture (mustard mixture will be very hot). Bake 10 additional minutes or until thermometer registers 145° (medium-rare). Cut rack between ribs, forming chops. Garnish with rosemary sprigs, if desired. Yield: 8 servings (serving size: 1 chop).

CALORIES 179 (34% from fat); FAT 6.8g (sat 2.5g, mono 1.8g, poly 1.3g); PROTEIN 28g; CARB 7.9g; FIBER 0.2g; CHOL 77mg; IRON 4.9mg; SODIUM 327mg; CALC 8mg

VENISON-VEGETABLE CHILI

(pictured on page 300)

Vegetable cooking spray
2 pounds lean, boned venison loin, cut into 1-inch cubes
2 tablespoons sliced green onions
1 cup diced red bell pepper
1 cup diced carrot
2 tablespoons minced jalapeño pepper
3 garlic cloves, minced
¼ cup masa harina or cornmeal
1 teaspoon ground cumin
½ cup tequila
1 teaspoon unsweetened cocoa
¾ teaspoon salt
¼ teaspoon pepper
⅛ teaspoon barbecue smoked seasoning (such as Hickory Liquid Smoke) (optional)
1 (14.5-ounce) can no-salt-added whole tomatoes, undrained and chopped
1 (14¼-ounce) can no-salt-added beef broth
1 (10-ounce) package frozen whole-kernel corn, thawed
½ cup chopped fresh cilantro

1. Place a large Dutch oven coated with cooking spray over medium-high heat until hot. Add venison; sauté 5 minutes, browning well on all sides. Remove meat from Dutch oven, and set aside. Wipe Dutch oven dry with a paper towel.
2. Coat Dutch oven with cooking spray; place over medium-high heat. Add onions and next 4 ingredients; sauté 5 minutes. Return venison to Dutch oven. Sprinkle with masa harina and cumin; cook, stirring constantly, 1 minute. Add tequila and next 7 ingredients; bring to a boil. Cover, reduce heat, and simmer 1 hour and 55 minutes or until venison is tender. Ladle chili into soup bowls; sprinkle with cilantro. Yield: 8 servings (serving size: 1 cup chili and 1 tablespoon cilantro).

CALORIES 249 (25% from fat); FAT 7g (sat 2.5g, mono 1.9g, poly 1.5g); PROTEIN 30g; CARB 16.6g; FIBER 2.3g; CHOL 77mg; IRON 6.1mg; SODIUM 296mg; CALC 43mg

---

THE KERR PACKAGE

Vegetables Take Center Stage

With this new technique, vegetables can be the stars of your plate.

If you, like me, occasionally experiment with vegetable-only meals, you may have noticed that without meat as the star attraction, the vegetables seem to drift around the plate. In short, the plate lacks focus, height, and drama. An effort to achieve all three elements leads to the creation of layered "sand castles" of flavors that I call MEVs, or "molded ethnic vegetables." I work with traditional European molds, but you can opt for 10-ounce ramekins.

MEXICAN MEV WITH BEANS, PEPPERS, AND JICAMA

2 (15-ounce) cans cannellini or other white beans
1 tablespoon vegetable oil
2 cups vertically sliced onion
1 to 1½ teaspoons bottled chipotle sauce or hot sauce
1 teaspoon dried savory
2 garlic cloves, minced
½ cup peeled, diced jicama
2 tablespoons minced fresh cilantro
1 (12-ounce) bottle roasted red bell peppers, drained
Vegetable cooking spray

1. Preheat oven to 350°.
2. Drain beans in a colander over a bowl, reserving ¼ cup bean liquid.
3. Heat oil in a large nonstick skillet over medium-high heat. Add onion; sauté 5 minutes. Add beans, chipotle sauce, savory, and garlic; sauté 5 minutes. Remove from heat. Place 2 cups bean mixture in a bowl; mash with a potato masher. Stir in remaining bean mixture, ¼ cup bean liquid, jicama, and cilantro.
4. Arrange bell peppers in bottom and up sides of 4 (10-ounce) ramekins coated with cooking spray. Divide bean mixture evenly among ramekins; place on a baking sheet. Bake at 350° for 20 minutes. Invert ramekins onto each of 4 plates. Yield: 4 servings.

CALORIES 313 (21% from fat); FAT 7.2g (sat 1.1g, mono 1.9g, poly 3.4g); PROTEIN 13.5g; CARB 50.2g; FIBER 6.2g; CHOL 0mg; IRON 4.5mg; SODIUM 480mg; CALC 97mg

---

READER RECIPES

Fall Harvest

In honor of autumn, our readers present a cornucopia of their favorite recipes.

SPINACH-AND-GRAPEFRUIT SALAD

With ready-to-serve, pre-packaged spinach, this family favorite takes no time at all.

–Carol Davanay,
Newport News, Virginia

2 tablespoons chopped pecans
8 cups torn spinach
2 cups red grapefruit sections (about 3 medium grapefruit)
2 cups sliced mushrooms (about 8 ounces)
¼ cup crumbled blue cheese
½ cup raspberry fat-free vinaigrette (such as Girard's)

1. Place pecans in a skillet; cook over medium heat 3 minutes or until lightly browned, shaking skillet frequently.
2. Place 2 cups spinach on each of 4 serving plates. Arrange ½ cup grapefruit and ½ cup mushrooms over spinach on each plate. Sprinkle each serving with 1 tablespoon cheese and 1½ teaspoons pecans; drizzle evenly with vinaigrette. Yield: 4 servings.

CALORIES 165 (28% from fat); FAT 5.2g (sat 1.6g, mono 2.2g, poly 0.9g); PROTEIN 6.4g; CARB 27.5g; FIBER 5.8g; CHOL 5mg; IRON 3.7mg; SODIUM 409mg; CALC 163mg

MUSHROOM-CHIVE PILAF

I created this recipe because I love the taste of mushrooms. My husband and I love it served with grilled swordfish. In the time it takes him to grill the fish, I can easily fix my side dish.

—Linda Kent-Jansons, San Jose, California

1 tablespoon olive oil
½ cup minced fresh onion
1 garlic clove, minced
2 cups low-salt chicken broth
½ teaspoon salt
½ teaspoon white pepper
1 cup uncooked basmati rice
¼ cup chopped chives
¼ cup thinly sliced green onions
1 (8-ounce) package mushrooms, chopped

1. Heat oil in a medium saucepan over medium-high heat. Add onion and garlic; sauté 2 minutes. Add broth, salt, and pepper. Bring to a boil; add rice. Cover, reduce heat, and simmer 35 minutes. Remove from heat; let stand 5 minutes. Stir in chives, green onions, and mushrooms. Yield: 6 servings (serving size: 1 cup).

CALORIES 161 (18% from fat); FAT 3.2g (sat 0.5g, mono 1.9g, poly 0.4g); PROTEIN 4.1g; CARB 29.1g; FIBER 1.2g; CHOL 0mg; IRON 2.3mg; SODIUM 226mg; CALC 20mg

URSULA SMITH'S PORK CHOPS AND SAUERKRAUT

This is a lighter version of a recipe that I used to watch my grandmother make. To lower the fat, I trim the fat from the pork chops and leave out the butter. My family loves it.

—Donna Sapienza, Littleton, Colorado

1 (14.5-ounce) can shredded sauerkraut, drained
1 tablespoon caraway seeds
¼ teaspoon ground cloves
6 (4-ounce) lean, boned center-cut loin pork chops (about 1 inch thick)
4 cups thinly sliced Granny Smith apple (about 2 medium)
½ teaspoon ground cinnamon

1. Preheat oven to 350°.
2. Arrange sauerkraut evenly in a 13 x 9-inch baking dish; sprinkle with caraway seeds and cloves. Place pork chops on sauerkraut; arrange apple slices on pork, and sprinkle with cinnamon. Cover and bake at 350° for 1 hour and 15 minutes or until pork is tender. Yield: 6 servings (serving size: 1 pork chop, ¼ cup sauerkraut, and about ½ cup apple slices).

CALORIES 210 (31% from fat); FAT 7.2g (sat 2.4g, mono 3.2g, poly 0.8g); PROTEIN 21.1g; CARB 14.3g; FIBER 4.8g; CHOL 60mg; IRON 2.8mg; SODIUM 483mg; CALC 20mg

SPICY BISTRO STEAK SUBS

(pictured on page 297)

Serve with baked potato chips, if desired.

—Maya Kline, Boise, Idaho

1 tablespoon stick margarine
2 garlic cloves, minced
1 pound thinly sliced lean deli roast beef
2 tablespoons ketchup
1 tablespoon plus 1 teaspoon Worcestershire sauce
½ teaspoon dried basil
½ teaspoon dried oregano
¼ teaspoon ground red pepper
1 (12-ounce) can dark beer
6 (2½-ounce) hoagie rolls with sesame seeds, cut in half lengthwise
Carrot curls and olives (optional)

1. Melt margarine in a large nonstick skillet over medium-high heat. Add garlic; sauté 2 minutes. Add roast beef and next 6 ingredients; bring to a boil. Reduce heat, and simmer 2 minutes, stirring frequently. Drain beef in a colander over a bowl, reserving sauce.
2. Divide roast beef evenly among roll bottoms; top with roll tops. Serve with reserved sauce. If desired, garnish sandwiches with carrot curls and olives. Yield: 6 servings (serving size: 1 sandwich and 3 tablespoons sauce).

CALORIES 345 (28% from fat); FAT 10.6g (sat 3.4g, mono 4.5g, poly 1.6g); PROTEIN 21.4g; CARB 40.6g; FIBER 1.6g; CHOL 2mg; IRON 3.8mg; SODIUM 938mg; CALC 67mg

> **MENU SUGGESTION**
>
> *Chicken and black-eyed pea ragoût**
>
> SKILLET CORN BREAD
>
> *Sauté ½ cup chopped onion in a non-stick skillet. Add 1½ cups shredded cooked chicken, 1 can pasta-style tomatoes, and 1 can black-eyed peas, drained. Heat thoroughly. Cut corn bread wedges in half horizontally. Place 1 corn bread wedge on a plate; top with ragoût and remaining corn bread wedge.

SKILLET CORN BREAD

My husband loves the fact that I like to cook, and he doesn't mind that I usually cook low-fat recipes. This light corn bread is one of his favorites.

—Janet Ramondetta, Casselberry, Florida

3 tablespoons margarine
½ cup chopped onion
½ cup chopped celery
1 cup all-purpose flour
1 cup yellow cornmeal
3 tablespoons sugar
2½ teaspoons baking powder
1 teaspoon rubbed sage
½ teaspoon salt
1 cup skim milk
1 large egg, lightly beaten
1 (11-ounce) can no-salt-added whole-kernel corn, drained

1. Preheat oven to 425°.
2. Melt margarine in a 9-inch cast-iron skillet over medium heat. Add onion and celery; sauté 3 minutes.
3. Combine flour and next 5 ingredients in a large bowl. Add milk, egg, and onion mixture, stirring just until moist. Stir in corn. Pour batter into skillet. Bake at 425° for 25 minutes or until a wooden pick inserted in center comes out clean. Yield: 10 servings (serving size: 1 wedge).

CALORIES 180 (23% from fat); FAT 4.6g (sat 0.9g, mono 1.8g, poly 1.3g); PROTEIN 4.6g; CARB 30.1g; FIBER 1.4g; CHOL 23mg; IRON 1.5mg; SODIUM 184mg; CALC 109mg

GARDEN-HARVEST VEGETABLES

I love to cook, and I have been doing it as long as I can remember. Lately, I have been changing old recipes so that they have less fat. This recipe is one of my grandmother's favorites that I've lightened.

—Annie Bayley, Chattaroy, Washington

Vegetable cooking spray
1   cup (½-inch-thick) sliced carrot
2   medium onions, each cut into
      8 wedges
3   cups (1-inch-thick) sliced
      zucchini
2   cups broccoli florets
4   large mushrooms, quartered
2   garlic cloves, minced
1   tablespoon dried parsley flakes
1   teaspoon dried rosemary
1   teaspoon dried tarragon
1   teaspoon chicken-flavored
      bouillon granules
¼   teaspoon salt
⅛   teaspoon pepper
¼   cup water
1   teaspoon cornstarch

1. Place a large nonstick skillet coated with cooking spray over medium-high heat. Add carrot and onions; sauté 8 minutes. Add zucchini and next 3 ingredients; sauté 5 minutes. Add parsley and next 5 ingredients; sauté 3 minutes. Combine water and cornstarch in a small bowl; add to skillet. Bring to a boil; cook, stirring constantly, 1 minute. Yield: 6 servings (serving size: 1 cup).

CALORIES 54 (12% from fat); FAT 0.7g (sat 0.1g, mono 0g, poly 0.2g); PROTEIN 2.9g; CARB 11.1g; FIBER 3g; CHOL 0mg; IRON 1.1mg; SODIUM 254mg; CALC 47mg

Color Me Dinner

The old adage that a colorful plate is a healthful one is truer than you think. So we got out the reds, yellows, oranges, and greens to create meals that look as good as they taste.

Whether in an impressionist painting or a Technicolor epic, there's no question that color attracts, draws you in. This is especially true of food, and it may be Mother Nature's way of getting you to eat healthfully.

Even if your mother wasn't a nutritionist, chances are she knew this. By simply including a colorful vegetable alongside the starch and meat, she was assured of serving her family a well-balanced meal. That's because vegetables (as well as fruits) are nutritional heavyweights that provide phytochemicals, antioxidants, and vitamins A and C.

But with today's haphazard eating styles and the popularity of one-dish meals, adding color to your plate can be a bit tricky. So we're here to help, especially because government surveys show that Americans are lucky to get even one or two servings of vegetables or fruit a day.

We dipped into nature's paintbox—the produce section of your supermarket—and carefully selected the most healthful vegetables and fruits we could find.

So tonight, don't think of cooking as just cooking—think of your dinner plate as your palette. Color it tasty. Color it healthful. Color it dinner.

HONEY MUSTARD-WHIPPED SWEET POTATOES

Serve this simple, creamy dish as a side to chicken or pork.

1   tablespoon margarine
½   cup sliced onion
3   medium-size sweet potatoes,
      peeled and cut into 1-inch
      pieces (about 1½ pounds)
1   tablespoon Dijon mustard
1   tablespoon honey
¼   teaspoon pepper
1   cup low-salt chicken broth

1. Melt margarine in a large saucepan over medium heat. Add onion and sweet potatoes; sauté 5 minutes. Add mustard and remaining ingredients; bring to a boil. Cover, reduce heat, and simmer 20 minutes or until sweet potatoes are very tender.
2. Place sweet potato mixture in a food processor; process until smooth. Yield: 4 servings (serving size: ¾ cup).

CALORIES 198 (18% from fat); FAT 4g (sat 0.7g, mono 1.3g, poly 1.1g); PROTEIN 3.1g; CARB 38.3g; FIBER 4.3g; CHOL 0mg; IRON 1.2mg; SODIUM 187mg; CALC 34mg

BUTTERNUT SQUASH WITH BARLEY STUFFING

2 (1-pound) butternut squash
1 tablespoon vegetable oil
1 cup diced red bell pepper
½ cup thinly sliced green onions
1 (10½-ounce) can low-salt chicken broth
1½ teaspoons rubbed sage
¾ cup uncooked pearl barley
2 tablespoons chopped fresh parsley
½ teaspoon salt
⅛ teaspoon pepper
½ cup (2 ounces) shredded part-skim mozzarella cheese

1. Preheat oven to 350°.
2. Cut each squash in half lengthwise; discard seeds and membranes. Place squash, cut sides down, on a baking sheet; bake at 350° for 35 minutes or until tender. Cool to touch. Scoop out pulp, leaving ¼-inch shells. Mash pulp to measure 2 cups; set aside.
3. Heat oil in a large saucepan over medium heat until hot. Add bell pepper and onions; sauté 5 minutes. Add broth and sage; bring to a boil. Stir in barley; return to a boil. Cover, reduce heat, and simmer 15 minutes. Uncover; cook 10 minutes or until most of liquid is absorbed. Remove from heat; stir in mashed squash, parsley, salt, and ⅛ teaspoon pepper. Divide mixture evenly among squash shells. Place on a baking sheet; bake at 350° for 15 minutes. Sprinkle evenly with cheese; bake 5 additional minutes or until cheese melts. Yield: 4 servings.

CALORIES 296 (21% from fat); FAT 7g (sat 2.2g, mono 1.7g, poly 2.1g); PROTEIN 10.2g; CARB 52.5g; FIBER 9g; CHOL 8mg; IRON 3.2mg; SODIUM 398mg; CALC 199mg

SPICY VEGETABLE RAGOÛT OVER POLENTA

Vegetable cooking spray
3 cups water
1 cup yellow cornmeal
⅓ cup grated fresh Romano cheese or Parmesan cheese
½ teaspoon salt, divided
½ teaspoon pepper
¼ cup chopped fresh cilantro
2 teaspoons olive oil
1 cup chopped onion
2 cups peeled, diced eggplant
1 cup diced yellow squash
½ cup diced carrot
1 jalapeño pepper, seeded and diced
1 tablespoon chili powder
1 (14.5-ounce) can whole tomatoes, undrained and chopped

1. Coat a 9-inch round cake pan with cooking spray; set aside.
2. Bring water to a boil in a large saucepan over medium-high heat. Reduce heat; add cornmeal, stirring constantly with a whisk. Cook 5 minutes, stirring frequently. Remove from heat; stir in cheese, ¼ teaspoon salt, ½ teaspoon pepper, and cilantro. Pour into prepared cake pan. Press plastic wrap onto surface; chill polenta 1 hour or until firm.
3. Heat oil in a large nonstick skillet over medium-high heat. Add onion; sauté 2 minutes. Add eggplant and next 3 ingredients; sauté 4 minutes. Stir in chili powder, tomatoes, and ¼ teaspoon salt; bring to a boil. Reduce heat; simmer 15 minutes.
4. Preheat broiler. Invert polenta onto a cutting board; cut into 4 wedges. Place on a baking sheet coated with cooking spray. Broil 5 minutes on 1 side or until golden. Serve ragoût over polenta. Yield: 4 servings (serving size: ¾ cup ragoût and 1 polenta wedge).

CALORIES 263 (24% from fat); FAT 6.9g (sat 2.5g, mono 2.8g, poly 0.8g); PROTEIN 9.5g; CARB 42.4g; FIBER 5.4g; CHOL 12mg; IRON 3mg; SODIUM 602mg; CALC 204mg

TARRAGON CHICKEN WITH ROASTED VEGETABLES

Serve this main dish with Honey Mustard-Whipped Sweet Potatoes.

4 (6-ounce) skinned chicken breast halves
3 tablespoons chopped fresh tarragon or 2 teaspoons dried tarragon
½ teaspoon salt
¼ teaspoon pepper
10 pearl onions, unpeeled
1 cup baby carrots (or carrots cut into 2-inch pieces)
1 cup trimmed Brussels sprouts, halved
1 tablespoon olive oil
2 plum tomatoes, quartered
1 teaspoon dried thyme
¼ teaspoon pepper
1 (15-ounce) bottle baby corn, drained

1. Preheat oven to 450°.
2. Sprinkle both sides of chicken breast halves with tarragon, salt, and ¼ teaspoon pepper; set aside.
3. Cook onions in boiling water 8 minutes; drain well. Cool to touch; peel. Place onions, carrot, and remaining 6 ingredients in a shallow baking dish; toss to coat. Arrange chicken on top of vegetable mixture. Bake at 450° for 20 minutes. Reduce oven temperature to 375°; bake 20 additional minutes. Yield: 4 servings (serving size: 1 chicken breast half and 1 cup vegetables).

CALORIES 402 (21% from fat); FAT 9.2g (sat 2g, mono 4.4g, poly 1.7g); PROTEIN 47.2g; CARB 35.3g; FIBER 4.1g; CHOL 116mg; IRON 3.6mg; SODIUM 707mg; CALC 92mg

- SPICY VEGETABLE RAGOÛT OVER POLENTA: *Joseph Phelps Vin du Grenache Mistral Rosé 1996 (California rosé), $12.50*

- CRAB-STUFFED POBLANO CHILES WITH MANGO SALSA: *Arrowood Viognier 1995 (Washington state white), $25 or The Hogue Cellars Fumé Blanc 1996 (Washington state white), $9*

- CURRIED LAMB-AND-LENTIL STEW: *Monte Volpe Sangiovese 1995 (California red), $15.99 or Hidden Cellars Sorcery 1995 (California red), $25*

SESAME BEEF STIR-FRY

(pictured on page 297)

With so many bell peppers, a serving of this recipe supplies three times the RDA of vitamin C.

1 (1-pound) lean flank steak
1 teaspoon five-spice powder
1 tablespoon dark sesame oil
1½ tablespoons peeled, minced fresh gingerroot
3 garlic cloves, minced
2 cups red bell pepper strips
2 cups yellow bell pepper strips
½ cup no-salt-added beef broth
3 tablespoons low-sodium soy sauce
1 tablespoon cornstarch
4 cups thinly sliced bok choy
1 tablespoon sesame seeds, toasted
¼ teaspoon salt
4 cups hot cooked rice

1. Trim fat from steak; rub surface of steak with five-spice powder. Slice diagonally across grain into thin strips.
2. Heat oil in a large nonstick skillet over medium heat. Add gingerroot and garlic; stir-fry 2 minutes. Add beef; stir-fry 4 minutes. Add bell peppers; stir-fry 2 minutes. Combine broth, soy sauce, and cornstarch in a small bowl. Add to beef mixture. Add bok choy; cook, stirring constantly, 1 minute or until bok choy wilts and mixture thickens. Remove from heat; stir in sesame seeds and salt. Serve over rice. Yield: 4 servings (serving size: 1 cup stir-fry and 1 cup rice).

CALORIES 469 (33% from fat); FAT 17.3g (sat 5.6g, mono 6.5g, poly 3.3g); PROTEIN 28.4g; CARB 48g; FIBER 3.1g; CHOL 57mg; IRON 6.8mg; SODIUM 867mg; CALC 132mg

CRAB-STUFFED POBLANO CHILES WITH MANGO SALSA

1 cup peeled, chopped mango
⅓ cup chopped red bell pepper
2 tablespoons chopped fresh cilantro
1 tablespoon balsamic vinegar or white wine vinegar
3 tablespoons grated fresh Romano cheese or Parmesan cheese, divided
1 teaspoon dried oregano
1 teaspoon Dijon mustard
⅛ teaspoon pepper
1 (15-ounce) carton fat-free ricotta cheese
1 (14-ounce) can quartered artichoke hearts, drained
1 (6-ounce) can lump crabmeat, drained
4 (5-inch) poblano chiles, halved lengthwise and seeded
Cilantro sprigs (optional)

1. Combine first 4 ingredients in a small bowl; stir well. Cover and chill.
2. Preheat oven to 350°.
3. Combine 2 tablespoons Romano cheese, oregano, and next 3 ingredients in a food processor; process until smooth. Spoon into a bowl; stir in artichokes and crabmeat. Divide mixture evenly among chile halves; sprinkle with 1 tablespoon Romano cheese. Place stuffed chiles on a baking sheet; bake at 350° for 30 minutes or until lightly browned. Serve chiles with mango salsa. Garnish with cilantro sprigs, if desired. Yield: 4 servings (serving size: 2 chile halves and ⅓ cup salsa).

Note: Substitute 4 red or green bell peppers for poblano chiles, if desired.

CALORIES 225 (10% from fat); FAT 2.4g (sat 1.1g, mono 0.6g, poly 0.4g); PROTEIN 29.5g; CARB 27.5g; FIBER 1.2g; CHOL 55mg; IRON 2.3mg; SODIUM 397mg; CALC 340mg

CURRIED LAMB-AND-LENTIL STEW

1½ pounds boned leg of lamb
1 tablespoon olive oil
½ cup chopped onion
½ cup chopped celery
2 garlic cloves, minced
1 tablespoon curry powder
1 teaspoon ground cumin
⅛ teaspoon ground red pepper
2 cups low-salt chicken broth
¾ cup lentils
1 (28-ounce) can crushed tomatoes, undrained
3½ cups chopped collards or spinach (about ¼ pound)
½ cup diced carrot
2 tablespoons chopped fresh cilantro
Cilantro sprigs (optional)

1. Trim fat from lamb; cut lamb into 1-inch cubes. Set lamb aside.
2. Heat oil in a Dutch oven over medium heat until hot. Add onion, celery, and garlic; sauté 2 minutes. Add lamb; sauté 5 minutes or until browned.
3. Add curry, cumin, and pepper to Dutch oven; stir well to coat. Add broth, lentils, and tomatoes; bring to a boil. Reduce heat; simmer, uncovered, 20 minutes, stirring occasionally. Add greens and carrot to Dutch oven; simmer 10 minutes or until lamb is tender. Remove from heat; stir in chopped cilantro. Garnish with cilantro sprigs, if desired. Yield: 6 servings (serving size: 1¼ cups stew).

CALORIES 309 (26% from fat); FAT 8.8g (sat 2.2g, mono 3.9g, poly 0.9g); PROTEIN 33.7g; CARB 25g; FIBER 5.7g; CHOL 73mg; IRON 6.9mg; SODIUM 311mg; CALC 115mg

SOUTHWEST ROASTED RED PEPPER BISQUE WITH CILANTRO CREAM

⅓ cup finely chopped fresh cilantro
¼ cup low-fat sour cream
2 teaspoons 2% low-fat milk
½ teaspoon salt
1½ pounds red bell peppers (about 3 large), roasted and peeled
2 teaspoons olive oil
2 cups chopped onion
½ cup chopped carrot
1 tablespoon tomato paste
½ teaspoon ground cumin
¼ teaspoon chili powder
Dash of ground red pepper
2 garlic cloves, minced
¾ cup cooked long-grain rice
½ cup water
2 (10½-ounce) cans low-salt chicken broth
½ cup 2% low-fat milk
¼ teaspoon salt
⅛ teaspoon black pepper

1. Combine first 4 ingredients in a small bowl; stir well, and set aside.
2. Chop bell peppers; set aside. Heat oil in a Dutch oven over medium heat. Add onion and carrot; sauté 8 minutes or until vegetables are lightly browned. Stir in bell peppers, tomato paste, and next 4 ingredients; cook 5 minutes, stirring frequently. Stir in rice, water, and broth, scraping Dutch oven to loosen browned bits. Bring to a boil; partially cover, reduce heat, and simmer 15 minutes.
3. Place broth mixture in a food processor; process until smooth. Return puree to Dutch oven; stir in ½ cup milk, ¼ teaspoon salt, and black pepper. Cook over medium heat until thoroughly heated (do not boil). Ladle bisque into bowls; top with cilantro cream mixture. Yield: 5 servings (serving size: 1 cup bisque and 2 teaspoons cilantro cream mixture).

CALORIES 167 (29% from fat); FAT 5.4g (sat 1.8g, mono 2.3g, poly 0.8g); PROTEIN 5.5g; CARB 26.1g; FIBER 4.3g; CHOL 7mg; IRON 3.3mg; SODIUM 426mg; CALC 84mg

GOOD IDEAS

Start Spreading the News

Today's fruit butters are effortless to make and in step with the times.

Unlike fruit preserves of old, these fruit butters don't require a perfect balance of sugar, pectin, and acid; careful timing; or temperature monitoring. You're free to add sugar and spices according to your taste. Cooking times need not be precise because they'll vary with the quantity you make, the juiciness of the fruit, and the intensity of the cooking heat. And it's difficult to overcook butters because if they become too thick, you can simply stir in more juice.

Fruit butters do require attentive stirring to prevent scorching, but this risk is minimized by using a heavy-bottomed pan. Best of all, you can make just a few jars at a time. This way, cooking takes just minutes, and you can skip the canning process by storing the jars in the refrigerator, where they'll keep for months.

CRANBERRY-MAPLE BUTTER

½ cup water
1 (12-ounce) bag fresh or frozen cranberries
½ cup maple syrup
¼ cup plus 2 tablespoons brown sugar
½ teaspoon ground cinnamon
½ teaspoon vanilla extract

1. Combine water and cranberries in a large saucepan. Bring to a boil; cover, reduce heat, and simmer 5 minutes or until cranberries pop. Place cranberry mixture in a blender or food processor; cover and process until smooth.
2. Combine cranberry mixture, maple syrup, sugar, and cinnamon in pan;

bring to a boil. Reduce heat; simmer, uncovered, 25 minutes or until mixture is thick, stirring frequently. Stir in vanilla. Cool. Store in an airtight container in the refrigerator up to 2 months. Yield: 1¾ cups (serving size: 1 tablespoon).

CALORIES 25 (0% from fat); FAT 0g; PROTEIN 0g; CARB 6.3g; FIBER 0.1g; CHOL 0mg; IRON 0.1mg; SODIUM 1mg; CALC 4mg

PENNSYLVANIA-DUTCH APPLE BUTTER

6½ cups peeled, chopped Granny Smith apple (about 2 pounds)
1¼ cups apple cider
¾ cup packed brown sugar
¾ teaspoon ground cinnamon
¼ teaspoon ground allspice
¼ teaspoon ground cloves
¼ teaspoon ground ginger

1. Combine apple and cider in a large saucepan or Dutch oven. Bring to a boil; cover, reduce heat, and simmer 40 minutes or until tender. Place apple mixture in a blender or food processor; cover and process until smooth.
2. Combine pureed apple mixture, sugar, and remaining ingredients in pan; bring to a boil. Reduce heat, and simmer, uncovered, 25 minutes or until mixture is thick, stirring frequently. Cool. Store in an airtight container in the refrigerator up to 2 months. Yield: 3 cups (serving size: 1 tablespoon).

CALORIES 25 (4% from fat); FAT 0.1g (sat 0.1g, mono 0g, poly 0g); PROTEIN 0g; CARB 6.4g; FIBER 0.4g; CHOL 0mg; IRON 0.1mg; SODIUM 2mg; CALC 5mg

PRUNE BREAKFAST BUTTER

1¾ cups boiling water
2 regular-size Earl Grey tea bags
½ pound pitted prunes
⅓ cup sugar
1 teaspoon grated lemon rind
½ teaspoon vanilla extract

1. Combine boiling water and tea bags in a medium bowl; cover and steep 5 minutes. Discard tea bags.
2. Combine tea and prunes in a large heavy saucepan. Bring to a boil; cover, reduce heat, and simmer 5 minutes or until tender. Place prune mixture in a blender; cover and process until smooth.
3. Combine prune mixture, sugar, and lemon rind in pan; bring to a boil. Reduce heat; simmer, uncovered, 20 minutes or until mixture is thick, stirring frequently. Stir in vanilla; cool. Store in an airtight container in the refrigerator up to 2 months. Yield: 1¾ cups (serving size: 1 tablespoon).

CALORIES 29 (0% from fat); FAT 0g; PROTEIN 0.2g; CARB 7.8g; FIBER 0.6g; CHOL 0mg; IRON 0.2mg; SODIUM 0mg; CALC 4mg

SPICED PLUM BUTTER

¾ cup orange juice
4 pounds plums, quartered
1 cup sugar
½ teaspoon ground cinnamon
¼ teaspoon ground allspice
¼ teaspoon ground ginger
⅛ teaspoon ground nutmeg
⅛ teaspoon ground cloves

1. Combine orange juice and plums in a large saucepan. Bring to a boil; cover, reduce heat, and simmer 30 minutes or until tender. Place mixture in a blender; cover and process until smooth. Press mixture through a fine sieve over a bowl; discard solids.
2. Combine plum mixture, sugar, and remaining ingredients in pan; bring to a boil. Reduce heat; simmer, uncovered, 1 hour or until thick, stirring frequently. Cool. Store in an airtight container in the refrigerator up to 2 months. Yield: 2½ cups (serving size: 1 tablespoon).

CALORIES 45 (6% from fat); FAT 0.3g (sat 0g, mono 0.2g, poly 0.1g); PROTEIN 0.4g; CARB 11.1g; FIBER 0.9g; CHOL 0mg; IRON 0.1mg; SODIUM 0mg; CALC 3mg

BEYOND BREAKFAST

Fruit butters contain virtually no fat and can enliven almost every kind of dish.

• Blend **Spiced Pear Butter** into a vinaigrette dressing using lemon juice, walnut oil, and black pepper; drizzle over a salad of greens, red onion, fresh pear slices, toasted walnuts, and blue cheese.

• Stir **Cranberry-Maple Butter** into a dressing using mustard, garlic, olive oil, raspberry vinegar, and dried crushed red pepper; drizzle over a salad of greens, toasted pecans, smoked turkey, and slices of apples and red onion.

• Mix **Pennsylvania-Dutch Apple Butter** with horseradish, lemon, and mayonnaise; spread on roast-beef sandwiches, and top with sauerkraut.

• Top smoked-turkey sandwiches with **Cranberry-Maple Butter** and reduced-fat Cheddar cheese.

• Roast chicken and spicy low-fat sausages in chicken stock flavored with garlic, mustard, and thyme; stir **Pennsylvania-Dutch Apple Butter** into the pan liquids.

• Blend **Pennsylvania-Dutch Apple Butter** with fresh rosemary, lemon juice, and coarsely ground black pepper; spoon over grilled center-cut pork chops.

• Use **Pennsylvania-Dutch Apple Butter** and maple syrup to flavor rice pudding.

SPICED PEAR BUTTER

Any type of pear will work in this recipe, but Bartletts are the best choice.

6 cups peeled, chopped ripe pear
   (about 2 pounds)
½ cup apple juice
1 cup sugar
¾ teaspoon ground cinnamon
¼ teaspoon ground cardamom
   (optional)
1 teaspoon vanilla extract

1. Combine pear and apple juice in a large saucepan or Dutch oven. Bring to a boil; cover, reduce heat, and simmer 45 minutes or until tender. Place pear mixture in a blender or food processor; cover and process until smooth.
2. Combine pureed pear mixture, sugar, cinnamon, and cardamom (if desired) in pan; bring to a boil. Reduce heat; simmer, uncovered, 55 minutes or until mixture is thick, stirring frequently. Stir in vanilla. Cool. Store in an airtight container in the refrigerator up to 2 months. Yield: 1¾ cups (serving size: 1 tablespoon).

CALORIES 42 (2% from fat); FAT 0.1g (sat 0g, mono 0g, poly 0.1g); PROTEIN 0.1g; CARB 10.7g; FIBER 0.7g; CHOL 0mg; IRON 0.1mg; SODIUM 0mg; CALC 4mg

SPICED SQUASH BUTTER

3 medium acorn squash or
   other winter squash (about
   3 pounds)
½ cup thawed apple juice
   concentrate, undiluted
¾ cup packed brown sugar
¼ teaspoon ground cinnamon
¼ teaspoon ground nutmeg
¼ teaspoon ground ginger
⅛ teaspoon ground cloves

1. Preheat oven to 400°.
2. Cut squash in half lengthwise; discard seeds and stringy pulp. Place squash, cut sides down, in a jelly-roll pan. Cover and bake at 400° for 1 hour or until tender. Cool. Scoop out pulp to equal 3 cups. Place pulp in a

blender or food processor; cover and process until smooth.
3. Combine pureed squash, apple juice, and remaining ingredients in a large saucepan or Dutch oven; bring to a boil. Reduce heat; simmer, uncovered, 45 minutes or until thick, stirring frequently. Cool. Store in an airtight container in the refrigerator up to 2 months. Yield: 2¾ cups (serving size: 1 tablespoon).

CALORIES 25 (0% from fat); FAT 0g; PROTEIN 0.2g; CARB 6.4g; FIBER 0.2g; CHOL 0mg; IRON 0.2mg; SODIUM 3mg; CALC 9mg

SWISS SCALLOPED POTATOES

2 medium leeks (about ¾
   pound)
2 tablespoons fresh lemon
   juice
2 teaspoons olive oil
½ teaspoon salt, divided
⅛ teaspoon pepper
Vegetable cooking spray
4 cups thinly sliced baking
   potatoes (about 1½ pounds)
1 cup skim milk
⅓ cup Spiced Pear Butter
   (page 318)
¾ cup (3 ounces) grated
   Gruyère cheese

1. Preheat oven to 500°.
2. Remove roots, outer leaves, and tops from leeks. Rinse under cold water; cut into 1½ x ½-inch strips.
3. Combine leeks, lemon juice, olive oil, ¼ teaspoon salt, and pepper in an 11 x 7-inch baking dish. Bake at 500° for 20 minutes or until leeks are tender, stirring once. Spoon leek mixture into a bowl; set aside. Reduce oven temperature to 350°.
4. Coat baking dish with cooking spray, and arrange half of potato slices in dish. Spread leek mixture over potato slices. Top with remaining potato slices; sprinkle with ¼ teaspoon salt.
5. Combine milk and Spiced Pear Butter in a small bowl, stirring with a whisk until smooth; pour over potato slices. Cover loosely with aluminum

foil; bake at 350° for 45 minutes. Uncover and bake 30 minutes. Sprinkle with cheese; bake 10 additional minutes. Yield: 6 servings (serving size: 1 cup).

CALORIES 248 (24% from fat); FAT 6.6g (sat 3g, mono 2.6g, poly 0.5g); PROTEIN 8.4g; CARB 40g; FIBER 2.8g; CHOL 17mg; IRON 1.5mg; SODIUM 279mg; CALC 234mg

AUTUMN RAGOÛT WITH ROASTED VEGETABLES

1 teaspoon grated lemon rind
3 tablespoons fresh lemon
   juice
2 teaspoons prepared mustard
2 teaspoons olive oil
1 teaspoon dried thyme
½ teaspoon salt
½ teaspoon pepper
4 garlic cloves, chopped
3 cups (1-inch) peeled, cubed
   butternut squash
2 cups (1-inch) peeled, cubed
   rutabaga
2 cups (1-inch) carrot pieces
1 small red onion, cut into
   1-inch pieces
1½ pounds skinned, boned
   chicken breast, cut into
   1-inch pieces
½ pound turkey kielbasa, cut
   into ½-inch pieces
2 cups (1-inch) pieces napa
   (Chinese) cabbage
2 cups low-salt chicken broth
½ cup apple juice
½ cup Pennsylvania-Dutch Apple
   Butter (page 317) or Spiced
   Pear Butter (page 318)
1 (15-ounce) can navy beans,
   drained

1. Preheat oven to 450°.
2. Combine first 8 ingredients in a 13 x 9-inch baking dish. Add squash and next 3 ingredients, tossing well. Bake at 450° for 30 minutes or until lightly browned, stirring occasionally. Remove from oven. Reduce oven temperature to 350°. Combine squash mixture, chicken, and remaining ingredients in a large ovenproof Dutch oven. Bake at 350° for 50 minutes or

until vegetables are tender, stirring occasionally. Yield: 10 servings (serving size: 1 cup).

CALORIES 231 (24% from fat); FAT 6.1g (sat 0.9g, mono 1.7g, poly 1.4g); PROTEIN 23.4g; CARB 25.1g; FIBER 3.7g; CHOL 62mg; IRON 2.6mg; SODIUM 543mg; CALC 93mg

PORK ROAST WITH PLUM GLAZE

1   (1½-pound) lean, rolled, boned pork loin roast
¼   cup plus 1 tablespoon Spiced Plum Butter (page 317)
2   tablespoons rice vinegar
2   tablespoons low-sodium soy sauce
2   teaspoons peeled, grated fresh gingerroot
1   teaspoon sesame oil
½   teaspoon five-spice powder (optional)
3   garlic cloves, crushed
Vegetable cooking spray
¼   cup water
Plum slices (optional)
Sage sprigs (optional)

1. Preheat oven to 425°.
2. Unroll roast; trim fat. Reroll roast, and secure at 1-inch intervals with heavy string. Combine Spiced Plum Butter and next 6 ingredients in a small bowl. Reserve ¼ cup plum mixture; set aside.
3. Place roast on a broiler pan coated with cooking spray. Insert a meat thermometer into thickest portion of roast. Brush 2 tablespoons remaining plum mixture over roast. Bake at 425° for 50 minutes or until meat thermometer registers 160° (slightly pink), basting occasionally with remaining plum mixture. Let stand 5 minutes before slicing.
4. Strain pan drippings through a sieve into a bowl, reserving 2 tablespoons drippings. Discard remaining liquid and solids. Combine reserved ¼ cup plum mixture, reserved 2 tablespoons drippings, and water in a small saucepan. Bring to a boil; reduce heat, and simmer 2 minutes. Serve sauce with roast. If desired, garnish with

plum slices and sage sprigs. Yield: 4 servings (serving size: 3 ounces pork and 2 tablespoons sauce).

CALORIES 253 (36% from fat); FAT 10.1g (sat 3.1g, mono 4.3g, poly 1.5g); PROTEIN 24.5g; CARB 15.7g; FIBER 1.2g; CHOL 68mg; IRON 1.2mg; SODIUM 316mg; CALC 21mg

┌─────────────────────────────────┐
│   MENU SUGGESTION   │
│   MOROCCAN-SPICED   │
│   LEG OF LAMB   │
│   *Orzo pilaf**   │
│   *Brussels sprouts*   │
│   *Combine 4 cups cooked orzo, ½ cup │
│   chopped red bell pepper, ½ cup feta │
│   cheese, and ¼ cup chopped parsley. │
└─────────────────────────────────┘

MOROCCAN-SPICED LEG OF LAMB

1   teaspoon salt
1   teaspoon coarsely ground black pepper
1   teaspoon ground ginger
1   teaspoon ground cinnamon
½   teaspoon ground cardamom
¼   teaspoon ground red pepper
1   (2½-pound) rolled, boned leg of lamb
1   tablespoon vegetable oil
1   cup chopped red onion
⅓   cup dry red wine
6   garlic cloves, chopped
1   (14¼-ounce) can fat-free beef broth
1   tablespoon all-purpose flour
2   tablespoons water
½   cup Spiced Pear Butter (page 318) or Spiced Plum Butter (page 317)

1. Combine first 6 ingredients in a small bowl; set aside.
2. Unroll roast; trim fat. Rub ginger mixture into folds and over surface of roast. Place roast in a large zip-top plastic bag; seal and marinate in refrigerator 12 to 24 hours, turning bag occasionally. Remove roast from bag; set aside.

3. Preheat oven to 325°.
4. Heat oil in an ovenproof Dutch oven over medium-high heat; add roast, browning on all sides. Add onion and next 3 ingredients; bring to a simmer. Insert meat thermometer into thickest portion of roast. Cover and bake at 325° for 50 minutes or until thermometer registers 145° (medium-rare), basting occasionally. Remove from Dutch oven; set aside, and keep warm.
5. Strain cooking liquid through a sieve into a bowl, and discard solids. Return cooking liquid to Dutch oven. Bring to a boil; cook 5 minutes or until reduced to 2 cups. Combine flour and water in a small bowl, stirring well with a whisk. Add flour mixture to cooking liquid in Dutch oven. Bring to a boil; cook, stirring constantly with a whisk, 1 minute or until slightly thick. Stir in Spiced Pear Butter; serve sauce with lamb. Yield: 8 servings (serving size: 3 ounces lamb and ¼ cup sauce).

CALORIES 225 (28% from fat); FAT 7g (sat 2.2g, mono 2.6g, poly 1.3g); PROTEIN 25.3g; CARB 14.8g; FIBER 1.3g; CHOL 73mg; IRON 2.6mg; SODIUM 383mg; CALC 26mg

Meal Ticket to Paradise

After a decade of effort, chef George Mavrothalassitis says Hawaii's light cuisine has finally arrived.

George Mavrothalassitis has been senior executive chef at Seasons restaurant at the Four Seasons Resort Maui at Wailea for the past two years. However, he still retains his passion for getting out of the kitchen and into the farm fields to see what's ready to harvest. With his emphasis on flavor, texture, and freshness, he's helped inspire Hawaii's light cuisine.

WARM PINEAPPLE TARTS WITH COCONUT SAUCE

This tart tastes best when served immediately.

⅓ cup coarsely chopped fresh pineapple
½ cup granulated sugar
½ cup light coconut milk
4 large egg yolks
1 tablespoon dark rum
16 sheets frozen phyllo dough, thawed
Butter-flavored vegetable cooking spray
2 tablespoons powdered sugar
1 large egg white
1½ medium pineapples, peeled and cored (about 2¾ pounds)
¼ cup granulated sugar

1. Place ⅓ cup chopped pineapple in a food processor; process until smooth. Combine pineapple puree, ½ cup granulated sugar, coconut milk, and egg yolks in a saucepan, stirring with a whisk until blended. Cook over medium heat, stirring constantly, about 6 minutes until thick (do not boil). Strain milk mixture through a sieve into a bowl, and discard solids. Stir in rum. Cover and chill.

2. Preheat oven to 325°.
3. Draw 2 (7-inch) circles on parchment paper. Cut out circles; set aside.
4. Place 1 phyllo sheet on a large cutting board or work surface (cover remaining dough to keep from drying); lightly coat with cooking spray. Working with 1 phyllo sheet at a time, coat 7 more phyllo sheets with cooking spray, placing one on top of the other. Place a sheet of plastic wrap on phyllo stack, pressing gently to seal sheets together; discard plastic wrap.
5. Place parchment circles over phyllo sheets. Cut 2 (7-inch) circles through phyllo layers, using the tip of a knife. Carefully place layered circles on a baking sheet coated with cooking spray; discard phyllo scraps. Repeat procedure with remaining 8 phyllo sheets.
6. Combine powdered sugar and egg white; brush over phyllo circles. Bake at 325° for 15 minutes.
7. Cut cored pineapples into quarters lengthwise. Cut each quarter into 1½-inch-long pieces. Cut each piece into ¼-inch-thick wedges lengthwise. Heat a nonstick skillet over medium-high heat until hot. Add pineapple; sauté 20 minutes or until pineapple begins to brown. Preheat broiler. Divide sautéed pineapple among tarts. Sprinkle 1 tablespoon granulated sugar over each tart. Broil 2½ minutes or until sugar melts. Drizzle with coconut sauce. Yield: 8 servings (serving size: ½ tart and about 3 tablespoons sauce).
Note: Coconut sauce may be prepared up to 1 day in advance.

CALORIES 287 (21% from fat); FAT 6.5g (sat 1.9g, mono 1.5g, poly 1.8g); PROTEIN 4.9g; CARB 52.2g; FIBER 1.3g; CHOL 109mg; IRON 1.9mg; SODIUM 201mg; CALC 22mg

November DECEMBER

The Gift of Gathering

When all is said and done, the holidays are about
friends and family getting together.
Let us help make your gatherings more special.

We thought hard about how we could best help you make the holidays as smooth and meaningful as possible. From Thanksgiving through New Year's Day, gatherings involve food, and plenty of it. Because these get-togethers are so special, the food should be, too. But considering all the demands that the holidays bring, who has time to plan several creative menus? So we devised an easy plan for your success.

The answer we came up with: holiday menus that can be mixed and matched, allowing you to spend more time with your family and guests.

MENU SUGGESTION

ROSEMARY-CRUSTED
RACK OF LAMB WITH
BALSAMIC SAUCE

BARLEY-AND-MUSHROOM
CASSEROLE

GLAZED BEETS AND
CABBAGE WITH
PEPPER-TOASTED PECANS

ORANGE-SCENTED
ROASTED
ROOT VEGETABLES

TIRAMISÙ ANGEL TORTE
page 361

ROSEMARY-CRUSTED RACK OF LAMB WITH BALSAMIC SAUCE

Ask your butcher for a French-cut rack of lamb (for which bones have been cleaned down to loin).

1 (1½-pound) French-cut lean rack of lamb (about 8 ribs)
3 tablespoons balsamic vinegar
1 tablespoon chopped fresh rosemary or 1 teaspoon dried rosemary, divided
2 garlic cloves, minced
⅛ teaspoon pepper
¼ cup fresh breadcrumbs
Vegetable cooking spray
½ teaspoon olive oil
¼ cup minced shallots
¼ cup dry white wine
½ cup low-salt chicken broth
2 teaspoons honey
½ teaspoon cornstarch
Thyme sprigs (optional)
Red grapes (optional)

1. Trim fat from lamb. Combine vinegar, 2 teaspoons rosemary, and garlic in a large zip-top plastic bag.

Add lamb to bag, and seal. Marinate in refrigerator for at least 6 to 12 hours, turning occasionally.
2. Preheat oven to 450°.
3. Remove lamb from bag, reserving marinade. Sprinkle lamb with pepper. Combine breadcrumbs and 1 teaspoon rosemary; pat breadcrumb mixture onto meaty side of lamb. Place lamb, meat side up, on a jelly-roll pan coated with cooking spray. Insert a meat thermometer into thickest part of lamb, making sure it does not touch bone. Bake at 450° for 20 minutes or until meat thermometer registers 145° (medium-rare) or to desired degree of doneness.
4. Heat oil in a large nonstick skillet over medium-high heat; add shallots, and sauté 4 minutes. Add wine and reserved marinade; bring to a boil. Reduce heat, and simmer, uncovered, 8 minutes or until liquid almost evaporates. Add chicken broth; bring to a boil. Reduce heat; simmer, uncovered, until reduced to ⅓ cup (about 5 minutes). Combine honey and cornstarch; add to broth mixture. Bring to a boil; cook, stirring constantly, 1 minute.
5. Slice rack into 8 chops. Serve sauce with lamb. If desired, garnish with thyme sprigs and red grapes. Yield: 4 servings (serving size: 2 lamb chops and about 2 teaspoons sauce).
Note: You can use ¾ cup low-salt chicken broth and omit wine, if desired.

CALORIES 208 (45% from fat); FAT 10.3g (sat 3.4g, mono 4.2g, poly 1g); PROTEIN 20.6g; CARB 7.7g; FIBER 0.2g; CHOL 65mg; IRON 2.2mg; SODIUM 87mg; CALC 25mg

BARLEY-AND-MUSHROOM CASSEROLE

Instead of rice, try this easy, high-fiber side dish. It has a robust, nutty flavor.

- 1 tablespoon stick margarine
- 1 (8-ounce) package presliced mushrooms
- 1 (3½-ounce) package shiitake mushrooms, stems removed and caps sliced
- 1 cup uncooked pearl barley
- 1 (1-ounce) envelope onion soup mix (such as Lipton Recipe Secrets)
- 4 cups water

1. Preheat oven to 350°.
2. Melt margarine in a medium non-stick skillet over medium-high heat. Add mushrooms; sauté 5 minutes or until tender.
3. Combine barley, soup mix, and water in a 3-quart casserole; stir in mushroom mixture. Cover and bake at 350° for 1 hour and 15 minutes or until liquid is almost absorbed. Yield: 6 servings (serving size: about ¾ cup).

CALORIES 161 (14% from fat); FAT 2.5g (sat 0.5g, mono 0.9g, poly 0.9g); PROTEIN 4.4g; CARB 31g; FIBER 5.9g; CHOL 0mg; IRON 1.5mg; SODIUM 434mg; CALC 13mg

GLAZED BEETS AND CABBAGE WITH PEPPER-TOASTED PECANS

- 1 teaspoon stick margarine
- 2 teaspoons sugar
- Dash of ground red pepper
- Dash of black pepper
- Dash of ground cinnamon
- ½ cup chopped pecans
- Vegetable cooking spray
- 3 (15-ounce) cans whole baby beets, undrained
- ¼ cup red currant jelly
- ¼ cup red wine vinegar
- ¼ teaspoon salt
- ⅛ teaspoon white pepper
- 1½ cups thinly sliced shallots
- 3 cups coarsely chopped red cabbage

1. Preheat oven to 325°.
2. Melt margarine in a small saucepan over medium heat. Add sugar and next 3 ingredients; cook, stirring constantly, 30 seconds. Remove from heat; stir in pecans. Spread pecan mixture onto a baking sheet coated with cooking spray. Bake at 325° for 8 minutes; cool. Set aside.
3. Drain beets in a colander over a bowl, reserving 3 tablespoons liquid. Combine reserved beet liquid, jelly, and next 3 ingredients. Cut beets in half; set aside.
4. Place a large nonstick skillet coated with cooking spray over medium-high heat until hot. Add shallots; sauté 4 minutes or until tender. Add cabbage, and sauté 10 minutes or until tender. Add jelly mixture and beets; bring to a boil. Reduce heat; simmer, uncovered, 5 minutes or until liquid is slightly thick. Spoon into a bowl; sprinkle with pecan mixture. Yield: 12 servings (serving size: ½ cup beets and 2 teaspoons pecans).

CALORIES 99 (21% from fat); FAT 2.3g (sat 0.2g, mono 1.2g, poly 0.6g); PROTEIN 2g; CARB 19.6g; FIBER 1.5g; CHOL 0mg; IRON 1mg; SODIUM 310mg; CALC 38mg

ORANGE-SCENTED ROASTED ROOT VEGETABLES

This no-fuss side dish roasts while you're tending to the rest of the meal.

- 4 cups (1-inch) cubes peeled sweet potato
- 3 cups (1-inch) cubes peeled rutabaga
- 2 cups (1-inch) sliced parsnip
- 1 tablespoon vegetable oil
- 2 medium onions, each cut into 8 wedges
- Vegetable cooking spray
- ⅓ cup packed brown sugar
- 2 tablespoons orange marmalade
- 2 tablespoons lemon juice
- 1 tablespoon sweet honey mustard
- ¼ teaspoon salt
- ⅛ teaspoon ground red pepper
- Dash of ground nutmeg

1. Preheat oven to 400°.
2. Combine first 5 ingredients in a bowl; toss. Arrange vegetables in a single layer in a shallow roasting pan coated with cooking spray. Bake at 400° for 45 minutes, stirring twice.
3. Combine sugar and remaining 6 ingredients in a small saucepan; bring to a boil. Reduce heat; simmer 1 minute. Pour mixture over vegetables; toss gently. Bake 15 additional minutes or until vegetables are tender. Yield: 7 servings (serving size: 1 cup).

CALORIES 229 (11% from fat); FAT 2.8g (sat 0.5g, mono 0.7g, poly 1.1g); PROTEIN 3g; CARB 50.7g; FIBER 4.9g; CHOL 0mg; IRON 1.4mg; SODIUM 148mg; CALC 84mg

MENU PLANNING PRIMER

These are the basic elements of creating interesting meals.

Most people say that meal planning is their tallest culinary hurdle. That's why we've assembled these recipes to give you menu ideas for the holidays. But we do encourage you to mix and match these favorites for your own holiday meals. And as you do, keep these elements in mind.

Plan for color. A variety of color gives a meal a pleasing appearance. But watch out for clashing colors. Just as in clothing, some colors in food don't work well together.

Plan for flavor. Too many strong flavors in a meal can overwhelm your taste buds. Likewise, a meal that has all bland flavors can bore your palate. Think about trying to balance sweet, savory, salty, and acidic flavors in each meal.

Plan for texture and consistency. Texture is how a food feels in our mouth—crisp, crunchy, chewy, or soft. Consistency is the food's density and firmness, as well as how it holds together on the plate. It's best to have a variety—too many crisp, crunchy, and chewy items can exhaust your jaw, while too many soft items can feel like mush in your mouth.

CREAMED-SPINACH GRATIN

Placing the creamed spinach in a casserole and topping it with sliced tomatoes gives the dish a bright, festive touch of red and green.

 1 (10-ounce) bag fresh spinach
    Vegetable cooking spray
 ⅔ cup chopped onion
 ¼ cup tub-style light cream cheese
 ½ teaspoon dried oregano
 ¼ teaspoon salt
 ¼ teaspoon pepper
 1 cup (¼-inch-thick) sliced tomato
 ¼ cup dry breadcrumbs
 2 tablespoons finely grated fresh Parmesan cheese

1. Preheat oven to 375°.
2. Remove large stems from spinach. Tear spinach into 1-inch pieces; place in a colander. Rinse spinach under cold water; drain. Set aside.
3. Place a large Dutch oven coated with cooking spray over medium heat until hot. Add onion; sauté 3 minutes. Add spinach; cover and cook 2 minutes or until spinach wilts. Add cream cheese and next 3 ingredients. Cook, uncovered, 1 additional minute or until cream cheese melts. Spoon spinach mixture into a 1-quart gratin dish or shallow casserole coated with cooking spray. Arrange tomato slices in a single layer over spinach; sprinkle with breadcrumbs and Parmesan cheese. Bake at 375° for 30 minutes or until golden. Yield: 6 servings (serving size: ½ cup).

CALORIES 72 (35% from fat); FAT 2.8g (sat 1.4g, mono 0.3g, poly 0.3g); PROTEIN 4.2g; CARB 8.5g; FIBER 2.8g; CHOL 7mg; IRON 1.8mg; SODIUM 265mg; CALC 105mg

---

> **MENU SUGGESTION**
>
> BEEF TENDERLOIN WITH BEAUJOLAIS JUS
>
> OYSTER DRESSING
>
> BRUSSELS SPROUTS-AND-RICE CASSEROLE
>
> HERBED FRUIT COMPOTE
>
> PUMPKIN PANACHE
>
> DARK-CHOCOLATE SOUFFLÉ CAKE
> page 352

BEEF TENDERLOIN WITH BEAUJOLAIS JUS

(pictured on page 333)

We recommend using a fairly good wine for the best flavor. If you have leftover beef, serve it on sandwiches with horseradish cream, which you can make by combining ¾ cup fat-free sour cream and 3 tablespoons prepared horseradish.

 1 (2¼-pound) beef tenderloin
 1 tablespoon plus 2 teaspoons minced fresh thyme, divided
 1 teaspoon salt
 ½ teaspoon coarsely ground pepper
 ½ cup dried porcini mushrooms (about ½ ounce)
 1 (750-milliliter) bottle Beaujolais or other light, fruity red wine
 1 (14¼-ounce) can fat-free beef broth
 2 garlic cloves, minced
 1 tablespoon water
 2 teaspoons cornstarch
 1 teaspoon olive oil
    Vegetable cooking spray

1. Trim fat from tenderloin. Combine 1 tablespoon fresh thyme, salt, and pepper; rub thyme mixture evenly over tenderloin. Cover tenderloin, and chill 2 hours.

2. Combine 2 teaspoons fresh thyme, mushrooms, and next 3 ingredients in a large saucepan; bring to a boil. Reduce heat, and simmer until reduced to 1½ cups (about 1 hour). Combine water and cornstarch; stir into wine mixture. Bring mixture to a boil; cook, stirring constantly, 1 minute. Remove wine mixture from heat; set aside, and keep warm.
3. Preheat oven to 400°.
4. Heat oil in a large nonstick skillet over medium-high heat. Add tenderloin, browning on all sides (about 12 minutes). Place tenderloin on rack of a broiler pan coated with cooking spray. Insert meat thermometer into thickest portion of tenderloin. Bake at 400° for 20 minutes or until thermometer registers 145° (medium-rare) to 160° (medium). Place tenderloin on a serving platter, and cover with aluminum foil. Let stand for 10 minutes. Serve with Beaujolais jus. Yield: 8 servings (serving size: 3 ounces beef and 3 tablespoons jus).

CALORIES 201 (39% from fat); FAT 8.6g (sat 3.2g, mono 3.5g, poly 0.4g); PROTEIN 25.7g; CARB 3.7g; FIBER 0.3g; CHOL 71mg; IRON 3.6mg; SODIUM 372mg; CALC 17mg

---

OYSTER DRESSING

(pictured on page 333)

 2 tablespoons margarine
 1½ cups chopped onion
 1 cup chopped green bell pepper
 ½ cup chopped celery
 2 garlic cloves, minced
 12 cups (1-inch) cubed French bread (about 1 pound)
 2 cups herb-seasoned stuffing mix
 ½ cup water
 2 tablespoons chopped fresh parsley
 1 teaspoon dried thyme
 1 teaspoon dried oregano
 4 (10-ounce) containers standard oysters, undrained
 1 cup chopped green onions
 ½ cup finely shredded Parmesan cheese
    Vegetable cooking spray

1. Preheat oven to 350°.
2. Melt margarine in a Dutch oven over medium-high heat. Add 1½ cups onion and next 3 ingredients; sauté 5 minutes or until tender. Add bread cubes and next 6 ingredients; cook, stirring constantly, 7 minutes or until oysters are done. Remove from heat; stir in green onions and cheese. Spoon into a 13 x 9-inch baking dish coated with cooking spray. Bake at 350° for 30 minutes. Yield: 12 servings (serving size: 1 cup).

CALORIES 290 (21% from fat); FAT 6.7g (sat 1.9g, mono 1.8g, poly 1.7g); PROTEIN 13.4g; CARB 43.1g; FIBER 1.8g; CHOL 49mg; IRON 6.8mg; SODIUM 739mg; CALC 128mg

BRUSSELS SPROUTS-AND-RICE CASSEROLE

(pictured on page 336)

1 (10-ounce) package frozen Brussels sprouts
¼ cup water
1 tablespoon stick margarine
2 tablespoons all-purpose flour
1½ cups 1% low-fat milk
¼ teaspoon salt
⅛ teaspoon white pepper
Vegetable cooking spray
1 cup cooked long-grain rice
1 ounce thinly sliced prosciutto or ham, cut into thin strips
¼ cup fresh breadcrumbs
2 tablespoons grated fresh Parmesan cheese

1. Preheat oven to 375°.
2. Combine Brussels sprouts and water in a saucepan; bring to a boil. Cover, reduce heat, and simmer 5 minutes. Uncover and cook 1 minute. Drain.
3. Melt margarine in a small saucepan over low heat; add flour, stirring with a whisk. Gradually add milk to saucepan. Bring to a boil; cook over medium heat, stirring constantly, 3 minutes or until thick and bubbly. Stir in salt and pepper.
4. Coat a 9-inch quiche or round baking dish with cooking spray. Pat rice into bottom of dish; arrange Brussels sprouts, stem sides down, on top of rice. Sprinkle Brussels sprouts with prosciutto; pour sauce over prosciutto. Combine breadcrumbs and cheese; sprinkle over sauce. Bake at 375° for 20 minutes or until lightly browned. Yield: 6 servings (serving size: about ½ cup).

CALORIES 133 (26% from fat); FAT 3.9g (sat 1.4g, mono 1.5g, poly 0.8g); PROTEIN 6.6g; CARB 18.5g; FIBER 2.6g; CHOL 7mg; IRON 1.2mg; SODIUM 280mg; CALC 129mg

HERBED FRUIT COMPOTE

(pictured on page 333)

This sweet-savory compote also goes well with Honey-Marsala Glazed Ham (page 330).

1 teaspoon olive oil
1½ cups chopped onion
2 cups water
½ cup chopped dried pears
½ cup chopped dried apricots
½ cup dried tart cherries
½ cup raisins
¼ cup sweet Marsala
2 tablespoons honey
¼ teaspoon dried thyme
¼ teaspoon dried rubbed sage

1. Heat oil in a large saucepan over medium heat. Add onion; cover and cook 10 minutes, stirring occasionally. Add water and remaining ingredients; bring to a boil. Reduce heat; simmer until thick (about 20 minutes). Pour into a bowl; cool. Yield: 3½ cups (serving size: ¼ cup).
Note: Apple juice may be substituted for Marsala, if desired.

CALORIES 80 (6% from fat); FAT 0.5g (sat 0.1g, mono 0.5g, poly 0.1g); PROTEIN 0.9g; CARB 20g; FIBER 1.4g; CHOL 0mg; IRON 0.7mg; SODIUM 7mg; CALC 15mg

PUMPKIN PANACHE

(pictured on page 333)

6 cups cauliflower florets
2 tablespoons grated Parmesan cheese, divided
½ teaspoon salt, divided
¼ teaspoon pepper, divided
Vegetable cooking spray
2 cups cooked, cubed fresh pumpkin or 1½ cups canned unsweetened pumpkin
¼ cup fat-free sour cream
⅓ cup fresh breadcrumbs
1 tablespoon minced fresh parsley

1. Preheat oven to 350°.
2. Arrange cauliflower in a steamer basket over boiling water. Cover and steam 4 minutes or until crisp-tender; drain. Combine cauliflower, 1 tablespoon cheese, ¼ teaspoon salt, and ⅛ teaspoon pepper in a 2-quart casserole coated with cooking spray; toss gently.
3. Place pumpkin in a food processor, and process until smooth. Add ¼ teaspoon salt, ⅛ teaspoon pepper, and sour cream; pulse until blended. Spoon pumpkin mixture over cauliflower. Combine 1 tablespoon cheese, breadcrumbs, and parsley; sprinkle over pumpkin mixture. Bake at 350° for 15 minutes. Yield: 6 servings (serving size: 1 cup).

CALORIES 57 (14% from fat); FAT 0.9g (sat 0.4g, mono 0.2g, poly 0.1g); PROTEIN 4g; CARB 9.5g; FIBER 2.9g; CHOL 1mg; IRON 1mg; SODIUM 261mg; CALC 64mg

ORANGE-AND-MAPLE ROASTED TURKEY WITH GIBLET GRAVY

(pictured on page 2)

¾ cup orange juice
¼ cup maple syrup
1 (12-pound) fresh or frozen and thawed whole turkey
1 tablespoon poultry seasoning
1 tablespoon grated orange rind
¼ teaspoon salt
¼ teaspoon pepper
1 medium orange, quartered
1 medium onion, quartered
Vegetable cooking spray
1 teaspoon margarine
½ cup water
2 (10½-ounce) cans low-salt chicken broth
2 tablespoons orange juice
1 tablespoon plus 2 teaspoons cornstarch
1 tablespoon maple syrup
¼ teaspoon grated orange rind
¼ teaspoon salt
⅛ teaspoon pepper
Fresh herbs (optional)
Red grapes (optional)

1. Combine ¾ cup orange juice and ¼ cup maple syrup in a small saucepan; bring just to a boil. Remove from heat; set aside.

2. Preheat oven to 375°.
3. Remove giblets (including liver) and neck from turkey; set aside. Rinse turkey thoroughly with cold water, and pat dry. Tie ends of legs to tail with string. Lift wing tips up and over back, and tuck under turkey. Sprinkle poultry seasoning and next 3 ingredients into body cavity and onto turkey. Stuff cavity with orange quarters and onion quarters. Place turkey on rack of a broiler pan coated with cooking spray. Insert meat thermometer into meaty part of thigh, making sure it does not touch bone. Bake at 375° for 45 minutes. Baste with orange juice mixture; cover loosely with aluminum foil. Bake an additional 2 hours and 15 minutes or until meat thermometer registers 180°, basting every 30 minutes. Let stand for 10 minutes; set pan and drippings aside.
4. While turkey is baking, melt margarine in a medium saucepan over medium-high heat. Add reserved giblets (not including liver) and neck; sauté 2 minutes or until browned on all sides. Add water and broth; bring to a boil. Cover, reduce heat, and simmer 45 minutes. Add liver; simmer 10 additional minutes. Remove giblets, neck, and liver from broth mixture; chop liver, and return to pan. Discard giblets and neck.
5. After turkey is done, add broth mixture to bottom of broiler pan, scraping pan to loosen browned bits. Strain mixture through a sieve over a bowl; discard solids. Remove fat from surface with a spoon. Pour broth mixture into saucepan; add 2 tablespoons orange juice and next 5 ingredients, stirring with a whisk until well-blended. Bring to a boil; cook 1 minute or until thick. Discard skin from turkey. Serve gravy with turkey. If desired, garnish with fresh herbs and grapes. Yield: 12 servings (serving size: 6 ounces turkey and ¼ cup gravy).

CALORIES 308 (15% from fat); FAT 5.1g (sat 1.6g, mono 1.2g, poly 1.4g); PROTEIN 52.8g; CARB 12g; FIBER 0.8g; CHOL 175mg; IRON 4.2mg; SODIUM 226mg; CALC 48mg

SWEET POTATO CASSEROLE WITH PRALINE TOPPING

For extra flavor, the streusel is stirred into the casserole plus sprinkled on top.

1 cup all-purpose flour
⅔ cup packed brown sugar
¼ cup chopped pecans, toasted
¼ cup stick margarine, melted
½ teaspoon ground cinnamon
4 medium-size sweet potatoes, peeled and halved (about 2½ pounds)
½ cup granulated sugar
1½ teaspoons vanilla extract
1 large egg white
1 (5-ounce) can evaporated skim milk
Vegetable cooking spray

1. Preheat oven to 350°.
2. Combine first 5 ingredients in a small bowl, stirring to form a streusel. Set aside.
3. Place potatoes in a Dutch oven; add water to cover. Bring to a boil; cover, reduce heat, and simmer 30 minutes or until very tender. Drain well; place in a large bowl, and mash. Stir in 1 cup streusel, granulated sugar, and next 3 ingredients. Spoon into a 2-quart casserole coated with cooking spray; top with remaining streusel. Bake at 350° for 45 minutes. Yield: 8 servings (serving size: ¾ cup).

CALORIES 376 (21% from fat); FAT 8.8g (sat 1.4g, mono 4.1g, poly 2.6g); PROTEIN 5.4g; CARB 70.1g; FIBER 3.8g; CHOL 1mg; IRON 1.9mg; SODIUM 115mg; CALC 97mg

CREAMY CAULIFLOWER BAKE

This side dish can be served as an alternative to mashed potatoes.

2 cups (1-inch) cubed French bread (about 3 [1-ounce] slices)
5 cups cauliflower florets
2 tablespoons reduced-calorie margarine, divided
Olive oil-flavored vegetable cooking spray
⅔ cup chopped onion
½ cup chopped green bell pepper
½ cup chopped red bell pepper
2 garlic cloves, minced
3 tablespoons water
½ teaspoon salt
⅛ teaspoon white pepper

1. Preheat broiler. Place bread cubes in a food processor; pulse until finely ground. Arrange breadcrumbs in a single layer on a jelly-roll pan; broil 2 minutes or until toasted, stirring after 1 minute. Set aside.
2. Arrange cauliflower in a steamer basket over boiling water. Cover and steam 13 minutes or until tender; set aside. Melt 1 tablespoon margarine in a nonstick skillet coated with cooking spray over medium-high heat. Add onion and next 3 ingredients; sauté 5 minutes or until tender. Combine onion mixture, cauliflower, 1 tablespoon margarine, water, salt, and white pepper in food processor; process until smooth, scraping sides of processor bowl occasionally.
3. Preheat oven to 375°.
4. Combine cauliflower mixture and 1½ cups breadcrumbs; spoon into a 1-quart casserole coated with cooking spray. Sprinkle with ½ cup breadcrumbs. Bake at 375° for 15 minutes or until thoroughly heated. Yield: 7 servings (serving size: ½ cup).

CALORIES 84 (29% from fat); FAT 2.7g (sat 0.8g, mono 1g, poly 0.9g); PROTEIN 2.9g; CARB 13.3g; FIBER 2.7g; CHOL 0mg; IRON 0.9mg; SODIUM 292mg; CALC 27mg

CRANBERRY-PORT RELISH

1 medium orange
2 cups port or other sweet red wine
1 bay leaf
3 whole cloves
½ cup sugar
1 (12-ounce) bag fresh or frozen cranberries

1. Carefully remove rind from orange, using a vegetable peeler and making sure not to get any of white pithy part of rind.
2. Combine orange rind, port, bay leaf, and cloves in a medium saucepan. Bring to a simmer over medium heat; cook 20 minutes or until reduced to 1 cup. Strain mixture through a sieve over a bowl; discard solids.
3. Return strained mixture to saucepan; stir in sugar. Add cranberries; cook over medium heat 10 minutes or until cranberries pop, stirring occasionally. Spoon into a bowl; cool. Yield: 2 cups (serving size: ¼ cup).

CALORIES 72 (1% from fat); FAT 0.1g (sat 0g, mono 0.1g, poly 0g); PROTEIN 0.3g; CARB 18.7g; FIBER 0.5g; CHOL 0mg; IRON 0.3mg; SODIUM 5mg; CALC 8mg

---

MENU SUGGESTION

PEPPER-ROASTED SALMON WITH MUSTARD-HERB CREAM SAUCE

ORANGE-SCENTED ROASTED ROOT VEGETABLES
page 323

CREAMED-SPINACH GRATIN
page 324

Whole-wheat rolls

APPLE-QUINCE CRISP
page 342

PEPPER-ROASTED SALMON WITH MUSTARD-HERB CREAM SAUCE

Tofu gives this sauce its rich, creamy texture. Make sure the fillet is one piece of fish; if your supermarket doesn't have a large seafood selection, you may need to call ahead to order it.

14 ounces light tofu, drained
1 garlic clove, peeled
⅓ cup fat-free sour cream
3 tablespoons Dijon mustard
1 tablespoon fresh lemon juice
½ cup chopped chives
¼ cup minced fresh dillweed
2 teaspoons coarsely ground mixed peppercorns, divided
1 (3-pound) salmon fillet
Olive oil-flavored vegetable cooking spray
1 teaspoon olive oil
¼ teaspoon salt
Rosemary sprigs (optional)

1. Place tofu and garlic in a food processor; process until smooth. Add sour cream, mustard, and lemon juice; process until blended. Stir in chives, dillweed, and ½ teaspoon ground peppercorns. Cover and chill.
2. Preheat oven to 450°.
3. Place salmon, skin side down, on a baking sheet coated with cooking spray. Brush fillet with oil; sprinkle with 1½ teaspoons ground peppercorns and salt. Bake at 450° for 12 minutes or until fish flakes easily when tested with a fork. Serve sauce with salmon. Garnish with rosemary sprigs, if desired. Yield: 8 servings (serving size: 5 ounces fish and ⅓ cup sauce).

CALORIES 290 (44% from fat); FAT 14.1g (sat 2.4g, mono 6.7g, poly 3.2g); PROTEIN 34.9g; CARB 2.7g; FIBER 0.9g; CHOL 99mg; IRON 1.5mg; SODIUM 365mg; CALC 41mg

VENISON MEDAILLONS WITH CHERRY-WINE SAUCE

This entrée is cooked on the stovetop and can be ready in less than 45 minutes. You can substitute 4-ounce beef tenderloin fillets for the venison steaks.

½   cup port or other sweet red wine
½   cup dried tart cherries
½   teaspoon dried thyme
1   (14¼-ounce) can fat-free beef broth
16   whole allspice
16   juniper berries (optional)
½   teaspoon salt, divided
⅛   teaspoon pepper
6   (4-ounce) venison tenderloin steaks (about 1½ inches thick)
Vegetable cooking spray
2   teaspoons margarine
½   cup minced shallots
2   garlic cloves, minced
2   teaspoons water
1   teaspoon cornstarch

1. Combine first 4 ingredients in a small saucepan. Bring to a boil. Remove from heat. Cover; set aside.
2. Place allspice and juniper berries, if desired, in a spice or coffee grinder; process until finely ground. Sprinkle ½ teaspoon allspice mixture, ¼ teaspoon salt, and pepper over venison. Coat a large nonstick skillet with cooking spray. Melt margarine in skillet over

medium-high heat. Add venison; cook 5 minutes on each side or until browned. Reduce heat to medium; cook 3 minutes on each side or to desired degree of doneness. Remove venison from skillet; keep warm.
3. Add shallots and garlic to skillet, sauté 2 minutes. Add cherry mixture, 1 teaspoon allspice mixture, and ¼ teaspoon salt; bring to a boil. Reduce heat; simmer, uncovered, until reduced to 1 cup (about 3 minutes). Combine water and cornstarch; add to cherry mixture. Bring to a boil; cook, stirring constantly, 1 minute. Serve sauce with venison. Yield: 6 servings (serving size: 3 ounces venison and 2 tablespoons sauce).

Note: You can substitute ½ cup cranberry juice for the port, if desired.

CALORIES 201 (18% from fat); FAT 4.1g (sat 1.3g, mono 1.6g, poly 1.1g); PROTEIN 25.6g; CARB 13.4g; FIBER 0.9g; CHOL 0mg; IRON 4.5mg; SODIUM 320mg; CALC 22mg

EYE OF ROUND WITH ROASTED-GARLIC SAUCE

Any leftover roast beef and garlic sauce can be used for French-dip sandwiches.

3   whole garlic heads
2   cups fat-free beef broth, divided
1   tablespoon plus 1 teaspoon dried marjoram, divided
1   teaspoon salt, divided
8   garlic cloves, peeled
2   large shallots, peeled
1   (4-pound) lean eye-of-round roast
½   teaspoon pepper
1   tablespoon brandy

1. Preheat oven to 350°.
2. Remove white papery skin from garlic heads (do not peel or separate cloves). Place garlic heads in a 1-quart baking dish; add ½ cup broth. Cover and bake at 350° for 1 hour. Cool 10 minutes; remove garlic heads, reserving cooking liquid. Separate cloves; squeeze to extract pulp, and discard skins. Place reserved cooking liquid,

garlic pulp, 1½ cups broth, 1 teaspoon marjoram, and ½ teaspoon salt in a food processor; process until smooth. Set garlic sauce aside.
3. Combine 1 tablespoon marjoram, ½ teaspoon salt, 8 garlic cloves, and shallots in a food processor; process to a coarse paste. Trim fat from roast; make ¾-inch-deep slits into roast. Spoon ¼ teaspoon marjoram paste into each slit; rub roast with remaining paste. Sprinkle roast with pepper. Cover and chill 1 hour.
4. Preheat oven to 325°.
5. Place roast on rack of a broiler pan; insert meat thermometer into thickest portion of roast. Bake at 325° for 2 hours or until thermometer registers 145° (medium-rare) or to desired degree of doneness. Place roast on a platter; cover with aluminum foil. Let stand 15 minutes. Set pan and drippings aside.
6. Add brandy and ½ cup garlic sauce to broiler pan, scraping pan to loosen browned bits. Combine brandy mixture and remaining garlic sauce in a saucepan; bring to a boil. Cut roast across grain into very thin slices; serve with warm garlic sauce. Yield: 16 servings (serving size: 3 ounces beef and 2 tablespoons sauce).

Note: Omit brandy, if desired.

CALORIES 180 (28% from fat); FAT 5.6g (sat 2.1g, mono 2.4g, poly 0.2g); PROTEIN 26.2g; CARB 4.8g; FIBER 0.3g; CHOL 59mg; IRON 2mg; SODIUM 211mg; CALC 32mg

HOLIDAY RICE PILAF

When the oven is jam-packed with your holiday fixings, this stovetop pilaf will be a relief.

1   tablespoon stick margarine
3   cups sliced mushrooms (about 8 ounces)
1   cup chopped red bell pepper
¾   cup sliced green onions
2   garlic cloves, minced
½   teaspoon salt
3   (10½-ounce) cans low-salt chicken broth
1   (12-ounce) package wild rice blend (such as Uncle Ben's)
⅓   cup chopped pecans, toasted

1. Melt margarine in a large nonstick skillet over medium-high heat. Add mushrooms and next 3 ingredients; sauté 5 minutes or until vegetables are tender. Set aside; keep warm.
2. Combine salt and broth in a large saucepan; bring to a boil. Add rice; cover, reduce heat, and simmer 25 minutes or until liquid is absorbed. Stir in mushroom mixture; cook 1 minute or until thoroughly heated. Stir in pecans. Yield: 14 servings (serving size: ½ cup).

CALORIES 121 (23% from fat); FAT 3.1g (sat 0.4g, mono 1.6g, poly 0.9g); PROTEIN 3.6g; CARB 20.7g; FIBER 1.2g; CHOL 0mg; IRON 0.7mg; SODIUM 232mg; CALC 15mg

RUTABAGA GRATIN

Vegetable cooking spray
1 cup vertically sliced onion
¼ cup all-purpose flour
2 cups 1% low-fat milk
½ cup (2 ounces) shredded Swiss cheese
½ teaspoon dried rubbed sage
¼ teaspoon garlic powder
⅛ teaspoon salt
⅛ teaspoon pepper
2 (15-ounce) cans diced rutabagas, drained
⅓ cup dry breadcrumbs

1. Preheat oven to 400°.
2. Place a nonstick skillet coated with cooking spray over medium heat until hot. Add onion; sauté 5 minutes or until tender. Stir in flour. Gradually add milk; cook, stirring constantly with a whisk, 10 minutes or until slightly thick. Remove mixture from heat; add cheese and next 4 ingredients, stirring until cheese melts. Stir in rutabagas.
3. Spoon into a 1½-quart shallow baking dish coated with cooking spray; sprinkle with breadcrumbs. Bake at 400° for 25 minutes or until golden. Let stand 5 minutes. Yield: 6 servings (serving size: 1 cup).

CALORIES 156 (23% from fat); FAT 4g (sat 2.3g, mono 1.1g, poly 0.2g); PROTEIN 8.1g; CARB 22.5g; FIBER 4.3g; CHOL 12mg; IRON 0.9mg; SODIUM 423mg; CALC 216mg

MENU SUGGESTION

BRAISED PORK ROAST WITH APPLE-BRANDY SAUCE

HASH BROWN CASSEROLE
page 330

CREAMED-SPINACH GRATIN
page 324

APPLE-GLAZED CARROTS WITH BACON
page 330

Whole-cranberry relish

TRIPLE-CORN SPOON BREAD
page 330

DOUBLE-CHOCOLATE CREAM TART
page 350

BRAISED PORK ROAST WITH APPLE-BRANDY SAUCE

Cooked in the same pan with the roast, the chunky apple-brandy sauce picks up the herb rub's savory flavors.

1 (2½-pound) rolled, boned pork loin roast
1 tablespoon dried rubbed sage
1½ teaspoons dried thyme
1 teaspoon salt, divided
½ teaspoon pepper, divided
Vegetable cooking spray
1 teaspoon margarine
2 cups chopped onion
½ cup chopped celery
½ cup thawed apple juice concentrate, undiluted
½ cup applejack (apple brandy)
1 (10½-ounce) can low-salt chicken broth
2⅔ cups peeled, chopped Granny Smith apple (about 1 pound)
1 tablespoon water
2 teaspoons cornstarch

1. Unroll roast; trim fat. Combine sage, thyme, ½ teaspoon salt, and ¼ teaspoon pepper; rub inside surface of roast with one-third of sage mixture. Reroll roast, securing at 1-inch intervals with heavy string. Rub outside surface of roast with remaining sage mixture.
2. Preheat oven to 425°.
3. Place a large Dutch oven coated with cooking spray over medium-high heat until hot. Add roast; brown on all sides. Remove roast from Dutch oven; set aside. Melt margarine in Dutch oven. Add onion and celery; sauté 5 minutes. Return roast to Dutch oven. Combine ½ teaspoon salt, ¼ teaspoon pepper, apple juice, applejack, and broth; pour over roast.
4. Insert a meat thermometer into thickest portion of roast. Cover and bake at 425° for 20 minutes. Reduce oven temperature to 325° (do not remove roast from oven); bake 30 minutes. Add apple; cover and bake 30 additional minutes or until meat thermometer registers 160° (slightly pink). Remove roast from Dutch oven, reserving apple mixture. Place roast on a platter; cover with aluminum foil. Let stand 10 minutes.
5. Combine water and cornstarch; stir into reserved apple mixture in Dutch oven. Bring mixture to a boil; cook 1 minute or until sauce is slightly thick. Serve sauce with pork. Yield: 8 servings (serving size: 3 ounces pork and ⅓ cup sauce).
Note: Use 1 cup apple juice concentrate and omit apple brandy, if desired.

CALORIES 259 (34% from fat); FAT 9.7g (sat 3.2g, mono 4.2g, poly 1.2g); PROTEIN 24.6g; CARB 18g; FIBER 2g; CHOL 68mg; IRON 1.9mg; SODIUM 396mg; CALC 34mg

HASH BROWN CASSEROLE

1 cup thinly sliced green onions
1 cup (4 ounces) shredded
   reduced-fat extra-sharp
   Cheddar cheese
2 tablespoons stick margarine,
   melted
¼ teaspoon pepper
1 (32-ounce) package frozen
   Southern-style hash brown
   potatoes, thawed
1 (16-ounce) carton fat-free sour
   cream
1 (10¾-ounce) can condensed
   reduced-fat, reduced-sodium
   cream of mushroom soup,
   undiluted
Vegetable cooking spray
½ teaspoon paprika

1. Preheat oven to 350°.
2. Combine first 7 ingredients in a large bowl; spoon into a 13 x 9-inch baking dish coated with cooking spray. Sprinkle with paprika. Bake at 350° for 1 hour or until bubbly. Yield: 9 servings (serving size: 1 cup).

CALORIES 146 (27% from fat); FAT 4.3g (sat 1.5g, mono 1.7g, poly 1g); PROTEIN 6.7g; CARB 17.8g; FIBER 0.7g; CHOL 8mg; IRON 0.7mg; SODIUM 224mg; CALC 105mg

APPLE-GLAZED CARROTS WITH BACON

2 bacon slices
1 cup chopped onion
2 (16-ounce) packages baby
   carrots
1½ cups apple cider
¼ cup packed brown sugar
¼ teaspoon ground red pepper
2 tablespoons chopped chives

1. Cook bacon slices in a small skillet over medium heat until crisp. Remove bacon from skillet, and crumble. Add onion to bacon drippings in skillet; sauté 3 minutes. Add carrots and next 3 ingredients; bring to a boil. Cook over medium heat 10 minutes or until carrots are tender. Do not drain.
2. Place carrot mixture in a large serving bowl. Sprinkle with crumbled bacon and chives. Yield: 8 servings (serving size: ¾ cup).

CALORIES 115 (9% from fat); FAT 1.2g (sat 0.4g, mono 0.4g, poly 0.2g); PROTEIN 2.1g; CARB 26g; FIBER 4.2g; CHOL 2mg; IRON 0.9mg; SODIUM 86mg; CALC 45mg

TRIPLE-CORN SPOON BREAD

This moist, slightly sweet dish is a cross between corn bread dressing and creamed corn.

1 cup fat-free sour cream
3 tablespoons stick margarine,
   melted
1 large egg
½ cup chopped onion
1 (15.25-ounce) can no-salt-
   added whole-kernel corn,
   undrained
1 (14¾-ounce) can no-salt-added
   cream-style corn
1 (8½-ounce) package corn
   muffin mix
Vegetable cooking spray

1. Preheat oven to 350°.
2. Combine first 3 ingredients in a large bowl; stir well with a whisk. Stir in onion and next 3 ingredients. Pour into an 8-inch square baking dish coated with cooking spray. Bake at 350° for 1 hour or until spoon bread is set and lightly browned. Yield: 8 servings.

CALORIES 262 (30% from fat); FAT 8.6g (sat 2.2g, mono 3g, poly 2.9g); PROTEIN 6.2g; CARB 39.3g; FIBER 1.6g; CHOL 28mg; IRON 1.2mg; SODIUM 322mg; CALC 15mg

MENU SUGGESTION
HONEY-MARSALA GLAZED
HAM

OYSTER DRESSING
page 324

CRANBERRY-AND-
APRICOT GLAZED SWEET
POTATOES

HERBED FRUIT COMPOTE
page 325

Collard greens

CRANBERRY ICE
page 362

HONEY-MARSALA GLAZED HAM

1 (10-pound) 33%-less-sodium
   smoked, fully cooked ham
   half
1 teaspoon ground allspice
Vegetable cooking spray
24 whole cloves
¼ cup honey
1 cup sweet Marsala, divided

1. Preheat oven to 275°.
2. Trim rind and excess fat from ham, leaving a ⅛-inch thick layer of fat. Score sides and top of ham in a diamond pattern; sprinkle allspice over ham. Place ham on rack of a broiler pan coated with cooking spray. Press cloves into ham; drizzle with honey. Bake at 275° for 30 minutes. Pour ½ cup Marsala over ham. Bake 30 minutes; baste with ½ cup Marsala. Bake an additional 1 hour and 10 minutes or until ham is thoroughly heated. Place ham on a platter; cover with aluminum foil. Let stand 15 minutes. Yield: 32 servings (serving size: 3 ounces).

CALORIES 169 (59% from fat); FAT 11g (sat 4g, mono 5.2g, poly 1g); PROTEIN 13g; CARB 4.3g; FIBER 0g; CHOL 50mg; IRON 0.8mg; SODIUM 860mg; CALC 1mg

CRANBERRY-AND-APRICOT GLAZED SWEET POTATOES

¾ cup water, divided
1⅔ cups chopped dried apricots (about 8 ounces)
¾ cup dried cranberries (about 3 ounces) or sweetened dried cranberries (such as Craisins)
1 (12-ounce) can apricot nectar
1 teaspoon grated orange rind
¼ cup orange juice
2 tablespoons stick margarine, melted
11 cups (¼-inch-thick) sliced peeled sweet potato (about 4 pounds)
Vegetable cooking spray
½ cup packed brown sugar, divided

1. Combine ½ cup water, apricots, cranberries, and nectar in a medium saucepan. Bring to a boil; cook 2 minutes. Remove from heat; cover and let stand 20 minutes. Drain apricot mixture in a colander over a bowl, reserving apricot mixture and cooking liquid. Add rind, orange juice, and margarine to cooking liquid; set aside.
2. Combine sweet potato and ¼ cup water in a 3-quart casserole. Cover with casserole lid; microwave at HIGH 18 minutes or until tender, stirring after 9 minutes. Drain well.
3. Preheat oven to 350°.
4. Arrange half of sweet potatoes in a 3-quart casserole coated with cooking spray; top with half of apricot mixture and ¼ cup sugar. Repeat procedure with remaining sweet potato, apricot mixture, and ¼ cup sugar. Pour reserved cooking liquid over sweet potato mixture. Bake, uncovered, at 350° for 30 minutes or until bubbly. Yield: 12 servings (serving size: ⅔ cup).

CALORIES 263 (9% from fat); FAT 2.5g (sat 0.5g, mono 0.9g, poly 0.7g); PROTEIN 3g; CARB 60g; FIBER 4.7g; CHOL 0mg; IRON 2mg; SODIUM 57mg; CALC 51mg

FLAVOR HITS

Pine and Dandy

Pine nuts give food a rich, buttery spark. And these Italian-inspired recipes will leave you pining for more.

Americans are most familiar with pine nuts in pesto sauce. Yet as Italians know, there is a variety of other uses for this buttery-tasting, ivory-colored nut. Also called *Indian nut, piñon, pignoli,* and *pignolia,* pine nuts are found inside pine cones, which must be heated so that the nuts can be removed. It's this labor-intensive process that makes them so expensive: in bulk, around $15 a pound, or nearly $22 a pound when bought in those little jars in the supermarket gourmet section.

Because pine nuts are so distinctive, even assertive, in taste, you use just a small amount in recipes. (They're not the kind of nut that you eat by the handful.) The nut's sweet, piny flavor goes extremely well with dried fruits (especially raisins), anchovies, capers, olive oil, and garlic, so it's no wonder Italians use them a lot in cooking.

PINE NUT-CRUSTED SNAPPER

2 (1-ounce) slices white bread, torn into pieces
¼ cup pine nuts, toasted
1 egg white
¼ teaspoon salt
⅛ teaspoon pepper
4 (6-ounce) skinned red snapper fillets or other firm white fish fillets
Vegetable cooking spray
2 teaspoons reduced-calorie margarine, melted
Lime wedges

1. Preheat oven to 400°.
2. Place bread in a food processor; process until crumbs are fine. Add pine nuts; pulse just until pine nuts are finely chopped. Place breadcrumb mixture in a shallow dish. Place egg white in a shallow bowl; beat with a whisk. Sprinkle salt and pepper over fish. Dip fish in egg white; dredge in breadcrumb mixture.
3. Place fish fillets on a baking sheet coated with cooking spray, and drizzle margarine over fish. Bake fish at 400° for 15 minutes or until outside is crispy and browned and fish flakes easily when tested with a fork. Serve fish with lime wedges. Yield: 4 servings.

CALORIES 283 (29% from fat); FAT 9.2g (sat 1.6g, mono 2.9g, poly 3.6g); PROTEIN 39.6g; CARB 11g; FIBER 0.9g; CHOL 63mg; IRON 1.7mg; SODIUM 365mg; CALC 75mg

PINE NUT-AND-RICE PILAF

2 teaspoons olive oil
1½ cups chopped onion
4 garlic cloves, minced
5 cups hot cooked rice
⅓ cup chopped fresh basil
⅓ cup pine nuts, toasted
½ teaspoon salt
¼ teaspoon pepper
Basil sprig (optional)

1. Heat olive oil in a large nonstick skillet over medium heat. Add onion and garlic; sauté 3 minutes or until tender. Combine onion mixture, rice, and next 4 ingredients in a bowl; toss well. Garnish with a basil sprig, if desired. Yield: 6 servings (serving size: 1 cup).

CALORIES 289 (29% from fat); FAT 9.3g (sat 1.4g, mono 3.9g, poly 3.3g); PROTEIN 5.5g; CARB 48.2g; FIBER 2.2g; CHOL 0mg; IRON 2mg; SODIUM 206mg; CALC 35mg

CROSTINI WITH ROASTED VEGETABLES AND PINE NUTS

1 large eggplant (about 1¼ pounds)
1 large green bell pepper (about ½ pound)
1 large red bell pepper (about ½ pound)
1 large yellow bell pepper (about ½ pound)
¼ cup pine nuts, toasted
1 teaspoon olive oil
¼ teaspoon ground red pepper
1 large garlic clove, minced
2 tablespoons balsamic vinegar
1 tablespoon capers
½ teaspoon sugar
¼ teaspoon salt
36 (¾-inch) slices French bread (about 1 pound), toasted

1. Preheat oven to 500°.
2. Pierce eggplant several times with a fork; place on an aluminum foil-lined baking sheet. Bake at 500° for 20 minutes or until tender. Cut eggplant in half lengthwise. Place in a colander; let stand 15 minutes. Peel eggplant. Cut into ½-inch cubes, and place in a medium bowl.
3. Preheat broiler. Cut bell peppers in half lengthwise; discard seeds and membranes. Place halves, skin sides up, on aluminum foil-lined baking sheet; flatten with hand. Broil 15 minutes or until blackened. Place in a heavy-duty, zip-top plastic bag, and seal. Let stand 15 minutes. Peel; cut into ½-inch pieces. Add bell peppers and pine nuts to eggplant; toss well.
4. Heat oil in a nonstick skillet over medium-high heat. Add ground red pepper and garlic; sauté 30 seconds. Add vinegar and next 3 ingredients. Bring to a boil; cook 30 seconds. Pour over eggplant mixture; toss. Marinate at room temperature for 2 hours.
5. Spoon 1 tablespoon eggplant mixture onto each bread slice. Serve immediately. Yield: 36 appetizers (serving size: 1 appetizer).

CALORIES 56 (19% from fat); FAT 1.2g (sat 0.2g, mono 0.5g, poly 0.4g); PROTEIN 1.9g; CARB 9.9g; FIBER 0.6g; CHOL 1mg; IRON 0.6mg; SODIUM 121mg; CALC 13mg

PENNE WITH ARUGULA PESTO

2 tablespoons pine nuts, toasted
2 large garlic cloves
4 cups trimmed arugula
¼ cup grated fresh Parmesan cheese
2 tablespoons water
2 teaspoons fresh lemon juice
⅛ teaspoon salt
2 tablespoons olive oil
5 cups hot cooked penne (tubular-shaped pasta)

1. Drop pine nuts and garlic through food chute with food processor on; process until minced. Add arugula and next 4 ingredients to food processor; process until finely minced. With food processor on, slowly pour olive oil through food chute, and process until well-blended. Combine pesto and pasta in a large bowl; toss well. Yield: 6 servings (serving size: 1 cup).
Note: Pesto can be prepared ahead of time and stored in a zip-top plastic bag in refrigerator for up to 1 week.

CALORIES 274 (29% from fat); FAT 8.8g (sat 1.8g, mono 4.3g, poly 1.9g); PROTEIN 9.2g; CARB 40.3g; FIBER 2.4g; CHOL 3mg; IRON 2.1mg; SODIUM 132mg; CALC 95mg

READ THE PINE PRINT

• Pine nuts are most commonly sold in vacuum-sealed glass jars alongside other nuts in the supermarket. You may also find them loose in bins, which allows you to purchase the amount you need. Just make sure the market has a brisk turnover to ensure that you're buying the freshest nuts.

• Like most nuts, pine nuts are rich in fat and can turn rancid quickly. Store them in an airtight container in the refrigerator up to one month or in the freezer for up to six months or longer. Chilling and freezing give them a "flabby" texture that can be improved by toasting.

• Toasting pine nuts heightens their piny flavor and restores crispness. Throw a handful into a skillet and toss over medium heat. Remove them from the heat when they're slightly lighter in color than you wish (the natural oil will continue to cook and take the nuts a shade darker). Or spread the pine nuts in a single layer in the bottom of a baking pan. Bake at 350° for 3 to 5 minutes or until they are uniformly golden, shaking the pan a couple of times. Immediately spread them out on a plate to cool.

Oyster Dressing, page 324
Beef Tenderloin with Beaujolais Jus, page 324

Pumpkin Panache, page 325
Herbed Fruit Compote, page 325

Dark-Chocolate Soufflé Cake, page 352

New England Baked Beans, page 348

An assortment of our slice-and-bake cookies, pages 355-357

Tortellini, White Bean, and Spinach Soup, page 339

Shrimp Newburg on Toast Points, page 370

Salad Greens with Cranberry Vinaigrette, page 370

Veal Paprikash, page 354

Quince-Glazed Cornish Hens, page 341

Quince-and-Hazelnut Stuffing, page 342

Brussels Sprouts-and-Rice Casserole, page 325

To a Soulful Year

*This updated menu can make your
New Year's even luckier.*

Traditional soul food might have been good for the spirit, but it was awfully tough on the body. Luckily, there's a major rethinking going on where this high-fat cuisine is concerned. Across the country, enthusiasts are incorporating its elements into new dishes, bringing it into sync with today's more healthful habits. Consider our version of hoppin' John, for instance. Instead of combining black-eyed peas with the usual salt pork or bacon, we've tossed them with pasta, prosciutto, and sun-dried tomatoes. If eating black-eyed peas on New Year's Day is supposed to bring you luck, imagine how lucky you'll be when you start off the year with this menu.

MENU

JOHN'S HOT-AND-
HOPPIN' CAVATAPPI

TURNIP GREENS WITH
CARAMELIZED ONIONS

PAN-ROASTED
CORN-AND-CUMIN
CORN BREAD
page 338

SWEET POTATO-BOURBON
TART
page 338

About 784 Calories and 20 grams of fat
(23% calories from fat)

JOHN'S HOT-AND-HOPPIN' CAVATAPPI

Be sure to use the hot pepper sauce that we call for because it contains whole peppers packed in vinegar. Using red-colored hot sauce won't yield good results.

    2 cups water
 1½ cups frozen black-eyed peas
    1 teaspoon dried thyme
    2 bay leaves
  ½ cup chopped sun-dried
        tomatoes, packed without oil
 1½ teaspoons hot pepper sauce
        (such as Cajun Chef)
    4 cups hot cooked cavatappi
        (about 6 ounces uncooked
        spiral-shaped pasta)
  ½ cup sliced green onions
  ½ cup chopped fresh parsley
    3 ounces very thinly sliced
        prosciutto or lean ham,
        chopped
  ¼ cup hot pepper sauce (such as
        Cajun Chef)
    1 tablespoon extra-virgin olive
        oil
  ½ teaspoon dry mustard
    2 tablespoons finely chopped
        fresh green chile or canned
        chopped green chiles, drained
    3 garlic cloves, minced

1. Combine first 4 ingredients in a large saucepan; bring to a boil. Cover, reduce heat, and simmer 15 minutes or until tender. Add tomatoes and 1½ teaspoons pepper sauce; simmer 5 minutes or until tomatoes are tender.

Drain black-eyed pea mixture in a colander over a bowl, reserving 2 tablespoons cooking liquid. Discard bay leaves.

2. Combine black-eyed pea mixture, pasta, and next 3 ingredients in a large bowl. Combine reserved cooking liquid, ¼ cup pepper sauce, and remaining 4 ingredients in a small bowl, stirring well with a whisk. Pour chile mixture over pasta mixture; toss well. Serve warm or at room temperature. Yield: 4 servings (serving size: 1½ cups).

CALORIES 246 (16% from fat); FAT 4.5g (sat 0.8g, mono 2.2g, poly 0.8g); PROTEIN 12.5g; CARB 40.2g; FIBER 2.7g; CHOL 8mg; IRON 3mg; SODIUM 443mg; CALC 51mg

---

TURNIP GREENS WITH CARAMELIZED ONIONS

    2 teaspoons stick margarine
    4 cups vertically sliced onion
    2 tablespoons brown sugar
  ½ teaspoon pepper
Vegetable cooking spray
    1 (2-pound) bag prepackaged
        turnip greens, coarsely
        chopped
Hot pepper sauce (optional)

1. Melt margarine in a large Dutch oven over medium-high heat. Add onion; sauté 7 minutes. Stir in sugar and ½ teaspoon pepper. Cover, reduce heat to medium-low, and cook 20 minutes or until onion is golden, stirring frequently. Remove from Dutch oven; set aside.

2. Place Dutch oven coated with cooking spray over medium-high heat until hot. Gradually add turnip greens, and cook 10 minutes or until wilted, stirring frequently. Add onion mixture to turnip greens; stir gently. Sprinkle with hot pepper sauce, if desired. Serve immediately. Yield: 6 servings (serving size: ¾ cup).

CALORIES 94 (19% from fat); FAT 2g (sat 0.4g, mono 0.6g, poly 0.6g); PROTEIN 3.2g; CARB 18.3g; FIBER 5.1g; CHOL 0mg; IRON 1.9mg; SODIUM 78mg; CALC 304mg

PAN-ROASTED CORN-AND-CUMIN CORN BREAD

Vegetable cooking spray
1 cup frozen whole-kernel corn, thawed
1 teaspoon ground cumin
2 tablespoons vegetable oil, divided
1 cup yellow cornmeal
¾ cup all-purpose flour
1½ teaspoons baking powder
¼ teaspoon baking soda
½ teaspoon salt
1 cup low-fat buttermilk
1 large egg

1. Preheat oven to 400°.
2. Place an 8-inch cast-iron skillet or ovenproof heavy skillet coated with cooking spray over medium heat until hot. Add corn and cumin; sauté 3 minutes or until corn is lightly browned. Place corn mixture in a large bowl; set aside.
3. Coat skillet with 2 teaspoons oil. Place in a 400° oven for 10 minutes or until hot. Add cornmeal and next 4 ingredients to corn mixture. Combine 1 tablespoon plus 1 teaspoon oil, buttermilk, and egg in a bowl; add to cornmeal mixture, stirring just until moist. Spoon into preheated skillet. Bake at 400° for 40 minutes or until a wooden pick inserted in center comes out clean. Yield: 8 servings (serving size: 1 wedge).

CALORIES 177 (25% from fat); FAT 4.9g (sat 1.1g, mono 1.5g, poly 1.9g); PROTEIN 5.1g; CARB 28.4g; FIBER 1.8g; CHOL 29mg; IRON 1.7mg; SODIUM 228mg; CALC 95mg

SWEET POTATO-BOURBON TART

2 tablespoons granulated sugar
2 tablespoons stick margarine
¼ teaspoon salt
1 ounce block-style fat-free cream cheese
1 teaspoon vanilla extract
1 large egg
1¼ cups all-purpose flour
4 medium-size sweet potatoes (about 2¼ pounds)
¾ cup packed brown sugar
3 tablespoons bourbon or ¼ teaspoon rum extract and 3 tablespoons water
2 tablespoons stick margarine
2 teaspoons vanilla extract
½ teaspoon ground cinnamon
¼ teaspoon salt
¼ teaspoon ground nutmeg
¼ teaspoon ground allspice
2 large eggs
Vegetable cooking spray
2 teaspoons water
1 large egg white, lightly beaten
¼ cup chopped pecans

1. Preheat oven to 400°.
2. Combine first 4 ingredients in a medium bowl; beat at medium speed of an electric mixer until light and creamy. Add vanilla and 1 egg; beat well. Gradually add flour, beating at low speed until moist. Press mixture gently into a 5-inch circle on heavy-duty plastic wrap; cover with additional plastic wrap. Chill 1 hour.
3. While dough chills, bake sweet potatoes at 400° for 55 minutes or until very tender. Cool. Reduce oven temperature to 350°. Peel potatoes; place potato pulp, brown sugar, and next 8 ingredients in a large bowl. Beat at medium speed of mixer until smooth.
4. Roll dough, still covered, into an 11-inch circle. Remove top sheet of plastic wrap, and fit dough, uncovered side down, into a 9-inch tart pan coated with cooking spray. Remove remaining sheet of plastic wrap. Spoon potato mixture into prepared crust. Combine 2 teaspoons water and egg white; brush edges of dough with egg white mixture. Sprinkle potato mixture with pecans. Bake at 350° for 1 hour or until puffy and set. Cool on a wire rack. Yield: 10 servings.

CALORIES 267 (29% from fat); FAT 8.5g (sat 1.6g, mono 3.9g, poly 2.3g); PROTEIN 5.3g; CARB 42.2g; FIBER 2g; CHOL 67mg; IRON 1.6mg; SODIUM 225mg; CALC 47mg

INSPIRED VEGETARIAN

A Bowlful of Cheer

Whether thick or broth-style, a peasant soup simmering on the stove is just what the holidays ordered.

There are many reasons why peasant-style soups are becoming more popular. The aroma of fresh ingredients simmering with one another comforts taste buds and warms souls. None of the valuable vitamins and minerals are discarded. And then there's the convenience: It's simple to throw ingredients into a pan to simmer almost unattended.

We're offering two distinct soup styles, one that's thick and hearty, and another that's a broth full of vegetables. Try experimenting with the various crouton recipes that are provided, too, because they go well with broth-style soups. If you have time, try the recipe for homemade vegetable broth rather than using the canned version.

BASIC HERB CROUTONS

Our herb croutons add flavor and texture when sprinkled on top of the soups.

4 cups (½-inch) cubed French bread (about 4 [1-ounce] slices)
Olive oil-flavored vegetable cooking spray
1 tablespoon dried Italian seasoning
½ teaspoon salt
½ teaspoon pepper

1. Preheat oven to 400°.
2. Place bread cubes on a jelly-roll pan; lightly coat bread cubes with cooking spray. Toss bread cubes with Italian seasoning, salt, and pepper. Bake bread cubes at 400° for 10 minutes or until golden. Yield: 16 servings (serving size: ¼ cup).

CALORIES 22 (8% from fat); FAT 0.2g (sat 0.1g, mono 0.1g, poly 0.1g); PROTEIN 0.7g; CARB 4.2g; FIBER 0.3g; CHOL 0mg; IRON 0.5mg; SODIUM 115mg; CALC 11mg

Cinnamon-Sugar Croutons:
Substitute 1 teaspoon cinnamon sugar (found in the spice section of your supermarket) for the Italian seasoning, salt, and pepper.

Mexican Croutons:
Substitute ½ teaspoon each chili powder, ground cumin, and dried oregano for the Italian seasoning, salt, and pepper.

Parmesan Croutons:
Substitute 2 tablespoons grated Parmesan cheese for the Italian seasoning.

FRESH VEGETABLE BROTH

This vegetable broth is used in all the soup recipes in this story.

  3 cups chopped onion
  2 cups chopped carrot
  2 cups chopped celery
  2 cups chopped parsnip
  1 cup chopped leek
 12 black peppercorns
  4 unpeeled garlic cloves
  3 bay leaves
  1 basil sprig
  1 thyme sprig
  1 rosemary sprig
  1 parsley sprig
  5 quarts cold water
  1 teaspoon salt

1. Combine all ingredients except salt in an 8-quart stockpot. Bring to a boil; reduce heat, and simmer, uncovered, 3 hours. Strain mixture through a cheesecloth-lined colander into a large bowl, pressing vegetables with the back of a spoon to remove as much liquid as possible; discard solids. Stir in salt. Yield: 12 cups (serving size: 1 cup).
Note: Store broth in the refrigerator in an airtight container for up to 1 week. Pour 2 cups broth into freezer-safe containers; freeze for up to 3 months.

CALORIES 7 (0% from fat); FAT 0g; PROTEIN 0.2g; CARB 1.6g; FIBER 0.3g; CHOL 0mg; IRON 0.1mg; SODIUM 199mg; CALC 5mg

TORTELLINI, WHITE BEAN, AND SPINACH SOUP

(pictured on page 335)

  1 teaspoon olive oil
  2 cups chopped onion
  ½ cup chopped red bell pepper
  1 teaspoon dried Italian seasoning
  3 garlic cloves, minced
  2 cups coarsely chopped spinach
  ⅔ cup water
  1 (16-ounce) can navy beans, drained
  2 cups Fresh Vegetable Broth or 1 (14½-ounce) can vegetable broth
  1 (14.5-ounce) can no-salt-added whole tomatoes, undrained and chopped
  1 (14-ounce) can quartered artichoke hearts, drained
  1 (9-ounce) package uncooked fresh cheese-filled tortellini
  ¼ cup grated fresh Parmesan cheese

1. Heat oil in a large Dutch oven over medium-high heat. Add onion and next 3 ingredients; sauté 5 minutes or until tender. Add spinach and next 5 ingredients; bring to a boil. Reduce heat; simmer 2 minutes. Add tortellini; cook until thoroughly heated. Sprinkle with cheese. Yield: 6 servings (serving size: 1½ cups soup and 2 teaspoons cheese).

CALORIES 281 (18% from fat); FAT 5.7g (sat 2.1g, mono 1.7g, poly 0.6g); PROTEIN 15g; CARB 43.9g; FIBER 4.2g; CHOL 23mg; IRON 2.8mg; SODIUM 562mg; CALC 158mg

CREAMY LIMA BEAN SOUP WITH PASTA

Any smaller-type pasta such as ditalini will work in this soup.

  2 teaspoons olive oil
  1 cup chopped onion
  1 cup chopped carrot
  3 garlic cloves, minced
  2 cups water
  3 thyme sprigs
  4 cups Fresh Vegetable Broth or 2 (14½-ounce) cans vegetable broth
  1 (16-ounce) package frozen baby lima beans
  ¼ cup chopped fresh basil
  1 tablespoon lemon juice
  ¾ teaspoon lemon pepper
  1 cup uncooked orecchiette pasta
  ½ cup chopped bottled roasted red bell peppers

1. Heat oil in a Dutch oven over medium-high heat. Add onion, carrot, and garlic; sauté 5 minutes. Add water and next 3 ingredients; bring to a boil. Cover, reduce heat, and simmer 15 minutes. Stir in basil, lemon juice, and lemon pepper. Place 3 cups soup in a blender; cover and process until smooth. Return pureed mixture to Dutch oven; bring to a boil. Add pasta; cook 15 minutes or until pasta is tender. Stir in bell peppers. Yield: 4 servings (serving size: 2 cups).

CALORIES 316 (11% from fat); FAT 4g (sat 0.6g, mono 2.2g, poly 0.6g); PROTEIN 13.6g; CARB 57.6g; FIBER 4.3g; CHOL 0mg; IRON 2.6mg; SODIUM 420mg; CALC 76mg

LENTIL SOUP

7½ cups Fresh Vegetable Broth
    (page 339) or water
1½ cups dried lentils
1 cup chopped onion
1 cup chopped carrot
½ cup chopped celery
½ cup chopped parsnip
2 tablespoons low-sodium soy
    sauce
2 teaspoons dried oregano
½ teaspoon salt

1. Combine broth and lentils in a large Dutch oven; bring to a boil. Cover, reduce heat, and simmer 30 minutes. Add onion and remaining 6 ingredients; cover and simmer 15 minutes. Yield: 6 servings (serving size: 1½ cups).

CALORIES 197 (3% from fat); FAT 0.6g (sat 0.1g, mono 0.1g, poly 0.3g); PROTEIN 14.5g; CARB 35.3g; FIBER 7.2g; CHOL 0mg; IRON 4.9mg; SODIUM 627mg; CALC 53mg

COUNTRY-FRENCH VEGETABLE SOUP

2 teaspoons olive oil
2 cups chopped green cabbage
1 cup chopped onion
1 cup (½-inch-thick) sliced
    carrot
1 cup sliced celery
1 cup diced red potato
1 teaspoon caraway seeds
1 cup water
4 cups Fresh Vegetable Broth
    (page 339) or 2 (14½-ounce)
    cans vegetable broth
1 cup drained canned chickpeas
    (garbanzo beans)
2 tablespoons minced fresh
    parsley
2 teaspoons chopped fresh
    dillweed or ½ teaspoon dried
    dillweed
½ teaspoon pepper

1. Heat oil in a Dutch oven over medium-high heat until hot. Add cabbage and next 5 ingredients; sauté 2 minutes. Add water and broth; bring to a boil. Cover, reduce heat, and simmer 30 minutes. Add chickpeas

and remaining ingredients; cook until thoroughly heated. Yield: 4 servings (serving size: 1¾ cups).

CALORIES 184 (20% from fat); FAT 4.1g (sat 0.7g, mono 2.3g, poly 0.8g); PROTEIN 5.7g; CARB 33.1g; FIBER 7.6g; CHOL 0mg; IRON 1.8mg; SODIUM 425mg; CALC 77mg

MEXICAN BUTTERNUT SQUASH SOUP

Try serving this zesty soup with quesadillas.

2 teaspoons olive oil
2 cups peeled, cubed butternut
    squash (about ¾ pound)
2 cups chopped onion
1 cup chopped red bell pepper
1 cup chopped celery
½ cup seeded, sliced poblano
    chile or 1 (4.5-ounce) can
    chopped green chiles
1 teaspoon dried oregano
1 teaspoon chili powder
4 cups Fresh Vegetable Broth
    (page 339) or 2 (14½-ounce)
    cans vegetable broth
1 (15.5-ounce) can white hominy
    or whole-kernel corn, drained
¼ cup fresh lime juice
2 tablespoons minced fresh
    cilantro

1. Heat oil in a large Dutch oven over medium-high heat. Add squash and next 6 ingredients; sauté 3 minutes. Add broth and hominy; bring to a boil. Reduce heat; simmer 35 minutes or until vegetables are tender. Stir in lime juice and cilantro. Yield: 4 servings (serving size: 1¾ cups).

CALORIES 161 (20% from fat); FAT 3.5g (sat 0.5g, mono 1.9g, poly 0.8g); PROTEIN 3.8g; CARB 31.7g; FIBER 6g; CHOL 0mg; IRON 2.2mg; SODIUM 389mg; CALC 76mg

BASQUE RICE-AND-KALE CHOWDER

2 teaspoons olive oil
1 cup chopped onion
1 cup chopped green bell pepper
½ cup chopped celery
⅓ cup sliced almonds
1 tablespoon Hungarian sweet
    paprika
2 bay leaves
1½ cups water
1 (14½-ounce) can stewed
    tomatoes, undrained and
    chopped
2 cups Fresh Vegetable Broth
    (page 339) or 1 (14½-ounce)
    can vegetable broth
2 cups chopped kale
1 cup cooked long-grain brown
    rice
⅔ cup drained canned chickpeas
    (garbanzo beans)
½ cup raisins

1. Heat oil in a large Dutch oven over medium-high heat. Add onion and next 5 ingredients; sauté 2 minutes. Add water, tomatoes, and broth; bring to a boil. Add kale and remaining ingredients; reduce heat, and simmer 10 minutes or until thoroughly heated. Discard bay leaves. Yield: 4 servings (serving size: 1¾ cups).

CALORIES 311 (25% from fat); FAT 8.7g (sat 1.1g, mono 4.9g, poly 1.9g); PROTEIN 8.9g; CARB 54.4g; FIBER 8.1g; CHOL 0mg; IRON 3.6mg; SODIUM 520mg; CALC 147mg

Quince Charming

Neither forbidden nor forgotten, quinces are being rediscovered by today's cooks.

Quinces are making a comeback and are in season starting in late autumn, just in time for the holidays. Unless picked tree-ripened in a warm climate, when their sugars have fully matured, quinces are not suitable for eating raw. They're best for cooking—poaching, baking, braising, or stewing. When subjected to heat, quinces undergo a mellow metamorphosis: Their acidic flavor becomes increasingly sweeter, and their yellow flesh becomes tender, pretty, and pink.

Because quinces maintain their shape during longer cooking times, the fruit is ideal for adding to all kinds of baked dishes, from puddings to stuffings. When incorporated into an apple crisp, for example, they not only contribute their own unique depth of flavor, but they also amplify the flavor of the apples. Quinces also provide an excellent complement to meat and a subtle taste boost to curry and chutney. And because of their high pectin content, quinces are particularly good for making jams, jellies, and marmalades.

SHRIMP-AND-QUINCE CURRY

This mellow, fragrant curry may be accompanied by Ginger-Quince Chutney (page 343).

- 1 tablespoon margarine
- 2 cups peeled, cored, diced quince (about 2 quinces)
- 1½ cups low-salt chicken broth, divided
- 1 cup chopped onion
- 2 tablespoons peeled, minced fresh gingerroot
- 1 tablespoon seeded, minced jalapeño pepper
- 2 garlic cloves, minced
- 2 tablespoons curry powder
- 2 cups canned crushed tomatoes with added puree, undrained
- 1 cup diced red bell pepper
- 1 cup diced yellow bell pepper
- ¼ cup dried currants
- 2 pounds medium-size shrimp, peeled and deveined
- 1 tablespoon water
- 2 teaspoons cornstarch
- ⅔ cup plain fat-free yogurt
- ½ teaspoon salt
- ¼ teaspoon black pepper
- 8 cups hot cooked rice
- 2 tablespoons sliced green onions

1. Melt margarine in a large non-stick skillet over medium-high heat. Add quince; sauté 3 minutes or until lightly browned. Add ½ cup broth and onion; simmer, uncovered, 12 minutes or until liquid evaporates. Add ginger-root, jalapeño pepper, and garlic; sauté 1 minute. Add curry powder, and sauté 1 minute. Add 1 cup broth and tomatoes. Bring to a boil; reduce heat, and simmer 15 minutes. Add bell peppers and currants; simmer 5 minutes. Add shrimp; simmer 4 minutes.

2. Combine water and cornstarch. Stir yogurt until smooth. Add cornstarch mixture, yogurt, salt, and ¼ teaspoon pepper to skillet. Bring to a simmer, and cook, stirring constantly, 1 minute or until mixture is slightly thick. Serve over rice, and sprinkle with green onions. Yield: 8 servings (serving size: 1 cup shrimp mixture and 1 cup rice).

CALORIES 411 (8% from fat); FAT 3.6g (sat 0.7g, mono 1.1g, poly 1g); PROTEIN 25.3g; CARB 68.7g; FIBER 3.6g; CHOL 166mg; IRON 6.5mg; SODIUM 471mg; CALC 140mg

QUINCE-GLAZED CORNISH HENS

(pictured on page 336)

- 3 (1¼-pound) Cornish hens
- ½ teaspoon salt
- ¼ teaspoon pepper
- Vegetable cooking spray
- ½ cup Ruby Quince Marmalade (page 343)
- 2 tablespoons lemon juice
- Rosemary sprigs (optional)

1. Preheat oven to 400°.

2. Remove and discard giblets and necks from hens. Rinse hens under cold water; pat dry. Remove skin, and trim excess fat. Working with 1 hen at a time, tie ends of legs together with string. Lift wing tips up and over back; tuck under hen. Combine salt and pepper; sprinkle over hens. Place hens on rack of a broiler pan coated with cooking spray; bake at 400° for 45 minutes.

3. Combine marmalade and lemon juice in a small saucepan; cook over medium heat 3 minutes. Place marmalade mixture in a blender; cover and process until smooth. Brush hens with marmalade mixture. Bake 15 additional minutes or until juices run clear, basting occasionally with marmalade mixture. Remove string; split hens in half lengthwise. Garnish with rosemary sprigs, if desired. Yield: 6 servings.

CALORIES 186 (18% from fat); FAT 3.8g (sat 0.9g, mono 1.2g, poly 0.9g); PROTEIN 21.9g; CARB 16g; FIBER 0.3g; CHOL 99mg; IRON 0.9mg; SODIUM 256mg; CALC 16mg

• When buying quinces, look for ones that are large, smooth, and fragrant; even though they have a hard skin, they do bruise easily.

• Quinces can be stored in the refrigerator for up to three weeks.

• Peeling a quince is more difficult than peeling an apple, but a vegetable peeler will do the job. After peeling, slice the flesh into quarters from stem to blossom end, then cut out the core. (Because the flesh is quite firm, you should peel or slice it with caution.)

• Depending on the size of the pieces, quinces become tender after a cooking time of about 20 to 25 minutes.

QUINCE-AND-HAZELNUT STUFFING

(pictured on page 336)

3   tablespoons hazelnuts
Vegetable cooking spray
3   cups peeled, cored, diced quince (about 3 quinces)
2   teaspoons brown sugar
¾   cup low-salt chicken broth, divided
¾   cup chopped green bell pepper
½   cup chopped onion
¾   teaspoon poultry seasoning
2   garlic cloves, minced
2¼   cups (½-inch) cubed French bread
½   teaspoon salt
⅛   teaspoon pepper

1. Preheat oven to 350°.
2. Place hazelnuts on a baking sheet. Bake at 350° for 15 minutes, stirring once. Turn nuts out onto a towel. Roll up towel; rub off skins. Coarsely chop nuts, and set aside.
3. Place a nonstick skillet coated with cooking spray over medium heat. Add quince, and sprinkle with sugar. Cook 15 minutes or until very brown, stirring frequently. Stir in ½ cup broth; bring to a boil. Reduce heat, and simmer, uncovered, 5 minutes or until quince is tender and liquid nearly evaporates. Add bell pepper, onions, poultry seasoning, and garlic; cook 3 additional minutes.
4. Remove skillet from heat; stir in ¼ cup broth, nuts, bread cubes, salt, and ⅛ teaspoon pepper. Spoon quince mixture into a 1-quart baking dish coated with cooking spray. Cover and bake at 350° for 30 minutes. Yield: 8 servings (serving size: ½ cup).

CALORIES 75 (30% from fat); FAT 2.5g (sat 0.2g, mono 1.6g, poly 0.3g); PROTEIN 1.7g; CARB 12.5g; FIBER 1.3g; CHOL 0mg; IRON 0.9mg; SODIUM 196mg; CALC 19mg

APPLE-QUINCE CRISP

7   cups peeled, sliced Granny Smith apple (about 2 pounds)
6   cups peeled, sliced quince (about 6 quinces)
¾   cup packed brown sugar
¼   cup water
2   teaspoons grated lemon rind
2   tablespoons fresh lemon juice
1   tablespoon cornstarch
1   teaspoon ground cinnamon
½   teaspoon ground nutmeg
Vegetable cooking spray
⅔   cup regular oats
2   tablespoons all-purpose flour
¼   cup packed brown sugar
2   tablespoons chilled stick margarine, cut into small pieces

1. Preheat oven to 400°.
2. Combine first 9 ingredients in a large bowl; toss well to coat. Spoon apple mixture into a 13 x 9-inch baking dish coated with cooking spray.
3. Place oats in a food processor, and pulse until coarsely ground. Add flour, ¼ cup brown sugar, and margarine; pulse 10 times or until mixture resembles coarse meal. Sprinkle over apple mixture.
4. Cover and bake at 400° for 30 minutes. Uncover and bake 20 minutes or until fruit is tender and topping is crisp. Serve warm or at room temperature. Yield: 12 servings (serving size: 1 cup).

CALORIES 162 (14% from fat); FAT 2.5g (sat 0.5g, mono 1g, poly 0.8g); PROTEIN 1.1g; CARB 36g; FIBER 2.6g; CHOL 0mg; IRON 0.9mg; SODIUM 31mg; CALC 27mg

QUINCE-AND-CRANBERRY BREAD PUDDING

¼   cup hazelnuts
1¼   cups skim milk
⅔   cup packed brown sugar
1   teaspoon ground cinnamon
1   teaspoon vanilla extract
½   teaspoon ground nutmeg
¼   teaspoon ground cardamom
2   large egg whites
1   large egg
6   cups (1-inch-thick) cubed French bread
Vegetable cooking spray
1   cup peeled, cored, diced quince (about 1 quince)
½   cup apple cider
¼   cup sweetened dried cranberries

1. Preheat oven to 350°.
2. Place hazelnuts on a baking sheet. Bake at 350° for 15 minutes, stirring once. Turn nuts out onto a towel. Roll up towel; rub off skins. Coarsely chop nuts; set aside.
3. Combine milk and next 7 ingredients in a bowl. Add bread cubes; toss to coat. Let stand 15 minutes.
4. Place a large nonstick skillet coated with cooking spray over medium heat until hot. Add quince; sauté 3 minutes. Add apple cider; reduce heat, and simmer 15 minutes or until liquid almost evaporates. Add quince, cranberries, and nuts to bread mixture; toss

gently to coat. Spoon into an 8-inch square baking dish coated with cooking spray. Bake at 350° for 35 minutes or until set. Let stand 5 minutes before serving. Yield: 6 servings.

CALORIES 329 (17% from fat); FAT 6.1g (sat 0.9g, mono 3.6g, poly 0.9g); PROTEIN 8.9g; CARB 60.6g; FIBER 1.5g; CHOL 39mg; IRON 2.2mg; SODIUM 321mg; CALC 129mg

RUBY QUINCE MARMALADE

This versatile, lemon-accented spread can be used as a glaze on roasted meat as well as a traditional topping for toast or an English muffin.

- 4 cups peeled, cored, chopped quince (about 4 quinces)
- 3 cups water
- 2 cups sugar
- ¼ cup (1-inch) julienne-cut lemon rind
- ¼ cup fresh lemon juice

1. Combine all ingredients in a large saucepan; bring to a boil. Reduce heat to medium; cook 1 hour and 15 minutes or until thick. (Mixture will continue to thicken as it cools.) Cool. Store marmalade in an airtight container in refrigerator up to 2 weeks. Yield: 2½ cups (serving size: 1 tablespoon).

CALORIES 44 (0% from fat); FAT 0g; PROTEIN 0.1g; CARB 11.6g; FIBER 0.2g; CHOL 0mg; IRON 0.1mg; SODIUM 1mg; CALC 2mg

GINGER-QUINCE CHUTNEY

- 4 cups peeled, cored, chopped quince (about 4 quinces)
- 1 cup sugar
- ½ cup dried currants
- ¼ cup peeled, grated fresh gingerroot
- ¼ cup cider vinegar

1. Combine all ingredients in a non-aluminum saucepan. Bring to a boil; partially cover. Reduce heat; simmer

35 minutes or until liquid almost evaporates. Yield: about 3 cups (serving size: 2 tablespoons).
Note: Store, covered, in refrigerator for up to 1 month.

CALORIES 50 (2% from fat); FAT 0.1g (sat 0g, mono 0.1g, poly 0g); PROTEIN 0.2g; CARB 13g; FIBER 0.3g; CHOL 0mg; IRON 0.2mg; SODIUM 2mg; CALC 5mg

THE KERR PACKAGE

A World of Flavor

Create bright new tastes by blending your own spices and herbs.

If we're to succeed at reducing the salt, fat, and sugar in the foods we enjoy, they must be replaced with flavors equally as satisfying. Otherwise, we'll be left with a vaguely deprived feeling. I believe these alternative tastes and flavors can best be achieved by "layering" combinations of herbs, spices, and other seasonings. Blends of flavors with global origins can engage your senses in a deep and satisfying way without depending on fats or salt. These "perfumes of the plate" can be store-bought blends or intriguing mixtures you blend yourself.

Now, to a busy cook this may seem a little far-fetched. But with a simple coffee grinder set aside for this use, you can toss in a handful of fresh, aromatic ingredients and spin them for a few seconds into a powder simply bursting with flavor and aroma.

Here's a simple recipe to get you started on this grand new experiment. It's a chicken dish with a flavoring mix that can be used in a variety of recipes.

MOROCCAN CHICKEN TAGINE

- 1 tablespoon plus 2 teaspoons cumin seeds
- 1 tablespoon plus 2 teaspoons coriander seeds
- 2½ teaspoons whole allspice
- 1 tablespoon plus 2 teaspoons ground nutmeg
- 2½ teaspoons ground ginger
- 1¼ teaspoons ground red pepper
- 1¼ teaspoons ground cinnamon
- 1 teaspoon olive oil
- 8 cups vertically sliced onion (about 2 pounds)
- ½ teaspoon salt
- 1½ teaspoons sugar
- ½ teaspoon black pepper
- 1 (10½-ounce) can low-salt chicken broth
- ¼ cup raisins
- 4 chicken thighs (about 1 pound), skinned
- 1 (15½-ounce) can chickpeas (garbanzo beans), drained
- 4 cups hot cooked couscous

1. Place first 3 ingredients in a spice or coffee grinder; process until finely ground. Combine cumin mixture, nutmeg, and next 3 ingredients; set aside.
2. Heat oil in an ovenproof Dutch oven over medium heat. Add onion and salt; cover and cook 10 minutes. Add 1 teaspoon cumin mixture, sugar, and black pepper; cover and cook 15 minutes. Add broth, and cook, uncovered, 30 minutes.
3. Preheat oven to 375°.
4. Add raisins, chicken, and chickpeas to Dutch oven; cover and bake at 375° for 30 minutes. Serve with couscous. Yield: 4 servings (serving size: 1 chicken thigh, about ⅔ cup onion mixture, and 1 cup couscous).
Note: Store remaining cumin mixture in an airtight container for up to 6 months.

CALORIES 543 (13% from fat); FAT 7.6g (sat 1.7g, mono 2.4g, poly 2.1g); PROTEIN 31.1g; CARB 91.6g; FIBER 10g; CHOL 58mg; IRON 5.5mg; SODIUM 548mg; CALC 121mg

It's a Wonderful Loaf

Sandwiches made with homemade breads are sure to earn notes of praise.

Sandwiches are a lot like presents: It's the packaging that gets the initial attention. Take, for example, a sandwich that's made with sliced, store-bought bread. As flavorful as the filling may be, the "packaging" doesn't say "special" like the look and taste of a sandwich made with homemade bread—and not just plain bread, either. Each of these breads is infused with such bold ingredients as olives, onions, or cheese. The recipes are also suitable for bread machines, and we offer a bread machine variation and filling suggestions for each one.

RED PEPPER-CHEESE BREAD

- 1 package active dry yeast
- 2 teaspoons sugar
- 1 cup warm water (105° to 115°)
- 3 cups bread flour, divided
- 2 teaspoons Dijon mustard
- 1 tablespoon vegetable oil
- ½ teaspoon salt
- ¼ to ½ teaspoon ground red pepper
- ¾ cup (3 ounces) shredded extra-sharp Cheddar cheese
- Vegetable cooking spray

1. Sprinkle yeast and sugar over 1 cup warm water in a large bowl; let stand 5 minutes. Add 1 cup flour, mustard, and next 3 ingredients; stir until smooth. Add 1¾ cups flour and cheese; stir to form a soft dough. Turn dough out onto a lightly floured surface. Knead until smooth and elastic (about 10 minutes), adding enough of remaining flour, 1 tablespoon at a time, to prevent dough from sticking to hands.

2. Place dough in a large bowl coated with cooking spray, turning to coat top. Cover and let rise in a warm place (85°), free from drafts, 1 hour or until doubled in bulk. Punch dough down; turn out onto a lightly floured surface.
3. Roll dough into a 14 x 7-inch rectangle. Roll up rectangle tightly, starting with a short edge, pressing firmly to eliminate air pockets; pinch seam and ends to seal. Place roll, seam side down, in a 9 x 5-inch loaf pan coated with cooking spray. Cover and let rise 1 hour or until doubled in bulk.
4. Preheat oven to 375°.
5. Uncover dough; bake at 375° for 35 minutes or until loaf sounds hollow when tapped. Remove from pan immediately; cool on a wire rack. Yield: 16 servings (serving size: 1 slice).

CALORIES 126 (22% from fat); FAT 3.1g (sat 1.3g, mono 0.8g, poly 0.7g); PROTEIN 4.6g; CARB 19.4g; FIBER 0.1g; CHOL 6mg; IRON 1.2mg; SODIUM 125mg; CALC 42mg

Bread Machine Variation:
Follow manufacturer's instructions for placing all dough ingredients in bread pan. Select cycle; start bread machine.

OATMEAL-ONION BATTER BREAD

This batter bread doesn't require kneading like standard yeast breads.

- 1¼ cups warm water (105° to 115°), divided
- 1 cup plus 1 teaspoon quick-cooking oats, divided
- 2 tablespoons brown sugar
- 1 package active dry yeast
- 3 cups all-purpose flour
- ¾ cup minced onion
- 2 tablespoons vegetable oil
- 1 teaspoon salt
- Vegetable cooking spray

1. Combine 1 cup warm water, ½ cup oats, and brown sugar in a small bowl.
2. Sprinkle yeast over ¼ cup warm water in a large bowl; let stand 5 minutes. Add oat mixture, ½ cup oats, flour, onion, oil, and salt; stir until well-blended. (Batter will be stiff.)

3. Cover and let rise in a warm place (85°), free from drafts, 45 minutes or until doubled in bulk. Stir batter well. Spoon into a 9 x 5-inch loaf pan coated with cooking spray. Sprinkle with 1 teaspoon oats. Cover and let rise 30 minutes or until doubled in bulk.
4. Preheat oven to 375°.
5. Uncover dough; bake at 375° for 50 minutes or until loaf sounds hollow when tapped. Remove bread from pan immediately, and cool on a wire rack. Yield: 16 servings (serving size: 1 slice).

CALORIES 143 (15% from fat); FAT 2.4g (sat 0.4g, mono 0.6g, poly 1.1g); PROTEIN 3.9g; CARB 26.2g; FIBER 1.5g; CHOL 0mg; IRON 1.6mg; SODIUM 148mg; CALC 10mg

Bread Machine Variation:
Follow manufacturer's instructions for placing all dough ingredients in bread pan. Select cycle; start bread machine.

OLIVE BREAD

- 1 package active dry yeast
- 2 teaspoons sugar
- ½ cup warm water (105° to 115°)
- 3 cups bread flour, divided
- ½ cup cornmeal
- ¾ cup plain fat-free yogurt
- ½ cup chopped green olives
- 1 tablespoon olive oil
- 1 teaspoon dried rosemary
- ¾ teaspoon salt
- Vegetable cooking spray

1. Sprinkle yeast and sugar over ½ cup warm water in a small bowl; let stand 5 minutes.
2. Combine yeast mixture, 1½ cups flour, cornmeal, and next 5 ingredients in a large bowl. Beat at medium speed of an electric mixer until blended. Add 1½ cups flour, stirring until a soft dough forms.
3. Turn dough out onto a lightly floured surface. Knead until smooth and elastic (about 8 minutes). Place dough in a large bowl coated with cooking spray, turning to coat top. Cover and let rise in a warm place (85°), free from drafts, 1 hour or until doubled in bulk.

4. Punch dough down; turn out onto a lightly floured surface. Let rest 5 minutes. Knead lightly. Roll dough into a 14 x 7-inch rectangle. Roll up rectangle, starting with a short edge, pressing firmly to eliminate air pockets; pinch seam and ends to seal. Place roll, seam side down, in a 9 x 5-inch loaf pan coated with cooking spray. Cover and let dough rise 45 minutes or until doubled in bulk.

5. Preheat oven to 375°.

6. Uncover dough; bake at 375° for 30 minutes or until loaf sounds hollow when tapped. Remove from pan immediately; cool on a wire rack. Yield: 16 servings (serving size: 1 slice).

CALORIES 127 (13% from fat); FAT 1.8g (sat 0.3g, mono 0.9g, poly 0.4g); PROTEIN 4.2g; CARB 23.3g; FIBER 0.7g; CHOL 0mg; IRON 1.5mg; SODIUM 158mg; CALC 30mg

Bread Machine Variation:
Follow manufacturer's instructions for placing all dough ingredients in bread pan. Select cycle; start bread machine.

GRAHAM-CRACKER BREAD

This bread is also wonderful toasted for breakfast.

 1 package active dry yeast
 ¼ cup warm water (105° to 115°)
 2 cups all-purpose flour
 ¾ cup cinnamon graham cracker crumbs (about 5 full cracker sheets)
 ½ cup whole-wheat flour
 2 tablespoons honey
 ½ teaspoon grated orange rind
 ½ teaspoon salt
 2 tablespoons chilled stick margarine, cut into small pieces
 ⅔ cup warm water (105° to 115°)
 2 tablespoons all-purpose flour
Vegetable cooking spray

1. Sprinkle yeast over ¼ cup warm water in a small bowl, and let stand 5 minutes.

2. Place 2 cups all-purpose flour and next 5 ingredients in a food processor; pulse 4 times or until blended. Add margarine; process 10 seconds. With processor on, slowly add yeast mixture and ⅔ cup warm water through food chute; process until combined. With processor on, add 2 tablespoons all-purpose flour through food chute, 1 tablespoon at a time, until dough leaves sides of bowl and forms a ball. Process 15 additional seconds.

3. Place dough in a large bowl coated with cooking spray, turning to coat top. Cover and let rise in a warm place (85°), free from drafts, 45 minutes or until doubled in bulk.

4. Punch dough down; divide into 3 equal portions. Working with one portion at a time (cover remaining dough to keep from drying), shape each portion into a 12-inch rope. Place 3 ropes lengthwise on a large baking sheet; pinch ends together at one end to seal. Braid ropes; pinch loose ends to seal. Place in an 8 x 4-inch loaf pan coated with cooking spray. Cover and let rise 45 minutes or until doubled in bulk.

5. Preheat oven to 375°.

6. Bake at 375° for 30 minutes or until loaf sounds hollow when tapped. Remove from pan immediately; cool on a wire rack. Yield: 16 servings (serving size: 1 slice).

CALORIES 115 (17% from fat); FAT 2.2g (sat 0.4g, mono 0.8g, poly 0.7g); PROTEIN 2.7g; CARB 21.3g; FIBER 1g; CHOL 0mg; IRON 1.2mg; SODIUM 120mg; CALC 7mg

Bread Machine Variation:
Increase second listing of water from ⅔ cup to 1 cup; follow manufacturer's instructions for placing all dough ingredients in bread pan. Select cycle; start bread machine.

SANDWICH IDEAS

RED PEPPER-CHEESE BREAD: The Dijon mustard and ground red pepper in this cheese bread accent the mild flavors of meat and poultry sandwiches.
- Sliced smoked turkey, lean ham, turkey bacon, tomatoes, and lettuce on toasted bread slices
- Sliced turkey and avocado with alfalfa sprouts
- Ham and asparagus topped with Cheddar cheese; broil until cheese melts

OATMEAL-ONION BATTER BREAD: Fillings with robust spices and ingredients go well with this coarse-textured bread.
- Curried egg salad
- Turkey bacon, tomato, and sharp Cheddar cheese

OLIVE BREAD: This bread has flavors and ingredients characteristic of Mediterranean cuisine. It goes well with simple fillings.
- Sliced turkey or roast beef topped with reduced-fat cheese, such as Swiss, Monterey Jack, or Cheddar; broil until cheese melts
- Grilled chicken breast or leftover slices of turkey, roasted red bell pepper strips, and sliced onion
- Sliced cucumbers, onions, tomatoes, and feta cheese tossed with fat-free Caesar dressing

GRAHAM-CRACKER BREAD: Because this bread is made with cinnamon graham crackers and honey, it pairs nicely with sweet fillings.
- Reduced-fat chunky peanut butter and your favorite fruit jam or homemade Ruby Quince Marmalade (page 343)
- Fruited chicken salad with raisins, dates, grape halves, or mandarin oranges
- A spread made with light cream cheese, orange marmalade, and chopped pecans

Bread Winners

When it comes to speed, quick breads always give a gold-medal performance.

These quick breads are unusual enough to be memorable, but not so far out that they're weird. They take very little effort to put together, and they freeze beautifully. You can bake a bunch, freeze them, then take one out and wrap it decoratively every time you think of someone who really needs a gift.

But you don't have to make them just to give away. You're bound to have houseguests at some point over the holidays, and these quick breads are ideal for brunch. Serve toasted Date-Nut-Carrot Bread alongside a bowl of vanilla yogurt, a choice of "mix-ins" (such as wheat germ, granola, or bran), and some fresh fruit, and you have a healthful, virtually effortless breakfast worthy of serving to company.

QUICK KICKS

Try toasting the bread the day after you make it or once you've taken it out of the freezer. You can also make a low-fat spread for it. Here are a few ideas.

• Soften Gorgonzola or blue cheese in the microwave; stir in fat-free plain yogurt, and cool. Serve with **Pear-and-Poppy Seed Loaf.**

• Spread light cream cheese mixed with a little honey and fat-free vanilla yogurt on **Date-Nut-Carrot Bread.**

• Drain fat-free plain yogurt for three hours, and mix with a little apricot fruit spread for **Apricot-Amaretto Bread.**

• Using your electric mixer, whip together light cream cheese and skim milk; add powdered sugar and vanilla, and spread over **Black Forest Bread.**

PEAR-AND-POPPY SEED LOAF

2¼ cups all-purpose flour
3 tablespoons poppy seeds
1½ teaspoons baking powder
1 teaspoon baking soda
½ teaspoon salt
⅛ teaspoon ground cardamom
1 cup peeled, chopped ripe pear
1 cup low-fat buttermilk
⅔ cup sugar
¼ cup honey
2 tablespoons stick margarine, melted
1 teaspoon vanilla extract
1 large egg
Vegetable cooking spray

1. Preheat oven to 350°.
2. Combine first 6 ingredients in a bowl. Stir in pear; make a well in center. Combine buttermilk and next 5 ingredients in a bowl; stir well with a whisk. Add to flour mixture; stir just until moist. Spoon into an 8 x 4-inch loaf pan coated with cooking spray.
3. Bake at 350° for 1 hour and 5 minutes or until a wooden pick inserted in center comes out clean. Cool 10 minutes in pan on a wire rack; remove from pan. Cool completely on wire rack. Yield: 14 servings (serving size: 1 slice).

CALORIES 173 (17% from fat); FAT 3.2g (sat 0.6g, mono 1g, poly 1.2g); PROTEIN 3.6g; CARB 33.2g; FIBER 1g; CHOL 16mg; IRON 1.3mg; SODIUM 217mg; CALC 84mg

DATE-NUT-CARROT BREAD

¾ cup hot water
½ cup pitted dates, chopped
½ cup golden raisins
1 cup shredded carrot
½ cup coarsely chopped walnuts
3 tablespoons vegetable oil
2 large eggs
1 large egg white
2 cups all-purpose flour
¾ cup sugar
1 tablespoon baking powder
1½ teaspoons ground cinnamon
½ teaspoon salt
Vegetable cooking spray

1. Preheat oven to 350°.
2. Combine first 3 ingredients in a bowl; let stand 15 minutes. Stir in carrot and next 4 ingredients. Combine flour and next 4 ingredients in a large bowl. Add carrot mixture to flour mixture, stirring just until moist. Spoon batter into an 8 x 4-inch loaf pan coated with cooking spray.
3. Bake at 350° for 1 hour and 5 minutes or until a wooden pick inserted in center comes out clean. Cool 10 minutes in pan on a wire rack; remove from pan. Cool completely on wire rack. Yield: 16 servings (serving size: 1 slice).

CALORIES 185 (28% from fat); FAT 5.7g (sat 0.9g, mono 1.5g, poly 2.9g); PROTEIN 3.9g; CARB 31.2g; FIBER 1.7g; CHOL 28mg; IRON 1.3mg; SODIUM 88mg; CALC 68mg

APRICOT-AMARETTO BREAD

2¼ cups all-purpose flour
2½ teaspoons baking powder
½ teaspoon baking soda
½ teaspoon salt
½ teaspoon ground allspice
½ cup chopped dried apricots
¼ cup toasted sliced almonds, divided
¾ cup sugar
¾ cup skim milk
¼ cup amaretto (almond-flavored liqueur)
3 tablespoons vegetable oil
½ teaspoon almond extract
1 large egg white
1 large egg
Vegetable cooking spray
1 tablespoon sugar

1. Preheat oven to 350°.
2. Combine first 5 ingredients in a large bowl. Stir in apricots and 3 tablespoons almonds; make a well in center of mixture. Combine ¾ cup sugar and next 6 ingredients in a bowl; add to flour mixture, stirring just until moist. Spoon batter into an 8 x 4-inch loaf pan coated with cooking spray. Sprinkle with 1 tablespoon almonds and 1 tablespoon sugar.

3. Bake at 350° for 45 minutes or until a wooden pick inserted in center comes out clean. Cool 10 minutes in pan on a wire rack; remove from pan. Cool completely on wire rack. Yield: 14 servings (serving size: 1 slice).
Note: For a nonalcoholic version, omit amaretto and increase skim milk to 1 cup; add ½ teaspoon almond extract.

CALORIES 188 (22% from fat); FAT 4.5g (sat 0.8g, mono 1.6g, poly 1.7g); PROTEIN 3.8g; CARB 33.7g; FIBER 0.9g; CHOL 16mg; IRON 1.4mg; SODIUM 149mg; CALC 77mg

DRIED-CRANBERRY SPICE BREAD

2¼　cups all-purpose flour
¾　cup sugar
¼　cup cornmeal
2　teaspoons baking soda
2　teaspoons ground cinnamon
1　teaspoon ground ginger
½　teaspoon ground allspice
½　teaspoon salt
¼　teaspoon ground nutmeg
1　cup dried cranberries
1　cup low-fat buttermilk
⅓　cup light molasses
2　tablespoons vegetable oil
2　large eggs
Vegetable cooking spray

1. Preheat oven to 350°.
2. Combine first 9 ingredients in a large bowl. Stir in cranberries, and make a well in center of mixture. Combine buttermilk and next 3 ingredients in a bowl; stir well with a whisk. Add buttermilk mixture to flour mixture, stirring just until moist. Spoon batter into a 9 x 5-inch loaf pan coated with cooking spray.
3. Bake at 350° for 1 hour or until a wooden pick inserted in center comes out clean. Cool 10 minutes in pan on a wire rack; remove from pan. Cool completely on wire rack. Yield: 16 servings (serving size: 1 slice).

CALORIES 185 (13% from fat); FAT 2.7g (sat 0.6g, mono 0.8g, poly 1g); PROTEIN 3.7g; CARB 37.4g; FIBER 1.2g; CHOL 28mg; IRON 1.6mg; SODIUM 259mg; CALC 46mg

BLACK FOREST BREAD

1¾　cups all-purpose flour
½　cup unsweetened cocoa
1　teaspoon baking soda
½　teaspoon salt
½　cup dried cranberries
1　tablespoon hot water
2　teaspoons instant coffee granules
¾　cup low-fat buttermilk
⅔　cup sugar
⅓　cup honey
2　tablespoons vegetable oil
2　teaspoons vanilla extract
1　large egg
Vegetable cooking spray

1. Preheat oven to 350°.
2. Combine first 4 ingredients in a large bowl. Stir in cranberries, and make a well in center of mixture. Combine water and coffee granules; add buttermilk and next 5 ingredients, stirring well with a whisk. Add to flour mixture, stirring just until moist. Spoon batter into an 8 x 4-inch loaf pan coated with cooking spray.
3. Bake at 350° for 50 minutes or until a wooden pick inserted in center comes out clean. Cool 10 minutes in pan on a wire rack; remove from pan. Cool completely on wire rack. Yield: 14 servings (serving size: 1 slice).

CALORIES 178 (15% from fat); FAT 3g (sat 0.8g, mono 0.7g, poly 1.1g); PROTEIN 3.7g; CARB 34.5g; FIBER 0.7g; CHOL 16mg; IRON 1.5mg; SODIUM 195mg; CALC 28mg

MAKING THE BREAD

• We tested all our recipes in shiny aluminum pans. If you're using a glass bread dish or a dark metal pan, decrease the oven temperature by 25 degrees, and bake the bread the same length of time.

• The breads should be cooled first, then covered in plastic wrap before being wrapped decoratively.

• To freeze bread, cool completely, then wrap in plastic wrap and then aluminum foil. Bread will freeze for up to one month.

Counting on Beans

Versatile and reliable, beans are always welcome when you're trying to feed hungry guests.

Deck the halls with boughs of . . . beans? Granted, beans aren't the same as cranberries or turkey, but they are dependable when it comes to feeding a crowd. With all the things you have to do, you need recipes that can be easily prepared and left to cook unattended. And to help you please a variety of palates, we're showcasing specialties from all over America.

LONGHORN CAVIAR

This Texas "caviar" is made from black-eyed peas. Make it one to three days ahead so the flavors will mellow.

1½　cups seeded, chopped tomato
⅓　cup thinly sliced green onions
2　tablespoons canned chopped green chiles
2　tablespoons white wine vinegar
1　tablespoon seeded, minced jalapeño pepper
1　tablespoon chopped fresh cilantro
1　teaspoon olive oil
¼　teaspoon salt
¼　teaspoon ground cumin
⅛　teaspoon pepper
1　garlic clove, minced
1　(15.8-ounce) can black-eyed peas, drained
Jalapeño slices (optional)
Cilantro sprigs (optional)

1. Combine first 12 ingredients in a bowl. Cover and chill. If desired, garnish with jalapeño slices and cilantro sprigs. Serve with baked tortilla chips. Yield: 3½ cups (serving size: ¼ cup).

CALORIES 31 (17% from fat); FAT 0.6g (sat 0.1g, mono 0.3g, poly 0.1g); PROTEIN 2g; CARB 5g; FIBER 0.7g; CHOL 0mg; IRON 0.5mg; SODIUM 105mg; CALC 10mg

CHICKPEA DIP

California's innovative food combinations inspired this dip made with yogurt and lemon juice. It can come in handy for impromptu gatherings. Serve it with pita triangles.

    3 garlic cloves
    ¼ cup plain low-fat yogurt
    1 tablespoon fresh lemon juice
    1 teaspoon olive oil
    ¼ teaspoon salt
    ¼ teaspoon paprika
    ⅛ teaspoon pepper
    1 (19-ounce) can chickpeas
       (garbanzo beans), drained

1. Drop garlic through food chute with food processor on, and process until minced. Add yogurt and remaining ingredients; process until smooth. Serve at room temperature. Yield: 2 cups (serving size: ¼ cup).

CALORIES 80 (18% from fat); FAT 1.7g (sat 0.1g, mono 0.2g, poly 0.1g); PROTEIN 4g; CARB 12.6g; FIBER 0.4g; CHOL 0mg; IRON 0.3mg; SODIUM 41mg; CALC 9mg

NEW ENGLAND BAKED BEANS

(pictured on page 334)

America's most famous bean dish was invented by the Puritan women of Boston. In addition to molasses and brown sugar, this version gets its sweet tang from barbecue sauce. Rather than salt pork, we used turkey bacon.

    3 cups dried Great Northern
       beans
    8 cups water
    1¼ cups chopped onion
    1 cup barbecue sauce
    ¾ cup packed brown sugar
    ¼ cup molasses
    1 tablespoon prepared mustard
    ½ teaspoon salt
    ¼ teaspoon pepper
    ⅛ teaspoon garlic powder
    4 slices turkey bacon, cut
       crosswise into ¼-inch
       strips

1. Sort and wash beans; place in a large ovenproof Dutch oven. Cover with water to 2 inches above beans, and bring to a boil. Cook 2 minutes. Remove from heat; cover and let stand 1 hour.
2. Drain beans; return to Dutch oven. Add 8 cups water and onion; bring to a boil. Cover, reduce heat, and simmer 2 hours or until beans are tender.
3. Preheat oven to 350°.
4. Drain bean mixture; return to Dutch oven. Add barbecue sauce and remaining ingredients; stir well. Cover and bake at 350° for 1 hour. Yield: 16 servings (serving size: ½ cup).

CALORIES 198 (11% from fat); FAT 2.5g (sat 0.6g, mono 1g, poly 0.7g); PROTEIN 9.6g; CARB 34.4g; FIBER 13.9g; CHOL 9mg; IRON 2.4mg; SODIUM 400mg; CALC 82mg

SOUTHWESTERN BEAN CASSEROLE

    1 teaspoon vegetable oil
       Vegetable cooking spray
    1 cup chopped onion
    2 garlic cloves, minced
    1 cup canned no-salt-added
       cream-style corn, divided
    ½ cup drained canned chopped
       green chiles, divided
    ½ cup bottled salsa
    ½ teaspoon salt
    ¼ teaspoon ground cumin
    ¼ teaspoon pepper
    2 (16-ounce) cans pinto beans,
       drained
    1 (14.5-ounce) can no-salt-added
       stewed tomatoes, undrained
    1 cup (4 ounces) shredded
       reduced-fat Cheddar cheese,
       divided
    ¾ cup yellow cornmeal
    ¼ cup all-purpose flour
    1 teaspoon sugar
    ¼ teaspoon salt
    ½ cup low-fat buttermilk
    ¼ cup vegetable oil
    2 egg whites, lightly beaten

1. Preheat oven to 375°.
2. Heat 1 teaspoon oil in a large saucepan coated with cooking spray over medium-high heat. Add onion and garlic; sauté 3 minutes. Add ½ cup corn, ¼ cup chiles, and next 6 ingredients; bring to a boil. Reduce heat, and simmer 15 minutes. Pour into a 13 x 9-inch baking dish coated with cooking spray; sprinkle with ½ cup cheese.
3. Combine cornmeal and next 3 ingredients in a medium bowl. Combine ½ cup corn, ¼ cup chiles, ½ cup cheese, buttermilk, ¼ cup oil, and egg whites; add to cornmeal mixture, stirring just until moist. Spread batter evenly over bean mixture. Bake casserole at 375° for 25 minutes or until corn bread is lightly browned. Yield: 7 servings (serving size: 1 cup).

CALORIES 376 (30% from fat); FAT 12.5g (sat 3.5g, mono 2.7g, poly 4.5g); PROTEIN 16.5g; CARB 51.3g; FIBER 5.2g; CHOL 11mg; IRON 3.6mg; SODIUM 680mg; CALC 225mg

SHOW-ME-STATE VEGETABLE-BEAN SOUP

    1 pound dried navy beans
    8 cups water
    ½ cup dry red wine
    2 teaspoons dried basil
    1½ teaspoons salt
    1 teaspoon dried marjoram
    ¼ teaspoon pepper
    2 cups chopped onion
    2 cups sliced zucchini
    1 cup chopped celery
    1 cup chopped red bell pepper
    1 cup sliced carrot
    6 garlic cloves, minced
    1 (6-ounce) can tomato paste
    ⅓ cup grated fresh Romano
       cheese

1. Sort and wash beans; place in a large Dutch oven. Cover with water to 2 inches above beans; bring to a boil. Cook 2 minutes. Remove from heat; cover and let stand 1 hour.
2. Drain beans; return to Dutch oven. Add 8 cups water and next 5 ingredients; bring to a boil. Cover, reduce heat, and simmer 1½ hours. Add onion and next 5 ingredients; simmer, uncovered, 50 minutes or until vegetables are tender. Stir in tomato paste; cook 10 additional minutes. Ladle into bowls, and sprinkle with cheese.

Yield: 10 servings (serving size: 1 cup soup and about 1½ teaspoons cheese).

CALORIES 227 (12% from fat); FAT 3g (sat 1.5g, mono 0.7g, poly 0.5g); PROTEIN 14.4g; CARB 38g; FIBER 6.8g; CHOL 8mg; IRON 4.1mg; SODIUM 419mg; CALC 187mg

SENATORIAL BEAN SOUP

For decades this soup has been served in the cafeteria of our nation's Capitol. If you prefer a smooth, creamy texture, puree all of the soup. It's even better when refrigerated several hours, and then reheated.

    1   cup dried navy beans
    2   tablespoons margarine
        Vegetable cooking spray
 2½   cups chopped leek
    2   cups sliced carrot
    1   cup thinly sliced celery
    1   cup diced cooked ham
        (such as Light & Lean)
    4   garlic cloves, minced
    8   cups water
    2   teaspoons chicken-flavored
        bouillon granules
    1   teaspoon beef-flavored
        bouillon granules
    1   teaspoon dried rubbed sage
    2   bay leaves

1. Sort and wash beans; place in a large Dutch oven. Cover with water to 2 inches above beans; bring to a boil. Cook 2 minutes. Remove from heat; cover and let stand 1 hour. Drain beans.
2. Melt margarine in Dutch oven coated with cooking spray over medium-high heat. Add leek and next 4 ingredients; sauté 10 minutes. Add beans, 8 cups water, and remaining 4 ingredients; bring to a boil. Cover, reduce heat, and simmer 1½ hours or until beans are very tender. Discard bay leaves.
3. Place half of soup in a blender; cover and process until smooth. Pour pureed mixture into remaining soup in Dutch oven; cook over medium-low heat 30 minutes. Yield: 8 servings (serving size: 1 cup).

CALORIES 174 (24% from fat); FAT 4.7g (sat 1.1g, mono 1.7g, poly 1.2g); PROTEIN 10g; CARB 24.5g; FIBER 4g; CHOL 9mg; IRON 2.5mg; SODIUM 525mg; CALC 77mg

The Gift of Chocolate

Here are our deep chocolate desserts that received our magazine's highest-rated taste scores.

These devilish indulgences are for devoted chocolate lovers only. But partake with abandon: Your little nutrition angel within will be delighted.

CHOCOLATE SILK CHEESECAKE

Using a food processor instead of a mixer makes this cheesecake creamier and smoother.

 ⅔   cup reduced-calorie chocolate
        wafer crumbs (about 20
        cookies)
    2   tablespoons sugar
    1   tablespoon stick margarine,
        melted
    1   tablespoon water
        Vegetable cooking spray
    3   ounces semisweet chocolate,
        chopped
    2   tablespoons skim milk
 1¼   cups sugar
    3   (8-ounce) blocks fat-free
        cream cheese
    1   (8-ounce) block ⅓-less-fat
        cream cheese (Neufchâtel)
    1   tablespoon vanilla extract
 ¼   teaspoon salt
    4   large egg whites
 ½   cup Dutch process or
        unsweetened cocoa
 ½   cup hot fudge topping
    1   cup low-fat sour cream

1. Preheat oven to 400°.
2. Combine first 4 ingredients in a bowl, tossing with a fork until blended. Press crumb mixture into bottom of a 9-inch springform pan coated with cooking spray. Bake at 400° for 8 minutes. Cool crust on a wire rack. Increase oven temperature to 525°.
3. Combine semisweet chocolate and milk in a bowl; microwave at HIGH 45 seconds or until chocolate melts, stirring after 30 seconds. Cool.
4. Combine 1¼ cups sugar and next 4 ingredients in a food processor; process just until smooth. Add egg whites; process until blended. Add chocolate mixture, cocoa, fudge topping, and sour cream; process until blended.
5. Spoon batter into prepared pan. Bake at 525° for 7 minutes. Reduce oven temperature to 250°, and bake 25 minutes or until almost set. (Cheesecake is done when the center barely moves when the pan is touched.) Remove cheesecake from oven; run a knife around outside edge, and cool to room temperature. Cover and chill at least 8 hours. Yield: 16 servings (serving size: 1 wedge).

CALORIES 261 (30% from fat); FAT 8.6g (sat 4.7g, mono 2.6g, poly 0.6g); PROTEIN 11g; CARB 35.8g; FIBER 0.1g; CHOL 26mg; IRON 0.9mg; SODIUM 455mg; CALC 161mg

EASY FUDGE LAYER CAKE

This recipe holds true to its name: It's supereasy to make.

Chocolate-Cream Cheese Frosting
Vegetable cooking spray
1¾ cups all-purpose flour
1¼ cups skim milk
⅔ cup granulated sugar
⅔ cup packed dark brown sugar
½ cup Dutch process or unsweetened cocoa
⅓ cup vegetable shortening
1 teaspoon baking powder
1 teaspoon baking soda
2 teaspoons vanilla extract
½ teaspoon salt
3 large eggs

1. Prepare Chocolate-Cream Cheese Frosting; cover and chill.
2. Preheat oven to 350°.
3. Coat 2 (8-inch) round cake pans with cooking spray; line bottoms of pans with wax paper. Coat wax paper with cooking spray; set pans aside.
4. Combine flour and remaining 10 ingredients in a large bowl; beat at low speed of an electric mixer 30 seconds or until ingredients are moist. Beat at medium speed 2 minutes or until well-blended.
5. Pour batter into prepared pans. Sharply tap pans once on the counter to remove air bubbles. Bake at 350° for 30 minutes or until cake springs back when touched lightly in center. Cool in pans on a wire rack 5 minutes. Loosen layers from sides of pans using a narrow metal spatula, and turn out onto wire racks. Peel off wax paper, and cool completely.
6. Place 1 cake layer on a plate, and spread with ½ cup Chocolate-Cream Cheese Frosting. Top with remaining cake layer; spread remaining frosting on sides and top of cake. Cover and chill at least 1 hour. Yield: 18 servings.

CALORIES 283 (24% from fat); FAT 7.7g (sat 2g, mono 1.3g, poly 0.6g); PROTEIN 5.4g; CARB 48.3g; FIBER 0.3g; CHOL 42mg; IRON 1.9mg; SODIUM 218mg; CALC 65mg

Chocolate-Cream Cheese Frosting:

½ (8-ounce) block ⅓-less-fat cream cheese (Neufchâtel)
2 tablespoons stick margarine, softened
3 tablespoons skim milk
3⅓ cups sifted powdered sugar
¾ cup Dutch process or unsweetened cocoa
⅛ teaspoon salt
1 teaspoon vanilla extract

1. Beat first 3 ingredients in a large bowl at high speed of an electric mixer until smooth. Combine sugar, cocoa, and salt; gradually add sugar mixture to cheese mixture, beating at low speed until well-blended. Add vanilla; beat well. Cover and chill. Yield: 1¾ cups.

DOUBLE-CHOCOLATE CREAM TART

(pictured on page 1)

The key to the creamy filling is the combination of fat-free sweetened condensed milk and light cream cheese with the cocoa.

1 cup all-purpose flour, divided
¼ cup ice water
1 tablespoon vanilla extract, divided
¾ cup Dutch process or unsweetened cocoa, divided
2 tablespoons sugar
¼ teaspoon salt
¼ cup vegetable shortening
Vegetable cooking spray
1 (14-ounce) can fat-free sweetened condensed milk
6 ounces ⅓-less-fat cream cheese (Neufchâtel), softened
1 large egg
1 large egg white
1½ cups frozen reduced-calorie whipped topping, thawed
1 ounce semisweet chocolate, finely chopped

1. Combine ¼ cup flour, ice water, and 1 teaspoon vanilla, stirring with a

whisk until well-blended; set aside. Combine ¾ cup flour, ¼ cup cocoa, sugar, and salt in a bowl; cut in shortening with a pastry blender or 2 knives until mixture resembles coarse meal. Add ice water mixture; toss with a fork until moist and crumbly (do not form a ball). Gently press mixture into a 4-inch circle on heavy-duty plastic wrap; cover with additional plastic wrap. Roll dough, still covered, into a 13-inch circle. Place dough in freezer 30 minutes or until plastic wrap can be easily removed.

2. Preheat oven to 350°.

3. Remove top sheet of plastic wrap; fit dough, uncovered side down, into a 10-inch round removable-bottom tart pan coated with cooking spray. Remove remaining sheet of plastic wrap. Fold edges under; flute. Pierce bottom and sides of dough with a fork; bake at 350° for 4 minutes. Cool on a wire rack. Place tart pan on a baking sheet; set aside.

4. Beat ½ cup cocoa and milk at medium speed of an electric mixer until blended. Add cheese; beat well. Add 2 teaspoons vanilla, egg, and egg white; beat just until smooth. Pour mixture into crust; bake tart at 350° for 25 minutes or until set. (Do not overbake.) Cool tart completely on a wire rack.

5. Spread whipped topping over tart; sprinkle with chopped chocolate. Yield: 12 servings (serving size: 1 wedge).

CALORIES 266 (33% from fat); FAT 9.7g (sat 3.8g, mono 0.4g, poly 0.5g); PROTEIN 7.8g; CARB 36.1g; FIBER 0.3g; CHOL 32mg; IRON 1.5mg; SODIUM 161mg; CALC 94mg

CHOCOLATE SOUFFLÉS WITH WHITE CHOCOLATE-RUM SAUCE

Butter-flavored vegetable cooking
    spray
2 tablespoons sugar
1½ cups skim milk
¾ cup sugar
⅔ cup Dutch process or
    unsweetened cocoa
3 tablespoons all-purpose flour
¼ teaspoon salt
1 ounce semisweet chocolate
3 large egg yolks
6 large egg whites
¼ teaspoon cream of tartar
⅓ cup sugar
1 (3-ounce) bar premium white
    chocolate, chopped
2 tablespoons skim milk
1 tablespoon white rum

1. Preheat oven to 400°.

2. Coat 8 (6-ounce) ramekins with cooking spray; sprinkle with 2 tablespoons sugar. Place on a baking sheet; set aside.

3. Combine 1½ cups milk and next 4 ingredients in a large saucepan; cook over medium-high heat, stirring constantly with a whisk, 5 minutes or until mixture thickens and comes to a boil. Cook, stirring constantly, 30 additional seconds. Remove from heat; add semisweet chocolate, stirring until melted. Gradually add chocolate mixture to egg yolks, stirring well. Return mixture to pan. Cook over medium heat, stirring constantly, 2 minutes. Spoon mixture into a large bowl; cool to room temperature, stirring occasionally.

4. Beat egg whites and cream of tartar at high speed of an electric mixer until foamy. Add ⅓ cup sugar, 1 tablespoon at a time, beating until stiff peaks form. Gently fold one-fourth of egg white mixture into chocolate mixture; gently fold in remaining egg white mixture. Spoon batter evenly into prepared ramekins. Bake at 400° for 20 minutes or until puffy and set.

5. Combine white chocolate and 2 tablespoons milk in a small saucepan; cook over low heat until chocolate

melts. Remove from heat; stir in rum. Cut into each soufflé with a spoon; pour 1 tablespoon sauce over each soufflé. Serve immediately. Yield: 8 servings.

CALORIES 289 (24% from fat); FAT 7.8g (sat 4.2g, mono 1.2g, poly 0.4g); PROTEIN 8.4g; CARB 46.4g; FIBER 0.1g; CHOL 84mg; IRON 1.8mg; SODIUM 157mg; CALC 101mg

FUDGY CHOCOLATE BROWNIES

The technique for these brownies is a bit unorthodox. When you add the sugar and cocoa to the melted chocolate, it forms a ball that's hard to stir. But stick with it; the end results are well worth it.

¼ cup plus 1 tablespoon stick
    margarine
1 ounce unsweetened chocolate
⅔ cup Dutch process or
    unsweetened cocoa
1½ cups sugar
3 large egg whites, lightly
    beaten
1 large egg, lightly beaten
1 cup all-purpose flour
½ teaspoon baking powder
Vegetable cooking spray

1. Preheat oven to 325°.

2. Melt margarine and chocolate in a large saucepan over medium heat. Stir in cocoa; cook 1 minute. Stir in sugar, and cook 1 minute (mixture will almost form a ball and be difficult to stir). Remove pan from heat; cool slightly. Combine egg whites and egg. Gradually add warm chocolate mixture to egg mixture, stirring with a whisk until well-blended. Combine flour and baking powder; add flour mixture to chocolate mixture, stirring well.

3. Spoon batter into a 9-inch square baking pan coated with cooking spray. Bake at 325° for 30 minutes (do not overbake). Cool on a wire rack. Yield: 20 servings.

CALORIES 132 (29% from fat); FAT 4.3g (sat 1.3g, mono 1.6g, poly 1g); PROTEIN 2.5g; CARB 21.7g; FIBER 0.2g; CHOL 11mg; IRON 0.9mg; SODIUM 46mg; CALC 16mg

DARK-CHOCOLATE SOUFFLÉ CAKE

(pictured on page 333)

Cake flour is a fine-textured, soft wheat flour with a high starch content, and usually comes in a box rather than a bag. It can be found with the cake mixes at the grocery.

Vegetable cooking spray
½ cup granulated sugar
½ cup packed dark brown sugar
¾ cup water
 1 tablespoon instant espresso or 2 tablespoons instant coffee granules
⅔ cup Dutch process or unsweetened cocoa
¼ teaspoon salt
 2 ounces semisweet chocolate, chopped
 2 ounces unsweetened chocolate, chopped
 2 tablespoons Kahlúa (coffee-flavored liqueur)
 3 large egg yolks
⅓ cup sifted cake flour (such as Swan's Down)
 6 large egg whites (at room temperature)
¼ teaspoon cream of tartar
⅓ cup granulated sugar
 1 tablespoon powdered sugar
¼ cup raspberries (optional)
Chocolate curls (optional)

1. Preheat oven to 300°.
2. Coat bottom of a 9-inch spring-form pan with cooking spray.
3. Combine ½ cup granulated sugar and next 3 ingredients in a large saucepan, stirring well; bring to a boil. Remove from heat; add cocoa and next 3 ingredients, stirring with a whisk until chocolate melts. Stir in Kahlúa and egg yolks. Stir in flour; cool to room temperature.
4. Beat egg whites and cream of tartar at high speed of an electric mixer until foamy. Add ⅓ cup granulated sugar, 1 tablespoon at a time, beating until stiff peaks form. Gently fold one-fourth of egg white mixture into chocolate mixture; repeat procedure with remaining egg white mixture, one-fourth at a time. Spoon into pan. Bake at 300° for 1 hour or until a wooden pick inserted in center comes out almost clean. Cool completely on a wire rack. Remove sides from pan; sift powdered sugar over cake. If desired, garnish with raspberries and chocolate curls. Yield: 12 servings (serving size: 1 wedge).
Note: You can substitute ¼ cup all-purpose flour for ⅓ cup cake flour.

CALORIES 205 (27% from fat); FAT 6.1g (sat 3.2g, mono 1.9g, poly 0.4g); PROTEIN 5g; CARB 34.2g; FIBER 0.2g; CHOL 55mg; IRON 2mg; SODIUM 91mg; CALC 31mg

BITTERSWEET CHOCOLATE PUDDING

3½ cups skim milk, divided
 1 cup Dutch process or unsweetened cocoa
 3 tablespoons cornstarch
¼ teaspoon salt
 1 cup sugar
 1 large egg, lightly beaten
 1 large egg yolk, lightly beaten
 2 ounces bittersweet chocolate, coarsely chopped
 1 tablespoon vanilla extract

1. Combine 1 cup milk, cocoa, cornstarch, and salt in a large bowl; stir well with a whisk. Set aside.
2. Cook 2½ cups milk in a large, heavy saucepan over medium-high heat to 180° or until tiny bubbles form around edge (do not boil). Remove from heat; stir in sugar with a whisk until sugar dissolves. Add cocoa mixture to pan, stirring until blended. Bring to a boil over medium heat; cook, stirring constantly, 2 minutes.
3. Combine egg and yolk in a bowl; stir well with a whisk. Gradually add milk mixture to egg mixture, stirring constantly. Return to pan. Cook over medium heat, stirring constantly, until thick (about 2 minutes). Remove from heat. Stir in chocolate and vanilla; stir until chocolate melts. Serve warm or chilled. Yield: 8 servings (serving size: ½ cup).

CALORIES 249 (18% from fat); FAT 5.1g (sat 2.7g, mono 1.3g, poly 0.3g); PROTEIN 8.3g; CARB 43g; FIBER 0g; CHOL 57mg; IRON 2.3mg; SODIUM 144mg; CALC 157mg

Hungarian Rhapsodies

That music you hear on the stove is the gentle simmering of Hungarian goulash, the perfect winter composition.

If ever there was a dish made to eat after coming in from the cold, it's Hungarian goulash. These stews are indeed gifts to be treasured because the recipes call for household staples such as onions, potatoes, carrots, and noodles. And they all share a common, colorful component: paprika. The cuts of meat are basic, be they ham, chicken, pork, or round steak. And as your life's hectic pace steps up, these dishes remain laid back. They only call for two basic cooking steps: Sautéing the vegetables and meat, then covering and simmering until they're tender.

KETTLE GOULASH

 1 tablespoon vegetable oil
 2 pounds lean, boned bottom round roast, cut into 1-inch cubes
 2 cups diced plum tomato
1½ cups vertically sliced red onion
 1 cup diced green bell pepper
 1 garlic clove, minced
 2 cups peeled, cubed red potato
⅓ cup dry red wine
¼ cup water
 1 tablespoon fresh lemon juice
1½ teaspoons paprika
 1 teaspoon caraway seeds
 1 teaspoon dried marjoram
½ teaspoon salt
½ teaspoon pepper
 1 (14¼-ounce) can fat-free beef broth

1. Heat oil in a large Dutch oven over medium-high heat. Add beef, and cook 5 minutes, browning on all sides. Remove beef from Dutch oven. Add tomato and next 3 ingredients to Dutch oven; sauté 10 minutes.

2. Return beef to Dutch oven; stir in potato and remaining ingredients. Bring to a boil; cover, reduce heat, and simmer 1½ hours or until beef is tender. Yield: 6 servings (serving size: 1 cup).

CALORIES 309 (26% from fat); FAT 8.9g (sat 2.7g, mono 3.2g, poly 1.6g); PROTEIN 36.8g; CARB 18.8g; FIBER 2.7g; CHOL 86mg; IRON 4.4mg; SODIUM 287mg; CALC 27mg

TRANSYLVANIAN GOULASH

3 chicken breast halves (about 1½ pounds), skinned
3 chicken drumsticks (about ¾ pound), skinned
3 chicken thighs (about ¾ pound), skinned
4 bacon slices
1 cup diced onion
1 garlic clove, minced
1 cup diced green bell pepper
2 (14.5-ounce) cans diced Italian-style tomatoes, undrained
½ cup dry red wine
1½ teaspoons paprika
¼ teaspoon salt
¼ teaspoon dried tarragon
¼ teaspoon pepper

1. Place first 3 ingredients in a Dutch oven; add water to cover. Bring to a boil; cover, reduce heat, and simmer 45 minutes or until tender. Drain chicken in a colander over a bowl, reserving 1 cup chicken broth. Remove chicken from bones; shred meat with 2 forks. Cover and chill.
2. Cook bacon in Dutch oven over medium-high heat until crisp; crumble and set aside.
3. Add onion and garlic to bacon drippings in Dutch oven; sauté 7 minutes or until lightly browned. Add bell pepper and tomatoes; cook over medium heat 30 minutes, stirring frequently. Stir in reserved chicken broth, wine, and remaining 4 ingredients; bring mixture to a boil. Partially cover, reduce heat, and simmer 30 minutes. Add shredded chicken; cook 15 minutes or until thoroughly heated. Ladle goulash into bowls, and sprinkle with

crumbled bacon. Yield: 8 servings (serving size: 1 cup).

CALORIES 280 (28% from fat); FAT 8.6g (sat 2.5g, mono 3.2g, poly 1.8g); PROTEIN 36.6g; CARB 13.1g; FIBER 1.2g; CHOL 105mg; IRON 2.2mg; SODIUM 820mg; CALC 57mg

PORK GOULASH

Vegetable cooking spray
1 (3-pound) lean, boned pork loin roast, cut into 1-inch pieces
2 bacon slices, chopped
1 cup diced onion
½ cup sliced carrot
½ cup sliced parsnip
1 cup tomato juice
1 cup beef broth
1 tablespoon brown sugar
2 teaspoons paprika
1 teaspoon salt
1 teaspoon dried marjoram
½ teaspoon pepper
1 (12-ounce) can light beer
6 cups coarsely chopped Savoy cabbage
3 cups peeled, cubed baking potato

1. Place a Dutch oven coated with cooking spray over medium-high heat until hot. Add pork; cook 5 minutes, browning on all sides. Drain; set aside.
2. Cook bacon in Dutch oven over medium heat until crisp. Add onion, carrot, and parsnip to Dutch oven; sauté 10 minutes or until tender. Return pork to Dutch oven. Add tomato juice and next 7 ingredients. Bring to a boil; cover, reduce heat, and simmer 1½ hours or until meat is tender, stirring occasionally. Add cabbage and potato; cover and simmer 30 minutes or until potato is tender. Yield: 8 servings (serving size: 1¼ cups).

CALORIES 325 (30% from fat); FAT 10.9g (sat 3.7g, mono 4.7g, poly 1.2g); PROTEIN 31.2g; CARB 23.3g; FIBER 2.5g; CHOL 84mg; IRON 2.2mg; SODIUM 749mg; CALC 51mg

CHICKEN PAPRIKASH

A paprikash is a goulash made with sour cream. For a shortcut, substitute 1½ pounds of ready-to-eat, roasted, skinned, boned chicken breasts (such as Tyson) for the cooked chicken. You can also use leftover roast turkey.

1 tablespoon reduced-calorie stick margarine
3 cups diced onion
½ cup diced green bell pepper
2 garlic cloves, minced
4 cups chopped cooked chicken (about 2 pounds)
1½ cups diced plum tomato
½ cup diced lean smoked ham
2 tablespoons all-purpose flour
2 teaspoons paprika
¼ teaspoon salt
⅛ teaspoon pepper
1 bay leaf
1 (10½-ounce) can low-salt chicken broth
1 cup uncooked medium egg noodles
½ cup low-fat sour cream

1. Melt margarine in a Dutch oven. Add onion, bell pepper, and garlic; sauté over medium heat 10 minutes or until tender. Add chicken, tomato, and diced ham; sauté 5 minutes. Stir in flour and next 4 ingredients.
2. Add broth; bring to a boil. Reduce heat, and simmer, uncovered, 15 minutes. Discard bay leaf. Stir in noodles; cover and cook 15 minutes or until noodles are tender. Remove from heat; stir in sour cream. Cook over low heat 5 minutes or until thoroughly heated. Yield: 7 servings (serving size: 1 cup).

CALORIES 290 (29% from fat); FAT 9.3g (sat 2.9g, mono 2.7g, poly 1.5g); PROTEIN 34.4g; CARB 16.2g; FIBER 2.4g; CHOL 100mg; IRON 2.4mg; SODIUM 322mg; CALC 55mg

VEAL PAPRIKASH

(pictured on page 336)

Lean, boned sirloin steak can be substituted for veal.

    1   tablespoon stick margarine,
        divided
        Vegetable cooking spray
    1   (2¼-pound) lean veal tip
        round roast, cut into 1-inch
        pieces
 1½   cups sliced carrot
    1   cup sliced onion
    1   garlic clove, minced
   ¼   cup all-purpose flour
    1   tablespoon paprika
   ½   teaspoon salt
   ½   teaspoon pepper
    1   cup low-salt chicken
        broth
    1   cup fat-free beef broth
   ½   cup dry white wine
    2   bay leaves
   ½   cup low-fat sour cream
 5¼   cups hot cooked medium egg
        noodles (about 3½ cups
        uncooked noodles)
        Chopped parsley (optional)

1. Melt 1 teaspoon margarine in a Dutch oven coated with cooking spray over medium-high heat. Add veal; cook 5 minutes, browning on all sides. Remove veal from Dutch oven; set aside.

2. Melt 2 teaspoons margarine in Dutch oven over medium heat. Add carrot, onion, and garlic; sauté 10 minutes or until tender. Stir in flour and next 3 ingredients. Stir in chicken broth and next 3 ingredients. Return meat to Dutch oven; bring to a boil. Cover, reduce heat, and simmer 1½ hours or until veal is tender, stirring occasionally. Discard bay leaves. Remove from heat; stir in sour cream. Cook over low heat 5 minutes or until thoroughly heated. Serve over noodles. Garnish with parsley, if desired. Yield: 7 servings (serving size: 1 cup stew and ¾ cup noodles).

CALORIES 423 (22% from fat); FAT 10.4g (sat 3.8g, mono 3.5g, poly 1.6g); PROTEIN 38.4g; CARB 39.2g; FIBER 4.1g; CHOL 166mg; IRON 3.8mg; SODIUM 320mg; CALC 57mg

---

LIGHTEN UP

International Appeal

From across the Atlantic comes an SOS to save a Chicken in Wine Cream Sauce that was adrift with fat and calories.

Requests to lighten up favorite recipes come from all over, including this SOS (save our sauce) from overseas. Claudia Burnett of Germany sent us a letter lamenting the heaviness of her native cuisine.

In our efforts to improve international culinary relations, we went to work. By skinning the chicken and using 1% low-fat milk and some light cream cheese to make the sauce, we succeeded more than a little bit. We lightened the recipe so that it has half the calories and only one-fifth the fat—that's about 66 fewer grams of fat per serving. But as dramatic as these numbers are, they would mean nothing if the recipe didn't stand up to the original in taste. As much as we loved it, we needed Claudia's approval. Her reply, "Wunderbar," said it all.

BEFORE & AFTER	
SERVING SIZE	
2 chicken thighs, ½ cup rice, and 1 cup sauce	
CALORIES	
994	444
FAT	
80.2g	14.5g
SATURATED FAT	
36.4g	4.4g
PERCENT OF TOTAL CALORIES	
73%	29%
CHOLESTEROL	
289mg	128mg

CHICKEN IN WINE CREAM SAUCE

    2   teaspoons dried oregano
    2   teaspoons dried basil
 1½   teaspoons dried rosemary
    1   teaspoon garlic powder
   ½   teaspoon salt
   ½   teaspoon pepper
   ¼   teaspoon paprika
    1   tablespoon plus 1 teaspoon
        olive oil, divided
    8   chicken thighs, skinned (about
        2¼ pounds)
        Vegetable cooking spray
   ⅓   cup all-purpose flour
 2¼   cups 1% low-fat milk
    1   cup dry white wine
    2   cups sliced mushrooms
   ¼   cup tub-style light cream
        cheese
    2   cups hot cooked wild rice
        Oregano sprigs (optional)
        Fresh cranberries (optional)

1. Combine first 7 ingredients and 2 teaspoons oil in a small bowl; rub over chicken. Heat 2 teaspoons oil in a large skillet coated with cooking spray over medium-high heat. Add chicken; cook 5 minutes on each side or until browned. Remove chicken from skillet; set aside.

2. Place flour in a bowl; gradually add milk and wine, stirring with a whisk until blended. Add mixture to skillet, scraping skillet to loosen browned bits; bring to a simmer. Return chicken to skillet; cover, reduce heat, and simmer 30 minutes or until chicken is done. Add mushrooms; cover and simmer 5 minutes. Remove chicken from skillet; cover and set aside.

3. Add cheese to skillet; cook, stirring constantly with a whisk, 5 minutes or until cheese melts. Place ½ cup rice on each of 4 plates. Top each with 2 chicken thighs and 1 cup sauce. If desired, garnish with oregano sprigs and cranberries. Yield: 4 servings.

CALORIES 444 (29% from fat); FAT 14.5g (sat 4.4g, mono 6.2g, poly 2.2g); PROTEIN 39.1g; CARB 39g; FIBER 2.5g; CHOL 128mg; IRON 4mg; SODIUM 568mg; CALC 246mg

Making the Rounds

Homemade cookies are a must during the holidays. With these slice-and-bake logs, you can whip up a batch in no time.

Wouldn't it be wonderful to have time to bake cookies with your kids or to offer a plate of warm, freshly baked cookies to friends who drop by during the holidays, or to just fill your home with an aroma guaranteed to melt the heart of even the grouchiest Grinch?

If baking cookies on anything other than an occasional basis seems like a fantasy in your time-pressed life, we've got a way for you to whip up a batch whenever the mood strikes—and in only 15 minutes.

Here are recipes for slice-and-bake cookies. You make the logs of dough, which are similar to the commercial brands sold on supermarket shelves but much tastier and far better for you. And the basic recipe is made from ingredients you probably have on hand; just mix them up, form the log, and keep it handy in your refrigerator or freezer. At a moment's notice, you can cut it into slices, pop them in the oven for 10 minutes, and serve them up on a plate.

LEMON-CORNMEAL ICEBOX COOKIES

¾ cup all-purpose flour
¼ cup yellow cornmeal
¼ teaspoon baking soda
⅛ teaspoon salt
¼ cup stick margarine, softened
¾ cup sugar
2 teaspoons grated lemon rind
1 teaspoon vanilla extract
1 large egg white
Vegetable cooking spray

1. Combine first 4 ingredients in a bowl, and set aside.
2. Beat margarine at medium speed of a mixer until light and fluffy. Gradually add sugar, beating until well-blended. Add lemon rind, vanilla extract, and egg white; beat well. Add flour mixture, and stir until well-blended. Turn dough out onto wax paper, and shape into a 6-inch log. Wrap log in wax paper, and freeze for 3 hours or until very firm.
3. Preheat oven to 350°.
4. Cut log into 24 (¼-inch) slices, and place slices 1 inch apart on a baking sheet coated with cooking spray. Bake at 350° for 8 to 10 minutes. Remove from sheet, and cool on wire racks. Yield: 2 dozen (serving size: 1 cookie).

CALORIES 62 (29% from fat); FAT 2g (sat 0.4g, mono 0.9g, poly 0.6g); PROTEIN 0.7g; CARB 10.4g; FIBER 0.2g; CHOL 0mg; IRON 0.2mg; SODIUM 50mg; CALC 2mg

BASIC ICEBOX SUGAR COOKIES

1 cup all-purpose flour
¼ teaspoon baking soda
⅛ teaspoon salt
¼ cup stick margarine, softened
⅔ cup sugar
1 teaspoon vanilla extract
1 large egg white
Vegetable cooking spray

1. Combine first 3 ingredients in a bowl, and set aside.
2. Beat margarine at medium speed of an electric mixer until light and fluffy. Gradually add sugar, beating until well-blended. Add vanilla and egg white; beat well. Add flour mixture; stir until well-blended. Turn dough out onto wax paper; shape into a 6-inch log. Wrap log in wax paper; freeze for 3 hours or until very firm.
3. Preheat oven to 350°.
4. Cut log into 24 (¼-inch) slices; place slices 1 inch apart on a baking sheet coated with cooking spray. Bake at 350° for 8 to 10 minutes. Remove from sheet; cool on wire racks. Yield: 2 dozen (serving size: 1 cookie).

CALORIES 59 (31% from fat); FAT 2g (sat 0.4g, mono 0.8g, poly 0.6g); PROTEIN 0.7g; CARB 9.6g; FIBER 0.1g; CHOL 0mg; IRON 0.2mg; SODIUM 50mg; CALC 2mg

DOUGH-RE-MI

Make it easy on yourself during this holiday season by having a batch of cookie dough in your refrigerator, ready to bake—just slice off as many cookies as you want. Our step-by-step instructions show you just how simple it is to make these low-fat treats.

❶ *Turn the cookie dough out onto a sheet of wax paper. Then, while working quickly, shape the dough into a 6-inch log.*

❷ *Wrap the dough log in wax paper, and form a compact roll; twist ends of wax paper securely. Freeze the log for 3 hours or until very firm.*

❸ *Immediately after taking the cookie dough from the freezer, unwrap the dough, and cut into ¼-inch slices with dental floss or a very sharp knife.*

Our pinwheel and striped cookies add pizazz to a platter of holiday goodies, ready in just minutes for those unexpected guests. Each variation makes about 4 dozen cookies.

First, prepare the doughs for Peanut Butter Icebox Cookies and Chocolate Icebox Cookies.

❶ *Roll each dough portion between 2 sheets of wax paper to form a 12-inch square (the dough is easier to roll at room temperature). Freeze dough for 15 minutes.*

❷ *Remove the wax paper, and stack dough portions one on top of the other. Roll together into a log, and wrap in wax paper. Freeze for 3 hours or until firm.*

❸ *Cut the dough log into ¼-inch slices with a piece of dental floss or a sharp knife. Place the slices on a cookie sheet, and bake at 350° for 10 minutes.*

PEANUT BUTTER ICEBOX COOKIES

     1 cup all-purpose flour
     ¼ teaspoon baking soda
     ⅛ teaspoon salt
     3 tablespoons stick margarine, softened
     2 tablespoons chunky peanut butter
     ½ cup packed brown sugar
     ¼ cup granulated sugar
     1 teaspoon vanilla extract
     1 large egg white
Vegetable cooking spray

1. Combine first 3 ingredients in a bowl, and set aside.
2. Beat margarine and peanut butter at medium speed of an electric mixer until light and fluffy. Gradually add sugars, beating until well-blended. Add vanilla and egg white; beat well. Add flour mixture; stir well. Turn dough out onto wax paper, and shape into a 6-inch log. Wrap log in wax paper, and freeze 3 hours or until firm.
3. Preheat oven to 350°.
4. Cut log into 24 (¼-inch) slices, and place slices 1 inch apart on a baking sheet coated with cooking spray. Bake at 350° for 8 to 10 minutes. Remove from sheet, and cool on wire racks. Yield: 2 dozen (serving size: 1 cookie).

CALORIES 69 (31% from fat); FAT 2.4g (sat 0.4g, mono 0.7g, poly 0.5g); PROTEIN 1.2g; CARB 10.8g; FIBER 0.2g; CHOL 9mg; IRON 0.4mg; SODIUM 53mg; CALC 7mg

Chocolate-Peanut Butter Variation:
Add 1 ounce of grated semisweet chocolate to flour mixture.

CHOCOLATE ICEBOX COOKIES

Rolling the dough in turbinado sugar gives the cookies a sugary edge. Turbinado sugar is a coarse, blond-colored sugar with a delicate molasses flavor; look for it in your grocery's baking section.

     ¾ cup all-purpose flour
     ¼ cup unsweetened cocoa
     ¼ teaspoon baking soda
     ⅛ teaspoon salt
     ¼ cup stick margarine, softened
     ⅔ cup granulated sugar
     1 teaspoon vanilla extract
     1 large egg white
     2 tablespoons turbinado sugar
Vegetable cooking spray

1. Combine first 4 ingredients in a bowl; set aside.
2. Beat margarine at medium speed of an electric mixer until light and fluffy. Gradually add granulated sugar, beating until well-blended. Add vanilla and egg white; beat well. Add flour mixture, and stir until well-blended. Turn dough out onto wax paper; shape into a 6-inch log. Wrap log in wax paper; freeze 3 hours or until very firm.
3. Preheat oven to 350°.
4. Roll log in turbinado sugar. Cut log into 24 (¼-inch) slices; place 1 inch apart on a baking sheet coated with cooking spray. Bake at 350° for 8 to 10 minutes. Remove from sheet; cool on wire racks. Yield: 2 dozen (serving size: 1 cookie).

CALORIES 61 (31% from fat); FAT 2.1g (sat 0.5g, mono 0.8g, poly 0.6g); PROTEIN 0.8g; CARB 9.8g; FIBER 0.1g; CHOL 0mg; IRON 0.4mg; SODIUM 51mg; CALC 3mg

Chocolate-Peppermint Variation:
Substitute 1 teaspoon of peppermint extract for vanilla extract.

CHOCOLATE-AND-VANILLA STRIPED COOKIES

Prepare the doughs for Chocolate Icebox Cookies and either Basic Icebox Sugar Cookies (page 355) or Brown Sugar Icebox Cookies. Shape each batch of dough into a 6-inch log, and wrap in wax paper. Freeze for 3 hours or until firm.

❶ *Cut each log lengthwise into 4 pieces.*

❷ *Make 2 stacks of dough, alternating chocolate and sugar-cookie dough. Wrap each stack in wax paper, and freeze 3 hours or until firm. Repeat procedure with the remaining chocolate and sugar-cookie dough pieces.*

❸ *Cut the dough logs into ¼-inch slices with a piece of dental floss or a sharp knife. Place the slices on a cookie sheet, and bake at 350° for 10 minutes.*

BROWN SUGAR ICEBOX COOKIES

1 cup all-purpose flour
¼ teaspoon baking soda
⅛ teaspoon salt
¼ cup stick margarine, softened
⅔ cup packed brown sugar
1 teaspoon vanilla extract
1 large egg white
Vegetable cooking spray

1. Combine first 3 ingredients in a bowl, and set aside.
2. Beat margarine at medium speed of an electric mixer until light and fluffy. Gradually add sugar, beating until well-blended. Add vanilla and egg white; beat well. Add flour mixture, and stir until well-blended. Turn dough out onto wax paper; shape into a 6-inch log. Wrap log in wax paper; freeze 3 hours or until very firm.
3. Preheat oven to 350°.
4. Cut log into 24 (¼-inch) slices, and place slices 1 inch apart on a baking sheet coated with cooking spray. Bake at 350° for 8 to 10 minutes. Remove from sheet; cool on wire racks. Yield: 2 dozen (serving size: 1 cookie).

CALORIES 60 (30% from fat); FAT 2g (sat 0.4g, mono 0.8g, poly 0.6g); PROTEIN 0.7g; CARB 10g; FIBER 0.1g; CHOL 0mg; IRON 0.4mg; SODIUM 52mg; CALC 7mg

Spice Variation:
Add ½ teaspoon ground cinnamon and ⅛ teaspoon ground cloves to flour mixture.

Freckled Chocolate Variation:
Add 1 ounce of grated semisweet chocolate to flour mixture.

Espresso Mocha Variation:
Add 2 teaspoons instant espresso granules or 4 teaspoons instant coffee granules to flour mixture.

HINTS & TIPS

• Too much flour will make these cookies bake up dry and crumbly. To measure flour correctly, lightly stir the flour, then spoon it into a dry measuring cup, leveling it off with the flat side of a knife.
• If the dough is too soft to shape into designs (such as pinwheels), simply chill until slightly firm.
• Each time you slice off a cookie from the log, turn log one quarter to prevent flattening on one side.
• Dough logs may be frozen up to one month, but be sure to double-wrap for extra protection.

FOR STARTERS

Dip the Light Fantastic

With these flavorful low-fat creations, you and your guests can dip to your heart's content.

Dips are a must for entertaining, but they can be sneaky. A little dip here, a little dip there, and before you know it, the fat and calories have piled up like snow in a blizzard. The following recipes, however, don't contribute to this dilemma: They're all flavorful, low-fat, and surprising. Because of ingredients such as toasted walnuts, sun-dried tomatoes, sweet potatoes, and tahini, they're far more interesting than the usual dips. To complete this healthful picture, do your dipping with baked tortilla chips, pita bread, or breadsticks. Dip, dip, hooray!

ROASTED-MUSHROOM, LENTIL, AND WALNUT PÂTÉ

2 cups water
1 cup dried lentils
¼ cup balsamic vinegar, divided
1 (8-ounce) package cremini mushrooms
1 tablespoon diced shallots
2 garlic cloves, minced
¾ cup coarsely chopped walnuts, toasted
½ cup chopped fresh basil
¼ teaspoon salt
⅛ teaspoon white pepper
Baked tortilla chips or pita bread (optional)

1. Preheat oven to 350°.
2. Combine water and lentils in a small saucepan; bring to a boil. Reduce heat; simmer 20 minutes or until lentils are soft.
3. Combine 2 tablespoons vinegar, mushrooms, shallots, and garlic in a bowl. Place on a jelly-roll pan, and bake at 350° for 15 minutes.
4. Combine lentils, mushroom mixture, 2 tablespoons vinegar, walnuts, and next 3 ingredients in a food processor; process until smooth. Serve with baked tortilla chips or pita bread, if desired. Yield: 3 cups (serving size: 1 tablespoon).

CALORIES 28 (39% from fat); FAT 1.2g (sat 0.1g, mono 0.3g, poly 0.8g); PROTEIN 1.8g; CARB 3g; FIBER 0.7g; CHOL 0mg; IRON 0.5mg; SODIUM 13mg; CALC 5mg

ROASTED SWEET POTATO DIP

3 cups peeled, chopped sweet potato (about 1 pound)
2½ cups chopped onion
1½ cups chopped carrot
1 tablespoon olive oil
¼ cup tahini (sesame-seed paste)
¼ teaspoon salt
⅛ teaspoon pepper
Breadsticks (optional)

1. Preheat oven to 350°.
2. Combine first 4 ingredients in a large bowl. Place potato mixture on a jelly-roll pan; bake at 350° for 1 hour or until sweet potatoes are tender.
3. Combine sweet potato mixture, tahini, salt, and pepper in a food processor; process until smooth. Serve with breadsticks, if desired. Yield: 3 cups (serving size: 1 tablespoon).

CALORIES 24 (38% from fat); FAT 1g (sat 0.1g, mono 0.5g, poly 0.3g); PROTEIN 0.5g; CARB 3.4g; FIBER 0.6g; CHOL 0mg; IRON 0.2mg; SODIUM 16mg; CALC 10mg

SUN-DRIED TOMATO DIP

1 (3-ounce) package sun-dried tomatoes, packed without oil (about 2 cups)
1 cup boiling water
⅓ cup fresh basil leaves (do not substitute dried basil)
2 tablespoons balsamic vinegar
2 tablespoons Italian-style tomato paste
1 tablespoon olive oil
⅛ teaspoon salt
⅛ teaspoon pepper
1 (15-ounce) can white beans, drained
1 garlic clove, minced
Pita chips or baked tortilla chips (optional)

1. Combine tomatoes and boiling water in a bowl; let stand 15 minutes or until soft. Drain tomatoes in a sieve over a bowl, reserving ½ cup soaking liquid.
2. Place tomatoes, reserved soaking liquid, basil, and next 7 ingredients in a food processor; process until smooth. Serve with pita chips or baked tortilla chips, if desired. Yield: 2½ cups (serving size: 1 tablespoon).

CALORIES 21 (26% from fat); FAT 0.6g (sat 0.1g, mono 0.3g, poly 0.1g); PROTEIN 1g; CARB 3.4g; FIBER 0.3g; CHOL 0mg; IRON 0.2mg; SODIUM 67mg; CALC 7mg

QUICK & EASY
WEEKNIGHTS

Shopping Break

Has holiday shopping got you run-down? Reenergize with these robust menus.

There's nothing like shopping to make you feel like a disarrayed sales rack. But you don't have to bow to the mall food court when your energy has been zapped by crowds and checkout lines. Instead, head home and indulge yourself with one of these healthful, flavorful menus. They'll not only recharge your vim and vigor, but can be made in less time than it takes to find your car in the mall's parking deck.

MENU

TANGY ROAST-BEEF
SANDWICHES

ROSEMARY POTATO
WEDGES

FROZEN YOGURT
WITH RUM-RAISIN SAUCE

(Serves 6)

TANGY ROAST-BEEF SANDWICHES

Prepare the horseradish spread ahead of time, and store it in the refrigerator until ready to use.

½ cup fat-free sour cream
4 ounces ⅓-less-fat cream cheese (Neufchâtel) (about ½ cup), softened
2 tablespoons prepared horseradish
1 (16-ounce) unsliced loaf French bread
¾ cup cranberry-raspberry crushed fruit (such as Ocean Spray)
¾ pound very thinly sliced reduced-fat deli roast beef (such as Healthy Choice)
1 cup alfalfa sprouts

1. Combine first 3 ingredients in a small bowl. Cover and chill.
2. Cut loaf in half horizontally. Spread sour cream mixture over cut sides of bread. Spread crushed fruit over bottom half of bread; top with roast beef, sprouts, and top half of bread. Cut into 6 pieces. Yield: 6 servings.

CALORIES 445 (18% from fat); FAT 8.7g (sat 4.4g, mono 2.2g, poly 1.1g); PROTEIN 23.1g; CARB 67.2g; FIBER 2.7g; CHOL 42mg; IRON 3.6mg; SODIUM 1,093mg; CALC 61mg

ROSEMARY POTATO WEDGES

5 red potatoes (about 1¾ pounds)
1 tablespoon olive oil
1 teaspoon dried rosemary
¼ teaspoon salt
¼ teaspoon pepper

1. Preheat oven to 450°.
2. Cut each potato lengthwise into 6 wedges. Pat dry with paper towels; place in an 11 x 7-inch baking dish. Drizzle with oil. Sprinkle with rosemary, salt, and pepper; toss well.
3. Bake at 450° for 30 minutes or until tender, stirring occasionally. Yield: 6 servings (serving size: 5 wedges).

CALORIES 119 (18% from fat); FAT 2.4g (sat 0.3g, mono 1.7g, poly 0.2g); PROTEIN 2.9g; CARB 22.1g; FIBER 2.4g; CHOL 0mg; IRON 1.8mg; SODIUM 107mg; CALC 20mg

FROZEN YOGURT WITH RUM-RAISIN SAUCE

The sauce can be made in advance and reheated in the microwave. Place it in a 2-cup glass measure; microwave at high 1 minute or until heated, stirring every 30 seconds.

⅓ cup packed brown sugar
2 tablespoons water
1 tablespoon stick margarine
1½ tablespoons all-purpose flour
1¼ cups 2% low-fat milk
⅓ cup raisins
½ teaspoon rum flavoring
3 cups low-fat vanilla frozen yogurt

1. Combine first 3 ingredients in a small saucepan over medium heat; cook 3 minutes or until margarine melts, stirring occasionally. Combine flour and milk in a small bowl; stir with a whisk. Add milk mixture and raisins to pan; stir well. Cook, stirring constantly, 5 minutes or until thick. Remove from heat; stir in rum flavoring. Serve over frozen yogurt. Yield: 6 servings (serving size: ½ cup frozen yogurt and ¼ cup sauce).

CALORIES 216 (22% from fat); FAT 4.8g (sat 2.4g, mono 1.1g, poly 1.2g); PROTEIN 5g; CARB 39.4g; FIBER 0.5g; CHOL 14mg; IRON 0.5mg; SODIUM 87mg; CALC 173mg

---

MENU

PAN-ROASTED PORK TENDERLOIN WITH OLIVES

Couscous with currants

GREEN BEANS PROVENÇALE

Sliced pears and cheese

(Serves 4)

PAN-ROASTED PORK TENDERLOIN WITH OLIVES

2 tablespoons sliced sun-dried tomatoes, packed without oil (about 6 pieces)
½ cup boiling water
¼ cup chopped green olives
¼ cup dry vermouth
2 tablespoons lemon juice
1 teaspoon chopped fresh rosemary or ¼ teaspoon dried rosemary
⅛ teaspoon dried crushed red pepper
2 garlic cloves, minced
1 (1-pound) pork tenderloin
¼ teaspoon black pepper
⅛ teaspoon salt
1 teaspoon olive oil
1 tablespoon water
1 teaspoon cornstarch
1 (10½-ounce) can low-salt chicken broth

1. Combine tomatoes and boiling water in a bowl. Cover; let stand 20 minutes or until soft. Stir in olives and next 5 ingredients.
2. Preheat oven to 400°.
3. Sprinkle pork with black pepper and salt. Heat oil in a 9-inch heavy ovenproof skillet over medium-high heat until hot. Add pork; cook 5 minutes, browning on all sides. Add tomato mixture; insert meat thermometer into thickest part of pork. Place skillet in oven; bake at 400° for 30 minutes or until thermometer registers 160° (slightly pink). Remove pork from skillet.
4. Combine 1 tablespoon water and cornstarch. Add cornstarch mixture and chicken broth to skillet. Bring to a boil over medium heat; reduce heat, and simmer 5 minutes or until slightly thick. Serve sauce with pork. Yield: 4 servings (serving size: 3 ounces pork and ¼ cup tomato-olive sauce).

CALORIES 143 (30% from fat); FAT 4.8g (sat 1.1g, mono 2.5g, poly 0.5g); PROTEIN 19.3g; CARB 5.5g; FIBER 0.4g; CHOL 55mg; IRON 1.9mg; SODIUM 275mg; CALC 25mg

GREEN BEANS PROVENÇALE

4 cups (2-inch) cut green beans (about ¾ pound)
1 teaspoon olive oil
½ cup sliced green onions
4 garlic cloves, crushed
2 cups plum tomato, seeded and thinly sliced (about ¾ pound)
2 tablespoons chopped fresh basil or 2 teaspoons dried basil
¼ teaspoon salt
⅛ teaspoon pepper

1. Arrange green beans in a steamer basket over boiling water; cover and steam 5 minutes or until tender. Drain.
2. Heat oil in a large nonstick skillet over medium-high heat. Add onions and garlic; sauté 1 minute. Add beans; sauté 3 minutes. Add tomato and remaining ingredients; sauté 2 minutes. Yield: 4 servings (serving size: 1 cup).

CALORIES 72 (20% from fat); FAT 1.6g (sat 0.2g, mono 0.9g, poly 0.3g); PROTEIN 3.2g; CARB 14g; FIBER 3.8g; CHOL 0mg; IRON 1.8mg; SODIUM 164mg; CALC 62mg

EGGS PIPÉRADE

Pipérade *is a dish from the Basque region of France that always includes tomatoes and bell peppers. This version with eggs is similar to a frittata. Cook the pipérade while the potatoes are roasting.*

1 teaspoon olive oil
¾ cup chopped red bell pepper
¾ cup chopped green bell pepper
1 garlic clove, minced
½ teaspoon dried thyme
¼ teaspoon salt
¼ to ½ teaspoon ground red pepper
1 (14.5-ounce) can diced tomatoes, undrained
4 large eggs, lightly beaten
1 tablespoon chopped fresh parsley (optional)

1. Heat oil in a large nonstick skillet over medium-high heat. Add bell peppers and garlic; sauté 5 minutes. Add thyme and next 3 ingredients; cover, reduce heat to medium, and cook 7 minutes or until bell peppers are tender. Uncover and cook 1 minute or until liquid almost evaporates. Gently stir in eggs; cover and cook 3 minutes or until set. Garnish with parsley, if desired. Cut into wedges. Yield: 4 servings.

CALORIES 134 (46% from fat); FAT 6.8g (sat 1.8g, mono 2.8g, poly 1g); PROTEIN 8.1g; CARB 10.7g; FIBER 1.4g; CHOL 221mg; IRON 2.2mg; SODIUM 476mg; CALC 67mg

ROASTED POTATOES

6 red potatoes, each cut into 8 wedges (about 1½ pounds)
1 tablespoon grated Parmesan cheese
1 tablespoon olive oil
2 teaspoons bottled real bacon bits
⅛ teaspoon pepper
Vegetable cooking spray

1. Preheat oven to 450°.
2. Combine first 5 ingredients in a medium bowl; toss well. Spoon potato mixture into an 11 x 7-inch baking dish coated with cooking spray. Bake at 450° for 35 minutes or until tender, stirring occasionally. Yield: 4 servings (serving size: 12 wedges).

CALORIES 214 (21% from fat); FAT 4.9g (sat 1g, mono 3g, poly 0.5g); PROTEIN 6g; CARB 37.8g; FIBER 4.1g; CHOL 2mg; IRON 3mg; SODIUM 63mg; CALC 47mg

SHERRIED PINE NUT ICE CREAM

2 tablespoons pine nuts, toasted
2 tablespoons cream sherry
2 cups vanilla fat-free ice cream, softened
¼ cup fat-free caramel-flavored sundae syrup

1. Stir pine nuts and sherry into ice cream. Drizzle caramel syrup evenly over each serving. Serve immediately. Yield: 4 servings (serving size: ½ cup ice cream mixture and 1 tablespoon syrup).

CALORIES 181 (12% from fat); FAT 2.5g (sat 0.4g, mono 1g, poly 1.1g); PROTEIN 5.2g; CARB 30.7g; FIBER 0.2g; CHOL 0mg; IRON 0.5mg; SODIUM 111mg; CALC 122mg

Grand Finales

From an Italian tiramisù to a cranberry sorbet, these desserts will end your holiday meals on a sweet note.

PEGGY SUE'S HONEY-CINNAMON DATE-NUT CAKE

The song "Peggy Sue" by Buddy Holly was one of my favorites in high school. So was this cake. I lightened the recipe and named my version after Mr. Holly's song. This way, I've brought back two of my favorites.
—Glee A. Erdelbrock, Toutle, Washington

½ cup stick margarine, softened
½ cup granulated sugar
½ cup packed brown sugar
1 cup evaporated skim milk
1 cup honey
½ cup applesauce
3 cups all-purpose flour
1½ teaspoons ground cinnamon
1 teaspoon baking soda
½ teaspoon salt
1 cup chopped pitted dates
¼ cup chopped walnuts, toasted
Vegetable cooking spray

1. Preheat oven to 350°.
2. Beat margarine and sugars at medium speed of an electric mixer until well-blended (about 5 minutes). Combine evaporated milk, honey, and applesauce; set aside. Combine flour and next 3 ingredients. Add flour mixture to margarine mixture alternately with honey mixture, beginning and ending with flour mixture. Stir in dates and walnuts.
3. Pour batter into a 13 x 9-inch baking pan coated with cooking spray. Bake at 350° for 55 minutes or until a wooden pick inserted in center comes out clean. Cool in pan on a wire rack. Yield: 16 servings.

CALORIES 248 (21% from fat); FAT 5.7g (sat 1g, mono 2.3g, poly 2.1g); PROTEIN 3.6g; CARB 47.7g; FIBER 1.5g; CHOL 1mg; IRON 1.3mg; SODIUM 193mg; CALC 53mg

WINTER-GARDEN FRUIT TART

I developed this recipe during a weight-reduction program. I know the freezing method used for the dough sounds a bit strange, but I can assure you that it makes handling the dough much easier. The crust comes out light and perfect every time.

—Diane Halferty,
Tucson, Arizona

 2 tablespoons butter
 ¼ cup vegetable oil
 2¼ cups all-purpose flour, divided
 2 tablespoons granulated sugar
 ½ teaspoon salt
 10 to 12 tablespoons skim milk
Vegetable cooking spray
 1 large egg white, lightly
    beaten
 ½ cup chopped pecans
 1 cup golden raisins
 ¾ cup plus 2 tablespoons
    granulated sugar
 ½ cup chopped dried apricots
 ½ cup packed brown sugar
 2 tablespoons cornstarch
 1 tablespoon grated orange rind
 1 teaspoon ground cinnamon
 ½ teaspoon ground nutmeg
 ½ teaspoon ground ginger
 1 (12-ounce) bag fresh or frozen
    cranberries
 ½ cup fresh orange juice
 1 tablespoon apricot preserves,
    melted

1. Place butter in a small saucepan; cook over medium heat 3 minutes or until lightly browned, stirring frequently. Pour browned butter into a small bowl. Stir in oil and 1 cup flour. Cover and freeze 30 minutes or until firm. Combine 1¼ cups flour, 2 tablespoons granulated sugar, and salt in a large bowl; set aside.
2. Preheat oven to 425°.
3. Break oil mixture into small pieces, and cut into flour mixture with a pastry blender or 2 knives until mixture resembles coarse meal. Sprinkle milk, 1 tablespoon at a time, over surface; toss with a fork until moist. Press mixture gently into a 6-inch circle on 2 sheets of slightly overlapping plastic wrap, and cover with additional sheets of plastic wrap. Roll dough, still covered, into a 13-inch circle.
4. Remove top sheets of plastic wrap; fit dough, uncovered side down, into an 11-inch tart pan coated with cooking spray. Remove remaining sheets of plastic wrap. Fold edges under, and press against sides of pan. Brush bottom of dough with egg white, and sprinkle with pecans; set aside. Combine raisins and next 9 ingredients in a large bowl; add orange juice, and stir well. Spoon fruit mixture into prepared crust. Brush edges of crust with preserves.
5. Place tart pan on a large baking sheet. Bake at 425° for 10 minutes. Reduce heat to 350° (do not remove tart from oven), and bake 30 additional minutes or until crust is golden. Cool tart on a wire rack. Yield: 16 servings (serving size: 1 wedge).

CALORIES 269 (26% from fat); FAT 7.7g (sat 1.8g, mono 3.0g, poly 2.4g); PROTEIN 3.2g; CARB 49.2g; FIBER 1.7g; CHOL 4mg; IRON 1.5mg; SODIUM 105mg; CALC 35mg

TIRAMISÙ ANGEL TORTE

I like to serve my tiramisù in a glass bowl or trifle dish and garnish it with shaved chocolate. That way, it looks as good as it tastes.

—Carolyn Lucarelli,
State College, Pennsylvania

 3 (8-ounce) cartons plain fat-free
    yogurt
 1 cup sugar, divided
 ½ cup water
 2 tablespoons instant espresso or
    ¼ cup instant coffee granules
 2 tablespoons Kahlúa (coffee-
    flavored liqueur)
 2 tablespoons skim milk
 ½ teaspoon vanilla extract
 1 (4-ounce) carton mascarpone
    cheese
 2 tablespoons unsweetened cocoa
 1 ounce bittersweet chocolate,
    grated
 1 (10-inch) round angel food
    cake

1. Place a colander in a 2-quart glass measure or medium bowl. Line colander with 4 layers of cheesecloth, allowing cheesecloth to extend over edges. Spoon yogurt into colander. Cover loosely with plastic wrap; refrigerate 12 hours. Spoon yogurt cheese into a bowl; discard liquid. Cover and refrigerate.
2. Combine ½ cup sugar, water, and espresso granules in a small saucepan; bring to a boil. Cook over medium heat 1 minute, stirring occasionally. Remove from heat, and stir in Kahlúa. Cool completely.
3. Combine yogurt cheese, ½ cup sugar, milk, vanilla, and mascarpone cheese; beat at medium speed of an electric mixer until smooth.
4. Combine cocoa and chocolate in a small bowl.
5. Cut angel food cake into 12 slices, using a serrated knife. Dip cake slices into espresso mixture; place 4 slices crosswise in a 9 x 5-inch loaf pan. Gently spread one-third of cheese mixture over cake layer, and sprinkle with one-third of cocoa mixture. Repeat procedure with remaining cake slices, cheese mixture, and cocoa mixture. Chill at least 2 hours. Yield: 10 servings (serving size: ¾ cup).

CALORIES 290 (20% from fat); FAT 6.5g (sat 3.4g, mono 1.8g, poly 0.3g); PROTEIN 15.9g; CARB 47.2g; FIBER 0g; CHOL 10mg; IRON 0.4mg; SODIUM 223mg; CALC 225mg

FUZZY-NAVEL BREAD PUDDING

Bread pudding was a favorite when I was growing up. My mother would use leftover cold biscuits and whatever sandwich bread she had around her kitchen. This version reflects my mother's bread combination.

—*Ruth Kent Cook, Batesville, Arkansas*

1 (17.3-ounce) can reduced-fat refrigerated buttermilk biscuits (such as Pillsbury Grands)
4½ cups (1-inch) cubed French bread (about 8 [1-ounce] slices)
1 cup raisins
½ cup packed brown sugar
1 large egg
2 cups skim milk
1 tablespoon lemon juice
1 teaspoon ground cinnamon
1 teaspoon vanilla extract
1 (20-ounce) can unsweetened crushed pineapple, undrained
Vegetable cooking spray
¼ cup reduced-calorie stick margarine
½ cup orange juice
¼ cup amaretto (almond-flavored liqueur)
1 (1-pound) box powdered sugar

1. Preheat oven to 375°.
2. Bake biscuits according to package directions; cool. Reduce oven temperature to 350°. Tear biscuits into 1-inch pieces. Combine torn biscuits, bread, and raisins in a large bowl.
3. Combine brown sugar and egg in a bowl; beat at medium speed of an electric mixer until blended. Add milk and next 3 ingredients; beat well. Add egg mixture and pineapple to bread mixture; stir until moist. Spoon into a 13 x 9-inch baking pan coated with cooking spray; bake at 350° for 30 minutes or until set and lightly browned.
4. Melt margarine in a saucepan over medium heat; add orange juice and amaretto. Gradually add powdered sugar; stir well with a whisk until sugar dissolves. Serve warm with bread pudding. Yield: 20 servings (serving size:

1 [2¼-inch] piece and about 2 tablespoons sauce).

CALORIES 294 (15% from fat); FAT 4.9g (sat 1.3g, mono 2.4g, poly 1.1g); PROTEIN 4.2g; CARB 58.1g; FIBER 1.3g; CHOL 12mg; IRON 1.3mg; SODIUM 355mg; CALC 64mg

TROPICAL SNAP-PUMPKIN PUDDING

I made up this recipe with my grandchildren in mind. I wanted to include fruit and wanted them to participate in the preparation. Their job was to crush the gingersnaps; it was quite a holiday ritual.

—*Peggy R. Thomas, Anchorage, Alaska*

2 (11-ounce) cans mandarin oranges in light syrup
¼ cup orange juice
1 (8-ounce) tub light cream cheese, softened
1 (15-ounce) can pumpkin
½ teaspoon ground cinnamon
¼ teaspoon ground ginger
⅛ teaspoon ground cloves
2 cups sifted powdered sugar
16 gingersnaps
1 cup frozen reduced-calorie whipped topping, thawed

1. Drain mandarin oranges; reserve 8 orange segments, and set aside remaining segments (about 2 cups).
2. Combine orange juice and cream cheese in a medium bowl; beat at medium speed of an electric mixer until smooth. Add pumpkin and next 3 ingredients; beat well. Gradually add sugar, and beat until well-blended.
3. Spoon ¼ cup pumpkin mixture into each of 8 ramekins or custard cups. Crush 1 gingersnap into large pieces with your hand, and sprinkle over each. Top each with ¼ cup orange segments and ¼ cup pumpkin mixture. Chill for at least 1 hour.
4. Top each serving with 1 crushed gingersnap, 2 tablespoons whipped topping, and 1 reserved orange segment. Yield: 8 servings.

CALORIES 328 (24% from fat); FAT 8.7g (sat 4.4g, mono 2.6g, poly 0.9g); PROTEIN 4.9g; CARB 59g; FIBER 2g; CHOL 23mg; IRON 1.8mg; SODIUM 194mg; CALC 89mg

CRANBERRY ICE

This recipe comes from a community cookbook printed in 1914 and has been a part of my Thanksgiving and Christmas dinners for many years. We serve this sorbet instead of the traditional cranberry sauce. My grandchildren just love it.

—*Katherine B. Holden, Murfreesboro, Tennessee*

8 cups water
4 cups fresh cranberries
3 cups sugar

1. Combine 8 cups water, fresh cranberries, and sugar in a Dutch oven; bring to a boil. Reduce heat, and cook 15 minutes or until all cranberries pop. Strain cranberry mixture through a fine sieve over a bowl, discarding solids. Cover and chill.
2. Pour cranberry mixture into freezer can of an ice-cream freezer; freeze according to manufacturer's instructions. Spoon cranberry ice into a freezer-safe container; cover and freeze 1 hour or until ready to serve. Yield: 10 cups (serving size: ½ cup).

CALORIES 125 (0% from fat); FAT 0g; PROTEIN 0.1g; CARB 32.4g; FIBER 0.2g; CHOL 0mg; IRON 0.1mg; SODIUM 0mg; CALC 2mg

CHERRIES IN THE SNOW

I like to use this recipe for special occasions. The colors are pretty, and it tastes like a heavy dessert. I end up giving out the recipe to almost everyone who tries it.

—*Pat Crawford, Brevard, North Carolina*

1 (8-ounce) tub fat-free cream cheese
1 cup sifted powdered sugar
1 (12-ounce) carton frozen reduced-calorie whipped topping, thawed
8 cups (1-inch) cubed angel food cake
1 (20-ounce) can light cherry pie filling

1. Beat cream cheese at medium speed of an electric mixer until smooth. Gradually add sugar, beating until blended. Gently fold in whipped topping.

2. Place half of cake cubes in a large glass bowl; top with half of cheese mixture. Spread half of cherry filling over cheese mixture. Repeat layers with remaining cake cubes, cheese mixture, and cherry filling. Cover and chill. Yield: 12 servings (serving size: 1 cup).

CALORIES 212 (17% from fat); FAT 3.9g (sat 2.5g, mono 0g, poly 1.3g); PROTEIN 5.5g; CARB 39g; FIBER 0g; CHOL 4mg; IRON 0.2mg; SODIUM 279mg; CALC 100mg

Reforming Arts

Florida's Clarita Garcia proves it's never too late to lighten.

Although Manuel A. "Manny" Garcia is a trained chef and longtime restaurateur, when his mother invited him to dinner, he wondered whether he was eating light or not. "She could fool me sometimes, but not always," he says, remembering the two years his mother spent testing low-fat traditional Spanish and Cuban recipes on her family. Those dishes are the basis of her latest cookbook, *Clarita's Cooking Lighter* (Seaside Publishing Inc., 1997).

This spicy dish, from her cookbook, contains an unusual medley of chicken, ham, and tomato flavors.

CHICKEN CREOLE

2 tablespoons olive oil
2 pounds skinned, boned chicken breast, cut into 1-inch cubes
1 cup (1-inch) cubes reduced-sodium ham
1 cup finely chopped onion
3 tablespoons minced fresh basil or 1 tablespoon dried basil
2 tablespoons minced fresh oregano or 2 teaspoons dried oregano
4 garlic cloves, minced
2 cups peeled, seeded, finely chopped tomato
1 cup dry white wine
½ cup thinly sliced carrot
¼ cup water
1 teaspoon hot sauce
½ teaspoon salt
½ teaspoon sugar
1 (8-ounce) can tomato sauce
1 (2-ounce) jar diced pimento
½ cup frozen green peas

1. Heat oil in a Dutch oven over medium heat until hot. Add chicken and ham; sauté 10 minutes or until chicken is browned. Remove chicken mixture from Dutch oven; set aside. Add onion and next 3 ingredients to Dutch oven; sauté 5 minutes or until onion is tender. Add tomato and next 8 ingredients; bring to a boil. Return chicken mixture to Dutch oven; cover, reduce heat, and simmer 40 minutes. Stir in peas; cook 2 minutes. Serve over rice. Yield: 6 servings (serving size: about 1½ cups).

CALORIES 294 (24% from fat); FAT 8g (sat 1.6g, mono 4.4g, poly 1.1g); PROTEIN 41.6g; CARB 13.4g; FIBER 2.3g; CHOL 99mg; IRON 2.5mg; SODIUM 738mg; CALC 53mg

Dinner without Elves

Let us be your helpers: We have eight quick meals with an ethnic kick.

For Santa, Christmas is the "ho ho ho" time of year. And why not? He's got helpers. But for most of us beyond the North Pole, Christmas is the "uh oh" time of year: "Uh oh, what am I going to cook for dinner?" Well, "uh oh" no more. We offer eight quick, simple dinner solutions to keep you and your family fed in between those holiday meals.

Each of these recipes relies on a combination of convenience products and fresh ingredients. With all of the spices, flavored sauces, and international food products that are available, it's easy to put an ethnic spin—Cajun, Caribbean, Italian, Mexican—on even the most mainstream of dishes.

JERK CHICKEN THIGHS

Preparation time: 10 minutes
Cooking time: 8 minutes

1½ teaspoons ground allspice
1 teaspoon ground cinnamon
½ teaspoon pepper
¼ teaspoon salt
¼ teaspoon ground nutmeg
¼ teaspoon ground mace
2 garlic cloves, crushed
1 pound skinned, boned chicken thighs
Vegetable cooking spray

1. Combine first 7 ingredients in a bowl. Rub chicken with spice mixture.

2. Prepare grill or broiler. Place chicken on grill rack or rack of a broiler pan coated with cooking spray; grill or broil 4 minutes on each side or until chicken is done. Yield: 4 servings (serving size: 3 ounces chicken).

CALORIES 187 (46% from fat); FAT 9.6g (sat 2.6g, mono 3.6g, poly 2.1g); PROTEIN 22.3g; CARB 1.8g; FIBER 0.4g; CHOL 81mg; IRON 1.4mg; SODIUM 223mg; CALC 27mg

CAJUN CHICKEN WITH OKRA

Preparation time: 12 minutes
Cooking time: 19 minutes

- 2 teaspoons vegetable oil
- 4 (4-ounce) skinned, boned chicken breast halves
- ⅔ cup low-salt chicken broth
- ¼ teaspoon salt
- ⅛ teaspoon dried crushed red pepper
- 1 (14½-ounce) can Cajun-style stewed tomatoes, undrained and chopped
- 2 garlic cloves, crushed
- 1 (10-ounce) package frozen cut okra, thawed
- 1½ tablespoons all-purpose flour
- 2 tablespoons water
- ¼ teaspoon hot sauce
- 2 cups cooked long-grain rice

1. Heat oil in a large nonstick skillet over medium-high heat until hot. Add chicken; cook 2 minutes on each side. Add broth and next 4 ingredients; cover, reduce heat, and simmer 8 minutes or until chicken is done. Add okra; simmer, covered, 3 minutes.
2. Combine flour and water in a small bowl, stirring with a whisk; add to skillet. Simmer, uncovered, 2 minutes or until thick. Stir in hot sauce. Serve over rice. Yield: 4 servings (serving size: 1 chicken breast half, ¾ cup sauce, and ½ cup rice).

CALORIES 326 (12% from fat); FAT 4.5g (sat 1g, mono 1g, poly 1.5g); PROTEIN 31.4g; CARB 39g; FIBER 1.6g; CHOL 67mg; IRON 2.8mg; SODIUM 505mg; CALC 119mg

MEDITERRANEAN CHICKEN WITH SALSA

A spicy breadcrumb coating and a bold sauce give this recipe a taste of Italy.
Preparation time: 10 minutes
Cooking time: 15 minutes

- ¾ cup bottled chunky salsa
- ⅓ cup diced plum tomato
- ⅓ cup diced zucchini
- 2 tablespoons chopped ripe olives
- 2 teaspoons capers
- 4 (4-ounce) skinned, boned chicken breast halves
- 2 tablespoons Italian-seasoned breadcrumbs
- 2 teaspoons olive oil
- 2 tablespoons water
- Black and green olives (optional)

1. Combine first 5 ingredients in a bowl, and set aside.
2. Sprinkle chicken with breadcrumbs. Heat oil in a large nonstick skillet over medium-high heat until hot. Add chicken, and cook 2 minutes on each side or until browned. Reduce heat to low; add water. Cover and cook 8 minutes or until chicken is done. Serve with salsa mixture. Garnish with olives, if desired. Yield: 4 servings (serving size: 1 chicken breast half and ⅓ cup salsa).

CALORIES 179 (22% from fat); FAT 4.4g (sat 0.8g, mono 2.4g, poly 0.7g); PROTEIN 27.6g; CARB 6.4g; FIBER 1.3g; CHOL 66mg; IRON 1.5mg; SODIUM 449mg; CALC 45mg

SICILIAN COD

Preparation time: 10 minutes
Cooking time: 25 minutes

- 2½ teaspoons olive oil, divided
- 3 cups sliced onion
- ½ cup red bell pepper strips
- 2 tablespoons golden raisins
- 2 tablespoons balsamic vinegar
- 2 teaspoons brown sugar
- ¼ teaspoon salt
- ⅛ teaspoon pepper
- 4 (6-ounce) cod fillets
- Olive oil-flavored vegetable cooking spray
- 1 tablespoon Italian-seasoned breadcrumbs
- ⅛ teaspoon salt

1. Preheat oven to 450°.
2. Heat 2 teaspoons oil in a large non-stick skillet over medium heat. Add onion and next 6 ingredients. Cover and cook 10 minutes or until onion is wilted, stirring occasionally. Set aside; keep warm.
3. Place fillets in a shallow baking dish coated with cooking spray. Brush fillets with ½ teaspoon oil; sprinkle with breadcrumbs and ⅛ teaspoon salt. Bake at 450° for 12 minutes or until fish flakes easily when tested with a fork. Serve onion mixture with fish. Yield: 4 servings (serving size: 5 ounces fish and ½ cup onion mixture).

CALORIES 230 (17% from fat); FAT 4.4g (sat 0.7g, mono 2.3g, poly 0.7g); PROTEIN 31.8g; CARB 15.1g; FIBER 2.1g; CHOL 73mg; IRON 1.3mg; SODIUM 361mg; CALC 52mg

PASTA WITH WHITE BEANS AND KALE

Preparation time: 15 minutes
Cooking time: 15 minutes

2½ cups uncooked radiatore
    (short, coiled pasta), rigatoni,
    or penne
 2 tablespoons olive oil, divided
 3 garlic cloves, minced
 1 (7-ounce) bottle roasted red
    bell peppers, drained and
    sliced
12 cups coarsely chopped kale
    (about ½ pound)
 1 (16-ounce) can cannellini
    beans or other white beans,
    drained
 2 tablespoons fresh lemon juice
 ¼ teaspoon coarsely ground
    pepper
 ¼ cup plus 2 tablespoons grated
    fresh Parmesan cheese

1. Cook pasta according to package directions, omitting salt and fat. Drain pasta in a sieve over a bowl, reserving ¼ cup cooking liquid; set pasta aside.
2. Heat 1 tablespoon oil in a large Dutch oven over medium heat. Add minced garlic and bell peppers; sauté 1 minute. Add chopped kale and cannellini beans; cover and cook 5 minutes or until kale is wilted, stirring occasionally. Add pasta, reserved cooking liquid, 1 tablespoon oil, lemon juice, and ¼ teaspoon pepper, stirring well. Spoon into serving bowls, and sprinkle with cheese. Yield: 6 servings (serving size: 1⅓ cups pasta and 1 tablespoon cheese).

CALORIES 349 (22% from fat); FAT 8.5g (sat 2g, mono 4.2g, poly 1.4g); PROTEIN 14.1g; CARB 54.7g; FIBER 3.4g; CHOL 5mg; IRON 3.9mg; SODIUM 289mg; CALC 170mg

PASTA MEXICANA

Preparation time: 8 minutes
Cooking time: 25 minutes

3½ cups uncooked farfalle
    (bow tie pasta)
 1 tablespoon reduced-calorie
    margarine
 2 garlic cloves, minced
 3 tablespoons all-purpose flour
 ½ teaspoon ground cumin
 ¼ teaspoon ground red pepper
 ¼ teaspoon salt
1½ cups skim milk
1¼ cups (5 ounces) shredded sharp
    Cheddar cheese
Vegetable cooking spray
 4 cups (¾-inch) sliced zucchini
    (about 2 medium)
 2 cups (¾-inch) cubed red bell
    pepper (about 2 medium)
 1 cup sliced green onions

1. Preheat oven to 350°.
2. Cook pasta according to package directions, omitting salt and fat.
3. Melt margarine in a small nonstick skillet over medium heat. Add garlic, and sauté 30 seconds. Stir in flour and next 3 ingredients; cook 1 minute. Gradually add milk; cook, stirring constantly, until thick and bubbly. Remove from heat; stir in cheese.
4. Place a large nonstick skillet coated with cooking spray over medium-high heat until hot. Add zucchini; cook 3 minutes. Add bell pepper; cook 1 minute. Combine pasta, zucchini mixture, and onions; spoon into a 13 x 9-inch baking dish coated with cooking spray. Spoon cheese sauce evenly over pasta mixture. Bake at 350° for 15 minutes or until bubbly. Yield: 6 servings (serving size: 1½ cups).

CALORIES 313 (29% from fat); FAT 10g (sat 5.4g, mono 2.7g, poly 1.1g); PROTEIN 15g; CARB 41.3g; FIBER 2.7g; CHOL 26mg; IRON 3.2mg; SODIUM 309mg; CALC 286mg

MEXICAN BLACK-BEAN CHILI

Preparation time: 15 minutes
Cooking time: 19 minutes

 1 cup diced onion
 1 cup diced green bell pepper
 1 pound ground chuck
1½ cups no-salt-added beef broth
 1 tablespoon chili powder
1½ teaspoons ground cumin
 ¾ teaspoon dried oregano
 ½ teaspoon salt
 ⅛ teaspoon pepper
 3 garlic cloves, crushed
 2 (14.5-ounce) cans no-salt-
    added diced tomatoes,
    undrained
 2 (15-ounce) cans black beans,
    drained
 ¼ cup plus 2 tablespoons fat-free
    sour cream
 ¼ cup plus 2 tablespoons chopped
    fresh cilantro

1. Place a large nonstick skillet over medium-high heat until hot. Add first 3 ingredients; cook until meat is browned, stirring to crumble. Drain mixture well.
2. Return meat mixture to skillet. Add broth and next 8 ingredients; bring to a boil. Reduce heat; simmer 15 minutes or until slightly thick, stirring occasionally.
3. Ladle into soup bowls; top with sour cream and cilantro. Yield: 6 servings (serving size: 1½ cups chili, 1 tablespoon sour cream, and 1 tablespoon cilantro).

CALORIES 346 (30% from fat); FAT 11.6g (sat 4.3g, mono 4.7g, poly 0.8g); PROTEIN 25.4g; CARB 35.5g; FIBER 5.5g; CHOL 44mg; IRON 4.9mg; SODIUM 529mg; CALC 103mg

CARIBBEAN RICE AND BEANS

Preparation time: 15 minutes
Cooking time: 15 minutes

⅔ cup water
⅔ cup uncooked instant rice
1 teaspoon vegetable oil
Vegetable cooking spray
1 cup chopped onion
½ cup chopped celery
½ cup diced green bell pepper
3 garlic cloves, minced
1 cup coarsely chopped tomato
⅛ teaspoon salt
¼ teaspoon dried crushed red pepper
¼ teaspoon ground cumin
¼ cup chopped fresh cilantro
1 (15-ounce) can black beans, drained
½ cup (2 ounces) shredded part-skim mozzarella cheese

1. Bring water to a boil in a saucepan; stir in rice. Cover, reduce heat, and simmer 5 minutes or until liquid is absorbed; set aside.
2. Heat oil in a large nonstick skillet coated with cooking spray over medium-high heat until hot. Add onion and next 3 ingredients; sauté 5 minutes or until tender. Add tomato and next 3 ingredients; sauté 2 minutes. Stir in cooked rice, cilantro, and black beans; cook for 1 minute or until thoroughly heated. Divide bean mixture evenly among 4 plates, and sprinkle with cheese. Yield: 4 servings (serving size: 1 cup bean mixture and 2 tablespoons cheese).

CALORIES 224 (18% from fat); FAT 4.4g (sat 1.8g, mono 1.1g, poly 0.9g); PROTEIN 11.4g; CARB 36.3g; FIBER 4.9g; CHOL 8mg; IRON 2.9mg; SODIUM 326mg; CALC 140mg

The Gift of Winter

There's much more to winter squash than beautiful packaging. Its many varieties inspire all kinds of creative recipes.

When cold weather comes, squash don't die on the vine. They just put on winter coats beautiful enough for the holidays. Now, if looks were all this fruit of the gourd family had going for it, no one would complain. But winter squash have far more to offer than being a table decoration. And during the holidays, when you have so many recipes to prepare, winter squash's versatility can rejuvenate your table. They can be served in a main dish, as the star of a side, or in a dessert. Loaded with nutrients, winter squash generally have a mellow, sweet flavor, but their numerous varieties display a range of subtle taste differences.

Besides providing recipes that show off each squash's flavor, we've included instructions for choosing, storing, cutting, and preparing this indigenous North American food.

Incidentally, when the colonists arrived here, they had never seen or tasted anything like fresh squash. For them, it was a major discovery. This holiday season, let it be one for you, too.

SPAGHETTI SQUASH SALAD

1 (3½-pound) spaghetti squash
3 tablespoons rice vinegar
1 tablespoon peeled, grated fresh gingerroot
2 teaspoons dark sesame oil
½ teaspoon salt
⅛ to ¼ teaspoon dried crushed red pepper
2 small cucumbers, peeled, halved lengthwise, and thinly sliced (about 2 cups)
1 cup diced red bell pepper
½ cup coarsely chopped fresh cilantro
1 tablespoon sesame seeds, toasted

1. Preheat oven to 350°.
2. Cut squash in half lengthwise, and discard seeds. Place squash, cut sides down, in a 13 x 9-inch baking dish; add water to dish to a depth of ½ inch. Bake at 350° for 45 minutes or until squash is tender when pierced with a fork.
3. Remove squash from water; cool. Scrape inside of squash with the tines of a fork to remove spaghetti-like strands to equal 4 cups.
4. Combine vinegar and next 4 ingredients, stirring well with a whisk. Combine 1 tablespoon vinaigrette and cucumbers; set aside.
5. Combine squash strands, bell pepper, cilantro, and remaining vinaigrette; toss well. Place squash mixture in a serving dish, and arrange cucumbers around edge of dish. Sprinkle salad with sesame seeds. Yield: 6 servings (serving size: ⅔ cup salad and ⅓ cup cucumbers).

CALORIES 68 (35% from fat); FAT 2.7g (sat 0.4g, mono 0.9g, poly 1.2g); PROTEIN 1.6g; CARB 10.3g; FIBER 2.3g; CHOL 0mg; IRON 1.3mg; SODIUM 221mg; CALC 53mg

SWEET DUMPLING SQUASH WITH CITRUS-HERB SAUCE

Most any small winter squash can be used in this recipe.

- 1 tablespoon grated lemon rind
- 1 tablespoon grated orange rind
- ½ cup water
- ¼ cup fresh lemon juice
- ¼ cup fresh orange juice
- 1½ tablespoons sugar
- ¼ teaspoon dried tarragon
- 1 tablespoon margarine
- ⅛ teaspoon white pepper
- 3 (1-pound) sweet dumpling squash or other winter squash

Tarragon sprigs (optional)

1. Preheat oven to 350°.
2. Combine first 7 ingredients in a small saucepan. Bring to a boil; reduce heat, and simmer until reduced to ½ cup (about 10 minutes). Remove from heat; stir in margarine and pepper. Keep warm.
3. Cut squash lengthwise into quarters, discarding seeds and stringy pulp. Place squash, cut sides down, on an aluminum foil-lined baking sheet. Bake at 350° for 30 minutes or until tender. Cool slightly. Scrape inside of squash with the tines of a fork; drizzle sauce over squash. Garnish with tarragon sprigs, if desired. Yield: 6 servings (serving size: 2 squash quarters and 4 teaspoons sauce).

CALORIES 101 (19% from fat); FAT 2.1g (sat 0.4g, mono 0.9g, poly 0.7g); PROTEIN 1.5g; CARB 22.4g; FIBER 2g; CHOL 0mg; IRON 1mg; SODIUM 27mg; CALC 59mg

KABOCHA SQUASH WITH FENNEL OVER COUSCOUS

- 2 teaspoons stick margarine
- ½ cup chopped onion
- 2 teaspoons peeled, minced fresh gingerroot
- 1 garlic clove, minced
- 2 cups peeled, cubed kabocha squash or other winter squash (about 1 pound)
- 1 cup plus 2 tablespoons chopped fennel bulb, divided
- 1½ teaspoons sugar
- ½ teaspoon salt, divided
- ¼ teaspoon fennel seeds
- ¾ cup fresh orange juice
- 1½ cups water, divided
- ¾ cup uncooked couscous
- 2 tablespoons chopped fennel fronds
- ½ teaspoon grated orange rind

1. Melt margarine in a large saucepan over medium-low heat. Add onion, gingerroot, and garlic; cook 3 minutes. Add squash, 1 cup fennel bulb, sugar, ¼ teaspoon salt, and fennel seeds; cover and cook 5 minutes. Uncover; cook 5 minutes. Add orange juice and ¼ cup water; cover, reduce heat, and simmer 20 minutes. Remove from heat; let stand, covered, 15 minutes.
2. Bring 1¼ cups water and ¼ teaspoon salt to a boil in a medium saucepan; gradually stir in 2 tablespoons fennel bulb, couscous, chopped fennel fronds, and orange rind. Remove couscous mixture from heat; cover and let stand 5 minutes. Fluff couscous with a fork. Serve squash mixture over couscous mixture. Yield: 4 servings (serving size: ½ cup squash and ½ cup couscous).

CALORIES 203 (11% from fat); FAT 2.5g (sat 0.4g, mono 0.9g, poly 0.7g); PROTEIN 5.9g; CARB 42.3g; FIBER 3g; CHOL 0mg; IRON 2.2mg; SODIUM 325mg; CALC 81mg

BUTTERNUT RISOTTO

- 4 cups low-salt chicken broth
- 1⅓ cups water
- 1 small leek, trimmed and cut in half lengthwise
- 1 tablespoon olive oil
- 1 cup thinly sliced celery
- 1½ cups uncooked Arborio rice or other short-grain rice
- 1 tablespoon thinly sliced fresh sage
- ⅓ cup dry white wine
- 4 cups (½-inch) peeled, cubed butternut squash or other winter squash (about 2 pounds)
- ½ teaspoon salt
- ⅓ cup grated fresh Parmesan cheese
- 2 teaspoons lemon juice
- ¼ teaspoon white pepper

1. Bring chicken broth and water to a simmer in a medium saucepan (do not boil). Keep broth mixture warm over low heat.
2. Cut leek crosswise into thin slices. Heat olive oil in a large saucepan over medium heat. Add leek and sliced celery; sauté 2 minutes. Add rice and sage; sauté 1 minute. Stir in wine, and cook, stirring constantly, 1 minute or until liquid is nearly absorbed. Stir in ½ cup broth mixture, squash, and salt; cook, stirring constantly, until liquid is nearly absorbed. Add remaining broth mixture, ½ cup at a time, stirring constantly; cook until each portion of broth mixture is absorbed before adding the next (about 20 minutes). Stir in cheese, lemon juice, and pepper. Yield: 6 servings (serving size: 1⅓ cups).

CALORIES 305 (17% from fat); FAT 5.7g (sat 1.9g, mono 2.6g, poly 0.5g); PROTEIN 8.7g; CARB 53.4g; FIBER 2.3g; CHOL 5mg; IRON 3.7mg; SODIUM 394mg; CALC 151mg

SQUASH, ANYONE?

Each squash has its own unique appearance and personality. Here's a look at some of our favorites.

ACORN: This squash has orange flesh and is mild and creamy. It's small to medium in size and has ribbed forest-green, marigold, or ivory skin.

BUTTERCUP: Similar to turban squash, this green or orange variety has a flavor reminiscent of a sweet potato. Shaped like a pasha's turban, it has a pale beanie on top that enlarges as the squash matures.

BUTTERNUT: The flesh of this variety is sweet, fruity, and orange. Look for large ones with evenly tan skin, a small ball end, and a thick neck.

HUBBARD: This term refers to a large group of fairly big to mammoth squash with a bumpy skin that can range in color from dark green to bright orange.

BUTTERCUP-HOMINY STEW

2 teaspoons cumin seeds
1 tablespoon vegetable oil
1 cup chopped red onion
1 teaspoon sugar
2 tablespoons all-purpose flour
1 tablespoon chili powder
1 garlic clove, minced
4 cups peeled, cubed buttercup squash or other winter squash (about 2 pounds)
2 cups water
1 (15.5-ounce) can yellow hominy or whole-kernel corn, drained
1 (10½-ounce) can beef broth
½ cup chopped green bell pepper
¼ cup minced fresh cilantro

1. Cook cumin seeds in a large saucepan over medium heat 1 minute or until toasted. Remove from pan.
2. Heat oil in saucepan over medium heat until hot. Add 1 teaspoon cumin seeds, onion, and sugar; sauté 5 minutes or until onion is lightly browned. Stir in flour, chili powder, and garlic. Add squash and next 3 ingredients; bring to a boil. Cover, reduce heat, and simmer 10 minutes. Uncover and simmer 10 additional minutes or until squash is very tender and stew thickens. Stir in 1 teaspoon cumin seeds, bell pepper, and cilantro. Yield: 4 servings (serving size: 1½ cups).

CALORIES 220 (19% from fat); FAT 4.8g (sat 0.8g, mono 1.4g, poly 2.3g); PROTEIN 8g; CARB 44.8g; FIBER 4.6g; CHOL 15mg; IRON 3.2mg; SODIUM 764mg; CALC 82mg

ORANGE-GLAZED ACORN SQUASH

This simple side dish goes well with lean ham, pork tenderloin, or roasted turkey.

3 medium acorn squash (about 1 pound each)
Vegetable cooking spray
3 tablespoons orange marmalade
1 tablespoon brown sugar
1 tablespoon lime juice
2 teaspoons low-sodium soy sauce
½ teaspoon vegetable oil
¼ teaspoon salt
Dash of ground red pepper

1. Preheat oven to 375°.
2. Cut squash crosswise into ¾-inch-thick slices, discarding seeds and stringy pulp. Arrange squash slices in a single layer on a large baking sheet coated with cooking spray. Bake at 375° for 15 minutes.
3. Combine orange marmalade and remaining 6 ingredients in a small bowl. Brush half of marmalade mixture over squash slices. Bake at 375° for 10 minutes. Brush with marmalade mixture, and bake 10 additional minutes. Transfer to a serving platter. Spoon remaining marmalade mixture over squash. Yield: 4 servings (serving size: 3 squash slices).

CALORIES 160 (12% from fat); FAT 2.1g (sat 0.4g, mono 0.5g, poly 0.9g); PROTEIN 2g; CARB 37.7g; FIBER 2.9g; CHOL 0mg; IRON 1.5mg; SODIUM 228mg; CALC 88mg

SQUASH KNOW-HOW

Some squash can be tasteless and fibrous. To get the best flavor, you'll want to follow these guidelines.
• Choose rock-solid, heavy winter squash with stems that are firm, full, and corky.
• If you can easily scrape off skin or press your nail into it, the squash is probably immature.
• Hard squash keep for weeks or more in a well-ventilated, cool, dry area.
• Don't refrigerate winter squash unless they're cut, in which case they should be wrapped in plastic wrap.

PUMPKIN FLAN WITH CARAMEL-ANISE SYRUP

Anise extract can be found in the spice section of your supermarket.

½ cup granulated sugar
2 tablespoons water
¼ to ½ teaspoon anise extract
Vegetable cooking spray
2 cups Pumpkin Puree or canned unsweetened pumpkin
½ cup packed brown sugar
3 tablespoons cornstarch
¼ teaspoon salt
¼ teaspoon ground cardamom
¼ teaspoon ground allspice
2 large eggs
1 large egg white
1 cup 2% low-fat milk
¼ cup dark rum
1 teaspoon vanilla extract
Star anise (optional)

1. Preheat oven to 350°.
2. Combine granulated sugar and water in a small heavy saucepan; cook over medium heat 8 minutes or until golden, stirring gently. Immediately stir in anise extract; pour into a 6½-cup metal ring mold coated with cooking spray, tipping quickly until caramelized syrup coats bottom of mold. Set aside.
3. Combine Pumpkin Puree and brown sugar in a blender or food processor; cover and process until smooth. Add cornstarch and next 5 ingredients; cover and process until smooth. Add milk, rum, and vanilla; cover and process until smooth. Pour into mold, and cover with aluminum foil. Place mold in a 13 x 9-inch baking pan; add hot water to pan to a depth of 1 inch.
4. Bake flan at 350° for 1 hour or until a knife inserted in center comes out clean. Remove mold from pan; cool, uncovered, on a wire rack. Cover and chill at least 3 hours.
5. Loosen edge of flan with a knife or rubber spatula. Place a plate upside down on top of mold; invert flan onto plate. Drizzle any remaining caramelized syrup over flan. Garnish with star anise, if desired. Yield: 8 servings (serving size: 1 wedge).

Note: If you don't have a 6½-cup ring mold, use a 9-inch round cake pan.

CALORIES 164 (11% from fat); FAT 2g (sat 0.8g, mono 0.7g, poly 0.2g); PROTEIN 3.5g; CARB 33.4g; FIBER 0.6g; CHOL 58mg; IRON 0.9mg; SODIUM 118mg; CALC 66mg

Pumpkin Puree:

2 (1½-pound) pumpkins
1 cup water, divided

1. Cut pumpkins lengthwise into quarters; remove seeds and stringy pulp. Arrange pumpkin, cut sides down, in 2 (2-quart) casseroles. Add ½ cup water to each casserole; cover and microwave at HIGH 15 minutes. Cool; peel pumpkins. Place pumpkin pulp in a food processor, and process until smooth or mash with a potato masher. Yield: 3 cups.
Note: Store remaining puree in a zip-top bag in the refrigerator up to 1 week or in the freezer up to 6 months.

BRUTE FORCE

While some large squash, such as butternut or turban, can be cut with a hefty knife or cleaver, some brutes need special handling. First, hack off the stem, then smack your sturdiest knife lengthwise into the squash. With a rubber mallet or rolling pin, gently hammer the knife where blade joins handle until the squash splits.

KABOCHA: This medium-size hard squash has a flattened-turban shape and a rough skin that ranges in color from jade green to tan. It has an unusually rich, sweet flesh.

SPAGHETTI SQUASH: Yellow, cream, or tan in color, this oblong-shaped squash contains mild, crisp, lightly sweet spaghetti-shaped strands. Larger squash have thicker strands and, often, more flavor.

SUGAR OR PIE PUMPKIN: The general term applies to small, round pumpkins—about 1 to 2 pounds each—of orange color and great variability. Their pulp ranges from dull and stringy to meaty and sweet.

SWEET DUMPLING: This solid, lobed, drumlike squash has a fine-grained, dry, corn-sweet pulp. The skin is ivory with pale gray-green stripes. They range in size from small (apple-size) to medium (melon-size).

TURBAN: This is the most flamboyantly colored, patterned, and shaped of winter squash. The pulp is creamy, moist, and a little bland.

Special Effects

These simple seafood menus will net you a holiday brunch with flair.

Breakfast can be a haphazard thing, and that's OK. Lunch can be "the usual," and that's OK, too. But brunch is another story. Brunch requires something special, sometimes even romantic. For the holidays, when elegance is usually the theme, we've created two seafood brunch menus for two.

Both menus are surprisingly easy to make. In fact, much of the preparation can be done in advance, so you can sleep late. And during this most hectic time of year, that's not "the usual."

MENU

SHRIMP NEWBURG ON TOAST POINTS

SALAD GREENS WITH CRANBERRY VINAIGRETTE

CARAMEL PEARS

About 553 calories and 14.7 grams of fat (24% calories from fat)

SHRIMP NEWBURG ON TOAST POINTS

(pictured on page 335)

    2   teaspoons olive oil, divided
    ¾   pound large shrimp, peeled and
          deveined
    2   cups sliced mushrooms
    ¾   cup 1% low-fat milk
    1   tablespoon all-purpose flour
    1   tablespoon dry sherry
    1   large egg yolk
    ¼   teaspoon salt
    Dash of ground red pepper
    Dash of black pepper
    4   (¾-ounce) slices whole-wheat
          bread, toasted
    2   teaspoons chopped chives

1. Heat 1 teaspoon oil in a large non-stick skillet over medium-high heat until hot. Add shrimp, and sauté 3 minutes. Remove shrimp from skillet; set aside, and keep warm.
2. Add 1 teaspoon oil to skillet. Add mushrooms; sauté 5 minutes. Combine milk and next 3 ingredients, stirring with a whisk until blended; add to mushrooms. Bring to a boil; reduce heat, and simmer, stirring constantly, until thick (about 3 minutes). Return shrimp to skillet; stir in salt and peppers.
3. Cut each toast slice in half diagonally. Arrange 4 toast triangles on each of 2 plates; top triangles with 1¼ cups shrimp mixture, and sprinkle with chives. Yield: 2 servings.

CALORIES 345 (30% from fat); FAT 11.5g (sat 2.6g, mono 5.1g, poly 2.1g); PROTEIN 35.2g; CARB 25.5g; FIBER 2g; CHOL 307mg; IRON 5.1mg; SODIUM 684mg; CALC 224mg

SALAD GREENS WITH CRANBERRY VINAIGRETTE

(pictured on page 335)

    1   tablespoon plus 1 teaspoon
          cranberry juice cocktail
    1   teaspoon extra-virgin olive oil
    ½   teaspoon sugar
    ½   teaspoon Dijon mustard
    ½   teaspoon red wine vinegar
    ⅛   teaspoon salt
    ⅛   teaspoon pepper
    2   cups torn romaine lettuce
    ½   cup julienne-cut zucchini

1. Combine first 7 ingredients in a small bowl; stir well with a whisk.
2. Combine lettuce and zucchini in a bowl; add vinaigrette, and toss. Yield: 2 servings (serving size: 1¼ cups).

CALORIES 46 (49% from fat); FAT 2.5g (sat 0.3g, mono 1.7g, poly 0.3g); PROTEIN 1.3g; CARB 5.1g; FIBER 1.1g; CHOL 0mg; IRON 0.8mg; SODIUM 190mg; CALC 26mg

CARAMEL PEARS

    ⅓   cup orange juice
    3   tablespoons brown sugar
    ⅛   teaspoon ground cinnamon
    Dash of ground cloves
    2   Bosc pears, peeled, cored, and
          cut into 1-inch-thick wedges
    2   tablespoons white rum
    Cinnamon sticks (optional)

1. Combine first 4 ingredients in a medium saucepan, and bring to a boil. Reduce heat, and simmer 5 minutes. Add pears, and cook until tender (about 10 minutes). Pour rum into saucepan. Cook 1 minute. Divide pears and sauce between 2 dishes. Garnish with cinnamon sticks, if desired. Yield: 2 servings.

CALORIES 162 (4% from fat); FAT 0.7g (sat 0g, mono 0.1g, poly 0.2g); PROTEIN 0.9g; CARB 41.4g; FIBER 4.2g; CHOL 0mg; IRON 0.7mg; SODIUM 6mg; CALC 34mg

---

PUTTING IT ALL TOGETHER

- Peel and devein shrimp the night before.
- Wash salad greens the night before; store in a zip-top plastic bag.
- Whisk vinaigrette the night before.
- Cook pears ahead of time; cover and store in refrigerator.

WINE PICKS

- SHRIMP NEWBURG ON TOAST POINTS: *Acacia Chardonnay Carneros 1995, (California white), $19 or Landmark Chardonnay 1995, (California white), $18*

- CARAMEL PEARS: *Eberle Muscat Canelli 1996, (dessert wine), $10*

CRAB RISOTTO

Serve this dish immediately.

- 2 cups low-salt chicken broth
- ¾ cup water
- 1 teaspoon olive oil
- 3 tablespoons finely chopped onion
- ¾ cup uncooked Arborio rice or other short-grain rice
- 3 tablespoons dry white wine
- 8 ounces lump crabmeat, drained and shell pieces removed
- 3 tablespoons minced fresh parsley
- ½ teaspoon dried basil
- 2 tablespoons grated Parmesan cheese

1. Heat chicken broth and water in a saucepan (do not boil). Keep warm over low heat.
2. Heat oil in a medium saucepan over medium-high heat. Add onion; sauté 2 minutes. Add rice; reduce heat to medium, and cook, stirring constantly, 3 minutes. Stir in wine; cook, stirring constantly, until liquid is nearly absorbed. Add broth mixture, ½ cup at a time, stirring constantly; cook until each portion of broth is absorbed before adding the next (about 20 minutes). Stir in crabmeat, parsley, and basil; cook, stirring constantly, 2 minutes or until thoroughly heated. Spoon onto plates; sprinkle with cheese. Yield: 2 servings (serving size: 1½ cups risotto and 1 tablespoon cheese).

CALORIES 453 (15% from fat); FAT 7.5g (sat 2.6g, mono 2.5g, poly 1g); PROTEIN 29.7g; CARB 64g; FIBER 1.6g; CHOL 103mg; IRON 5.8mg; SODIUM 452mg; CALC 193mg

SAVORY RED PEPPER-CORNMEAL SCONES

- ⅔ cup all-purpose flour
- ⅓ cup yellow cornmeal
- 1 tablespoon sugar
- ½ teaspoon ground cumin
- ½ teaspoon baking powder
- ¼ teaspoon baking soda
- ⅛ teaspoon salt
- 2 tablespoons chilled stick margarine, cut into small pieces
- ⅓ cup diced red bell pepper
- ⅓ cup fat-free buttermilk
- Vegetable cooking spray

1. Preheat oven to 400°.
2. Combine first 7 ingredients in a bowl; cut in margarine with a pastry blender or 2 knives until mixture resembles coarse meal. Add bell pepper and buttermilk; stir just until moist.
3. Pat dough into a 6-inch circle on a baking sheet coated with cooking spray, and cut into 4 wedges. Bake at 400° for 20 minutes or until golden. Serve warm. Yield: 4 servings (serving size: 1 wedge).

CALORIES 193 (30% from fat); FAT 6.4g (sat 1.2g, mono 2.6g, poly 2g); PROTEIN 4.1g; CARB 29.9g; FIBER 1.4g; CHOL 1mg; IRON 1.8mg; SODIUM 239mg; CALC 67mg

BROWN SUGAR-BALSAMIC GLAZED ORANGES

- 2 medium navel oranges (about 1 pound)
- 2 tablespoons brown sugar
- 1 tablespoon balsamic vinegar

1. Peel oranges, and cut each crosswise into ¼-inch-thick slices. Divide oranges evenly between 2 plates. Combine brown sugar and vinegar; drizzle vinegar mixture over oranges. Cover and marinate in refrigerator 2 hours. Yield: 2 servings.

CALORIES 111 (1% from fat); FAT 0.1g (sat 0g, mono 0g, poly 0g); PROTEIN 1.7g; CARB 28.3g; FIBER 7.3g; CHOL 0mg; IRON 0.4mg; SODIUM 5mg; CALC 74mg

THE ENLIGHTENED CHEF

Peak-Performance Cooking

See how two chefs worked out the fat in their renowned sports club's light menus.

For the chef team at Manhattan's Reebok Sports Club/NY, part of the job is staying in shape. "We have to," says Sous-Chef Will Collins, "just to keep up with the members."

Though Executive Chef Jim Ackard goes for weight training, and Collins swims laps in the club's pool, the real endurance test begins in their kitchen.

At The Grill—the club's white-tablecloth restaurant—the chefs express their talents in high gear. The focus is on texture and flavor. For the latter, they start with homemade vegetable broth for most of their cooking. The lineup of fresh, low-fat fare includes all the hottest healthful picks. Wraps, vegetarian sushi rolls, muffins and breads, salads, and smoothies are created to satisfy, not stuff.

SEARED DUCK BREAST WITH BULGUR SALAD AND ORANGE DRESSING

"We wanted to do duck as healthfully as possible. That way someone could enjoy this dish as much as a typical roast duck. But without so many calories from fat," says Ackard.

    1   cup homemade or canned
          vegetable broth
    ½   cup uncooked bulgur or
          cracked wheat
    2   cups (½-inch) cubes peeled
          sweet potato
  Vegetable cooking spray
    ¼   cup dried cranberries
    1   cup boiling water
    1   cup coarsely chopped gourmet
          salad greens
    ½   teaspoon salt, divided
    ½   teaspoon pepper, divided
    ¼   cup thawed frozen orange juice
          concentrate, undiluted
    2   teaspoons olive oil
    1   teaspoon chopped shallots
    1   teaspoon water
    4   (8-ounce) duck breast halves

1. Bring vegetable broth to a boil in a saucepan; add bulgur. Cover and let stand 30 minutes. Fluff with a fork; set aside.

2. Preheat oven to 400°.

3. Place sweet potato on a baking sheet coated with cooking spray. Bake at 400° for 15 minutes or until tender, stirring occasionally. While potato is baking, combine cranberries and boiling water in a bowl; cover and let stand 15 minutes. Drain well.

4. Combine bulgur, sweet potato, cranberries, and salad greens in a bowl; sprinkle with ¼ teaspoon salt and ¼ teaspoon pepper. Toss well; cover and chill.

5. Combine orange juice concentrate and next 3 ingredients in a blender; cover and process until smooth. Set aside.

6. Wrap handle of a large ovenproof nonstick skillet with aluminum foil; place skillet coated with cooking spray over medium-high heat until hot. Sprinkle duck with ¼ teaspoon salt and ¼ teaspoon pepper. Place duck, skin side down, in skillet; reduce heat to medium, and cook 20 minutes or until skin is browned (pour off fat frequently). Place skillet in oven; bake at 400° for 10 minutes or to desired degree of doneness. Remove and discard skin; slice duck into ¼-inch-wide strips.

7. Arrange bulgur salad and duck on individual serving plates; drizzle with orange dressing. Yield: 4 servings (serving size: 3 ounces duck, 1 cup salad, and 1 tablespoon vinaigrette).

Note: Substitute pork tenderloin or chicken breasts for the duck, if desired.

CALORIES 385 (29% from fat); FAT 12.6g (sat 4g, mono 4.9g, poly 1.6g); PROTEIN 24.3g; CARB 44.5g; FIBER 6.1g; CHOL 76mg; IRON 3.6mg; SODIUM 614mg; CALC 48mg

QUACK FIXES

We've arranged the Seared Duck Breast with the bulgur mixture and drizzled it with citrus dressing for a marvelous blending of flavors. While we're serving the duck as a main-dish salad, here are some suggestions for quick accompaniments when serving duck as a main-dish entrée.

• The strong flavor of duck pairs nicely with plain, hearty breads, including low-fat biscuits, French bread, or crusty dinner rolls.

• Typically, tangy relishes or chutneys go well with duck. (For the same type of flavor combination, we've used the orange dressing to complement this salad.)

• Other classic accompaniments: cabbage, turnips, chestnuts, mushrooms, onions, or rice.

Month-by-Month Index

General Recipe Index

Menu Index

Each menu includes recipes from the magazine and appropriate generic items to round out the meal.
Refer to the page number with each menu to locate the recipe.

Acknowledgments and Credits

CONTRIBUTING RECIPE
DEVELOPERS:

Kimberly Ahto
Pat Baird
Carol M. Bareuther
Bruce Beck
Mark Bittman
Leslye Michlin Borden
Susan S. Bradley
Jennifer Brulé
Holly Berkowitz Clegg
Christine Day
Sandra Day
Abby Duchin Dinces
Dave DiResta
Brooke Dojny
Linda W. Eckhardt
Janet Fletcher
Jim Fobel
Joanne Foran
Linda Gassenheimer
Sam Gugino
Barbara C. Heiken
Nancy Hughes
Barbara Jakacki
Telia Johnson
Vanessa Taylor Johnson
Jeanne Kelley

Jean Kressy
Louis Lanza
Sharon Lerch
Susan Herrmann Loomis
Marcy Marceau
Judy Monroe
Patty Neeley
Lou Seibert Pappasi
Greg Patent
Steven Petusevsky
Paul Piccuito
Steven Raichlen
Jane Ingrassia Reinsel
Sharon Sanders
Chris Schlesinger
Elizabeth Schneider
Marie Simmons
Nina Simonds
Eric Skokan
Kathleen Desmond Stang
Eileen Stukane
Elizabeth Taliaferro
Jennifer Viegas
Robin Vitetta
Robb Walsh
Kenneth Wapner
Ann Willan
John Willoughby

CONTRIBUTING PHOTO STYLISTS:

Connie Formby: page 263
Susan Herrmann Loomis: pages 261, 262

CONTRIBUTING PHOTOGRAPHERS:

Brit Huckabay: pages 169, 206, 368-369
Randy Mayor: pages 39, 74, 109, 110,
111, 170, 207
Susan Salinger: page 205

RECIPE CREDITS:

Emu Fillets with Quandong-Chile Glaze
(page 164) reprinted with permission
from *A Taste of Australia: The Bathers
Pavilion Cookbook,* by Victoria Alexander
and Genevieve Harris.
© 1995 Ten Speed Press, P.O. Box 7123,
Berkeley, CA 94707.

Chicken Creole (page 363) reprinted
with permission from *Clarita's Cooking
Lighter,* by Clarita Garcia.
© 1997 Seaside Publishing Inc.,
P.O. Box 14441,
St. Petersburg, FL 33733.

METRIC EQUIVALENTS

The recipes that appear in this cookbook use the standard United States method
for measuring liquid and dry or solid ingredients (teaspoons, tablespoons, and cups).
The information in the following charts is provided to help cooks outside the U.S.
successfully use these recipes. All equivalents are approximate.

EQUIVALENTS FOR DIFFERENT TYPES OF INGREDIENTS

A standard cup measure of a dry or solid ingredient will
vary in weight depending on the type of ingredient.
A standard cup of liquid is the same volume for any type of
liquid. Use the following chart when converting standard
cup measures to grams (weight) or milliliters (volume).

Standard Cup	Fine Powder (ex. flour)	Grain (ex. rice)	Granular (ex. sugar)	Liquid Solids (ex. butter)	Liquid (ex. milk)
1	140 g	150 g	190 g	200 g	240 ml
¾	105 g	113 g	143 g	150 g	180 ml
⅔	93 g	100 g	125 g	133 g	160 ml
½	70 g	75 g	95 g	100 g	120 ml
⅓	47 g	50 g	63 g	67 g	80 ml
¼	35 g	38 g	48 g	50 g	60 ml
⅛	18 g	19 g	24 g	25 g	30 ml

DRY INGREDIENTS BY WEIGHT
(To convert ounces to grams, multiply the number of ounces by 30.)

1 oz	=	¹⁄₁₆ lb	=	30 g
4 oz	=	¼ lb	=	120 g
8 oz	=	½ lb	=	240 g
12 oz	=	¾ lb	=	360 g
16 oz	=	1 lb	=	480 g

LENGTH
(To convert inches to centimeters, multiply the number of inches by 2.5.)

1 in				=	2.5 cm		
6 in	=	½ ft		=	15 cm		
12 in	=	1 ft		=	30 cm		
36 in	=	3 ft	= 1 yd	=	90 cm		
40 in				=	100 cm	=	1 m

LIQUID INGREDIENTS BY VOLUME

¼ tsp					=	1 ml	
½ tsp					=	2 ml	
1 tsp					=	5 ml	
3 tsp	=	1 tbls		= ½ fl oz	=	15 ml	
		2 tbls	= ⅛ cup	= 1 fl oz	=	30 ml	
		4 tbls	= ¼ cup	= 2 fl oz	=	60 ml	
		5⅓ tbls	= ⅓ cup	= 3 fl oz	=	80 ml	
		8 tbls	= ½ cup	= 4 fl oz	=	120 ml	
		10⅔ tbls	= ⅔ cup	= 5 fl oz	=	160 ml	
		12 tbls	= ¾ cup	= 6 fl oz	=	180 ml	
		16 tbls	= 1 cup	= 8 fl oz	=	240 ml	
		1 pt	= 2 cups	= 16 fl oz	=	480 ml	
		1 qt	= 4 cups	= 32 fl oz	=	960 ml	
				33 fl oz	=	1000 ml	= 1 l

COOKING/OVEN TEMPERATURES

	Fahrenheit	Celcius	Gas Mark
Freeze Water	32° F	0° C	
Room Temperature	68° F	20° C	
Boil Water	212° F	100° C	
Bake	325° F	160° C	3
	350° F	180° C	4
	375° F	190° C	5
	400° F	200° C	6
	425° F	220° C	7
	450° F	230° C	8
Broil			Grill